HEATH
Physics

David G. Martindale
Robert W. Heath
William W. Konrad
Robert R. Macnaughton
Mark A. Carle

Dr. Philip C. Eastman
Physics Consultant

D.C. Heath and Company
Lexington, Massachusetts / Toronto, Ontario

Heath Physics Program

Pupil's Edition
Teacher's Guide
Laboratory Manual
Laboratory Manual, Teacher's Edition
Computer Test Bank
Computer Test Bank, Teacher's Guide

Editorial Development: Joel Reid Gendler, Virginia A. Flook, Roland E. Boucher, Toby Klang
Project and Cover Design: Susan Geer
Design Assistance: Irene Elios, Rick Rizzotto
Marketing Manager: Richard G. Ravich
Production: Pamela L. Wing
Editorial Services: Marianna Frew Palmer, K. Kirschbaum Harvie
Readability Testing: Swinburne Readability Laboratory
Laboratory Safety Consultant: Jay A. Young, Ph.D.
Cover Photograph: Fiber optic bundle. Simon Fraser/Science Photo Library (Photo Researchers, Inc.)

D.C. Heath gratefully acknowledges the comments and suggestions of the following teachers:

Ann Brandon
West Joliet Township High School
Joliet, IL

Max Hollon
Evansville North High School
Evansville, IN

Douglas Nauman
George Washington High School
Cedar Rapids, IA

Dr. Henry Razzaboni
Burlington High School
Burlington, MA

Terese Keogh
Freeport High School
Freeport, NY

Steven Brown
William Vitez
Berea High School
Berea, OH

Edward Leshinskie
Pottstown Senior High School
Pottstown, PA

Melody McCollum
Kris Whelan
Lake Highlands High School
Richardson, TX

Robert Severson
Lake Washington High School
Kirkland, WA

Published simultaneously in Canada
Printed in the United States of America
International Standard Book Code Number 0-669-25793-1

89 - DCI - 03 02 01

Contents

8 Thermal Energy 224

9 Fluids 266

10 The Properties and Behavior of Waves

306

11 The Production and Properties of Sound

348

12 The Interference of Sound Waves — 374

13 Light Rays and Reflection — 408

14 Curved Mirrors

436

15 Refraction of Light

462

19   Current Electricity   566

20   Electric Circuits   584

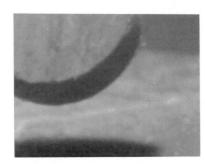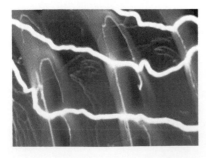

24 Investigating New Rays   **706**

25 Investigating the Atom   **732**

26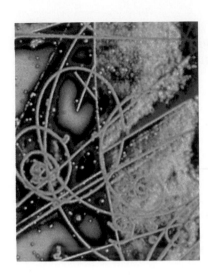

Investigating the Nucleus

27

Nuclear Energy

Appendices

Investigations

Special Features

Physics Connects . . .

Technology

Careers

Chapter Introduction Photographs

To the Student

Physics is so fundamental a subject that there is scarcely an area of modern life unaffected by it. The impact of physics on society can be seen in most of society's products, processes, and services. For example, the communications industry evolved almost entirely because of research by physicists. The telephone, satellite television, transistors, integrated circuits, fiber optics, cable television, and laser disks all depend on the laws of physics. In the medical field, the applications of physics are familiar to everyone: X-rays, CAT scans, ultrasonic diagnosis, radiation therapy, hearing aids, pacemakers, and laser scalpels. All have a basis in physical principles. Communications, medicine, and many other fields—such as geology, energy, transportation, and astronomy—are extremely important in today's technological society.

The authors of this text believe that learning thrives on direct personal experience, and to let you take part actively, **66 laboratory investigations** have been included in this text. The authors have also noticed that students must be able to solve related numerical problems in order to grasp a concept in physics. The ability to do this gives you a feeling of real competence. If you are like most students, you will find numerical problems worrisome, so **Sample and Practice Problems** have been included all through the book, as well as extra problems in the Chapter Review at the end of most chapters. Answers are given for every problem that has a numerical answer.

The study of physics begins with an introduction to the basic skills and techniques of the study of motion, which will lead to a grasp of the concept of energy and the reasons for the universal concern about our limited energy resources (Chapters 1–7). Then heat energy and the behavior of fluids (Chapters 8–9) are studied. Next, wave phenomena, especially sound, are examined, followed by a study of geometric optics and color (Chapters 10–17). Electricity and magnetism are next (Chapters 18–23). Study is concluded with a look at recent developments in modern physics that have changed the way of looking at the atom and have put nuclear energy at the service of humanity (Chapters 24–27).

The authors know the joy and satisfaction that come from greater awareness and understanding of the physical world and wish you luck as you set out to capture these rewards for yourself.

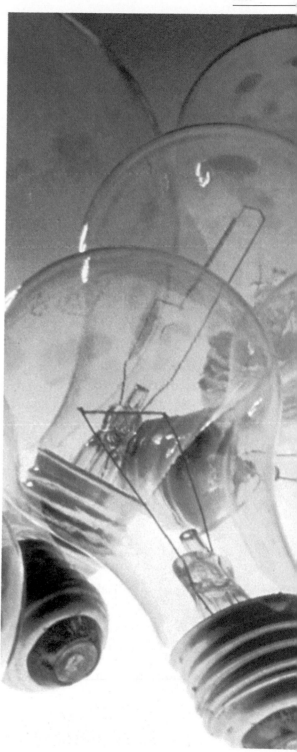

Safety in the Laboratory

A physics laboratory is a place where discovery leads to knowledge and understanding. It is also a place where caution is essential for your safety and the safety of others. Your knowledge of and adherence to safe laboratory practices are important factors in avoiding accidents. The following information describes some basic rules for safe laboratory work. Read the rules thoroughly and observe them in the laboratory.

1. Locate and learn to use all laboratory safety equipment.

2. Never eat, drink, chew gum, or apply cosmetics in the laboratory. Do not store food or beverages in the lab area.

3. Never do a lab investigation without your teacher's supervision.

4. Read all parts of a lab investigation before you begin work. Follow your teacher's directions completely.

5. Never run, push, play, or fool around in the laboratory.

6. Keep your work area clean and uncluttered. Store items such as books and purses in designated areas. Keep glassware and containers of chemicals away from the edges of your lab bench.

7. Turn off all electric equipment, water, and gas when not in use.

8. Pay attention to safety **CAUTIONS.** Wear safety goggles and a lab apron whenever you use heat, chemicals, solutions, glassware, or other dangerous materials.

9. Dress properly for the laboratory. Do not wear loose-fitting sleeves, bulky outerwear, dangling jewelry, or open-toed shoes. Tie back long hair and tuck in scarves when you use heat or chemicals.

10. Never touch a hot object with your bare hands. Use a clamp, tongs, or heat-resistant gloves when handling hot objects.

11. Use care in handling electrical equipment. Do not touch electrical equipment with wet hands or use it near water. Check for frayed cords, loose connections, or broken wires. Do not touch bare wires. Make sure cords do not dangle from work tables. Disconnect appliances from outlets by pulling on the plug, not on the cord.

12. Use care when working with chemicals. Keep all chemicals away from your face and off your skin. Keep your hands away from your face while working with chemicals. If a chemical gets in your eyes or on your skin or clothing, wash it off immediately with plenty of water. Tell your teacher what happened.

13. Report accidents to your teacher immediately. Do not touch broken, cracked, or chipped glassware.

14. Always clean your equipment work space after you finish a lab investigation. Always wash your hands with soap and water before leaving the laboratory.

Safety in the Laboratory

Throughout the Chapter Investigations in *Heath Physics,* you will see a variety of symbols relating to safe laboratory procedures. These symbols and their meanings are shown in the table that follows. Study this information and be familiar with all cautions in an investigation before you begin your work.

Wear safety goggles and lab aprons. Investigation involves chemicals, hot materials, lab burners, or the possibility of broken glass.

Extreme care is needed. Investigation involves heating or handling equipment that could burn you. Use heat-resistant gloves, a clamp, or tongs to handle hot equipment.

Danger of cuts exists. Investigation involves scissors, wire cutters, pins, or other sharp instruments.

Investigation involves the use of electrical equipment, such as electric lamps and hot plates.

Extreme care is needed. Investigation involves hot plates, lab burners, lighted matches, or flammable liquids with explosive vapors.

The arrow alerts you to additional, specific safety procedures in an Investigation. Always discuss safety cautions with your teacher before you begin work.

Extreme care is needed. Investigation involves chemicals that may be irritating, corrosive, flammable, or poisonous. Avoid spills. Avoid touching the chemicals directly.

Investigation involves using radioactive materials. Use tongs to handle the samples. Follow the directions of your teacher.

Simple Motion

Chapter Objectives

- **Distinguish** *between vector and scalar quantities.*

- **Calculate** *displacement, given the initial and final positions.*

- **Explain** *what is meant by uniform motion.*

- **Distinguish** *between displacement and position and between velocity and speed.*

- **Relate** *velocity, displacement, and time in equations describing uniform motion.*

- **Analyze** *a position-time graph of uniform motion to determine velocity.*

- **Calculate** *average speed, given distance and time or given a position-time graph.*

- **Measure** *positions, using a paper tape made with a recording timer, and* **make a graph** *of the motion.*

- **Determine** *the velocity at any point on a curved position-time graph.*

Introduction

Few things in our universe are at rest. Most are in constant motion, whether it be planets orbiting suns, electrons in atoms, or birds in the sky. Describing these motions mathematically is the first step towards understanding them.

If you have your driver's license you may identify with the situation in the photograph. The driver will be worried that she is going over the speed limit. With radar, the police officer can tell the car's speed as it approaches the cruiser. His radar unit measures the speed precisely and records it in kilometers per hour. If the car is going over the speed limit, the officer will stop the driver, tell her what speed she was travelling, and probably ticket her. He will not care why the driver was speeding.

Our study of motion begins by describing it as accurately as possible. Like the police officer, we will not yet worry about the "why?", or cause, of the car's motion. The branch of physics that deals with describing the motion of objects is called **kinematics**. With an understanding of kinematics, we will go on to study why objects move as they do—a study known as **dynamics**—in a later chapter.

1.1 Vectors and Scalars

To develop some of the vocabulary used when describing motion, consider this problem. Suppose someone tells you that a valuable diamond is hidden in the room where you are standing. You are also given one of the following bits of information:
(a) It is in the carpet, two meters (2 m) from where you are standing.
(b) It is 2 m away from you.
(c) It is on the carpet, 2 m north of where you are standing.
Which bit of information would be most helpful? Which would be least helpful? Let us analyze the implications of each:
(a) You would have to search the carpet along the circumference of a circle with a radius of 2 m and with you at its center.
(b) You would have to search all points that were 2 m from you, including those above and below the floor.
(c) Providing you know which direction is north, you should find the diamond quickly.

A specific direction is an important piece of information. Quantities in physics are generally divided into two types—vector quantities and scalar quantities. **Vector quantities** have a size (or magnitude), a unit, and a direction. The situation we just studied involved a vector quantity. Some examples of vector quantities are: a displacement of 2.0 m[N]; a velocity of 80 km/h[E]; a force of 40 N[W]. **Scalar quantities**, on the other hand, have only a magnitude and a unit. Some examples of scalar quantities are: a distance of 2.0 m; a speed of 80 km/h; a time of 3.2 h.

N is the symbol for newton, the unit of force in SI.

By convention, directions are enclosed in square brackets.

*P*ractice

1. Organize the following quantities into two groups: vector quantities and scalar quantities. Also identify the physical quantity that each measures. For example, the quantity sixteen years (16 a) is a scalar quantity since it measures time and has no direction.
50 km/h, 6 km[N], 2000 kg/m³, 6 centuries, 800 kg, 1.0 kg/week, 20 m/s[S], 400 N[down]

a = annum

1.2 Position and Displacement

Suppose you are driving east on a straight highway along which numbered markers are spaced 1.0 km apart. Each marker pinpoints a specific position. You look out the car window and note that you are at marker number 5. A short time later you reach marker number 16. Your displacement during that time interval is 11 km[E].

Displacement describes both the magnitude and direction of a change in position. Most of our discussion of motion will involve that which occurs along a straight line. We could therefore represent it using a number line:

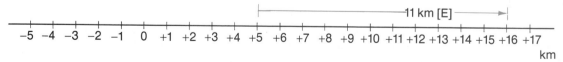

Consider the highway as a number line and the 0 km marker as the center of town. Positive numbers on the line represent east; negative numbers represent west.

In the example above, the initial position was +5 km and the final position was +16 km. Then the displacement, or change in position, was +11 km.

The arrow used to represent a vector quantity is called a vector.

We will use the symbol $\vec{d}$ for position and the symbol $\overrightarrow{\Delta d}$ for displacement. The arrow above the two symbols shows that they represent vector quantities. The Δ sign is the Greek letter *delta*, and is commonly used in mathematics and science to represent "change in", "increase of", "decrease of", or "interval". We could represent the relationship between displacement and position this way:

$$\overrightarrow{\Delta d} = \vec{d}_2 - \vec{d}_1$$

where $\vec{d}_1$ is the initial position

$\vec{d}_2$ is the final position

$\overrightarrow{\Delta d}$ is the displacement

The following sample problems refer to the number line or highway introduced on the preceding page. Consider the highway as a number line and the 0 km marker as the center of a town. The negative numbers on the number line represent positions west of the town.

Sample Problems

1. Find the displacement for a driver who started at marker +3 km and ended at marker −4 km.

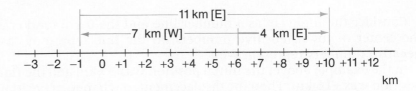

$$\overrightarrow{\Delta d} = \vec{d}_2 - \vec{d}_1$$
$$= -4 \text{ km} - (+3 \text{ km})$$
$$= -4 \text{ km} - 3 \text{ km}$$
$$= -7 \text{ km, or } 7 \text{ km[W]}$$

2. Find the displacement for a cyclist who starts at marker +6 km, moves to −1 km, and then proceeds to marker +10 km.

Remember that the displacement for an interval is simply the difference between the final position and the initial position.

Therefore, the displacement can be found as follows:

$$\vec{\Delta d} = \vec{d}_2 - \vec{d}_1$$
$$= +10 \text{ km} - (+6 \text{ km})$$
$$= +10 \text{ km} - 6 \text{ km}$$
$$= +4 \text{ km, or } 4 \text{ km[E]}$$

Practice

Use a number line to determine the displacements for the following changes in position:
1. −4 km to +5 km
2. −4 km to −9 km
3. +5 km to +11 km
4. +3 km to −5 km to +7 km
5. +8 km to −8 km
6. +2 km to −3 km to +3 km
7. 4 km[E] to 10 km[W]
8. 23 km[W] to 2 km[W]

1.3 Distance and Displacement

The displacement from +2 km to +8 km is +6 km, but what is the distance travelled? Distance is a scalar quantity for which direction is not specified. In this case, the distance travelled is simply 6 km. A displacement from position +3 km to −4 km is equal to −7 km. The distance travelled in this case is 7 km. A displacement from +2 km to −6 km and then to +7 km is +5 km. The distance travelled, however, is 8 km + 13 km, or 21 km. The distance travelled includes the *total* length of path, not simply the difference between the final and initial positions.

Practice

For each of the problems in the previous practice exercise, determine the distance travelled.

1.4 Uniform Motion

You see movement around you every day, but have you ever considered what moving objects represent the simplest kind of motion? You may think a leaf falling from a tree is such an example.

An elevator is a good example of an object that approximates uniform motion as it moves from one floor to another.

First, however, we must define the word "simple." The simplest motion possible should be easy to describe in precise terms. That is, we should be able to predict accurately the object's path and its location at various times along the path. A falling leaf takes a unique and unpredictable path. It therefore does not pass this test.

Physicists consider the simplest possible motion to be that which follows a straight line in a specific direction at a constant speed. When both the speed and direction remain the same, we say the velocity is constant. Such a motion is sometimes referred to as **uniform motion**.

Velocity is defined as the displacement of an object in a unit of time. When motion is uniform, we can write a simple equation that relates the velocity, the displacement, and the time as follows:

$$\vec{v} = \frac{\vec{\Delta d}}{\Delta t}$$

where $\vec{v}$ is the uniform velocity

$\vec{\Delta d}$ is the displacement

Δt is the time interval

Sample Problems

1. What is the velocity of a runner who runs 96 m[N] in 12 s?

$$\vec{\Delta d} = 96 \text{ m[N]}$$
$$\Delta t = 12 \text{ s}$$
$$\vec{v} = ?$$
$$\vec{v} = \frac{\vec{\Delta d}}{\Delta t}$$
$$= \frac{96 \text{ m[N]}}{12 \text{ s}}$$
$$= 8.0 \text{ m/s[N]}$$

Therefore the runner has a velocity of 8.0 m/s[N].

2. An air traffic controller notices that a distant aircraft has a velocity of 360 km/h[SW]. What displacement will the plane experience in the 25 s period before the controller checks its position again?

$$\vec{v} = 360 \text{ km/h[SW]}$$
$$\Delta t = 25 \text{ s}$$
$$\vec{\Delta d} = ?$$

Before calculating the displacement, convert the time to hours or the velocity to metres per second. A positive sign is used to indicate the direction [SW].

$$\vec{v} = \frac{+360 \text{ km}}{1.00 \text{ h}}$$

$$= \frac{360\ 000 \text{ m}}{3600 \text{ s}}$$

$$= \frac{+100 \text{ m}}{1 \text{ s}}, \text{ or } 100 \text{ m/s[SW]}$$

Another way to convert units is:

$$360 \ \frac{\cancel{km}}{\cancel{h}} \times \frac{1000 \text{ m}}{1\cancel{km}} \times \frac{\cancel{h}}{3600 \text{ s}}$$

$$= 100 \text{ m/s}$$

Notice how the units divide to give you the correct final units.

$$\vec{\Delta d} = \vec{v}\ \Delta t$$

$$= (+100 \text{ m/s})(25 \text{ s})$$

$$= +2500 \text{ m, or } 2.5 \text{ km[SW]}$$

Therefore the plane's displacement is 2.5 km[SW].

Practice

1. What is the velocity of an airplane that experiences a displacement of 580 m[N] in 2.5 s?
2. A car has a velocity of 105 km/h[N]. What is its displacement if it travels at this velocity for 2.5 h?
3. What velocity is required for a truck moving along the highway to experience a displacement of 400 m[W] in a time of 20 s? Express your answer in meters per second and in kilometers per hour.
4. How long would it take a dolphin swimming at 8.0 m/s[E] to travel 208 m[E]?

1.5 Speed and Velocity

Speed is a scalar quantity while velocity is a vector quantity. Speed is defined as the distance covered in a unit of time.

$$\textbf{speed} = \frac{\textbf{distance}}{\textbf{time}} \quad \text{or} \quad v = \frac{\Delta d}{\Delta t}$$

where v is the speed,
        Δd is the distance,
and Δt is the time interval.

The following sample problem illustrates the difference between speed and velocity.

Sample Problems

Suppose a car travels with uniform motion from a position of 2.0 km[N] to a position of 20 km[S] in 0.50 h. Find the car's
(a) displacement,
(b) velocity,
(c) distance travelled, and
(d) speed.
  In this case (+) will be used for north and (−) will be used for south.

(a) $\vec{d}_1 = +2.0$ km
  $\vec{d}_2 = -20$ km
  $\Delta t = 0.50$ h
  $\vec{\Delta d} = \vec{d}_2 - \vec{d}_1$
      $= -20$ km $-$ (+2.0 km)
      $= -22$ km, or 22 km[S]

Therefore, the car's displacement was 22 km[S].

(b) $\vec{v} = \dfrac{\vec{\Delta d}}{\Delta t}$

   $= \dfrac{-22 \text{ km}}{0.5 \text{ h}}$

   $= -44$ km/h, or 44 km/h[S]

Therefore, the car's velocity was 44 km/h[S].

(c) The distance travelled by the car is 2.0 km + 20 km, or 22 km.

(d) $v = \dfrac{\Delta d}{\Delta t}$

   $= \dfrac{22 \text{ km}}{0.5 \text{ h}}$

   $= 44$ km/h

Therefore, the car's speed was 44 km/h .

  Note that since the car does not change direction, the distance is the same as the magnitude of the displacement, and the speed is the same as the magnitude of the velocity.

Practice

1. What is the speed of a train that travels a distance of 480 km in 8.0 h?
2. An ant moves a distance of 39.4 cm in 7.3 s. What is its speed?
3. A goalkeeper for a hockey team has a reaction time of 0.40 s. A puck travelling at 25 m/s bounces off an opposing player's pads without slowing down. How far away must this occur to give the goalkeeper a chance to make a save?

The highest speed officially recorded for a wheeled vehicle was achieved by Richard Noble of Great Britain on October 4, 1983 at a site in the Black Rock Desert in Nevada. He was driving a jet-engined car called "Thrust 2" and reached a speed of 1013.5 km/h.

4. A tourist travelling along a straight section of highway late at night has the car set on cruise control. At 11:30 p.m. he notices a sign which says "Houston 100 km". At midnight he notices another sign which reads "Houston 40 km". If the tourist is located directly west of Houston on both occasions, find:
   (a) his displacement for the half hour interval stated,
   (b) his velocity, and
   (c) his speed.

1.6 Graphing Motion

A useful way to describe an object's motion is to graph it. Consider a car moving with a velocity of 20 m/s[E]. Assume that the car starts from a position of 0 m. Since its velocity is uniform we can use the equation $\vec{\Delta d} = \vec{v}\Delta t$ to determine its displacement at one-second intervals. The chart in the margin shows these values. The direction [E] is assumed to be positive.

Plotting time on the horizontal axis and position on the vertical axis results in this graph:

Time (s)	Position (m)
0	0
1	20
2	40
3	60
4	80

As in mathematics, when no sign is written a positive sign is assumed.

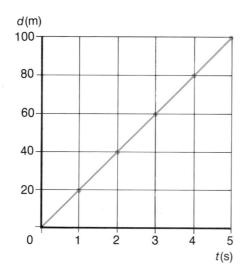

When graphing a vector quantity, like position, no vector arrow is shown above the symbol. This is because the graph itself indicates the vector nature of the data and an arrow would therefore be redundant. This practice will be used throughout the text whenever vector quantities are graphed.

The graph's straight line is significant. Whenever a graph of position versus time is a straight line, we know that the object is travelling with uniform velocity.

Let's look at the following graph to see what we can learn.

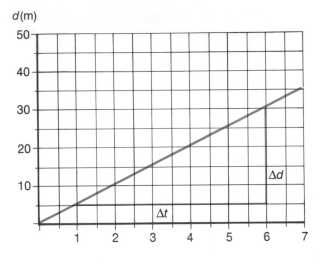

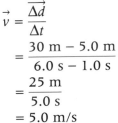

We don't have a data table for this graph but we could easily generate one from it. For example, the position at 3.0 s is 15 m and the position of 25 m is reached at 5.0 s. How can we determine the velocity of the object from the graph? We can see that its displacement for the time interval from 1.0 s to 6.0 s is 25 m. Using the relationship developed earlier, we can determine its velocity.

$$\vec{v} = \frac{\overrightarrow{\Delta d}}{\Delta t}$$

$$= \frac{30 \text{ m} - 5.0 \text{ m}}{6.0 \text{ s} - 1.0 \text{ s}}$$

$$= \frac{25 \text{ m}}{5.0 \text{ s}}$$

$$= 5.0 \text{ m/s}$$

Therefore, the velocity is 5.0 m/s.

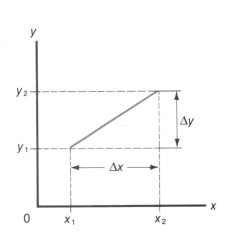

In mathematics, the slope of a straight line is calculated as follows:

$$\text{slope} = \frac{\Delta y}{\Delta x}$$

where $\Delta y = y_2 - y_1$ and
$\Delta x = x_2 - x_1$

We can look at the graphed data in another way. The displacement $\overrightarrow{\Delta d}$ is the rise of the line, and the time interval Δt is the run. From your study of mathematics you will recognize that rise/run gives us the property of a line referred to as slope.

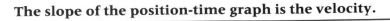

The slope of the position-time graph is the velocity.

Practice

1. This position-time graph shows the positions of several runners at various times. Determine the velocity of each of the runners.

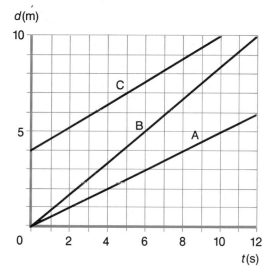

2. This position-time graph represents the motion of a dog running along a railway track.

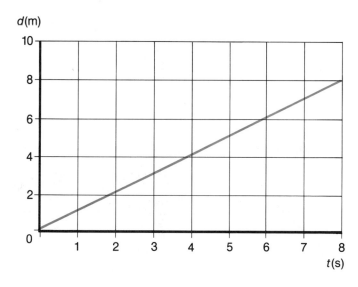

(a) What is the dog's position at 4.0 s?
(b) What is the dog's displacement between 2.0 s and 5.0 s?
(c) What is the velocity of the dog?

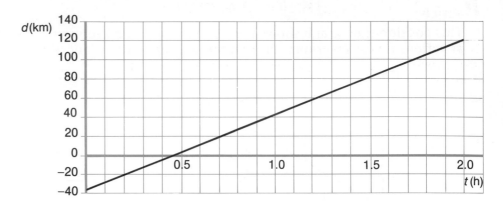

3. The position-time graph above represents the motion of a car along a section of straight highway. The car starts south of a town at a marker labelled 40 km[S]. Two hours later it is located at a marker north of town marked 120 km[N].

   (a) What is the displacement of the car during the 2.0 h period?

   (b) What is the velocity of the car for the 2.0 h interval?

   (c) At what time does the car pass the 0 marker?

4. The slope of a graph is an important characteristic of many types of graphs. For each graph below determine its slope. Include both the units and value of the slope in your answer.

(a)
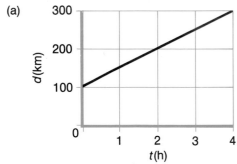

(b)
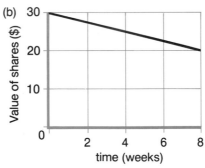

(c)
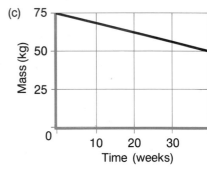

(d)
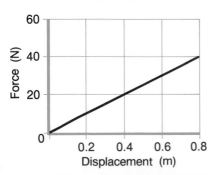

(e)
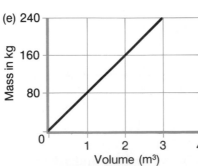

(f)
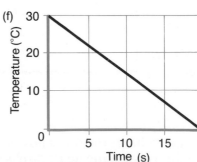

1.7 Motion at Different Velocities

Only a few things move with uniform motion for long periods of time. Generally they speed up or slow down or change direction. For now, let us consider an example in which one uniform velocity changes abruptly to a different velocity.

Sample Problems

The following position-time graph depicts the motion of a jogger moving along a straight path.

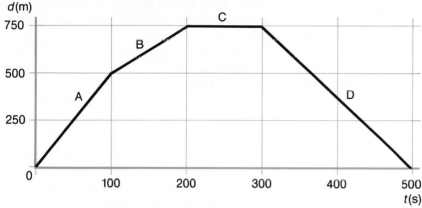

Examine the graph to answer the following questions.
(a) When was the jogger running the fastest?
(b) What was the farthest point reached by the jogger?
(c) When, if ever, did the jogger rest?
(d) State the jogger's displacement for the following time intervals.
   (i)   0 to 200 s
   (ii)   100 s to 300 s
   (iii) 300 s to 500 s
   (iv) 0 to 500 s
(e) Find the velocity for each of the lettered sections A, B, C, and D.
(f) What was the total distance travelled by the jogger?

Solutions
(a) Since the slope of a position-time graph gives the velocity, we know that the greater the slope, the greater the velocity. Since section A has the steepest slope, it represents the interval during which the jogger ran fastest.

(b) Between 200 s and 300 s the jogger's position remained at 750 m from her starting point and then she started back. Therefore, the farthest point reached was 750 m.

(c) The position of the jogger doesn't change between 200 and 300 s. Therefore she must have been resting during this time interval.

(d) Remember that if we know the positions we can find the displacement by using the relationship:

$$\overrightarrow{\Delta d} = \vec{d}_2 - \vec{d}_1$$

Therefore, the displacement for each of the specified intervals may be determined as follows:

(i) For the interval 0 to 200 s

$$\overrightarrow{\Delta d} = 750 \text{ m} - 0 \text{ m}$$
$$= 750 \text{ m}$$

(ii) For the interval 100 s to 300 s

$$\overrightarrow{\Delta d} = 750 \text{ m} - 500 \text{ m}$$
$$= 250 \text{ m}$$

(iii) For the interval 300 s to 500 s

$$\overrightarrow{\Delta d} = 0 \text{ m} - 750 \text{ m}$$
$$= -750 \text{ m}$$

(iv) For the interval 0 to 500 s

$$\overrightarrow{\Delta d} = 0 \text{ m} - 0 \text{ m}$$
$$= 0 \text{ m}$$

(e) The slope of each section gives the velocity for that interval, or:

$$\vec{v} = \frac{\overrightarrow{\Delta d}}{\Delta t}$$

For section A

$$\vec{v} = \frac{500 \text{ m}}{100 \text{ s}}$$
$$= 5.00 \text{ m/s}$$

For section B

$$\vec{v} = \frac{750 \text{ m} - 500 \text{ m}}{200 \text{ s} - 100 \text{ s}}$$
$$= \frac{250 \text{ m}}{100 \text{ s}}$$
$$= 2.50 \text{ m/s}$$

For section C

$$\vec{v} = \frac{750 \text{ m} - 750 \text{ m}}{300 \text{ s} - 200 \text{ s}}$$
$$= \frac{0 \text{ m}}{100 \text{ s}}$$
$$= 0 \text{ m/s}$$

For section D
$$\vec{v} = \frac{0\text{ m} - 750\text{ m}}{500\text{ s} - 300\text{ s}}$$
$$= \frac{-750\text{ m}}{200\text{ s}}$$
$$= -3.75\text{ m/s}$$

The negative sign in this case means that the jogger is moving in the opposite direction to sections A and B. In sections A and B she moves away from her starting position. She rests in section C and returns to her starting position in section D.

(f) To find the total distance travelled by the jogger, the distance travelled away from the starting point is added to the distance travelled on the return trip.
$$\Delta d_{total} = \Delta d_A + \Delta d_B + \Delta d_C + \Delta d_D$$
$$= 500\text{ m} + 250\text{ m} + 0 + 750\text{ m}$$
$$= 1500\text{ m}$$

If the jogger maintained a negative velocity she would eventually move past her starting point. A negative velocity indicates movement in the direction designated as negative.

Practice

This position-time graph shows the motion of a delivery truck whose driver is trying to find a certain house on a long straight street.

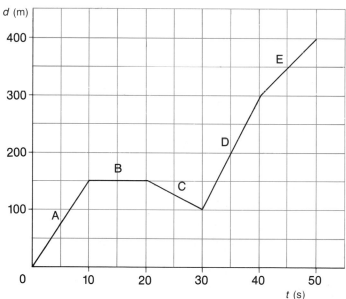

1. What is the truck's position at each of the following times?
   (a) 10 s   (b) 15 s   (c) 30 s   (d) 45 s   (e) 50 s
2. What is the truck's velocity in each of the lettered intervals?

3. What is the displacement for the following time intervals?
   (a) 0 to 20 s
   (b) 0 to 30 s
   (c) 0 to 50 s
4. What is the distance travelled during the following intervals?
   (a) 0 to 20 s
   (b) 0 to 30 s
   (c) 0 to 50 s

1.8 Average Velocity and Average Speed

The position-time graphs we have examined up to this point have consisted of straight lines or straight-line sections. The slope of the line gives us the velocity. If the velocity changes, and especially if it changes frequently, it is useful to be able to calculate the average velocity for a specific time interval. Average velocity is defined as follows:

$$\text{average velocity} = \frac{\text{total displacement}}{\text{time interval}}$$

$$\vec{v}_{av} = \frac{\overrightarrow{\Delta d}}{\Delta t}$$

Similarly, average speed is defined as follows:

$$\text{average speed} = \frac{\text{total distance}}{\text{time interval}}$$

$$v_{av} = \frac{\Delta d_{total}}{\Delta t}$$

The following sample problems will illustrate how average velocity and average speed are calculated, and how these quantities differ.

Sample Problems

1. A soccer player warming up for a game jogs along a track. He jogs 50 m[N] and then jogs 30 m back toward his starting point before stopping to talk to his coach. If he jogged for 20 s, determine the following:
   (a) his average velocity,
   (b) his average speed.

(a) To find his average velocity we need to find his displacement first. We will use + for north.

$$\overrightarrow{\Delta d} = \vec{d}_2 - \vec{d}_1$$
$$= 20 \text{ m} - 0 \text{ m}$$
$$= 20 \text{ m}$$

Now we can calculate the average velocity.

$$\vec{v}_{av} = \frac{\overrightarrow{\Delta d}}{\Delta t}$$
$$= \frac{20 \text{ m}}{20 \text{ s}}$$
$$= 1.0 \text{ m/s}$$

The soccer player had an average velocity of 1.0 m/s in the positive direction, or 1.0 m/s[N].

(b) To find his average speed we need to know how far he ran. Since he ran 50 m in one direction and then 30 m back toward his starting point, he ran a total of 80 m.

$$v_{av} = \frac{\Delta d_{total}}{\Delta t}$$
$$= \frac{80 \text{ m}}{20 \text{ s}}$$
$$= 4.0 \text{ m/s}$$

The player had an average speed of 4.0 m/s. Note that in this case the magnitude of the average velocity is different than the value of the average speed.

2.

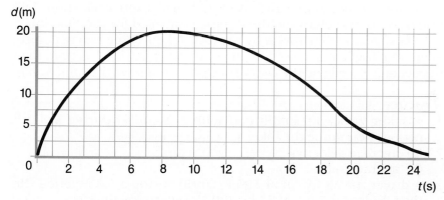

The graph above represents the motion of a dog running along a fenced-in run attached to its kennel. For the time interval from 4.0 s to 20 s, determine the dog's
(a) average velocity,
(b) average speed.

(a) The displacement for the time interval between 4.0 and 20 s is:

$$\overrightarrow{\Delta d} = \vec{d}_2 - \vec{d}_1$$
$$= 5 \text{ m} - 15 \text{ m}$$
$$= -10 \text{ m}$$

Therefore

$$\vec{v}_{av} = \frac{\overrightarrow{\Delta d}}{\Delta t}$$

$$= \frac{-10 \text{ m}}{16 \text{ s}}$$

$$= -0.63 \text{ m/s}$$

The average velocity is −0.63 m/s. This is also the slope of the line joining the two points in question.

When you use a position-time graph to find the average velocity, remember the following rule:

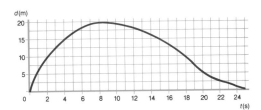

The average velocity is equal to the slope of the straight line joining two points on a position-time graph.

(b) To find the average speed we must determine the distance first. The dog travelled from a position of 15 m to 20 m and then back to 5 m. This represents a distance of 5 m + 15 m, or 20 m.

$$v_{av} = \frac{\Delta d_{total}}{\Delta t}$$

$$= \frac{20 \text{ m}}{16 \text{ s}}$$

$$= 1.25 \text{ m/s, or } 1.3 \text{ m/s}$$

The dog's average speed for the time interval in question is 1.25 m/s. To determine the average speed from a position-time graph, we must determine the distance travelled for the time interval specified and then divide by the time taken. If the moving object keeps moving in one direction and never changes its direction, then the average speed and the average velocity will have the same value.

Practice

1. A hiker walks 5.0 km[E] and then 8.0 km[W] during a 3.0 h period. Determine the hiker's
   (a) average velocity,
   (b) average speed.
2. A driver travels by car at 100 km/h[E] during a 1.0 h period. He then drives for 2.0 h at 82 km/h[W]. Determine the car's
   (a) resulting displacement,
   (b) average velocity,
   (c) distance travelled, and
   (d) average speed.

3.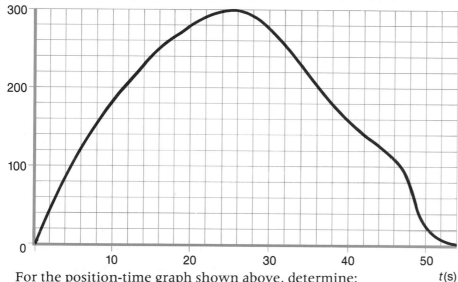

For the position-time graph shown above, determine:
(a) the average velocity for the intervals
    (i)   0 s to 40 s, and
    (ii) 20 s to 50 s.
(b) the average speed for the intervals
    (i)   0 s to 40 s, and
    (ii) 20 s to 50 s.

1.9 Velocity at a Point

When an object's velocity changes, we say that the object is accelerating. We will take a closer look at acceleration in the next chapter.

Given a position-time graph of a moving object, how can we determine the object's velocity when the velocity constantly changes?

The position-time graph for a moving car, illustrated in the margin, shows an example of increasing velocity. Initially, the graph line is horizontal and indicates that the car is at rest. As the car starts to move and increases its velocity, the slope of the curve increases as time increases. To determine the velocity at point A on the graph, we must determine the slope of the graph at that moment.

To this point, we have dealt only with straight-line graphs. To find the slope of a curve at a specific point requires an extra step. Through point A, draw a straight line that has the same slope as the graph at point A. If the line is drawn at the wrong angle, it will cross the graph at point A. The line you want just touches the graph at point A. Such a line is called a **tangent**.

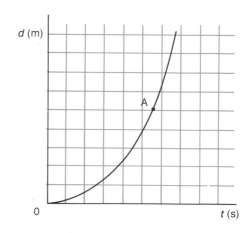

Find the slope of this tangent and you will have the velocity of the car.

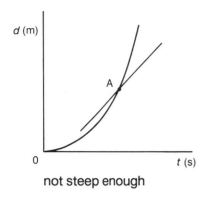

not steep enough

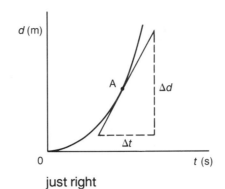

just right

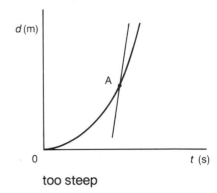

too steep

Velocity is equal to the slope of the tangent to a position-time graph.

Sample Problems

On the following position-time graph, find the velocity at points A, B, and C by finding the slope of the tangent to the graph at each of the points.

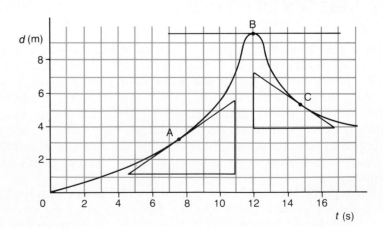

For point A: $\vec{v} = \dfrac{\overrightarrow{\Delta d}}{\Delta t}$

$= \dfrac{4.4 \text{ m}}{6.3 \text{ s}}$

$= 0.70 \text{ m/s}$

For point B: $\vec{v} = \dfrac{\overrightarrow{\Delta d}}{\Delta t}$

$= \dfrac{0 \text{ m}}{10 \text{ s}}$

$= 0 \text{ m/s}$

For point C: $\vec{v} = \dfrac{\overrightarrow{\Delta d}}{\Delta t}$

$= \dfrac{-3.2 \text{ m}}{4.5 \text{ s}}$

$= -0.71 \text{ m/s}$

t(s)	$\vec{d}$(m)
0	0
0.5	0.5
1.0	1.2
1.5	2.0
2.0	3.0
2.5	4.1
3.0	5.3
3.5	6.9
4.0	8.7
4.5	10.7
5.0	13.0
5.5	15.0
6.0	16.1
6.5	16.9
7.0	17.3
7.5	17.8
8.0	17.9
8.5	18.0
9.0	18.0
9.5	17.8
10.0	17.6
10.5	17.2
11.0	16.8
11.5	16.3
12.0	15.7
12.5	14.9
13.0	14.0

Practice

Plot a graph of the data tabulated in the margin.
1. What is the average velocity for the first 5.0 s?
2. What is the average velocity from the 2.0 s mark to the 13.0 s mark?
3. At what time is the velocity zero? How can you tell?
4. What are the velocities at each of the following times?
   (a) 3.0 s   (b) 6.5 s   (c) 11.0 s

Investigations

Preamble:

Recording Timers

In many of the investigations of motion that follow, you will be using a recording timer like the one in the photograph. A moving arm, driven by an electromagnet, strikes a metal block at a high frequency. A long strip of ticker tape, attached at one end to the moving object under study, slides between the moving arm and the metal block. A circular piece of carbon paper, attached so that it can rotate, makes a dot on the ticker tape every time the moving arm strikes it. In this way, a complete record is made of the motion. An

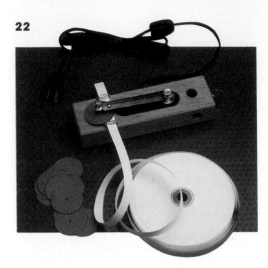

The unit for frequency is named after Heinrich Hertz (1857-1894). In 1887, when he was 30 years old, he discovered how to generate high-frequency radio waves.

analysis of the marks on the paper tape will give information about distance, time, speed, and acceleration.

Examine your timer carefully. Does it work in the same way as the one shown? Follow your teacher's directions and be sure to connect your timer correctly to the power supply. When you turn your timer on, it should make a regular sound.

Period and Frequency

When an object like a recording timer makes repeated motions, the basic motion that is repeated over and over again is called a **cycle**. The time required for one cycle is called the **period** (T). The number of cycles in a specific time interval (usually a second) is called the **frequency** (f). The SI unit for frequency is the **hertz** (Hz), where 1 Hz = 1 cycle/s. Mathematically, the period and the frequency are related:

$$f = \frac{\text{cycles}}{\Delta t}$$
$$T = \frac{\Delta t}{\text{cycles}}$$

From the above relationships it is also obvious that period and frequency are reciprocals of each other, that is

$$f = \frac{1}{T} \text{ or } T = \frac{1}{f}$$

For example, a recording timer makes 125 dots in 2.5 s. What are (a) its period and (b) its frequency?

(a) Period

$$T = \frac{2.5 \text{ s}}{125}$$
$$= 0.020 \text{ s}$$

(b) Frequency

$$f = \frac{125}{2.5 \text{ s}} \qquad \text{or} \qquad f = \frac{1}{T}$$
$$= 50 \text{ s}^{-1} \qquad\qquad = \frac{1}{0.020 \text{ s}}$$
$$= 50 \text{ Hz} \qquad\qquad = 50 \text{ Hz}$$

*P*ractice

1. A recording timer makes 540 dots in 4.0 s. What is its period?
2. A recording timer has a period of 0.025 s. How many dots does it make in 0.80 s?
3. A recording timer has a frequency of 25 Hz. How many dots does it make in 0.20 s?
4. A recording timer makes 465 dots in 8.5 s.
   (a) Calculate its period.
   (b) Its actual period is 0.020 s. Calculate the percentage error.

Investigation 1.1: The Period of a Recording Timer

Problem:
What are the period and the frequency of the recording timer?

Materials:
recording timer
power supply
2 m ticker tape
carbon paper disc
stopwatch

Procedure:
1. Connect the timer to the power supply.
2. Attach the carbon paper disc, carbon side up, to the timer.
3. Thread one end of the paper tape into the timer, over the carbon paper disc.
4. Make the tape as follows: One person starts pulling the tape through the timer at a steady rate. Another person then switches on the power supply and starts a stopwatch at the same instant. Turn the power supply off in 3.0 s.

Observations:
In a data table, record the number of dots and the time for the run, in seconds. Calculate and record the frequency and the period of the timer.

Questions:
1. Why is it important in this investigation not to pull the tape too quickly?
2. Why is it equally important not to pull the tape too slowly?
3. Does it matter whether the dots are unevenly spaced along the tape? What would that indicate?

4. The period of many recording timers is $\frac{1}{60}$ s, or 0.017 s. If this is true for your timer (your teacher can tell you whether it is), calculate the percentage error in your measurement of the period. (See Appendix I.)
5. What are the major sources of error that could affect your measurements and your calculation of the period? How could you allow for each of these sources of error, so as to obtain a more accurate value for the period?

Conclusion:

Each investigation must have a conclusion. The conclusion is the best answer you can give to the problem posed at the start of the investigation. If the answer is a number, as in this investigation, it is a good idea whenever possible to give its percentage error as well. After you have done each investigation, you should come to a conclusion and include it in your written report.

Investigation 1.2: Uniform Motion

Problem:

Is it possible for a person to move with uniform motion?

Materials:

recording timer
1 m ticker tape

Procedure:

1. Set up the timer and thread one end of the tape into it.
2. Holding on to the end of the tape, walk several steps while your partner operates the timer. Pull the tape as smoothly and steadily as possible.
3. Analyze the tape as follows:
   (a) Select a convenient unit of time. A timer may have a period of $\frac{1}{60}$ s. Then six dots would represent 0.10 s, a convenient unit.
   (b) Draw a line across the tape through the first dot on the tape.
   (c) Draw a line through every sixth dot all the way along the tape.

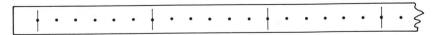

(d) Determine the position at the end of each 0.10 s interval. This is done by measuring from the first dot to the end of the interval in question.

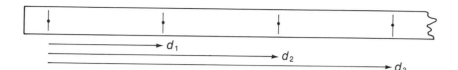

If the recording timer you are using vibrates at a frequency other than 60 Hz, it will take a different amount of time to make 6 ticks.

4. Record this information in a data table similar to this:

Time (s)	0	0.10	0.20	0.30	0.40	0.50	0.60		1.40	1.50
Position	0									

5. Construct a position-time graph, plotting time horizontally and position vertically. Make the graph as large as possible.

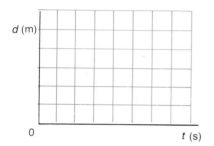

Questions:
1. Was your velocity uniform? How can you tell?
2. Find the average velocity for your motion.
3. How would the graph change if you repeated the experiment but moved more quickly? More slowly?

Investigation 1.3: Uniform Motion

Problem:
What type of motion does a glider on an air track exhibit?

Materials:
air track with gliders and accessories
Polaroid camera
opaque projector
light stroboscope

Procedure:
1. Level the air track by adjusting it so that the glider does not drift when the air is turned on.
2. Using some plasticine, mount a drinking straw vertically on the glider so that it is perpendicular to the glider's surface.
3. Obtain a picture of the moving glider by following this procedure:
   (a) Make sure the camera is mounted securely on a tripod and positioned in front of the air track. The shutter speed of the camera should be set on time exposure.

(b) Darken the room and turn on the stroboscope so that it flashes several times a second.

(c) Give the glider a push so that it moves at moderate speed along the air track.

(d) Wait till the glider rebounds from one end of the track. At that instant press the shutter release on the camera and hold it down until the glider reaches the other end of the air track.

(e) Process the picture.

4. To aid in the analysis of the picture, tape it to a stiff material like a file folder and insert it into an opaque projector.

5. Focus the image on a piece of paper taped to the wall.

6. Construct a data table with the following headings:

Time (flashes)	Position (cm)

Assume that the first image of a straw occurred at time 0 flashes. The next image will then have occurred at time 1 flash, the next at time 2 flashes, etc. To determine the value of the position at 1 flash, simply measure from the first image of the straw to the second image. To determine the position at 2 flashes, measure the distance from the first straw to the third straw. Record all positions in this way to complete the data table.

7. Construct a position-time graph for the glider. Plot time in flashes on the horizontal axis and position in centimeters on the vertical axis.

The distances measured in the enlarged photograph projected on the wall are very likely different from those that actually occurred. If you wish to determine the actual distances, you will need to include a reference length such as a meter stick in the photograph.

Measuring time in flashes instead of in seconds makes the analysis much simpler. Remember, we are just interested in whether or not the glider moved with uniform motion. The actual value of the velocity in meters per second is not relevant in this investigation.

Use this photograph to conduct the analysis if you do not have the equipment to produce your own.

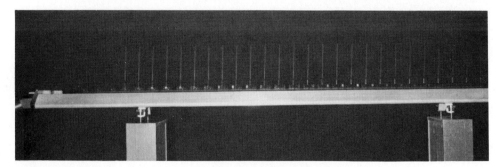

Questions:

1. Is the motion of the glider uniform? How can you tell?
2. Determine the average velocity of the glider. Be sure to state the units for velocity.
3. How would the graph of the motion change if the glider were moving with a greater velocity?
4. If we wished to determine the average velocity of the glider in meters per second, what additional information would we need to know?

Investigation 1.4: A Challenge

Using the materials available in the physics laboratory, design a procedure to determine how far you can run in two seconds if you start from rest. After your instructor has approved your design, carry out the investigation.

▶ **CAUTION: Write your procedure as a series of steps. Be sure to include the safety precautions you will use in the procedure.**

Chapter Summary

1. Vector quantities have a magnitude, a unit, and a direction.
2. Scalar quantities have a magnitude and a unit.
3. Displacement is a vector quantity that is a measure of the change in position.
4. Distance is a scalar quantity, that is, a measure of the length of path.
5. Uniform motion is motion at constant velocity.
6. Velocity is a vector quantity which may be found by using the following relationship if the velocity is uniform:
$$\text{velocity} = \frac{\text{displacement}}{\text{time}}$$
7. Speed is a scalar quantity which may be found by using the following relationship if the speed is uniform:
$$\text{speed} = \frac{\text{distance}}{\text{time}}$$
8. The position-time graph for an object moving with uniform motion is a straight line. The slope of the straight line gives the velocity of the object.
9. A negative slope on a straight line position-time graph indicates motion in a negative direction at constant velocity.
10. For any motion, the average velocity is the displacement for the time interval divided by the length of the time interval, or $\vec{v}_{av} = \frac{\vec{\Delta d}}{\Delta t}$. On a position-time graph it is the slope of the line joining points on the curve at the two times in question.
11. For any motion, the average speed is the distance for the time interval divided by the length of the time, or $v_{av} = \frac{\Delta d_{total}}{\Delta t}$.

12. The velocity at any point on a curved position-time graph is equal to the slope of the tangent to the curve at that point.

Chapter Review

Discussion

1. Very few objects exhibit perfectly uniform motion as it was defined in this chapter. Suggest why a study of kinematics should begin with a study of uniform motion.

2. Which of the following are examples of uniform motion? In those cases where the motion is not uniform, suggest why it is not.
   (a) A feather drifts downward at a constant speed in a quiet room.
   (b) A leaf falls from a tree.
   (c) A rock is dropped from the edge of a bridge and allowed to fall to the water below.
   (d) A satellite orbits the earth at a constant speed.
   (e) An elevator moves from the second to the eleventh floor at a constant speed.
   (f) A car travels along a straight section of expressway with its cruise control set at 100 km/h.

3. Classify each of the following quantities as vector or scalar: displacement, speed, velocity, distance, time, average speed, average velocity.

4. Sketch a position-time graph for a sprinter who runs as fast as she can until she crosses the finish line, and then slows down and jogs at a constant speed for a while longer to cool down.

5. A boy runs as fast as he can to a corner store two blocks from his home. After making a purchase he runs home, again running as fast as he can. Use the position-time graph in the margin to answer these questions:
   (a) When did the boy run faster, on the way to the store or on the way home? Explain your answer.
   (b) Assume that the reason for the difference in speeds is that in one case the boy was running uphill and in the other downhill. Which is at the higher elevation, the home or the store? Explain your answer.

6. Under what conditions will the magnitude of the displacement for a moving object be the same as the distance it travels?

7. Sketch position-time graphs for each of the following:
   (a) A sky diver jumping from an aircraft finds that her velocity increases rapidly at first, but that after falling for about ten seconds her velocity becomes constant.
   (b) The engine of a rapidly moving snowmobile stalls, causing the snowmobile to slide gradually to a stop.

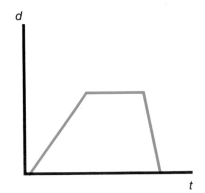

8. All cars are equipped with a speedometer and an odometer. Do these instruments measure vector or scalar quantities? Give a reason for your answer.

9. None of the following could be a position-time graph for a moving object. Explain why in each case.

(a)

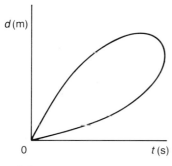

(b)

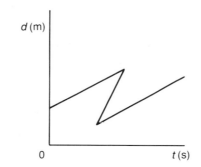

(c)

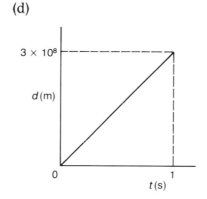

(d)

Problems

10. How long does it take for a motorboat travelling at 40 km/h to cross a lake that is 2.0 km wide?

11. The sun is located a distance of 1.49×10^{11} m from the Earth. Light travels at 3.00×10^8 m/s. How much time will elapse between the time a solar flare erupts from the surface of the sun and the time it is seen by an astronomer on Earth?

12. Here are some world record times for various track and field events.

Race	Time (s)	Held by
(a) 200 m	19.72	Pietro Mennea (Italy)
(b) 400 m	43.29	Butch Reynolds (United States)
(c) 800 m	101.8	Sebastian Coe (England)

Solar flares are eruptions of hot material from the sun's surface.

Calculate the average speed for each of the three runners. Suggest why the average speeds vary as they do.

13. Viking I, the first spacecraft to land on Mars, travelled 7.00×10^8 km in 303 d. Calculate its average speed, in kilometers per second.

14. How long does it take a girl, riding her bike at 2.50 m/s, to travel 1800 m?

15. How far will a man travel in 15 min, driving his car down the highway at 24 m/s?

16. The speed limit on expressways is 100 km/h. If you see something on the road ahead of you, as you are driving along, it usually takes about 1.0 s to fully apply the brakes. How far will the car travel in that time, in meters?

17. The speed limit on suburban roads is 50 km/h. You are travelling at the limit when an empty paper bag blows onto the road from behind a parked car 5.0 m in front of you. If you maintain your velocity how long will it be before you hit it?

18. A marathon runner in training runs 22 km[N] and then 32 km[S]. Assuming the entire run takes 4.2 h, answer the following questions:
    (a) What is the runner's position at the end of the run?
    (b) What is the total displacement for the run?
    (c) What is the average velocity?
    (d) What is the total distance travelled?
    (e) What is the average speed?

19. Calculate the velocity of the object in each of these position-time graphs.
    (a)   (b)

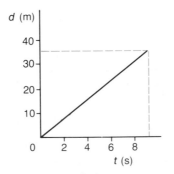
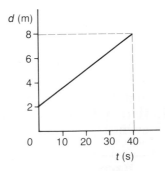

According to SI, meters per second should be used for all speeds and velocities.

(c)

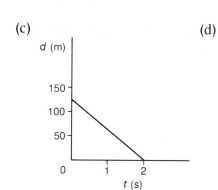

(d)

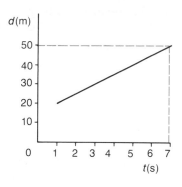

20. Calculate the velocity of this automobile in each part of its trip.

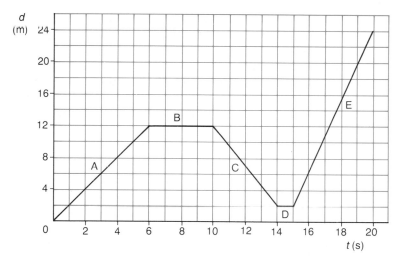

21. A light plane leaves Albany, New York and flies 80 km due south toward Kingston, New York. After arriving over Kingston the pilot is informed that the navigational equipment at the airport is malfunctioning. He is advised to land at an airport near Hudson, New York, located 18 km to the north of Kingston. The trip from Albany to Kingston takes 20 minutes, and the trip from Kingston back to the airport near Hudson takes 8.0 min.

(a) What is the total distance travelled by the airplane?

(b) What is the total displacement for the airplane?

(c) What is the average velocity for the airplane in travelling from

   (i)   Albany to Kingston?

   (ii) Kingston to Hudson?

   (iii) Albany to Kingston?

(d) What is the average speed for the entire trip?

22. This position-time graph shows the motion of a commuter train from station A to B and back again.

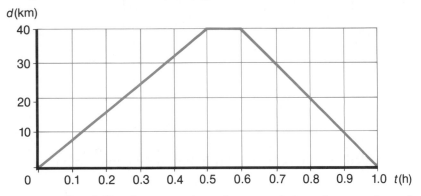

Answer the following questions by examining the graph and carrying out the calculations required.
(a) How far apart are A and B?
(b) How long did the commuter train remain at station B?
(c) How fast was the train going on its way to station B, and on its return to A?
(d) What is the displacement of the train for the interval 0 h to 1.0 h?
(e) If a passenger falls asleep on the train and makes the round trip, what is the total distance travelled?

23. Draw a position-time graph for a runner who moves at 5.0 m/s for 10 s, then at 2.0 m/s for 20 s, then at −9.0 m/s for 10 s.

24. Draw a position-time graph using the following data:

d (km)	0	0.5	1.0	1.5	2.2	3.2	4.2	5.2	5.7	5.8	5.8
t (h)	0	0.1	0.2	0.3	0.4	0.5	0.6	0.7	0.8	0.9	1.0

How fast was the object moving after
(a) 0.10 h?   (b) 0.50 h?   (c) 1.00 h?
What was the average velocity for
(d) the first 0.50 h?   (e) the last 0.50 h?   (f) the whole hour?

25. (a) Harry gives Sam a 30 m head start in the 100 m dash. Harry can run at 10 m/s, while Sam only runs at 6.0 m/s. Draw a position-time graph for a 100 m dash, plotting both runners.
    (b) Does Harry win? If so, at what time and place does he catch up to Sam?
    (c) How much of a head start would Sam need to win the race?

26. A rocket took off straight up, heading for the moon. The following data were recorded. Draw a position-time graph.

d (m)	0	10	80	270	640	1250	2160	3430	5120	7290	10 000	13 300
t (s)	0	1	2	3	4	5	6	7	8	9	10	11

(a) What was the average velocity for the first 6.00 s?

(b) What was the velocity exactly 6.00 s from the start of the trip?

(c) What was the average velocity for the 11th second? (10.0 s to 11.0 s)

(d) What was the velocity 10.5 s after the start of the trip?

27. Austin is about 50 km from San Marcos. A freight train starts out from San Marcos for Austin at 50 km/h. At the same time, a passenger train leaves Austin for San Marcos at 75 km/h. How much time passes before they meet one another, in minutes?

28. Two trains, each 1.0 km long, are heading towards each other at 50 km/h. At a certain moment, their locomotives are right beside one another (they are on parallel tracks). How much time passes before their cabooses are beside one another, in minutes?

29. A boy runs out the door and starts down the road for school at 10 km/h. Six minutes later, his mother discovers that he has forgotten his lunch, and she runs after him at 14 km/h.

(a) How far does he get in 6.0 min?

(b) How long does it take her to catch him, in minutes?

(c) How far from home is he when she catches him?

page 18
1. (a) 1.0 km/h[W]   (b) 4.3 km/h
2. (a) 64 km[W]   (b) 21 km[W]
   (c) 264 km   (d) 88 km
3. (a) (i)   4.0 m/s   (ii) -8.7 m/s
   (b) (i)   11 m/s   (ii) 10 m/s

page 21
1. 2.6 m/s
2. 1.0 m/s
3. 0
4. (a) 2.6 m/s   (b) 1.5 m/s
   (c) -1.1 m/s

page 23
1. 7.4×10^{-3} s
2. 32
3. 5
4. (a) 1.8×10^{-2} s   (b) -10%

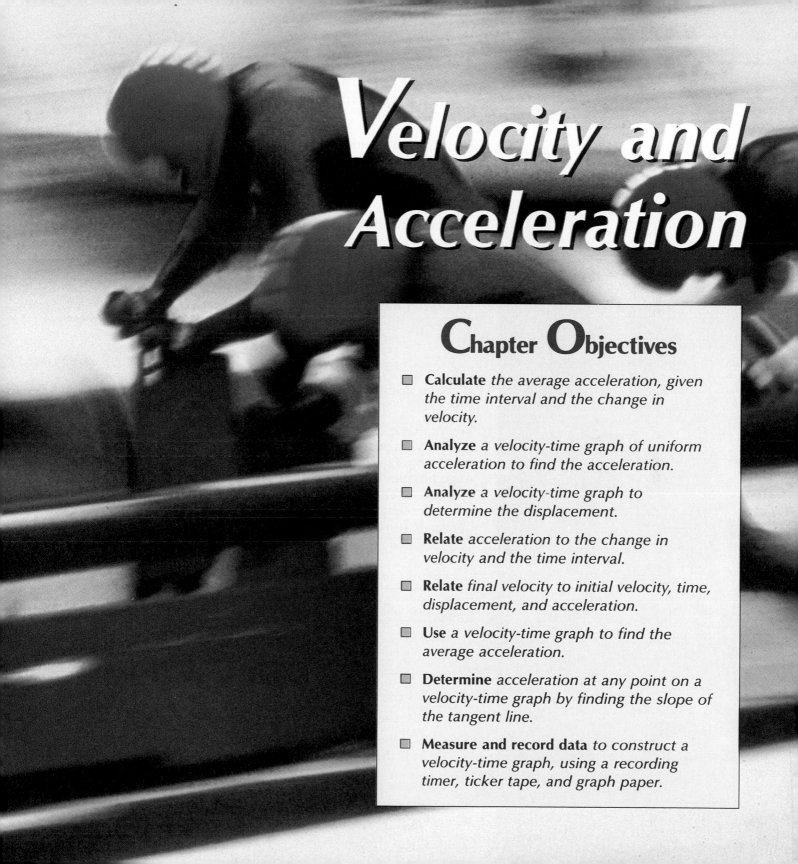

Velocity and Acceleration

Chapter Objectives

- **Calculate** *the average acceleration, given the time interval and the change in velocity.*

- **Analyze** *a velocity-time graph of uniform acceleration to find the acceleration.*

- **Analyze** *a velocity-time graph to determine the displacement.*

- **Relate** *acceleration to the change in velocity and the time interval.*

- **Relate** *final velocity to initial velocity, time, displacement, and acceleration.*

- **Use** *a velocity-time graph to find the average acceleration.*

- **Determine** *acceleration at any point on a velocity-time graph by finding the slope of the tangent line.*

- **Measure and record data** *to construct a velocity-time graph, using a recording timer, ticker tape, and graph paper.*

Introduction

By means of position-time graphs, we can analyze the motion of objects with either constant or changing velocities. By calculating the slope of these graphs, we can determine what the velocity is, and whether it is increasing or decreasing. The next step is to determine the rate at which the velocity increases or decreases. This is called the **acceleration** of the object. Two cars may both be able to reach a velocity of 120 km/h, but one may be able to reach it twice as quickly as the other. One may accelerate steadily while the other's acceleration varies. In this chapter, you will learn what is meant by acceleration, what unit is used to measure it, and how to measure the acceleration of ordinary moving objects.

2.1 Acceleration

You probably already have an idea of what the term "acceleration" means. Most people think of it as an increase in velocity. A car that is increasing its velocity is definitely accelerating. Physicists, though, use a broader definition of the term. They consider *any* change in velocity to be an acceleration. Because the time interval during which acceleration occurs is also important, acceleration, or the rate of change of velocity, may be expressed as:

$$\text{acceleration} = \frac{\textbf{change in velocity}}{\textbf{time interval}}$$

We can calculate acceleration with this mathematical equation:

$$\vec{a} = \frac{\overrightarrow{\Delta v}}{\Delta t} \text{ or } \vec{a} = \frac{\vec{v}_2 - \vec{v}_1}{\Delta t}$$

where $\vec{a}$ is the acceleration

$\vec{v}_1$ is the initial velocity

$\vec{v}_2$ is the final velocity

Δt is the time interval

This equation is used in the following sample problems. Note that acceleration is measured as kilometers per hour per second, (km/h)/s; or meters per second per second, (m/s)/s or m/s².

> If the acceleration is not uniform, this expression will give the value of the average acceleration.

Sample Problems

1. A car accelerates at a constant rate from 40 km/h[E] to 90 km/h[E] in 5.0 s. What is its acceleration?

$$\vec{a} = \frac{\vec{v}_2 - \vec{v}_1}{\Delta t}$$

$$= \frac{90 \text{ km/h[E]} - 40 \text{ km/h[E]}}{5.0 \text{ s}}$$

$$= \frac{50 \text{ km/h[E]}}{5.0 \text{ s}}$$

$$= 10 \text{ (km/h)/s[E]}$$

The car is accelerating at a uniform rate of 10 (km/h)/s[E]. This means that its velocity increases by 10 km/h[E] each second.

2. A runner starting from rest reaches a velocity of 9.6 m/s in 2.0 s. What is her average acceleration?

$$\vec{a} = \frac{\vec{v}_2 - \vec{v}_1}{\Delta t}$$

$$= \frac{9.6 \text{ m/s} - 0}{2.0 \text{ s}}$$

$$= 4.8 \text{ (m/s)/s, or } 4.8 \text{ m/s}^2 \text{ in a positive direction}$$

This means that on the average, her velocity increases by 4.8 m/s each second.

> The preferred SI unit for acceleration is meters per second squared (m/s²). There may be situations where other units, such as kilometers per hour per second, are more appropriate.

3. A baseball player running at 8.0 m/s[W] slides into third base, coming to rest in 1.6 s. What is his average acceleration?

$$\vec{a} = \frac{\vec{v}_2 - \vec{v}_1}{\Delta t}$$

$$= \frac{0 - 8 \text{ m/s[W]}}{1.6 \text{ s}}$$

$$a = \frac{-8.0 \text{ m/s[W]}}{1.6 \text{ s}}$$

$$= -5.0 \text{ m/s}^2\text{[W], or } 5.0 \text{ m/s}^2\text{[E]}$$

> Notice that the final velocity is zero, since he ends up at rest.

Sample problem 3 shows that when an object slows down, its acceleration is in the opposite direction to its velocity. Although we usually call slowing down **deceleration**, it is easier to think of it as an acceleration in the opposite direction to the velocity.

Practice

1. A cyclist accelerates from 5.0 m/s[S] to 15 m/s[S] in 4.0 s. What is his acceleration?
2. A jet plane accelerates from rest to 750 km/h in 2.2 min. What is its average acceleration?
3. A runner accelerates from 0.52 m/s to 0.78 m/s in 0.50 s. What is her acceleration?
4. A driver entering the outskirts of a city takes her foot off the accelerator so that her car slows down from 90 km/h to 50 km/h in 10 s. Find the car's average acceleration.
5. A boy rolls a ball up a hill giving it a velocity of 4.5 m/s[N]. Five seconds later the ball is rolling down the hill with a velocity of 1.5 m/s[S]. What is the ball's acceleration?

2.2 Velocity-Time Graphs and Acceleration

Position-time graphs are useful for representing the motion of objects travelling at a constant velocity or changing from one constant velocity to another, but the motion of objects whose velocity is constantly changing is better represented by a velocity-time graph. To draw a velocity-time graph you need a record of the velocity of an object at different times. For example, you could sit in the back seat of a car with a stopwatch, look over the driver's

Time (s)	Velocity (km/h)
0	0
5	10
10	20
15	30
20	40
25	50
30	60

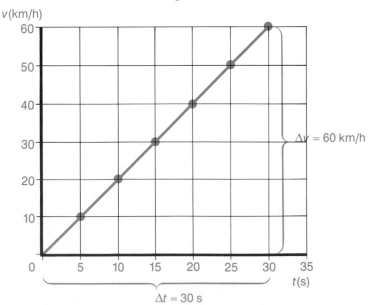

shoulder at the speedometer, and record the speed of the car every five seconds. Using these data, you could produce a velocity-time graph such as the one on the preceding page.

It is readily apparent that the graph is a straight line and that it represents an increase in velocity. On closer examination, you will see that the car increased its velocity by 10 km/h during each five-second interval. This is an acceleration of 2.0 (km/h)/s. Since the acceleration for each interval is the same, the graph illustrates uniform acceleration. You will find that whenever a velocity-time graph is a straight line, it represents uniform acceleration.

Applying the equation $\vec{a} = \overrightarrow{\Delta v}/\Delta t$ to the graph for the time interval 0 to 30 s results in:

$$\vec{a} = \frac{60 \text{ km/h} - 0}{30 \text{ s}}$$
$$= 2.0 \text{ (km/h)/s}$$

To determine acceleration from a velocity versus time graph, you simply calculate its slope. Note that $\overrightarrow{\Delta v}$ is the rise and Δt is the run.

Acceleration is equal to the slope of a velocity-time graph.

Sample Problems

1. Use the velocity-time graph in the margin to determine this object's acceleration for
   (a) the first 10 s of its motion, and
   (b) the time interval of 10 s to 15 s.

(a)
$$\overrightarrow{\Delta v} = 25 \text{ m/s} - 0 \text{ m/s}$$
$$= 25 \text{ m/s}$$
$$\Delta t = 10 \text{ s}$$
$$\vec{a} = \frac{\overrightarrow{\Delta v}}{\Delta t}$$
$$= \frac{25 \text{ m/s}}{10 \text{ s}}$$
$$= 2.5 \text{ m/s}^2$$

(b)
$$\vec{a} = \frac{\overrightarrow{\Delta v}}{\Delta t}$$
$$= \frac{30 \text{ m/s} - 25 \text{ m/s}}{5.0 \text{ s}}$$
$$= 1.0 \text{ m/s}^2$$

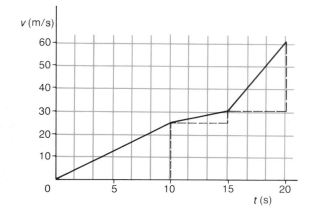

Practice

1. Calculate the acceleration of the object in the sample problem for the time interval 15 s to 20 s.
2. The graph below shows the motion of a car accelerating from a stop at an intersection.
   (a) How fast was the car moving at the following times: 2.0 s, 4.0 s, 15.0 s?
   (b) Determine the acceleration during the following time intervals: 0 to 4.0 s, 4.0 s to 10.0 s, 10.0 s to 15.0 s.

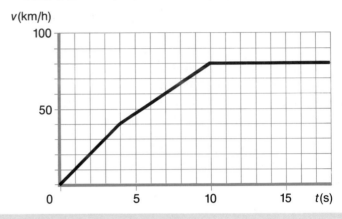

2.3 Positive, Negative, and Zero Accelerations

Large negative accelerations are experienced when cars and passengers are stopped abruptly in an accident, assuming that the car's velocity at the moment of impact is positive.

Examine the velocity-time graph at the top of the next page. On it you will find examples of three different kinds of acceleration. The object starts off from rest (at zero velocity) and accelerates steadily for a while. After 10 s, it stops accelerating and then travels at a constant velocity for 10 s. The slope of this part of the graph is zero, telling you that the acceleration is zero. Now the object slows down. In each second, it loses the same amount of velocity. The slope of the graph in this section is negative, making the acceleration negative. The acceleration for each section is:

A: $\overrightarrow{\Delta v} = 20$ m/s
$\Delta t = 10$ s
$\overrightarrow{a} = \dfrac{20 \text{ m/s}}{10 \text{ s}}$
$= +2.0$ m/s²
(increasing velocity)

B: $\overrightarrow{\Delta v} = 0$ m/s
$\Delta t = 10$ s
$\overrightarrow{a} = \dfrac{0 \text{ m/s}}{10 \text{ s}}$
$= 0$ m/s²
(constant velocity)

C: $\overrightarrow{\Delta v} = -20$ m/s
$\Delta t = 8.0$ s
$\overrightarrow{a} = \dfrac{-20 \text{ m/s}}{8.0 \text{ s}}$
$= -2.5$ m/s²
(decreasing velocity)

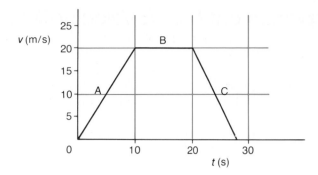

If line segment C were extended so that it went below the time axis, the acceleration would still be negative. However, the object would now be moving faster and faster in a negative direction.

Practice

1. For each lettered section on the graph in the margin, calculate the acceleration of the object.
2. Construct a velocity-time graph for
   (a) a car that starts from rest and accelerates at 8 (km/h)/s for 10 s.
   (b) a runner who runs at a constant velocity of 8.0 m/s for 5.0 s, then slows down at a uniform rate and stops in 2.0 s.
3. Copy the graph below in your notebook. On the same axes, construct a line showing the motion of an object with an acceleration
   (a) two times that of the original line on the graph, and
   (b) half that of the original line on the graph.

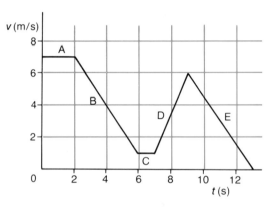

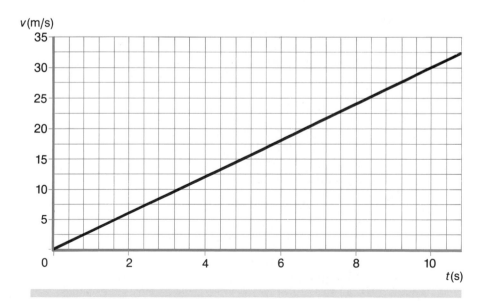

2.4 Displacement from a Velocity-Time Graph

A velocity-time graph indicates the velocity of a moving object at various times. The slope of a velocity-time graph gives the object's acceleration as well. You can also use velocity-time graphs to determine a third property of motion—displacement. Consider the following examples.

Sample Problems

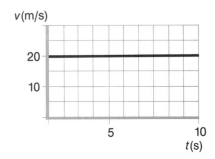

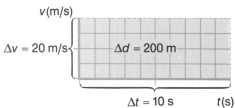

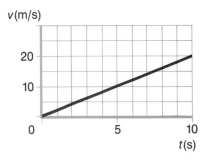

1. The graph in the margin shows the motion of a car for a 10 s interval. What is the displacement of the car during this time interval?

   The graph shows a uniform velocity of 20 m/s for 10 s. We know from Chapter 1 that the displacement for an object moving with uniform velocity can be found by using the equation

   $$\vec{\Delta d} = \vec{v}\Delta t$$

   In this case
   $$\vec{v} = 20 \text{ m/s}$$
   $$\Delta t = 10 \text{ s}$$

   then
   $$\vec{\Delta d} = (20 \text{ m/s})(10 \text{ s})$$
   $$= 200 \text{ m}$$

   We could also look at this solution in another way. Observe that $\vec{v}$ and Δt are actually the length and width of the rectangle formed by the graph line and the time axis. The product of these two quantities gives us the area of the rectangle.

2. The graph in the margin shows the velocity of a ball that starts from rest and rolls down a long hill. What is the ball's displacement after 10 s?

   Since this graph does not involve uniform motion, we cannot use $\vec{\Delta d} = \vec{v}\Delta t$. As in the previous example, the area between the time axis and the graph line represents the displacement for the interval. In this case the shape is a triangle. You'll recall that the area of a triangle equals $\frac{1}{2} \times$ base $\times$ height.

   $$\vec{\Delta d} = \text{area of} \triangle = \frac{1}{2}bh$$

   $$= \left(\frac{1}{2}\right)(10 \text{ s})(20 \text{ m/s})$$

   $$= 100 \text{ m}$$

   Therefore, the ball had a displacement of 100 m after it had rolled for 10 s.

We can apply this approach to more complex velocity-time graphs consisting of several straight-line sections.

3. The graph in the margin shows the motion of a dog running along the side of a straight road for a 16 s interval. What is its displacement for that time interval?

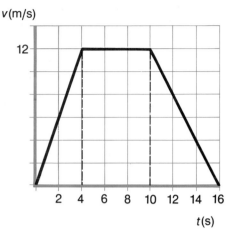

v(m/s)

Again, we can find the displacement by finding the area under the graph line. Since the figure is complex, we can divide it into three figures, as shown by the black, dotted lines, to simplify the task. To find the total displacement, we find the total of the three areas.

$$\vec{\Delta d} = \text{area}\ (\triangle + \square + \triangle)$$

$$= \left(\frac{1}{2}\right)(4.0\ \text{s})(12\ \text{m/s}) + (6.0\ \text{s})(12\ \text{m/s}) + \left(\frac{1}{2}\right)(6.0\ \text{s})(12\ \text{m/s})$$

$$= 24\ \text{m} + 72\ \text{m} + 36\ \text{m}$$

$$= 132\ \text{m}$$

Therefore, the dog has a displacement of 132 m for the interval.

These problems illustrate that the area under the velocity-time graph is equivalent to the displacement during the time interval. This is valid in all cases, whatever the shape of the velocity-time graph.

The displacement in any interval is given by the area under the velocity-time graph for that interval.

Practice

1. Find the displacement represented by each of the following velocity-time graphs.

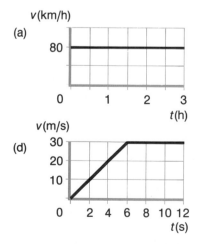

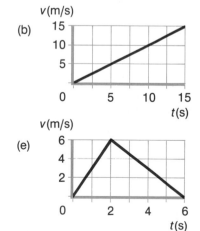

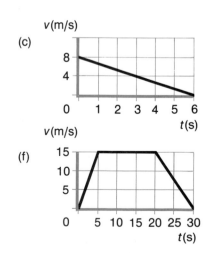

2. For each of the graphs shown in question 1, write a sentence to describe the motion.
3. What graphs in question 1 show a negative acceleration? Specify the time interval during which the acceleration was negative and determine its value in each case.

2.5 Equations for Motion with Uniform Acceleration

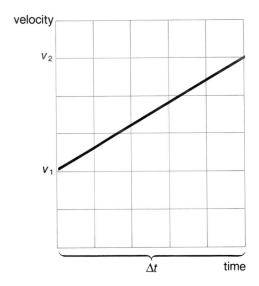

We know that a graph is an effective way to represent motion. Velocity-time graphs, for example, give information about the velocity, acceleration, and displacement of a moving object. We can also use a mathematical equation to describe an object's motion. We will limit our study to equations for motion that involve uniform acceleration.

The graph in the margin shows the motion of an object that is accelerating uniformly. It starts with a velocity $\vec{v}_1$ and reaches a velocity of $\vec{v}_2$ after a time interval Δt. We already know that the acceleration can be found as follows:

$$\vec{a} = \frac{\overrightarrow{\Delta v}}{\Delta t}$$

Since we know

$$\overrightarrow{\Delta v} = \vec{v}_2 - \vec{v}_1$$

then we can write

$$\vec{a} = \frac{\vec{v}_2 - \vec{v}_1}{\Delta t}$$

This equation can be rearranged algebraically to give:

$$\vec{a}\Delta t = \vec{v}_2 - \vec{v}_1$$

or

$$\vec{v}_2 = \vec{v}_1 + \vec{a}\Delta t$$

Note that $\vec{a} \Delta t$ is the same as $\overrightarrow{\Delta v}$. Therefore, the equation can also be thought of as: final velocity = initial velocity + change in velocity.

We know that the displacement is given by the area between the line on the graph and the time axis.

$$\overrightarrow{\Delta d} = \text{area} \square + \text{area} \triangle$$

$$= \vec{v}_1\Delta t + \frac{1}{2}(\vec{v}_2 - \vec{v}_1)\Delta t$$

But we showed that $\vec{v}_2 - \vec{v}_1 = \vec{a}\Delta t$
Therefore,

$$\overrightarrow{\Delta d} = \vec{v}_1\Delta t + \frac{1}{2}\vec{a}(\Delta t)^2$$

An alternate expression for displacement results from a slightly different algebraic manipulation. Starting with the same expression as before, it is:

$$\vec{\Delta d} = \vec{v}_1 \Delta t + \frac{1}{2}(\vec{v}_2 - \vec{v}_1)(\Delta t)$$

$$= \frac{2\vec{v}_1 \Delta t + \vec{v}_2 \Delta t - \vec{v}_1 \Delta t}{2}$$

$$= \frac{\vec{v}_1 \Delta t + \vec{v}_2 \Delta t}{2}$$

$$\vec{\Delta d} = \frac{(\vec{v}_1 + \vec{v}_2)}{2}\Delta t$$

When describing vector quantities, the vector notation sometimes appears cumbersome and unnecessary. When the direction of motion is obvious and does not change, the vector notation may be omitted for the sake of simplicity. In this chapter, all motion is in a straight line, so for the remaining examples vector notation will be omitted. Vectors in the direction of the initial velocity will be assumed to be positive, and those in the opposite direction, negative.

Sample Problems

1. A ball rolling down a hill at 4.0 m/s accelerates at 2.0 m/s². What is its velocity 5.0 s later?

To solve motion problems of this type, it helps to summarize the given information in algebraic form. This summary is shown below.

$$v_1 = 4.0 \text{ m/s}$$
$$a = 2.0 \text{ m/s}^2$$
$$\Delta t = 5.0 \text{ s}$$
$$v_2 = ?$$

To solve the problem we can use one of the equations developed for uniform acceleration. It must contain v_2 as the only variable for which the value is not known. The equation which will provide the solution is

$$v_2 = v_1 + a\Delta t$$

Substituting the values into this equation yields

$$v_2 = 4.0 \text{ m/s} + (2.0 \text{ m/s}^2)(5.0 \text{ s})$$
$$= 4.0 \text{ m/s} + 10 \text{ m/s}$$
$$= 14 \text{ m/s}$$

The ball reaches a velocity of 14 m/s in 5.0 s.

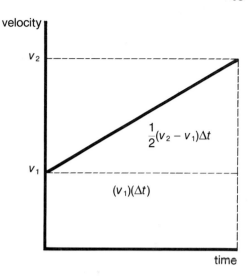

In Chapter 1 we found that the average velocity may be calculated by using the expression

$$\vec{v}_{av} = \frac{\vec{\Delta d}}{\Delta t}$$

Note also that

$$\vec{\Delta d} = \vec{v}_{av}\Delta t$$

If the acceleration is uniform, and only if it is uniform, the following expression is also valid.

$$\vec{v}_{av} = \frac{\vec{v}_1 + \vec{v}_2}{2}$$

2. A car travelling at 10 m/s accelerates at 4.0 m/s² for 8.0 s. What is its displacement during this interval?

$$v_1 = 10 \text{ m/s}$$
$$a = 4.0 \text{ m/s}^2$$
$$\Delta t = 8.0 \text{ s}$$
$$\Delta d = ?$$

$$\Delta d = v_1 \Delta t + \frac{1}{2} a (\Delta t)^2$$

$$= (10 \text{ m/s})(8.0 \text{ s}) + \frac{1}{2} (4.0 \text{ m/s}^2)(8.0 \text{ s})^2$$

$$= 80 \text{ m} + (2.0 \text{ m/s}^2)(64 \text{ s}^2)$$

$$= 80 \text{ m} + 128 \text{ m}$$

$$= 208 \text{ m, or } 2.1 \times 10^2 \text{ m}$$

The car's displacement for 8.0 s is 2.1×10^2 m.

3. A car accelerating at 5.0 m/s² has a displacement of 114 m in 6.0 s. What was its velocity at the beginning of the interval?

$$v_1 = ?$$
$$a = 5.0 \text{ m/s}^2$$
$$\Delta t = 6.0 \text{ s}$$
$$\Delta d = 114 \text{ m}$$

The equation that we can use to solve this question doesn't have the unknown variable on the left side. That is not a problem because the equation can be manipulated algebraically to solve for v_1 in one of two ways. We can either substitute the values and solve for v_1:

$$\Delta d = v_1 \Delta t + \frac{1}{2} a (\Delta t)^2$$

$$114 \text{ m} = v_1 (6.0 \text{ s}) + \frac{1}{2} (5.0 \text{ m/s}^2)(6.0 \text{ s})^2$$

$$114 \text{ m} = (6.0 \text{ s})v_1 + 90 \text{ m}$$

$$24 \text{ m} = (6.0 \text{ s})v_1$$

$$v_1 = 4.0 \text{ m/s}$$

or rearrange the equation before substituting the values.

$$\Delta d = v_1 \Delta t + \frac{1}{2} a (\Delta t)^2$$

$$\Delta d - \frac{1}{2} a (\Delta t)^2 = v_1 \Delta t$$

$$\frac{\Delta d - \frac{1}{2} a (\Delta t)^2}{\Delta t} = v_1$$

$$\frac{114 \text{ m} - \frac{1}{2}(5.0 \text{ m/s}^2)(6.0 \text{ s})^2}{6.0 \text{ s}} = v_1$$

$$\frac{114 \text{ m} - 90 \text{ m}}{6.0 \text{ s}} = v_1$$

$$\frac{24 \text{ m}}{6.0 \text{ s}} = v_1$$

$$4.0 \text{ m/s} = v_1$$

The car had a velocity of 4.0 m/s when it started to accelerate.

4. A ball rolls at an initial velocity of 4.0 m/s up a hill. Five seconds later it is rolling down the hill at 6.0 m/s². Find the following:
   (a) its acceleration.
   (b) its displacement at 5.0 s.

(a) Assuming "up" the hill is positive and "down" the hill is negative, then:

$$v_1 = 4.0 \text{ m/s}$$
$$v_2 = -6.0 \text{ m/s}$$
$$\Delta t - 5.0 \text{ s}$$
$$a = ?$$

$$a = \frac{v_2 - v_1}{\Delta t}$$

$$= \frac{-6.0 \text{ m/s} - 4.0 \text{ m/s}}{5.0 \text{ s}}$$

$$= \frac{-10 \text{ m/s}}{5.0 \text{ s}}$$

$$= -2.0 \text{ m/s}^2, \text{ or } 2.0 \text{ m/s}^2[\text{down}]$$

The ball has an acceleration of 2.0 m/s² [down].

(b) We can use the information from (a) to solve this question.

$$\Delta d = \frac{(v_1 + v_2)\Delta t}{2}$$

$$= \frac{(4.0 \text{ m/s} + (-6.0 \text{ m/s}))}{2} (5.0 \text{ s})$$

$$= \frac{(-2.0 \text{ m/s})}{2} (5.0 \text{ s})$$

$$= -5.0 \text{ m, or } 5.0 \text{ m[down]}$$

The ball is 5.0 m down the hill from its starting point after 5.0 s.

*P*ractice

1. A horse running at 4.0 m/s accelerates uniformly to a velocity of 18 m/s in 4.0 s. What is its displacement during the 4.0 s time interval?
2. A car acquires a velocity of 32 m/s by accelerating at 4.0 m/s² for 5.0 s. What was its initial velocity?

3. A ball falling from rest is located 45 m below its starting point 3.0 s later. Assuming that its acceleration is uniform, what is its value?
4. The brakes are applied on a car travelling at 30 m/s. The car stops in 3.0 s.
   (a) What is its displacement during this time?
   (b) What is the car's average acceleration?
5. How long will it take a truck travelling at 35 m/s to stop if it accelerates at -5.0 m/s^2?
6. A landing plane accelerates at -1.5 m/s^2 for 1.0 min until it stops. How fast was it going before it started to slow down?
7. A car hitting a tree loses 40.0 m/s in 0.100 s. What is its acceleration?
8. A skier accelerates at 1.20 m/s^2 down an icy slope, starting from 2.0 m/s. What is her displacement in
   (a) 5.0 s? (b) 10.0 s? (c) 15.0 s?
9. What is the acceleration of an object that accelerates steadily from rest, travelling 10 m in 10 s?
10. How long does it take an airplane, accelerating from rest at 5.0 m/s^2 to travel a distance of 360 m?
11. A rocket is moving forward at 120 m/s. When its retro rockets are fired it experiences an acceleration of -8.0 m/s^2. If these rockets are fired for 20 s, determine:
    (a) the final velocity of the rocket.
    (b) the displacement of the rocket.

2.6 Changing Acceleration

To this point we have studied velocity-time graphs that are straight lines and represent objects moving with constant acceleration. Like velocity, acceleration is not always constant. It can both increase and decrease. Consider a car accelerating from rest. At first, it accelerates quickly. Later, its velocity increases at a lower rate. Eventually, the car's acceleration will be zero, having reached a constant velocity.

We know that the velocity-time graph of an object moving with constant acceleration is a straight line. When acceleration is not constant, the velocity-time graph is a curve and it has a different value at each point along the curve. To find the average acceleration for any interval, we must find the two points that correspond to the beginning and end of the interval. Joining the two points with a straight line results in a slope that gives us the average acceleration.

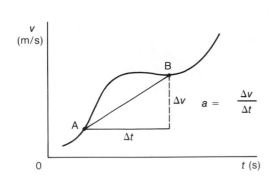

Average acceleration for an interval is equal to the slope of the line joining the two points on a velocity-time graph.

To find the acceleration at a particular moment in time, we use the same technique that we used in Chapter 1. That is, we draw a tangent to the curve at the time in question and calculate its slope.

Acceleration at a particular instant is equal to the slope of the tangent to a velocity-time graph at the time in question.

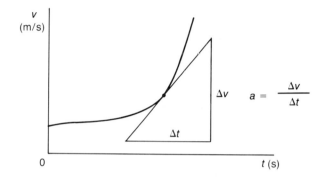

The equation for each of the above is expressed:

$$a = \frac{\Delta v}{\Delta t}$$

Sample Problems

You can see that the graph on the next page has a straight-line section where the acceleration is constant. It also has a curved section where the acceleration is continually changing. We will use the graph to find:
(a) the acceleration for the straight-line portion from 0 s to 9 s
(b) the average acceleration for the interval 12 s to 20 s
(c) the acceleration at 17.4 s.

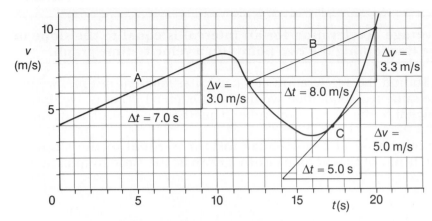

(a) The acceleration in section A is constant. Its value is the slope of the line segment A and is given by

$$a = \frac{\Delta v}{\Delta t} = \frac{3.0 \text{ m/s}}{7.0 \text{ s}} = 0.43 \text{ m/s}^2$$

(b) The velocity between 12 and 20 s is not uniform. It decreases and then increases again. The average acceleration between these two times is the slope of the line segment B, and is given by:

$$a = \frac{\Delta v}{\Delta t} = \frac{3.3 \text{ m/s}}{8.0 \text{ s}} = 0.41 \text{ m/s}^2$$

(c) The velocity around 17.4 s is increasing and so is the acceleration. The acceleration at 17.4 s is the slope of the tangent that has been drawn at point C, and is given by:

$$a = \frac{\Delta v}{\Delta t} = \frac{5.0 \text{ m/s}}{5.0 \text{ s}} = 1.0 \text{ m/s}^2$$

*P*ractice

Examine the following velocity-time graph.

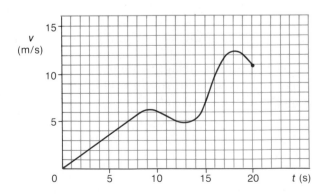

1. At what times is the acceleration zero?
2. What is the acceleration for the first 7.0 s?
3. What is the average acceleration for each of the following time intervals?
   (a) 5.0 s to 15.0 s
   (b) 9.0 s to 13.0 s
   (c) 15.0 s to 20.0 s
4. What is the acceleration at each of the following times?
   (a) 15.0 s
   (b) 11.0 s
   (c) 17.0 s

Dragsters that race over a distance of only 0.4 km accelerate rapidly for the entire race.

Investigations

Investigation 2.1: Motion on an Inclined Plane

Problem:
What type of motion does a cart released from rest on an inclined plane experience?

Materials:
recording timer
2 m ticker tape
cart
ramp

Procedure:
1. Set up the ramp, making it steep enough that the cart will speed up considerably on the way down. Use the recording timer to make a record of this motion on a 2 m length of ticker tape.
2. To analyze the tape, divide it into convenient time intervals, as indicated in Section 1.4. In this investigation, however, measure the displacement travelled during each interval, and not the total displacement for the trip.
3. If each time interval consists of six dots, each representing $\frac{1}{60}$ s, then each interval lasts for 0.10 s (6 × $\frac{1}{60}$ s = 0.10 s). Use this time to calculate the velocity for each interval.
4. Prepare a data table such as this:

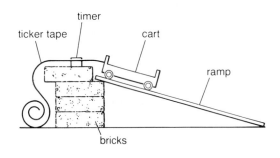

If your timer does not make 60 vibrations each second, six dots will represent a time other than 0.10 s.

Time	t (s)	0.1	0.2	0.3	0.4	0.5	0.6	0.7
Displacement during interval	Δd (cm)							
Average velocity for interval	v (cm/s)							

5. Record your displacement and time measurements in the data table. Complete the table by calculating the average velocity for each interval.
6. Use this table to plot a velocity-time graph, with time plotted horizontally, as before.
7. Examine the plotted points and try to decide what shape of graph they imply. Then draw either a smooth curve or the straight line which best fits the plotted data.

Here, you are plotting the velocity at the end of each time interval. In fact, the average velocity would be more accurately described as the velocity "in the middle of" each time interval, assuming the acceleration is constant.

Questions:
1. Describe the cart's motion as it rolled down the slope.
2. Use the graph to determine the cart's acceleration. Record and keep your calculations.

Investigation 2.2: Chain Sliding from a Desktop

Problem:
What type of motion is experienced by a chain sliding from a desk?

Materials:
recording timer
2 m ticker tape
1 m chain with 2-3 cm links

Procedure:
1. Attach the paper tape to one end of the chain. Place the chain at right angles to the edge of the desk, with its free end hanging over the edge. Connect the recording timer to the paper tape.
2. Pull the hanging end of the chain over the edge of the desk until the chain starts to move by itself. Immediately start the timer, shutting it off as soon as all of the chain has left the desk. For your graph, use only the part of the tape where the chain is falling under its own weight with some of the chain still on the desk. This usually means discarding parts at the beginning and end of the tape.
3. Divide the tape into convenient time intervals (use 0.1 s if possible) and make the necessary measurements to draw a velocity-time graph.
4. Join the first and last points on your graph with a straight line and calculate its slope. This tells you the average acceleration of the chain during its motion.

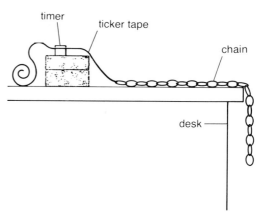

Questions:
1. Is the slope of the line increasing, constant, or decreasing?
2. Is this an example of increasing, constant, or decreasing acceleration?
3. How do you calculate the average acceleration of an object whose acceleration is not constant?
4. Classify each of the following graphs as representing constant, increasing, or decreasing acceleration.

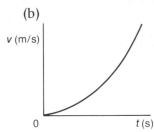

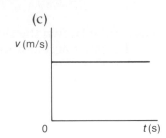

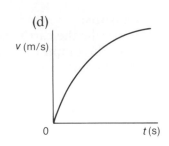

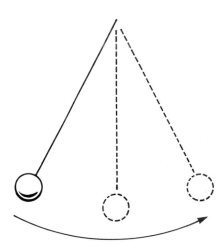

Investigation 2.3: Motion of a Pendulum

Preamble:
In this investigation, you will study and record the motion of a pendulum on both position- and velocity-time graphs. To start a pendulum, you move it to one side and release it. At the instant when you let go of it, its velocity is zero, but its acceleration is not. After all, if an object had both zero velocity and zero acceleration, it could never start moving. It would have to stay at rest.

The pendulum then accelerates down to the bottom of its swing, reaching its maximum velocity. Is this also the point of maximum acceleration? Consider that it has just finished speeding up and is now going to slow down. What is the value of its acceleration?

After passing the midpoint of its trip, the pendulum rises, slows down, and stops. How does its final acceleration compare with its initial acceleration? How does its velocity on one side of the midpoint compare with its velocity at the same distance on the other side of the midpoint?

Other questions can be answered by comparing your results with the graphs of others with pendulums of different amplitudes. The amplitude is the maximum distance the pendulum is displaced from the rest position. How does the amplitude affect the maximum velocity and the acceleration? What is the effect of the amplitude on the period of the pendulum?

Before you do the investigation, predict the pendulum's motion and sketch the position- and velocity-time graphs you think will result.

Problem:
How do both velocity and acceleration vary as a pendulum swings?

Materials:
recording timer
large pendulum (at least 2 m long)
2 m ticker tape

Procedure:

1. Feed the paper tape into the timer. Move the pendulum bob over to the timer and attach it to the paper tape. Release the bob and record only its forward motion as it moves away.
2. Draw both position-time and velocity-time graphs of the motion. On the position-time graph, mark the positions of both zero and maximum velocity. On the velocity-time graph, mark the positions of both maximum and zero acceleration.

Assume that the pendulum bob moves forward in a straight line.

Questions:

1. What is the average velocity of the pendulum?
2. What is the average acceleration of the pendulum?
3. What is the period of the pendulum?
4. What is the maximum velocity of the pendulum?
5. What is the initial acceleration of the pendulum?
6. What is the final acceleration of the pendulum?
7. Is the velocity-time graph symmetrical? What does this indicate about the velocities and accelerations on opposite sides of the midpoint?

Chapter Summary

1. Acceleration is the rate of change of velocity and is expressed mathematically as

$$\vec{a} = \frac{\vec{\Delta v}}{\Delta t} \quad \text{or} \quad \vec{a} = \frac{\vec{v}_2 - \vec{v}_1}{\Delta t}$$

2. On velocity-time graphs, a straight line shows that an object has a constant acceleration. The acceleration of the object is equal to the slope of the velocity-time graph.
3. A negative slope on a velocity-time graph means that the velocity is decreasing if the object is moving in a positive direction.
4. The area under the velocity-time graph gives the displacement.
5. Three equations for motion with uniform acceleration are:

$$\vec{v}_2 = \vec{v}_1 + \vec{a}\Delta t$$

$$\vec{\Delta d} = \left(\frac{\vec{v}_1 + \vec{v}_2}{2}\right)\Delta t$$

$$\vec{\Delta d} = \vec{v}_1\Delta t + \frac{1}{2}\vec{a}(\Delta t)^2$$

6. If the motion is in a straight line, the vector notation may be omitted and positive and negative signs used instead.

7. A curved velocity-time graph indicates changing acceleration. The average acceleration for an interval may be found by finding the slope of the straight line joining the two points on the curve in question.

8. The acceleration at any point on a curved velocity-time graph is the slope of the tangent to the curve at that point.

9. To construct a velocity-time graph from a ticker tape recording, mark the tape into lengths of the same time interval. The displacement for each interval divided by the time gives the average velocity for that interval. Plotting the average velocity for each interval versus the time will yield a velocity-time graph.

Chapter Review

Discussion

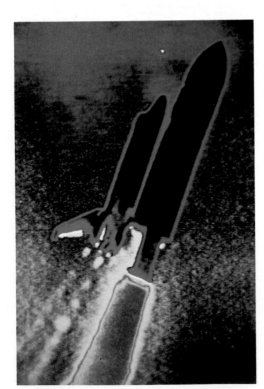
Infrared photo of the space shuttle accelerating during lift-off.

1. In this chapter we have used meters/(second)^2 and (kilometers/hour)/second as units for acceleration. Suggest three additional units that could be used to measure acceleration in the SI system of units.

2. A girl's school is directly down the street from where she lives. In riding her bicycle to school she accelerates uniformly from rest to a moderate velocity, and then maintains this velocity until she gets near the school. She then decelerates uniformly until she stops. Sketch a velocity-time graph for her motion.

3. A rocket accelerates slowly immediately after lift-off, but then begins to accelerate more and more rapidly as it rises. Sketch a velocity-time graph for the motion of the rocket.

4. Describe one situation in which this equation would not be valid:

$$\Delta d = v_1 \Delta t + \frac{1}{2} a (\Delta t)^2$$

5. Is it possible for an object to have a velocity of zero at the same instant that it has an acceleration that is not zero? Explain your answer and support it with examples.

6. In this chapter we derived three equations that could be used for motion involving uniform acceleration. What will each of these equations simplify to if
(a) the object travels with uniform velocity?
(b) the object starts from rest?

7. Two equations in addition to the ones we derived for motion involving uniform acceleration are

$$v_2^2 = v_1^2 + 2a\Delta d$$

$$\Delta d = v_2\Delta t - \frac{1}{2}a(\Delta t)^2$$

Derive these equations using the three equations developed in this chapter as your starting point.

8. Two students sitting in the rear seats of different cars make the following observations. Student A observes the speedometer every 5 s for a 30 s interval. She notices that the speedometer reads 10 km/h more each time she observes it. Student B observes the speedometer each time the car passes a telephone pole. He does this over a distance of 1.5 km. He notices that the speedometer in his vehicle also reads 10 km/h more each time he observes it.

(a) State which student is experiencing uniform acceleration. Give a reason for your answer.

(b) Is it possible that the two students were experiencing the same acceleration? Explain your answer.

Problems

9. A dragster accelerates from 0 to 90 m/s in 6.0 s. What is its acceleration?

10. The driver of a truck moving at 18 m/s applies the brakes and stops it in 4.0 s. What is the truck's acceleration?

11. A car accelerates from rest to 8.8 m/s in 3.0 s in first gear, then changes into second gear. After 8.0 s from the start of the trip, the car reaches 22.0 m/s and is shifted into third gear. After 7.0 s in third gear, it reaches 41.8 m/s. Calculate the average acceleration in each gear.

12. Draw the velocity-time graph of the motion of a bus that accelerates from rest at 1.0 m/s² for 6.0 s, then continues on at a constant speed for 6.0 s, then accelerates at −2.0 m/s² for 3.0 s.

13. An arrow shot straight up into the air at 50 m/s accelerates at −10 m/s². Draw a velocity-time graph of this motion from the time the arrow leaves the bow until it reaches maximum height.

14. Here is the velocity-time graph of a trip on a bicycle.

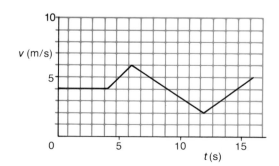

(a) How fast is the bicycle moving at each of the following times?

(i) 4.0 s   (ii) 6.0 s   (iii) 10.0 s   (iv) 12.0 s

(b) What is the acceleration of the bicycle at each of these times?

(i) 2.0 s   (ii) 5.0 s   (iii) 7.0 s   (iv) 14.0 s

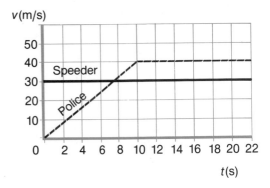

v(m/s)

(c) What is the bicycle's displacement at the following times?
  (i)   4.0 s   (ii) 12.0 s   (iii) 16.0 s

15. A speeder passes a stationary police cruiser. The police officer spots the speeder and pursues him. The graph in the margin shows the velocity of the two vehicles as a function of time. Assume that at time $t = 0$ s the speeder passes the stationary cruiser.
  (a) What is the police cruiser's acceleration?
  (b) What is the displacement for each of the two vehicles at 10 s?
  (c) How far apart are the two vehicles at 10 s?
  (d) At what time will the police cruiser pass the speeder?

16. A rocket accelerates at 40 m/s^2 for 3.0 min. What is its change in velocity?

17. How long will it take a falling rock, accelerating at 10 m/s^2, to reach 112 m/s, if it starts from rest?

18. A car enters a tunnel at 24 m/s and accelerates steadily at 2.0 m/s^2. At what velocity does it leave the tunnel, 8.0 s later?

19. A motorcycle stuntwoman accelerates from rest to a maximum velocity of 35.2 m/s at the top of the take-off ramp, then swoops up and over 20 cars. Calculate how long it takes her to accelerate, at an acceleration of 8.8 m/s^2.

20. Two runners accelerate uniformly from rest at 1.40 m/s^2 for 8.00 s.
  (a) What is their final velocity?
  (b) What is their average velocity?
  (c) How far do they travel?

21. A ball accelerates steadily down a ramp, starting from rest. It goes 2.0 m in 4.0 s.
  (a) What is its average velocity?
  (b) What is its final velocity?
  (c) What is its acceleration?

22. A car accelerates from rest at 6.00 m/s^2. What distance does it travel between 10.0 s and 15.0 s?

23. A skier accelerates steadily down a hill from 3.50 m/s to 11.40 m/s in 4.20 s.
  (a) What is the average velocity for the interval?
  (b) What is the displacement?

24. Runner A runs at 6.0 m/s for 10 s. Runner B accelerates from 4.0 m/s to 10.0 m/s, steadily, in 10 s.
  (a) How far does runner A go?
  (b) How far does runner B go?
  (c) How much farther does runner B travel than runner A?

25. A motorcycle moving at 12 m/s[W] accelerates at 6.0 m/s^2[W]. How long will it take to experience a displacement of 63 m[W]?

26. A baseball player catches a ball moving at 24 m/s. Upon striking the player's glove, the ball moves 12 cm as it comes to rest. Assume uniform acceleration in answering these questions:
    (a) How long did it take the ball to come to rest after striking the glove?
    (b) What was the ball's acceleration as it came to rest?
27. A ball pushed along a slope has an initial velocity of 10 m/s[up]. Its acceleration is 2.0 m/s²[down].
    (a) After its release, what is the ball's velocity at: 2.0 s, 5.0 s, 8.0 s?
    (b) What is the ball's displacement at: 2.0 s, 5.0 s, 8.0 s?
28. An astronaut on the moon throws a wrench straight up at 4.0 m/s. Three seconds later it falls downwards at a velocity of 0.8 m/s.
    (a) What was the acceleration of the wrench after it left the astronaut's hand?
    (b) How high above the point from which it was released was the wrench at 3.0 s?
    (c) How long would it take the wrench to return to the position from which it was thrown?
29. At the Los Alamos National Laboratory in New Mexico protons are accelerated from rest to a velocity of 2.5×10^8 m/s in an accelerator that is 0.80 km long.
    (a) What is the protons' average acceleration?
    (b) How long do the protons take to travel the length of the accelerator?
30. Jack and Jill ran down the hill. Both started from rest and accelerated steadily. Jack accelerated at 0.25 m/s² and Jill at 0.30 m/s². After running for 20 s, Jill fell down.
    (a) How far did Jill get before she fell?
    (b) How far had Jack travelled when Jill fell?
    (c) How fast was Jack running when Jill fell?
    (d) How long (to the nearest second) was it after Jill fell that Jack ran into her and broke his crown?

In actual fact the protons would achieve over 90% of their final velocity in the first few meters of travel. Assuming constant acceleration for part (b), your answer will only be a rough estimate of the required time.

page 38
1. 2.5 m/s²[S]
2. 3.4 × 10² (km/h)/min
3. 0.52 m/s²
4. −4.0 (km/h)/s
5. 1.2 m/s²[S]

page 40
1. 6 m/s²
2. (a) 20 km/h, 40 km/h, 80 km/h
   (b) 10 (km/h)/s, 6.7 (km/h)/s, 0

page 41
1. A 0, B −1.5 m/s², C 0, D 2.5 m/s²,
   E −1.5 m/s²

page 43
1. (a) 240 km   (b) 113 m   (c) 24 m
   (d) 270 m   (e) 18 m   (f) 338 m
3. (c) −1.3 m/s²   (e) −1.5 m/s²
   (f) −1.5 m/s²

page 47
 1. 44 m
 2. 12 m/s
 3. 10 m/s²
 4. (a) 45 m   (b) −10 m/s²
 5. 7.0 s
 6. 90 m/s
 7. −400 m/s²
 8. (a) 25 m   (b) 80 m   (c) 165 m
 9. 0.20 m/s²
10. 12 s
11. −40 m/s, 8.0 × 10² m

page 50
1. 9.2 s, 12.7 s, 18.1 s
2. 0.71 m/s²
3. (a) 0.33 m/s²
   (b) −0.35 m/s²   (c) 0.71 m/s²
4. (a) 2.8 m/s²   (b) 0.53 m/s²
   (c) 1.3 m/s²

31.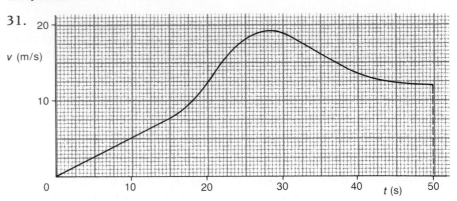

The graph shows the motion of a small bird flying down a long, straight, narrow cage.
(a) What is the bird's acceleration for the first 10 s of the trip?
(b) At what time is the bird's acceleration at its maximum?
(c) What is this maximum acceleration?
(d) At what time(s) is the bird's acceleration zero?
(e) At what time(s) is the bird's velocity zero?

Acceleration and The Human Body

Over the centuries people have found many ways to apply forces to accelerate themselves. People ride horses, sail ships, drive cars and ride rockets. The magnitude of the acceleration a body experiences is directly proportional to the magnitude of the force acting on it. Large accelerations require large forces. For example, for a major league pitcher to throw a fastball requires a much larger force than you might use to toss a baseball to a friend.

The amount of acceleration that humans can withstand is limited. The rockets that place the space shuttle into orbit must not reach an acceleration that will incapacitate or kill the astronauts who are inside. Nevertheless, the rocket must accelerate to a velocity that is great enough to allow the space shuttle to achieve a stable orbit about the Earth. As a result, the astronauts sit in rocket couches designed so that they can withstand accelerations far greater than those we encounter everyday.

Astronauts being launched into orbit experience an acceleration of about 100 m/s² for several seconds. If the astronauts sat in a vertical position during the launch, the blood would move from their heads and they would faint. For this reason they lie in a horizontal position during the launch.

What is the maximum acceleration the human body can withstand? The answer depends on factors that include the duration of the acceleration and the physical condition of the person.

Experiments have shown that the human body can withstand an

How fast can a person accelerate? The photograph shows Florence Griffith-Joyner, the U.S. sprinter who won the 100-meter dash at the 1988 Olympics in Seoul, South Korea. One key to any sprinter's success is the ability to accelerate rapidly out of the starting block and to reach top speed as quickly as possible. At the 1988 Olympic trials, Griffith-Joyner set a world record of 10.49 s in the 100-m dash. We can estimate that she experienced an average acceleration of 1.82 m/s² during the race. Actually, her acceleration as she left the starting block was quite a bit greater.

acceleration of about 300 m/s² for approximately 0.5 s. Very high accelerations are experienced by a moving body that is brought to rest in a very short distance. The Guinness Book of World Records documents several examples of this type of acceleration. For example, the race car driver, David Purley, survived a deceleration or negative acceleration from 172 km/h to 0 while travelling a mere 66 cm. This resulted in an acceleration of about 1730 m/s². As a result of this experience he suffered 29 fractures, 3 dislocations, and 6 subsequent heart stoppages.

Another example of a high acceleration rate is that experienced by divers of the Pentecost Islands, New Hebrides, who dive from a platform with a vine tied to their ankles. When they reach the end of the vine they are brought to rest in a short distance just above the ground. In one documented case the diver's speed, when he reached the end of the vine, was 15 m/s. The rate of negative acceleration was estimated to be 1070 m/s²!

Vectors

Chapter Objectives

- **Draw** displacement and velocity vectors to scale, given their magnitude and direction.

- **Add** vectors, using vector diagrams.

- **Solve** relative motion problems, using vector diagrams.

- **Relate** the centripetal acceleration of an object moving with uniform circular motion to the radius of the circle and the object's velocity.

- **Relate** centripetal acceleration, period of motion, and the radius of the object's path in uniform circular motion problems.

Introduction

Recall that vector quantities require a magnitude, a unit, and a direction for a complete description. Examples include displacement, velocity, and acceleration. Scalar quantities, on the other hand, require only a magnitude and a unit. Speed, distance, and time, for example, are scalar quantities.

In the first two chapters we studied motion along a straight line only. In real life, however, most motion does not occur in a straight line. This chapter will introduce motion in two dimensions. In addition, we will look at various methods of calculation using vector quantities.

3.1 Vector Diagrams

Vector quantities are often represented in diagrams by arrows called vectors. The length of the arrow indicates the vector's magnitude in the direction in which the arrow is pointing. The following displacement vectors represent magnitudes that are larger than the pages of this book. They are therefore drawn on a reduced scale. This will be the case with most vectors we encounter.

	Distance	Displacement
Symbol	Δd	$\overrightarrow{\Delta d}$
Example	10 km	5 km[E]

[N] north
[E] east
[W] west
[S] south
Square brackets indicate the direction for a vector quantity. To go [E30°S], you face east, then turn 30° towards the south.

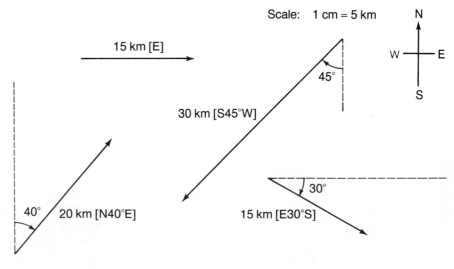

3.2 Vector Addition

If you went on a trip of 30 km[N], followed by a trip of 40 km[E], the sum of the distances you travelled is 70 km.

However, you would not be 70 km from your starting point. Your displacement from that point may be obtained from a vector diagram by "adding" together the two displacement vectors. The first step is to set up a proper scale and a set of directions.

(a) To add vectors, draw both of them to the same scale and connect them tip to tail.

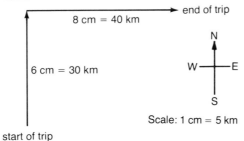

start of trip

Here $\vec{\Delta d_1}$ = 30 km[N]
$\vec{\Delta d_2}$ = 40 km[E]
The total displacement of these two, $\vec{\Delta d}_{total}$, is shown as:
$$\vec{\Delta d_3} = \vec{\Delta d_1} + \vec{\Delta d_2}$$
This equation tells you to add the two vectors together using a vector diagram, and not just to add their magnitudes together.

(b) Now, draw a vector from the tail of the first to the tip of the second displacement vector. This represents the total displacement. Measure the length and direction of this vector and calculate the displacement, using the scale. The total displacement is 50 km[N53°E].

The magnitude of this displacement may be written as $|\vec{\Delta d}|$ = 50 km. Note that its value is different from the distance travelled.

If we have more than two vectors, the procedure for addition is the same. The vectors are drawn to scale and are added tip to tail, one after the other. The vector sum is the vector drawn from the tail of the first to the tip of the last vector.

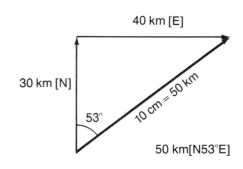

*P*ractice

1. What is the total displacement of a trip in which a person travels 10 km[N] and then 24 km[E]?
2. What is the total displacement of a trip of 50 km[W] followed by a trip of 100 km[N30°E]?
3. What is the total displacement of a trip of 100 km[N30°E] followed by a trip of 50 km[W]? What is significant about the result? What is significant about the result when compared to the answer for question 2?
4. A small boy goes to a store 2 blocks[N], 3 blocks[E], 1 block[S], 5 blocks[W], 4 blocks[S], and then 2 blocks[E]. What is the total displacement of his trip?

3.3 Speed and Velocity

You know from our work in Chapter 1 that the speed of a car, measured on its speedometer, is a scalar quantity. The car could be going east or west, uphill or downhill. The speedometer does not indicate direction. You will also recall that the combination of speed and direction is called velocity, a vector quantity.

Velocity vectors can also be represented by arrows. Look at these vector diagrams. All that is needed is a proper scale and a north-pointing arrow to establish direction. Velocity vectors are added together in exactly the same way as displacement vectors. As you will see, the vector diagrams that are produced are useful in a wide variety of boat, balloon, and airplane navigation problems.

	Speed	Velocity
Symbol	v	$\vec{v}$
Example	25 km/h	100 km/h[W]

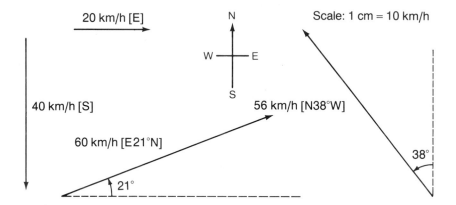

3.4 Velocity Vectors in One Dimension

Let's consider a situation that involves velocity vectors in one dimension.

A passenger walking inside a moving train has different velocities relative to the train and the ground. On a train moving at 20 km/h[E], seated passengers are at rest relative to the train, but are moving at 20 km/h[E] relative to the ground. If a passenger on this train walks towards the front of the train at a normal pace, say, 3 km/h, the passenger's velocity is 3 km/h[E] relative to the train and 23 km/h[E] relative to the ground. The passenger's velocity relative to the ground is found by adding his or her velocity relative to the train and the train's velocity relative to the ground.

We can use a vector diagram to carry out this calculation. Note the following symbols:

$_p\vec{v}_t$ = velocity of passenger relative to the train

$_t\vec{v}_g$ = velocity of train relative to the ground

$_p\vec{v}_g$ = velocity of passenger relative to the ground

$_p v_g = 23$ km/h [E]

$_p v_t = 3$ km/h [E]　　　　　　　　　　$_t v_g = 20$ km/h [E]

Scale: 1 cm = 2 km/h

To add vectors that are in the same direction, combine them by adding their magnitudes together.

$$_p\vec{v}_g = {}_p\vec{v}_t + {}_t\vec{v}_g$$
$$= 20 \text{ km/h[E]} + 3 \text{ km/h[E]}$$
$$= 23 \text{ km/h[E]}$$

If a passenger walks towards the back of the train with a velocity of 3 km/h[W], the passenger's velocity relative to the ground is 17 km/h[E]. This velocity is found in the same way as in the previous example, by adding the passenger's velocity relative to the train and the train's velocity relative to the ground.

$_t v_g = 20$ km/h [E]

$_p v_t = 3$ km/h [W]　　　　　　　$_p v_g = 17$ km/h [E]

Scale: 1 cm = 2 km/h

To add vectors that are in opposite directions, change the sign of one vector so that they have the same direction, and add their magnitudes.

$$_p\vec{v}_g = {}_p\vec{v}_t + {}_t\vec{v}_g$$
$$= 20 \text{ km/h[E]} + 3 \text{ km/h[W]}$$
$$= 20 \text{ km/h[E]} - 3 \text{ km/h[E]}$$
$$= 17 \text{ km/h[E]}$$

Note that by changing the sign *and* the direction, the vector is equivalent to the original vector. That is, 3 km/h[E] is the same velocity as −3 km/h[W].

When all vectors in a problem lie along the same line, we can use the technique introduced in Chapter 1. We assign a positive sign to one direction and a negative sign to the opposite direction. For example, assuming east is positive and west is negative, the above problem could be solved like this:

$$_p\vec{v}_g = {}_p\vec{v}_t + {}_t\vec{v}_g$$
$$= +20 \text{ km/h} + (-3 \text{ km/h})$$
$$= +17 \text{ km/h, or } 17 \text{ km/h[E]}$$

In symbols like this the pre-subscript denotes the object that is moving. The post-subscript denotes the frame of reference with respect to which the object is moving.

In problems such as this a simple chain rule correctly relates the different relative velocities.

$$_p\vec{v}_g = {}_p v_t + {}_t v_g$$

In vector diagrams the vector itself indicates that the quantity has direction. Vector signs are therefore omitted from the symbols.

$$_p\vec{v}_g = {}_p v_t + {}_t v_g$$

Practice

1. A baseball pitcher is warming up as he travels to a game by plane. The plane is flying at 400 km/h[W] relative to the ground. The pitcher throws a ball at 150 km/h relative to the airplane. What is the ball's velocity relative to the ground, if the pitcher throws the ball towards
   (a) the front of the plane?
   (b) the rear of the plane?
2. A jet plane travelling horizontally at 1200 km/h relative to the ground fires a rocket forwards at 1100 km/h relative to itself. What is the velocity of the rocket relative to the ground?
3. A bowler is practising his game on a railway flatcar travelling at 50 km/h[N] relative to the ground. If the ball's velocity relative to the flatcar is 60 km/h[S], what is its velocity relative to the ground?
4. A boat is travelling upstream at 5 km/h[N] relative to the shore. If there is a current of 7 km/h[S], what is the boat's velocity relative to the water?

3.5 Velocity Vectors in Two Dimensions

The principles we have established are also valid in situations that involve two dimensions. Consider this one.

A swimmer jumps into a river and swims for the opposite shore. Her velocity relative to the water is 4.0 km/h[N]. The current in the river is 3.0 km/h[E]. Because of the current she doesn't actually go north, but moves at an angle to the bank of the river. To find the swimmer's velocity relative to the ground, add her velocity relative to the water and the velocity of the water relative to the bank. Let "s" stand for the swimmer, "w" for the water, and "g" for the ground:

$\vec{_sv_g}$ = velocity of swimmer relative to ground
$\vec{_sv_w}$ = velocity of swimmer relative to water
$\vec{_wv_g}$ = velocity of water relative to ground (current)

Although the vectors do not lie along the same straight line, the chain rule established in the previous section still applies. The correct relationship is:

$$\vec{_sv_g} = \vec{_sv_w} + \vec{_wv_g}$$

To solve this problem you could construct a diagram like the one below. To do so would require the following steps:

(a) Choose a scale and indicate directions.

(b) Draw the vector $_s\vec{v}_w$.

(c) Starting at the tip of $_s\vec{v}_w$ draw the vector $_w\vec{v}_g$.

(d) Draw the vector $_s\vec{v}_g$ by joining the tail of $_s\vec{v}_w$ and the tip of $_w\vec{v}_g$. You could then use such a diagram to measure velocity. In this problem, the swimmer's velocity relative to the ground, or $_s\vec{v}_g$, is 5.0 km/h[N37°E].

It's often helpful to draw the velocity vectors for a question before drawing the vector diagram that shows how they're related. For this problem, the individual vectors look like this:

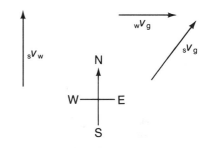

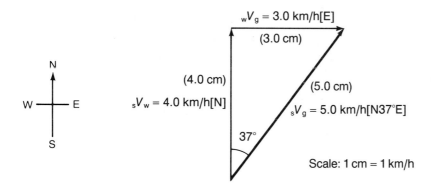

You could also solve this problem using the Pythagorean theorem. There are two ways, therefore, to find answers to problems using vector diagrams. You can draw

1. an accurate scale diagram and take measurements from it, or
2. a diagram that is roughly to scale and use algebra and trigonometry to find an answer.

Practice

1. A swimmer jumps into a river and swims straight for the other side at 1.5 km/h[N] relative to the water. There is a current in the river of 2.0 km/h[W]. What is the swimmer's velocity relative to the shore?

2. A conductor in a train travelling at 12.0 km/h[N] walks across the aisle at 5.0 km/h[E] relative to the train. What is his velocity relative to the ground?

3. A mouse is crawling inside a cart which is being pushed across the deck of a moving boat. The mouse is moving at 0.5 m/s[E] relative to the cart. The cart is travelling at 1.2 m/s[E] relative to the surface of the boat, and the boat is moving at 4.0 m/s[N] relative to the water. What is the velocity of the mouse relative to the water?

3.6 Airplane Navigation Problems

Vector diagrams are useful in solving a wide variety of navigation problems. The principles that we established for swimmers and boats in the previous section are also valid for aircraft. Flying objects are affected by the wind in the same way that floating or swimming objects are carried downstream by the current.

An airplane that can fly at 250 km/h in still air will only travel over the ground at 200 km/h if flying into a 50 km/h wind. Flying in the same direction as this wind will increase the plane's ground velocity to 300 km/h.

The plane's velocity relative to the ground is found by adding the plane's velocity relative to the air and the velocity of the air relative to the ground. Pilots have special names for each of these vectors, as shown in the table.

Symbol	Velocity vector	Speed	Direction
$\vec{_pv_a}$	plane's velocity relative to air	air speed	heading
$\vec{_av_g}$	wind velocity (velocity of air relative to ground)	wind speed	wind direction
$\vec{_pv_g}$	plane's velocity relative to ground	ground speed	track

The relationship between the vectors is stated as:

$$\vec{_pv_g} = \vec{_pv_a} + \vec{_av_g}$$

Air navigation problems are solved with vector diagrams in exactly the same way as river-crossing problems. The vectors in this section, however, will not always be at right angles to one another as they were in the previous examples.

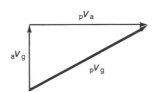

$$_a\vec{V_g} + _p\vec{V_a} = _p\vec{V_g}$$

Use this vector relationship stated above to solve these sample problems.

Sample Problems

1. An airplane has a velocity of 240 km/h[E] relative to the air. An 80 km/h wind is blowing towards the south. Calculate the velocity of the airplane relative to the ground.
   We can state that:
   $$\vec{_pV_g} = \vec{_pV_a} + \vec{_aV_g}$$
   $$= 240 \text{ km/h[E]} + 80 \text{ km/h[S]}$$

   Since the vectors to be added do not both lie along the same straight line a vector diagram is required. The vector diagram in the margin shows the solution. The tail of the second vector is placed at the tip of the first. The resultant vector then goes from the tail of the first vector to the tip of the second. Measuring this vector gives the magnitude of the resultant velocity and the angle at its tail gives its direction.

   The velocity of the plane relative to the ground is 253 km/h[E18°S].

2. A pilot wants to fly due west. The airplane has a velocity of 200 km/h relative to the air. There is a 62 km/h wind blowing to the north. Determine the heading the pilot should use and the velocity of the plane relative to the ground.

   Since the wind will tend to carry the plane northward the pilot must aim slightly towards the south to compensate for the wind. Draw a dotted line to represent the east→west direction. Draw the wind velocity vector $\vec{_aV_g}$ so that its tip is located on the dotted line. Then draw a second vector $\vec{_pV_a}$ 10 cm long (200 km/h) so that its tip is on the tail of the first vector and its tail is on the dotted line. The resultant vector, $\vec{_pV_g}$, goes from the tail of $\vec{_pV_a}$ to the tip of $\vec{_aV_g}$.
   By measurement we see that the resultant velocity is 190 km/h and the heading should be [W18°S].

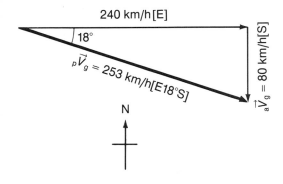

Scale: 1 cm = 40 km/h

A wind of 20 km/h[N] is called a "south wind" because it blows from the south.

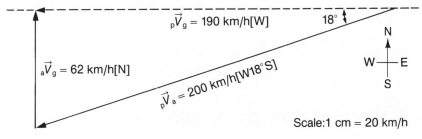

Practice

1. A plane has a velocity of 300 km/h relative to the air. If the pilot points the plane straight north, when there is a wind of 80 km/h blowing towards the west, what will the resultant velocity of the plane be?

2. An airplane pilot checks her instruments and finds that the speed of the plane relative to the air is 325 km/h. The instruments also show that the plane is pointed in a direction [S30°W]. A radio report indicates that the wind velocity is 80 km/h[W]. What is the velocity of the plane relative to the ground as it is recorded by an air traffic controller in a nearby airport?

3. A blimp pilot wants to travel north. The blimp can move at 26 km/h in still air. There is a wind of 10 km/h[E].
   (a) What is the heading? (That is, which way should the pilot point the blimp?)
   (b) How fast will the blimp travel relative to the ground?

4. An airplane pilot wants to fly east. The plane has a velocity of 500 km/h relative to the air. A wind is blowing at 50.0 km/h[N]. Calculate
   (a) the proper heading,
   (b) the magnitude of the plane's velocity relative to the ground.

3.7 Uniform Circular Motion

The examples of acceleration we have considered so far have involved a change of speed. Is it possible to have an acceleration when an object's speed is constant? The answer is yes. Since velocity is a vector quantity, when an object moving at a constant speed changes direction, a change in velocity occurs.

A ball being swung around on a string at a uniform speed provides a simple example of this type of acceleration. The strobe photograph in the margin shows images of the moving ball that are equally spaced in both time and position. Suppose the ball is moving in a horizontal circle and in a clockwise direction. When it is in the "twelve o'clock" position, it is moving toward the east. When the ball is at the "three o'clock" position, it is moving toward the south. During the entire movement of the ball around the circle, it is always changing its direction of motion. Since the velocity is constantly changing direction, the ball must be accelerating, even though the speed remains constant.

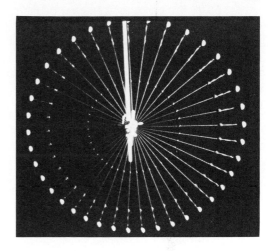

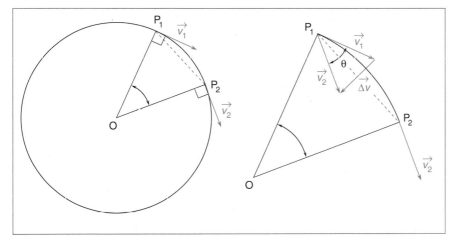

To calculate the average acceleration of the ball, we need to determine the change of velocity during the time interval Δt. In the left diagram above, the ball moves from position P_1 to position P_2 during the time interval Δt. The arrows $\vec{v}_1$ and $\vec{v}_2$ represent the velocities of the ball at these two positions. At any instant in time, the velocity of the ball is tangent to the circular path and perpendicular to a radius drawn to its location.

During the time interval Δt, a change in velocity, $\Delta \vec{v}$, must be added to $\vec{v}_1$ to produce the new velocity of the ball, $\vec{v}_2$. Positioning $\vec{v}_1$ and $\Delta \vec{v}$ tip to tail in a vector diagram (above right) gives $\vec{v}_2$. The change in direction of the velocity is shown by the angle θ, between $\vec{v}_1$ and $\vec{v}_2$.

Because the velocity vectors at P_1 and P_2 are perpendicular to their respective radii, angle P_1OP_2 equals angle θ. Therefore, the triangle formed by $\vec{v}_1$, $\vec{v}_2$, and $\Delta \vec{v}$ is similar to triangle P_1OP_2. Therefore:

$$\frac{\Delta v}{\text{chord } P_1P_2} = \frac{v_1}{R}$$

For a small angle Θ, chord P_1P_2 is nearly the same length as arc P_1P_2. Using this approximation, we can write the equation:

$$\frac{\Delta v}{\text{arc } P_1P_2} = \frac{v_1}{R}$$

Since arc length P_1P_2 is the actual distance the ball travels in time interval Δt at speed v, then arc length $P_1P_2 = v\Delta t$. Thus:

$$\frac{\Delta v}{v\Delta t} = \frac{v}{R}$$

or

$$\frac{\Delta v}{\Delta t} = \frac{v^2}{R}$$

$$a = \frac{v^2}{R}$$

This equation gives the acceleration of an object travelling in a circular path with a uniform speed. It has been derived for the case when angle Θ is very small—that is, when the time interval Δt of the velocity change is very small. The approximation becomes better and better as Δt becomes smaller. In other words, the equation above gives the acceleration of the object at any instant along its circular path. But what is the direction of the acceleration? Look again at the vector diagram on the previous page. Notice that Δv points towards the center of the circle. The inward acceleration is called **centripetal acceleration.** The name *centripetal* comes from the Greek expression for "center seeking."

$$a_c = \frac{v^2}{R}$$

Even though these cars move at a constant speed, they are accelerating. The direction of acceleration is inward, toward the center of the track.

Sample Problems

1. A car turns a circular curve with a speed of 20 m/s. If the radius of the curve is 100 m, what is the centripetal acceleration of the car?

$$a_c = \frac{v^2}{R}$$

$$= \frac{(20 \text{ m/s})^2}{(100 \text{ m})}$$

$$a_c = 4.0 \text{ m/s}^2$$

2. A ball on a string swings in a horizontal circle of radius 2.0 m. If its centripetal acceleration is 15 m/s², what is the speed of the ball?

$$a_c = \frac{v^2}{R}$$

Therefore, $v = \sqrt{a_c R}$

$$= \sqrt{(15 \text{ m/s}^2)(2.0 \text{ m})}$$

$$v = 5.5 \text{ m/s}$$

For most objects moving at a constant speed in a circular path, it is easier to measure the period of motion than to measure the speed. Since $v = \dfrac{\Delta d}{\Delta t}$, and Δd is the circumference of the circle, then $v = \dfrac{2\pi R}{T}$, where T is the period of motion (Δt for one circumference of the circle).   Therefore, $a_c = \dfrac{v^2}{R}$

$$= \frac{(2\pi R/T)^2}{R}$$

$$a_c = \frac{4\pi^2 R}{T^2}$$

Sample Problems

1. What is the centripetal acceleration of a small girl standing at the outer edge of a carousel with a radius of 2.0 m, which makes one complete rotation in 6.0 s?

$$a_c = \frac{4\pi^2 R}{T^2}$$

$$= \frac{4\pi^2 (2.0 \text{ m})}{(6.0 \text{ s})^2}$$

$$a_c = 2.2 \text{ m/s}^2$$

2. An airplane flies in a horizontal circle of radius 500 m. If its centripetal acceleration is 20 m/s^2, how long does it take to complete the circle?

$$a_c = \frac{4\pi^2 R}{T^2}$$

$$\text{thus, } T^2 = \frac{4\pi^2 R}{a_c}$$

$$T = \sqrt{\frac{4\pi^2 R}{a_c}}$$

$$= \sqrt{\frac{4\pi^2(500 \text{ m})}{(20 \text{ m/s}^2)}}$$

$$T = 31 \text{ s}$$

Practice

1. What is the centripetal acceleration of a toy race car travelling around a circular track of radius 0.75 m with a speed of 4.5 m/s?
2. What is the speed of a locomotive that travels around a circular curve of radius 250 m with a centripetal acceleration of 1.5 m/s^2?
3. Patrons on an amusement park ride called the Rotor stand with their backs against the wall of a revolving cylinder. If the cylinder has a radius of 4.0 m and completes a rotation every 2.5 s, what is the centripetal acceleration of the riders?
4. NASA places communication satellites into Earth orbits with radii of about 42 000 km. If the centripetal acceleration of one such satellite was 0.22 m/s^2, what is the period of motion for this satellite?

Testing for Centripetal Acceleration

There is an interesting demonstration you can try to show that an object moving in a circle at constant speed is indeed accelerating.

Get a jar with a tightly fitting screw-on lid and cement a small loop of copper wire to the center of the inside of the lid. Tie one end of a short string to the loop and the other end to a cork. Fill the jar with water, screw on the lid, and turn the jar upside down.

This instrument is called an accelerometer. When the jar is stationary, the cork is straight up and down. Accelerate the jar horizontally. The cork always points in the direction of the acceleration. Try it a few more times to make sure.

Now for the test. Hold the jar at arm's length and turn round and round at a steady speed. Which way should the cork point? What should happen if there is really no acceleration at all?

You could also use a helium balloon to demonstrate centripetal acceleration. With a friend, take the balloon for a drive in a car with the windows closed. Have your friend hold the balloon on a string so that it moves freely. The balloon will act as an accelerometer and will "lean" in the direction of the car's acceleration.

Incidentally, both the cork in the jar and the balloon on the string indicate the magnitude of the acceleration. The angle between the string and the vertical position is actually a measure of the magnitude of the acceleration.

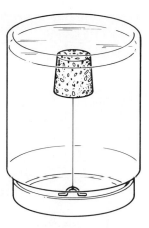

A jam-jar accelerometer

➡ CAUTION: Make sure the balloon cannot move to block the driver's forward or rearview vision.

Chapter Summary

1. Scalar quantities have magnitude only.
2. Vector quantities have both magnitude and direction.
3. Displacement is a vector quantity that includes a direction and a distance.
4. Velocity is a vector quantity that includes a direction and a speed.
5. Acceleration is a vector quantity. It therefore requires a direction for a complete description.
6. Vector quantities are represented by arrows called vectors. The arrow's length is proportional to the magnitude of the quantity. The arrow's direction indicates the quantity's direction.
7. Vectors are added by joining them head to tail. The vector sum is represented by an arrow drawn from the tail of the first vector to the head of the last vector.
8. In navigation problems, an object's resultant velocity relative to the ground is the vector sum of the velocity relative to the air or water and the velocity of the air or water relative to the ground.
9. An object moving at a uniform speed in a circle has an acceleration towards the center of the circle. This is called a centripetal acceleration. Two equations for centripetal acceleration are

$$a_c = \frac{v^2}{R} \text{ and } a_c = \frac{4\pi^2 R}{T^2}$$

Chapter Review

Discussion

1. Why do airplane pilots prefer to land and take off by heading into the wind?
2. Satellites are often launched so that they orbit the earth from west to east. What advantage is there in selecting this direction instead of east to west?
3. Sometimes when you sit in a car at a traffic light and look at the car beside you, you feel that you are moving backwards. In fact, your vehicle is at rest on the pavement. How is this possible?
4. Suppose you are being carried along by the wind as you ride in a hot air balloon. The wind velocity is 40 km/h[S]. You hold up a small flag. In which direction will the flag point?
5. An airplane pilot points his plane due east. A wind is blowing from the north. Assuming his destination is due east from the starting point, explain why the pilot will not reach it.
6. A girl is capable of swimming at 3.0 m/s in still water. She jumps into a river in which the current is 4.0 m/s. Is it possible for her to reach a point directly across the river from her starting point? Explain your answer.
7. Imagine that you are twirling a stone attached to a string in a horizontal circle about you. If you lengthen the string so that the radius of the circle is two times longer but do not change the period of motion, how does the centripetal acceleration of the rock change?

Problems

8. A boat sails 120 km[E60°N], then 60 km[W]. What is its displacement?
9. A balloon drifts 20 km[S60°E], then its engines are turned on and it flies 20 km[S60°W]. What is its total displacement?
10. A man inside a plane flying at 400 km/h[W] fires a gun eastwards. The muzzle velocity of the gun is 450 km/h. What is the velocity of the bullet relative to the ground?
11. A streetcar accelerates from rest at 2.5 m/s²[W]. A woman inside the streetcar is walking at 2.0 m/s[E] relative to the streetcar. What is her velocity relative to the ground at:
    (a) 0 s?   (b) 1.0 s?   (c) 2.0 s?   (d) 3.0 s?   (e) 4.0 s?

12. A man is walking inside a railway boxcar at 3.0 m/s[N] relative to the boxcar. The boxcar is rolling along a ferryboat at 5.0 m/s[S] relative to the ferryboat. The ferryboat is heading north at 4.0 m/s. What is the velocity of the man relative to (a) the ferryboat? (b) the water?

13. A boy and a girl both swim at 3.0 m/s. They jump into a river 1.0 km across, with a current of 2.0 m/s[E].
    (a) The boy faces due north at all times. What is his velocity relative to the ground?
    (b) The girl swims so that she ends up directly across from her starting point. What is her velocity relative to the ground?
    (c) How many minutes does each take to cross the river?
    (d) How far apart are the boy and girl when they reach the opposite bank?

14. A motorboat is headed [E30°N] with its engine set to move the boat at 30 km/h in still water. There is a current of 15 km/h[S]. What is the velocity of the boat relative to the shore?

15. A boy in a car moving at 10 km/h[N] wants to throw a ball to a girl standing on the right-hand side of the road. He is able to throw the ball at 20 km/h. He wants the ball to go straight east, directly to her.
    (a) Relative to the car, which way should he throw the ball in order to do this?
    (b) Relative to the ground, how fast will the ball travel to reach her?

16. A pilot wants to fly north. The plane has an air speed of 350 km/h. There is a 25 km/h wind blowing to the west.
    (a) What is the plane's velocity relative to the ground?
    (b) What is its heading?

17. A small plane is flying east at 100 km/h relative to the air, in a wind blowing at 20 km/h[S].
    (a) What is the plane's speed relative to the ground?
    (b) What is its track?

18. A pilot flies 300 km[E] and then back home 300 km[W] at an air speed of 300 km/h. A 30 km/h wind is blowing to the east.
    (a) What is the pilot's velocity relative to the ground for each leg of the trip?
    (b) What is the time for each leg of the trip, in minutes?
    (c) How long would the trip take if there were no wind, in minutes?

19. A ball rolls up a hill, starting at 10 m/s[up] and accelerating at 3.0 m/s^2[down]. What is its velocity after
    (a) 1.0 s? (b) 3.0 s? (c) 4.0 s?

20. A ship travels at 30 km/h[N30°E] for 10 h, and then at 20 km/h[W60°S] for 17 h. What is its total displacement?

21. A man is standing on the deck of a freighter heading north at 10 km/h. He measures the wind velocity and gets a reading of 10 km/h[E]. What is the actual wind velocity?
22. A pilot wants to fly a huge square path over the ground, 100 km[N], 100 km [W], 100 km[S], and then 100 km[E]. Her plane has an air speed of 100 km/h. A 50 km/h wind is blowing to the south. For each leg of the trip, calculate
    (a) the ground speed,
    (b) the heading,
    (c) the time, in minutes.
    (d) What would the saving in time if there were no wind?
23. A wheel with a radius of 50 cm is rolling along the ground at 10 m/s[E]. That is, the center point of the wheel is moving at 10 m/s[E].
    (a) What are the velocities of the top, bottom, front, and back points of the wheel, relative to its center?
    (b) What are the velocities of those four points relative to the ground?
    (c) In what direction are each of those four points accelerating?
24. A car, travelling at 25 m/s around a circular curve, has a centripetal acceleration of 8.3 m/s². What is the radius of the curve?
25. A traditional wristwatch has a second hand measuring 1.2 cm from center to tip. What is the centripetal acceleration of the tip of the second hand?
26. The moon, an Earth satellite with a period of about 27.3 days and a nearly circular orbit, has a centripetal acceleration of 2.7×10^{-3} m/s². What is the average distance from the Earth to the moon?

Meet Arlene Yakeley . . . Air Traffic Controller

Arlene works at an air traffic control center, where she is a Team Supervisor. Her job involves keeping track of and giving instructions to aircraft as they pass through a certain controlled airspace.

Q. How did you become an air traffic controller?
A. I actually started as a meteorologist. I saw some literature about meteorology in the guidance office at high school and thought it looked interesting—not an ordinary desk job. Then I went to college to study meteorology. After becoming involved in doing weather briefing for aviation, I decided to apply to be an air traffic controller.

Q. What's involved in being accepted for the program?
A. You take aptitude tests and are interviewed. Then, if you're accepted, you take a training course. The overall training takes about two years before you are licensed.

Q. How is the knowledge of physics involved in your work?
A. We're constantly dealing with the three factors of time, distance, and speed and how they interact. We have to figure out how long it will take any aircraft to reach a point that conflicts with another aircraft. We also need to understand the physics involved in flight. For example, centrifugal forces affect how fast an aircraft can turn—it takes longer to turn at a higher speed.

Q. What qualities make a good air traffic controller?
A. This is something constantly being investigated. New tests are being developed to assess exactly what qualities are required. Some that I know of are—the ability to tolerate stress and make quick decisions, ability in math and physics and spatial aptitude, and having a lot of personal confidence and a good memory.

Q. How does memory fit it?
A. You must remember which aircraft are your responsibility, what their destinations, their altitudes, and their speeds are, the type and characteristics of each aircraft, and what heading you've been assigned. This all has to be in your head while you work, and when it's very busy you might be remembering all of this information for about 25 different aircraft.

Q. At what point do you become involved with the aircraft?
A. Once the plane has taken off it appears on our radar screen. The airline pilot files a flight plan that indicates the "airways" that are to be used, the cruising altitude, the estimated time en route, and so on. If the plane is flying in my sector, in other words, the airspace that I'm in charge of, I get this information. It comes to the controller who is working on the data position—part of the two person team controlling each sector.

Q. How do you work as a team?
A. One controller sits at the data position board with the estimates on expected aircraft. The other sits in front of a radarscope where there is also a panel of phone lines and radio frequencies. Our main job is to provide vertical and horizontal separations between each aircraft—we call this a "block" of protected airspace.

Q. How big is this block of airspace?
A. We watch the radar screen to see that the aircraft are eight kilometers away from each other or separated by 300 m in altitude.

Q. Do you communicate with the pilots all the time?
A. Yes. We speak to the pilots on radio frequencies directing them as they fly through our airspace and we speak to other controllers on dedicated phone lines. When an aircraft is moving out of our sector we communicate with the controller in the area that the aircraft is moving into.

Q. Why do you like your job?
A. I like the independence. When you're working, you have a very responsible position and you are in charge. You make your own decisions. I feel a sense of accomplishment, particularly after a busy period when I've solved a lot of problems.

4

Bodies in Free Fall

Chapter Objectives

☐ **Measure and record data** of the motion of a freely falling object and **determine** the acceleration due to gravity, using a velocity-time graph.

☐ **State** the value of the acceleration due to gravity of a freely falling object near the surface of the Earth.

☐ **Relate** the time interval, the initial velocity, the final velocity, and the displacement in free-fall problems.

☐ **Relate** the length of a pendulum to its period of vibration and the acceleration due to gravity.

☐ **Describe** methods that can be used to determine the acceleration due to gravity.

Aristotle (384-322 B.C.)

Galileo Galilei (1564-1642)

Introduction

In the first few chapters you learned some of the skills required to describe motion. We will now use some of those skills to analyze the motion of objects, or "bodies", in free fall. A free fall refers to any body falling under the influence of gravity alone. For example, a parachute produces a "drag" on a falling body. A fall resisted by a parachute would not be a free fall. The only force that acts on a freely falling body—for example, a stone dropped from a tree—is gravity. In considering the stone's fall, several questions may come to mind. Does the stone fall with uniform motion? With uniform acceleration? Or is it a combination of the two? Which objects fall faster—heavy or light ones? These and other questions will form the focus of our work in this chapter.

4.1 How Do Things Fall?

To begin, let us consider how people have responded to this question over time. Aristotle, who lived in the third century B.C., believed that objects would fall at a constant speed and that the speed would depend on the mass of the object. In other words, the speed of a falling object would be proportional to its mass. A two-kilogram stone, for example, would fall twice as fast as a one-kilogram stone.

Aristotle's understanding of the behavior of freely falling objects went unchallenged for nearly 2000 years. For one reason, it is difficult to tell by observation alone the type of motion an object exhibits. For another, theories that seemed reasonable had not been tested by experiment.

Galileo Galilei, the great Italian scientist, finally did challenge Aristotle's ideas at the beginning of the seventeenth century. Galileo reasoned that an object of similar shape with twice the mass of another object would not fall at twice the rate if dropped from the same height. In addition, he hypothesized that objects do not fall at a constant speed, but accelerate.

To test his hypotheses, Galileo devised a clever experiment. To do so, he had to overcome a severe limitation. To that point in history no precision timing devices had been perfected—not even the pendulum clock. His solution involved rolling a ball down an inclined plane. He reasoned that the ball's motion would be the same as that of a freely falling body. The motion, however, would occur at a slower rate because of the inclined plane. This, he believed, would simply "dilute" the force of gravity and make it possible to measure the time intervals as the motion occurred. He used a container with a hole in it as a timer. He measured time by finding the mass of water that ran through the hole during the time interval it took the ball to roll down the slope. He then applied the following equation to the motion:

$$\Delta d = v_1 \Delta t + \frac{1}{2}a(\Delta t)^2$$

Assuming that $v_1 = 0$, we can rearrange the equation as follows:

$$\Delta d = 0 + \frac{1}{2}a(\Delta t)^2$$

$$a = \frac{2\Delta d}{(\Delta t)^2}$$

Many consider Galileo to be the father of modern science. He was the first to develop his theories using the results of experiments he devised to test them.

Since all of the problems in this chapter involve motion along a line, we will once again omit the vector signs above the variables in the equations.

Another way of stating Galileo's result is that

$$\frac{2\Delta d_1}{(\Delta t_1)^2} = \frac{2\Delta d_2}{(\Delta t_2)^2} = \frac{2\Delta d_3}{(\Delta t_3)^2}$$

Galileo and his inclined plane

For a slope inclined at a particular angle, Galileo found that the ratio on the right side of this equation was a constant. He concluded, then, that the ball in his experiment, rolling as it was under the effect of diluted gravity, experienced uniform acceleration. In addition, he concluded that the ball would have a constant acceleration if it were dropped and allowed to fall freely. The acceleration would be greater, though, than for the ball rolling down the incline.

Aristotle's ideas were so entrenched that Galileo had difficulty persuading others that objects fall with uniform acceleration, not uniform motion. To convince those who doubted his logic, Galileo devised a clever thought experiment that used Aristotle's own logic to disprove the Greek philosopher's hypothesis.

Galileo's argument suggested the following. Consider two bodies of different mass. According to Aristotle the heavier mass would fall faster than the lighter one. Based on this theory, Galileo reasoned that if the two masses were joined together with a string, the heavier mass would speed up the lighter mass, and the lighter mass would slow down the heavier mass. He pointed out that this would cause the speed of the combined masses to be between the speeds of the two masses when they fell independently. But when the two masses were joined, he noted, they would actually create a heavier mass, which, according to Aristotle's theory, would fall faster than either of the two separate masses. This contradiction showed the flaw in Aristotle's theory.

It is possible that over the years, Galileo's thought experiment has been represented symbolically by the story of how Galileo dropped two objects from the Leaning Tower of Pisa. Seemingly, however, this story has no basis in historical fact.

Galileo changed how we view falling objects, but, perhaps more importantly, he changed how we view the scientific process. He was the first scientist to design experiments to test his hypotheses and develop his theories. Today, all scientific ideas are subject to rigorous testing before they are accepted by the scientific community. That doesn't mean that theories are never again questioned. They are considered sound, however, until new scientific evidence leads to new experiments and, sometimes, revised or new theories.

Galileo's discoveries and his use of mathematics to solve physical problems set the stage for the great English physicist and mathematician, Isaac Newton.

Legend has it that Galileo dropped two objects of different mass from the Leaning Tower of Pisa and found that they hit the ground at the same time. Historians are quite certain that Galileo did not conduct such an experiment. There is evidence, however, that a Dutch scientist, Simon Stevinus (1548-1620) did something like that a few years before Galileo began conducting his experiments.

4.2 Free Fall Analyzed

We are no longer handicapped by the lack of technology that Galileo experienced. Several investigations at the end of this chapter will help you see what happens to objects in free fall. In the meantime, we can make some preliminary conclusions using the photograph in the margin.

This photo was taken by setting the camera on time exposure. The apparatus was set up in a dark room where a light stroboscope flashed at a constant rate. The shutter of the camera was opened and the ball was dropped. Each time the light strobe flashed, an image of the ball formed on the film. (See Investigation 4.3 for a detailed analysis.)

The photograph shows that the distance the ball travels between successive flashes gets successively larger. This means that the ball is accelerating. A detailed analysis would show that the acceleration is constant and that it has a value of 9.8 m/s². Do all masses fall with the same acceleration? We would have to say that it depends on the situation.

Look at the strobe photograph on the next page of two balls of different mass dropped from the same level. We can see that in this portion of the fall the balls have the same acceleration. Would they, however, continue to accelerate at the same rate *beyond* the distance shown in the photograph? And would we get similar results with other pairs of objects?

We know that a feather doesn't accelerate as fast as a rock. As a matter of fact, it may not accelerate at all. What is the problem here?

Galileo explained that for very light objects or for objects with a large surface area compared to their mass, the air resistance they experience causes them to accelerate less. In fact, when air resistance is large enough, an object will stop accelerating and fall at a constant speed. So, in a sense, Aristotle was actually correct. There *are* situations in which bodies fall with a constant velocity.

An object falling through the atmosphere eventually reaches a velocity where air resistance is great enough to prevent further acceleration. A sky diver, for example, will reach this **terminal velocity** after about 10 s of fall. As a result, we must be careful to qualify our statements. In situations where air resistance can be ignored, a body will fall with an acceleration of 9.8 m/s². Galileo himself suggested that if all the air were to be removed, then all objects, including feathers, would have the same acceleration. You can test these ideas by performing Investigations 4.1 and 4.2.

Acceleration due to gravity is such an important quantity in physics that it has its own symbol—g. Near the surface of planet Earth, the value of g is 9.8 m/s². As we move away from the Earth's

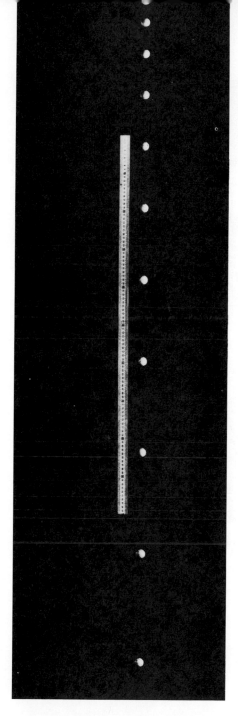

A strobe photograph of a falling ball. The time between flashes is 0.050 s.

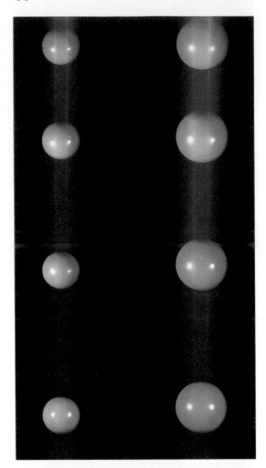

The strobe photograph above shows two balls of different mass dropped at same instant.

surface, the value of g decreases. Since the elevation above sea level varies from place to place, the value of g varies slightly at different locations. In this text, however, you can assume that $g = 9.8$ m/s^2, unless told otherwise. The direction of the acceleration due to gravity is *always* down toward the center of the Earth.

Sample Problems

(*Note*: Since freely falling bodies experience uniform acceleration, the equations we derived in Chapter 2 also apply when solving free fall problems. A common convention is to designate down as negative and up as positive.)

1. A girl throws a rock straight down from a bridge at 15 m/s. How fast is it going 3.0 s later?

   We know from the question that
   $$v_1 = 15 \text{ m/s[down]} = -15 \text{ m/s}$$
   $$\Delta t = 3.0 \text{ s}$$

   However, since the rock is in free fall, the instant it leaves the girl's hand we can also assume that
   $$a = g = 9.8 \text{m/s}^2\text{[down]} = -9.8 \text{ m/s}^2$$

   To find the velocity of the rock, we use the equation
   $$v_2 = v_1 + a\Delta t$$
   $$= -15 \text{ m/s} + (-9.8 \text{ m/s}^2) \, (3.0 \text{ s})$$
   $$= -15 \text{ m/s} + -29.4 \text{ m/s}$$
   $$= -44.4 \text{ m/s, or } 44 \text{ m/s[down]}$$

   Therefore, the rock acquires a velocity of 44 m/s[down] in 3.0 s.

2. An egg drops through a hole in the bottom of a nest. How far does it fall in 1.0 s?

   Assuming that the egg is in free fall after leaving the nest, we can state the following:
   $$v_1 = 0$$
   $$\Delta t = 1.0 \text{ s}$$
   $$a = 9.8 \text{ m/s}^2\text{[down]} = -9.8 \text{ m/s}^2$$

   $$\Delta d = v_1 \Delta t + \frac{1}{2} a(\Delta t)^2$$

   $$= (0) \, (1.0 \text{ s}) + \left(\frac{1}{2}\right) (-9.8 \text{ m/s}^2) \, (1.0 \text{ s})^2$$

   $$= -4.9 \text{ m, or } 4.9 \text{ m[down]}$$

   Therefore, the egg falls 4.9 m in 1.0 s.

3. A girl throws a baseball straight up at 15 m/s. What is the ball's velocity 2.0 s later?

$$v_1 = 15 \text{ m/s[up]} = 15 \text{ m/s}$$
$$a = 9.8 \text{ m/s}^2\text{[down]} = -9.8 \text{ m/s}^2$$
$$\Delta t = 2.0 \text{ s}$$

$$v_2 = v_1 + a\Delta t$$
$$= 15 \text{ m/s} + (-9.8 \text{ m/s}^2)\ (2.0 \text{ s})$$
$$= 15 \text{ m/s} - 19.6 \text{ m/s}$$
$$= -4.6 \text{ m/s}$$

After 2.0 s the ball is moving downward at 4.6 m/s.

*P*ractice

1. What velocity does a freely falling object reach after 4.0 s if it starts from rest?
2. A boy throws a rock into a deep well with a velocity of 10 m/s[down]. What is the velocity of the rock 2.5 s later?
3. A prankster drops a water-filled balloon from the balcony of a high-rise. How long docs it take for the balloon to fall 44.1 m?
4. A girl uses a slingshot to fire a stone straight up at 24 m/s. What is the stone's velocity 3.0 s later? What is its displacement 3.0 s after it was fired?

The 1968 Summer Olympics were held in Mexico City which has a high elevation. As a result, the value of g is slightly less than at most locations on Earth. The air also is a little thinner. In which events would the high elevation make it easier for athletes to set new world records?

4.3 Gravity and the Pendulum

You can make a simple pendulum by attaching a small, heavy mass, such as a few large washers, to the end of a long piece of string. Fasten the other end of the string to something sturdy, and start the pendulum swinging.

The **period** of the pendulum is the time required for one complete cycle; the pendulum must cross from one side of its swing to the other and back again. The mass at the end of the string is called the **bob**. The pendulum's **amplitude** is the maximum sideways displacement of the bob from its rest position.

The period of the pendulum depends on its length, and on g. The mass of the bob doesn't matter, as long as it is not too small. Nor does the amplitude, as long as it is not too large. Also, as long as the bob is compact and dense, air resistance will not affect the pendulum significantly.

If $\qquad T = 2\pi\sqrt{\dfrac{L}{g}}$

(first square both sides)

then $\qquad T^2 = 4\pi^2\dfrac{L}{g}$

(now multiply both sides by g)

and $\qquad gT^2 = 4\pi^2 L$

(now divide both sides by T^2)

so that $\qquad g = \dfrac{4\pi^2 L}{T^2}$

The equation for calculating the period of a pendulum is:

$$T = 2\pi\sqrt{\dfrac{L}{g}}$$

where T is the period of the pendulum, in seconds

$\qquad L$ is the length of the pendulum, measured from the top end of the string to the center of the bob, in meters

$\qquad g$ is the acceleration due to gravity, in meters per second squared

$\qquad \pi = 3.14$

Using the above relationship and taking measurements of the period and length of the pendulum, it is possible to determine the value of g.

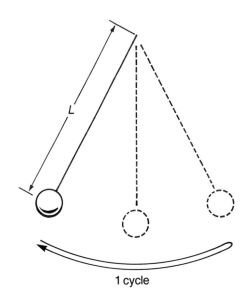

1 cycle

Sample Problems

What is the period of a pendulum 1.0 m long?

$$T = 2\pi\sqrt{\dfrac{L}{g}}$$

$$= 2\pi\sqrt{\dfrac{1.0 \text{ m}}{9.8 \text{ m/s}^2}}$$

$$= 2\pi\sqrt{0.102 \text{ s}^2}$$

$$= 2(3.14)\,(0.319 \text{ s})$$

$$= 2.0 \text{ s}$$

A pendulum 1.0 m long is used in some grandfather clocks. Each half cycle marks one second. A clockwork motor gives the pendulum a small push at the right moment during each swing, to keep it going.

Practice

1. What is the period of a pendulum
   (a) 4.0 m long? (b) 9.0 m long? (c) 16.0 m long?
2. What is the period of a 1.0 m pendulum on the moon, where g is one-sixth of that on Earth?
3. How long must a pendulum be to have a period of 1.0 s?
4. What is the acceleration due to gravity on the planet Mars if a 2.5 m pendulum on that planet has a period of 5.19 s?

4.4 Gravimetry

The study of acceleration due to gravity, and the measurement of this acceleration, is a major part of the science of gravimetry. The most accurate measurements are made at the International Bureau of Weights and Measures (BIPM), in France. Three methods have been used.

Starting in 1888, g was calculated by measuring the periods of pendulums. The best value obtained by this method for the local acceleration due to gravity is 9.809 398 m/s^2. This method is no longer used because it does not allow for changes in the length of a pendulum as it swings back and forth; even a steel pendulum will stretch a little.

The second method, initiated in 1951, involves photographing a falling meterstick made of platinum and iridium, graduated in millimeters. The stick falls inside a cylindrical vacuum chamber to eliminate air resistance. An illuminated scale on the stick gives out light flashes at regular intervals. The chamber's temperature is measured to allow for any expansion or contraction of the scale. For each fall, a camera records about 50 images that are analyzed to provide the value of g, which is 9.809 280 m/s^2.

The third method, in use since 1960, involves launching an object upwards by means of an elastic band and allowing it to fall. Three mirrors are arranged at each end of the projectile, and a constant laser light is reflected constantly from the object as it moves. The distance the object falls is then measured in terms of the wavelength of the light to an accuracy of about 10^{-9} m. Again, to ensure accuracy, the apparatus is enclosed in a vacuum chamber and cushioned to prevent vibration from the ground and from the shock of landing.

The results obtained since 1966 show an average value for g of 9.809 260 m/s^2, slightly less than the value obtained by the earlier methods. The new, more accurate, measurements show that g varies from time to time by about 0.000 000 4 m/s^2. The origin of these variations is not yet known.

Investigations

Investigation 4.1: Gravity

Problem:
What factors influence the motion of falling objects?

Materials:
this book
a large rubber stopper
a piece of paper slightly smaller than the cover of this book

Procedure:
1. The mass of this book is many times the mass of the rubber stopper. Hold the book horizontally at exactly the same height as the stopper and release them both simultaneously. Drop the book carefully so that it lands flat on its cover, and not on a corner. Note whether there is any great difference between the times the book and the stopper take to fall. Repeat several times to make sure of your observations.
2. Drop the book and the piece of paper, both held horizontally, from the same height. Then shield the piece of paper from the air flow by placing it on top of the book, hold the book and paper horizontally, and drop them again. Compare the rates at which they fall each time.
3. Crumple the paper into a tiny ball and drop it side by side with the book. Note what happens.

Questions:
1. Why does the ball of paper keep up with the book, whereas the sheet of paper does not?
2. What is the rule for falling objects, when there is little or no air resistance?
3. According to your results, if you dropped a bus and an apple from the same height, which would hit the Earth first? Explain.

Investigation 4.2: Falling Objects and Air

Problem:
How does the presence of air affect the rate at which a body falls?

Materials:
vacuum pump
glass tube
special fittings or stoppers
styrofoam
coin

 CAUTION: Put on your safety goggles.

 CAUTION: Use a safety shield to confine flying glass in the event that the glass tube implodes.

Procedure:
1. Obtain a glass tube similar to the one in the illustration.
2. Insert a coin and a piece of styrofoam into the tube.
3. Hold the tube vertically so that the coin and styrofoam both slide to one end.
4. Now flip the tube over quickly so that the styrofoam and coin fall to the other end. Repeat this several times to see in which order they hit the bottom.
5. Now attach the tube to the vacuum pump and pump the air from the tube. When as much air has been removed as possible, close the valve to keep air from entering the tube. (You may close the valve by attaching a pinch clamp to the hose joining the tube and pump.)
6. Again flip the tube as before to see how the styrofoam and coin fall.

Questions:
1. Describe and account for the different results when air was and was not present in the tube.
2. Pretend that the Earth has no atmosphere. What will you predict about the acceleration of falling objects, regardless of their shape and mass?

Investigation 4.3: Motion of a Freely Falling Object

(Method I)

Problem:
What type of motion is experienced by an object in free fall?

Materials:
ball bearing
strobe light
Polaroid camera and tripod
meterstick
magnifier with scale (00.1 mm graduation)

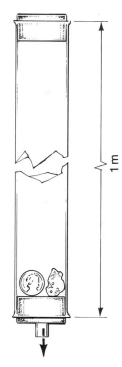

to vacuum pump

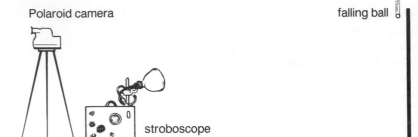

Polaroid camera

falling ball

stroboscope

CAUTION: The strobe light is fragile and hot. Wear safety goggles and handle with care.

Procedure:
1. Set the camera on a tripod several meters away from the ball bearing. (The ball bearing's fall should fill the picture frame, and its path should be just to the side of the meterstick.)
2. Set the camera on time exposure. (If the camera adjusts the exposure time automatically, put a piece of black tape over the electronic eye.) Now focus the camera on the bearing and meterstick.
3. Set the strobe light at a convenient frequency of about 10 Hz (ten flashes per second). To analyze the motion you will need to know the strobe frequency as accurately as possible.
4. To take the picture proceed as follows:
   (a) Darken the room and turn on the stroboscope.
   (b) Hold down the shutter release button to open the shutter.
   (c) Drop the bearing.
   (d) The instant the bearing hits the floor, release the shutter.
   (e) Develop the picture.
5. If the procedure has worked correctly, your picture should look similar to the one on page 87.
6. Use a ruler to measure the length of the meterstick on the print.
7. Determine the scale factor to be used with all the following measurements. The scale factor is

$$\frac{\text{actual length of meterstick, or } 1000 \text{ mm}}{\text{length of meterstick on print, (in mm)}}$$

Suppose the image of the meterstick is 40 mm long. The scale factor will then be

$$\frac{1000 \text{ mm}}{40 \text{ mm}}, \text{ or } 25.$$

To convert any measurement in the photograph into its actual length, multiply it by the scale factor. In our example the scale factor is 25, but you will need to calculate it for your own photograph.

If hand magnifiers of the type described in the experiment are not available, you can make measurements as follows. Enlarge the photograph with an opaque projector. Project the photograph onto a large piece of paper and mark the position of the images in the photograph. Ensure that you also note the position of the ends of the meterstick on the paper. To analyze the motion, simply make the measurements from the markings on the paper.

8. Prepare and complete a data table. Use a hand magnifier with a built-in scale to determine the displacement for each interval.

Time	t (s)					
Displacement measured for interval	Δd (mm)					
Actual displacement for interval	Δd (cm)					
Actual average velocity for interval	v (cm/s)					

9. Construct a velocity-time graph for the motion.

Questions:
1. What does the shape of the graph tell you about the motion of a freely falling object?
2. Use the slope of the graph to calculate the acceleration in meters per second squared.
3. The accepted value of g is about 9.8 m/s². What is the percentage error of your measurement?
4. Could you have used a styrofoam ball in this investigation? Explain your answer.

Note: If you do not have the photographic equipment required for this experiment, use the photograph on page 87.

Investigation 4.4: Motion of a Freely Falling Body

(Method II)

Problem:
What type of motion is experienced by a freely falling body?

Materials:
recording timer
paper tape
1 kg mass
masking tape
power supply
connecting wires

A challenge: Use the listed materials to design and conduct an experiment to answer the problem posed above.
Hints:
• The procedure will be similar to the one used in Investigation 2.1.
• Use a time interval of $\frac{1}{30}$ s instead of $\frac{1}{10}$ s. (This will only be feasible if your timer operates at 60 vibrations/s, or 60 Hz.)

CAUTION: Write your procedure as a series of steps. Be sure to include the safety precautions you will use. Ask your instructor to approve your plans before carrying out your investigation.

Chapter 4

Investigation 4.5: Gravity and the Pendulum

Problem:
What is the value of g as calculated from the period of a pendulum?

Materials:
1.5 m string
6 large washers
stopwatch
meterstick

The divers are in free fall.

Procedure:
1. Make a pendulum about 1.5 m long, and measure its length carefully in meters. Measure from the top end of the pendulum to the center of the bob.
2. Start the pendulum swinging and measure the time for 20 complete cycles.
3. Calculate the time for one cycle.
4. Calculate g, using:
$$g = \frac{4\pi^2 L}{T^2}$$
5. Repeat, using two other lengths, say, 1.0 m and 0.5 m.
6. Calculate your average value of g.
7. Calculate your percentage error for g.
8. If you have time, see whether the period is affected by the use of nine or twelve washers for the bob, instead of six.
9. Of all the methods to find g, which is the most accurate?

Chapter Summary

1. When air resistance is minimal, all freely falling objects have the same downwards acceleration.
2. A ball rolling down an incline has a uniform acceleration.
3. Acceleration due to gravity is approximately constant near the Earth's surface, and has a value of:
$$g = 9.8 \text{ m/s}^2$$
4. The equations derived for uniform acceleration in Chapter 2 apply to freely falling objects.
5. The period of a pendulum is given by:
$$T = 2\pi\sqrt{\frac{L}{g}}$$

Chapter Review

Discussion

1. Galileo argued that by using an inclined plane he was "diluting gravity". What criticism could you make about this assumption?

2. Apollo astronaut David Scott performed a simple experiment on the moon's surface on July 31, 1972. He dropped a feather and a hammer at the same instant and from the same height.
   (a) Keeping in mind that the moon has no atmosphere, predict what Scott and millions of television viewers observed.
   (b) What prediction would Galileo have made? Aristotle?

3. Sketch a velocity-time graph for an object that falls from rest. Assume that it accelerates uniformly at the beginning and then gradually decreases its acceleration until it falls with uniform velocity (similar to a skydiver's fall before the parachute opens).

4. Galileo showed mathematically that the distance a freely falling body falls in successive equal time intervals is in the ratio of $1:3:5:7...$. If Galileo was correct, what should you hear if the device shown in the margin is dropped?

   (You may wish to perform this test. If you record it on a tape recorder at high speed and play it back on low speed, you'll be able to check Galileo's prediction more accurately.)

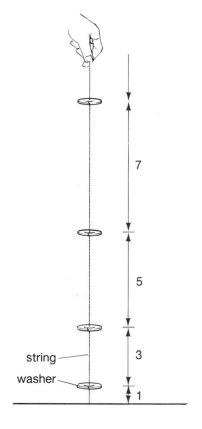

Problems

Use: $g = 9.80$ m/s^2

5. A tourist drops a rock from rest from a guard rail at an observation point overlooking a valley. What is the velocity of the rock at the following times:
   (a) 2.0 s?   (b) 6.0 s?

6. Determine the displacement for the rock in question 5 at:
   (a) 2.0 s   (b) 6.0 s

7. Suppose the tourist in question 5 threw the rock with an initial velocity of 8.0 m/s[down]. Determine the velocity and displacement of the rock at:
   (a) 2.0 s   (b) 6.0 s

8. The acceleration due to gravity on the moon is about 1.6 m/s^2. How long would it take the hammer referred to in question 2 to hit the surface of the moon, if it was dropped from a height of 1.8 m?

Numerical Answers to
Practice Problems

page 89
1. 39 m/s[down]
2. 35 m/s[down]
3. 3.0 s
4. 5.4 m/s[down]
   28 m[up]

page 90
1. (a) 4.0 s
   (b) 6.0 s
   (b) 8.0 s
2. 4.9 s
3. 0.25 m
4. 3.7 m/s²

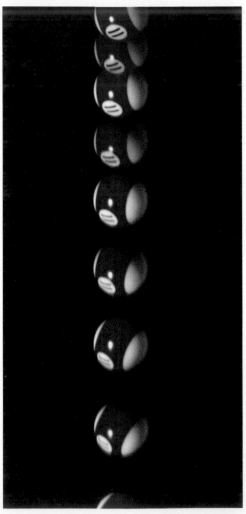

9. The Sears Tower in Chicago is 443 m high.
   (a) How long would it take a rock, dropped from the top, to reach the ground?
   (b) How fast would the rock be moving as it hit the ground (in meters per second and kilometers per hour)?
   (c) Would the rock actually reach the speed calculated in (b)? Discuss.
10. How much farther does a freely falling object fall in 10 s than in 1.0 s? (Divide one distance by the other to get a ratio.)
11. An astronaut arrives on a planet where the unit for time is a ces and the unit for distance is a tem. She drops a rock from a height of 20 tem and finds that it hits the ground in 2.0 ces.
   (a) Assuming that freely falling objects accelerate uniformly on this planet, determine the acceleration due to gravity near its surface.
   (b) With what velocity did the rock hit the ground?
   (c) If 1 ces = 2.50 s and 1 tem = 2.0 m what is the acceleration due to gravity in SI units?
12. A helicopter hovering above a forest fire dumps a large bucket of water. How far does the water fall
   (a) in the first 3.0 s?
   (b) during the third second?
13. A flower pot falls from a balcony ledge to the sidewalk below. If the flower pot falls a distance of 30 m, find
   (a) the time it takes to hit the sidewalk.
   (b) the velocity when the pot hits the sidewalk.
14. (a) A stone is fired straight up with a velocity of 29.4 m/s. Find its displacement and velocity at 1.0 s intervals between 0 and 6.0 s.
   (b) Using the answers for (a), construct position-time and velocity-time graphs for the stone.
15. A girl throws a pebble into a deep well at 4.0 m/s[down]. It hits the water in 2.0 s.
   (a) How far below the ground is the water's surface?
   (b) What is the pebble's average velocity?
   (c) How soon after it is thrown does the pebble actually acquire the velocity calculated in (b)?
   (d) What is the velocity of the pebble when it hits the water?
16. (a) Tarzan swings from one tree to the next using a vine 4.0 m long. If he swings through exactly half a cycle, how long does it take him to move from tree to tree?
   (b) An astronaut on the moon swings on a rope that is 4.0 m long. If the value of g on the moon is 1.6 m/s², how long does it take for the astronaut to swing through the same distance as Tarzan in question (a)?

Meet Diana Gonzalez . . . Teacher

Diana is a science teacher in San Antonio, Texas. She has taught students from the junior high school level through high school. She has also participated in several interesting summer programs.

Q. When did you first become interested in science?

A. I distinctly remember becoming excited about science in tenth grade. The course was biology, and I had a terrific teacher. I especially enjoyed lab work and using equipment such as the microscope. I also enjoyed chemistry, physics, and several courses in mathematics. I have found that a strong math background is very useful in science.

Q. When did you first become interested in teaching science?

A. Throughout my high school years, I tutored my friends in math and science. I found it rewarding to help my peers with their homework in subjects such as geometry and physics. My interest in tutoring carried over into college.

Q. What did you study in college?

I enrolled at the University of Texas as a science major. I was once considering a career in either pharmacy or medicine. I took many different science courses, including several lab courses.

Q. How did this lead to a teaching career?

A. Toward the end of my college program, I switched my major to education. After my experience as a tutor, it had become clear that teaching was what I enjoyed most. My strong science background quickly began to pay in the classroom. I was able to supplement my courses with discussions of my own experiences in the laboratory and in the field. I soon was comfortable with my new career.

Q. What type of teaching certification do you hold?

A. I hold a certificate in Composite Science, which means I can teach just about any science subject. My favorite subject areas include physics and geology. This year I am teaching earth science.

Q. Do you feel there is a shortage of science teachers?

A. There is a shortage of qualified teachers in many subject areas, including science. There is a particular shortage of teachers who have a strong science background in laboratory and field work. It is difficult for teachers to use hands-on science instruction when they have no hands-on experience.

Q. What do you enjoy most about teaching?

A. I really enjoy the daily contact with students. It is especially rewarding to see students apply what they have learned.

Q. Can you describe the summer programs you took?

A. One summer, I attended a summer institute sponsored by the National Science Foundation. We hiked Big Bend in West Texas and studied the geologic formations. I found the experience particularly useful when I began teaching earth science. The next summer, I taught *Physics and Chemistry Laboratory Management* under a new government science grant designed to help minority students prepare for college. Specifically, I taught laboratory courses in physics and chemistry. We found that the laboratory setting was an excellent way to strengthen the students' science backgrounds.

Q. What are your long-range goals?

A. I intend to get my master's degree in science education. I will remain in the classroom for a few more years. One of my goals is to spend some time teaching at the elementary grades. I am concerned about how children's attitudes toward science change as they move through the grades. By broadening my experience, I hope to reach some conclusions about how science education can be improved. Eventually, I would like to become a supervisor of science education.

Q. What advice do you have for students who are thinking about a career in science teaching?

A. They should get as much science background as possible, including work in the laboratory and in the field. There is more to science education than content. Students need exposure to the processes of science. There is one other key factor. Students must learn to be more accepting of the diversity in our population.

5

Forces

Chapter Objectives

- **Distinguish** *between mass and weight and* **measure** *each, using the correct units.*

- **Relate** *the gravitational field strength to the force on an object and its mass.*

- **Explain** *variations in the Earth's gravitational field strength due to latitude and height above sea level.*

- **Calculate** *the force of gravity on an object as its distance from the Earth changes.*

- **Calculate** *the gravitational field strength at a given distance from the Earth's center.*

- **Relate** *the gravitational field strength to the acceleration of a freely falling body.*

- **Calculate** *the force of gravity between two objects, given their masses and the distance between their centers.*

- **Relate** *the force on a spring to the spring constant and the spring's deformation.*

- **Relate** *the force of friction to the normal force and the coefficient of friction.*

- **List** *two factors that do not significantly affect friction and two factors that do.*

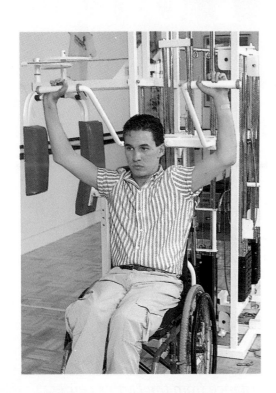

Introduction

The simple definition of a **force** is a push or a pull. Forces make things happen. They speed things up, slow them down, push them around corners and up hills. Forces can also distort matter by compressing, stretching, or twisting. This chapter will deal with the study of forces—the agents that objects use to interact with one another.

5.1 Kinds of Force

Though there seem to be a great many different kinds of forces, physicists believe that there are at most four basic forces: the force of gravity, the electric force, the strong nuclear force, and the weak nuclear force.

The **force of gravity** is important for large objects like stars, planets, and moons. It holds them together and controls their motions in the same way that it controls the motion of falling objects.

The **electric force** is the force between electric charges. It is the force that holds atoms and molecules together, making diamonds hard and rubber weak. It tenses muscles and explodes sticks of dynamite. Even the force of magnetism is electric—produced by electric charge in motion. Indeed, most common forces are electric.

The strong and weak nuclear forces act between the particles that form the nucleus of an atom. This nucleus contains positively charged and neutral particles called protons and neutrons, respectively. The **strong nuclear force** holds the protons together, even when they are influenced by the electric force of repulsion. This nuclear force is a short-range force but is much stronger than the electric force. It is significant only when the particles are close together.

Besides the proton and the neutron, there are many more "elementary" particles. The electron is but one of the others. Many of these particles, including the neutron, are unstable and break up. The **weak nuclear force** is responsible for this.

Physicists are now working on "unified field theories", which, they hope, will replace the four forces with a single force. Scientists constantly search for ways to simplify and reduce the number of laws that govern the universe.

Measuring Force

The SI unit of force is the **newton** (N), named after the famous English physicist, Isaac Newton. Forces are often measured by means of a spring balance calibrated in newtons. To see how much force a newton represents, obtain a spring balance and pull on it until it reads 1 N. Use the spring balance to find the force of gravity pulling on a 100 g mass. If your school has a newton bathroom scale, stand on it to find the force of gravity pulling down on you in newtons.

5.2 The Force of Gravity

The Earth is surrounded by a gravitational force field. This means that every mass large or small feels a force pulling it towards the Earth, no matter where it is in the space on or above the Earth's surface. The **gravitational field strength** is the amount of force acting on each kilogram of mass, and is therefore measured in newtons per kilogram (N/kg). The gravitational field strength is not the same everywhere. It depends on how close the object is to the center of the Earth—it is greater in valleys and less on mountaintops.

The simplest way to measure the gravitational force acting on a mass is to suspend that mass from a spring balance calibrated in newtons. The table below shows data that were collected in this way.

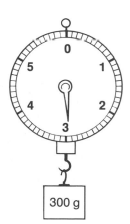

Mass (kg)	Force of gravity (N)
0	0
10	98
20	196
30	294
40	392
50	490

When the data are plotted on a graph, we get the following result.

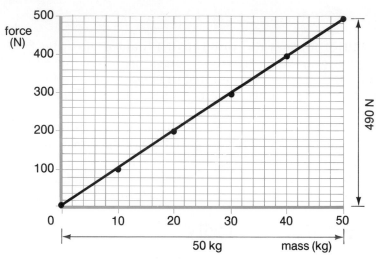

The gravitational field surrounding the Earth (not to scale)

Gravitational field strength is a vector quantity whose direction is always toward the center of the Earth.
$\vec{g}$ = 9.8 N/kg[toward center of Earth]
However, since the direction is understood, the vector notation is usually omitted.

Notice that the graph is a straight line. The slope of the line can be found by dividing the rise by the run.

$$\text{slope} = \frac{490 \text{ N}}{50 \text{ kg}}$$
$$= 9.8 \text{ N/kg}$$

The slope gives us the gravitational field strength in newtons per kilogram. Notice that this measurement is numerically equal to the acceleration due to gravity in meters per second squared. This will be explained fully in Chapter 6. Because the gravitational field strength and the acceleration due to gravity are numerically equal, the same symbol, g, is used for both. Therefore, at the surface of the Earth,

g = 9.8 N/kg, or g = 9.8 m/s²

Since the graph yields a straight line though the origin, the equation for that line is

$F_g = mg$

where F_g is the force of gravity on an object, in newtons
m is the mass of the object, in kilograms
g is the gravitational field strength, in newtons per kilogram

Sample Problems

What is the force of gravity on a 1250 kg automobile?

$$F_g = mg$$
$$= (1250 \text{ kg})(9.8 \text{ N/kg})$$
$$= 1.2 \times 10^4 \text{ N}$$

Practice

1. What is the force of gravity on a 4.5 kg block of concrete?
2. What is the mass of an object that is pulled down by a force of gravity of 167 N at the Earth's surface?
3. The force of gravity on a 250 kg spacecraft on the moon is 408 N. What is the gravitational field strength there?
4. At what rate would a freely falling object accelerate near the surface of the moon?

Mass and Weight

Weight is a commonly used term that is often confused with mass. Weight and mass are quite different things.

"**Mass**" is used to describe the amount of matter in an object. It is measured in kilograms. As long as the amount of matter in an object remains the same, its mass stays the same. The label on a kilogram of hamburger should say "mass: 1 kg".

"**Weight**" is used to describe the force of gravity on an object. Since gravity is a force, weight is measured in newtons, not in kilograms. Since the force of gravity can vary, the weight of an object will also vary, depending on its location. On the Earth's surface an object's weight does not vary much, but astronauts on a trip to the moon find their weight slowly decreasing towards zero.

Even with a massive spacesuit, an astronaut can jump higher on the moon than on the Earth.

Astronaut's location	Astronaut's mass	Force of gravity on astronaut
on the surface of the Earth	60 kg	590 N
150 km above the Earth	60 kg	560 N
$\frac{9}{10}$ of the way to the moon	60 kg	0 N
on the surface of the moon	60 kg	98 N

Note that the point about $\frac{9}{10}$ of the way to the moon is special. There, the pull of the Earth is balanced by the pull of the moon to give a net weight of zero.

To avoid confusion it is better to use the phrase "force of gravity" than the word "weight". In general, this will be the practice in this text.

Newton was the first to explain how the rotation of the Earth produces a bulging out at the equator. You feel the same effect on a merry-go-round moving quickly. The merry-go-round is actually pulling you in toward the center but you get the sensation that there is a force which is trying to push you outward. Physicists refer to this apparent force as a fictitious force. The Earth seems solid enough, but even it slowly gave way to the immense forces involved. The effect is greatest at the equator because the speed of the turning Earth is greatest there. The Earth's equatorial circumference is

$$C = 2\pi r$$
$$= 2\pi(6.378 \times 10^6 \text{ km})$$
$$= 4.0 \times 10^7 \text{ m}$$
$$= 4.0 \times 10^4 \text{ km}$$

Any point on the equator travels around the circumference in about 24 h. Therefore, the approximate speed of rotation of a point on the equator is

$$v = \frac{\Delta d}{\Delta t}$$
$$= \frac{4.0 \times 10^4 \text{ km}}{24 \text{ h}}$$
$$= 1.7 \times 10^3 \text{ km/h}$$

This is a very large speed. It is 17 times as great as the speed limit on major highways.

Distance to center of Earth (Earth radii)	Force of gravity (N)
1	900
2	225
3	100
4	56
5	36
6	25
7	18
8	14
10	9
30	1

5.3 Variations in Gravitational Field Strength

The Earth is not a sphere. Because it rotates on a axis through its north and south poles, it bulges out slightly at the equator. A sled located at the north pole would be about 21 km closer to the center of the Earth than a boat floating in the ocean at the equator. As a result, the gravitational field strength at the north pole is slightly greater than the gravitational field strength at the equator, as shown in the table.

Latitude (°)	g^* (N/kg)	Distance to center (km)*
0 (equator)	9.7805	6378
15	9.7839	6377
30	9.7934	6373
45	9.8063	6367
60	9.8192	6362
75	9.8287	6358
90 (north pole)	9.8322	6357

*all measurements made at sea level

The height above sea level also affects the gravitational field strength, as shown below. Again, the farther from the center of the Earth you get, the smaller the gravitational field strength becomes.

Location	Latitude (°)	g at sea level (N/kg)	Altitude (m)	g (N/kg)
Chicago	42°	9.8035	182	9.8029
Mount Everest	28	9.7919	8848	9.7647
Dead Sea	32	9.7950	−397	9.7962

The tables show that the gravitational field strength for different locations on the Earth's surface varies, but only slightly. To one decimal place, the value of g is 9.8 N/kg everywhere. Usually we consider g to be constant on the Earth's surface. We sometimes refer to this as the gravitational field constant.

On the other hand, farther out in space, the value of g decreases considerably. The table to the left shows the force of gravity on an object at various distances from the center of the Earth. The force of gravity on this object is 900 N at the Earth's surface.

The table shows that the force of gravity on an object depends on its distance from the Earth, decreasing as the distance increases. An object on the Earth's surface is about 6400 km from its center. At twice this distance from the center, the force of gravity on the object is not one-half as much, but $(\frac{1}{2})^2$, or $\frac{1}{4}$ as much. At 10 times the distance, the force is reduced to $(\frac{1}{10})^2$ or $\frac{1}{100}$ of its original value. This is called the **Inverse Square Law for Gravity.** The force depends inversely on the square of the distance from the Earth's center. Inverse square laws turn up often in physics, describing such things as light intensity, magnetism, and electric forces, as well as gravity.

Mathematically the inverse square law for gravitational force may be expressed as

$$F \propto \frac{1}{d^2}$$

or as

$$\frac{F_1}{F_2} = \frac{d_2{}^2}{d_1{}^2}$$

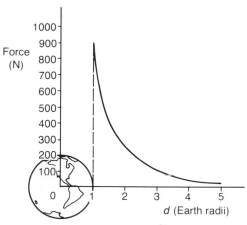

The force of gravity on a 92 kg object at various distances from the Earth

Sample Problems

The force of gravity on a rocket 10 000 km from the center of the Earth is 900 N. What will the force of gravity on the rocket be when it is 30 000 km from the center of the Earth?

$$F_1 = 900 \text{ N}$$
$$d_1 = 10\ 000 \text{ km}$$
$$d_2 = 30\ 000 \text{ km}$$
$$\frac{F_1}{F_2} = \frac{(d_2)^2}{(d_1)^2}$$
$$\frac{900 \text{ N}}{F_2} = \frac{(30\ 000 \text{ km})^2}{(10\ 000 \text{ km})^2}$$
$$\frac{900 \text{ N}}{F_2} = \frac{9}{1}$$
$$F_2 = 100 \text{N}$$

When the distance increases to 30 000 km from the center of the Earth, the force drops to 100N.

Another way of expressing the relationship between gravitational force and distance from the center of the Earth is

$$F \times d^2 = \text{constant, or}$$
$$F_1 \times d_1{}^2 = F_2 \times d_2{}^2$$

Applying this relationship to the problem yields

$$900 \text{ N} \times (10\ 000 \text{ km})^2 = F_2 \times (30\ 000 \text{ km})^2$$

$$900 \text{ N} \times \frac{(10\ 000 \text{ km})^2}{(30\ 000 \text{ km})^2} = F_2$$
$$100 \text{ N} = F_2$$

Practice

1. The force of gravity on the average person is about 700 N at the Earth's surface. Calculate the force of gravity on a person at 10 times that distance from the Earth's center.

2. If the Earth's radius is 6400 km, calculate the force of gravity on a 100 000 kg space station situated

(a) on the Earth's surface.

(b) 128 000 km from the center of the Earth

(c) 384 000 km from the center of the Earth (about the distance to the moon).

(d) 1.5×10^8 km from the Earth's center (about the distance to the sun).

3. The force of gravity on a meteorite approaching the Earth is 50 000 N at a certain point. Calculate the force of gravity on the meteorite when it reaches a point one-quarter of this distance from the center of the Earth.

4. The gravitational field stength is also governed by an inverse square law. What is the gravitational field stength 200 km above the Earth's surface, the altitude of many piloted space flights?

5.4 Satellites in Orbit and Projectiles

It was Newton who first saw the connection between falling objects, projectiles, and satellites in orbit. The example he gave is still as good an explanation of this relationship as any.

Imagine a large cannon on the top of a high mountain firing cannon balls horizontally at greater and greater speeds. At first the cannon balls fall quickly to the ground. As their initial speed increases, the cannon balls travel farther and farther.

At very high speeds a new factor affects the distance. Since the Earth is round, it curves downwards. The cannon balls must travel down and around before landing.

When a certain critical speed is reached, the cannon ball's path curves downwards at the same rate as the Earth's curvature. The cannon ball is then in orbit, perpetually falling towards the Earth, but never landing.

A satellite in circular orbit 100 km above the Earth's surface travels at about 7900 m/s (or 28 400 km/h), and takes about 86 min for each orbit.

The first artificial Earth satellite, Sputnik, launched from the Soviet Union on October 4, 1957, was a spherical metal instrument package 60 cm in diameter with a mass of 83.5 kg. Its orbit was elliptical, with a perigee, or closest approach to the Earth, of 228 km, an apogee of 946 km, and an orbital period of about 96 min. Slowed by air resistance in the upper atmosphere, it descended towards the Earth after about three months and burned up, vaporized by the heat generated by air resistance in the denser air.

5.5 The Law of Universal Gravitation

You may have already heard the story of Newton, the apple, the moon, and the force of gravity. To explain both the motion of the falling apple and the orbiting of the moon, he concluded that the Earth must exert a force of attraction on all objects around it, a force that decreases as an object's distance from the Earth increases.

Now, if the Earth attracts people and apples, what about the moon? If an apple were dropped near the surface of the moon, wouldn't it fall to the moon? What holds the atmospheres of Jupiter and Saturn in? Surely these planets are surrounded by gravitational fields too!

If you hold two apples side by side and let go, they will both fall to the Earth. What would happen if you tried this deep in outer space, far from the Earth or any other large object? Would the apples fall towards each other? Why should large objects have a force of attraction but not small ones?

Newton decided that every apple, every rock, every particle in the universe attracts, and is attracted to, every other particle in the universe. The strength of the attraction depends on the masses of the objects and on the distance between them. The equation Newton gave for this force is:

$$F = \frac{Gm_1m_2}{d^2}$$

where F is the force of attraction between any two objects, in newtons

m_1 is the mass of one object, in kilograms

m_2 is the mass of the other object, in kilograms

d is the distance between the objects measured center to center, in meters

$G = 6.67 \times 10^{-11}$ N · m²/kg²

There are several important points here. First, there are two equal but opposite forces present. The Earth pulls down on the moon; the moon pulls up on the Earth with an equal force. At the Earth's surface, the Earth pulls down on a 1 kg mass with a force of 9.8 N. Newton's equation also requires that the 1 kg mass pull upwards on the Earth with a force of 9.8 N.

Second, the forces of attraction are governed by an inverse square law. If an object is moved 10 times as far from the center of the Earth as the Earth's surface, the force of gravity is reduced to $(\frac{1}{10})^2$, or $\frac{1}{100}$ of what it was at the Earth's surface. The forces decrease rapidly as objects move apart.

Watching an apple fall from a tree caused Newton to wonder if the force that caused the apple to fall also affected the moon. However, the apple he observed did not hit him on the head, contrary to the many cartoons that have propagated this myth over the years.

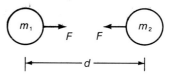

Newton obtained an approximate value for G, the universal gravitation constant, by estimating the mass of the Earth. Henry Cavendish found a much more accurate value of 6.67×10^{-11} N · m²/kg² in 1798. He measured the extremely small force of gravitational attraction between two small spheres on a rod 2 m long and much larger spheres placed near them as illustrated in the diagram below.

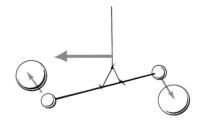

On the other hand, there is no value of d, no matter how great, that would reduce the forces of attraction to zero. Every object in the universe exerts a force on all other objects, near or far.

Third, the value of the constant, G, is small. The force of gravity is significant only if one or both of the objects is massive. It takes the whole Earth, with a mass of 5.98×10^{24} kg, to exert 9.8 N of force on a 1 kg mass. The force operating between relatively small objects, such as two cars on the road, is not worth considering.

Sample Problems

What is the force of attraction between two apples, each with a mass of 0.50 kg, held so that their centers are 10 cm apart?

$$m_1 = m_2 = 0.50 \text{ kg}$$
$$d = 10 \text{ cm} = 0.10 \text{ m}$$
$$G = 6.67 \times 10^{-11} \text{ N} \cdot \text{m}^2/\text{kg}^2$$
$$F = \frac{Gm_1m_2}{d^2}$$
$$= \frac{(6.67 \times 10^{-11} \text{ N} \cdot \text{m}^2/\text{kg}^2)\,(0.50 \text{ kg})\,(0.50 \text{ kg})}{(0.10 \text{ m})^2}$$
$$= 1.7 \times 10^{-9} \text{ N}$$

The force of gravity between small objects is not zero, but it is too small for ordinary measuring instruments and is insignificant for practical purposes.

Practice

1. What is the force of attraction (gravitational!) between a 60 kg girl and a 70 kg boy whose centers are 1.0 m apart?
2. What is the force of attraction between two 2000 kg cars side by side whose centers are 2.5 m apart?
3. What is the force of gravity acting on a 1.00 kg mass 20 000 km from the center of the Earth?

5.6 Hooke's Law

When forces are applied to an object, the dimensions of the object tend to change. For example, if opposite forces are applied to both ends of a spring, it stretches or compresses. When the forces are removed, the spring returns to its original length. If an object returns to its original dimensions after the applied force is removed, we say that the object is **elastic.**

The British scientist Robert Hooke was one of the first to study the elasticity of matter. In 1678, he published his now famous statement of Hooke's Law.

> **The amount of deformation of an elastic object is proportional to the forces applied to deform it.**

We will study Hooke's Law as it applies to a simple, coiled spring, fixed at one end and either stretched or compressed by an applied force at the other end. We will call the deformation of the spring x; i.e., x is the amount by which it is stretched or compressed from its normal length. A graph of F versus x has the form shown.

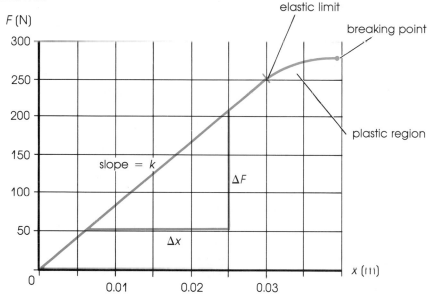

The F-x graph is a straight line up to a point called the elastic limit of the spring. If the spring is deformed beyond this limit, the graph is no longer linear, and the spring may not return to its original shape after the force is removed. If deformed too far beyond the elastic limit, the spring may permanently stretch or fracture.

For the linear portion of the graph, the constant slope is given by

$$k = \text{rise/run} = F/x$$

and the equation relating force and deformation (extension or compression) is

> $$F = kx$$

where F is the forced exerted on the deformed spring, in newtons
$\quad$ x is the amount of deformation of the spring, in meters
$\quad$ k is the force constant of the spring, in newtons per meter

We can distinguish between compressions of the spring and extensions of it by adopting a simple sign convention. When the spring is compressed, both x and F are negative $(-)$; when the spring is stretched, both x and F are positive $(+)$. Notice that the force exerted on the spring and the deformation of the spring are in the same direction, making k always positive.

For the spring whose F-x graph is shown on the previous page,

$$k = \frac{\Delta F}{\Delta x}$$
$$= \frac{160 \text{ N} - 80 \text{ N}}{0.02 \text{ m} - 0.01 \text{ m}}$$
$$= \frac{80 \text{ N}}{0.01 \text{ m}}$$
$$= 8.0 \times 10^3 \text{ N/m}$$

Sample Problems

A spring whose force constant is 48 N/m has a 0.25 kg mass suspended from it. What is the extension of the spring?

If the spring obeys Hooke's Law,

$$F = kx$$
$$\text{therefore } x = F/k$$
$$\text{but } F = mg$$
$$= (0.25 \text{ kg}) (9.8 \text{ N kg})$$
$$= 2.4 \text{ N}$$
$$\text{Therefore } x = \frac{2.4 \text{ N}}{48 \text{ N/m}}$$
$$= 0.050 \text{ m, or 5.0 cm}$$

Practice

1. What force is necessary to stretch a spring whose force constant is 120 N/m by an amount of 30 m?
2. A spring with a force constant of 600 N/m is used in a scale for weighing fish. What is the mass of a fish that stretches the spring 7.5 cm from its normal length?
3. A spring in a pogo stick is compressed 12 cm when a 40 kg boy stands on the stick. What is the force constant for the pogo stick spring?

5.7 Frictional Forces

There are various kinds of friction. There is **static friction**, the force that keeps a stone from slipping down a sloping roof, and there is **sliding friction**, the force opposing a toboggan sliding down a hill. There is **rolling friction**, the force resisting the motion of a bicycle wheel, as well as the resistance of fluids such as air or water that oppose the motion of aircraft and boats. **Frictional forces nearly always act opposite to the direction of motion.**

Most frictional forces are complex, depending on the nature of the materials involved and the size, shape, and speed of the moving object. We shall consider only the force of friction acting on an object sliding along a horizontal surface.

The Coefficient of Friction

The coefficient of friction is a number used to calculate the force of friction acting on a sliding object. The equation for the coefficient of friction is

$$\mu = \frac{F_f}{F_N}$$

where F_f is the force of friction, in newtons
F_N is the force pushing two surfaces together, in newtons (it acts at right angles to the surfaces)
μ is the coefficient of friction, and has no units
A rearrangement of this equation will give the equation for calculating the force of friction.

$$F_f = \mu F_N$$

The force of friction depends on μ, the coefficient of friction, which is determined by the two materials in contact and their smoothness and cleanness, and by the force pushing the surfaces together, which is called the **normal** force. "Normal" means perpendicular. If the surfaces are horizontal, the normal force will simply be equal in value to the force of gravity on the object. The following table shows the value of the coefficient of friction for a number of surfaces.

Sliding friction is also known as kinetic friction.

The force of friction between the tires and the pavement is an example of rolling friction. Can you find other examples of rolling friction in the photo?

For a block pulled across a rough table top

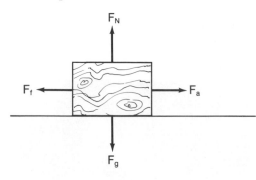

F_g is the force of gravity on the object.
F_N is the normal force exerted by the table on the block.
F_a is the applied force.
F_f is the force of friction.

To find the value of F_f the frictional force, one simply finds the value of F_a the applied force required to slide the block along a level surface at a constant speed. This will be more fully explained in the next chapter.

Materials	μ (coefficient of sliding friction)
oak on oak, dry	0.30
steel on steel, dry	0.41
greasy	0.12
steel on ice	0.01
rubber on asphalt, dry	1.07
wet	0.95
rubber on concrete, dry	1.02
wet	0.97
rubber on ice	0.005
leather on oak, dry	0.50

Sample Problems

1. It takes 50 N to pull a 6.0 kg object along a desk at constant speed. What is the coefficient of friction?

$$\mu = \frac{F_f}{F_N}$$
$$= \frac{F_f}{mg} \quad (\text{since } F_N = F_g = mg)$$
$$= \frac{50 \text{ N}}{(6.0 \text{ kg}) (9.8 \text{ N/kg})}$$
$$= 0.85$$

2. The coefficient of sliding friction between two materials is 0.35. A 5.0 kg object made of one material is being pulled along a table made of another material. What is the force of friction?

$$F_f = \mu F_N$$
$$= \mu mg \quad (\text{since } F_N = F_g = mg)$$
$$= (0.35) (5.0 \text{ kg}) (9.8 \text{ N/kg})$$
$$= 17 \text{ N}$$

Practice

1. A 70 kg hockey player glides across the ice on steel skates. What is the force of friction acting on the skater?
2. The driver of a 1500 kg car applies the brakes on a concrete road. Calculate the force of friction (a) on a dry road and (b) on a wet road.
3. A worker for a moving company places a 250 kg trunk on a piece of carpeting and slides it across the floor by exerting a horizontal force of 425 N on the trunk.

(a) What is the coefficient of sliding friction?

(b) What is likely to happen to the coefficient of sliding friction if another 50 kg trunk is placed on top of the 250 kg trunk?

(c) What horizontal force must the mover apply to move the combination of two trunks?

5.8 Adding Force Vectors

In real life, objects are often acted upon by a number of forces simultaneously. In order to carry out an analysis in cases like this, physicists find it useful to determine the resultant force. This resultant force is also called the **net force** or the **unbalanced force**. The symbol used is $\vec{F}_{net}$.

Force is a vector quantity. This means that it has both magnitude and direction. The resultant force, or net force, on an object is the vector sum of all the forces acting on that object. The rules for vector addition established in Chapter 3 also apply to force vectors. Consider the following sample problems.

The terms "unbalanced force" and "net force" are both frequently used in physics texts to describe the resultant force. In this text we will therefore use both of these terms so that you become familiar with them.

A diagram that shows all the forces acting on a body is called a "free body diagram". Free body diagrams are a useful aid in solving all motion problems.

Sample Problems

1. Forces of 10 N[E] and 20 N[E] are acting on a block of wood. What is the unbalanced force acting on the block?

    The following expression gives the correct relationship between the force vectors:

    $$\vec{F}_{net} = \vec{F}_1 + \vec{F}_2$$

    To add the two force vectors, place the tail of one vector at the tip of the other.

    $F_1 = 10N[E]$ $F_2 = 20N[E]$

    $F_{net} = 30N[E]$

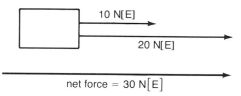

The resultant vector is represented by a vector drawn from the tail of the first vector to the tip of the second vector.

In a simple example like this, in which the two vectors to be added are in the same direction, the magnitude of the vector sum is the same as the arithmetic sum.

2. Two children pull in opposite directions on a toy. One pulls with a force of 20 N[E] and the other pulls with a force of 5 N[W]. What is the net force acting on the toy?

Since the forces again act along the same line, the resultant force may be calculated as follows:

$$\vec{F}_{net} = \vec{F}_1 + \vec{F}_2$$
$$= 20 \text{ N[E]} + 5 \text{ N[W]}$$
$$= 20 \text{ N[E]} - 5 \text{ N[E]} \quad \text{(where east is positive)}$$
$$= 15 \text{ N[E]}$$

Again, however, the result may also be obtained by using a vector diagram.

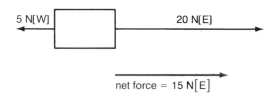

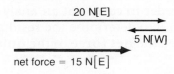

As indicated earlier, you can solve vector addition problems in one of two ways:
1. by using an accurately drawn scale diagram;
2. by using a sketch roughly to scale, and then using algebra and trigonometry.

For Sample problem 3 we could determine the answer as follows:
$$(30 \text{ N})^2 + (40 \text{ N})^2 = (F_{net})^2$$
$$900 \text{ N}^2 + 1600 \text{ N}^2 = (F_{net})^2$$
$$2500 \text{ N}^2 = (F_{net})^2$$
$$F_{net} = 50 \text{ N}$$
$$\tan \theta = \frac{40 \text{ N}}{30 \text{ N}}$$
$$\tan \theta = 1.33$$
$$\theta = 53°$$

Therefore the resultant force is 50 N[N53°E].

3. Let's consider an example in which the forces do not act along the same line. A trunk is acted upon by forces of 30 N[N] and 40 N[E]. Find the unbalanced force acting on the trunk.

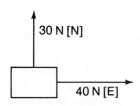

This time a mathematical solution obtained by inspecting the problem is much more difficult. The addition of the vectors, however, proceeds as before.

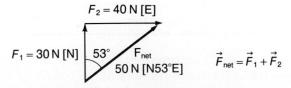

Using a scale diagram or the Pythagorean Theorem, the resultant force has a magnitude of 50 N. Its direction is determined by finding the angle at the tail of the net force vector. Since the value of this angle is 53°, a complete description of the resulting net force is 50 N[N53°E].

Practice

1. The diagrams below show forces acting on various objects. For each case determine the net force and state its value.

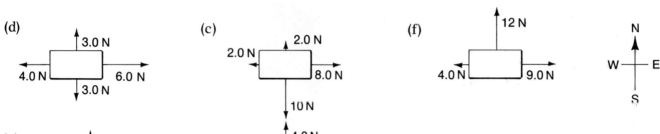

(a)

6.0 N 8.0 N

(b)

6.0 N
4.0 N

(c)

30 N 25 N

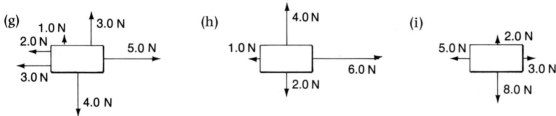

(d)

3.0 N
4.0 N 6.0 N
3.0 N

(c)

2.0 N
2.0 N 8.0 N
10 N

(f)

12 N
4.0 N 9.0 N

N
W — E
S

(g)

1.0 N 3.0 N
2.0 N
5.0 N
3.0 N
4.0 N

(h)

4.0 N
1.0 N
6.0 N
2.0 N

(i)

2.0 N
5.0 N
3.0 N
8.0 N

2. (a) A child is pulling a wagon along a sidewalk. At a particular instant the child is exerting a horizontal force of 10 N[W] on the wagon. Frictional resistance amounts to 8.0 N. Draw a diagram of the wagon showing both forces acting on it. Determine the unbalanced force acting on the wagon.

   (b) There are at least two additional forces acting on the wagon described in (a). Add them to your diagram and write a sentence describing each of them.

3. Two children playing on the beach are pulling on an inner tube. One exerts a force of 45 N[N]. The other exerts a force of 60 N[SW]. What is the net force acting on the tube?

The Sensation of "Weightlessness"

Astronauts experience the sensation of "weightlessness" while orbiting the Earth in the space shuttle. But are they truly "weightless?" The weight of an object is defined as the force of gravity acting on it. At the height the shuttle orbits the Earth, the force of gravity acting on the astronauts and the shuttle is about 90% of what it is on Earth's surface. It is this force that keeps the shuttle in orbit about the Earth. The astronauts experience "weightlessness", not because there is a lower force of gravity acting on them, but because there is no force acting upwards on them.

If an astronaut stood on a bathroom scale while in orbit the scale would read zero—the scale would be accelerating toward the Earth at the same rate as the astronaut. To help understand this, imagine what a bathroom scale would read if you were standing on it in an elevator, and the cable supporting the elevator suddenly broke. The result would be the same. Anytime a person is in free fall the sensation that he or she experiences is similar to that of the astronauts, when in orbit.

When you jump to the ground from a height, you momentarily experience free fall. There is virtually no force acting upward on you as the force of gravity pulls you down to the Earth. But, the time interval is so short that the sensation doesn't really have time to take effect. During training the interval of free fall or "weightlessness" is extended for astronauts. They are placed in the cargo hold of a large military transport plane. First the plane climbs to a high altitude. Then it dives to gain speed. Next, it pulls into a large parabolic path and into a dive (as illustrated).

It is while in this parabolic path and final dive that the plane is in free fall for about 30 s and the astronauts can "float" around inside the cargo hold, experience the sensation of "weightlessness".

There are exciting ways in which you can briefly experience free fall yourself. Large amusement parks usually have some rides in which passengers experience free fall or near free fall conditions. For example, the steep fall experienced by most roller coasters after they have climbed to the very top of the ride comes close to being free fall. In another ride passengers ride slowly to the top of a tower in an enclosed carriage and then drop freely through a distance of about 30 m before slowing down and coming to rest. While in free fall for a few seconds, the passengers experience the same sensation that astronauts experience during their orbit of the Earth. If a ride likes this makes you feel ill, then chances are you would not like being an astronaut. While in space, you would experience the same conditions over a much longer time period.

Another example of partial "weightlessness" is an experience that everyone has had while on a swing. When you reach the top of the swing and start back on your way down, you experience a split second of partial "weightlessness". If you were sitting on a bathroom scale while you were swinging, you could actually calculate what fraction of your weight you appear to lose at the top of the arc. But, remember the bathroom scale only measures the force supporting your body. The only way to lose weight and be truly "weightless" is to turn off gravity—an impossibility.

Investigations

Investigation 5.1: Mass and the Force of Gravity

Problem: How does the force of gravity acting on an object depend on its mass?

Materials:
spring balance calibrated in newtons (0 N to 5 N)
five 100 g masses

Procedure:
1. Make sure the spring balance reads zero with no mass attached. If it does not, ask your teacher to fix it, or make a note of the reading so that you can correct the readings you make in the investigation.
2. Hang various combinations of 100 g masses (from one to five) on the spring balance, and measure the force of gravity each time. Jiggle the balance before each reading to make sure it doesn't stick. Record your observations in a data table drawn up in your notebook.
3. Plot a graph of force versus mass, with mass plotted horizontally. This graph should be a straight line. Use a ruler to draw the best straight line possible, as close to, or through, as many points as possible. Don't forget to plot the point (0,0) as part of your graph.

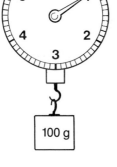

Questions:
1. Determine the slope of your graph. This is the value of the gravitational field strength. What are the units of this slope? You have seen this value before in connection with gravity, but with different units. What were those units?
2. Make up an equation for calculating F_g the force of gravity, when you are given m, the mass of the object, and g, the gravitational field strength.
3. If you did this investigation on top of Mount Everest, would the line be straight? Would it have the same slope? Explain your answers.

Investigation 5.2: Sliding Friction

Problem:
What factors affect the force of friction on a sliding wooden block?

Materials:
3 wooden blocks
spring balance

Procedure:
1. Measure the length, width, and height of a block. Calculate the area of each face.
2. Use the spring balance to find the force of gravity on the block, in newtons.
3. Pull one block along the desk on its largest face at a steady speed, and record the force required.
4. Repeat, using piles of two and three blocks, at the same speed as in step 3.
5. Pull one block along, first on its edge and then on its end, again at the same speed. Record the force required each time.
6. Pull one block along, first at half the original speed and then at twice the original speed. Record the force required each time.

Questions:
1. Does the speed of the block have a significant effect on the force of friction? For example, to go twice as fast, do you have to apply twice the force?
2. Does the area in contact with the desk affect the force of friction significantly? When the area is twice as much, does the force double, or halve, or remain the same?
3. When you double or triple the number of blocks, what happens to the force of friction?
4. The coefficient of friction, represented by the Greek letter μ, is calculated by dividing the force of friction between the two surfaces by the force pushing the two surfaces together, both expressed in newtons. In this experiment, the force pushing the two surfaces together is the force of gravity. Calculate the coefficient of friction for each of the above cases.
5. Find the average value of the coefficient of friction for the kind of wood you are using, sliding on the kind of desk you have. Each different combination of materials will have its own coefficient of friction.
6. If you were to make the desk or the block smoother, what effect would this have on the coefficient of friction?
7. Try repeating some of the measurements using a different surface such as the floor.

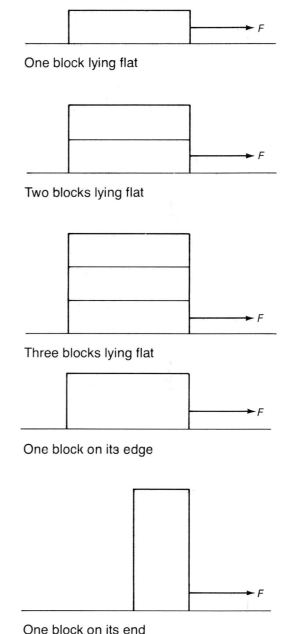

One block lying flat

Two blocks lying flat

Three blocks lying flat

One block on its edge

One block on its end

Chapter Summary

1. Force is a push or pull on an object, measured in newtons.
2. Mass is the amount of matter in an object.
3. The gravitational field strength g at a given point is the force of gravity on each kilogram of mass at that point.
4. At the surface of the Earth, $g = 9.8$ N/kg.
5. The gravitational field strength at a given point and the acceleration of a freely falling object at that point have the same value.

$$g = 9.8 \text{ N/kg} = 9.8 \text{ m/s}^2 \text{ at the Earth's surface}$$

6. The force of gravity, F_g, on a mass, m, is found by the equation

$$F_g = mg$$

7. The gravitational field strength, g, is inversely proportional to the square of the distance to the center of the Earth, d.

$$g \propto \frac{1}{d^2}$$

   As a result, gravitational force is also inversely proportional to the square of the distance.

$$F \propto \frac{1}{d^2}, \text{ or } \frac{F_1}{F_2} = \frac{d_2{}^2}{d_1{}^2}$$

8. According to Newton's Law of Universal Gravitation, there is a force of gravitational attraction between every pair of masses in the universe. This force varies directly with the magnitude of each mass, and inversely with the square of the distance between them.

$$F = \frac{Gm_1m_2}{d_2}, \text{ where } G = 6.67 \times 10^{-11} \text{ N} \cdot \text{m}^2/\text{kg}^2$$

9. Hooke's Law, which takes the form $F = kx$, relates the deformation of a spring to the force applied to the spring. Hooke's Law applies only for deformations less than the elastic limit.
10. Sliding friction depends on the roughness of the surfaces and on the force pushing them together. It does not depend significantly on the speed of the motion (if the speed is low) or on the area in contact (if the normal force stays the same.)
11. The coefficient of sliding friction is μ, where

$$\mu = \frac{F_f}{F_N}$$

12. When adding forces along the same straight line, consider all the forces in one direction as being positive, and all the forces in the opposite direction as being negative; then add them all together to find the unbalanced, or net, force.
13. A vector diagram is needed to find the net force when the forces are not in the same or opposite directions.

The planet Saturn

Chapter Review

Use $g = 9.8$ N/kg near the Earth's surface.

Discussion

1. Describe briefly the four basic forces that physicists believe can account for all known forces.
2. (a) What is meant by the term, "unified field theory"?
   (b) Refer to a science journal and report on the progress being made toward a "unified field theory".
3. In response to a test question a student writes the following sentence. "Gravity is 9.8 N." What is wrong with this answer?
4. If one watches a videotape of the Apollo astronauts on the moon, it seems that they are moving about in slow motion. Explain why this is the case.
5. Why is the gravitational field strength halfway up Mount Everest the same as at sea level at the equator?
6. Why is the gravitational field strength at the south pole less than the field strength at the north pole?
7. Scientists collecting data from a space probe that is moving towards the surface of a distant planet determine that the acceleration due to gravity near the surface of that planet is 12.8 m/s². What is the gravitational field strength near the surface of the planet?
8. Is it possible for a body somewhere in the universe to have no forces whatsoever acting on it? Explain your answer.
9. If you wanted to reduce the number of forces acting on your body to a minimum, what would you have to do?
10. Suppose you decided to make some spending money by purchasing precious materials like gold at one altitude and selling it for the same price in dollars per newton at another altitude. In this situation is "Buy low and sell high" a good sales strategy?
11. Friction may be a help in some situations and a hindrance in others. Describe two examples for each situation. For those situations where friction is undesirable, what efforts are made to reduce it as much as possible? For those situations where friction is desirable, how is it increased?

Problems

12. What is the force of gravity at the Earth's surface on each of the following masses?
    (a) 75.0 kg   (b) 454 g   (c) 2.00 metric tons
13. What is the weight of each of the following masses at the Earth's surface?
    (a) 25 g   (b) 102 kg   (c) 12 mg
14. Use these forces of gravity to determine the masses of the objects on which they act.
    (a) 0.98   (b) 100 N   (c) 62 N   (d) 44.5×10^6 N
15. Copy and complete the following chart. Assume that the same object is used on each of the three planets.

Planet	Mass on planet's surface (kg)	Force of gravity on this mass (N)	g - gravitational field strength at surface (N/kg)
(a) Mercury	57	188	—
(b) Venus	—	462	—
(c) Jupiter	—	—	26

16. An astronaut on the surface of Mars finds that a rock accelerates at 3.6 m/s² when it is dropped. She also finds that a newton scale reads 180 N when she steps on it.
    (a) What is her mass as determined on the surface of Mars?
    (b) What would the newton scales read if she stepped on it on Earth?
    (c) What would her mass be on Earth?
17. The force of gravity on an astronaut is 600 N at the Earth's surface. What is the force of gravity on him at each of the following distances from the center of the Earth, measured in multiples of the Earth's radius?
    (a) 2   (b) 5   (c) 10   (d) 20
18. The force of gravity on a spacecraft some distance from the Earth is 800 N. What would that force be if its distance to the Earth's center were
    (a) one-half as great?   (b) one-third as great?   (c) one-tenth as great?   (d) one-quarter as great?
19. A 20 kg object out in space is attracted to the Earth by a force of gravity of 100 N. How fast will this object accelerate towards the Earth, if it is falling freely?

20. Two of the largest oil tankers in the world, the *Batilus* and the *Bellaya,* have masses of 492 000 t, fully loaded. If they were moored side by side, 1.0 m apart, their centers would be 64 m apart. Calculate the force of gravity between them.

21. Sirius is the brightest star in the night sky. It has a radius of 2.5×10^9 m and a mass of 5.0×10^{31} kg. What is the gravitational force on a 1.0 kg mass at its surface?

22. Sirius B is a white dwarf star, in orbit around Sirius, with a mass of 2.0×10^{30} kg (approximately the mass of the sun), and a radius of 2.4×10^7 m (approximately one-thirtieth of the radius of the sun).
    (a) What is the force on a 1.0 kg mass on the surface of Sirius B?
    (b) What is the acceleration due to gravity on the surface of Sirius B?

23. In a Hooke's Law experiment, a force of 160 N produces a stretch of 8.00 cm in a spring. What is the spring constant?

24. A 100 N force stretches a spring from 12 cm to 14 cm. What will be the length of the spring when a force of 500 N is applied, assuming that the spring remains within its elastic limit?

25. A 20.0 kg toboggan is pulled along at a constant speed by a horizontal force of 30.0 N.
    (a) What is the force of gravity on the toboggan?
    (b) What is the coefficient of friction?
    (c) How much force is needed to pull the toboggan if two 60.0 kg girls are sitting on it?

26. It takes a 5.0 N horizontal force to pull a 2.0 kg object along the ground at a constant speed. What is the coefficient of friction?

27. How much horizontal force does it take to pull a 100 kg packing crate along a rough floor at a constant speed, given each of the following coefficients of friction?
    (a) 0.10   (b) 0.20   (c) 0.50

28. If the coefficient of friction is 0.25, how much horizontal force is needed to pull each of the following masses along a rough desk at a constant speed?
    (a) 25 kg   (b) 15 kg   (c) 200 g

29. Find the unbalanced force for each of the following combinations of forces.
    (a) 20 N[E], 30 N[W], 50 N[E]
    (b) 27.3N[N], 2.8 N[S], 13.5N[S]
    (c) 50 N[E], 20 N[W], 5 N[E], 35 N[W]
    (d) 100 N[S], 80 N[W], 30 N[N], 10 N[E]

30. Three teenagers are playing with a huge "earthball". At a particular instant, one person exerts a force of 400 N[N], the second a force of 300 N[S], and the third a force of 200 N[E]. What is the unbalanced force acting on the ball at that instant?

Numberical Answers to Practice Problems

page 105
1. 44 N
2. 17 kg
3. 1.63 N/kg
4. 1.63 m/s^2

page 108
1. 7.0 N
2. (a) 9.8×10^5 N
   (b) 2.5×10^3 N
   (c) 2.7×10^2 N
   (d) 1.8×10^{-3} N
3. 8.0×10^5 N
4. 9.2 N/kg

page 110
1. 2.8×10^{-7} N
2. 4.3×10^{-5} N
3. 1.00 N

page 112
1. 36 N
2. 4.6 kg
3. 3.3×10^3 N/m

page 114
1. 6.9 N
2. (a) 1.5×10^4 N
   (b) 1.4×10^4 N
3. (a) 0.173
   (c) 5.1×10^2 N

page 117
1. (a) 2.0 N[E]
   (b) 2.0 N[N]
   (c) 5 N[W]
   (d) 2.0 N[E]
   (e) 10 N[S37°E]
   (f) 13 N[E67°N]
   (g) 0
   (h) 5.4 N[E22°N]
   (i) 6.3 N[W72°S]
3. 42.5 N[N87°W]

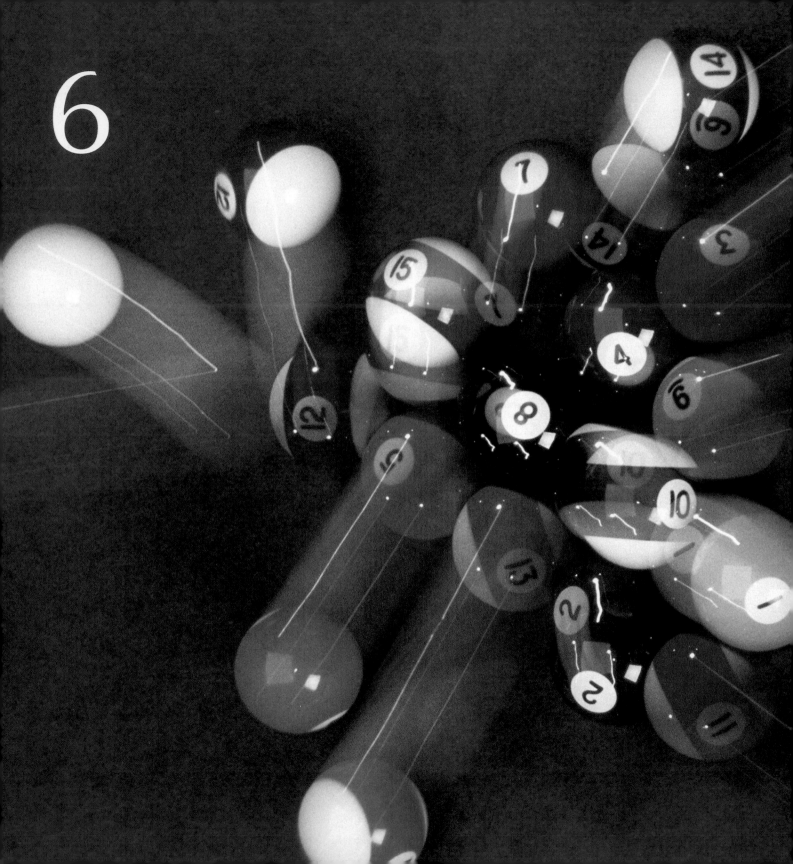

Chapter Objectives

- **State** *Newton's three Laws of Motion.*

- **Explain** *events from everyday experience in terms of Newton's Laws of Motion.*

- **Construct and interpret** *a free body diagram from the forces acting on a body.*

- **Relate** *the net force acting on an object to the mass and the acceleration.*

- **Solve** *motion problems using Newton's Second Law.*

- **Determine** *the magnitude and direction of the reaction force, given any force.*

- **Calculate** *an object's momentum, given its mass and velocity.*

- **Relate** *the change in momentum of an object to the force acting on it and the time interval.*

- **Solve** *motion problems, using the Law of Conservation of Momentum.*

In this chapter, you will study the laws of motion developed by Isaac Newton (1642–1727). Newton's Laws of Motion apply universally, from the motion of the galaxies to the motion of subatomic particles.

Introduction

In Chapters 1 to 4 we dealt with the description of motion. We found that measurements and calculations of displacement, velocity, and acceleration make it possible to describe the motion of an object as it moves from one point to another. The branch of physics that deals with the description of motion is called **kinematics**, from the Greek word *kinema*, meaning motion.

In Chapter 5 we introduced the concept of force. As defined in Chapter 5, a force tends to cause motion. The branch of physics that deals with the causes of motion is called **dynamics**, from the Greek word *dynamis*, meaning power. In this chapter we will begin the study of dynamics.

6.1 Galileo Looks at Force and Motion

People have been curious about the causes of motion for over 2000 years, but a systematic approach to dynamics began only during the time of Galileo Galilei (1564-1642) and Isaac Newton (1642-1727).

The Greeks, about the time of Aristotle (384-322 B.C.), observed that, in everyday situations, it requires a continuous pushing or pulling to keep an object such as a rolling stone moving. When the pushing or pulling is no longer applied, the stone comes to rest. The early Greek law of motion was simple: a constant force was required to produce a constant velocity. If the force was increased, the object moved faster. If the force was decreased, the object moved more slowly. If the force was removed, the object stopped.

These statements seem logical, but they are incorrect. Nevertheless, the assumptions they were based on endured for nearly 2000 years, until the great Italian physicist Galileo explained the relationship between force and motion more accurately. Galileo devised two simple thought experiments about motion on inclined planes to explain his theory.

In his first thought experiment, he reasoned that since a ball rolling down a slope speeds up and a ball rolling up a slope slows down, then a ball rolling across a horizontal, non-sloping surface neither slows down nor speeds up but continues to move with a constant velocity, indefinitely.

Galileo did, of course, observe that a ball rolling along a horizontal surface eventually stops, but he assumed correctly that the ball was being slowed down by friction, or "resistance", as he called it.

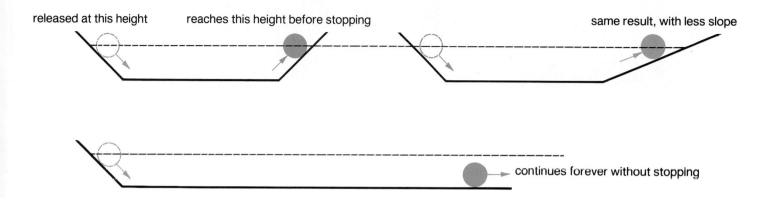

released at this height   reaches this height before stopping   same result, with less slope

continues forever without stopping

In his second thought experiment, Galileo reasoned that if the slope of the rising plane was decreased to make it less steep than the descending slope, the ball would roll farther along this slope, stopping when it reached the height from which it was released on the first slope (see diagram). The fact that the ball did not quite reach that height he attributed, once again, to friction. He concluded, logically, that if the slope of the second plane was zero, the ball, once rolling, would continue forever with no loss of speed, in an attempt to reach its original height.

This reasoning showed great imagination. After all, there is no such thing as a frictionless surface. Also, it was in direct conflict with Aristotelian physics, which enjoyed general acceptance at the time. In contrast with previous beliefs, Galileo argued that it is just as "natural" for an object to move with a constant speed as it is for it to be at rest.

We now have the technology to illustrate what Galileo could only visualize. There are devices available that can slide along a smooth surface with almost no friction. One of them consists of a circular metal disk, or "puck", with a small hole through its center. Gas is pumped through the little hole at a pressure sufficient to raise the puck off the table a millimeter or so. The puck slides along the table on a cushion of gas. In one type of puck designed for this purpose, the gas is air from an inflated balloon attached to it. Another type has a small electric air pump mounted on it, to pump air through the little hole.

Many of the so-called disagreements between Galileo and Aristotle are due to differences in their use of language, i.e., their different interpretations of the same word or phrase. For example, Galileo identified friction as a force while Aristotle considered it to be "natural" and therefore not a force.

These "frictionless" pucks float on a cushion of air provided by the attached balloons.

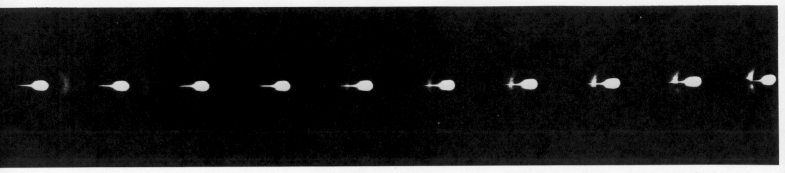

This strobe photograph is of a "frictionless" puck with a built-in flashing light. Can you tell which way the puck is going?

The strobe photograph shows one of these pucks moving across a smooth, level surface. You can see, by measuring the distances travelled in equal time intervals, that the speed is quite constant, and in a straight line.

Once an object, such as the frictionless puck, is moving, it needs no force to keep it moving, as long as no other force acts on it. Galileo explained his theory of motion by stating that every object possesses a property that Newton later called inertia. **Inertia** is that property that causes a body to resist changes in its state of motion. Suppose, for example, you are standing in the aisle of a stationary bus. As the bus starts to move, your body wants to stay at rest because of its inertia. As a result you may fall toward the rear of the bus unless you brace yourself. When the bus reaches a uniform velocity you have no trouble standing in the aisle, because you are also moving with uniform velocity. Suppose the bus driver suddenly applies the brakes. The bus will slow down. Your body, however, has a tendency to keep moving because of its inertia. Again you will need to brace yourself or you will fall toward the front of the bus. The amount of inertia an object possesses depends directly on its mass: the greater the mass, the greater the inertia the body possesses.

6.2 Newton's First Law (The Law of Inertia)

Galileo published his ideas about motion early in the 17th century. Scientists all over Europe accepted them almost immediately. Isaac Newton summarized his own work and that of Galileo in his book *Principia Mathematica*, published in 1687. Newton described what Galileo had discovered about inertia much the same way Galileo had described it. Because it was included with Newton's other laws of motion, it is often referred to as Newton's First Law. It may be stated in either of these ways:

When no external, unbalanced force acts on an object, its velocity remains constant.

or

If no net force acts on an object, it maintains its state of rest or its constant speed in a straight line.

This famous and important law has several significant implications that should be understood:

- An external force is required to change the velocity of an object. Internal forces have no effect on an object's motion. For example, a driver pushing on the dashboard of his car does not cause the car's velocity to change.
- The external force must be unbalanced; that is, two equal opposing forces acting on an object will not change its velocity. For an object's velocity to change, the vector sum of the applied forces on the object must be different than zero.
- Objects at rest remain at rest unless acted upon by an external unbalanced force. For example, a ball on a horizontal floor will remain at rest forever unless something pushes it.
- Moving objects continue to move in a straight line at a constant speed unless acted upon by an external unbalanced force. For example, a car moving into a flat icy curve will tend to continue in a straight line, off the side of the road.

Newton also used the concept of inertia to explain the motion of objects. There are many examples of objects that resist a change in their motion, due to inertia. Consider those that follow.

- When a car stops suddenly, a passenger in the front seat (not wearing a seat belt) continues to move forward (due to the passenger's inertia) and collides with the car's windshield. It is Newton's first law that explains the importance of seat belts. A car's brakes will stop a car, but will not stop you from moving forward.

Newton wrote in Latin: "LAW I: Every body continues in its state of rest, or of uniform motion in a straight line, unless it is compelled to change that state by forces impressed upon it."

Aristotle's description of motion was abandoned primarily because it was not as simple as Galileo's and Newton's: it required more assumptions and divided motion into more categories, each with its own description.

Isaac Newton was born on Christmas Day in 1642. He was a frail baby, and was raised by his grandmother after his widowed mother remarried when he was 2 years old. He had a difficult childhood, and it is thought that this may have contributed to his neurotic tendencies later in life. He became very violent whenever his ideas were challenged, and it is known that he suffered at least two nervous breakdowns.

While at Cambridge (1661-1665) Newton easily mastered science and mathematics, and began to develop some new concepts in mathematics. Probably his most productive period was just after his graduation from Cambridge. England was struck by the plague and tens of thousands died. Schools were closed and pupils were sent home, forcing Newton to work quietly at home, where he developed many of the fundamental laws of physics as well as several important mathematical theorems. Because of his reluctance to publish his research, Newton's work was initially known to only a small circle of friends and acquaintances. In 1669, the professor of mathematics at Cambridge gave up his position to Newton, to enable Newton to devote more time to his theories. His greatest work, *Principia Mathematica*, was published in 1687. Most of the major ideas found in Chapters 5 and 6 are found in the *Principia* where they are developed in more detail and rigor. This work made Newton internationally famous.

Newton never married, cared little about clothes or food, and was known to laugh only once—at a friend who complained he did not see the value of geometry.

Without a seat belt, the "dummy" continues moving forward when the car crashes.

• Were you to flip a coin straight up into the air in a car travelling at constant speed, it would appear to come straight back down again. In fact, if the coin is in the air for 0.5 s, and the car is travelling at 50 km/h, the coin will travel almost 7 m horizontally while in the air. The force applied to the coin is vertical. There is no force acting horizontally on the coin, which "maintains a constant speed" horizontally, keeping up with your hand and the car. You can imagine what would happen if the car stopped abruptly while the coin was in the air. It would hit the front of the car at 50 km/h.

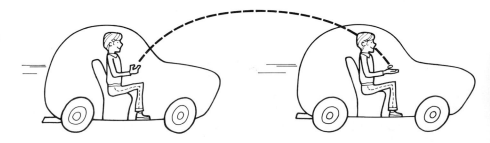

• Cut a small square of cardboard 4 cm by 4 cm. Balance the card on one index finger. Now place a nickel on the card so that it balances, too. Aim carefully, then flick one corner of the card with the other index finger. If you hit the corner squarely, the card will spin out from under the nickel, leaving the nickel balanced on your finger. The force is applied to the card, not the nickel. The nickel "maintains its state of rest".

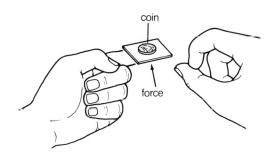
coin

force

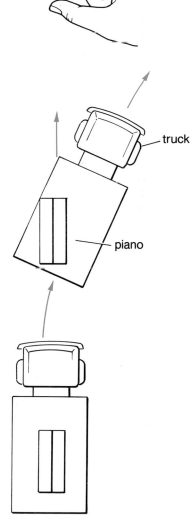
truck

piano

Sample Problems

Suppose you are helping a friend move from one residence to another. The friend asks you to stand in the back of a pickup truck to hold a piano because there is no rope available to tie it down. Explain why you should refuse this request. Your answer should show that you understand the reasoning used by Galileo and Newton.

Since the piano has a large mass, it also has a great deal of inertia. If the pickup truck starts suddenly, the piano trying to stay in its state of rest could roll off the back of the truck. If the truck stops suddenly, the piano will have a tendency to keep moving. Anyone standing between the cab of the pickup and the piano could be crushed. Similarly, if the truck turns a corner, the piano will tend to continue moving in a straight line, while the truck takes the curve. A person standing beside the piano could be injured in this case. The diagram in the margin illustrates this point.

Practice

1. Construction workers are warned not to leave their hard hats on the rear window ledge of their cars. Explain why.

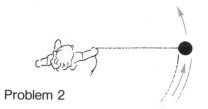

Problem 2

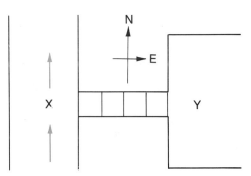

Problem 3

In the text, when an unbalanced force is part of a free body diagram, it will be shown as a force vector unattached to the body being considered. All vectors representing forces acting on the body will be connected to the body.

You can also think of the "unbalanced force", or "net force", as the vector sum of all the forces acting on the object.

Chapter 6

2. A boy looks down from an apartment building to see a girl twirling a ball on a string around her head. If the string breaks while in the position shown in the diagram, what path will the ball take? Explain your answer.

3. A delivery boy throws newspapers onto his customers' front porches. At a particular instant, the boy is riding due north at a constant speed and aims a newspaper to land on a customer's porch at Y. He throws the paper so that it travels due east relative to him. For the newspaper to reach its intended destination, should he throw it before he gets to, the instant he reaches, or after he has passed point X? Explain the reasons for your answer.

Free Body Diagrams

When analyzing many problems, it is frequently helpful to draw a diagram on which all the forces acting on an object are shown as force vectors. As we explained briefly in Chapter 5, such a diagram is called a free body diagram.

Sample Problems

For each of the following, determine the magnitude and direction of the net, or unbalanced, force. State which objects could be at rest or could be moving with a uniform velocity.

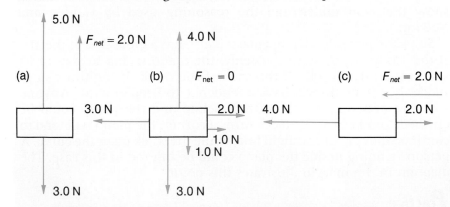

Only object (b) could be at rest or moving with uniform velocity because it is the only one in which the unbalanced force is 0.

Practice

1. Determine the magnitude and direction of the net force for each of the following. State in which case the object could be at rest.

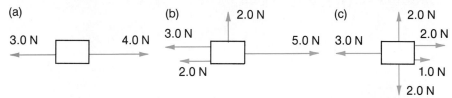

(a) 3.0 N ← ☐ → 4.0 N

(b) 2.0 N ↑, 3.0 N ←, 5.0 N →, 2.0 N ↓

(c) 2.0 N ↑, 2.0 N →, 3.0 N ←, 2.0 N →, 1.0 N →, 2.0 N ↓

2. A jet plane is travelling at a constant speed in a straight line in level flight. What does this tell you about the forces acting on it? Draw a free body diagram of the plane, showing all the forces acting on it.

3. A woman pushes a refrigerator across the floor at a steady speed of 20 cm/s. If she has to push with a horizontal force of 400 N to keep it moving, is the force of friction on the refrigerator
   (a) more than 400 N? (b) less than 400 N? (c) 400 N?
   Explain your answer.

4. A 1200 kg boat accelerates steadily at 0.05 m/s² in a straight line. Are the forces on this boat balanced or unbalanced?

6.3 Newton's Second Law: Motion with Unbalanced Forces

When an unbalanced force acts on an object, it seems reasonable that the object will not have a constant velocity but will accelerate. Investigation 6.1 will give you an understanding of the relationship between an unbalanced force and the resulting motion. For now, the following simple exercise will give you some insight into this relationship.

You will need a dynamics cart, a meterstick, and a long elastic band. Loop the elastic over the peg at the front of the cart. Hold the cart steady with one hand as you stretch the band about 20 cm. Release the cart, keeping the band stretched at 20 cm. (This provides a constant, unbalanced force.) You should find that you will have to increase your speed as you run beside the cart to keep up with it.

Notice that the cart accelerated in the direction in which you applied the constant force. Were you to analyze this process by collecting data, you would find the cart's acceleration to be uniform.

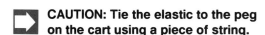

CAUTION: Tie the elastic to the peg on the cart using a piece of string.

What do you think would happen if you repeated the experiment using two identical elastic bands in parallel? With careful analysis, you'd find that when an unbalanced force is doubled, the resulting acceleration is doubled, too. We can write this mathematically as:

$$\vec{a} \propto \vec{F}, \text{ where } m \text{ is constant}$$

A third factor can affect the situation. Let's return to a single elastic band, but repeat the process using two carts, one on top of the other. What do you think would happen? The cart accelerates, of course, but more slowly. When a force remains constant, but the mass increases, the acceleration decreases. In this case, where the mass doubles, the acceleration is half as great as before. Mathematically, the relationship can be expressed as:

$$\vec{a} \propto \frac{1}{m}, \text{ where } \vec{F} \text{ is constant}$$

The ideas in this section can be summarized to create Newton's Second Law:

If an unbalanced force acts on an object, the object accelerates in the direction of the force.
The acceleration varies directly with the unbalanced force.
The acceleration varies inversely with the mass of the object.

Newton wrote: "LAW II: The change of motion is proportional to the motive force impressed, and is made in the direction of the straight line in which the force is impressed."

We can combine the two proportionality statements to form a third proportionality statement,

$$\vec{a} \propto \frac{\vec{F}}{m}$$

or insert a proportionality constant, k, to produce

$$\vec{a} = \frac{k\vec{F}}{m}$$

which is more commonly written as

$$k\vec{F} = m\vec{a}$$

In SI units, mass is measured in kilograms and acceleration is measured in meters per second squared. The equation is most simple when k is assigned a value of 1. Given this value we can solve the equation to see what units F must have.

$$k\vec{F} = m\vec{a}$$

$$1|F| = (kg)(m/s^2)$$

We can see that F must have units of kilograms times meters per second squared if k has a value of 1.

You will recall that we introduced the newton as the unit of force in Chapter 5. In actual fact one newton is equal to one kilogram meter per second squared. We can now properly define the newton as follows:

---

1 N is the force that, when applied to a mass of 1 kg, produces an acceleration of 1 m/s².

$$1 \text{ N} = 1 \text{ kg} \cdot \text{m/s}^2$$

As SI units are used throughout this text, instead of using $k\vec{F} = m\vec{a}$ for Newton's Second Law, we can write $\vec{F}_{net} = m\vec{a}$ because $k = 1$. The subscript, *net*, reminds us that it is the net, or unbalanced, force that determines the acceleration.

Mathematically, then, Newton's Second Law is:

$$\vec{F}_{net} = m\vec{a}$$

This relationship is illustrated in the following sample problems.

Chapter 5 pointed out that the gravitational field strength in newtons per kilogram is always identical to the acceleration of a freely falling body in meters per second squared. We can now see why. Since $1 \text{ N} = 1 \text{ kg} \cdot \text{m/s}^2$, the expressions newtons per kilogram and meters per second squared are dimensionally equivalent.

Sample Problems

1. What is the acceleration of a 70 kg skater, acted upon by an unbalanced force of 161 N[W]?

$$\vec{a} = \frac{\vec{F}_{net}}{m}$$

$$= \frac{161 \text{ N[W]}}{70 \text{ kg}}$$

$$= 2.3 \text{ m/s}^2\text{[W]}$$

Therefore the skater accelerates at 2.3 m/s²[W].

2. A worker applies a force of 360 N[E] on a trunk of mass 50 kg. If frictional resistance amounts to 340 N, what is the resulting acceleration of the trunk?

It's often useful to construct a free body diagram (see margin) to solve problems of this type. We can draw a rectangle to represent the trunk. The 360 N applied force is shown as a vector acting on the trunk in an easterly direction. Since the frictional resistance opposes the motion, it acts as an applied force in the opposite direction. The information can then be summarized as follows:

$$\vec{F}_{net} = 20 \text{ N[E]}$$

$$m = 50 \text{ kg}$$

$$\vec{a} = \frac{\vec{F}_{net}}{m}$$

$$= \frac{20 \text{ N[E]}}{50 \text{ kg}}$$

$$= 0.40 \text{ m/s}^2\text{[E]}$$

Therefore the trunk will accelerate at 0.40 m/s²[E].

3. A boy pushes horizontally on a 10 kg wagon and it accelerates at 2.5 m/s². If frictional forces total 50 N, what force must he be exerting on it? When no direction is specified for the acceleration or the net force, you can assume that they are in the positive direction.

$$m = 10 \text{ kg}$$

$$\vec{a} = 2.5 \text{ m/s}^2$$

$$\vec{F}_{net} = m\vec{a}$$

$$= (10 \text{ kg}) (2.5 \text{ m/s}^2)$$

$$= 25 \text{ N}$$

The net force is 25 N. We can use a free body diagram to help determine the force that the boy applies.

$F_{net} = 20$ N

$F_f = 340$ N $F_a = 360$ N

$F_N = 490$ N

$F_g = 490$ N

The normal force, F_N, and the force of gravity, F_g, are also shown in this diagram. If you are certain that the forces acting on the object in a vertical direction balance each other, it is acceptable to omit them from the free body diagram.

Note that a wiggly arrow is used to denote the acceleration vector in the free body diagram. We have done this to avoid confusion when both a force vector and an acceleration vector are needed in a free body diagram. We will use this convention in this text. Also note that F_{net} is shown unattached to the wagon. This is because it represents the vector sum of all contact forces acting on the wagon.

$F_{net} = 25$ N $a = 2.5$ m/s²

$F_f = 50$ N $F_a = ?$

or, expressed mathematically

$$\vec{F}_{net} = \vec{F}_a + \vec{F}_f$$ where $\vec{F}_a$ is the applied force and
$$25\ N = \vec{F}_a - 50\ N$$ $\vec{F}_f$ is the force of friction
$$\vec{F}_a = 75\ N$$

To produce the required unbalanced force of 25 N, the boy must exert a force of 75 N in the direction in which the wagon is accelerating.

Practice

1. The net force on a 5.0 kg bowling ball is 20 N. What is its acceleration?
2. A baseball hit by a bat with an average force of 1000 N accelerates at 4.0×10^3 m/s². What is the ball's mass?
3. What unbalanced force is needed to accelerate a 3.0×10^4 kg spacecraft at 2.5 m/s²?
4. How much applied force is needed to accelerate a 2.0 kg block of wood at 4.0 m/s² along a rough table, against a 10 N force of friction?
5. A jet plane pilot decides to accelerate horizontally. If the thrust of the engines is increased to 50 000 N at a time when the air resistance (or drag) acting on the 4000 kg plane amounts to 30 000 N, what will be the plane's acceleration?

6.4 Newton's Third Law

When you blow up a balloon and release it, air rushes from the open nozzle and causes it to move off in the opposite direction. A skater, standing at the side of a skating rink, pushes against the boards and glides off in the other direction, towards the center of the ice. A soldier places a rifle against his shoulder and pulls the trigger. As the bullet speeds from the muzzle, the rifle is driven backward into the soldier's shoulder by the recoil.

These familiar situations are examples of a phenomenon that Newton summarized in his work on motion. We now call it Newton's Third Law of Motion:

For every action force, there exists a reaction force that is equal in magnitude but opposite in direction.

or

If object A exerts a force on object B, then object B exerts a force equal in magnitude, but opposite in direction, on object A.

Newton's original version is: "LAW III: To every action there is always opposed an equal reaction; or, the mutual actions of two bodies upon each other are always equal, and directed to contrary parts." In the discussion that followed, he added: "If you press a stone with your finger, the finger is also pressed by the stone. If a horse draws a stone tied to a rope, the horse (if I may say so) will be equally drawn back towards the stone."

Another way of looking at Newton's Third Law is realizing that you cannot touch someone else without being touched in return.

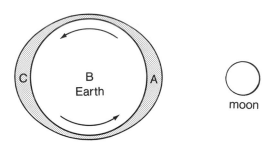

Diagram is a top view, looking down on the north pole of the earth.

At some locations, such as the Bay of Fundy in Nova Scotia, Canada, there are extreme changes in sea level at high and low tide.

In the preceding example above, when the skater pushes against the boards of the rink (action force), the boards push back on the skater with an equal force but in the opposite direction (reaction force). This force causes the skater to move in the opposite direction from the one in which she originally pushed. Mathematically, we can write:

$$\vec{F}_{\text{skater-on-boards}} = -\vec{F}_{\text{boards-on-skater}}$$
$$\text{(action force)} \quad \text{(reaction force)}$$

Similarly, the reaction force of a bullet backward on the rifle causes the rifle to move backward into the soldier's shoulder. The reaction force of the air pushing on the inner surface of the balloon causes it to move in the direction opposite to the escaping air.

In each of these cases, it is the reaction force that causes the described motion. No force in nature exists without its equal and opposite reaction force.

One of the most striking action-reaction pairs is found in the Earth-moon system. We know that the Earth exerts a force on the moon: that the moon orbits the Earth. We also know that the moon exerts a force back on the Earth: the moon's gravitational pull on the Earth causes tides. Observe the diagram that shows the two high tides in a 24-h period. The moon attracts the water at A more strongly than it attracts the Earth at B because the water is closer to the moon than the Earth. As the water is free to move, its level is raised on the side closest to the moon and a high tide is created. Similarly, the moon attracts the Earth at B more strongly than the water at C. The latter is on the side of the Earth opposite the moon. In a sense the water at C is "left behind" because there is less force on it than on an equivalent mass of earth. Consequently a high tide results at C.

These examples illustrate a basic truth about the world around us—forces exist in pairs. A single force is impossible. There is always a corresponding reaction force. You may wonder how an unbalanced force can act on an object if all forces occur in equal but opposite pairs. You must recognize that action and reaction forces always act on *different* bodies. Consider the skater and the boards. The skater's force acts on the boards. The boards' reaction force acts on the skater. Were we to draw a free body diagram of the skater, we would only show the force exerted on her by the boards. Two other forces act on the skater. Earth exerts a downward gravitational force on her, and the ice exerts an upward force on her. In the diagram, we see that the unbalanced force acts on the skater towards the left, causing an acceleration in that direction.

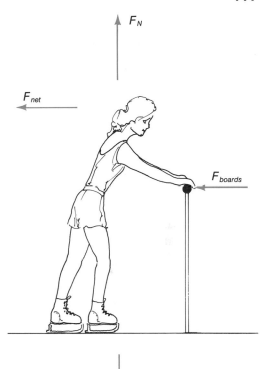

Sample Problems

1. A tractor exerts a force of 2000 N[W] on a trailer. Describe the reaction force.
   The trailer exerts a force of 2000 N[E] on the tractor.
2. A 10 kg bowling ball is at rest on the floor.
   (a) Draw a free body diagram for the ball.
   (b) Describe each of the forces acting on the ball.
   (c) For each of the forces described in (b), describe the corresponding reaction force.
   (a) To calculate the force of gravity on a mass, we use the relationship developed in Chapter 5, $F_g = mg$.

$$\vec{F_g} = m\vec{g}$$
$$= (10 \text{ kg}) (9.8 \text{ N/kg[down]})$$
$$= 98 \text{N[down]}$$

Since the ball remains at rest, we know that the forces acting on it are balanced. Therefore, the floor must exert a force of 98 N[up] on the ball. The free body diagram in the margin illustrates this.
(b) and (c)

Action	Reaction
a force of 98 N exerted downward by the Earth on the ball	a force of 98 N exerted upward by the ball on the Earth
a force of 98 N exerted upward by the floor on the ball	a force of 98 N exerted downward by the ball on the floor

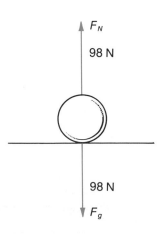

*P*ractice

1. Write a description of the reaction force for each of the following forces.
    (a) When a football player kicks a football, his foot exerts a force of 500 N[N] on the ball.
    (b) A book pushes down on a desk with a force of 25 N.
    (c) A crane exerts a force of 6000 N[up] on a steel girder that it is lifting.
    (d) A gun exerts a force of 1000 N[E] on a bullet when the bullet is fired.
    (e) The Earth pulls down on an apple with a force of 5 N.
2. A skydiver of mass 60 kg attempting a publicity stunt jumps from the edge of the CN tower.
    (a) Draw a free body diagram for the skydiver in the instant after he jumps. (Assume that at this point his velocity is near zero so that air resistance is still negligible.)
    (b) Write a description for the force acting on him.
    (c) Describe the reaction force for the force described in (b).
3. An astronaut is stranded 10 m from a space station that is orbiting the Earth. Explain what she could do to return to the space station. Assume that the jet pack used to propel her is out of fuel, but that it can be removed without endangering her.
4. A man wants to test a rope. He ties one end to a telephone pole and the other to a horse. The horse pulls as hard as it can, but is not strong enough to break the rope. The man replaces the telephone pole with a second horse of identical strength. Assume the two horses pull in opposite directions as hard as they can. Will the rope break? Explain your answer.

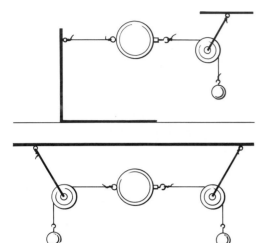

The demonstration above may help you understand question 4. All the masses are identical. Before you set up the demonstration, predict what the reading on each spring scale will be.

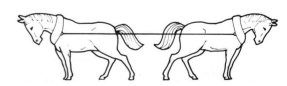

An Action-Reaction Problem

In the following illustration of Newton's Third Law we can calculate the size of the action force and reaction force separately.

Consider the situation shown in the diagram in the margin. A force of 60 N[E] acts on a combination of two boxes that are next to each other on a frictionless surface.

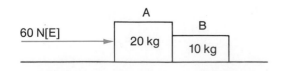

Find:
(a) the acceleration of the boxes.
(b) the force exerted by box A on box B.
(c) the force exerted by box B on box A.

(a) To find the acceleration of the boxes, we can simply think of them as being one mass. The free body diagram in the margin shows all the information given in the question.

$$\vec{a} = \frac{\vec{F}_{net}}{m}$$

$$= \frac{60 \text{ N[E]}}{30 \text{ kg}}$$

$$= 2.0 \text{ m/s}^2\text{[E]}$$

Therefore, the system accelerates at 2.0 m/s²[E].

(b) To find the force exerted by A on B, we need to construct a free body diagram for B. (Remember that a free body diagram for an object shows all the forces acting on it.)

Since the force exerted by A on B is the only force acting in a horizontal direction, it must be the unbalanced force.

$$\vec{F}_{net} = m\vec{a}$$

$$= (10 \text{ kg}) (2.0 \text{ m/s}^2\text{[E]})$$

$$= 20 \text{ N[E]}$$

The force exerted by A on B is 20 N[E]. Are you surprised to see that the 60 N exerted on A is not all transferred to B? If you think about it you will realize that this is not possible. If it were, then B would accelerate at 6.0 m/s² instead of at 2.0 m/s².

(c) To find the force exerted by B on A, construct a free body diagram for A. We find the net force acting on A first.

$$\vec{F}_{net} = m\vec{a}$$

$$= (20 \text{ kg}) (2 \text{ m/s}^2\text{[E]})$$

$$= 40 \text{ N[E]}$$

Since the net force is 40 N[E] and the force being applied on A is 60 N[E], B must be pushing back on A with a force of 20 N[W].

You can see that the answers obtained for (b) and (c) constitute an action-reaction pair. If we changed the masses of A and B and the applied force, we would get different values. We would always find, though, that the force exerted by B on A is *equal* and *opposite* to that exerted by A on B.

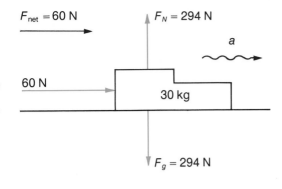

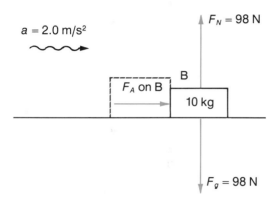

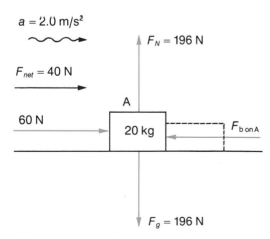

This example shows clearly that action and reaction forces act on different bodies.

"Tension" is a word that physicists and engineers use to describe the force exerted by a rope or rigid member that "pulls" on another object. It may also be referred to as a *tensile force*.

*P*ractice

1. Two toboggans are connected by a rope. The first toboggan has a mass of 60 kg and the second has a mass of 40 kg. The two toboggans are pulled by a rope connected to the first toboggan. If the force exerted on the rope is 250 N[E], and friction between the toboggans and the ice can be ignored, find:
   (a) the acceleration of the toboggans.
   (b) the tension in the rope connecting the toboggans.

2. Suppose a third toboggan of mass 25 kg is connected to the second toboggan in question 1. Find:
   (a) the acceleration of the system of three toboggans.
   (b) the force exerted by toboggan one on toboggan two.
   (c) the force exerted by the second toboggan on the last one.

Applying Newton's Third Law

We see evidence of Newton's Third Law around us all the time. The following are but a few applications. With the exception of rockets, they are things you could likely witness every day.

Walking

Note that in this case, friction acts in the direction of motion, since it is the force responsible for your acceleration.

When you walk, you push with your feet, but your feet do not push on you. They push on the ground and are not responsible for your movement. We need to find a force that acts forwards, and acts on you. This force is the reaction force of the ground. Your feet push backwards on the ground and the ground pushes you forwards. The next time someone asks you why you can walk, tell them the ground pushes you forwards.

Driving

When a car moves forwards, the engine turns the driveshaft, the driveshaft turns the wheels, and the wheels push backwards on the ground. If you have ever stood behind a car accelerating on gravel, you will appreciate this. Why does the car move forwards? The ground pushes it forwards, because of the reaction force to the force of the turning wheels.

Consider what happens to a car on slippery ice. There is nothing wrong with the car's engine, but it can't make the car go forwards. Because the ice is slippery, the wheels cannot exert much force of friction on the ground. Consequently, the ground cannot exert much force of friction on the wheels, either.

Swimming

In swimming, you push backwards on the water. The water's reaction force pushes you forwards.

Flying

A propeller on a plane pushes air backwards, like a giant fan. This air pushes forwards on the propeller, which moves ahead, dragging the plane along behind it.

Rockets

The burning, or combustion, of fuel in a rocket's engine produces gases. These gases are forced out at great speed and exert an equal and opposite force on the rocket. When a rocket is launched, the force on the exhaust gases causes them to move in one direction. The gases react on the rocket and force it to accelerate in the opposite direction. In other words, the rocket accelerates in one direction by throwing mass in the opposite direction. The greater the mass, and the faster it's thrown, the greater the resulting force on the rocket.

A massive amount of fuel is used to place a space shuttle in orbit. The fuel tank and the solid fuel rocket boosters are larger and heavier than the shuttle itself.

6.5 Using Newton's Laws

A knowledge of Newton's Laws can be used together with concepts developed in earlier chapters to solve motion problems.

Sample Problems

1. A boy gives his sister a ride on a sled by exerting a force of 300 N[E]. Frictional resistance amounts to 200 N. If the sister and sled have a combined mass of 50 kg, and if the boy starts from rest and pushes for 5.0 s, find the following:
   (a) the sled's acceleration.
   (b) the velocity attained by the sled in 5.0 s.
   (c) the distance travelled by the sled in 5.0 s.

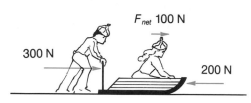

(a) We can summarize the information given in the problem as follows:

$$\vec{v_1} = 0$$
$$\Delta t = 5.0 \text{ s}$$
$$\vec{a} = ?$$

A free body diagram will help in the solution.

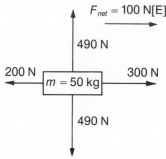

Assume that east is positive.

$$\vec{F}_{net} = \vec{F}_1 + \vec{F}_2$$
$$= 300 \text{ N} - 200 \text{ N}$$
$$= 100 \text{ N}$$

$$\vec{F}_{net} = m\vec{a}$$
$$100 \text{ N} = (50 \text{ kg}) \vec{a}$$
$$\vec{a} = \frac{100 \text{ N}}{50 \text{ kg}}$$
$$= 2.0 \text{ m/s}^2$$

The sled accelerates at 2.0 m/s²[E].

(b) We can use the information summarized for part (a) as well as the fact that the acceleration is 2.0 m/s²[E].

$$\vec{v_2} = \vec{v_1} + \vec{a}\Delta t$$
$$= 0 + (2.0 \text{ m/s}^2)(5.0 \text{ s})$$
$$= 10 \text{ m/s}$$

The sled acquires a velocity of 10 m/s[E] in 5.0 s.

(c) Using the information given in the question and the answers to parts (a) and (b), we actually have more than one way of finding the answer to (c). Only one solution is given.

$$\vec{\Delta d} = \vec{v_1}\Delta t + \frac{1}{2}\vec{a}(\Delta t)^2$$

$$= 0 + \left(\frac{1}{2}\right)(2.0 \text{ m/s}^2)(5.0 \text{ s})^2$$

$$= 25 \text{ m, or } 25 \text{ m[E]}$$

The sled's displacement for the 5.0 s interval that it is pushed is 25 m[E].

2. An automobile travelling at 72 km/h hits a tree. The driver who has a mass of 55 kg comes to rest in 0.10 s after the impact.
   (a) What is the average force that acts on the driver?
   (b) What distance does the driver travel after the car first hits the tree?

(a) Summarizing the information given:

$$\vec{v}_1 = 72 \text{ km/h}$$
$$\Delta t = 0.10 \text{ s}$$
$$m = 55 \text{ kg}$$
$$\vec{v}_2 = 0$$

Before proceeding, the value of $\vec{v}_1$ must be converted to meters per second.

$$\vec{v}_1 = \left(\frac{72 \text{ km}}{1 \text{ h}}\right)\left(\frac{1000 \text{ m}}{1 \text{ km}}\right)\left(\frac{1 \text{ h}}{3600 \text{ s}}\right)$$
$$= 20 \text{ m/s}$$
$$\vec{a} = \frac{\vec{v}_2 - \vec{v}_1}{\Delta t}$$
$$= \frac{0 - 20 \text{ m/s}}{0.10 \text{ s}}$$
$$= -200 \text{ m/s}^2$$
$$\vec{F}_{net} = m\vec{a}$$
$$= (55 \text{ kg})(-200 \text{ m/s}^2)$$
$$= -11\ 000 \text{ N, or } -1.1 \times 10^4 \text{ N}$$

The solution assumes constant acceleration as the car comes to rest.

The front portion of the car collapses as the driver is brought to rest.

The negative value for force means that the force on the driver acted in a direction opposite to that in which the car was travelling.

(b)
$$= \left(\frac{\vec{v}_1 + \vec{v}_2}{2}\right)\Delta t$$
$$= \left(\frac{20 \text{ m/s} + 0}{2}\right)(0.10 \text{ s})$$
$$= 1.0 \text{ m}$$

The driver travels a distance of 1.0 m after the car hits the tree.

3. A skydiver, complete with parachute, has a mass of 70 kg. A short time after the skydiver jumps from the aircraft, the force of air resistance acting on him is 520 N. What is his acceleration at that instant?

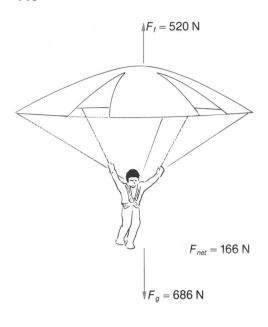

$F_f = 520$ N

$F_{net} = 166$ N

$F_g = 686$ N

A free body diagram is helpful when analyzing this type of problem. One for this sample problem is shown in the margin. Up will be considered positive and down negative.

$$\vec{F_g} = m\vec{g}$$
$$= (70 \text{ kg}) \, (-9.8 \text{ N/kg})$$
$$= -686 \text{ N}$$
$$\vec{F}_{net} = \vec{F_g} + \vec{F_f}$$
$$= -686 \text{ N} + 520 \text{ N}$$
$$= -166 \text{ N}$$

$$\vec{a} = \frac{\vec{F}_{net}}{m}$$
$$= \frac{-166 \text{ N}}{72 \text{ kg}}$$
$$= -2.3 \text{ m/s}^2, \text{ or } 2.3 \text{ m/s}^2[\text{down}]$$

At the instant specified, the skydiver will have an acceleration of 2.3 m/s²[down].

*P*ractice

1. Two children are arguing over a toy. One pulls on the toy with a force of 32 N[N]. The other pulls with a force of 30 N[S]. If the toy has a mass of 500 g, what will be its resulting acceleration?
2. A tennis player is practicing by hitting a ball against a brick wall. The ball has a mass of 84 g and is travelling at 32 m/s when it hits the racquet. If its velocity is reduced to zero, 0.010 s after it hits the racquet, determine the average force exerted by the racquet on the ball during this phase of its motion.
3. A swimmer releases a 20 kg rock from rest under water. If the resistance and buoyancy provided by the water is 150 N, how long will it take for the rock to fall 1.0 m?
4. A little girl has a toy of mass 312 g on the end of a string. She holds the string so that the toy hangs below her hand. She then exerts a force upward on the string of 3.80 N.
   (a) What is the unbalanced force acting on the toy?
   (b) What is the toy's acceleration?

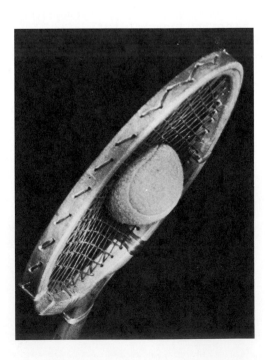

6.6 Motion and Momentum

As you have seen in previous sections, Newton's Laws are used when examining many problems in motion. They explain why some objects are stationary, why others move, and why some accelerate. Examples of forces and the changes in motion they cause can be seen everywhere. It is easy to observe a change in velocity when two football players collide or when a golf ball is struck. The change in direction that occurs when a rubber ball bounces against a wall is also a velocity change.

When forces act on these objects, the resulting acceleration is not as easy to measure as the changes in velocity. In fact, Newton's original thinking on motion was not in terms of an object's acceleration. Rather, Newton described an object's motion by combining the mass and velocity of the moving object. He called this expression the object's quantity of motion. We now call this quantity **momentum** and give it the symbol $\vec{p}$. The momentum of a moving object is given by the equation:

$$\vec{p} = m\vec{v}$$

where $\vec{p}$ is the object's momentum, in kilogram meters per second
m is its mass, in kilograms
$\vec{v}$ is its velocity, in meters per second

Combining information about the mass and velocity of an object gives us a way of comparing the motion of objects. For instance, a school bus and a car travelling at the same speed would have different amounts of momentum because they have different masses. Because of its larger mass, the school bus has more momentum. With this greater momentum, it would be more difficult to change the motion of the bus than to change the motion of the car.

Momentum is a vector quantity whose direction is always the same as that of the object's velocity. The unit of momentum, kilogram meter per second (kg · m/s), is a derived unit and has no special name.

Sample Problems

What is the momentum of a 1000 kg car moving at 15 m/s[E]?
$$\vec{p} = m\vec{v}$$
$$= (1000 \text{ kg})(15 \text{ m/s[E]})$$
$$= 1.5 \times 10^4 \text{ kg} \cdot \text{m/s[E]}$$

In simple problems involving momentum, the direction of the moving object is often not stated. Usually, the direction is not significant to the understanding of the problem and we assume it is just "forward".

Practice

1. Calculate the momentum of each of the following objects:
   (a) a 0.50 kg ball thrown upward with a velocity of 30 m/s
   (b) a 2000 kg railway car moving south at 10 m/s
   (c) an electron of mass 9.1×10^{-31} kg, moving at a velocity of 1.0×10^7 m/s
   (d) the Earth, of mass 6.0×10^{24} kg, moving along its solar orbit with a velocity of 3.0×10^4 m/s
2. The momentum of a 7.3 kg shot is 22 kg · m/s[forward]. What is its velocity?
3. A bullet travelling at 900 m/s has a momentum of 4.5 kg · m/s. What is its mass?

6.7 Momentum and Impulse

Newton's laws can also be written in terms of momentum changes rather than acceleration. Newton's Second Law, $\vec{F} = m\vec{a}$, can be expressed as:

$$\vec{F} = \frac{m \, \Delta \vec{v}}{\Delta t}$$

Thus,
$$\vec{F} = \frac{m \, (\vec{v_2} - \vec{v_1})}{\Delta t}$$

or
$$\vec{F} = \frac{m\vec{v_2} - m\vec{v_1}}{\Delta t}$$

If the mass of the object does not change when the force is applied to it, the Second Law can be written as:

$$\vec{F} = \frac{\Delta \, (m\vec{v})}{\Delta t}$$

or
$$\vec{F} = \frac{\Delta \vec{p}}{\Delta t}$$

Multiplying both sides of this equation by Δt gives:

$$\vec{F}\Delta t = \Delta \vec{p}$$

$$\vec{F}\Delta t = \Delta \vec{p} = m\vec{v_2} - m\vec{v_1}$$

To change the momentum of an object, two quantities are important—the force applied to the object and the length of time the force is applied. To give a golf ball its maximum momentum, you must hit the ball hard and follow through with your swing. Following through on the swing keeps the club in contact with the ball as long as possible. This increases the time the force is exerted on the ball. The product $\vec{F}\Delta t$ is named "impulse."

$$\textbf{impulse} = \vec{F}\Delta t$$

where $\vec{F}$ is the average net force acting on an object, in newtons
Δt is the time for which the force acts, in seconds

The unit for impulse is the newton second (N · s), and impulse is a vector quantity whose direction is the same as the direction of the net force causing the impulse.

Whenever there is an impact or collision between objects, the impulse has great significance. In a collision, the car and its passengers change momentum rapidly as the car comes to a stop. In a car where a passenger is not protected by an air bag or a seat belt, the passenger might strike the hard dashboard and come to a stop very quickly—possibly within 0.07 seconds. (See "Wear Your Seat Belt" on page 165.) In a similar collision, a passenger protected by an air bag would undergo the same change in momentum and impulse. But the inflated air bag brings the passenger to a stop much more slowly. Even though the product $F\Delta t$ is the same, a greater Δt means that F will be much smaller.

A force of 40 N acting for 4 s has the same impulse as a force of 20 N acting for 8 s. In each case, the product is 160 kg · m/s. The graphs below will help you visualize this.

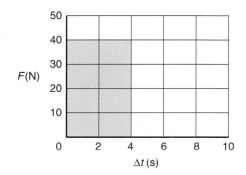

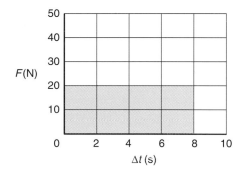

Sample Problems

1. What average force will stop a 1000 kg car in 1.5 s if the car is moving at 22 m/s?

$$\vec{F}\Delta t = m\vec{v}_2 - m\vec{v}_1$$

Therefore, $\vec{F} = \dfrac{m\vec{v}_2 - m\vec{v}_1}{\Delta t}$

$$= \frac{(1000\ \text{kg})(0\ \text{m/s}) - (1000\ \text{kg})(22\ \text{m/s})}{1.5\ \text{s}}$$

$$= \frac{-22\ 000\ \text{kg} \cdot \text{m/s}}{1.5\ \text{s}}$$

$$= -1.5 \times 10^4\ \text{N}$$

The negative sign indicates that the direction of the force is opposite to that of the car's initial velocity. This force could also be expressed as: $\vec{F} = 1.5 \times 10^4$ N[backwards]

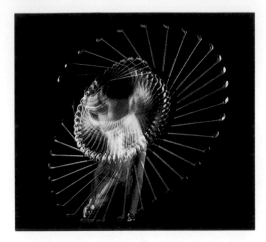

2. What is the impulse given to a golf ball by a club if they are in contact for 0.0050 s, during which time the club exerts an average force of 500 N on the ball?

$$\text{impulse} = \vec{F}\Delta t$$
$$= (500 \text{ N})(0.0050 \text{ s})$$
$$= 2.5 \text{ N} \cdot \text{s [forwards]}$$

In situations where the colliding or interacting objects move in a straight line, the vector notation for momentum and impulse may be omitted. As before, directions forwards and backwards can be indicated by using plus and minus signs. Even so, not all interactions are one-dimensional, and the vector property of momentum and impulse is very important.

*P*ractice

1. What impulse is exerted in each of the following cases?
   (a) a force of 25 N[E] on a dynamics cart for 3.2 s
   (b) a hockey stick exerting a force of 120 N on a puck during the 0.05 s they are in contact
   (c) the Earth pulling down on a 12 kg rock during the 3.0 s it takes to fall from a cliff
2. A billiard ball of mass 200 g rolls towards the right-hand cushion of a billiard table at 2.0 m/s and rebounds straight back at 2.0 m/s.
   (a) What is its change in momentum as a result of hitting the cushion?
   (b) What impulse is given to the ball by the cushion?
3. A 2.0 kg skateboard is rolling across a smooth, flat floor when a small girl kicks it, causing it to speed up to 4.5 m/s in 0.50 s without changing direction. If the average force exerted by the girl on the skateboard in its direction of motion was 6.0 N, with what initial velocity was it moving?

Perhaps the first person to publish a statement regarding impulse and momentum was John Wallis, an English mathematician. His findings concerning conservation of momentum were published in 1670 in a book called *Mechanica* and formed the basis for Newton's later statement in his *Principia*.

6.8 Conservation of Momentum

During the 17th century, Newton and others before him measured the momentum of colliding objects before and after the collision. They discovered a very interesting phenomenon: the total momentum of the colliding objects was the same before and after a collision.

For example, imagine two marbles rolling along the floor and colliding with each other. Each of their motions and momentum will change, but the total sum of their momentum will not change.

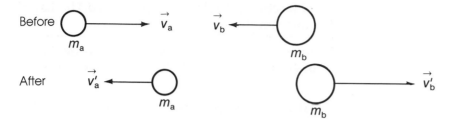

This result can be explained by applying Newton's Third Law. When any two objects collide, they exert equal and opposite forces on each other.

$$\vec{F}_{a \text{ on } b} = -\vec{F}_{b \text{ on } a}$$

Combining this with Newton's Second Law gives

$$m_b\,\vec{a}_b = -m_a\,\vec{a}_a$$

The acceleration and velocity change of each object occurs during the time Δt that the objects are in contact. Rewriting the above equation using $\vec{a} = \dfrac{\Delta \vec{v}}{\Delta t}$ gives:

$$m_b\,\frac{\Delta \vec{v}_b}{\Delta t} = -m_a\,\frac{\Delta \vec{v}_a}{\Delta t}$$

$$m_b\left(\frac{\vec{v}_b' - \vec{v}_b}{\Delta t}\right) = -m_a\left(\frac{\vec{v}_a' - \vec{v}_a}{\Delta t}\right)$$

$$\frac{m_b\vec{v}_b' - m_b\vec{v}_b}{\Delta t} = \frac{-m_a\vec{v}_a' + m_a\vec{v}_a}{\Delta t}$$

The terms $m_b\vec{v}_b'$ and $m_a\vec{v}_a'$ are the momenta of the two objects after they collide. Multiplying both sides of the equation by the amount of time of the collision, Δt, and rearranging terms yields the following expression:

$$m_a\vec{v}_a + m_b\vec{v}_b = m_a\vec{v}_a' + m_b\vec{v}_b'$$

To avoid confusion, the subscripts a and b are used to distinguish between the two objects in a collision. The prime designation is used to indicate the motion *after* the collision.

The total momentum of the two objects is the same before and after they interact. We say that the total momentum is conserved. Conservation of momentum is not limited to just two objects. It can be extended to any group, or system, of interacting objects that are free from external forces. This relationship is called The Law of Conservation of Momentum. It says:

If the net external force acting on a system of objects is zero, then the total momentum of the system remains unchanged.

$$\text{If } \vec{F}_{net} = 0,\ \Delta \vec{p}_{total} = 0$$

or

$$\vec{p}_{total} = \vec{p}'_{total}$$

The Law of Conservation of Momentum is one of the most important laws in science. It can be used to explain what happens when objects collide. For instance, conservation of momentum explains the movement of billiard balls after a collision or the scattering of bowling pins by a bowling ball. It can be used to describe the movement and behavior of gas molecules. The basic structure of the atom and the mass of particles within the atom were determined through momentum measurement during collisions and deflections of these small bits of matter.

Conservation of momentum works just as well to describe explosions. Consider, for instance, the interaction that occurs when a

During any collision, careful analysis will reveal that the total momentum of the "system" has been conserved. In this case, the bowling ball transfers some of its momentum to the pins.

bullet is fired from a rifle. Before an explosion of gunpowder drives the bullet out of the gun, the gun and the bullet are both at rest. Their total momentum is zero. After the explosion, the bullet moves out of the gun at a great velocity. Its momentum is forwards, away from the rifle. The rifle recoils, moving backwards. Both the rifle and the bullet will have equal amounts of momentum. The momentum of the gun and the bullet are in opposite directions, however. The vector quantities cancel each other, and the total momentum remains zero.

Exactly the same principle applies in rocket propulsion. Small amounts of gas (the bullets) arc cjcctcd at high vclocity from the tail of the rocket (the rifle). The massive rocket increases its velocity forwards to keep the momentum of the system unchanged.

The Law of Conservation of Momentum even works for interactions between objects that do not seem to touch each other. The gravitational effects of the Earth on the moon, the moon on the Earth (tides), and the attraction of distant stars all obey the principles of momentum conservation.

Sample Problems

1. A loaded railway car of mass 6000 kg is rolling to the right at 2.0 m/s when it collides and couples with an empty freight car of mass 3000 kg, rolling to the left on the same track at 3.0 m/s. What is their speed and direction of the pair after the collision?

Since momentum is a vector quantity, directions are significant. We will assume that velocities to the right are positive, and to the left negative. Primed symbols indicate the value of each quantity *after* collision.

Before the collision,

$$\vec{p}_a = m_a \vec{v}_a$$
$$= (6000 \text{ kg})(2.0 \text{ m/s})$$
$$= 1.2 \times 10^4 \text{ kg} \cdot \text{m/s}$$
$$\vec{p}_b = m_b \vec{v}_b$$
$$= (3000 \text{ kg})(- 3.0 \text{ m/s})$$
$$= -9.0 \times 10^3 \text{ kg} \cdot \text{m/s}$$

Therefore $\vec{p}_{total} = \vec{p}_a + \vec{p}_b$
$$= 1.2 \times 10^4 \text{ kg} \cdot \text{m/s} + (-9.0 \times 10^3 \text{ kg} \cdot \text{m/s})$$
$$= 3.0 \times 10^3 \text{ kg} \cdot \text{m/s}$$

After the collision,

$$\vec{p}'_{total} = (m_a + m_b) \vec{v}'_{ab} = (9000 \text{ kg}) \vec{v}'_{ab}$$

Since the total of outside forces on the cars is 0, $\vec{\Delta p} = 0$.

Therefore $\vec{p}'_{total} = \vec{p}_{total}$

$\quad$ (9000 kg) $\vec{v}'_{ab} = 3.0 \times 10^3$ kg $\cdot$ m/s

$\qquad\qquad\vec{v}'_{ab} = 0.33$ m/s[right]

Thus, the pair of coupled cars moved off to the right (positive direction) at a speed of 0.33 m/s.

2. Calculate the recoil velocity of an unconstrained rifle of mass 5.0 kg after it shoots a 50 g bullet at a speed of 300 m/s.

Since the rifle is unrestrained by any force, there are no net outside forces on the system.

$$\vec{\Delta p} = 0$$

$$\vec{p}_{total} = \vec{p}'_{total}$$

$$\vec{p}_b + \vec{p}_r = \vec{p}'_b + \vec{p}'_r \qquad \text{where r and b represent the}$$
$$\text{rifle and bullet respectively}$$

$$m_b\vec{v}_b + m_r\vec{v}_r = m_b\vec{v}'_b + m_r\vec{v}'_r$$

If the bullet is assumed to be shot in the positive direction,
$$(0.050 \text{ kg}) (0) + (5.0 \text{ kg}) (0) = (0.050 \text{ kg})(300 \text{ m/s}) + (5.0 \text{ kg})v'_r$$

$$v'_r = \frac{-15 \text{ kg} \cdot \text{m/s}}{5.0 \text{ kg}}$$
$$= -3.0 \text{ m/s}$$

Note that, because of its much larger mass, the speed of the rifle is much less than the speed of the bullet. The negative sign indicates that the rifle's velocity and its momentum is in the opposite direction to that of the bullet.

3. A competition is held between two teams of physics students, each team made up of three members, and each member having a mass of 60 kg. The teams will take turns climbing onto a cart and jumping off. They want to see whose cart will be moved fastest by propelling it with a jump. They will start at the west end of a cart of mass 120 kg that is free to roll without friction on a level, east-west track. The plan is to run east along the cart and then jump off with a velocity of 10 m/s, with respect to the cart. **(Do not attempt this experiment yourself.)**

The first team decides that its three members will run and jump off together. The second team decides that one member will depart according to the rules, followed by the second, and then, finally, the third.

Calculate the final velocity of the cart for each team, and discuss the results.

Assume that vectors to the east are positive and omit vector notation.

For the first team: Let the velocity acquired by the cart with respect to the Earth be V. The velocity of the three students relative to the Earth, v, will be $10 + V$.

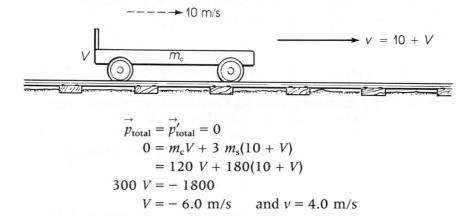

$$\vec{p}_{\text{total}} = \vec{p}'_{\text{total}} = 0$$
$$0 = m_c V + 3\, m_s(10 + V)$$
$$= 120\, V + 180(10 + V)$$
$$300\, V = -1800$$
$$V = -6.0 \text{ m/s} \quad \text{and } v = 4.0 \text{ m/s}$$

Note: The negative sign for V indicates a velocity to the west.
For the second team: Let the velocity of the cart after each successive student has jumped be V_1, V_2, and V_3, and let the velocities of the three students relative to the Earth be v_1, v_2, and v_3.

After the first student has jumped,

$$\vec{p}_{\text{total}} = \vec{p}'_{\text{total}} = 0$$
$$0 = m_c V_1 + 2\, m_s V_1 + m_s(10 + V_1)$$
$$= 120\, V_1 + 120\, V_1 + 60(10 + V_1)$$
$$300\, V_1 = -600$$
$$V_1 = -2.0 \text{ m/s, or } 2.0 \text{ m/s[W], and } v_1 = 8.0 \text{ m/s}$$

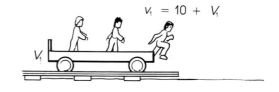

After the second student has jumped,

$$0 = m_c V_2 + m_s V_2 + m_s(10 + V_2) + m_s v_1$$
$$= 120\, V_2 + 60\, V_2 + 60(10 + V_2) + 60(8.0)$$
$$240\, V_2 = -1080$$
$$V_2 = -4.5 \text{ m/s, or } 4.5 \text{ m/s[W], and } v_2 = 5.5 \text{ m/s}$$

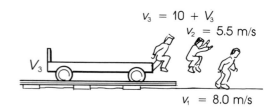

Finally, after the third student has jumped,

$$0 = m_c V_3 + m_s(10 + V_3) + m_s v_2 + m_s v_1$$
$$= 120\, V_3 + 60(10 + V_3) + 60(5.5) + 60(8.0)$$
$$180\, V_3 = -1410$$
$$V_3 = -7.8 \text{ m/s, or } 7.8 \text{ m/s[W], and } v_3 = 2.2 \text{ m/s}$$

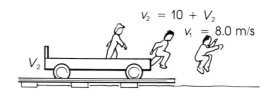

Of course, as the rocket engines expel exhaust gases backwards to provide forward momentum, the mass of the rocket slowly decreases. For that reason, the last kilogram of gases ejected produces the greatest increase in velocity.

As can be seen from the result, the team that chose to have its members jump separately was able to give the cart a greater velocity in the opposite direction. This is what happens in a rocket as the engines burn and eject mass in continuous small amounts, instead of ejecting it all in one large burst.

*P*ractice

(All velocities are relative to the Earth unless otherwise specified.)

1. A 5000 kg boxcar moving at 5.2 m/s on a level, frictionless track, runs into a stationary 8000 kg tank car. If they hook together in the collision, how fast will they be moving afterwards?

2. A 75 kg girl running at 3.0 m/s jumps onto a sled that has a mass of 10 kg and that is already moving in the same direction as the girl, at 2.0 m/s. What will be the final velocity of the girl and the sled, assuming that the sled is on level snow and that there is no friction?

3. A 100 g ball moving at a constant velocity of 200 cm/s strikes a 400 g ball that is at rest. After the collision, the first ball rebounds straight back at 120 cm/s. Calculate the final velocity of the second ball.

4. A 25 kg object moving with a velocity of 3.0 m/s to the right collides with a 15 kg object moving to the left at 6.0 m/s. Find the velocity of the 25 kg object after the collision, if the 15 kg object (a) continues to move to the left but at only 0.30 m/s, (b) rebounds to the right at 0.45 m/s, and (c) sticks together with the 25 kg object.

5. A 1.5 kg wooden trolley on wheels is stationary on a horizontal, frictionless track. What will be the final velocity of the trolley if a bullet of mass 2.0 g is fired into it with a horizontal velocity of 300 m/s along the direction of the track? (The bullet remains embedded in the trolley.)

6. An experimental rocket sled on a level, frictionless track has a mass of 1.4×10^4 kg. For propulsion, it expels gases from its rocket engines at a rate of 10 kg/s and at an exhaust speed of 2.5×10^4 m/s relative to the rocket. For how many seconds must the engines burn in order that the sled acquire a velocity of 50 m/s starting from rest? You may ignore the small decrease in mass of the sled and the small speed of the rocket compared to the exhaust gas.

Investigations

Investigation 6.1: Newton's Second Law

Preamble:
In the following investigation, carts of different masses will be accelerated by varying amounts of force. The carts have low-friction roller skate wheels. If the frictional force is very small, the unbalanced force will be almost exactly equal to the force applied to accelerate the cart.

The first mass to be accelerated is a cart and three 200 g masses. The diagram below shows that two of the masses are on the cart and one is attached to the cart by means of a string which passes over a pulley.

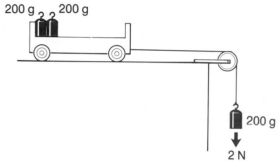

Gravity exerts a force of (0.200 kg)(9.8 N/kg), or about 2.0 N, on the 200 g mass suspended by the string. If the cart is released and allowed to accelerate, this 2.0 N force will not change. The 200 g mass moving downward and the cart and masses moving to the right have accelerations that are equal in magnitude. By attaching a paper tape to the cart and allowing the tape to pass through a recording timer, we can determine the kind of motion that occurs when a constant unbalanced force acts on a mass.

To double the force accelerating the system, we simply transfer a 200 g mass from the cart to the end of the string. The total mass being accelerated has not changed, however. It is still one cart and three 200 g masses.

To triple the force accelerating the system, the last 200 g mass is transferred from the cart to the end of the string.

Suppose we wished to double the total mass being accelerated without changing the unbalanced force that is acting. We simply add another cart and three more 200 g masses.

Three times the original mass would be a total of three carts and nine 200 g masses.

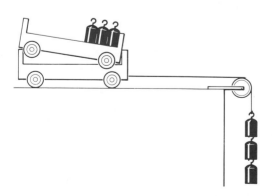

Vector signs have been omitted here for the sake of simplicity.

Instead of plotting a velocity-time graph for each tape produced in the experiment, it is possible to determine the average acceleration as follows.

Given:

$$\Delta d = v_1 \Delta t + \frac{1}{2}a(\Delta t)^2$$

and

$$v_1 = 0$$

(For each trial in the experiment the value of v_1 is 0.)

then

$$\Delta d = \frac{1}{2}a(\Delta t)^2$$

This expression can then be rearranged to give:

$$a = \frac{2\Delta d}{(\Delta t)^2}$$

The magnitude of the cart's acceleration in the horizontal direction is equal to the magnitude of the acceleration of the mass in a downward direction.

The acceleration can then be determined by measuring the distance travelled, doubling it, and dividing it by the square of the time taken. If the acceleration is not uniform, this calculation will yield the average acceleration.

Problems:
(a) Is the acceleration produced by a constant unbalanced force uniform?
(b) How does an increase in the magnitude of the unbalanced force affect the acceleration if the mass is kept constant?
(c) How does an increase in the mass of an object affect the acceleration if the unbalanced force is kept constant?

Materials:
3 carts
nine 200 g masses
recording timer
paper tape
pulley and string
clamp for pulley
matches
retort stand
table

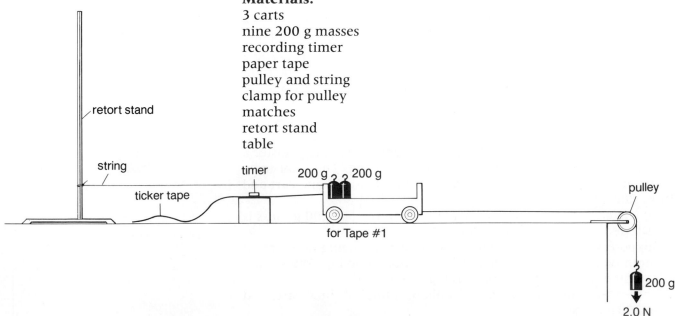

retort stand

string

ticker tape

timer   200 g 200 g

pulley

for Tape #1

200 g

2.0 N

Procedure:

1. Find the mass of each of the carts you will use.
2. Set up the apparatus as shown in the diagram. (Make sure that the length of paper tape is a few centimeters less than the distance between the 200 g mass hanging over the pulley and the floor.) The string on the left side of the cart will hold the cart until you are ready to begin the experiment.
3. Start the timer. Burn the string near the retort stand to release the cart. Catch the cart before it hits the pulley. Label the tape you produce "tape 1".
4. Analyze the tape and show the data you have collected. Construct a velocity-time graph for the motion of the cart and masses. (See Investigation 2.1, if necessary.)
5. Repeat steps 1 to 3 to produce four more tapes. Use the cart and mass arrangements shown in the series of diagrams in the margin. Note that for tapes 2 and 3, the total mass is the same as tape 1, but the force is greater. For tapes 4 and 5, the force is the same as for tape 3, but the total mass is increased for each one.
6. Determine the average acceleration for tape 1 by using the velocity-time graph you constructed.
7. For each of tapes 2 to 5: (a) Mark convenient time intervals starting with the first dot on each tape, e.g., 30 dots = $30 \times \frac{1}{60}$ s = 0.50 s. (b) Measure the distance travelled in this time. (c) Calculate the car's acceleration. (d) Record your calculation results in a chart similar to this:

Tape	Force (N)	Mass (kg)	Acceleration (m/s²)	Mass × Acceleration
1	2			
2	4			
3	6			
4	6			
5	6			

8. From the chart in step 7, note that there were three trials for which the mass was constant but the force changed. Construct a data table with the following headings:

Force (N)	Acceleration (m/s²)

Use the table to construct a graph of acceleration versus force. After plotting the data, which will consist of three points, draw the best straight line.

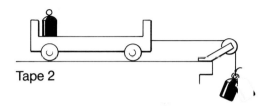

Tape 2

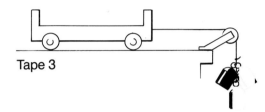

Tape 3

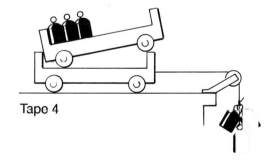

Tape 4

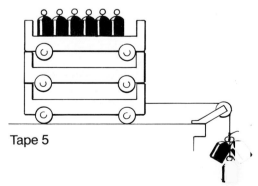

Tape 5

9. Once again, note from the chart in step 7 that there were three trials for which the force was constant but mass changed. Construct a data table with the following headings:

Mass (kg)	Acceleration (m/s²)

Use the table to construct a graph of acceleration versus mass. After plotting the data, which will consist of three points, draw the best smooth curve.

10. Use the chart from step 7 to construct a graph of force versus mass times acceleration, the product of mass and acceleration, for all cases.

Questions:

1. What type of acceleration results when a constant unbalanced force acts on a mass?
2. How does an object's acceleration change when the unbalanced force acting on it is doubled?
3. What is the relationship between an object's acceleration and the unbalanced force acting on it?
4. How does acceleration change when the mass of an object is doubled, but the unbalanced force acting on it remains constant?
5. What relationship exists between the mass of an object and its acceleration?
6. What is the relationship between the unbalanced force acting on an object and *ma*, the product of its mass and its acceleration?
7. If a 1 N force accelerates one cart at 0.5 m/s², what acceleration will a 5 N force produce on a stack of five carts?

Investigation 6.2: Testing Newton's Laws

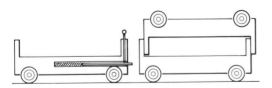

Preamble:
It is possible to test all three of Newton's laws of motion in one investigation, using spring-loaded carts. These carts have a spring-loaded plunger that can be depressed and locked in the "loaded" position, ready to fire when a wooden "trigger" is struck by a meter-stick. A kind of explosion can be created by placing a loaded cart against one or more other carts. When the spring is released, the carts move off in opposite directions, at various speeds, according to the laws of motion.

Newton's Third Law of Motion

When the spring in the first cart is released, its plunger pushes on the second cart with a certain force. According to Newton's third law of motion, the second cart should push back with an equal force. Also, the two forces should act for exactly the same length of time while the carts are in contact.

Newton's Second Law of Motion

The acceleration of each of the carts is determined by its mass and the force acting on it. Since the forces on the carts are equal, their accelerations are determined by their masses. Three stacked carts should have one-third of the acceleration of a single cart. Since the forces act for the same length of time, the single cart should reach three times the speed of the three carts.

Newton's First Law of Motion

Once the spring stops pushing, the carts should continue to move across the desk at a constant speed, provided that friction is minimal.

In the next investigation, you will examine such explosions between carts. You can test your predictions by using two bricks, one at either end of the desk. You must set up the carts and the bricks so that the carts collide with the bricks simultaneously. This example will show you what we mean.

Three carts repel a single cart. If the single cart travels 45 cm to hit its brick, how far must the other carts travel?

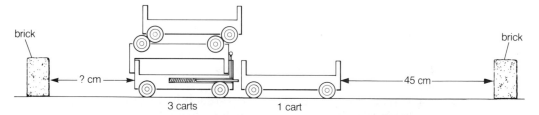

The cart with three times the mass of a single cart will have one-third the acceleration and a final speed one-third as great. Moving at a constant speed, it will travel only one-third as far as the single cart in the same time. Its brick must be placed $\frac{45 \text{ cm}}{3}$, or 15 cm, away.

In the same way, you can predict and test explosions between any number of carts.

Problem:
Do Newton's laws work for exploding carts?

Materials:
4 spring-loaded carts
2 bricks
meterstick
desk or table

Procedure:
1. Set a stack of carts on the desk next to a single cart. Place bricks at opposite ends of the desk so that the carts will hit them simultaneously. You might put one brick 40 cm from the stacked cart. Then, use Newton's laws of motion to predict the distance the single cart should travel. Record this prediction in a data table.

Number of carts in stack	Distance stack of carts travels (cm)	Predicted distance single cart will travel (cm)	Actual distance single cart travels (cm)	Error (%)
1				
2				
3				

2. Release the spring in the single cart by hitting the trigger with the meterstick. Do the carts hit their bricks simultaneously? If they do not, move the brick hit by the single cart until they do. Record this distance and calculate the percentage error between your predicted distance and the actual distance.
3. Repeat, using a different number of carts in the stack.
4. Calculate the average percentage error of the experiment.

Questions:
1. In this explosion, when a large mass and a small mass travel out in opposite directions, which mass
   (a) has the greater speed?
   (b) travels the greater distance to reach its brick?
   (c) takes the longer time to reach its brick?
2. What is the relationship between the ratio of the masses of the two carts and the ratio of their speeds?

Wear Your Seat Belt

Do you wear your seat belt every time you ride in a car? If not, your life may be in peril! Careful study of car crashes has revealed the following split second account of a car travelling at 90 km/h hitting a solid tree.

0 s—The front bumper of the car makes initial contact with the tree. The rest of the car, including the driver, is still moving at 90 km/h.

0.01 s—The front bumper and grill have collapsed. Slivers of the material making up the bumper have penetrated the trunk of the tree to a depth of 3 to 4 cm.

0.02 s—The grill disintegrates completely. The hood of the car crumples and rises as it smashes into the windshield. The rear wheels, still spinning, leave the ground. The front fenders crumple and rear car body begins to come forward past the front doors of the car. The driver continues to move forward with the car's initial speed and his legs, which are ramrod straight, snap at the knee joints.

The force exerted by the tree has stopped the front of the car and is now affecting the rest of the car, with the rate of deceleration or "negative acceleration" declining as one goes to the rear of the car.

0.03 s—The driver's body rises off the seat. His head nears the sun-visor and his chest moves towards the steering wheel. His broken knees press into the dashboard. His grip on the steering wheel causes it to bend and the steering assembly begins to collapse.

0.04 s—The front 60 cm of the car is now completely demolished. The rear end of the car, however, is still travelling at an estimated 55 km/h. The engine slams into the tree trunk, causing the rear of the car to rise high in the air. The driver, however, is still travelling close to his original speed of 90 km/h.

0.05 s—The driver's chest strikes the steering column and the dashboard at a speed of nearly 90 km/h. The impact collapses the chest, driving his ribs into his lungs and the surrounding arteries. His chest cavity begins to fill with blood.

0.06 s—The negative acceleration experienced by the driver is so great that his shoes are ripped off even though they are tightly laced. But his forward motion continues until his head smashes into the windshield. The rear end of the car and the wheels, still spinning, dig into the ground and the car's forward motion nears zero.

0.07 s—The entire body of the car is now smashed out of shape. Hinges tear and doors spring open. The seat rams forward applying an additional force on the driver. Shock has probably stopped his heart, and he will die in less than 1.0 s.

Car manufacturers try to design vehicles in which the passenger compartment will remain intact during the collision. In order to enable the passenger compartment to come to rest over as great a distance as possible, they try to design the vehicle so that the front part of the car will collapse in a controlled way under impact. This increases the stopping distance of the passenger compartment, thereby cushioning the impact to some extent. If you are not wearing your seat belt this margin of safety is wasted.

The best way for you to prevent injuries like those described is to drive with great care and to wear a seat belt. Wearing a seat belt is not a guarantee that you will survive such a violent collision, but it will certainly improve your chances.

Chapter Summary

1. Newton's First Law of Motion: If no net force acts on an object, it maintains its state of rest or its constant speed in a straight line.
2. Newton's Second Law of Motion: If an unbalanced force acts on an object, the object accelerates in the direction of the force. The acceleration varies directly with the unbalanced force and inversely with the mass of the object.

$$\vec{F}_{net} = m\,\vec{a}$$

3. One newton is the unbalanced force that accelerates a one kilogram object at one meter per second squared.

$$1\ N = 1\ kg \cdot m/s^2$$

4. Newton's Third Law of Motion: For every action force, there is an equal and opposite reaction force.
5. The momentum of an object is the product of its mass and velocity. An object's momentum is changed by applying an impulse.

$$\vec{F}\Delta t = \Delta\vec{p} = m\vec{v}_2 - m\vec{v}_1$$

6. The Law of Conservation of Momentum states: If the net external force acting on a system of objects is zero, then the total momentum of the system remains unchanged. For two interacting bodies, this can be written

$$m_a\vec{v}_a + m_b\vec{v}_b = m_a\vec{v}_a' + m_b\vec{v}_b'$$

Chapter Review

1. Use Newton's first law of motion to explain what will happen in situations (a), (b), and (c). Then describe what will happen in situation (d) and explain why it is different.
   (a) A car attempts to stop at a traffic light on an icy street.
   (b) A truck attempts to turn a corner on an icy expressway.
   (c) A passenger in a car does not have the seat belt buckled when the car runs into a snowdrift.
   (d) An airline passenger attempts to sip a cup of coffee when the force of gravity suddenly pulls the airplane down one meter.

2. For which of the following situations does the unbalanced force have a value of zero?
   (a) A ball rolls down a hill at an ever-increasing speed.
   (b) A car travels on a straight, level road at 100 km/h.
   (c) A boulder falls from the edge of a cliff to the lake below.
   (d) A book is at rest on a shelf.
   (e) A communications satellite is located in an orbit such that it remains in the same spot above the Earth at all times.

3. For each of the situations in question 2 where the unbalanced force was not zero, describe the source of the unbalanced force.

4. A student performs an experiment to study the relationship between applied force and acceleration on a dynamics cart. After applying five different forces and determining the resulting acceleration, the student plots a graph of acceleration versus applied force and obtains the result shown in the margin.
   (a) Explain why the graph doesn't pass through the origin.
   (b) How would the graph change if the experiment were repeated using a surface where friction between the cart and the surface were greater?
   (c) What was the value of the frictional force that acted upon the cart when the student carried out the investigation?

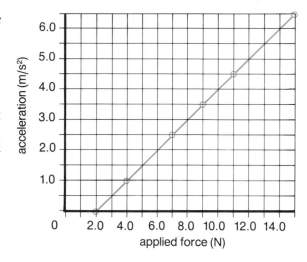

5. The Earth exerts a force of 20 000 N on a satellite that is orbiting 8000 m above the surface. What force does the satellite exert on the Earth?

6. A large loaded truck strikes a stationary compact car.
   (a) How do the forces experienced by the two vehicles during the collision compare?
   (b) Explain why the driver of the compact car would likely experience more serious injuries that the driver of the truck.

7. You are a passenger in a small rowboat. You are about to step from the boat onto a nearby dock. Explain why you may end up in the water instead.

8. According to Newton's Third Law, when a horse pulls on a cart, the cart pulls back with an equal force on the horse. If, in fact, the cart pulls back on the horse as hard as the horse pulls forward on the cart, how is it possible for the horse to move the cart?

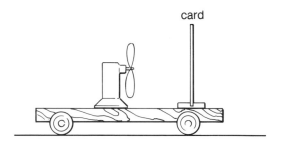

9. The cart shown in the margin has a battery-operated fan on it. It also was a slot into which a card can be inserted. Predict and explain what will happen if the fan is turned on when the card is
   (a) absent,
   (b) present.

10. Use Newton's Laws to explain why each of the following statements is correct. For each case, indicate which of the three laws best explains the situation.
    (a) It takes longer for a car to accelerate from 0 to 100 km/h if it has five passengers in it than when it has only one.
    (b) Many a novice hunter has experienced a sore shoulder after firing a shotgun.
    (c) Subway cars provide posts and overhead rails for standing passengers to hold.

11. A man is pushing a car along a level road at a constant velocity of 2.0 m/s with a horizontal force of 243 N. The total force acting on the car in the opposite direction, including road friction and air resistance, is one of the following. Which one?
    (a) slightly more than 243 N (b) exactly equal to 243 N
    (c) slightly less than 243 N

12. (a) A common misconception is that a rocket does not work as well in empty space because there is nothing for the exhaust gases to push against. Explain what is wrong with this reasoning.
    b) Two identical rockets are fired. One is at the Earth's surface and the other is just above the Earth's atmosphere. How do their accelerations compare? Assume that both are pointing away from the center of the Earth. Explain your reason.

13. A 50 kg woman is standing on a level floor. Draw a free body diagram to show the two forces acting on her. Are these forces an action-reaction pair? Explain your answer.

14. A heavy mass is suspended from a string as shown in the diagram. An identical string is tied to the bottom of the mass. Predict and explain what will happen if you take the lower string and
    (a) jerk it down quickly,
    (b) pull it down slowly.
    You may wish to try this activity. If you do, don't let the heavy mass land on your hand.

15. An astronaut is stranded in space a short distance from his spacecraft. Explain how he might use the Law of Conservation of Momentum to travel safely to his ship. Describe what he does at both the beginning and end of this travel.

16. Describe the beneficial effects of "air bags" used in modern cars to cushion passengers from collisions with the dashboard during an accident. Explain from the point of view of impulse and momentum.

Problems

17. Draw a free body diagram to determine the unbalanced force acting on the underlined object in each of the following situations:
    (a) A pail of water of mass 8.0 kg falls from the platform of a window washer to the sidewalk below. (Assume that air resistance is negligible.)
    (b) A water skier is being pulled directly behind a motorboat at a constant velocity of 20 m/s. The tension in the horizontal rope is 520 N.
    (c) An elevator, including passengers, has a mass of 1000 kg. The cable attached to the elevator exerts an upward force of 12 000 N. Friction opposing the motion of the elevator is 1500 N.

18. What unbalanced force would be required to accelerate a 0.50 kg grapefruit at:
    (a) 4.0 m/s²? (b) 8.0 m/s²?

19. What acceleration would an unbalanced force of 84 N produce on each of the following masses?
    (a) 4.2 kg (b) 8.4 kg

20. A 1200 kg car travelling at 50 km/h experiences an air resistance of 5000 N and road friction of 2200 N. If the wheels push with a force of 7500 N, what is the car's acceleration?

21. Two boys, one with a mass of 60 kg and the other with a mass of 90 kg, are standing side by side in the middle of an ice rink. One of them pushes the other with a force of 360 N for 0.10 s. Assuming that the ice surface is frictionless:
    (a) what is the acceleration of each boy?
    (b) what speed will each boy reach after the 0.10 s?
    (c) does it matter which boy did the pushing?

22. An 1100 kg car accelerates from rest at 3.4 m/s².
    (a) What is the unbalanced force acting on it?
    (b) If the horizontal force exerted on the wheels by the road is 5600 N, what force must be resisting the motion of the car? Use a free body diagram to illustrate your answer.

23. A block of wood of mass 6.0 kg slides along a skating rink at 12.5 m/s[W]. The block slides onto a rough section of ice that exerts a 30 N force of friction on the block of wood. Calculate:
    (a) the acceleration of the block of wood.
    (b) the time it takes the block of wood to stop.
    (c) how far the block slides after friction begins to act on it.

Numerical Answers to Practice Problems

page 135
1. (a) 1.0 N[right]
   (b) 2.0 N[up]
   (c) 0
3. 400 N

page 139
1. 4.0 m/s²
2. 0.25 kg
3. 7.5 × 10⁴ N
4. 18 N
5. 5.0 m/s²

page 144
1. (a) 2.5 m/s²[E]
   (b) 1.0 × 10² N
2. (a) 2.0 m/s²[E]
   (b) 1.3 × 10² N[E]
   (c) 5.0 × 10¹ N[E]

page 148
1. 4.0 m/s²
2. 2.7 × 10² N
3. 0.93 s
4. (a) 0.74 N
   (b) 2.4 m/s²

page 160
1. (a) 15 kg · m/s [upwards]
   (b) 2.0 × 10⁴ kg · m/s [S]
   (c) 9.1 × 10⁻²⁴ kg · m/s [forwards]
   (d) 1.8 × 10²⁹ kg · m/s [forwards]
2. 3.0 m/s [forwards]
3. 0.0050 kg, or 5.0 g

page 162
1. (a) 80 N · s [E]
   (b) 6 N · s [forwards]
   (c) 3.5 × 10² N · s [down]
2. (a) −0.80 kg · m/s [right]
   (b) 0.80 kg · m/s [left]
3. 3.0 m/s [forwards]

page 168
1. 2.0 m/s [forwards]
2. 2.9 m/s [forwards]
3. 80.0 cm/s [forwards]
4. (a) 0.42 m/s [left]
   (b) 0.87 m/s [left]
   (c) 0.38 m/s [left]
5. 0.40 m/s [forwards]
6. 2.8 s

24. A car is travelling along an expressway at 90 km/h. The driver spots a stalled car and some traffic congestion on the road ahead, and so applies the brakes. The braking action causes a frictional force of 8400 N to act on the 1050 kg car.
    (a) What is the acceleration of the car when the brakes are applied?
    (b) How long does it take for the car to stop?
    (c) How far does the car travel while it is braking?
25. A force of 36 N gives a mass m_1 an acceleration of 4.0 m/s². The same force gives a mass m_2 an acceleration of 12 m/s². What acceleration will this force give to m_1 and m_2 if the two masses are fastened together?
26. What change in velocity would be produced by an unbalanced force of 2.0×10^4 N acting for 6.0 s on a 2.0×10^3 kg dragster?
27. Calculate the unbalanced force acting on a 4000 kg truck that changes its velocity from 22.0 m/s[N] to 8.00 m/s[N] in 3.50 s.
28. How long does it take a 50 kg rider on a 10 kg bicycle to accelerate from rest to 4.0 m/s[E] if the unbalanced force acting on the bicycle is 48 N[E]?
29. A 0.50 kg model rocket accelerates at a constant rate from 20 m/s[up] to 45 m/s[up] in 0.70 s. Calculate the unbalanced force acting on it.
30. A 0.2 kg sponge is dropped from rest, pulled down by gravity. How fast will it be travelling in 6.0 s, if a 0.5 N force of air resistance acts on it?
31. A fully loaded Saturn V rocket has a mass of 2.92×10^6 kg. Its engines have a thrust of 3.34×10^7 N.
    (a) What is the downward force of gravity on the rocket at blast-off?
    (b) What is the unbalanced force on the rocket at blast-off?
    (c) What is the acceleration of the rocket as it leaves the launching platform?
    (d) As the rocket travels upwards, the engine thrust remains constant, but the mass of the rocket decreases. Why?
    (e) Does the acceleration of the rocket increase, decrease, or remain the same as the engines continue to fire?
32. Calculate the initial acceleration of a 13 140 kg V-2 rocket bomb fired vertically upwards, if the thrust of its engines is 2.63×10^5 N. Then calculate the rocket's acceleration near "burn-out", when its mass is only 4170 kg. This rocket does not go very high; at burn-out, it is still in the region where the gravitational field strength is 9.8 N/kg.

33. For the diagrams in the margin, assume that each person has a mass of 60 kg. Determine the reading on each of the spring scales. Assume that the pulleys are frictionless, and that the balances are light enough not to affect the reading significantly.

34. What is the speed of an 1800 kg car with a momentum of 3.0×10^4 kg · m/s?
35. A 1.5×10^3 kg car accelerates from rest at 4.0 m/s² for 6.0 s. (a) What momentum does it acquire in that time? (b) What was the impulse exerted on it?
36. A golf club exerts an average force of 7.2×10^3 N on a ball for the 5.0×10^{-4} s they are in contact.
    (a) Calculate the impulse of the impact on the ball.
    (b) If the ball has a mass of 45 g, what velocity will it have as it leaves the club face?

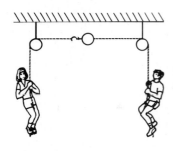

37. A 300 g ball is struck by a bat with an impact that lasts 0.020 s. If the ball moves through the air towards the bat at 50 m/s and leaves at 100 m/s in the opposite direction, calculate the average force exerted by the bat on the ball.
38. A toy rocket develops an average forward thrust of 4.0 N when the velocity of the exhaust gases relative to the engine is 30 m/s. Calculate the mass of gases ejected per second.
39. A stationary Volkswagen Rabbit of mass 1.0×10^3 kg is rammed from behind by a Ford Escort of mass 1.2×10^3 kg, travelling 20 m/s on an icy road. If they lock bumpers in the collision, how fast will the pair move forward?

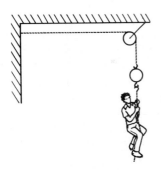

40. An arrow travelling at 40 m/s strikes and imbeds itself in a 400 g apple at rest. The apple with the arrow in it moves off horizontally at 10 m/s after the impact. What is the mass of the arrow?
41. (a) A soft target of mass 999.9 kg lies on a horizontal sheet of ice. A 0.10 kg bullet is fired with a speed of 1000 m/s. How fast does the target slide after being hit?
    (b) Another target, of mass 990 kg, is hit by a bullet from the same gun. In this case, the bullet hits a steel belt surrounding the target and bounces straight back with negligible change in speed. How fast does the target slide after being hit?

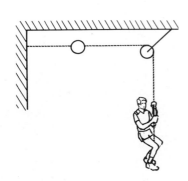

7

Work, Power, and Energy

7.1 Work

The term work has a specific meaning in physics. **Work** is done on an object whenever a force makes that object move—when a car's engine makes the car accelerate, when a crane lifts a steel beam for a new building, when an archer bends a bow as the arrow is pulled back, and when the bow releases the arrow. Work is also being done when a chicken is roasted in an oven, although in this case it is not so obvious what the force is, and what is being made to move. On the other hand, even though you may perspire when holding a heavy object on your shoulder, you are not doing any work on that object because you are not moving it.

Measuring Work

The standard amount, or unit, of work is called a **joule** (J).You can do 1 J of work by pushing on a small object with a force of exactly 1 N, moving that object exactly 1 m.

If you move the same object twice as far, you will have done twice as much work. The amount of work done varies directly with the actual displacement of the object.

If you use twice as much force to move the object through the original displacement, again you will have done twice as much work. The amount of work done varies directly with the amount of force acting on the object.

Here are the results of an imaginary experiment using work (W), displacement ($\vec{\Delta d}$), and force ($\vec{F}$).

The ball of a wrecking crane does work on a building

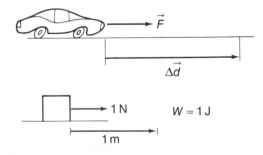

The displacement is in the direction of the force.

Force $\vec{F}$ (N)	Displacement $\vec{\Delta d}$ (m)	Work W (J)
1	1	1
1	2	2
1	5	5
2	1	2
5	1	5
2	2	4
5	5	25

In each case, the amount of work done is calculated by multiplying the force that was applied by the displacement of the object.

$$W = \vec{F} \cdot \vec{\Delta d}$$

where $\vec{F}$ is the force applied, in newtons

$\vec{\Delta d}$ is the displacement of the object in meters

W is the work done, in joules

Although it is the product of two vectors, work itself is a scalar quantity. The full implications of this fact will be left for more advanced study in physics. In this text, all numerical problems involving work deal with situations where the force is parallel to the displacement. It will therefore be acceptable to omit the vector signs and use the expression

$$W = F\Delta d$$

There are also situations in which there may be motion or force or both, but no work is done. For example, once set in motion, an object on a frictionless surface continues to move. Consider the glider on the air track in the photo below. Once pushed it glides along the track with no appreciable decrease in speed. Work is required to start the glider but not to keep it moving.

The joule is named after James Prescott Joule (1818-1889), owner of a Manchester brewery, who was determined to prove that heat was not "caloric fluid" (a substance) but a form of energy that could be produced by doing work. He found that the heat produced by stirring water or mercury is proportional to the amount of work done in the stirring. For more details see Chapter 8.

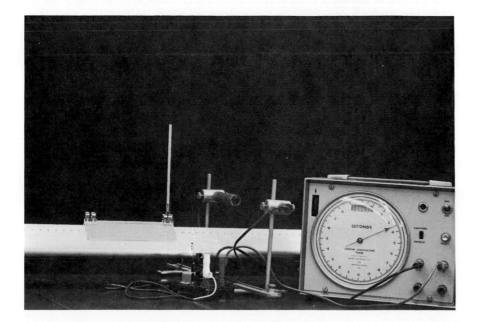

Mathematically we would say that the force of the skater on his partner has no component in the direction of motion. Therefore no work is done.

You may have experienced this example. You are in a car that is stuck in a snowbank. You ask some of your friends to push you out. They push as hard as they can but the car doesn't budge. In this case, a force is applied, but no work is done as the car does not move.

A third example is shown in the margin. A figure skater glides along the ice, holding his partner above his head. In this case, there is motion and a force, but the force does no work. Why? Because the vertical force exerted upward by the skater on his partner does not result in any vertical motion of the partner. Work was done in the lifting but not in the holding of the partner. Whenever the force applied on the object is perpendicular to the motion of the object, no work is done on the object.

Most of the situations we will study involve work done on an object when a force, applied to the object, causes it to move in the direction of the force. The sample problems will illustrate this.

Sample Problems

1. How much work is done by a boy pushing a car with a force of 800 N for a distance of 200 m?

$$W = F\Delta d$$
$$= (800 \text{ N}) (200 \text{ m})$$
$$= 1.60 \times 10^5 \text{ J}$$

The boy does 1.6×10^5 J of work.

2. How much work is done by a girl pushing a 96 kg refrigerator across a floor a distance of 1.2 m, using a force of 350 N? The force of friction opposing the motion of the refrigerator is 350 N.

In the expression for work, $W = F\Delta d$, the F stands for the applied force, not the unbalanced force. Though the applied force is balanced by the force of friction, once the girl has started moving the refrigerator, the values for F substituted in the equation is still 350 N.

$$W = F\Delta d$$
$$= (350 \text{ N}) (1.2 \text{ m})$$
$$= 420 \text{ J, or } 4.2 \times 10^2 \text{ J}$$

Therefore the girl does 4.2×10^2 J of work on the refrigerator.

3. A camper uses a rope and pail to get water from a well. If the pail with water has a mass of 20 kg and if it is raised a vertical distance of 3.5 m, how much work is done by the camper?

The free body diagram in the margin will help you solve the problem.

Note that according to the laws of motion, you only need to balance the force of gravity in order to keep an object moving straight up at a constant speed. Of course, a force slightly larger than the force of gravity is needed at the beginning to start the movement, and a force slightly less is needed as the object stops. The small amount of extra work at the beginning is offset by the slight reduction at the end. For our purposes, when something is being lifted in our problems, we will assume that the force needed is equal to the force of gravity on the object, and that it is constant for the whole interval.

$$F_g = mg$$
$$= (20 \text{ kg})(9.8 \text{ N/kg})$$
$$= 2.0 \times 10^2 \text{ N}$$
$$W = F\Delta d$$
$$= (2.0 \times 10^2 \text{ N}) (3.5 \text{ m})$$
$$= 7.0 \times 10^2 \text{ J}$$

The camper does 7.0×10^2 J of work in lifting the pail of water from the well.

The girl does 4.2×10^2 J of work on the refrigerator. The frictional force also does work on the refrigerator. The work done in this case is $(-350 \text{ N})(1.2 \text{ m})$, or -4.2×10^2 J. The negative sign indicates that the displacement and the force are in opposite directions.

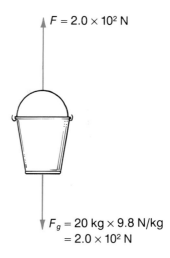

$F = 2.0 \times 10^2$ N

$F_g = 20 \text{ kg} \times 9.8 \text{ N/kg}$
$= 2.0 \times 10^2$ N

$= 2.0 \times 10^2$ N

Practice

1. A force of 20 N was used to push a box 8.0 m along the floor. How much work was done?
2. A 2.0 kg puck accelerated at 5.0 m/s² for 0.50 m across a frictionless air hockey table. How much work was done on the puck?
3. A bulldozer pushed a large rock with a force of 5000 N at 2.0 m/s for 20 s. How much work was done by the bulldozer?

4. A 71 kg window washer stands on a 179 kg platform suspended on the side of a building. If an electric motor raises the platform 58 m up the side of the building, how much work is done by the motor?

7.2 Power

In 1782, James Watt (1736-1819) introduced a new, improved version of the steam engine that changed its status from that of a minor gadget to that of a universal work horse. First used to pump water from coal mines, it soon powered steamships, locomotives, shovels, tractors, cars, and any number of mechanical devices.

In 1807, Robert Fulton, the American inventor, launched the first commercially successful steamboat.

George Stephenson built the first practical steam locomotive in 1814. The 7 t engine pulled 48 t at a speed of 25 km/h from Darlington to Stockton, in the north of England.

The watt described here is the same unit of power that describes electrical devices such as a 60 W light bulb.

"Work" and "power" are often used interchangeably in everyday life, but in physics each has a distinct meaning. **Power** is defined as the rate at which work is done. The machine that can do a certain amount of work the fastest is developing the most power.

For machines working steadily, the power is calculated by dividing the work done by the time taken to do the work. The standard amount of power is a joule per second, which, in SI units, is one watt (W), that is 1 J/s = 1 W

$$P = \frac{W}{\Delta t}$$

where W is the work done, in joules
Δt is the time taken, in seconds
P is the power, in watts

Sample Problems

1. What is the power of a bulldozer that does 5.5×10^4 J of work in 1.1 s?

$$W = 5.5 \times 10^4 \text{ J}$$
$$\Delta t = 1.1 \text{ s}$$
$$P = ?$$
$$P = \frac{W}{\Delta t}$$
$$= \frac{5.5 \times 10^4 \text{ J}}{1.1 \text{ s}}$$
$$= 5.0 \times 10^4 \text{ W}$$

Therefore the bulldozer develops 5.0×10^4 W of power.

2. How much power is developed by a 60 kg boy running up a 4.5 m high flight of stairs in 4.0 s?

Horsepower is a unit for power still commonly used in some industries. One horsepower is equivalent to 746 W.

$$F_g = mg$$
$$= (60 \text{ kg}) (9.8 \text{ N/kg})$$
$$= 588 \text{ N}$$
$$W = F\Delta d$$
$$= (588 \text{ N}) (4.5 \text{ m})$$
$$= 2646 \text{ J}$$
$$P = \frac{W}{\Delta t}$$
$$= \frac{2646 \text{ J}}{4.0 \text{ s}}$$
$$= 660 \text{ W, or } 6.6 \times 10^2 \text{ W}$$

The boy develops 6.6×10^2 W of power.

He is doing work on himself against the force of gravity.

Practice

1. How much power does a crane develop, doing 6.0×10^4 J of work in 5.00 min?
2. How long does it takes a 2.5 kW electric motor to do 7.5×10^4 J of work?
3. How much work can a 500 W electric mixer do in 2.5 min?
4. How much power is developed by a 50 kg girl running up a 3.00 m high flight of stairs in 2.50 s?
5. How long will it take the girl in question 4 to run up a flight of stairs 4.5 m high?
6. A boy who can generate 500 W runs up a flight of stairs in 5.0 s. How high are the stairs if the boy has a mass of 62 kg?

The world's highest free standing structure is the CN Tower in Toronto, Ontario. A record for climbing its 1760 steps was set in August, 1980 by Michael Round who climbed the steps in 10 min and 10 s. Try estimating his average power during the climb.

7.3 Another Unit for Work

The SI unit for work is the joule, which is the amount of work done by a force of 1 N pushing an object for a distance of 1 m. The joule is a very small quantity of work. Even a small machine, such as the fan on a furnace, does several million joules of work in a day.

There is a larger unit that is used to measure work called the kilowatt hour. It is the amount of work done by a machine with a power of 1 kW, in 1 h.

To calculate the work done in 1 h by a machine working at a rate of 1 kW, we will use the equation:

$$P = \frac{W}{\Delta t}$$

This means that

$$W = P\Delta t$$

Now, to calculate the work done in each of the units:

$P = 1$ kW	or	$P = 1000$ W
$\Delta t = 1$ h	or	$\Delta t = 3600$ s
$W = P\Delta t$	or	$W = P\Delta t$
$= (1$ kW$)(1$ h$)$		$= (1000$ W$)(3600$ s$)$
$= 1$ kW $\cdot$ h		$= 3\ 600\ 000$ J

$$1\ \textbf{kW} \cdot \textbf{h} = 3\ \textbf{600}\ \textbf{000}\ \textbf{J}$$
$$= \textbf{3.6}\ \textbf{MJ}$$

When amounts of work are to be calculated in kilowatt hours, it is simpler to use kilowatts instead of watts for the power and hours instead of seconds for time. The units of work will then be kilowatt hours instead of joules.

Kilowatt hours are commonly used to measure energy, especially electrical energy. Eventually, however, the megajoule will be used for large amounts of energy.

$$1\ \text{MJ} = 10^6\ \text{J}$$

Sample Problems

How much work in kilowatt hours is done by a 25 kW water pump running steadily for a week?

$$
\begin{aligned}
W &= P\Delta t \\
&= (25\ \text{kW})(7 \times 24)\ \text{h} \\
&= (25\ \text{kW})(168\ \text{h}) \\
&= 4.2 \times 10^3\ \text{kW} \cdot \text{h}
\end{aligned}
$$

Practice

1. How much work (in kilowatt hours) is done by a 6000 W electric generator, running 8.0 h a day for a year?
2. How long (in hours) will it take a 500 W power drill to do 100 kW $\cdot$ h of work?
3. How much power is being developed by a machine that can do 600 kW $\cdot$ h of work in 12 h?

7.4 Energy

No machine can operate without fuel. Just as gasoline is the fuel for automobiles, food is the fuel for the human body. Food gives you the ability to do work; it gives you energy. **Energy** is the ability to do work.

This is not the complete story. Suppose that you do some work on a large rock, by lifting it straight up into the air. You have used some of your energy supply. But that energy has not vanished. It has not been "used up", but transferred (most of it) to the rock. And the rock can now do something it could not do before. If you let go of it, it will fall back to its original position, and, as it falls, it can do work. It might be made to push down on a lever, lifting some other object. Or you could tie a rope to the rock and run the rope over a pulley, so that, as it fell, the rock would lift some other object or pull it along the ground. Each time work is done, energy is transferred from the object doing the work to the object being worked on. **Work** is the transfer of energy.

It is convenient to measure both work and energy in the same unit, the joule. If you do 5000 J of work on an object, you have transferred 5000 J of your energy to it. Doing work on an object increases its energy. Mathematically, this is expressed as:

$$W = \Delta E$$

where W is the work done on an object, in joules
ΔE is the change in energy of the object, in joules

Earlier in this chapter we considered a number of situations in which a force caused an object to move. At that time we stated that work was being done on the object. We could also have stated that energy was being transferred to the object. But what about a situation in which the only force acting on the object is friction, which causes the object to slow down? Consider the following example.

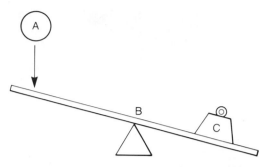

When falling object A does work on lever B, which does work on object C, energy is transferred from A to B to C.

Sample Problems

A clerk gives a plastic bin of groceries a push along the floor. An average frictional force of 52 N causes the bin to come to rest after sliding 1.9 m. How much work is done by the force of friction?

In this case most of the bin's energy is being transferred as heat to the surface it is sliding on. The friction causes the bin to lose energy. For this reason, the work being done is considered to be negative work—the energy transfer is from, instead of to, the object. As the direction of the frictional force is opposite to the displacement, it is given a negative value. The value obtained for work is also negative.

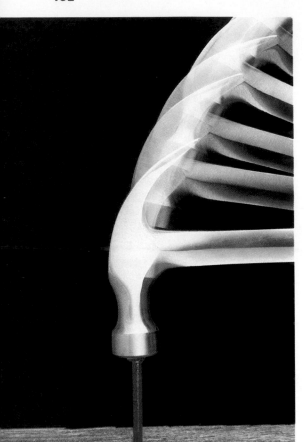

A hammer utilizes gravitational potential energy.

$$F = -52 \text{ N}$$
$$\Delta d = 1.9 \text{ m}$$
$$W = F\Delta d$$
$$W = -52 \text{ N} \times 1.9 \text{ m}$$
$$W = -99 \text{ J}$$

Therefore the work done on the bin by the floor is −99 J. This means that 99 J of energy is transferred from the bin.

*P*ractice

1. A car is moving along at 80 km/h when the brakes are applied. The frictional force generated by the brakes amounts to 4500 N and acts over a distance of 50 m. Determine the work done on the car. Does the energy of the car increase or decrease as a result of the braking action?
2. What frictional force is required to reduce the energy of a curling rock by 240 J over a distance of 12 m?

Kinds of Energy

Energy is transferred when work is done, but it is also, usually, transformed from one kind of energy to another. There are many kinds of energy, some obvious, and some not so obvious. It took many scientists many years to discover the various forms we know. The secret is to remember that anything that can do work has energy. The following is a description of the more important kinds of energy.

1. **Gravitational Potential Energy:** Any raised object, such as the rock you lifted, has energy and can do work as it falls. A pile driver works on this principle. The potential energy stored in the mass can be used to drive a huge beam (pile) into the ground.
2. **Kinetic Energy:** Any moving object, such as a fast-moving baseball, has energy and can do work on any object it hits. For example, a moving hammer does work when it drives a nail into a board.

 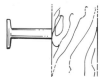

3. **Heat Energy:** Hot objects have energy and can do work. It is easiest to show this with a very hot object, such as a boiler full of superheated steam, but even water at room temperature can do work under certain circumstances.

4. **Radiant Energy:** The radiant energy produced by the sun can be shown to do work in a number of ways. Ordinarily, heat energy is produced when sunlight is absorbed. When light strikes a photo-cell, electrical energy is produced. However, in a famous experiment, a tiny piece of metal foil in a vacuum was made to move by a beam of light shining on it. The beam of light did work, so it must have had energy.

5. **Chemical Potential Energy:** Atoms join together in various combinations to form many different kinds of molecules, involving varying amounts of energy. In chemical reactions, new arrangements of atoms are formed and energy is absorbed or released. A stick of dynamite releases chemical energy and can do work when it explodes. You release chemical energy when you burn coal, flex a muscle, or turn on a flashlight.

The paddle wheel in the glass bulb above rotates when exposed to sunlight. The sun's energy is absorbed by the black side of the paddle wheel. This causes the air next to it to heat up. The expanding air forces the paddle wheel to move. If the glass bulb were completely evacuated, and if all friction between the paddle wheel and the shaft on which it is mounted were eliminated, it would turn in the opposite direction when exposed to strong light. Can you guess why?

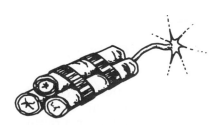

6. **Elastic Energy:** Some objects that are compressed, stretched, or twisted can do work as they return to their original shape and therefore have energy. Examples are: the twisted rubber band of a model airplane, and the bent bow that results when an archer pulls back an arrow.

7. **Electrical Energy:** Electric currents make motors turn and lights flash. There are electric clocks and dishwashers, elevators, streetcars, pencil sharpeners, and VCRs. Almost every conceivable kind of work can be done by electricity. Even our bodies use electrical impulses to send messages back and forth. Electric charges can do work as they move through a circuit.

8. **Nuclear Energy:** The nucleus of every atom has energy. The energy released by the fission of a kilogram of uranium atoms in a nuclear reactor is more than the energy released in the burning of thousands of tons of coal in a conventional thermal generating station.

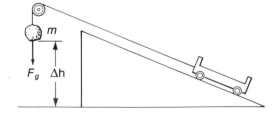

7.5 Gravitational Potential Energy

Imagine a rock with a mass, m, tied to the end of a long rope. The rope runs up over a pulley and the other end is tied to another object, or to a spring, or perhaps to a wagon on a ramp.

If you let go of the rock, it will fall, pulling on the rope, and do work on the object tied to the rope. The rock will pull downwards with a force equal to the force of gravity, if it falls at constant speed.

The work done by the rock depends on how far it falls. Suppose that it falls a distance, Δh. Then the work done will be:

$$W = F\Delta d \qquad \text{Since} \quad F = mg$$
$$= (mg)(\Delta h) \qquad \text{and} \quad d = \Delta h$$
$$= mg\,\Delta h$$

This is also the amount of energy that will be transferred to whatever is attached to the other end of the rope, provided that the rope and the pulley are frictionless. The higher the rock is lifted in the first place, the more work it will be able to do, and the more energy will be stored in it. When the rock falls, this energy is released.

Some of the lost potential energy may be used to increase the kinetic energy of the rock itself.

The energy stored in an object due to its distance above the surface of the Earth is called **gravitational potential energy,** E_g. The change in gravitational potential energy of an object is given by the equation:

$$\Delta E_g = mg\,\Delta h$$

$\Delta h = h_{final} - h_{initial}$

where m is the mass of the object, in kilograms
g is the gravitational field strength, in newtons per kilogram
Δh is the vertical displacement the object is moved, in meters
ΔE_g is the object's change in gravitational potential energy, in joules

Sample Problems

1. How much gravitational potential energy does a 4.0 kg rock gain if it is lifted 25 m?

$$\Delta E_g = mg\,\Delta h$$
$$= (4.0 \text{ kg}) (9.80 \text{ N/kg}) (25 \text{ m})$$
$$= 9.8 \times 10^2 \text{ J}$$

2. How much potential energy is lost by a 61.2 kg boy falling 0.500 m out of bed?

$$\Delta E_g = mg\,\Delta h$$
$$= (61.2 \text{ kg}) (9.80 \text{ N/kg}) (-0.500 \text{ m})$$
$$= -300 \text{ J}$$

A negative change in energy is a decrease in energy, so the boy must lose 300 J of gravitational potential energy.

The expression $\Delta E_g = mg\,\Delta h$ can only be used to calculate changes in gravitational potential energy near the surface of the Earth. For very large values of Δh such as 1×10^6 m, the expression is no longer accurate because the value of g decreases gradually as one moves away from the Earth's surface.

Practice

1. A crane lifts a 1500 kg car 20 m straight up.
   (a) How much potential energy does the car gain?
   (b) How much energy does the crane transfer to the car?
   (c) How much work does the crane do?
2. A 0.0400 kg rubber ball drops from a height of 5.00 m to the ground and bounces back to a height of 3.00 m.
   (a) How much potential energy does the ball lose on the trip down?
   (b) How much potential energy does the ball regain on the trip back up?

Relative Potential Energy

The equation just developed may be used to determine the change in an object's potential energy as it is moved towards or away from the Earth.

In practice, it is useful to select a position at which an object's potential energy is considered to be zero. Usually we pick the lowest point in the problem. The potential energy at any other point is measured relative to the zero position. As a result, the equation for the gravitational potential energy is:

$$E_g = mgh$$

where h is measured vertically from the zero position.

Sample Problems

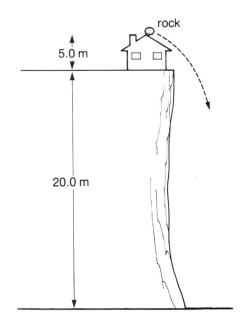

A 10.0 kg rock is on top of a house 5.00 m high on the edge of a cliff 20.0 m high. What is the gravitational potential energy of the rock relative to
(a) the roof of the house?
(b) the floor of the house?
(c) the bottom of the cliff?

(a) The zero point is the top of the house.
$$E_g = mgh$$
$$= (10.0 \text{ kg}) (9.80 \text{ N/kg}) (0 \text{ m})$$
$$= 0 \text{ J relative to the top of the house}$$

(b) The zero point is the floor of the house.
$$E_g = mgh$$
$$= (10.0 \text{ kg}) (9.80 \text{ N/kg}) (5.00 \text{ m})$$
$$= 490 \text{ J relative to the floor of the house}$$

The main advantage in picking a low level as a reference level is that it enables one to avoid negative numbers.

(c) The zero point is the bottom of the cliff.
$E_g = mgh$
$= (10.0 \text{ kg}) (9.80 \text{ N/kg}) (25.0 \text{ m})$
$= 2450 \text{ J}$
$= 2.45 \times 10^3 \text{ J}$ relative to the bottom of the cliff

$P_{ractice}$

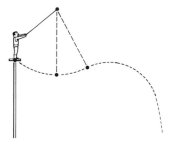

1. A man on a flying trapeze stands on a platform 20 m above the ground holding the trapeze. The trapeze is 10 m long and is attached to the roof 26 m above the ground. The man swings down and lets go of the rope on the upswing. He has a mass of 60 kg. Calculate his potential energy relative to the ground when he is at each of the following heights.
   (a) 20 m (on platform)
   (b) 16 m (bottom of swing)
   (c) 18 m (lets go of trapeze)
   (d) 9.0 m (halfway to ground)
2. Repeat the previous question, calculating his potential energy relative to a point 16 m above the ground.

Remember, the distance, h, in the equation $E_g = mgh$ is the vertical straight-line distance of the object above the chosen reference plane, since the force of gravity is always vertical.

7.6 Kinetic Energy

Kinetic energy is the energy of a moving object. A curling stone moving down the ice will be able to do work on other stones because it is moving. The amount of kinetic energy in the stone depends on how fast it is moving, and on its mass. A hockey puck moving down the ice at the same speed could do very little work on the stones.

The kinetic energy of any object is a result of work having been done on it. If we could determine how much work it took to accelerate a curling stone up to a certain speed, then we would know how much kinetic energy had been given to it.

Imagine a curling stone with mass, m, accelerated by a curler with a force, F, pushing on it for a displacement, Δd, down a frictionless ice surface.

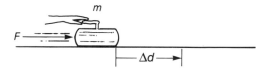

Force F acts over displacement Δd on curling stone, mass m.

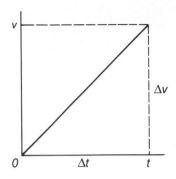

The work done on the curling stone by the curler is
$$W = F\Delta d$$
The relationship between the force, the mass of the stone, and the acceleration of the stone, since there is no friction, is:
$$F = ma$$
By substitution, we now have:
$$W = (ma)\Delta d$$
$$= ma\,\Delta d$$
The speed-time graph of an object accelerating from rest is a straight line for a constant acceleration.

The speed of the stone changes from 0 to v in the time interval Δt. The acceleration is the slope of the graph:
$$a = \frac{\Delta v}{\Delta t}$$
$$= \frac{(v - 0)}{(t - 0)}$$
$$= \frac{v}{t}$$
The displacement of the accelerating curling stone is:
$$\Delta d = \left(\frac{v_1 + v_2}{2}\right)\Delta t$$
$$= \left(\frac{0 + v}{2}\right)(t - 0)$$
$$= \frac{vt}{2}$$
Now we substitute into the equation for work:
$$W = ma\,\Delta d$$
$$= m\left(\frac{v}{t}\right)\left(\frac{vt}{2}\right)$$
$$= \frac{1}{2}mv^2$$

Doing work on the object by accelerating it has transferred energy to it. The only change between the object now and before the work was done on it is its increased speed. The energy the stone now has is energy of motion, or **kinetic energy**, written as E_k.

$$E_k = \frac{1}{2}mv^2$$

where m is the mass of the object, in kilograms
v is the speed of the object, in meters per second
E_k is the kinetic energy, in joules

Note that the units on the right side of the equation reduce to joules.
$$(kg)\,(m/s)^2 = kg(m^2/s^2)$$
$$= \left(\frac{kg \cdot m}{s^2}\right)(m)$$
$$= N \cdot m$$
$$= J$$

In the relationship $E_k = \frac{1}{2}\,mv^2$, v is the speed, not the velocity. When a velocity is given, use its magnitude and ignore the direction.

Sample Problems

1. What is the kinetic energy of a 6.0 kg curling stone sliding at 4.0 m/s?

$$E_k = \frac{1}{2}mv^2$$

$$= \frac{1}{2}(6.0 \text{ kg})(4.0 \text{ m/s})^2$$

$$= 48 \text{ J}$$

Therefore, the kinetic energy of the curling stone is 48 J.

2. What is the speed of a 5.44 kg shotput if its kinetic energy is 68 J?

$$m = 5.44 \text{ kg}$$
$$E_k = 68 \text{ J}$$

$$E_k = \frac{1}{2}mv^2$$

$$68 \text{ J} = \frac{1}{2}(5.44 \text{ kg})(v^2)$$

$$v^2 = \frac{68 \text{ J}}{2.72 \text{ kg}}$$

$$= 25 \text{ m}^2/\text{s}^2$$

$$v = 5.0 \text{ m/s}$$

The shotput must have a speed of 5.0 m/s.

Practice

1. What is the kinetic energy of a 0.500 kg ball thrown at 30.0 m/s?
2. What is the kinetic energy of a 25.0 g bullet travelling at 3600 km/h?
3. What is the mass of an object travelling at 20 m/s with a kinetic energy of 4000 J?
4. What is the speed of a 1.5 kg rock falling with a kinetic energy of 48 J?
5. A 0.50 kg rubber ball is thrown into the air. At a height of 20 m above the ground, it is travelling at 15 m/s.
   (a) What is the ball's kinetic energy?
   (b) What is its gravitational potential energy relative to the ground?
   (c) How much work was done by someone at ground level throwing the ball up into the air?
   (d) What was the speed of the ball when it left the ground?
6. How much work is required to accelerate a 150 kg motorbike from 10 m/s to 20 m/s?

7.7 Conservation of Energy

Imagine a large rock inside a tall vacuum chamber. The rock is released at the top of the chamber and falls, accelerating at 9.8 m/s². As it falls, its gravitational potential energy decreases, and its kinetic energy increases. (Fortunately, there is no air resistance in a vacuum, and no heat energy is produced.) Is the increase in kinetic energy equal to the decrease in potential energy?

Object with mass m falling in a vacuum

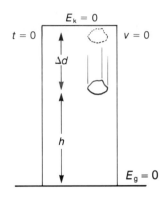

Suppose that the rock has a mass of 0.500 kg, that it falls from a height of 78.4 m, and that its gravitational potential energy is zero at the bottom of the chamber.

1. Since the rock falls from rest with an acceleration of 9.80 m/s², its speed at time, Δt, can be obtained as follows:
$$v_2 = v_1 + a\Delta t$$
$$= 0 + 9.80 \text{ m/s}^2 \Delta t$$
$$= 9.80 \text{ m/s}^2 \Delta t$$

2. The distance fallen at time Δt will be:
$$\Delta d = v_1 \Delta t + \frac{1}{2} a(\Delta t)^2$$
$$= 0 + \frac{1}{2} (9.80 \text{ m/s}^2) (\Delta t)^2$$
$$= (4.90 \text{ m/s}^2) (\Delta t)^2$$

3. The height above the ground at time Δt will be:
$$h = 78.4 \text{ m} - \Delta d$$

4. Its kinetic energy will be:
$$E_k = \frac{1}{2} mv^2$$

5. Its gravitational potential energy will be:
$$E_g = mgh$$

6. Its total energy will be:
$$E_T = E_k + E_g$$

The table summarizes the results of all the calculations for the fall of the rock.

time Δt (s)	1 speed v (m/s)	2 distance fallen Δd (m)	3 height h (m)	4 kinetic energy E_k (J)	5 potential energy E_g (J)	6 total energy E_T (J)
0	0	0	78.4	0	384	384
1	9.80	4.90	73.5	24.0	360	384
2	19.6	19.6	58.8	96.0	288	384
3	29.4	44.1	34.3	216	168	384
4	39.2	78.4	0	384	0	384

Since the total amount of energy remained constant, the potential energy lost as the rock fell was converted into kinetic energy. This appears to happen during every kind of energy transfer or transformation, even though more than these two kinds of energy may be involved. This principle is called the Law of Conservation of Energy.

In any transfer or transformation of energy, the total amount of energy remains constant.

Friction and air resistance are present in most real-life situations. When a leaf falls from a tree, the gravitational potential energy it had before its fall turns partly into kinetic energy. Due to the air resistance experienced by the falling leaf, some of the energy is converted to heat energy, too. Sometimes, the friction and air resistance are negligible. Some examples include a dense object with a small surface area falling for a short distance; a child swinging on a swing; and a hockey puck fired at a high speed from the blue line to the goal. When friction and air resistance are negligible we can assume that not only the total energy but also the total mechanical energy is conserved. **Total mechanical energy** is the sum of the kinetic and potential energies.

Sample Problems

1. A 56 kg diver runs and dives from the edge of a cliff into the water which is located 4.0 m below. If she is moving at 8.0 m/s the instant she leaves the cliff, determine the following:
   (a) her gravitational potential energy relative to the water surface when she leaves the cliff

The Law of Conservation of Energy was proposed by Heinrich von Helmholtz (1821-1894) in 1847, suggesting that energy could be neither created nor destroyed.

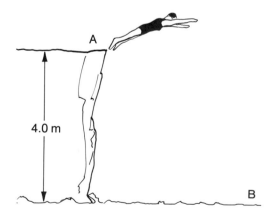

(b) her kinetic energy when she leaves the cliff
(c) her total mechanical energy relative to the water surface when she leaves the cliff
(d) her total mechanical energy relative to the water surface just before she enters the water below
(e) the speed at which she enters the water

(a) In solving problems where friction and air resistance are small enough to be ignored, it is important to recognize that mechanical energy is conserved. It is also important to realize that the gravitational potential energy and the kinetic energy will change as the person or object moves. Therefore, it is imperative that we specify the location that is being dealt with at the moment. In the diagram the two positions that are referred to in the question are labelled as A and B.

At position A:
$$v = 8.0 \text{ m/s}$$
$$h = 4.0 \text{ m}$$
$$g = 9.8 \text{ N/kg}$$
$$m = 56 \text{ kg}$$ If the water surface is considered to be zero potential energy, then
$$E_g = mgh$$
$$= (56 \text{ kg}) (9.8 \text{ N/kg}) (4.0 \text{ m})$$
$$= 2.2 \times 10^3 \text{ J}$$

The gravitational potential energy of the diver the instant she leaves the cliff is 2.2×10^3 J, relative to the water surface.

(b) The kinetic energy at position A can be determined by using the following relationship:
$$E_k = \frac{1}{2}mv^2$$
$$= \left(\frac{1}{2}\right) (56 \text{ kg}) (8.0 \text{ m/s})^2$$
$$= (28 \text{ kg}) (64 \text{ m}^2/\text{s}^2)$$
$$= 1.8 \times 10^3 \text{ J}$$

The diver has a kinetic energy of 1.8×10^3 J the instant she leaves the cliff.

Notice that the direction of v is not specified, and that this information is not required to find the kinetic energy.

(c) The total mechanical energy of the diver at position A is simply the sum of the potential energy and kinetic energy at A.
$$E_T = E_g + E_k$$
$$= 2.2 \times 10^3 \text{ J} + 1.8 \times 10^3 \text{ J}$$
$$= 4.0 \times 10^3 \text{ J}$$

The total mechanical energy when the diver leaves the cliff is 4.0×10^3 J relative to the water surface.

(d) The total mechanical energy remains constant if friction and air resistance can be ignored. Therefore the total mechanical energy of the diver the instant she enters the water is still 4.0×10^3 J.

(e) To find the speed of the diver the instant she enters the water we can reason as follows.

At position B:

$$E_T = 4.0 \times 10^3 \text{ J}$$
$$E_g = 0 \text{ (diver is at reference level)}$$
$$E_T = E_k + E_g$$
$$4.0 \times 10^3 \text{ J} = \frac{1}{2} mv^2 + mgh$$
$$= \left(\frac{1}{2}\right)(56 \text{ kg})v^2 + 0 \text{ J}$$
$$= (28 \text{ kg})v^2$$
$$v^2 = \frac{4.0 \times 10^3 \text{ J}}{28 \text{ kg}}$$
$$= 1.4 \times 10^2 \text{ J/kg}$$
$$v = 12 \text{ m/s}$$

Therefore the diver enters the water at 12 m/s.

You may wish to rearrange the expression before substituting values.

$$E_k = \frac{1}{2} mv^2$$
$$v^2 = \frac{2E_k}{m}$$
$$= \frac{2(4.0 \times 10^3 \text{ J})}{56 \text{ kg}}$$
$$= 1.4 \times 10^2 \text{ J/kg}$$
$$v = 12 \text{ m/s}$$

2. A child throws a 0.200 kg rock at a tree. When the rock leaves the child's hand, it is moving at 20 m/s and is located 1.5 m above the ground.

(a) Find the total mechanical energy of the rock.

(b) How high above the ground does the rock strike the tree if it is moving at 10 m/s at the instant it hits the tree?

(a) It is realistic to assume that air resistance is negligible in this case. Therefore the total mechanical energy will remain constant. It can be calculated at the instant the rock is released because we have enough information to find the potential and kinetic energy. If ground level is chosen as the reference level then at the instant of release:

$$m = 0.200 \text{ kg}$$
$$g = 9.8 \text{ N/kg}$$
$$v = 20 \text{ m/s}$$
$$h = 1.5 \text{ m}$$
$$E_T = E_k + E_g$$
$$= \frac{1}{2} mv^2 + mgh$$
$$= \left(\frac{1}{2}\right)(0.200 \text{ kg}) (20 \text{ m/s})^2 +$$
$$(0.200 \text{ kg})(9.8 \text{ N/kg})(1.5 \text{ m})$$
$$= 42.94 \text{ J, or } 43 \text{ J}$$

The total mechanical energy of the rock at release is 43 J.

(b) At the instant the rock is travelling at 10 m/s, it still has a total mechanical energy of 43 J. This information is useful in determining the height as shown below:

$$E_T = E_k + E_g$$

$$43 \text{ J} = \frac{1}{2}mv^2 + mgh$$

$$43 \text{ J} = \left(\frac{1}{2}\right)(0.200 \text{ kg})(10 \text{ m/s})^2 + (0.200 \text{ kg})(9.8 \text{ N/kg})h$$

$$43 \text{ J} = 10 \text{ J} + (1.96 \text{ N/kg})h$$
$$(1.96 \text{ N/kg})h = 33 \text{ J}$$
$$h = 17 \text{ m}$$

Therefore the rock is 17 m above the ground when it strikes the tree.

Practice

1. A 300 kg snowmobile is travelling at 16 m/s when it comes to the edge of a small cliff. Since there is a deep fluffy snowdrift 2.5 m below the cliff, the driver doesn't slow down but goes over the edge without changing speed.
   (a) What is the total mechanical energy of the snowmobile when it leaves the edge of the cliff? (Specify the reference level you are using for gravitational potential energy.)
   (b) How fast is the snowmobile going when it lands on the snowdrift?
2. Several children, pretending that they are playing in the jungle, suspend a rope from an overhead tree limb. A child of mass 40 kg running at 8.0 m/s grabs the rope and swings off the level ground.
   (a) What maximum height does the child reach?
   (b) How fast would a 30 kg child have to run to reach the same height as the 40 kg child?
3. An amusement park has a slide for which participants are given a cloth sack to sit on. The top of the slide is 6.0 m high.
   (a) Determine the speed attained at the bottom of the slide by a 30 kg child. Assume that the child starts from rest and make the unrealistic assumption that friction can be ignored in this case.
   (b) Repeat your calculations for (a), but this time assume that 80% of the gravitational potential energy that the child has at the top of the slide is required to overcome friction, and is therefore lost as heat energy.

7.8 Machines

Machines are mechanical devices that help do work. Machines make work easier by redirecting or changing the sizes of forces. A wide variety of machines have been developed to make jobs easier. Cranes lifting freight, tractors pulling farm equipment, bulldozers pushing mounds of earth, a huge compactor crushing used cars—these represent a few of the many complex mechanical devices that aid people in doing work.

The operation of a machine can be explained using the Law of Conservation of Energy. When operating a machine, you do work to use the machine. The machine then does work to move another object. With negligible friction, the energy to operate the machine (work input) equals the energy provided by the machine (work output).

$$\text{energy input} = \text{energy output}$$

or

$$W_{\text{input}} = W_{\text{output}}$$

$$F_{\text{input}}\Delta d_{\text{input}} = F_{\text{output}}\Delta d_{\text{output}}$$

Machines do not save work. Energy must be conserved. However, machines can make work easier. In many machines, we trade motion (when the input distance is larger than the output distance) for force (when the output force is larger than the input force). Even the most complex mechanical equipment follows this simple relationship.

The illustration in the margin shows the advantage of a machine. Pushing down on the end furthest from the pivot lifts the block only a small distance. From the Law of Conservation of Energy we know that the product $F\Delta d$ is the same on both the input and output sides. A small input force pushing the bar down a long distance produces a large output force that moves the block up a short distance. Applying an input force of 25 N though a distance of 1 m could exert an output force of 250 N to move the object 0.1 m.

Simple Machines

A complex machine, like a crane or bulldozer, is made up of many combinations of simpler machines. These simple machines can be classified into six types.

1. Lever
A lever is a length of rigid material, like a bar, which pivots around a fixed point. This point is called the fulcrum. Levers are classified by the position of the fulcrum.

Often we refer to the "mechanical advantage" of a machine. The mechanical advantage is the ratio of the output force to the input force.

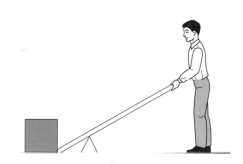

Lifting a heavy block is made easier by using a machine, in this case, a straight bar.

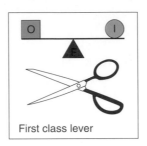
First class lever

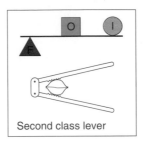
Second class lever

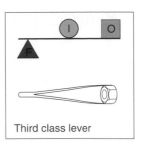
Third class lever

First-class levers have the fulcrum (F) between the input (I) and output (O) forces. Laboratory balances, pliers, and scissors are examples of first-class levers. Second-class levers apply the output force between the fulcrum and input force. Second-class levers can be seen in wheelbarrows and nutcrackers. Third-class levers have the input force applied between the fulcrum and the output force. Examples of third-class levers include hammers, tweezers, and snow shovels. Every limb of your body is a third-class lever!

2. Wheel and axle
When a wheel is solidly attached to an axle, they turn together. This combination acts in the same manner as a second-class lever. A small input force applied to the outer edge of the wheel turns the smaller axle with a larger force. Door knobs, hand cranks, and automobile cam shafts are examples.

3. Pulley
A pulley is also an example of a lever that rotates around a fixed point. Often, pulleys are used to redirect forces rather than increase them. The pulley at the top of a flagpole is an example.

4. Inclined Plane
The inclined plane, or ramp, may be the simplest of all machines. A ramp lets someone do the work necessary to raise a heavy object by allowing the object to be pushed along a long inclined surface. The longer the incline, the smaller the necessary input force.

5. Wedge
The wedge is a moving inclined plane. As a wedge moves through material, it cuts or forces the material apart. Knives, nails, saws, can openers—even zippers—are examples of wedges.

6. Screw
The screw is an inclined plane wrapped around a cylinder. As a screw is turned, material moves up or down the length of the screw. Screws are often used as fasteners. Screws used in jacks can lift cars, trucks, and even buildings.

A ramp is an inclined plane.

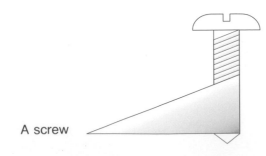
A screw

7.9 Efficiency

According to the Law of Conservation of Energy, the amount of energy present before an energy transformation is equal to the amount of energy present after that energy transformation. Unfortunately, sometimes some of the energy is not in a useful form and is wasted. Some transformations are more efficient than others. The efficiency of an energy transformation is calculated as follows:

$$\text{efficiency} = \frac{\textbf{useful energy output}}{\textbf{energy input}} \times \textbf{100\%}$$

Automobiles are highly inefficient. Suppose that an amount of fuel containing 1000 J of chemical energy is used by an automobile's engine. In an internal combustion engine, the fuel is vaporized and mixed with air, then drawn into a cylinder containing a piston. A spark from the spark plug ignites the fuel mixture, producing very high temperatures and pressures. The pressure of the gases pushes down on the piston, which turns the crankshaft, and thus, through the transmission, turns the wheels to make the car move forwards. If you were to calculate the work done by multiplying the force of the wheels moving the car by the car's displacement, you would get far less than the original 1000 J. Perhaps only 100 J remains. The rest is lost as heat energy.

Much of this heat is carried away by the exhaust gases. When the exploded fuel gases have done their job, they are pushed out through the exhaust valve, which opens as the piston starts moving back up the cylinder.

Some of the heat is conducted through the walls of the cylinders to the rest of the engine. To keep the engine from getting too hot, a mixture of water and anti-freeze is pumped through special passages inside the engine to pick up heat and carry it to the car's radiator, where a large fan blows air past the mixture to cool it down. Not only is this heat energy lost, but energy is used to run the water pump and the fan.

As the energy is transferred to the car's driving wheels, friction in the crankshaft bearings, transmission, differential, and wheel bearings generates more heat energy, decreasing the useful energy available.

By the time all these losses have been subtracted, perhaps only 250 of the 1000 J reaches the transmission and only 100 J is delivered to the wheels. The other 900 J is lost as heat.

The efficiency of the car is $\frac{100 \text{ J}}{1000 \text{ J}} \times 100\%$, or 10%.

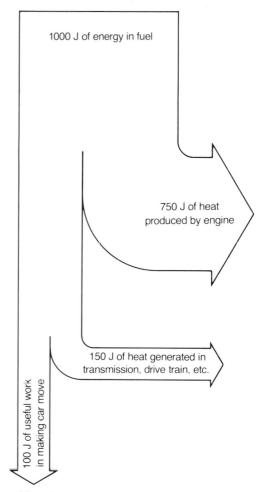

1000 J of energy in fuel

750 J of heat produced by engine

150 J of heat generated in transmission, drive train, etc.

100 J of useful work in making car move

Heat loss in a typical car

Some losses, such as the heat given off to the surroundings by the engine, are unavoidable.

Engineers the world over are always seeking ways to reduce energy consumption. Making machines more efficient is one way of doing this.

Sample Problems

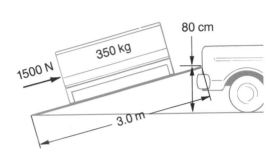

A family uses several planks to slide a 350 kg piano onto the back of a pickup truck. The box in the back of the pickup is 80 cm above the ground and the planks are 3.0 m long. If an average force of 1500 N is required to slide the piano up the planks, find:
(a) the work done in loading the piano.
(b) the efficiency of the planks as a simple machine to load the piano.

(a)
$$F = 1500 \text{ N}$$
$$\Delta d = 3.0 \text{ m}$$
$$W = F\Delta d$$
$$= 1500 \text{ N} \times 3.0 \text{ m}$$
$$= 4.5 \times 10^3 \text{ J}$$

The work done, or the actual energy input in loading the piano, is 4.5×10^3 J.

(b) The useful energy output in this case is the increase in gravitational potential energy of the piano in moving from ground level onto the back of the truck.

The useful work done (or the energy output) is
$$W = \Delta E_g = mg\Delta h$$
$$= (350 \text{ kg}) (9.8 \text{ N/kg}) (0.80 \text{ m})$$
$$= 2.7 \times 10^3 \text{ J}$$

The efficiency is found by using the expression
$$\text{efficiency} = \frac{\text{useful energy output}}{\text{energy input}} \times 100\%$$
$$= \frac{2.7 \times 10^3 \text{ J}}{4.5 \times 10^3 \text{ J}} \times 100\%$$
$$= 60\%$$

The planks are 60% efficient when used as a machine to load the piano onto the pickup truck.

Notice, however, that the planks let them get the job done. A direct lift onto the truck was probably impossible.

Practice

1. Several friends use a simple rope and pulley to raise a tree house from the ground into a tree. The mass of the tree house is 150 kg. By pulling together, the friends manage to exert an average force of 1.6×10^3 N as they raise the tree house a distance of 3.2 m above the ground.
   (a) Find the work done in raising the tree house.

(b) How much "useful work" is done?

(c) What is the efficiency of the rope and pulley in raising the tree house?

(d) Suggest why the efficiency of this simple machine is not 100%.

2. A container factory uses a 370 W motor to operate a conveyor belt that lifts containers from one floor to another. To raise 250 1-kg containers a vertical distance of 3.6 m, the motor runs for 45 s.

(a) Determine the useful energy output.

(b) How much energy does the motor use?

(c) What is the efficiency of the motorized conveyor system?

7.10 Energy and Society

Few of us would want to change our lifestyle. We are so used to the comforts of modern living—central heating, refrigerators, hot and cold running water, and cars are but a few—that we take them for granted. We probably would not choose to give up luxury items such as air conditioning, automatic dishwashers, stereo systems, and microwave ovens.

Consider what it would have been like in primitive times—hunting for food with bows and arrows, or spears; huddling around an open fire in a dark, damp cave as protection from cold temperatures, wind, and rain. Even since the time when your grandparents were young, our living conditions have changed remarkably.

We have learned how to change our environment to suit our tastes and needs. Only recently, however, have we begun to realize the tremendous price, in energy and material, that we and the rest of the world are paying and will continue to pay for our ingenuity.

Energy Consumption

A million years ago, primitive people derived energy only from the food they ate. This might have amounted to 8 MJ/d per person. Later, hunters used wood for heat and cooking as well, increasing consumption to 22 MJ/d per person. By 5000 B.C., farmers grew crops and used some animal energy to bring the per capita consumption up to about 50 MJ/d. Advanced farmers in Northern Europe, by around 1400 A.D., were using coal for heating, animals for transportation, plus water and wind power to run simple machines. This

Modern society depends on huge quantities of energy.

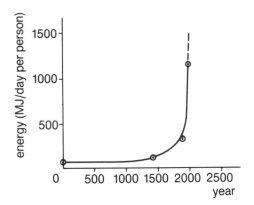

brought the total energy consumption up to 110 MJ/d per person.

The Industrial Revolution began at the end of the 18th century with the invention of the steam engine and the blast furnace. Coal mines, kept dry by steam pumps, produced coal for steam locomotives, ships, and other machines. Blast furnaces provided steel for construction. Energy consumption rose to 325 MJ/d per person by 1875.

The 20th century has seen coal largely replaced by oil, natural gas, and electricity. Hydroelectric, thermal, and now nuclear power plants generate most of our electricity. Diesel replaced steam locomotives, and cars replaced the horse and buggy. A virtual revolution in electricity and electronics has produced the electric light, the phonograph, and the telephone; then radio and television; later pocket calculators and kitchen gadgets; now home computers and VCRs. We've sent people into space and to visit the moon. Energy consumption in the United States is, at the time of printing, about 920 MJ/d per person.

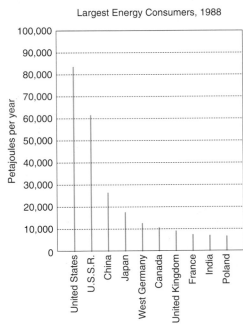

Largest Energy Consumers, 1988

World Energy Consumption

Energy consumption on a per capita basis is much lower in developing than in industrialized countries. Although the latter have only a small portion of the world's population, they consume 80% of the world's energy. The United States is a world leader in this regard. While in 1988 the energy consumed worldwide exceeded 33×10^{13} MJ, the United States alone consumed 8.4×10^{13} MJ. This represents 25% of world consumption. The graph in the margin identifies the 10 largest consuming nations and their total energy consumption. Notice that the United States, the U.S.S.R., and China consumed almost 50% of the energy produced worldwide.

Events of the seventies caused the industrialized world to take warning, however. World oil prices jumped from $2.50 to $9.50 a barrel in 1973–74. They jumped again from $17.50 in 1979 to $29.50 in 1981. Oil was so expensive that Western nations were forced to cut consumption by about 15% in four years. Efforts to find and implement more fuel-efficient vehicles and better insulated housing increased. Oil prices fell drastically in 1986, once again encouraging consumption. More recently oil prices have again been on the rise. At the time of printing, world oil prices were approaching 1981 levels.

The Increasing Demand for Energy

The graph in the margin shows the total projected annual United States energy consumption for the period from 1990 to 2010. The graph shows that despite the implementation of current conservation plans, government planners believe energy consumption will continue to increase. Further, the graph indicates that the United States will continue to depend on petroleum-based products as a major source of energy, despite the volatile history of world oil prices. Encouragingly, renewable resources are projected to become a larger and larger percentage of total energy consumed. As our national consciousness is raised towards energy conservation, recycling, and preserving our environment, we may find that the total energy consumed may not increase as much as projected.

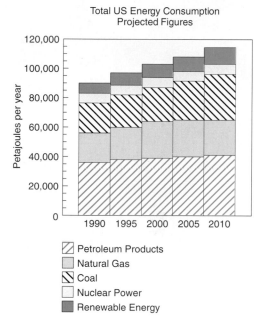

Total US Energy Consumption
Projected Figures

Petroleum Products
Natural Gas
Coal
Nuclear Power
Renewable Energy

*P*ractice

1. What fuel did coal replace as the primary fuel?
2. What replaced coal as the primary fuel?
3. Examine the graph on total U.S. Energy Consumption and answer the following questions:
   (a) Determine the average change in energy demand in petajoules per year between 1990 and 2010.
   (b) List some energy sources that would come under the category of "renewable".
   (c) In 1990, the population of the United States was approximately 250,000,000. Determine the per capita energy consumption for the United States for 1990.

The metric prefix "peta" means 10^{15}.

7.11 Sources of Energy

Sources of energy are classified as renewable or nonrenewable. Renewable sources can be replenished or replaced within a human lifetime. They would include sources such as solar, wind, biomass, and tides. Nonrenewable sources cannot be replaced within a human lifetime. Once consumed, such a source is considered to be depleted. Examples include coal, oil, natural gas, and uranium.

We tend to forget that the Earth is in a state of constant change. Every place where coal and oil are found today was once the bottom of an ancient sea. What will the world look like by the time the next batch of fossil fuel is ready?

1 barrel = 159 L

World Fossil Fuel Reserves	
	%
coal	88.8
natural gas	4.7
crude oil	5.2
tar sands oil	0.8
shale oil	0.5
	100.0

Chapter 7

Petroleum

Petroleum reserves found throughout the world were formed millions of years ago when microscopic organisms died and were quickly covered with mud and sediment. Petroleum pumped from the ground is called crude oil. Based on differences in the boiling points of its components, crude oil can be separated into gas, gasoline, kerosene, heating oil, and lubricating oil. The residue from this process is used to produce asphalt and paraffin wax.

Petroleum has an extremely high energy content for its mass. When burned, a large amount of chemical energy is released. Over the years, the United States has grown highly dependent on petroleum-based products.

Texas is by far the largest domestic crude-oil supplier. Oil fields discovered in Texas during the 1930's originally held more oil than has been discovered in the entire history of any other state except California. California ranks second in crude oil discovered, with 15% of the U.S. total. Alaskan oil flowing through the Trans-Alaska Pipeline to the lower continental states is a third major domestic source of crude oil. Domestic crude-oil production has been decreasing since 1985 because of a reduction in drilling and the depletion of older oil fields.

Unfortunately domestic oil alone cannot meet our energy needs. The United States has had a history of fluctuating dependence on foreign oil. During the late 1970's, net imports reached a peak of 46.5% of the total petroleum products supplied. Imports dropped to 27.3% of the total supplied in 1985. It is interesting to note that this pattern corresponds to world oil prices during the same periods. As of 1989, U.S. dependence on foreign oil had increased to 41.6%.

Natural Gas

Like petroleum, natural gas was formed millions of years ago and is trapped in underground reserves. Natural gas is often produced along with oil, but it can also be produced deep underground by the intense heating of coal. Natural-gas reserves in this country are found in Texas, Louisiana, and the Gulf of Mexico. The most common natural gas is methane, which is used primarily for home heating and cooking. Of the 18 780 billion cubic feet consumed in this country in 1988, 25% was used residentially. Another 3% was used in the operation of pipelines that transport natural gas.

Coal

It is believed that coal was formed millions of years ago from the compression of land plants in swampy environments. There are several different types of coal—each one having gone through longer, more intense compression than the next. The most compressed form of coal, anthracite, is also the most efficient. This hard, shiny black substance burns without smoke and has an extremely high energy-per-mass content.

The United States has just over 30% of the world's known recoverable coal reserves. Most of them are found in the Appalachian states, such as Pennsylvania, Kentucky, Ohio, and West Virginia. In 1988, 18% of worldwide coal production was in the United States.

Of the coal produced in this country, approximately 90% is also consumed in this country. Electric utility companies are the major users of coal. Only 0.7% of the coal used in 1988 was used commercially or residentially.

Methods used for obtaining coal include strip mining—whereby coal reserves just beneath the surface are stripped away—and shaft mining—whereby coal deposits deep beneath the Earth's surface are removed. While strip mining is less expensive and safer than shaft mining, there are serious environmental concerns associated with strip mining. Not only is the landscape temporarily scarred by the procedure, but sulfur-rich wastes released during strip mining can contaminate nearby streams.

Strip mining for coal

Gravitational Potential Energy

At hydroelectric plants, the gravitational potential energy of water is converted into kinetic energy. The kinetic energy of moving water is used to drive large turbines, which in turn generate large amounts of electricity.

It is estimated that hydroelectric power generates about 25% of the world's electricity. In the United States, hydroelectric power accounts for only about 10% of the energy we consume. However, based on the estimated rate of the flow of water, hydrologists have calculated a theoretical potential of 200×10^6 kilowatts of power waiting to be tapped.

While hydroelectric power is renewable and clean, there are problems associated with its use. From an environmental point of view damage can occur from the damming of rivers and the building of reservoirs. Technically electric power can be transmitted efficiently over long distances, but construction of transmission lines is an expensive undertaking.

The Glenn Canyon Dam on Lake Powell in Arizona

Nuclear Energy

Nuclear power reactors are discussed in more detail in Chapter 27.

In the United States, most electricity is produced from the burning of fossil fuels, such as oil, gas, and coal. Since fossil fuels are nonrenewable and demand for electricity is increasing, other sources of energy are necessary. In 1973, only 4.5% of our electricity came from nuclear power; today the figure has increased to 19%. Most nuclear power plants utilize uranium as fuel. As is true of fossil fuels, however, the supplies of uranium will not last forever.

Despite extensive precautions to maintain safety in the nuclear power industry, there are problems for which better solutions are being tested. Public concern arises from two main environmental dangers—the possibility of radioactive substances leaking from nuclear sites and the safe disposal of spent fuel. The effects of the 1986 accident in Chernobyl bear testimony to the potential devastation that a poorly designed or managed reactor could bring about.

The sun produces its energy by a process known as fusion. Hydrogen atoms are forced together at extreme pressures and temperatures to form helium atoms, and they release energy. Scientists have been able to produce fusion by aiming laser beams at tiny fuel pellets containing hydrogen. If a process can be perfected for doing this on a large scale, it could solve all our energy problems. The necessary fuel, hydrogen, is found in every molecule of water. (See Chapter 27 for more details.)

A nuclear power plant

*P*ractice

1. List five renewable and four non-renewable sources of energy.
2. What are the consequences of increased U.S. dependence on foreign oil?
3. Why do fossil fuels have such a high ratio of energy to mass?

4. What are the advantages of oil and natural gas over coal for home heating?
5. Describe all the transformations of energy that take place in producing electricity from hydroelectric power.
6. To replace the electrical energy generated from coal, oil, and gas would require about five times the present nuclear-generating capacity. At present, we use about 10^7 kg of uranium per year. How much uranium would we use per year if all our nonnuclear power plants were converted to nuclear plants?
7. Compare the five energy sources described in this section.
    (a) What are some pros and cons of each energy source?
    (b) What would be your recommendations if it were your job to plan the future use of these sources in the United States?

7.12 The Flow of Energy

Clearly, alternative sources of energy will have to be found to meet the predicted future demand in the United States. We are using our remaining coal, gas, oil, and uranium at an ever-increasing rate. The major renewable source of energy, falling water, is already being almost fully exploited.

To see what other kinds of energy are available, let us examine the flow of energy to and from the Earth's surface, as shown in the chart on the following page.

More than 99% of the incoming energy comes from the sun as solar radiation. About 30% of this radiation is reflected immediately back out into space, while another 47% is absorbed by the oceans, continents, and atmosphere, and converted into heat energy. Another 23% is used in the water cycle to evaporate water that will later fall as rain or snow. A small fraction drives the winds, waves, and currents. An even smaller fraction is used in photosynthesis, to supply energy to growing plants. A small fraction of this last amount of energy may eventually be found as oil, gas, or coal. These fossil fuels are formed by the action of extreme temperature and pressure on dead plants and animals buried deep beneath the Earth's surface.

The sun and the moon both make another energy source possible. The forces of gravity with which these objects pull on the oceans generate tidal energy in the form of tides and tidal currents.

The only other flow of energy to the Earth's surface comes from its interior as heat. The center of the Earth is a large mass of molten iron. As it cools, heat is conducted upwards to the surface.

In addition, heat is being generated throughout the Earth by the decay of radioactive elements. This heat is also conducted upwards.

At the surface we see evidence of this underground activity in volcanoes and hot springs. In a volcano, molten rock is escaping upwards through cracks in the rocks from deep underground. In hot springs, surface water seeps down into hot underground formations where it is heated, often far above its boiling point. The heated water returns to the surface as steam, or hot water.

The total rate of energy flow to the Earth's surface is about 1.2×10^{17} W, after subtracting the radiation reflected back immediately into space. In a day, this would amount to 1.04×10^{16} MJ of energy. In 1989, there were about 5.2 billion people on the Earth. Each person's daily share of that energy would equal 2.0×10^6 MJ if it could be completely transformed into useable forms of energy.

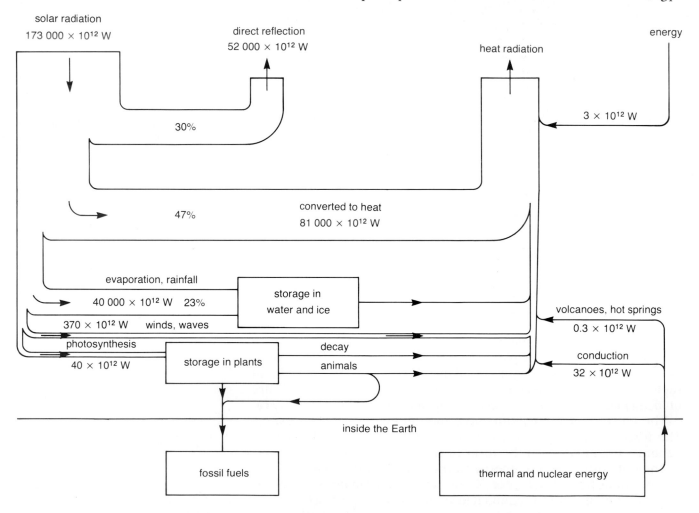

The flow of energy

7.13 Alternate Sources of Energy

Tidal Energy

An energy source that has not been harnessed to any great extent is the energy of ocean tides and tidal currents. The world's first tidal generating station was built at the mouth of the Rance River in Brittany, France. Water passes through gates in a large dam as the tide comes in. At high tide, the gates are closed and the water is trapped. About three hours after high tide, the water is allowed to start escaping through a powerhouse in which it turns turbines that generate electricity. There are 24 generators, capable of producing a total of 240 MW of electric power.

The Bay of Fundy in Canada is a promising site for tidal power. The difference between high and low tide is about 15 m, the biggest difference for any location in the world. North America's first tidal-generating plant was built there in the early 1980s. This plant is rated at 20 MW. Because of its large size, the Bay of Fundy has considerable potential for further development.

The tidal generating plant at the Bay of Fundy

Wave Energy

There have been many ambitious schemes for extracting energy from ocean waves, but none have so far been implemented. The latest, put forward by a group in Scotland, would involve the construction of a floating wave machine offshore. Moving segments would pump water into a floating generator to produce electric power. Such an installation might be extremely useful in the United States in view of our thousands of kilometers of coastline.

Wind Energy

Windmills were in use thousands of years ago, transforming the energy of the wind into useful work. At the end of the 19th century, in northern Europe, some 24 000 were in operation. Most of them were eventually replaced by steam engines.

In the early part of this century, thousands of windmills were in operation in rural North America, some of them capable of generating as much as 3000 W of electric power. They disappeared gradually as electric transmission lines were extended throughout the country.

Average wind speed	(km/h)
Anchorage, AK	10.9
Atlanta, GA	14.6
Chattanooga, TN	9.9
Galveston, TX	17.6
Minneapolis, MN	16.8
Mt. Washington, NH	56.2
New York, NY	15.0
San Francisco, CA	13.9
St. Louis, MO	15.5

Wind turbines

Recently, people have started to buy wind generators for their cottages, homes, or farms. A typical system includes a small generator and some storage batteries. The generator charges the batteries whenever the wind is blowing.

In areas where high-speed winds blow in a consistent direction, wind farms, which consist of 50 or more giant wind turbines, have been constructed. Areas such as the Pacific Northwest and central California are well suited for wind farms.

Biomass Energy

Biomass energy is the chemical potential energy that is stored in plants and animals. Some useful sources of biomass energy are wood, crop wastes, animal wastes, forestry waste, and garbage.

In India, thousands of methane-gas digesters use a mixture of animal manure and crop waste to generate methane gas for home heating and cooking. The sludge that remains is an excellent fertilizer. Some experiments have been carried out with digesters suitable for large livestock farms. While this process will never be a major power producer, it is feasible and it does have a useful by-product.

Alcohol is produced by the action of yeast on sugar and starch, which is found in sugar cane, beets, potatoes, corn, and wheat. In Brazil, suppliers have been mixing alcohol with gasoline for a number of years.

Heating municipal solid wastes in the absence of oxygen, a process called "pyrolysis", or destructive distillation, produces a mixture of gases and liquids that can be processed into fuels. Solid-waste landfills are reaching their capacity in certain regions of the country. Pyrolysis may be a partial solution to the problem of solid-waste disposal.

Gasification is the burning of biomass material in a controlled supply of air to produce fuel gases. Here the heat energy is supplied by the partial burning. The process has long been used with coal, coke, and charcoal, especially in Great Britain. Small biomass generators have been built for cars, trucks, and buses; they work best in constant-speed operation such as cross-country trucking.

Finally, the United States should be able to provide a large amount of wood for burning in stoves and furnaces. As the cost of fossil fuels rises, the cost of firewood may become more reasonable. Newer, improved designs for fireplaces, grates, and stoves have greatly increased efficiencies.

Geothermal Energy

More and more countries are starting to install power plants that make use of geothermal energy—the energy of hot springs and geysers.

Steam from geysers can be used to drive turbines and generate electricity. Such plants have been built in Italy, Australia, New Zealand, Iceland, and the United States. A plant at Lardarello, Italy, is able to generate 370 MW of power. A plant in California produces 396 MW of electric power.

Geothermal energy

Solar Energy

The average solar power received at ground level in the United States varies from about 150 W/m² in Seattle, Washington, to about 250 W/m² in Houston, Texas. Most of this energy is absorbed as heat during the day and radiated back out into space at night. If this solar energy could be captured and converted to electrical energy by some kind of solar panel working at 100% efficiency, our energy needs could be fully satisfied. Unfortunately, commercial solar cells are now only about 8–10% efficient. Thus, for many practical applications, they are not yet economical.

Many scientists believe that solar energy will find its greatest use on a small scale, for heating homes and offices and producing hot water. Much of the energy consumed in northern portions of this country is used to heat living and working areas and to produce hot water. Despite cold winters in these regions, solar energy could supplement gas, oil, and electricity.

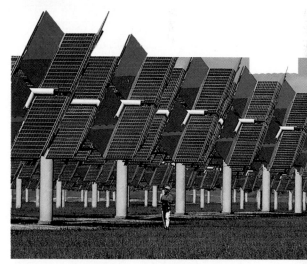

These solar collectors at the Carissa Plains power station use photovoltaic cells to produce electricity.

*P*ractice

1. List the alternative forms of energy that are under development and have been discussed in this chapter.
2. List some possible harmful effects to the environment of:
   (a) nuclear power plants
   (b) coal-fired thermal power plants
   (c) tidal generating stations
   (d) hydroelectric power stations
3. Which of the renewable energy forms described in this chapter are the most feasible for your community? Give reasons for your answer.
4. List some reasons why renewable energy sources are not adopted on a large scale throughout the country.

Investigations

Investigation 7.1: Power Running Up Stairs

Problem:
What is the maximum power that a physics student can develop running up stairs?

Materials:
physics student(s)
kilogram bathroom scales
meterstick
stopwatch

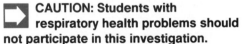
CAUTION: Students with respiratory health problems should not participate in this investigation.

Procedure:
1. Measure the mass of the physics student (or students, if you want to make this a competition), in kilograms. Set up a suitable table in your notebook and start recording your data.
2. Calculate the force of gravity on the student, using $F_g = mg$. Use this value for force in your work calculation.
3. Measure the height of one step. Count the number of steps and multiply to find the vertical height the student will rise, in meters.
4. With the stopwatch, measure the time the student takes to run up the stairs, from a standing start, in seconds.
5. Calculate the power developed.

Questions:
1. What are the physical characteristics of the more powerful students in your class? Do they tend to be tall, strong, heavy, or a combination of these?
2. In which sports must a person be able to generate a lot of force? Do much work? Develop great power?

Investigation 7.2: The Pendulum and Mechanical Energy

Problem:
Is mechanical energy conserved when a pendulum swings?

Materials:
large mass (about 5 kg)
strong string or wire
ceiling hook
millisecond timer (or computer)
light source

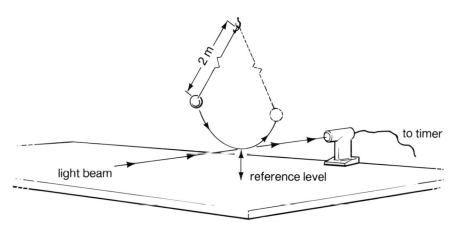

Procedure:

1. Construct a pendulum by attaching a 5 kg mass (or whatever size you have available) to a strong string or wire about 2 m long. Attach the string or wire to a secure hook in the ceiling.
2. Measure the distance from the floor or a table to the bottom of the pendulum bob. The elevation you measure from will be your reference point for determining the gravitational potential energy of the pendulum bob.
3. Set up the timer using a photocell and light beam so that the beam will break when the bob is in the lowest part of its swing. The timer will then record the time at which the beam is broken to the nearest millisecond.
4. Draw the pendulum aside and set the timer to zero.
5. While the pendulum bob is held aside, have someone measure the height of the bob from the reference level.
6. Release the pendulum and allow it to swing through the light beam. Have someone catch it on the other side of its swing.
7. Note the time interval for which the light beam was broken by the pendulum bob.
8. Measure the diameter of the pendulum bob, making sure to measure the bob in the area where it broke the beam.

If the bob is not spherical, measure the height from the reference level to the middle of the bottom side.

The average speed calculated in this step is the average for a very short time interval. For that reason we can assume that it is also the speed the pendulum has the instant it is at the bottom of its swing.

9. Determine the average speed of the pendulum bob at the lowest point in its swing by using the time for which the beam was broken and the diameter of the bob.
10. Calculate the gravitational potential energy of the pendulum bob when it is held aside, and when it swings through the lowest point in its cycle.
11. Assume that mechanical energy was conserved, and calculate what the speed of the bob should have been at the bottom of the swing if our assumption is correct.
12. Compare the result you obtained in step 9 with the result obtained in step 11.

Questions:
1. Was mechanical energy conserved during one swing of the pendulum? Justify your answer.
2. We know that any pendulum will eventually stop swinging. Explain how the mechanical energy gradually disappears.

Investigation 7.3: The Inclined Plane
Problem:
What is the efficiency of an inclined plane used to raise a cart?

Materials:
inclined plane
newton spring balance
dynamics cart
measuring tape or meter stick
several bricks or books

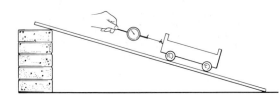

Procedure:
1. Set up the apparatus as shown in the diagram.
2. Use the newton spring balance to determine the force required to lift the dynamics cart vertically. (If this goes beyond the capacity of the newton scales, find the mass of the cart in kilograms and calculate the force required, using $F_g = mg$.)
3. Measure the length of the inclined plane and how high it will raise the cart when it is pulled up the ramp.
4. Attach the newton balance to the cart and determine the average force required to pull the cart up the ramp.
5. Calculate the work done in pulling the cart up the incline. (This is the energy input.)
6. Calculate the work that would be required to lift the cart straight up through the height of the inclined plane. (This is the useful energy output.)

7. Determine the efficiency of the inclined plane using the relationship

$$\text{efficiency} = \frac{\text{useful energy output}}{\text{energy input}} \times 100\%$$

Questions:
1. What is the efficiency of the inclined plane as it was used for this task?
2. What could you do to increase the efficiency of the inclined plane?
3. What is the maximum value the efficiency could theoretically have? Explain why efficiencies higher than this are impossible.

Investigation 7.4: Total Energy of a Toy Car

Preamble:
The Law of Conservation of Energy was arrived at by experiment. One interaction after another was studied; energies were measured and totalled. When the total energy was not constant, invariably a new form of energy was discovered to account for the difference.

This investigation involves a strobe photograph of a toy car moving down a curved ramp. Measurements of the distance travelled between dots will enable you to calculate the speed and the kinetic energy of the car at various times. Measurements of the car's height above the desk at these same times will enable you to calculate the corresponding gravitational potential energy. Adding these results together will give the total mechanical energy.

Problem:
Is the total mechanical energy of a toy car on a ramp constant?

Materials:
accurate metric scale
onionskin paper

Procedure:
1. Draw a straight line across a sheet of onionskin paper to serve as a zero line for potential energy.
2. Place the onionskin paper over the photograph with the straight line lined up with the lower edge of the photograph. Assume that the lower edge of the photograph is horizontal.
3. Put a small dot in the center of the little square on the top of each image of the car.
4. Number the dots, as shown in the photograph.

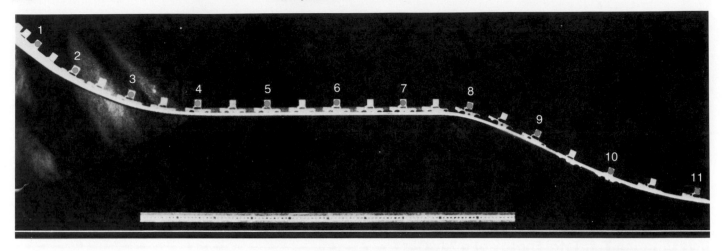

5. Measure the height above the zero line of each numbered dot and correct for the scale of the photograph (1 cm represents 10 cm). Set up a table in your notebook and record your observations.

Interval	h (m)	Δd (m)	v (m/s)	E_g (J)	E_k (J)	$E_T = E_g + E_k$ (J)
1						
2						

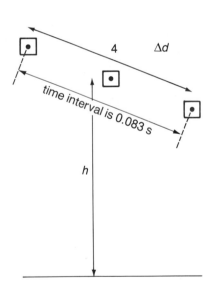

6. Measure the distance travelled between the two dots on either side of each numbered dot, and correct for the scale of the photograph.
7. Divide each distance travelled by the time interval. The time between dots is 0.0415 s. The time interval here is 2 × 0.0415 s, or 0.083 s. This gives you the average speed for each numbered interval.
8. Calculate the kinetic energy, the potential energy, and the total energy for each numbered interval. The mass of the car is 100 g.
9. On a single set of axes, draw graphs of each type of energy plotted against time.

Questions:
1. What should the graph of total mechanical energy against time look like if the sum of kinetic and potential energies is constant?
2. What percentage of the sum of the original kinetic energy and potential energy remains at the end of the trip?
3. What other energy transformations could have taken place as the car went down the ramp?

Extra kinetic energy is in the spinning wheels but not much, since their mass is small.

Meet Caesar Wheeler . . . Civil Engineer

Caesar worked for several years for a large engineering design and consulting firm. In that capacity, he worked on several major construction projects in the United States and around the world.

Q. What does a civil engineer do?
A. A civil engineer helps plan and supervise large construction projects, such as bridges, tunnels, power plants, factories, and skyscrapers. Engineers spend a great deal of time evaluating and preparing a site even before the actual construction begins.

Q. Why did you become an engineer?
A. I have always been interested in building things and studying how things work. In choosing my college program, I realized that engineering offered many different career opportunities.

Q. What type of preparation is required to become an engineer?
A. Many colleges and universities offer a 4-year program for engineering majors. In most of these programs, the first 2 years involve coursework in several different areas, with a strong emphasis on science, mathematics and English. In the last 2 years, the courses became more highly specialized—including courses such as surveying, hydraulics, structures.

Q. Do engineers need to have any specific credentials?
Requirements vary from state to state; however, each state requires that an engineer be registered before they are allowed to work on a major construction project. In order to become registered in most states, a person must be a graduate of an accredited engineering program, have several years of experience, and pass a state examination to receive a license.

Q. What are some of the different types of engineers and what do they do?
A. Some of the most familiar types of engineers include industrial engineers and mechanical engineers. An industrial engineer may design a new factory or help a company select the best equipment and people to improve the delivery of goods and services. A mechanical engineer may design and develop machines and engines. Mechanical engineers also test their designs and frequently supervise the implementation of a machine that they have designed.

Q. What are some of the newer fields of engineering?
A. Modern technology has led to the emergence of several specialized fields of engineering. For example, electrical engineers design and develop electrical and electronic equipment; computer engineers design computer systems; nuclear engineers design and operate nuclear power plants; and bio-medical engineers develop health-related products, such as hearing aids and artificial limbs.

Q. Do you work closely with other engineers?
I frequently work with or consult with other types of engineers. Projects frequently require different types of engineering expertise. In fact, large projects may require an entire team of engineers and technicians.

Q. What types of projects have you worked on?
A. Most of my experience has been in the preparation of sites for major construction projects. A great deal of testing and planning is done before the actual construction begins. Good site preparation is essential for the success of any construction project. One recent project involved the site preparation of storm water drainage systems for a large industrial complex. Large projects can take months or even years to complete.

Q. What do you like best about your work?
I enjoy the challenge of solving difficult problems. Since each new project has its own unique characteristics, it is rewarding to be able to apply my knowledge and expertise to new situations.

Q. What advice would you have for young people who are interested in a career in engineering?
I would encourage them to take their high school program seriously and get a strong background in math and science. They should explore several different college programs and several areas of specialization before choosing a particular field.

Chapter Summary

1. Work done on an object is calculated by multiplying the applied force by the displacement the object experiences in the direction of the force. If the force is in newtons and the displacement is in meters, the work done will be in joules.

$$W = F\Delta d \qquad 1 \text{ J} = \text{N} \cdot \text{m}$$

2. Power is the rate at which work is done. It is determined by dividing the work done by the time required. If the work is in joules and the time in seconds, the power will be in watts.

$$P = \frac{W}{\Delta t} \qquad 1 \text{ W} = 1 \text{ J/s}$$

3. Two units frequently used to measure work are joules and kilowatt hours.

$$1 \text{ kW} \cdot \text{h} = 3.6 \times 10^6 \text{ J}$$

4. Energy is the ability to do work.
5. Work is the transfer of energy. $\quad W = \Delta E$
6. Friction often does negative work on an object because it removes energy from it.
7. Gravitational potential energy is the energy of an object raised above the Earth's surface.

$$E_g = mgh$$

8. Kinetic energy is the energy of a moving object.

$$E_k = \frac{1}{2}mv^2$$

9. According to the Law of Conservation of Energy, in any transfer or transformation of energy, the total amount of energy remains constant. However, it may be in any one of a number of different forms.
10. In situations where friction and air resistance are small enough to be ignored and where no other energy is added to the system, the total mechanical energy is conserved.
11. Machines are mechanical devices that help do work. They make jobs easier by redirecting and changing the size of forces. When friction is negligible, work input to operate a machine equals work output of the machine.
12. The efficiency of an energy transformation is calculated from the energy input and the useful energy output. Useful energy is the energy that is actually used for some purpose and not wasted.

$$\text{efficiency} = \frac{\text{useful energy output}}{\text{energy input}} \times 100\%$$

Chapter Review

Discussion

1. Give an example of a situation in which:
    (a) a force is acting but there is no motion and therefore no work done.
    (b) a force is acting, but the displacement is perpendicular to the force and therefore no work is done.
    (c) there is motion, but since no force is acting to cause the motion, no work is done.

2. Suppose you have a contest in your class to see who can develop the most power in climbing a flight of stairs. Describe the physical characteristics of the person who would have the best chance of winning the contest.

3. When friction causes a moving object to slow down, it is doing negative work on the object. Explain why the work done by friction is viewed in this way.

4. A pendulum is drawn aside so that the center of the bob is at position A as shown. A horizontal rod is positioned at B so that when the pendulum is released the string catches at B, forcing the bob to swing in an arc that has a smaller radius. How will the height to which the bob swings on the right side of B compare to *h*? Explain your answer.

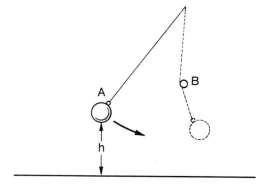

5. An engineer uses a single car to test the roller coaster track, shown in the diagram in the margin . In answering the following questions, assume that friction can be ignored and the speed at A is 0. In each case, give a reason for your answer.
    (a) Where is the gravitational potential energy the greatest?
    (b) Where is the kinetic energy the greatest?
    (c) Where is the speed the greatest?
    (d) Give a written description of what happens to the speed of the car as it rolls from A to B and so on to E.

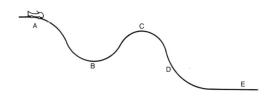

6. Most satellites circle the Earth in elliptical orbits so that they are not always the same distance from the Earth. (An ellipse is an oval shape.) A satellite in a stable elliptical orbit has a total

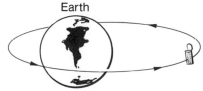

Satellite in elliptical orbit

The Earth is *not* at the center of the ellipse.

mechanical energy which remains constant. At what point in the orbit would the speed of the satellite be greatest? At what point would it be least? Explain your reasoning.

7. A small automobile jack has an output force that is 50 times larger than the input force that operates it. How does the input energy to operate the jack compare to the output energy?

8. Explain why it is impossible to have a motor that is 100% efficient.

9. Suppose you are a planner for an electrical utility company. You wish to build a hydroelectric power plant. Describe briefly the main factors you would have to consider in selecting a site for such a development.

10. The use of more flexible poles in pole vaulting has resulted in athletes being able to jump higher. By consulting the appropriate sources, estimate to what extent improved technology has affected the heights jumped by pole vaulters. Document your estimate with quotations from the references you have consulted.

11. One suggestion that has been made for efficient travel between two cities some distance apart is to link them with a straight tunnel bored through the Earth itself. Passengers would then travel through a portion of the Earth's core rather than travel along the circumference. Using energy relationships, explain why this approach should greatly decrease the fuel required to get from one city to the other.

12. When the speed of an object doubles, by what factor does its kinetic energy change?

13. Two balls with the same mass, one of wood and the other a Ping-Pong ball partly filled with sand, are rolled along a desk. The wooden ball rolls along nicely, but the Ping-Pong ball stops in a few centimeters. What happened to its kinetic energy? Was the kinetic energy changed to heat energy by the force of friction between the ball and the desk? Explain your answer.

14. Derive an expression for the speed v acquired by a mass m allowed to fall freely from rest through a height h at a location where the gravitational field strength is g. Assume that air resistance can be ignored.

15. A 60 kg man and a 40 kg girl sit on identical swings. They are then each given a push so that in both cases the swings move through the same angle from the vertical. How will their speeds compare as they swing through the bottom of the cycle? Explain your answer.

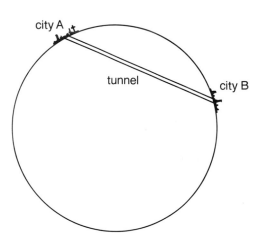

city A

tunnel

city B

Problems

Use $g = 9.80$ N/kg.
Assume applied forces act horizontally unless stated otherwise.

16. Calculate the work done by a 0.47 N force pushing a pencil 0.26 m.
17. Calculate the work done by a 0.47 N force pushing a 0.026 kg pencil 0.26 m against a force of friction of 0.23 N.
18. Calculate the work done by a 2.4 N force pushing a 400 g sandwich across a table 0.75 m wide.
19. How far will a mother push a 20.0 kg baby carriage, using a force of 62 N, while she does 2920 J of work?
20. How much work must be done to lift a 20 kg sack of potatoes vertically 6.5 m?
21. If a small motor does 520 J of work to move a toy car 260 m, what force does it exert?
22. A girl pushes her little brother on his sled with a force of 300 N for 750 m. How much work does she do if the force of friction acting on the sled is (a) 200 N,　(b) 300 N?
23. A 75.0 kg man pushes on a 500 000 t wall for 250 s but it does not move. How much work does he do on the wall?
24. A boy on a bicycle drags a wagon full of newspapers at 0.80 m/s for 30 min using a force of 40 N. How much work has the boy done?

An example of a wheel and axle

25. A power mower does 9.00×10^5 J of work in 0.500 h. What power does it develop?
26. How long would it take a 500 W electric motor to do 1.50×10^5 J of work?
27. How much work can a 22 kW car engine do in 60 s
    (a) if it is 100% efficient?　(b) if it is 30% efficient?
28. A force of 5.0 N moves a 6.0 kg object along a rough floor at a constant speed of 2.5 m/s.
    (a) How much work is done in 25 s by the force?
    (b) What power is being developed?
    (c) What force of friction is acting on the object?
29. The motor for an elevator can produce 2200 W of power. The elevator has a mass of 1100 kg complete with contents. At what constant speed will the elevator rise?
30. A 1500 kg car accelerates uniformly from rest to a speed of 100 km/h in 10.0 s.
    (a) What is the car's acceleration?
    (b) What is the car's displacement?
    (c) How much work is done on the car during this 10 s interval?
    (d) What average power is required to produce this motion?
31. A chair lift takes skiers to the top of a mountain that is 300 m high. The average mass of a skier complete with equipment is

80 kg. The chair lift can deliver three skiers to the top of the mountain every 30 s.
   (a) Determine the power required to carry out this task. (Assume the skiers join the lift at full speed.)
   (b) If friction increases the power required by 25%, what power must the motors running the lift be able to deliver?

32. What is the gravitational potential energy of a 61.2 kg person standing on the roof of a 10-story building, relative to each of the following levels? (Each story is 2.50 m high.)
   (a) the tenth floor
   (b) the sixth floor
   (c) the first floor

33. A 10 000 kg airplane lands, descending a vertical distance of 10 km while travelling 100 km measured along the ground. What is the plane's loss of potential energy?

34. A coconut falls out of a tree 12.0 m above the ground and hits a bystander 1.80 m tall on top of the head. It bounces back up 0.50 m before falling to the ground. If the mass of the coconut is 2.00 kg, calculate the potential energy of the coconut relative to the ground at each of the following times.
   (a) while it is still in the tree
   (b) when it hits the bystander on the head
   (c) when it bounces up to its maximum height
   (d) when it lands on the ground
   (e) when it rolls into a groundhog hole and falls 2.50 m to the bottom of the hole

35. Engineers have long dreamed of harnessing the tides in the Bay of Fundy. Although in places the difference between high tide and low tide can be as much as 17 m, the average change in height for the entire bay is about 4.0 m. The bay has the same area as a rectangle that is about 300 km long and 65 km wide. Water has a density of 1000 kg/m^3.
   (a) Calculate the volume of water and the mass of water that flows out of the bay between high tide and low tide.
   (b) Determine the loss in gravitational potential energy when the water flows out of the bay. Assume that the decrease in gravitational potential energy is equal to that of the mass calculated in (a) being lowered a distance of 2.0 m.
   (c) If half the gravitational potential energy lost when the tide flows out could be converted to electricity over a 6 h period, determine the amount of electrical power that would be generated.

36. Calculate the kinetic energy of a 45 g golf ball travelling at:
   (a) 20 m/s   (b) 60 m/s

This assumption is necessary because it represents the average change in height for the water.

37. How fast must a 1000 kg car be moving to have a kinetic energy of:
    (a) 2.0×10^3 J? (b) 2.0×10^5 J? (c) 1.0 kW·h?

38. How high would you have to lift a 1000 kg car to give it a potential energy of:
    (a) 2.0×10^3 J? (b) 2.00×10^5 J? (c) 1.00 kW·h?

39. A 50 kg cyclist on a 10 kg bicycle speeds up from 5.0 m/s to 10.0 m/s.
    (a) What was the total kinetic energy before accelerating?
    (b) What was the total kinetic energy after accelerating?
    (c) How much work was done to increase the kinetic energy of the cyclist?
    (d) Is it more work to speed up from 0 to 5.0 m/s than from 5.0 to 10.0 m/s?

40. At the moment when a shotputter releases a 5.00 kg shot, the shot is 2.00 m above the ground and travelling at 15.0 m/s. It reaches a maximum height of 8.00 m above the ground and then falls to the ground. Assume that air resistance is negligible.
    (a) What was the potential energy of the shot as it left the hand, relative to the ground?
    (b) What was the kinetic energy of the shot as it left the hand?
    (c) What was the total mechanical energy of the shot as it left the hand?
    (d) What was the total mechanical energy of the shot as it reached its maximum height?
    (e) What was the potential energy of the shot at its maximum height?
    (f) What was the kinetic energy of the shot at its maximum height?
    (g) What was the kinetic energy of the shot just as it struck the ground?

41.

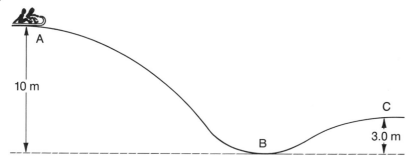

Some children go tobogganing on an icy hill. They start from rest at the top of the hill as shown in the diagram. The toboggan

and children have a combined mass of 90 kg. If friction is small enough to be ignored, determine:
(a) the total mechanical energy of the toboggan at A.
(b) the speed of the toboggan at B.
(c) the speed of the toboggan at C.

42. A boy fires a 60 g pebble with his slingshot. The pebble leaves the slingshot at 35 m/s.
    (a) How high above the slingshot will the pebble rise if it is fired straight up?
    (b) If the pebble is fired so that it goes in an arc and has a speed of 10 m/s at its maximum height, what will the maximum height be?
    (c) At what speed would an 80 g pebble have to be fired to reach the same height as the pebble in (a)? Assume that the 80 g pebble is also fired straight up.

43. A high jumper of mass 55 kg wishes to jump over a bar 1.8 m above the ground. Her center of mass is located 1.0 m above the ground. (We can imagine that all of her mass is located at this point for calculation purposes.)
    (a) If she wishes to clear the bar while travelling at a speed of 0.4 m/s, how fast must she be travelling the instant her feet leave the ground?
    (b) She lands on her back on a foam pad that is 40 cm thick. At what speed will she be travelling when she first makes contact with the pad?
    (c) Shortly after she lands she will be at rest. What has happened to the mechanical energy she had moments earlier?

44. A child of mass *m* slides down a slide 5.0 m high. The child's speed at the bottom of the slide is 3.0 m/s.
    (a) What percent of the mechanical energy that the child had at the top of the slide has not been converted to kinetic energy?
    (b) What feature of the slide determines the percentage of mechanical energy that is converted to other forms of energy?

45. A rodeo rider is riding a bucking bronco when he is thrown off. At the instant he leaves the horse he is located 1.6 m above the ground and is moving straight up at 4.0 m/s.
    (a) What maximum height above the ground does the rider reach?
    (b) At what speed will the rider hit the ground?

Numerical Answers to Practice Problems

page 177
1. 1.6×10^2 J
2. 5.0 J
3. 2.0×10^5 J
4. 1.4×10^5 J

page 179
1. 2.0×10^2 W
2. 30 s
3. 7.5×10^4 J
4. 5.9×10^2 W
5. 3.7 s
6. 4.1 m

page 180
1. 1.8×10^4 kW·h
2. 200 h
3. 50 kW

46. It is estimated that one kilogram of fat will provide 3.8×10^7 J of energy. A 60 kg mountain climber decides to climb a mountain 4000 m high.
    (a) How much work does the climber do against gravity in climbing to the top of the mountain?
    (b) If the body's efficiency in converting energy stored as fat to mechanical energy is 25%, determine the amount of fat the climber will use up in providing the energy required to work against gravity.

47. Suppose that each person in a particular family uses energy at an average rate of about 2 kW. (This figure includes energy used outside the home.) On a bright sunny day, the solar energy striking a horizontal surface provides power at a rate of 200 W/m². If a solar collector can capture 20% of the energy striking it, how large a collector in square meters is required to supply the energy requirements of a family of five during the daylight hours of a sunny day?

page 182
1. -2.3×10^5 J
2. -20 N

page 186
1. (a) 2.9×10^5 J   (b) 2.9×10^5 J
   (c) 2.9×10^5 J
2. (a) 1.96 J   (b) 1.18 J

page 187
1. (a) 1.2×10^4 J
   (b) 9.4×10^3 J
   (c) 1.1×10^4 J
   (d) 5.3×10^3 J
2. 2.4×10^3 J, 0, 1.2×10^3 J, -4.1×10^3 J

page 189
1. 225 J
2. 1.25×10^4 J
3. 20 kg
4. 8.0 m/s
5. (a) 56 J   (b) 98 J
   (c) 1.5×10^2 J   (d) 25 m/s
6. 2.3×10^4 J

page 194
1. (a) 4.6×10^4 J   (b) 17 m/s
2. (a) 3.3 m   (b) 8.0 m/s
3. (a) 11 m/s   (b) 4.9 m/s

page 198
1. (a) 5.1×10^3 J
   (b) 4.7×10^3 J
   (c) 92%
2. (a) 8.8×10^3 J
   (b) 1.7×10^4 J
   (c) 52%

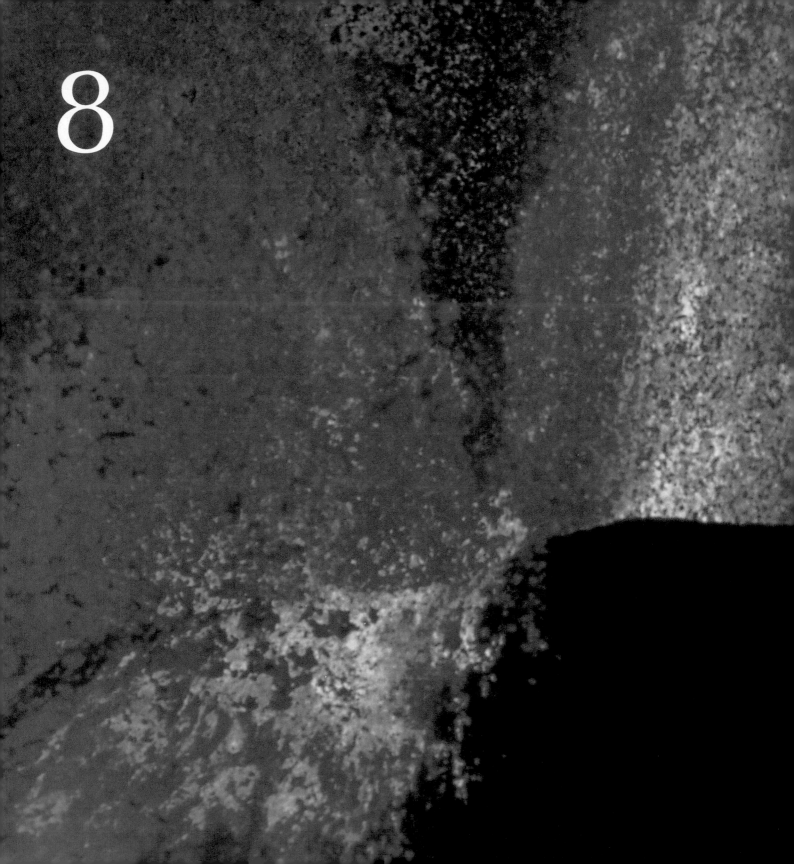

Thermal Energy

Chapter Objectives

- ☐ **Describe** *the Kinetic Molecular Theory.*

- ☐ **Relate** *change in size to the temperature change and the coefficient of expansion.*

- ☐ **Distinguish** *between temperature and heat.*

- ☐ **State** *three factors that affect the quantity of heat gained or lost by an object.*

- ☐ **Relate** *the temperature change to heat energy, mass, and specific heat capacity.*

- ☐ **Predict** *the final temperature when two substances at different temperatures are mixed.*

- ☐ **Measure** *heat capacity using a calorimeter.*

- ☐ **Explain** *latent heat and changes of state, using the Kinetic Molecular Theory.*

- ☐ **Relate** *heat energy to mass and latent heat.*

- ☐ **Explain** *heat engines and refrigerators.*

- ☐ **Calculate** *RSI values for a specific wall or ceiling, using tables of RSI values.*

- ☐ **Explain** *the principles of solar heating.*

Introduction

Rub your hands together quickly and they will become warm. Apply the brakes on a speeding car and they will soon heat up. These and other examples suggest that energy of motion, or kinetic energy, can be converted into heat, or **thermal energy**. The nature of this transfer at the molecular level, the factors that affect the transfer, and the results of the transfer are the topics of this chapter. All of us should understand some properties of thermal energy. It is involved in all aspects of our everyday lives—from cooking our food to keeping us warm on a cold winter night.

8.1 Kinetic Theory of Matter

Democritus, the Greek philosopher, was the first to suggest that all matter is made up of small particles called atoms. Democritus's theory did not receive experimental support until John Dalton (1766-1844) showed that the atomic theory supported the Law of Definite Proportions. (A more detailed discussion of this law is left for a chemistry course.) Robert Brown provided direct evidence for the existence of atoms and molecules. In 1827 he was viewing, through a microscope, some pollen grains suspended in water. He noticed that the individual pollen grains were moving about in a random manner. At first, he believed that a hidden force or life within the pollen grains caused their movement. However, when he studied non-living dye particles under the same conditions, he found the same erratic motion in individual particles of the dye. This motion is now known as **Brownian Motion**.

At the time of his discovery, Brown could not put forward an explanation for the motion of the particles. It was only after the development of the Kinetic Molecular Theory some twenty years later that the motion could be properly explained. Brownian Motion is explained if one assumes that the atoms or molecules in a substance are constantly moving. The movement Brown observed occurred when rapidly moving water molecules, too small to be seen through the microscope, collided with the individual particles of pollen and dye.

Other scientists provided strong evidence for the atomic theory around the turn of the twentieth century. In 1905, Albert Einstein

Although usually associated with Brownian Motion, Robert Brown (1773-1853) made a second major discovery in his capacity as a botanist. Brown was the naturalist on the 1801 voyage to the newly-discovered continent of Australia. He returned in 1805 with over 4000 species of plants, which he classified. He then discovered that a regular feature of all plant cells was a small body he called the *nucleus*, from the Latin, meaning "little nut".

developed mathematical models based on the evidence of Brownian Motion. He estimated that the diameter of a typical atom would be about 10^{-11} m. Today, scientists generally accept the **Kinetic Molecular Theory** as valid. Some of the features of this theory are listed below.

- All matter is made of atoms that may join together to form molecules.
- Atoms and molecules are in a constant state of motion.
- Atoms and molecules exert forces on one another that are electrical in nature. The forces are attractive when the atoms and molecules are near one another. But if the atoms and molecules are too close together, the force becomes repulsive. As a result, atoms and molecules maintain a minimum separation from one another.
- In a solid, the attractive forces between the atoms and molecules are strong enough to cause them to vibrate about a more or less fixed position. (Recall that most solids are rigid.)
- In a liquid, the atoms and molecules move about more quickly, or the attractive forces between them are weaker. As a result, they can change position while still bound together. (Recall that a liquid takes the shape of its container, but has a fixed volume.)
- In a gas, the atoms and molecules move about very quickly, or the attractive forces between them are very weak. As a result, the atoms and molecules do not stay together and tend to move out in all directions. (Recall that a gas completely fills its container.)
- Molecules have two forms of energy—potential, because of the electrical forces holding them together, and kinetic, because of their motion. The total thermal energy of a substance equals the sum of the potential and kinetic energies of its molecules.

These, then, are some of the general characteristics of the Kinetic Molecular Theory. We will be using these concepts throughout the chapter.

(a) 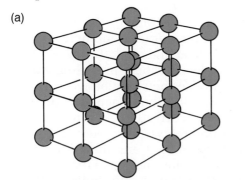   (b) 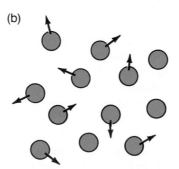   (c)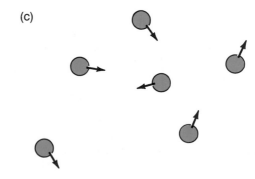

Atomic arrangements in (a) a crystalline solid, (b) a liquid, (c) a gas

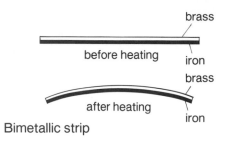

Bimetallic strip

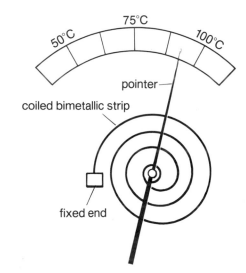

Bimetallic thermometer

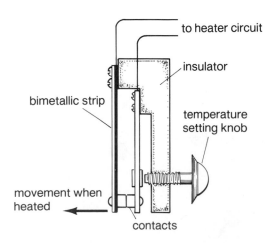

Thermostat

8.2 Temperature

In everyday usage, temperature is simply a measure of how hot or cold a substance is. In physics, temperature is defined from the standpoint of kinetic theory. When a substance is hot it has a higher concentration of kinetic energy than when it is cold. **Temperature** is actually a measure of the average kinetic energy of the atoms and molecules in a substance. The instrument designed to measure temperature is the thermometer.

Thermometers vary widely in their design and construction. But each is based on the property that temperature changes cause measurable changes in matter. Most common thermometers are based on the property that materials expand when heated and contract when cooled. In a liquid thermometer, a liquid, such as alcohol, expands when heated and rises up a hollow glass tube. A scale is attached to the glass tube from which temperatures are read. Other thermometers use bimetallic strips, made from two dissimilar metals. As the temperature changes, the two metals in the bimetallic strip expand or contract at different rates, and the strip bends. The larger the bend, the greater the temperature. The bimetallic strips are often coiled, with one end fixed and the other attached to a pointer (see diagram).

Other properties of matter are also used to create special thermometers. The electric thermometer and the pyrometer are two examples. The electric thermometer uses the principle that electrical resistance changes with changes in temperature. The pyrometer converts changes in a hot object's colour into temperature readings. It is commonly used in making steel.

All thermometers have a common numerical scale from which temperature is measured, or read. The most common scale in use today is the **Celsius scale**, sometimes called the centigrade scale. The Celsius scale has one hundred equal divisions between the freezing and boiling points of water—the two fixed points upon which the scale is arbitrarily based. For example, the following procedure could be used to calibrate a mercury thermometer. First, place the bulb in a mixture of ice and water and mark the level of the mercury in the glass tube 0°C. Then place the bulb in boiling water and mark the level 100°C. Finally, divide the space between these two fixed points into one hundred equal divisions. Each division will be 1°C. When a thermometer has been correctly calibrated, it can then be used to calibrate other thermometers.

It is important to note that all thermometers are limited to some extent by the physical properties of the material used to make them. For example, mercury freezes at −39°C and alcohol boils at 78°C.

While this book refers to the Celsius scale exclusively, the **Kelvin scale**, adopted in 1954, warrants mention. The illustration in the margin compares the two systems. You can see that the magnitude of both the Kelvin and the Celsius degree is the same. The absolute zero of temperature, or 0 K on the Kelvin scale, marks a minimum of kinetic energy, and as a result molecular energy is at a minimum (but not zero!) The freezing point of water is 273 K. Therefore K = °C + 273. The Kelvin equivalent for 10°C would therefore be 283 K. Note that the degree symbol (°) is *not* used with Kelvin degrees.

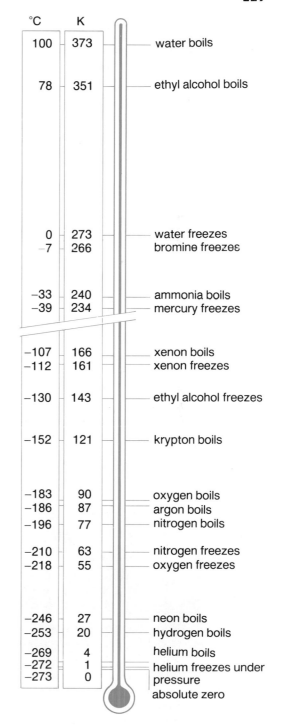

8.3 Thermal Expansion

As we've discussed above, thermal expansion provides a means of measuring temperature. On an atomic scale, thermal expansion occurs because the average distance between molecules increases as their thermal energy increases. The amount of expansion or contraction varies, however, depending on the substance.

Solid objects expand in all directions (length, width, and thickness) when temperature rises. The change in length, or **linear expansion**, provides a measure of the expansion of the whole object. For most solids, a change in length (ΔL) is directly proportional to a change in temperature (ΔT). An iron rod, for example, increases in length by twice as much when heated from 20°C to 180°C ($\Delta T = 160°C$) as it would from 20°C to 100°C ($\Delta T = 80°C$). This relationship is stated mathematically as $\Delta L \propto \Delta T$.

As one might expect, a change in length is also proportional to the original length of an object (L_0). That is, if 1 m and 2 m rods are both heated through the same temperature change, the 2 m rod will expand twice as much. This relationship is stated mathematically as $\Delta L \propto L_0$.

When the two proportionalities are combined and a proportionality constant k is added, they can be written as an equation, as follows: $\Delta L = kL_0 \Delta T$. The proportionality constant k in this relationship has a specific meaning and is replaced by the symbol α (alpha). The equation for linear expansion now becomes:

$$\Delta L = \alpha L_0 \Delta T$$

where ΔL is the change in length, in meters

α is the coefficient of linear expansion, in $°C^{-1}$

L_0 is the original length, in meters

ΔT is the temperature change, in degrees Celsius

The former name for the Celsius scale was the centigrade scale. Centigrade means "divided into 100 degrees". In 1948 the centigrade scale was officially renamed after Anders Celsius (1701-1744), who developed it. Centigrade and Celsius units are therefore equal. Celsius, a Swedish astronomer, also studied the aurora borealis, or northern lights, and was the first to associate this phenomenon with changes in the Earth's magnetic field. (See Chapter 21.)

For values of the coefficients of expansion for some common substances, see the chart on the next page. In common applications the values for different temperature ranges vary so slightly that they may be considered constant.

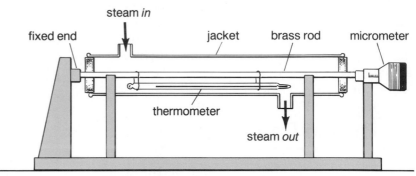

Measurement of thermal expansion

Engineers and architects must always allow for thermal expansion when designing any structure. If they ignore the thermal expansion of the materials used in construction, their structures may be in peril. The thermal expansion of steel and concrete can produce tremendous forces. Allowances for expansion are necessary in large bridge structures (see photograph). Expansion joints must be placed in concrete sidewalks and highways to allow room for expansion.

Just as linear expansion occurs in most solids, **volume expansion** occurs in most liquids when temperature increases. The relationship for volume expansion is similar to the one for linear expansion:

$$\Delta V = \beta V_0 \Delta T$$

where ΔV is the change in volume, in cubic meters
β is the coefficient of volume expansion in $°C^{-1}$
V_0 is the original volume, in cubic meters
ΔT is the temperature change, in degrees Celsius.
The value of β for some materials is given in the chart on the next page. Note that the coefficients of volume expansion for liquids are typically larger than those for solids.

An expansion joint in a bridge allows the steel beams of the bridge to thermally expand and contract without causing damage.

Expansion space left between two railway rails.

Continuous welded rails, without expansion spaces, are now used on many major railway lines. The rails are clamped so securely to the railway ties that they cannot change length. This does not mean that they do not expand and contract; they do—but only in width and height, not in length.

Coefficients of Thermal Expansion

Substance	Coefficient of linear expansion (α) ($\times 10^{-6}$ °C^{-1})	Coefficient of volume expansion (β) ($\times 10^{-6}$ °C^{-1})
aluminum	24	
brass	19	
concrete	10-14	
copper	17	
glass (window)	9.0	
glass (pyrex)	3.3	
granite	8.3	
ice	50	
lead	27	
oak (along fiber)	5	
(across fiber)	54	
steel or iron	12	
ethyl alcohol		1100
gasoline		950
mercury		182
water		210
air and most gases		3400

*The values for liquids and gases assume constant pressure.

Sample Problems

1. A steel I-beam used in the construction of a bridge is 9.2 m long at 20°C. On a hot summer day the temperature rises to 40°C. What is the change in the beam's length due to linear expansion?

At one time "degrees Celsius"
represented a point on the temperature
scale and "Celsius degrees" represented
a temperature change. In SI, we use only
"degrees Celsius" in both cases.

$$L_0 = 9.2 \text{ m}, \Delta T = T_2 - T_1 = 40°C - 20°C = 20°C,$$
$$\text{and } \alpha = 1.2 \times 10^{-5} \text{ °C}^{-1}$$
$$\Delta L = L_0 \alpha \Delta T$$
$$= (9.2 \text{ m})(1.2 \times 10^{-5} \text{ °C}^{-1})(20°C)$$
$$= 2.2 \times 10^{-3} \text{ m}$$

This change may not seem like much. But imagine the force that the beam would exert if prevented from expanding. The forces for this beam would exceed 5.3×10^5 N!

It can be estimated that the tank's volume will increase by approximately 3.6×10^{-5} m³, about 1.5% of the volume change for the gasoline.

2. A gasoline tank in a typical car has a capacity of 60 L at 20°C. If the tank is filled to the top, how much gasoline will overflow if the car is left in the sun and the gasoline reaches a temperature of 45°C? (Ignore the small expansion of the tank itself.)
$$V_0 = 60 \text{ L}, \Delta T = T_2 - T_1 = 45°C - 20°C = 25°C,$$
$$\text{and } \beta = 9.5 \times 10^{-4} \text{ °C}^{-1}$$
$$\Delta V = \beta V_0 \Delta T$$
$$= (9.5 \times 10^{-4} \text{ °C}^{-1})(60 \text{ L})(25°C)$$
$$= 1.4 \text{ L}$$

Since the gasoline expands by 1.4 L, this is the approximate amount that would be spilled on the road.

Practice

1. A brass wire is 0.500 m long at 20°C. If heated to 50°C, what change in length would occur?
2. A gap must be left between the ends of steel railroad rails to prevent stress. A 12.0 m rail is laid at 20°C. What gap is necessary so that the rails would just touch at 45°C?
3. A house has a volume of 500 m³ at 20°C. How much air enters or leaves the house if the temperature falls to 0°C? Which way does the air flow?
4. In an experiment to determine the coefficient of linear expansion for aluminum, a 0.50 m rod is heated from 20°C to 100°C. The increase in length is found to be 0.0096 mm. What is the coefficient of linear expansion for aluminum?

Most substances contract uniformly as their temperature decreases. Water, however, is unusual in that it does not exhibit this property. The volume versus temperature graph for water in the margin on the next page shows that the volume of water decreases as it is cooled from room temperature. However, when the temperature of water reaches 4°C its volume begins to increase. This means that water actually has a maximum density at 4°C. Most liquids reach their maximum density at their freezing point.

This **anomalous behavior** of water explains why the water in lakes and rivers freezes first at the surface. As the water cools below

4°C, the increase in volume decreases the density of the cooler water ($D = m/V$). The cooler, less dense water moves to the surface, while the more dense 4°C water sinks. As a result, the surface water freezes first because it reaches 0°C first. The water below the ice in a deep pond or a lake never freezes, and the fish and plant life are able to survive the winter (see diagram below).

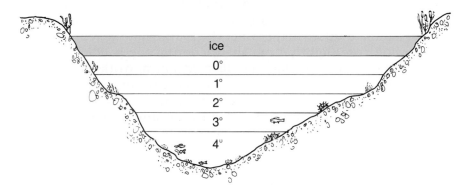

Temperatures in an ice-covered pond

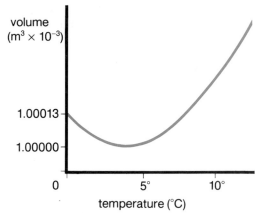

Volume of 1.00000 kg of water as a function of temperature

One other exception is rubber. When heated, rubber does not expand, it contracts. You may have noticed this in a chemistry laboratory. It's difficult to remove a warm rubber tube from a glass tube because the rubber contracts on the glass.

8.4 Thermal Energy

In everyday life we use the term "heat" quite loosely. In science we must define heat more precisely. Recall from Section 8.1 that thermal energy is the sum of the potential and kinetic energies of the atoms and molecules in a substance. When an electric stove element heats up, the average kinetic energy of its molecules increases as the temperature rises. When a pot of cold water is placed on a hot stove element, there is contact between the molecules with high kinetic energy in the element and the molecules with low kinetic energy in the pot and the water. The temperature of the pot and water rises as the energy is transferred from the element to them. Similarly, if the pot were placed in crushed ice, the molecules with higher kinetic energy in the pot and water would lose some of their energy to molecules with lower kinetic energy in the ice. In both cases, the energy flows from the object with the higher temperature to the one with the lower temperature. **Heat** is defined as the thermal energy that flows from one object to another due to a difference in their temperatures.

James Prescott Joule (1818–1889) was a self-educated British brewer who had a keen interest in the subject of measurement. Even in his teens he was publishing papers concerning heat and electric motors. When he was 22 he worked out the relationship between the rate of heat flow and electric current. ($E = I^2 R\Delta t$: see Section 20.6.) While managing the family brewery, he spent ten years conducting experiments on energy. When he first made his ideas public, in 1847, they were not accepted by the academic community. He persevered, nevertheless, and two years later gained the support of William Thompson, later Lord Kelvin, after whom the Kelvin degree was named. Fully recognized by 1849, Joule went on to become a member of the Royal Society and president of the British Association for the Advancement of Science. The fact that he was never a professor and remained a brewer all his life did not seem to matter in the democratic world of science.

In 1847, James Joule (1818-1889) proposed what is now known as the First Law of Thermodynamics—also called the Law of Conservation of Energy. According to this law, the heat energy absorbed by a body equals the change in the internal energy of that body plus the work done by that body on its surroundings. Joule performed a series of experiments to show that heat, like work, represents a transfer of energy. One of his experiments is illustrated below. In this experiment, the two falling masses caused the paddles in the insulated tank to rotate in the water. He found that the temperature of the water rose slightly from the friction of the paddles moving through the water. By comparing the mechanical work done by the falling masses and the temperature rise in the water, he was able to show the relationship between mechanical work and heat energy. Before stating this relationship, we must examine the factors that affect the quantity of heat energy in a substance.

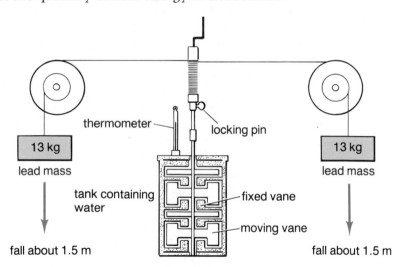

Joule's experiment to show the relationship between mechanical work and heat energy

One obvious factor is the temperature. Since temperature is an indirect measure of the kinetic energy of the molecules in a substance, the higher the temperature, the greater the thermal energy in the substance. Another factor is the mass. The larger the mass, the greater the number of molecules present—each with its own thermal energy. The last factor is not so apparent. Different substances are made up of different atoms and molecules so that their thermal properties vary. This thermal property, called the specific heat capacity, also affects the amount of heat energy in a substance.

Specific heat capacity is defined as the quantity of heat required to raise the temperature of 1 kg of a substance by 1°C. The units of specific heat capacity are joules per kilogram times degrees Celsius. The specific heat capacity of water, for example, is 4.2×10^3 J/kg · °C. This means that 4.2×10^3 J of heat energy is required to change the temperature of 1 kg of water 1°C. Using this value, we can determine the quantity of heat required to raise the temperature of 50 kg of water from 20°C to 90°C. Since 4.2×10^3 J is required to raise the temperature of 1 kg of water 1°C, it follows that $(4.2 \times 10^3$ J$)$ $(50$ kg$)(70$°C$)$, or 1.5×10^7 J, is required to raise the temperature of 50 kg through a temperature change of 70°C.

We can summarize this in a general equation as follows.

$$E_H = mc\Delta T$$

where E_H is the heat energy gained or lost, in joules
m is the mass, in kilograms
ΔT is the temperature change, in degrees Celsius
c is the specific heat capacity, in joules per kilogram degree Celsius

Applying this relationship to the above example, we can write:

$$\begin{aligned}
E_H &= mc\Delta T \\
&= (50 \text{ kg})(4.2 \times 10^3 \text{ J/kg} \cdot °\text{C})(70°\text{C}) \\
&= 1.47 \times 10^7 \text{ J, or } 1.5 \times 10^7 \text{ J}
\end{aligned}$$

The specific heat capacities of various common materials are provided in the table in the margin. These values are determined experimentally, using a technique similar to that followed in Investigation 8.3. In general, the greater the specific heat capacity, the greater the amount of heat required to change the temperature of a unit mass of a substance. For example, the specific heat capacity of iron is 4.5×10^2 J/kg · °C, whereas that of water is 4.2×10^3 J/kg · °C. This means that almost ten times more heat is needed for a 1°C rise in temperature of 1 kg of water than for 1 kg of iron. The following examples will demonstrate the application of these concepts.

Actually, the scientific definition of the specific heat capacity of water is that 4.2×10^3 J of heat energy is necessary to raise the temperature of 1 kg of water from 14.5°C to 15.5°C. This narrow temperature range is specified since the energy required varies slightly for different temperature ranges. But the differences are less than 1% in the 0°C to 100°C range. As a result, the variation can be ignored for most practical purposes.

Specific Heat Capacities of Various Materials	
Substance	**Specific heat capacity (c) (J/kg · °C)**
aluminum	9.0×10^2
brass	3.8×10^2
copper	3.9×10^2
glass (crown)	6.7×10^2
(pyrex)	7.8×10^2
gold	1.3×10^2
iron	4.5×10^2
lead	1.3×10^2
sand	8.0×10^2
silver	2.3×10^2
alcohol (ethyl)	2.3×10^2
alcohol (methyl)	2.5×10^2
glycerine	2.4×10^2
mercury	1.4×10^2
nitrogen (liquid)	1.1×10^2
water (liquid)	4.2×10^3
water (ice)	2.1×10^3
water (steam)	2.0×10^3
air	1.0×10^3

Values in most cases must be regarded as average values.

The original unit for heat, still used by many people today, is the *calorie*. The calorie is defined as the amount of heat energy necessary to raise the temperature of 1 g of water 1°C. More often used is the kilocalorie (kcal), or Calorie (with a capital C), which is defined as the heat required to raise the temperature of 1 kg of water 1°C. The Calorie is still commonly used to measure food energies. It is of particular interest to dieters.

The relationship between mechanical energy in joules and heat energy in calories is:

$$4.2 \text{ J} = 1 \text{ cal}$$
$$4.2 \times 10^3 \text{ J} = 1 \text{ kcal}$$
$$1 \text{ kcal} = 1 \text{ Calorie}$$

The only exception to this procedure is the case where one of the temperature values is unknown. See Sample problem 3.

Note that when one of the values in a temperature change is unknown, the absolute signs are removed and the sign of temperature change is used.

Sample Problems

1. How much heat energy is required to heat 2.0 kg of copper from 30°C to 80°C?

$$m = 2.0 \text{ kg}$$
$$\Delta T = T_2 - T_1 = 80°C - 30°C = 50°C$$
$$c = 3.9 \times 10^2 \text{ J/kg} \cdot °C \text{ (from table)}$$

$$E_H = mc\Delta T$$
$$= (2.0 \text{ kg})(3.9 \times 10^2 \text{ J/kg} \cdot °C)(50°C)$$
$$= 3.9 \times 10^4 \text{ J}$$

Therefore 3.9×10^4 J of heat energy is needed.

2. How much heat energy is lost when 54 g of iron is cooled from 90°C to 10°C?

$$m = 54 \text{ g} = 0.054 \text{ kg}$$
$$c = 4.5 \times 10^2 \text{ J/kg} \cdot °C \text{ (from table)}$$
$$\Delta T = T_2 - T_1 = 10°C - 90°C = -80°C$$

But, for most temperature changes we take the absolute value to simplify the mathematics. That is,

$$\Delta T = |T_2 - T_1| = |10°C - 90°C| = 80°C$$

$$E_H = mc\Delta T$$
$$= (0.054 \text{ kg})(4.5 \times 10^2 \text{ J/kg} \cdot °C)(80°C)$$
$$= 1.9 \times 10^3 \text{ J}$$

Therefore 1.9×10^3 J of heat energy is lost as the iron cools.

3. 3.0×10^4 J of heat energy is transferred to a 1 kg block of aluminum initially at 10°C. What will be its final temperature?

$$E_H = 3.0 \times 10^4 \text{ J}$$
$$m = 1.0 \text{ kg}$$
$$c = 9.0 \times 10^2 \text{ J/kg} \cdot °C \text{ (from table)}$$

$$E_H = mc\Delta T$$
$$\text{or } \Delta T = \frac{E_H}{mc}$$

$$= \frac{3.0 \times 10^4 \text{ J}}{(1.0 \text{ kg})(9.0 \times 10^2 \text{ J/kg} \cdot °C)}$$
$$= 33°C$$

As heat energy is added, ΔT will be $+33°C$.
Thus the final temperature will be:

$$\Delta T = T_2 - T_1$$
$$T_2 = T_1 + \Delta T$$
$$= 10°C + 33°C$$
$$= 43°C$$

Practice

1. How much heat energy is lost by 3.0 kg of water when it cools from 80°C to 10°C?
2. A 300 g piece of aluminum is heated from 30°C to 150°C. What amount of heat energy is absorbed?
3. Determine the temperature change in each of the following.
   (a) 10 kg of water loses 232 kJ of heat energy.
   (b) 500 g of copper gains 1.96 kJ of heat energy.
4. After 2.0 kg of mercury gained 2.52×10^4 J of heat energy, its final temperature was 130°C. What was its initial temperature?

The term "heat capacity" is sometimes used in calculations that do not involve mass. Heat capacity is defined as the quantity of heat energy required to raise an object's temperature 1°C. Its units are joules per degree Celsius.
To calculate heat capacity, find the product of the specific heat capacity and the mass. Stated mathematically, heat capacity $(J/°C) = c\,(J/kg \cdot °C)m\,(kg)$. As mass is usually a variable in applications of heat energy, *specific* heat capacity is the more appropriate term to use.

8.5 Heat Exchange in Mixtures

The Law of Conservation of Energy states that "in any transfer or transformation of energy, the total amount of energy remains constant". When two substances at different temperatures are mixed together, the warmer substance loses heat to the cooler substance. This is true provided that no heat energy is lost or gained to the surroundings. From the Law of Conservation of Energy,

---

heat lost = heat gained
E_H **lost = E_H gained**

The sample problems illustrate this concept.

Sample Problems

1. How much water at 100°C must be added to 1.0 kg of water at 10°C to give a final temperature of 37°C?

Given:
  warm water: cold water:
   $m_w = ?$ $m_c = 1.0$ kg
   $c_w = 4.2 \times 10^3$ J/kg · °C $c_c = 4.2 \times 10^3$ J/kg · °C
   $\Delta T_w = |T_2 - T_1|$ $\Delta T_c = |T_2 - T_1|$
       $= |37°C - 100°C| = 63°C$ $= |37°C - 10°C| = 27°C$
   E_H lost by the warm water $= E_H$ gained by the cold water
$$m_w c_w \Delta T_w = m_c c_c \Delta T_c$$
$$(m_w)(4.2 \times 10^3 \text{ J/kg} \cdot °C)(63°C) = (1.0 \text{ kg})(4.2 \times 10^3 \text{ J/kg} \cdot °C)(27°C)$$
$$m_w = 0.43 \text{ kg}$$

2. A brass kilogram mass at 88°C is submerged in 0.44 kg of water at 6°C. The final temperature is 20°C. Find the specific heat capacity of the brass.

brass:
$m_b = 1.0$ kg
$\Delta T_b = |20°C - 88°C| = 68°C$
$c_b = ?$

water:
$m_w = 0.44$ kg
$\Delta T_w = |6°C - 20°C| = 14°C$
$c_w = 4.2 \times 10^3$ J/kg·°C

$$E_H \text{ lost} = E_H \text{ gained}$$
$$m_b c_b \Delta T_b = m_w c_w \Delta T_w$$
$$(1.0 \text{ kg})(c_b)(68°C) = (0.44 \text{ kg})(4.2 \times 10^3 \text{ J/kg·°C})(14°C)$$
$$c_b = 3.8 \times 10^2 \text{ J/kg·°C}$$

Therefore the specific heat capacity of brass is 3.8×10^2 J/kg·°C.

3. A 125 g pyrex glass mug at 20°C is filled with 200 g of coffee at 90°C. Assuming that all heat lost by the coffee is transferred to the mug, what will be the final temperature of the coffee?
Let the final temperature of the coffee and the mug be T_2. Assume that the specific heat capacity of coffee is that of water.

*It is obvious that T_2 lies between 20°C and 90°C. For the coffee, ΔT_2 equals $|T_2 - 90°C|$ which equals $90°C - T_2$. The latter expression gives a positive value and makes the mathematics easier. Similarly, we use the expression $T_2 - 20°C$ for the glass mug.

coffee:
$m_c = 200$ g $= 0.200$ kg
$c_c = 4.2 \times 10^3$ J/kg·°C
*$\Delta T_c = 90°C - T_2$

glass mug:
$m_g = 125$ g $= 0.125$ kg
$c_g = 7.8 \times 10^2$ J/kg·°C (from
*$\Delta T_g = T_2 - 20°C$ table)

$$E_H \text{ lost by the coffee} = E_H \text{ gained by the mug}$$
$$m_c c_c \Delta T_c = m_g c_g \Delta T_g$$
$$(0.200 \text{ kg})(4.2 \times 10^3 \text{ J/kg·°C})(90°C - T_2)$$
$$= (0.125 \text{ kg})(7.8 \times 10^2 \text{ J/kg·°C})(T_2 - 20°C)$$
$$75\,600 - 840T_2 = 97.5T_2 - 1950$$
$$77\,550 = 937.5T_2$$
$$T_2 = 82.7°C, \text{ or } 83°C$$

Therefore the final temperature of the coffee (and the mug) will be 83°C.

Calorimetry

Calorimetry is the precise measurement of heat exchange. The vessel used to make these precise measurements is called a **calorimeter**. Calorimeters employ the technique of mixtures outlined above, and are most commonly used to determine the specific heat capacities of substances.

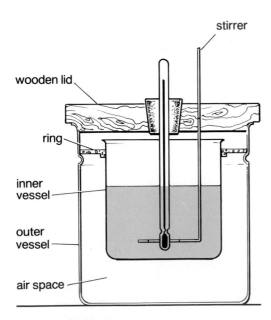

stirrer

wooden lid

ring

inner vessel

outer vessel

air space

Aluminum calorimeter

The calorimeter is designed to ensure that virtually all the heat exchange occurs within its vessel, not with its surroundings. Both the inner and outer vessels are shiny to reduce heat radiation and absorption loss. The fiber ring that separates the two vessels and the wooden or fiber lid are poor conductors of heat. The air space between the two vessels provides yet more insulation, as air is a poor conductor of heat.

Typically, a hot sample of the substance whose specific heat capacity is unknown is placed in cold water in the inner cup. The specific heat capacity of the substance can be found by taking careful measurements of the masses of the water, the sample of the substance, and the calorimeter, and measurements of the temperature of both the water and the substance before and after mixing them in the vessel. The actual calculation of specific heat capacity is illustrated in the sample problem below, and in Investigation 8.3.

Sample Problems

1. In an investigation, 0.500 kg of lead at 100°C is placed in 0.200 kg of water at 20°C contained in an aluminum calorimeter with a mass of 0.400 kg. The final temperature of lead, water, and calorimeter is 24°C. Find the specific heat of the lead.

lead:
$m_1 = 0.500$ kg
$c_1 = ?$
$\Delta T_1 = |24°C - 100°C| = 76°C$

water:
$m_w = 0.200$ kg
$c_w = 4.2 \times 10^3$ J/kg·°C
$\Delta T_w = |24°C - 20°C| = 4°C$

calorimeter:
$m_c = 0.40$ kg
$c_c = 9.0 \times 10^2$ J/kg·°C
$\Delta T_c = |24°C - 20°C| = 4°C$

$$E_H \text{ lost by lead} = E_H \text{ gained by water} + E_H \text{ gained by calorimeter}$$
$$m_1 c_1 \Delta T_1 = m_w c_w \Delta T_w + m_c c_c \Delta T_c$$
$$(0.500 \text{ kg})(c_2)(76°C) = (0.200 \text{ kg})(4.2 \times 10^3 \text{ J/kg·°C})(4°C)$$
$$+ (0.400 \text{ kg})(9.0 \times 10^2 \text{ J/kg·°C})(4°C)$$
$$(38 \text{ kg·°C})c_1 = 3360 \text{ J} + 1440 \text{ J}$$
$$c_1 = 1.26 \times 10^2 \text{ J/kg·°C, or } 1.3 \times 10^2 \text{ J/kg·°C}$$

Therefore the specific heat capacity of the lead was 1.3×10^2 J/kg·°C.

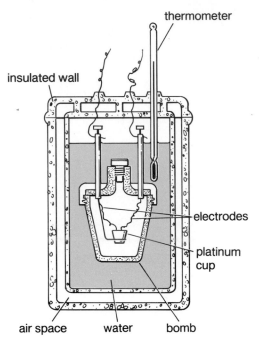

Bomb calorimeter

1590 kJ is equivalent to 380 Calories, the unit found on many food packages and in diet books. (4.2 kJ = 1 Calorie)

Specific Heats of Combustion

Substance	Specific heat of combustion (kJ/kg)
fuels	
alcohol (ethyl)	3.0×10^4
coal	3.2×10^4
gasoline	4.7×10^4
hydrogen	1.4×10^5
methane	5.5×10^4
wood (pine)	2.1×10^4
Food	
bread (whole wheat)	1.0×10^4
beef (sirloin)	9.1×10^4
egg (boiled)	6.8×10^3
egg (fried)	9.1×10^3
milk (whole)	2.9×10^3
peanuts	2.5×10^4
potato (boiled)	3.2×10^3
potato chips	2.4×10^4

Bomb Calorimeter

The bomb calorimeter is a specially designed calorimeter used to determine the energy content of foods and fats. A carefully measured sample of the food to be tested is placed in the platinum cup. The sample is ignited electrically and burns. The heat absorbed by the inner container, the cup, and the water is carefully measured. Performing a calculation similar to that in Sample problem 4 results in an accurate value for the energy content, or heat of combustion, of the food. For example, a 10 g sample of cake may release 159 kJ when burned in the bomb calorimeter. This means that the energy value of a 100 g piece of cake will be 1590 kJ.

Practice

(For these questions, we assume that no heat is lost to, or gained from, the surroundings.)

1. A 13.5 g spoon at 20°C is completely submerged in a plastic foam cup containing 200 g of hot water at 90°C. If the temperature of the water is lowered 1°C, what is the specific heat capacity of the spoon?

2. When 100 g of a metal at 94°C is placed in 100 g of water at 10°C, the final temperature of the water is 17°C. Calculate the specific heat capacity of the metal.

3. When 1.0 kg of water at 100°C is mixed with 2.0 kg of water at 20°C, what is the final temperature of the mixture?

4. What mass of copper at 90°C, when added to 200 g of water at 15°C contained in a 100 g aluminum calorimeter, will give a final temperature of 25°C?

5. A scientist wants to determine the specific heat capacity of a new alloy. A 100 g sample is heated to 480°C and then quickly placed in 250 g of water at 20°C, contained in a 200 g aluminum calorimeter cup. The final temperature of the alloy is 36°C. Calculate its specific heat capacity.

8.6 Change of State and Latent Heat

The addition or removal of heat from an object does not always change its temperature. The temperature versus time graph on the next page, for example, shows the change in temperature as heat is

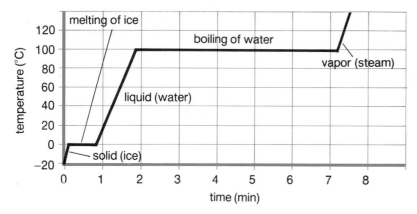

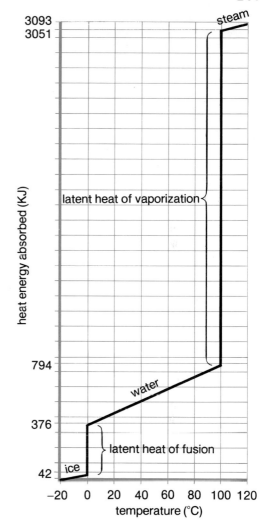

Graph of heat absorbed versus temperature for 1.0 kg of ice as its temperature is raised from −20°C to 120°C

added to water at a constant rate. The temperature of the water increases from −20°C to form steam at 120°C over 7.5 min. Note that the temperature of the water remains virtually constant at the melting point, where the ice changes to water, and at the boiling point, where the water changes to steam. The heat energy absorbed versus temperature graph in the margin shows that at both fixed points an extra quantity of heat energy is required to produce a change in state. The Kinetic Molecular Theory explains this behavior.

In a solid, the molecules are held together by electrical forces, commonly referred to as intermolecular bonds. When molecules gain energy, their motion increases about their equilibrium positions. When enough energy is added to a solid, the intermolecular bonds break and it becomes a liquid. In the liquid state the molecules are relatively free to move, although they are still bound to one another. When enough heat energy is added to the liquid, the distance between the molecules becomes great enough for them to become gas molecules. Liquids vaporize at all temperatures, not just at the boiling point. Some molecules at the surface of the liquid may acquire enough energy from collisions with other molecules to leave the liquid and form a vapor. (When water boils, gas bubbles form first near the bottom of the container, where the temperature is usually the highest.)

At certain fixed points on the temperature scale the addition of heat energy does not increase the temperature of a substance. Instead the additional energy is used to produce a change of state. At these points the energy weakens or breaks the intermolecular

Boiling occurs within a liquid when the vapor pressure in the liquid is equal to the atmospheric pressure on the surface of the liquid.

bonds. The temperature remains constant because only the potential energy of the molecules changes as a result of the changes in the relative positions of the molecules. The speed of the molecular motion does not change. Once all the molecules have changed state, a further addition of heat will cause the temperature to rise again.

The heat energy involved in a change in state is called the **latent heat** (ℓ). Naturally the quantity of heat involved depends not only on the latent heat, but also on the mass of the substance. That is,

$$E_L = m\,\ell$$

where E_L is the heat transferred, in joules

m is the mass, in kilograms

ℓ is the latent heat, in joules per kilogram

The latent heat of fusion (ℓ_f) is the heat energy required to melt 1 kg of a substance to form a liquid, or it is the quantity of heat given off when 1 kg of a liquid changes to a solid. For example, the latent heat of fusion for water is 3.3×10^5 J/kg. This means that 3.3×10^5 J of thermal energy is required to change 1 kg of ice at 0°C to water at 0°C. The latent heat of vaporization (ℓ_v) is the heat energy required to change 1 kg of a liquid to a vapor, or it is the energy given off when 1 kg of a vapor condenses to form a liquid. The latent heat of vaporization of water is 2.3×10^6 J/kg, which means that 2.3×10^6 J of energy is lost when 1 kg of steam changes to 1 kg of water at 100°C, the boiling point of water. Notice that the latent heat of vaporization for water is nearly seven times larger than that for fusion. The values for the latent heat of selected materials are provided in the table below. The sample problems demonstrate the use of the latent heat relationship.

Substance	Melting point (°C)	Latent heat of fusion (J/kg)	Boiling point (°C)	Latent heat of vaporization (J/kg)
water	0	3.3×10^5	100	2.3×10^6
alcohol (ethyl)	−130	1.4×10^4	78	8.5×10^5
alcohol (methyl)	−97.8	6.8×10^4	64.7	1.1×10^6
lead	327	2.5×10^4	1780	8.7×10^5
nitrogen	−209.9	2.5×10^4	−196.8	2.0×10^5
oxygen	−218.9	1.4×10^4	−183	2.1×10^5
silver	961	8.8×10^4	1950	

Sample Problems

1. How much heat energy is required to change
   (a) 2.0 kg of ice at 0°C to water at 0°C?
   (b) 500 g of water at 100°C to steam at 100°C?

(a) $E_L = m\ell_f$
$$= (2.0 \text{ kg})(3.3 \times 10^5 \text{ J/kg})$$
$$= 6.6 \times 10^5 \text{ J}$$

Therefore 6.6×10^5 J of heat energy is required to change the ice to water.

(b) $E_L = m\ell_v$
$$= (0.500 \text{ kg})(2.3 \times 10^6 \text{ J/kg})$$
$$= 1.15 \times 10^6 \text{ J/kg, or } 1.2 \times 10^6 \text{ J/kg}$$

Therefore 1.2×10^6 J of heat energy are required to change the water to steam.

2. How much heat does a refrigerator freezer have to remove from 1.5 kg of water at 20°C to make ice at −10°C?

mass of ice (m_i) = mass of water (m_w) = 1.5 kg
$$c_i = 2.1 \times 10^3 \text{ J/kg} \cdot °\text{C}$$
$$c_w = 4.2 \times 10^3 \text{ J/kg} \cdot °\text{C}$$
$$\ell_f = 3.3 \times 10^5 \text{ J/kg}$$
$$\Delta T_w = |T_2 - T_1| = |0°\text{C} - 20°\text{C}| = 20°\text{C}$$
$$\Delta T_i = |T_2 - T_1| = |-10°\text{C} - 0°\text{C}| = 10°\text{C}$$

Note that the specific heat capacities of ice and steam are different from that of water.

$$E_{total} = E_w + E_f + E_i$$
$$= m_w c_w \Delta T_w + m_w \ell_f + m_i c_i \Delta T_i$$
$$= (1.5 \text{ kg})(4.2 \times 10^3 \text{ J/kg} \cdot °\text{C})(20°\text{C}) + (1.5 \text{ kg})(3.3 \times 10^5 \text{ J/kg})$$
$$+ (1.5 \text{ kg})(2.1 \times 10^3 \text{ J/kg} \cdot °\text{C})(10°\text{C})$$
$$= 1.25 \times 10^5 \text{ J} + 4.95 \times 10^5 \text{ J} + 3.15 \times 10^4 \text{ J}$$
$$= 6.56 \times 10^5 \text{ J, or } 6.6 \times 10^3 \text{ J}$$

Therefore the total amount of heat that the refrigerator removes from the ice is 6.6×10^5 J.

3. What will be the final temperature if 1.0 kg of water at 20°C is heated by the condensation of 30 g of steam at 100°C?

$$m_w = 1.0 \text{ kg}, m_s = 30 \text{ g} = 3.0 \times 10^{-2} \text{ kg}$$
$$\ell_v = 2.3 \times 10^6 \text{ J/kg}$$
$$c_w = 4.2 \times 10^3 \text{ J/kg} \cdot °\text{C}$$

Let T_2 be the final temperature of the water.

$$\Delta T_{w_1} = T_2 - 20°\text{C}$$
$$\Delta T_{w_2} = 100°\text{C} - T_2 \text{ (water from condensed steam)}$$

E_H lost by steam + E_H lost by water from condensed steam
$$= E_H \text{ gained by water}$$

It is obvious that T_2 lies between 100°C and 20°C. For the water from the steam, ΔT_{w_2} equals $|T_2 - 100°\text{C}|$ which equals $100°\text{C} - T_2$. The latter expression gives a positive value for ΔT_{w_2}, making the mathematics easier. Similarly, for the cooler water, the expression we use for ΔT_{w_1} is $T_2 - 20°\text{C}$.

$$m\ell_v + m_{w_2}c_w\Delta T_{w_2} = m_{w_1}c_w\Delta T_{w_1}$$
$$(3.0 \times 10^{-2}\ kg)(2.3 \times 10^6 J/kg)$$
$$+ (3.0 \times 10^{-2}\ kg)(4.2 \times 10^3\ J/kg \cdot {}^\circ C)(100^\circ C - T_2)$$
$$= (1.0\ kg)(4.2 \times 10^3\ J/kg \cdot {}^\circ C)(T_2 - 20^\circ C)$$
$$6.9 \times 10^4\ J + 1.26 \times 10^4\ J - (1.26 \times 10^2\ J/{}^\circ C)\ T_2$$
$$= (4.2 \times 10^3\ J/{}^\circ C)T_2 - 8.4 \times 10^4\ J$$
$$(4.33 \times 10^3\ J/{}^\circ C)\ T_2 = 1.66 \times 10^3\ J$$
$$T_2 = 38.4^\circ C,\ or\ 38^\circ C$$

Therefore the final temperature of the water will be 38°C.

Practice

1. The mass of a typical ice cube is approximately 25 g. How much heat must be added to the ice cube to melt it? Assume the temperature remains at 0°C throughout.
2. How much heat is lost when 100 g of steam at 100°C condenses and cools to water at 80°C?
3. How much heat is required to convert 100 g of ice at −20°C to steam at 110°C?
4. When 15.0 g of ice at 0°C is melted in 100 g of water at 20.0°C, the final temperature is 9.5°C. Find the heat of fusion of ice, based on these data.
5. Steam at 100°C is condensed in 200 g of water at 25°C. How much steam will be required to raise the temperature of the water in the cup to 50°C?

8.7 Thermodynamics, Heat, and Work

Thermodynamics comes from the Latin words meaning "motions of heat".

The branch of physics that deals with the relationships between heat and other forms of energy is called **thermodynamics**. In Section 8.5 we showed how the Law of the Conservation of Energy is applied to heat exchange in mixtures. Basically, the First Law of Thermodynamics is simply a restatement of the Law of the Conservation of Energy. In Chapter 7 we learned that the terms work and energy can be used interchangeably. The **First Law of Thermodynamics** can thus be stated:

The quantity of heat energy transferred to a system is equal to the work done by the system plus the change in the internal energy of the system.

To gain some insight into the Second Law of Thermodynamics we must first study the operation of some heat engines.

A **heat engine** is a device that changes heat energy into mechanical work. The basic concept behind all heat engines, whether steam, gasoline, or jet engines, involves three characteristic operations:
1. the absorption of heat energy at a high temperature;
2. the transformation of some of the heat energy to mechanical energy;
3. the release of heat energy at a lower temperature.

These principles are illustrated in the schematic diagram in the margin. The high and low temperatures, T_H and T_L, represent the operating temperatures of the engine. By the First Law of Thermodynamics,

$$E_H = E_L + W$$

where E_H represents the quantity of thermal energy flowing in at the higher temperature

F_L represents the quantity of thermal energy flowing out at the lower temperature

W represents the mechanical work done by the heat engine

In a modern steam turbine, high-pressure, high-temperature steam from a boiler is directed at a series of turbine blades, causing them to rotate. This rotation is transferred by a shaft to do useful work, such as turning the propeller of an ocean liner or turning generators at an electric power plant. The steam is exhausted from the turbine chamber. Otherwise, pressure on both sides of the blades would remain the same and stop the motion. A decrease in pressure on the exhaust side of the turbine chamber is accomplished by cooling the steam until it condenses to water. This is what occurs in a large electrical power plant. The energy to create the steam may come from the burning of coal, oil, or natural gas, or it may come from a nuclear power reactor. The steam is condensed in a heat exchanger cooled by water from a lake or river or a large cooling tower.

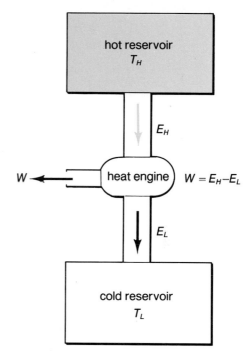

Schematic diagram of the operation of a heat engine

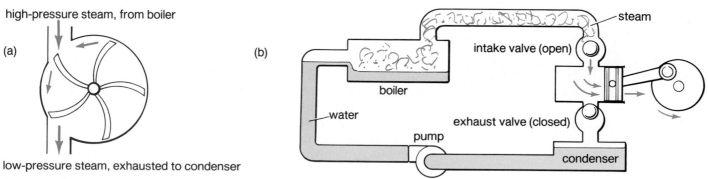

Steam Engines: (a) turbine type (b) reciprocating piston type

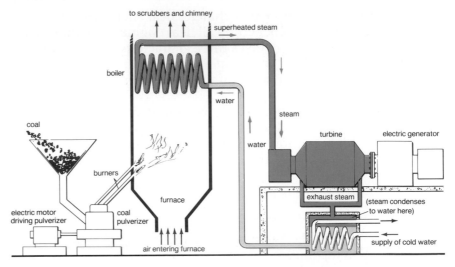

Diagram of a steam station in which electricity is generated. Pulverized coal is burned in a furnace. The water passing through the steam generator absorbs heat released by the fire and is converted into steam. This steam is superheated and is led to the turbine. The exhaust steam condenses to water in the condenser. The water then flows back to the steam generator.

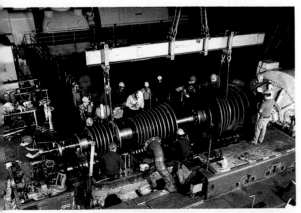

Wheel and shaft of a giant steam turbine in the assembly stage. The wheel, called a rotor, will make 1800 rev/min as steam rushes through its blades.

Much the same conditions exist in the historic piston-type reciprocating steam engine. Hot steam passes through an intake valve and expands against a piston connected to a driveshaft. As the piston moves down the cylinder, the driveshaft rotates. This motion is transferred to do mechanical work such as moving a steam railroad engine. The piston moves back up the cylinder to the original position, forcing the steam out the exhaust valve. Again, if the pressure is not lower on the exhaust side of the engine, the piston will not be able to move back up the cylinder and it will stop.

Steam engines illustrate the principle common to all heat engines: there must be a temperature difference in a heat engine for it to operate.

The first practical steam engine was developed by James Watt in 1774. Soon steam engines were used everywhere, accelerating the historical period now known as the Industrial Revolution. By observing the operation of steam engines and other phenomena, it became clear to scientists that heat always flows naturally from a hot object to a cold object. It also became clear that heat energy cannot flow naturally from a cold to a hotter region. These facts were first summarized by R. Clausius (1822-1888). This statement became known as the **Second Law of Thermodynamics**.

Heat flows naturally from a hot object to a cold object; heat will not flow naturally from a cold object to a hot object.

Work must be done on a system to make heat flow from a cold to a hot region. As the diagram in the margin shows, $E_L + W = E_H$. This is the process that occurs in refrigerators, air conditioners, and heat pumps. Let us examine the operation of a refrigerator first.

The basic parts of a typical refrigerator are: a compressor, condensing coils, an expansion valve, cooling or evaporating coils, and a working fluid, usually freon-12. These are connected together as illustrated. In a typical home refrigerator, the cooling coils are located inside the refrigerator or freezer, the compressor is mounted at the bottom, and the condensing coils are located outside of the refrigerator on the back or on the side.

When any gas is compressed, its temperature increases. You have probably noticed this when you touch the cylinder of a bicycle pump. It becomes hot when it is used to pump up a tire. When freon vapor is compressed, it becomes a hot vapor. Then it enters the condensing coils. By the time it arrives at the end of these coils it has lost this heat, and has condensed to a liquid. The latent heat of vaporization, absorbed by the coils, is given off to the air outside the refrigerator. Emerging as a liquid under pressure, it "sprays" through the expansion valve into an area of lower pressure in the cooling coils. To vaporize, the droplets of liquid freon require heat. This heat is absorbed through the walls of the cooling coil from

The Second Law of Thermodynamics can also be stated as Law of Entropy, which states that "the available energy in the universe is diminishing". Ask your teacher what entropy and the Law of Entropy mean.

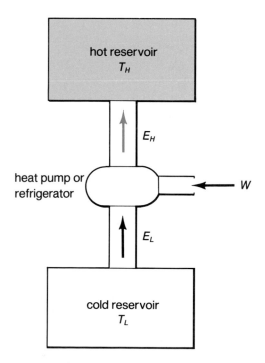

Schematic diagram of a heat pump or refrigerator

cooling coils

inside refrigerator

low-pressure vapor

hot, pressurized vapor

outside refrigerator

condensing coils

compressor

low pressure cool fluid

expansion valve

high pressure cool liquid

Typical refrigerator

A heat pump can deliver much more heat energy to a house than the electrical energy it uses. E_H can be three or four times as large as W, but this factor rapidly drops towards unity as the temperature difference increases.

the food and other objects in the refrigerator, adjacent to the cooling coils. The absorbed heat is used to evaporate the freon liquid to a vapor. The vapor leaves the cooling coils and re-enters the compressor, where the cycle starts again. Simply put, the refrigerator takes heat from the inside of the refrigerator and gives it off through the cooling coils, outside the refrigerator.

An air conditioner operates in much the same manner except that the cooling coils are located inside a building, and the condenser coils, which give off heat, are located outside. A heat pump is essentially an air conditioner working backwards. The cooling coils are outside the building and the condensing coils are inside. In this way, heat is extracted from the air outside and released inside, even when the temperature outside is below freezing. A heat pump usually has a reversible system so that it can heat a house in winter and act as an air conditioner during the summer.

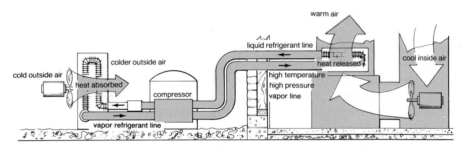

Heat pump

You might expect, based on the First Law of Thermodynamics, that it should be possible to build a perfect heat engine that converts all the heat it receives into mechanical work. For reasons we cannot discuss in a text at this level, such a perfect engine cannot be constructed. Similarly, it is impossible to create a perfect refrigerator in which no mechanical work is required to move the heat from a low to a high temperature region. In fact, both of these facts are considered restatements of the Second Law of Thermodynamics.

The Second Law of Thermodynamics says, in essence, that energy can only be lost, never gained, when converted from one form to another. The First Law says that energy is conserved.

It is a theoretical and an experimental fact that absolute zero is impossible to attain. This is known as the Third Law of Thermodynamics.

There is no device that can transform its heat input completely into work.

There is no heat pump that can transfer heat energy from a low temperature region to a higher temperature region without the application of work.

The principles described here apply to all heat engines. The Earth's atmosphere is like a giant heat engine. Radiant energy from the sun raises the temperature of the land and water. Weather occurs when this heat moves from regions of high temperature to those of low temperature within the atmosphere.

The human body is also similar to a heat engine. Before exercising, your body contains its normal amount of heat energy. When you exercise, work is done by your muscles and heat is released to your body. Your body temperature would quickly rise as well, except that you breathe faster and perspire, giving off the excess heat. This keeps your body temperature relatively constant.

These last two examples are not usually considered to be heat engines, but as they involve heat and work, in reality they are. It is obvious that in the world around us there are many other devices and systems that involve the laws of thermodynamics.

"NOW, IN THE SECOND LAW OF THERMODYNAMICS..."

8.8 Conservation of Heat Energy in the Home

Buildings in many countries of the world require a heating system in winter. As we have just discussed, heat energy tends to flow from warm areas to cold areas. To conserve energy, buildings should be constructed to reduce this flow.

Heat energy flows via three separate processes, namely, conduction, convection, and radiation. Conduction involves a transfer of heat energy from one part to another part of the same object, or from one object to another, provided they are in contact. Some materials conduct better than others. Convection involves the transfer of heat energy by the movement of a heated material such as air. In the process of radiation, a warm object radiates heat energy in exactly the same way that the sun radiates heat—infrared radiation is given off. (See Chapter 17.) Maintaining heat in homes primarily involves conduction and convection.

Heat loss through walls and ceilings of a building depends on several factors. One of these is the temperature difference between the inside and outside of the house. The flow of heat energy is directly proportional to the temperature difference. As seen in the example in the margin, when a thermostat is lowered from 22°C to 18°C, the amount of heat loss is reduced. If, for example, the thermostat is lowered to 15°C at night or when the house is unoccupied, the savings could be as high as 30%, other factors remaining the same.

The word conduction comes from the Latin meaning "to lead together".

The word convection comes from the Latin meaning "to carry together".

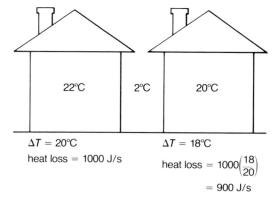

$\Delta T = 20°C$
heat loss = 1000 J/s

$\Delta T = 18°C$
heat loss = $1000\left(\dfrac{18}{20}\right)$
= 900 J/s

Lowering the thermostat saves heat energy.

SI units are still not commonly used in the construction industry. To convert R-values to SI, use the following equation:

$$RSI = \frac{R\text{-value}}{5.678}$$

For example, to convert R-20 to SI,

$$RSI = \frac{R\text{-}20}{5.678}$$
$$= 3.52$$

A second factor influencing the flow of heat energy is the thermal resistance (RSI) of the insulation in the walls and ceilings. The thermal resistance depends on the substance used and its thickness. The higher the resistance value, the less heat energy will pass through the insulating material. The RSI-values for various materials are listed in the chart below.

Material	Thickness (cm)	Thermal resistance (RSI)
brick	10	0.08
gypsum board	10	0.46
plywood	10	0.88
fiberglass	10	2.11
plastic foam (white)	10	2.82
plastic foam (SM blue)	10	3.47
plastic foam (Glasclap)	10	3.05
rock wool	10	2.11
cellulose fiber	10	2.29
vermiculite	10	1.59
air space	2-10	0.18

Strangely, the RSI-value of an air space does not depend greatly on the width of the space.

When a wall is constructed of more than one material, the RSI-values of the components are added together. Just a few years ago, walls were built with little or no insulation, and ceilings were given less than half the insulation used in new homes today. As seen in the data provided in the margin on the next page, the walls in the new house have over six times the insulation value, letting through only one-sixth as much heat energy. The ceilings in a newer house will let through about one-third as much heat energy as the ceilings of the house built in the 1950s. Increasing the thickness of the insulation in the walls and ceiling can significantly lower the cost of heating a home.

A significant portion of each wall is composed of windows. The RSI-value of single-pane glass is about 0.18. Double-pane windows and storm windows have an RSI-value of 0.36, but still let through nine times as much heat energy as the equivalent wall area. The windows and doors can be responsible for as much as 25% of the total loss in heat energy in a home.

The above factors relate mostly to heat losses due to conduction. Higher RSI-values also reduce convection losses, but another important factor is the "tightness" of the building. To make a building more airtight, an air-vapor barrier, usually polyethylene film, is installed on the heated side of the insulation. The barrier prevents warm, moist air from entering cold areas in the walls by convection.

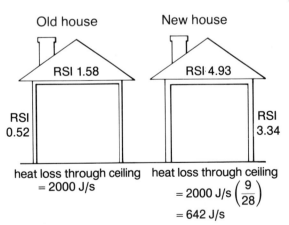

Old house   New house

RSI 1.58   RSI 4.93

RSI 0.52   RSI 3.34

heat loss through ceiling = 2000 J/s

heat loss through ceiling
$$= 2000 \text{ J/s} \left(\frac{9}{28}\right)$$
$$= 642 \text{ J/s}$$

More insulation reduces heat loss.

It is not always possible to install a barrier in older homes, but a program to seal air leaks in walls and ceilings can reduce heat losses. Electrical outlets and fixtures, openings in the walls or ceilings and around door and window frames should all be sealed, and weather stripping applied around doors.

Some new homes are designed to be very airtight, but this can create new problems. Smoke, carbon monoxide and other contaminants can build up to unsafe levels. There must always be a source of fresh air for these homes. This would appear to be counter-productive from the standpoint of heat energy. It is possible to install air-to-air heat exchangers that use the stale outgoing air to warm up the fresh, incoming air, thereby recovering up to 80% of the heat energy.

Applying just some of the factors discussed in this section can significantly reduce the loss of heat energy in the home and lower home heating costs.

*P*ractice

1. On a day when it is 6°C outside, what percentage of the regular fuel used would you save by lowering the thermostat setting from 21°C to 18°C?
2. What is the RSI-value of each of the following?
   (a) 20 cm of brick
   (b) 5.0 cm of plastic foam (white)
   (c) 15 cm of fiberglass
   (d) 7.0 cm of cellulose fiber
3. The space inside the walls of an older home is usually about 9.0 cm deep. If this could be filled with vermiculite, by how much would the RSI-value of the wall be increased?

Typical wall

New house

	RSI
10 cm brick	0.08
3.8 cm plastic foam (SM blue)	1.32
8 cm fiberglass	1.83
2 cm gypsum board	0.09
	3.32

1950 house

	RSI
10 cm brick	0.08
2 cm plywood	0.18
air space	0.18
2 cm gypsum board	0.09
	0.53

Typical ceiling

New house

	RSI
2 cm gypsum board	0.08
23 cm fiberglass	4.86
	4.94

1950 house

	RSI
2 cm gypsum board	0.08
6.5 cm fiberglass	1.49
	1.57

8.9 *A*pplications: Solar Homes

Many types of solar-heated homes have been built in the U.S. One such heating system consists of an array of solar radiation collecting panels on the roof and a large water storage tank in the basement. When the sun is shining, water is pumped from the tank up through pipes into the solar panels. The water is heated as it passes through the solar panels. It then returns through a second set of pipes to the tank. The water's temperature in the storage tank may reach 50°C or more.

Solar collector panels used for heating water

When heat is needed, hot water is pumped from the storage tank into a coil of piping in the furnace called a heat exchanger. Inside the furnace, a fan blows cold air past the heat exchanger. The water gives up some of its heat energy to the air. The air is then conducted through ducts to all parts of the house, and the cooler water returns through pipes from the heat exchanger to the storage tank.

A tank holding 20 m³ of water can store enough heat for a single-family home for three to five cloudy days, except during the coldest part of the winter. For emergencies, most solar homes have some form of auxiliary heating.

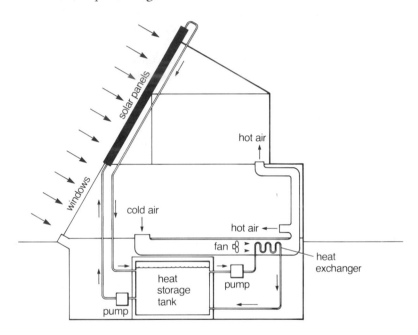

A typical solar heating system

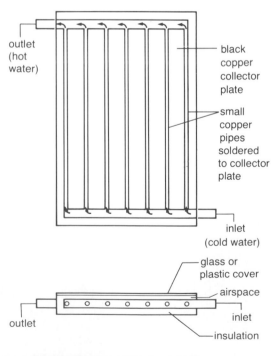

A typical solar collector panel

The solar radiation collector panels are designed to absorb and hold as much heat energy as possible from the incoming radiation. A typical collector panel is a copper plate, 1 m by 2 m, painted black to absorb solar radiation. Copper pipes run vertically up the plate every 10 cm or so, carrying water to absorb heat from the plate. These small copper pipes are joined to a larger pipe across the bottom of the panel, where the water enters, and to a larger pipe across the top of the panel, where the water leaves. The back of the collector plate is insulated to keep the heat in, and the front is covered by a thin sheet of transparent plastic or glass to allow the sun's radiation to enter.

The sheet of plastic reduces heat transfer back out of the panel by conduction, convection, and radiation. The air trapped between the plastic sheet and the collector plate is a poor conductor of heat. Little heat is lost through conduction. Convection occurs when hot air rises and cold air takes its place. If the top end of the panel were open, the hot air would escape up and out by convection. The plastic sheet prevents this from happening.

All hot objects radiate energy. In this case, the solar energy can pass through the plastic sheet as it enters, but the radiation from the collector plate is infrared radiation and cannot pass back out through the plastic sheet. This is called the "greenhouse effect"; the same property of glass and plastic is used to keep a greenhouse warmer than its surroundings, to promote plant growth.

The solar home pictured here has other features designed to conserve energy. Large windows on the south side of the house allow solar radiation to enter and heat the living and dining areas directly. Drapes on the windows trap the heat inside at night and keep it out in the summertime.

The kitchen is on the north side of the house. The heat from the stove, refrigerator, and other appliances helps to keep it warm.

The few windows on the east, west, and north sides of the house are small to reduce heat loss.

The insulation in the walls and roof is two to three times as thick as in a normal house. This keeps the heat out in the summertime as well as keeping it in in the winter.

Solar homes are expensive to build, beyond the reach of all but a few families. It is possible that future mass production of the components will decrease the costs. In the meantime, many of the features found in solar homes can be used to reduce the energy demands of a house with a conventional heating system. We do know that solar heating works!

A solar-heated home

*P*ractice

1. Calculate the average power received from the sun by 60 m² of solar panels on the roof of a solar home if the average solar power received at ground level is 300 W/m².
2. If the system is only 10% efficient, how much heat energy will be stored in the storage tank on a sunny 10 h day?
3. The storage tank holds 2×10^4 kg of water. What temperature change would one day's input of solar energy produce in the water in the storage tank?

The north side of a solar-heated home has few windows.

In another design, air is used instead of water. The storage tank in the basement is filled with fist-sized rocks. A fan blows air up into the panels to be heated, then down to the basement to heat the rocks. Water holds considerably more heat per kilogram than rock at the same temperature, but water may be more difficult to handle than air.

Investigations

Investigation 8.1: Coefficient of Linear Expansion

Problem:
What is the coefficient of linear expansion of a solid rod?

Materials:
linear expansion apparatus
thermometer (0°C–100°C)
meterstick
steam generator
rubber tubing
50 cm rods (e.g., aluminum, iron, copper)

Caution: This investigation utilizes live steam under pressure. To avoid steam burns wear protective gloves and safety glasses at all times. Never expose your skin to steam.

Linear expansion apparatus

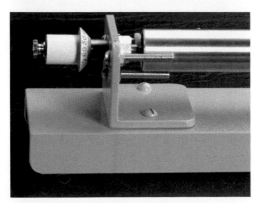

Micrometer gauge at free end

CAUTION: If a thermometer breaks, do not touch it or try to clean it up. Notify your instructor.

Procedure:
1. Measure the length of the rod to the nearest millimeter (L_0).
2. Set up the apparatus and have your teacher check it.
3. Adjust the screw mechanism so that the micrometer gauge is just in contact with the free end of the rod. Record the reading (L_1).
4. Set the screw back at least 3 mm to allow for the expansion of the rod.
5. Record the initial temperature of the rod (T_1).
6. Pass steam through the apparatus for a minimum of five minutes.
7. At the end of this time record the final temperature (T_2) of the rod.
8. Before removing the steam, adjust the micrometer screw until contact is made with the free end of the rod. Record the new reading (L_2).
9. If time allows, repeat the investigation using a rod made from a different material. If not, obtain the results from another group in the class.
10. Using your data from the experiment, determine the expansion (ΔL) and temperature change (ΔT).
11. Determine the coefficient of linear expansion for the material, using the relationship $\Delta L = \alpha L_0 \Delta T$.

Questions:
1. Using the values found in the table on page 231, determine the percentage error for each material tested. Comment on the reasons for the error.
2. You have determined the mean coefficient of linear expansion for a specific temperature range. Why is the value restricted to a specific temperature range, and why is the word "mean" used?

Investigation 8.2: Heat and Work

Problem:
What is the efficiency of an electrical immersion heater?

Materials:
large plastic foam cup
thermometer (0°C–100°C)
immersion heater
stopwatch

Procedure:
1. Find the mass of the empty plastic foam cup.
2. Add room temperature water to the cup until it is approximately two thirds full.
3. Find the mass of the cup containing the water.
4. Record the initial temperature of the water, leaving the thermometer in the water.
5. Carefully place the immersion heater in the cup, without touching the thermometer.
6. Plug in the immersion heater and start the stopwatch the instant the heater is plugged in.
7. Heat the water until the temperature has approximately doubled. Turn off the heater and stop the stopwatch. Record the time interval. Do not remove the immersion heater.
8. Stir the water gently, allowing the water to reach its highest temperature. Record the temperature.
9. Record the power rating of the immersion heater in watts.

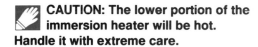 **CAUTION: The lower portion of the immersion heater will be hot. Handle it with extreme care.**

Calculations:
10. The quantity of heat energy produced by the immersion heater is determined by multiplying the power rating (in watts) by the time (in seconds), that is, $E_H = P\Delta t$.
11. Find the quantity of heat energy gained by the water. Use the relationship $E_H = mc\Delta T$.

12. Compare the values for steps 10 and 11, and determine the efficiency of the energy transfer.

Questions:
1. What assumptions are being made in step 10?
2. Why was the immersion heater left in the water, even after it was disconnected? (step 7)

Investigation 8.3: Specific Heat Capacity

Problem:
What is the specific heat capacity of a solid?

Materials:
quantity of metal shot (e.g., copper, aluminum)
balance
200 mL beaker
retort stand, ring, gauze
Bunsen burner (or electric immersion heater)
test tube clamp
calorimeter
2 thermometers (0°C–100°C)

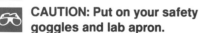

CAUTION: Put on your safety goggles and lab apron.

CAUTION: Do not reach over the flame of a Bunsen burner.
Constrain long hair and loose clothing.

CAUTION: If a thermometer breaks, do not touch it or try to clean it up.
Notify your instructor.

Procedure:
1. Half fill the test tube with metal shot, and place it in the water.
2. Heat the water with the Bunsen burner while continuing with steps 3 to 6.
3. Find the mass of the inner cup of the calorimeter and the stirrer (if used).
4. Half fill the inner cup with water that is slightly below room temperature.
5. Find the mass of the inner cup and the water, then determine the water's mass.
6. Place the inner cup in the calorimeter and secure the lid. Stir the contents and measure the temperature of the water.
7. By now the water in the beaker should be boiling. When the temperature stops rising, record the temperature of the hot metal shot.
8. Carefully remove the themometer from the shot. Gently pour the shot into the water in the calorimeter's inner cup. Replace the lid, stir the mixture, and record its maximum temperature. **(CAUTION: Excessive stirring could break the thermometer if you use it as a stirrer.)**

9. Find the mass of the calorimeter cup, water, and contents. Determine the mass of the shot.
10. Ask your teacher for the specific heat capacity of the calorimeter's inner cup.
11. Record all your observations in a table or chart.
12. Under the heading "Calculations", determine and record the following:
    (a) the mass of the cold water
    (b) the mass of the metal shot
    (c) the temperature change of the water
    (d) the temperature change of the calorimeter
    (e) the temperature change of the metal shot
    (f) the heat gained by the water
    (g) the heat gained by the calorimeter
    (h) the specific heat capacity of the metal

Questions:
1. Collect other values for the specific heat capacity for the metal, you used. Determine the average value for the metal, and the experimental error.
2. What are the sources of error in this investigation?
3. The cold water was initially a few degrees lower than room temperature. Why is this desirable?

Investigation 8.4: Latent Heat of Fusion

Problem:
What is the latent heat of fusion of ice?

Materials:
2 identical insulated cups (plastic foam)
retort stand, gauze, ring clamp
Bunsen burner (or electric immersion heater)
thermometer (0°C—100°C)
250 mL beaker
beaker tongs
100 mL graduated cylinder
balance
ice cube

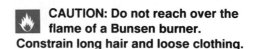

CAUTION: Put on your safety goggles and lab apron.

CAUTION: Do not reach over the flame of a Bunsen burner.
Constrain long hair and loose clothing.

Procedure:
1. Set up the apparatus.
2. Add 100 mL of water to the beaker and heat to approximately 75°C. Do not boil.

3. Find the mass of one of the insulated cups.
4. Dry one ice cube and add it to the cup. Measure and record the mass of the cup plus the ice cube.
5. Using the beaker tongs, pour the hot water into the second empty cup. Measure and record its temperature.
6. Carefully pour the hot water into the cup containing the ice cube, taking care that no water splashes out of the cup.
7. Stir the mixture gently with the thermometer until all the ice has melted. At that point quickly measure and record the mixture's final temperature.
8. Find the new mass of the cup and its contents.
9. Under the heading "Calculations", determine and record the following:
   (a) the mass of the ice cube
   (b) the mass of the hot water
   (c) the change in temperature of the hot water
   (d) the change in temperature of the melted ice water
   (e) the heat lost by the hot water
   (f) the heat gained by the melted ice water
   (g) the heat gained by ice when melting
   (h) the latent heat of fusion of ice

Questions:
1. Compare your value for the latent heat of fusion of ice with the accepted value by determining the experimental error.
2. Why did you dry the ice cube in step 4?
3. List other sources of error in this investigation, and suggest ways to reduce them.

Investigation 8.5: Latent Heat of Vaporization

Problem:
It is your problem to design and implement a method to determine the latent heat of vaporization of water.

Materials:
as illustrated
(CAUTION: Boiling water and live steam can cause very severe burns. Special care is necessary.)

 CAUTION: Stir gently. Do not break the thermometer.

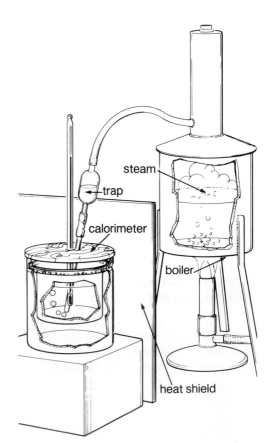
steam
trap
calorimeter
boiler
heat shield

Investigation Design:
1. Write a clear statement of the problem under the heading "Problem".
2. Under the heading "Procedure", list in order the steps you would follow to solve the problem.
3. Submit your procedure to your teacher for approval before commencing the investigation.

Investigation Report:
1. Perform the investigation by following the steps outlined in your procedure.
2. Under the heading "Observations", record the results of all your measurements.
3. Under the heading "Calculations", show the relevant calculations and equations used.
4. Under the heading "Conclusions", provide the answer to your problem, and comment on its validity by discussing possible sources of experimental error.

CAUTION: Be sure to include the safety precautions you will follow.

Chapter Summary

1. The Kinetic Molecular Theory of matter can be used to explain the thermal energy, temperature, and changes of state of a substance.
2. Temperature is an indirect measure of the average kinetic energy of the atoms and molecules in a substance.
3. Thermal energy refers to the total kinetic and potential energy of all the atoms and molecules in a substance.
4. The SI scale of thermometry uses the Celsius degree. The fixed points on this scale are the freezing and boiling points of water. A Kelvin degree (K) is equivalent to a Celsius degree (°C).
5. The thermal expansion or contraction of an object depends on three factors, namely, the initial size of the object, the temperature change, and the type of material. Linear expansion is given by the relationship $\Delta L = \alpha L_0 \Delta T$; the expression for volume expansion is $\Delta V = \beta V_0 \Delta T$.
6. The phenomena of expansion and contraction have many practical applications, and must be considered in the design of most structures.

7. The thermal expansion of water differs from that of most other substances. It contracts as it is cooled to 4°C, but from 4°C to 0°C it expands.

8. Heat is a measure of the amount of thermal energy that flows from one body to another because of a difference in temperature.

9. The SI unit of heat energy is the joule. To change the temperature of 1 kg of water by 1°C requires 4.2 kJ of energy.

10. The specific heat capacity (c) of a substance is the energy required to change the temperature of 1 kg of the substance by 1°C.

11. According to the Law of Conservation of Energy, when two substances at different temperatures are mixed, the heat energy lost by one is equal to the heat energy gained by the other. This is the basis of calorimetry, the quantitative measurement of heat exchange.

12. When a substance changes state, an exchange of energy occurs without a temperature change. Latent heat is the amount of energy required to produce a change in state of 1 kg of a substance.

13. The latent heat of fusion is the heat required to melt 1 kg of a solid to form a liquid at its melting point. It is also the energy given off when the substance changes from a liquid to a solid.

14. The latent heat of vaporization is the heat required to change 1 kg of a liquid to form a vapor at its boiling point. It is also the energy given off when the substance changes from a vapor to a liquid.

15. The First Law of Thermodynamics states that the quantity of heat energy transferred to a system is equal to the work done by the system plus the change in the internal energy of the system.

16. The Second Law of Thermodynamics states that heat flows naturally from a hot to a cold region, but not the reverse.

17. The heat flow through an insulated wall varies inversely with the RSI-value of the wall, directly with the area of the wall, and directly with the temperature difference between the outside and the inside of the wall.

Chapter Review

Discussion

1. Distinguish between heat capacity and specific heat capacity.
2. Using the Kinetic Molecular Theory, explain each of the following.
   (a) What is the difference between evaporation and boiling?
   (b) How can you boil a liquid without heating it? Why is this possible?
3. Why is it easier to loosen the metal lid on a glass jar after heating it under hot water?
4. Why should you not loosen a brass nut on an aluminum bolt by heating? How would you loosen it?
5. It is possible to heat a cold kitchen by opening the oven door, but it is not possible to cool the room by opening the refrigerator door. Why?
6. Given an equal mass of aluminum and brass, which would require more heat energy if the temperature of each were raised the same number of degrees?
7. If equal masses of copper and iron at 90°C were placed in equal volumes of water at the same initial temperature, would the final temperature be the same for each mixture? Explain your answer.
8. What is the relationship between the density and the specific heat capacity of a pure substance. Check your prediction by looking up the values for at least five elements and plotting a graph of specific heat capacity versus density.
9. Usually winds blow onshore from a large body of water during the day and offshore during the evening. Explain this using your knowledge of specific heat capacities.
10. In a solar heating system the energy gained during the day is usually stored in large tanks for use at night. A mixture of water and ethylene glycol is often used in the system. Why is neither pure water nor pure ethylene glycol used?
11. In winter the ground may be frozen, but large bodies of water such as the Great Lakes usually are not. Why?
12. When a frost warning is issued in regions such as Florida, the fruit growers often direct water on the fruit trees all night. Why does this procedure tend to reduce the destruction of sensitive plants due to freezing?
13. Why does steam produce more severe burns on exposed skin than would the same amount of boiling water?

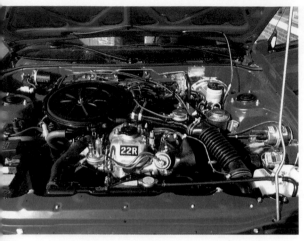

A gasoline engine

14. "For a heat engine to operate there must be a temperature difference." In a minimum of 200 words, explain how this principle is applied in one of the following heat engines: a gasoline engine, a diesel engine, a jet engine.

15. You are asked to design the heating and air conditioning requirements for a computer classroom. After doing some research, report on the sources of heat in such a room and estimate the heat produced by each.

16. The ocean contains an enormous amount of thermal energy. It is not practical to put this energy to useful work. Explain.

Problems

17. A rod 1.0 m long expands 0.50 mm when heated from 20°C to 84°C. What is the coefficient of linear expansion of the material from which the rod is made?

18. A steel measuring tape is calibrated at 20°C. A reading of 32.10 m is measured when it is used to find the length of a building. If the temperature is 5°C, what is the actual length of the building at that temperature?

19. A metal rod has a length of 100 cm at 200°C. At what temperature will the length be 99.8 cm if the coefficient of linear expansion of the material in the rod is 2.0×10^{-5} °C^{-1}?

20. A bimetallic compound strip of brass and iron is 10 cm long at 20°C. It is held horizontally with the iron on top. When heated over a Bunsen flame the temperature of the brass is 800°C and the iron 750°C. Calculate the difference in lengths of the iron and the brass. (Ignore the effects of bending.)

21. An iron rim is mounted on a wooden wheel by heating it so that it expands larger than the circumference of the wooden wheel. When cooled in place, it contracts tightly on the rim. The outside diameter of a wooden wheel is 1.000 m. An iron rim has an inside diameter of 0.996 m at 20°C. To what temperature must the iron rim be heated in order for it to just fit the wheel?

22. A beaker is filled to the brim with 250 cm^3 of ethyl alcohol at 15°C. How much will overflow at 30°C? (Assume that the beaker does not expand significantly.)

23. A mercury thermometer has a uniform capillary bore with an area of cross section of 1.0×10^{-3} mm^2. The volume of mercury in the bulb is 1.0 mm^3. Neglecting the expansion of the glass in the thermometer, by how much would the height of the mercury in the bore change if the temperature increased by 60°C?

24. How much heat is required to raise the temperature of 2.0 kg of water from 25°C to 80°C?

25. How much heat is lost when 1.00 kg of copper cools from 90°C to 20°C?
26. What will be the temperature change in each of the following?
    (a) 10.0 kg of water loses 456 kJ.
    (b) 4.80 kg of ethyl alcohol gains 12.6 kJ.
27. A 6.0 g pellet of lead at 30°C gains 36.8 J of heat. What will be its final temperature?
28. When 2.1×10^3 J of heat is added to 100 g of a substance, its temperature increases from 15°C to 40°C. What is the specific heat capacity of the substance?
29. A 70 kg person is on a diet that provides 8.36×10^6 J (2000 Calories) daily. If a corresponding amount of heat were added to 70 kg of water at 37°C, what would be its final temperature?
30. How much water at 80°C must be added to 200 g of water at 10°C to give a final temperature of 36°C?
31. When 0.500 kg of water at 90°C is added to 1.00 kg of water at 10°C, what is the final temperature?
32. A copper calorimeter cup with a mass of 100 g contains 96 g of water at 13°C. If 70 g of a substance at 84°C is dropped into the calorimeter, the temperature increases to 20°C. Find the specific heat capacity of the substance.
33. Someone pours 150 g of heated lead shot into a 250 g aluminum calorimeter cup that contains 200 g of water at 25°C. The final temperature is 28°C. What was the initial temperature of the lead shot?
34. How long does it take a 1000 W electric kettle to bring 1.0 L of water to the boiling point if the initial temperature of the water is 15°C and the kettle is made of 400 g of iron? Assume that no water is boiled, that no heat is lost to the surroundings, and that the kettle is 100% efficient.
35. A farmer drives a 100 g iron spike with a 2.0 kg sledge hammer. The sledge hammer moves at 3.0 m/s and comes to rest on the spike after each swing. Assuming all the energy is absorbed by the nail and ignoring the work done by the nail, how much would its temperature rise after 10 successive swings?
36. A waterfall is 50 m high. If all of the gravitational potential energy of the water at the top of the falls were converted to heat energy at the bottom of the falls, what would be the increase in the temperature of the water at the bottom? (Hint: Consider one kilogram of water going over the waterfall.)
37. How much heat is given off when 300 g of water at 0°C freezes to ice at 0°C?
38. How much heat is required to convert 100 g of ice at −10°C to water at 50°C?
39. What will be the final temperature if 1.9×10^2 kJ of heat is added to 0.50 kg of ice at 0°C?

According to physics folklore, Joule even took time on his honeymoon to take temperature measurements at several European waterfalls.

40. A 70 kg hockey player moving at 8.0 m/s stops quickly. How much ice melts due to the friction between the player's skates and the ice? Assume that only 60% of the energy lost by the skater goes to melting the ice, and that the temperature of the ice is 0°C.

41. A 200 g piece of ice at −10°C is placed in 200 g of water at 50°C. After a few minutes the ice-water mixture reaches thermal equilibrium. How much water is there in the mixture now?

42. How much heat is required to:
    (a) convert 50 g of water at 100°C to steam at 100°C?
    (b) change 50 g of water at 80°C to steam at 120°C?
    (c) change 100 g of ice at −10°C to steam at 130°C?

43. To what temperature will 100 g of water at 24°C be heated by the condensation of 3.0 g of steam at 100°C?

44. During an aerobics exercise class, a person gives off 1.2×10^6 J of heat energy in 45 min. Assuming all this energy is used to evaporate water from the skin, how much water is lost?

45. In an investigation to measure the heat of vaporization of water, some students collected the following data:
    mass of aluminum calorimeter = 126.0 g
    mass of calorimeter + water = 286.0 g
    mass of calorimeter + water + steam water = 296.1 g
    initial temperature of water = 8°C
    final temperature of water = 40°C
    Find the heat of vaporization of water.

46. An ice-water mixture has a mass of 180 g and is contained in a 100 g aluminum calorimeter. When 35 g of steam at 100°C is condensed in the water, the temperature rises to 50°C. How much ice was in the container initially?

47. Accidentally 0.20 kg of water at 0°C is poured into a large thermos containing liquid nitrogen at −196°C. If the heat of vaporization of nitrogen is 2.0×10^5 J/kg, how much nitrogen vaporizes?

48. Natural gas (methane) has a heat of combustion of 5.5×10^7 J/kg.
    (a) How much gas is required to heat a house that requires 2.0×10^9 kJ for the whole winter? Assume that the furnace is 80% efficient.
    (b) If the density of methane is 7.2×10^{-7} kg/L, calculate the volume of gas used.
    (c) If natural gas costs on average $0.23/m³, how much did it cost to heat the house?

49. A 2.0 g sample of a substance is placed in a bomb calorimeter with an iron combustion chamber whose mass is 80 g. Surrounding the combustion chamber is 200 g of water initially at 15°C. When the sample is completely burned, the final temperature of the water and combustion chamber is 65°C. What is the specific heat of combustion of the substance?

Numerical Answers to Practice Problems

page 232
1. 2.9×10^{-4} m
2. 3.6×10^{-3} m
3. 34 m³
4. 24×10^{-6} °C^{-1}

page 237
1. 8.8×10^5 J
2. 3.2×10^4 J
3. (a) 5.5°C   (b) 10°C
4. 40°C

page 240
1. 9.0×10^2 J/kg · °C
2. 3.8×10^2 J/kg · °C
3. 47°C
4. 3.2×10^{-1} kg
5. 4.4×10^2 J

page 244
1. 8.3×10^3 J
2. 4.1×10^4 J
3. 3.1×10^5 J
4. 2.5×10^5 J
5. 8.4×10^{-3} kg

page 251
1. 20%
2. (a) 0.16   (b) 1.41
   (c) 3.17   (d) 1.60
3. 1.25

page 253
1. 1.8×10^4 W
2. 6.5×10^7 J
3. 0.77°C

Fluids

Most of us would describe glass as a solid. Yet, images seen through old windows are often distorted because the glass has become thicker near the bottom. Scientists believe that the glass flows, albeit very slowly, under the influence of gravity.

Introduction

You have already learned that there are three states, or phases, of matter: solid, liquid, and gas. These three states are easily distinguishable by their properties. Solids have a fixed shape and a definite volume; even a large force will not change the shape or volume of a solid very much. A liquid will adapt quickly to the shape of its container but, like a solid, its volume will not change much even under the application of a large force. A gas has neither a fixed shape nor a definite volume; it will expand indefinitely to fill the volume and shape of its container. Since liquids and gases do not maintain a fixed shape, they are said to have the ability to "flow", and together they are referred to as **fluids**.

Fluids, particularly air and water, play an important part in our everyday lives. The properties of fluids enable us to move across and beneath the surface of bodies of water and above the surface of the Earth through the atmosphere. Because they form the basis of all hydraulic and pneumatic devices, fluids are essential to our modern industrial processes. This chapter will introduce you to some of the basic properties of fluids and the very significant role they play in our technological society.

In your study of mechanics, you were able to describe the motion of objects that were acted upon by known forces. However, using the concepts of force and mass presents complications when applied to fluids. A given mass of fluid does not have a fixed shape; it is not rigid. The concepts of density and pressure are more useful when describing the properties of fluids at rest or in motion.

9.1 Density and Relative Density

We often hear expressions like this: "as light as a feather", "as heavy as lead". It is clear that equal volumes of different substances can vary considerably in mass. As a measure of this property, we define **density** as the mass per unit volume of a substance. Mathematically,

$$\rho = \frac{m}{V}$$

where m is the mass, in kilograms

V is the volume, in cubic meters

ρ is the density, in kilograms per cubic meter

For small objects whose mass and volume are more readily measured in grams and cubic centimeters, density is commonly expressed in grams per cubic centimeter, so that

$$1\,kg/m^3 = 1000\ g/(100\ cm)^3$$
$$= 10^{-3}\ g/cm^3$$

Thus, densities of 2.0×10^3 kg/m³ and 2.0 g/cm³ are equivalent. The table in the margin gives values for the densities of some common substances.

The **relative density** of a solid or liquid is defined as the ratio of its density to the density of pure water, at 4°C. Conveniently, the density of pure water at 4°C is 1.0×10^3 kg/m³, or 1.0 g/cm³. Stated mathematically,

$$\text{relative density} = \frac{\text{density of substance}}{\text{density of water}}$$
$$= \frac{\text{density of substance (in kg/m}^3)}{1.0 \times 10^3\ \text{kg/m}^3}$$
$$= \frac{\text{density of substance (in g/cm}^3)}{1.0\ \text{g/cm}^3}$$

We can see that the relative density of any substance is a number, without units.

For example, the density of mercury is

$$\rho_{mercury} = 13.6 \times 10^3\ \text{kg/m}^3, \text{ or } 13.6\ \text{g/cm}^3$$

Therefore, the relative density of mercury is 13.6.

The following sample problems will illustrate the applications of this concept.

The Greek letter ρ, pronounced "rho", is used universally as the symbol for density.

Densities of Common Substances (in kilograms per cubic meter)

aluminum	2.70×10^3
iron, steel	7.8×10^3
copper	8.9×10^3
lead	11.3×10^3
gold	19.3×10^3
concrete	2.3×10^3
granite	2.7×10^3
wood	$0.3{-}0.9 \times 10^3$
glass	2.6×10^3
ice	0.917×10^3
water (4°C)	1.0×10^3
sea water	1.03×10^3
mercury	13.6×10^3
alcohol	0.79×10^3
gasoline	0.68×10^3
air	1.29
helium	0.179
steam	0.60

Relative density is also called specific gravity. We think you will agree that relative density conveys more clearly the meaning of the quantity.

Sample Problems

1. A shot used in shot-put has a mass of 7.3 kg and a volume of 6.5×10^{-4} m^3.
   (a) What are its density and relative density?

$$\rho = \frac{m}{V}$$

$$= \frac{7.3 \text{ kg}}{6.5 \times 10^{-4} \text{ m}^3}$$
$$= 1.1 \times 10^4 \text{ kg/m}^3$$
$$= 11 \text{ g/cm}^3$$

$$\text{relative density} = \frac{\text{density of metal}}{\text{density of water}}$$
$$= \frac{1.1 \times 10^4 \text{ kg/m}^3}{1.0 \times 10^3 \text{ kg/m}^3}$$
$$= 11$$

   (b) Of what metal is the shot made?
   Using the tables on page 269, we can assume that the metal is probably lead, since its density is given as 11.3×10^3 kg/m^3, or 11.3 g/cm^3.

2. Kerosene has a relative density of 0.82. What volume of kerosene has a mass of 6.4 kg?
   The density of kerosene is

$$\rho_{\text{kerosene}} = 0.82 \, (\rho_{\text{water}})$$
$$= 0.82 \, (1.0 \times 10^3 \text{ kg/m}^3)$$
$$= 8.2 \times 10^2 \text{ kg/m}^3$$

Then, the volume will be

$$V = \frac{m}{\rho}$$

$$= \frac{6.4 \text{ kg}}{8.2 \times 10^2 \text{ kg/m}^3}$$
$$= 7.8 \times 10^{-3} \text{ m}^3$$

The volume of a sphere is $\frac{4}{3}\pi r^3$.

Practice

(Use the table of densities on page 269, if needed.)
1. What is the volume of an iceberg whose mass is 3.6×10^5 kg?
2. The Earth has a mass of 6.0×10^{24} kg and a radius of 6.4×10^6 m. What is its average density?
3. (a) Calculate the mass of a four-liter jug of antifreeze (ignore the mass of the plastic container) if the density of antifreeze is 8.0×10^2 kg/m^3.
   (b) Calculate the density of a mixture of 40% antifreeze and 60% water, if there is a 5% decrease in total volume when they are mixed.

4. What is the approximate mass of air in a house whose floor area is 185 m² and whose interior walls are 2.5 m high?
5. A bottle has a mass of 24.20 g when empty and 86.54 g when completely filled with water. When emptied and completely filled again with carbon tetrachloride, its mass is 123.94 g. What is the relative density of carbon tetrachloride?

Although we have been considering the densities of all three states of matter, the densities of liquids and gases have particular significance in the study of fluids. Notice, from the table on page 269, that for the most part solids have relative densities greater than 1, liquids have relative densities around 1, and gases have relative densities much less than 1. We will see how the relative densities of solids, liquids, and gases are related when we study buoyancy later in this chapter.

9.2 Pressure in Fluids

Although the term *pressure* has many everyday implications, its meaning is exact in physics. **Pressure** is defined as the force acting perpendicular to a unit area.
Mathematically,

$$p = \frac{F}{A}$$

where F is the force acting perpendicular to a given area, in newtons

A is the area, in square meters

p is the pressure, in pascals, or newtons per square meter

To honor Blaise Pascal for his pioneering work with pressure, the SI unit for pressure has been designated the pascal (Pa).

1 Pa is the pressure when a force of 1 N acts perpendicular to an area of 1 m². (1 Pa = 1 N/m²)

The following problem will illustrate the use of this relationship.

Blaise Pascal (1623-1662)
Pascal, born in Clermont-Ferrand, France, was a child prodigy, who published a geometry book when he was 16, and invented a mechanical calculator by age 19. Working with the famed mathematician Fermat, Pascal laid the groundwork for the study of probability and statistics.

In physics, Pascal discovered that any pressure exerted on a fluid in a closed container would be transmitted, undiminished, throughout the fluid. By sending his brother-in-law up into the mountains with a mercury barometer, he also verified Torricelli's prediction that atmospheric pressure would decrease with altitude.

Pascal later abandoned mathematics and physics and turned his attention to meditation and religious writings. A lifelong sufferer from stomach disorders, he died at the young age of 39.

A pressure of 1 Pa is very small. A dime resting on a table exerts a pressure of about 88 Pa. A more practical unit of pressure is the kilopascal (kPa).

$$1 \text{ kPa} = 1000 \text{ Pa}$$
$$= 1000 \text{ N/m}^2$$

Snowshoes enable a person to walk on the surface of deep snow by distributing the snow's reaction to the force of gravity on the person over a much larger area than just the soles of the feet. The pressure created is then small enough that it can be supported by the snow. Large-area "flotation tires" on vehicles used on soft terrain employ the same principle.

Sample Problems

A physics textbook has a mass of 1.2 kg, and its cover measures 22 cm by 24 cm. It is 3.5 cm thick. What pressure does it exert on your desk when lying (a) flat, and (b) on its spine?

$$F = mg$$
$$= (1.2 \text{ kg}) (9.8 \text{ N/kg})$$
$$= 11.8 \text{ N}$$

(a) When lying flat on the desk,

$$A_1 = lw$$
$$= (0.24 \text{ m}) (0.22 \text{ m})$$
$$= 5.28 \times 10^{-2} \text{ m}^2$$

Then,

$$p_1 = \frac{F}{A_1}$$
$$= \frac{11.8 \text{ N}}{5.28 \times 10^{-2} \text{ m}^2}$$
$$= 2.2 \times 10^2 \text{ N/m}^2, \text{ or } 2.2 \times 10^2 \text{ Pa}$$

(b) When lying on its spine,

$$A_2 = lt$$
$$= (0.24 \text{ m}) (0.035 \text{ m})$$
$$= 8.4 \times 10^{-3} \text{ m}^2$$

And,

$$p_2 = \frac{F}{A_2}$$
$$= \frac{11.8 \text{ N}}{8.4 \times 10^{-3} \text{ m}^2}$$
$$= 1.4 \times 10^3 \text{ N/m}^2, \text{ or } 1.4 \times 10^3 \text{ Pa}$$

Notice that the book exerts a greater pressure on the desk when the area in contact is smaller.

Practice

1. The gauge on a pressure cooker indicates that the pressure inside is 3.0×10^5 Pa. If the pot has a circular cross-section and an inside diameter of 24 cm, what total force is acting upward on the lid?
2. The arm of a record player is adjusted to exert a downward force on the stylus equivalent to the force of gravity on a 1.0 g mass. If the tip of the stylus has a circular cross-section, with a diameter of 1.5×10^{-5} m, calculate the pressure it exerts on the record groove.
3. Calculate the pressure exerted on the floor by a 60 kg girl, standing on both feet, if each of her soles has an area of 240 cm². What does the pressure become if she balances on one foot?
4. A car has a mass of 1250 kg. Each tire's pressure is 210 kPa. Assuming perfectly flexible thin tires and equal sharing of the load, what is the area of each tire in contact with the road?

The concept of pressure is particularly significant in understanding the behavior of fluids at rest. Consider two tanks of water, each of depth 1.0 m, but with cross-sectional areas of 1.0 m² and 4.0 m², respectively, as shown:

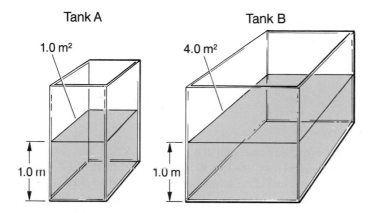

The pressure exerted by the water on the bottom of each of the tanks can be calculated, as follows:

For tank A,
$$F_A = m_A g = (\rho_W V_A)g$$
$$= (1.0 \times 10^3 \text{ kg/m}^3)(1.0 \text{ m}^3)(9.8 \text{ N/kg})$$
$$= 9.8 \times 10^3 \text{ N}$$
$$p_A = \frac{F_A}{A_A} = \frac{9.8 \times 10^3 \text{ N}}{1.0 \text{ m}^2}$$
$$= 9.8 \times 10^3 \text{ N/m}^2$$

For tank B,
$$F_B = m_B g = (\rho_W V_B)g$$
$$= (1.0 \times 10^3 \text{ kg/m}^3)(4.0 \text{ m}^3)(9.8 \text{ N/kg})$$
$$= 39.2 \times 10^3 \text{ N}$$
$$p_B = \frac{F_B}{A_B} = \frac{39.2 \times 10^3 \text{ N}}{4.0 \text{ m}^2}$$
$$= 9.8 \times 10^3 \text{ N/m}^2$$

Notice that the pressure exerted on the bottom of each tank is the same, regardless of the size of the tank. In fact, the shape of the tank is also of no significance, as the sketches in the margin indicate. *The pressure depends only on the depth and density of liquid in the tank.* Of course, as the depth increases, the pressure increases also, as any scuba diver will verify.

A fluid also exerts its pressure equally in all directions. Consider a very small, imaginary cube of a fluid situated at a depth, d, in a container of the fluid at rest, as shown on the next page:

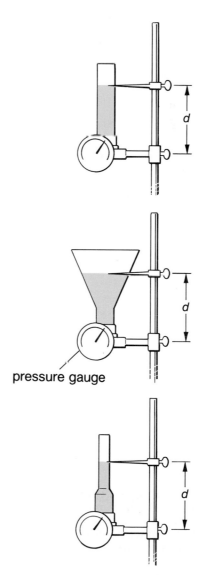

pressure gauge

The pressure at a given depth in a liquid does not depend on the shape of the container.

Assume the very small cube has negligible mass.

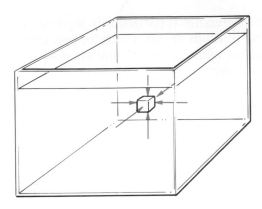

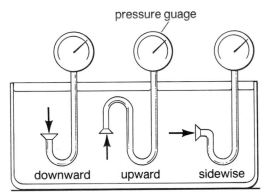

pressure guage

downward   upward   sidewise

The pressure at a given depth in a liquid is exerted equally in all directions.

The downward pressure of the fluid above on the top of the cube must be balanced by an equal upward pressure on the bottom. Otherwise there would be a net force on the cube that would make it move up or down. This is true for the pressures on the front and back plus the sides of the cube, too. Since the fluid is at rest and no part of it is moving, all of these pressures must be equal. The sketch shows an experimental verification of the equality of these pressures.

An additional property of a fluid at rest, whose explanation goes beyond the scope of this book, is that fluids exert their pressure perpendicular to any surface they touch. That is, a fluid can only push directly against a surface, and never along it.

In summary, then:
• The pressure at equal depths in a given fluid is equal.
• The pressure is exerted equally in all directions.
• The pressure is exerted perpendicular to any surface with which the fluid is in contact.

The next sample problem will show how we can calculate the pressure at a specific depth in a given liquid.

The pressure at a given depth in a fluid may be measured with a pressure-sensitive device and is called a gauge pressure. You will learn more about gauge pressures on page 277.

Sample Problems

Calculate the pressure at a depth of 2.0 m in a swimming pool.

Consider an imaginary plane 1.0 m by 1.0 m at a depth of 2.0 m in the swimming pool, as shown on the next page. The pressure at this depth is due to the downward force of the column of water above the plane.

The volume of this column of water, V, is
$$V = lwh$$
$$= (1.0 \text{ m})(1.0 \text{ m})(2.0 \text{ m})$$
$$= 2.0 \text{ m}^3$$

And its mass, m, is given by
$$m = \rho_w V$$
$$= (1.0 \times 10^3 \text{ kg/m}^3)(2.0 \text{ m}^3)$$
$$= 2.0 \times 10^3 \text{ kg}$$
The force of gravity on this column of water is
$$F_g = mg$$
$$= (2.0 \times 10^3 \text{ kg})(9.8 \text{ N/kg})$$
$$= 1.96 \times 10^4 \text{ N}$$
Thus, the pressure exerted on the plane, at a depth of 2.0 m is
$$p = \frac{F}{A}$$
$$= \frac{1.96 \times 10^4 \text{ N}}{1.0 \text{ m}^2}$$
$$= 1.96 \times 10^4 \text{ N/m}^2, \text{ or } 2.0 \times 10^4 \text{ Pa}$$

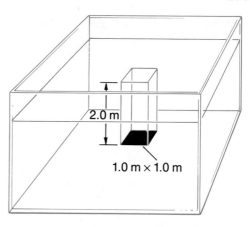

The pressure at a specific depth in any fluid is expressed as

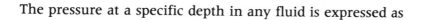

$$p = \rho g d$$

where p is the fluid pressure, in pascals
  ρ is the density of the fluid, in kilograms per cubic meter
  g is the gravitational field strength, in newtons per kilogram
  d is the fluid depth, in meters
This equation is only valid for fluids whose density remains constant over the depth, d, and for depths over which g remains constant. Most liquids are virtually incompressible—their densities remain essentially constant and do not vary with depth. Gases, on the other hand, are compressible. For example, at sea level the density of the Earth's atmosphere is about 1.22 kg/m³, whereas at an altitude of 10 km its density is only 0.425 kg/m³.

Sample Problems

Determine the pressure in a gasoline storage tank at a depth of 8.0 m, if the relative density of gasoline is 0.70.
  For gasoline, $\rho = (0.70)(1.00 \times 10^3 \text{ kg/m}^3)$
$$= 7.0 \times 10^2 \text{ kg/m}^3$$
Then $p = \rho g d$
$$= (7.0 \times 10^2 \text{ kg/m}^3)(9.8 \text{ N/kg})(8.0 \text{ m})$$
$$= 5.5 \times 10^4 \text{ Pa}$$

For the more general problem, to calculate the pressure at a depth d, in a fluid of density ρ:

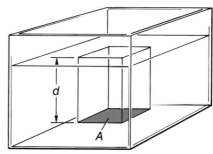

Volume of fluid column is
$$V = dA$$
Mass of fluid column is
$$m = \rho V = \rho dA$$
Force of gravity on fluid column is
$$F_g = mg = \rho dAg$$
Therefore, the pressure at depth d is
$$p = \frac{F}{A}$$
$$= \frac{\rho dAg}{A}$$
$$p = \rho g d$$

Although it sounds as though it relates only to water, the pressure below a column of any fluid at rest is called "hydrostatic pressure".

We don't normally notice atmospheric pressure pushing in on us because our bodies have an internal pressure that just balances it. Our ears, however, are sensitive to changes in atmospheric pressure. As the altitude increases, atmospheric pressure on the eardrum from the outside decreases. Normal pressure on the inside of the eardrum causes a force on the eardrum, and it bulges out, resulting in some minor discomfort or pain. Fortunately the ears "pop" as pressure behind the ear decreases until it is once again equal to the outside pressure. Swallowing or chewing gum assists the ears to "pop".

Meteorologists, in order to predict the weather, keep a close watch on changes in atmospheric pressure. Generally, high pressure indicates fair weather, while low pressure often precedes a storm.

Practice

1. With what pressure would a saline solution, of relative density 1.02, be forced into a patient's vein if the surface of fluid in the intravenous bottle were held 0.80 m above the needle?
2. What height of water tower is required to produce a faucet pressure of 3.5×10^5 Pa?
3. Alvin, the underwater exploration vehicle that photographed the Titanic, descended to a depth of 4000 m in sea water of average density 1.03×10^3 kg/m³. If its camera port were circular, of radius 15 cm, what total force would it have to withstand?

Atmospheric Pressure

Air, the name given to the mixture of gases in our atmosphere, is a fluid and exerts a pressure. Being at sea level is like being at the bottom of a column of air approximately 160 km high, called the atmosphere. Atmospheric pressure cannot be calculated using the equation $p = \rho g d$, since the value of g varies over the 160 km height of the atmosphere. Also, ρ varies from a value of 1.22 kg/m³ at sea level, to a value of nearly zero at the top edge of the atmosphere.

Normal atmospheric pressure may be measured, however, using a simple device called a **barometer**. A barometer is a thin, strong-walled glass tube, sealed at one end and open at the other. The tube is completely filled with a liquid and then carefully inverted in a reservoir of the same liquid that is open to the atmosphere. This is illustrated below, using mercury.

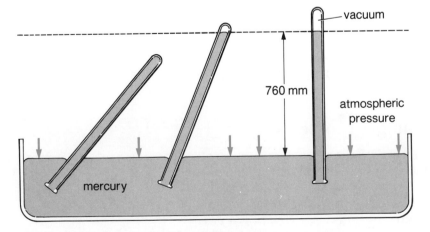

Some of the liquid in the tube will flow back into the reservoir, leaving a column of liquid in the tube with a vacuum (no pressure)

above it. A column of liquid of this height exerts a pressure at the level of the surface of the liquid in the reservoir. This pressure is just equal to the downward pressure of the atmosphere, causing the liquid to come to rest.

Because of its high density, mercury (Hg) is the most common liquid used in barometers. Atmospheric pressure varies, and by taking many measurements, it has been determined that average atmospheric pressure at sea level supports a column of mercury that is 760 mm high. The **atmosphere**, abbreviated atm, is often used as a unit of pressure and is equated to the height of mercury column it will support.

$$1 \text{ atm} = 760 \text{ mm Hg}$$
$$= \rho g d, \text{ for the mercury column}$$
$$= (13.6 \times 10^3 \text{ kg/m}^3)(9.8 \text{ N/kg})(0.760 \text{ m})$$
$$= 101.3 \times 10^3 \text{ N/m}^2$$
$$= 101.3 \text{ kPa, or } 1.0 \times 10^2 \text{ kPa}$$

Measuring Pressure in Fluids

In measuring and referring to fluid pressures, one must always be careful to distinguish between absolute pressure and gauge pressure. **Absolute pressure** is the total pressure, including atmospheric pressure, to which all objects at the Earth's surface are subjected. **Gauge pressure** is any additional pressure over and above atmospheric pressure. An example will illustrate.

Sample Problems

Calculate the absolute pressure and the gauge pressure in a fresh water lake at a depth of 50 m.

The pressure exerted on the surface of the lake is normal atmospheric pressure, 1.0×10^5 Pa. The additional gauge water pressure at a depth of 50 m is given by:

$$p = \rho g d$$
$$= (1.0 \times 10^3 \text{ kg/m}^3)(9.8 \text{ N/kg})(50 \text{ m})$$
$$= 4.9 \times 10^5 \text{ Pa}$$

This is the gauge pressure at a depth of 50 m. The absolute pressure at a depth of 50 m is the sum of the atmospheric pressure and the gauge hydrostatic pressure:

$$p_{absolute} = p_{atmospheric} + p_{gauge}$$
$$= 1.0 \times 10^5 \text{ Pa} + 4.9 \times 10^5 \text{ Pa}$$
$$= 5.9 \times 10^5 \text{ Pa}$$

It is more convenient to measure atmospheric pressure with an aneroid barometer. An enclosed chamber with thin, flexible metal walls expands and contracts as atmospheric pressure decreases or increases. As the pressure changes, a pointer attached to this chamber moves back and forth across a scale calibrated in kilopascals.

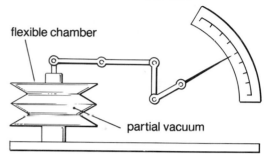

flexible chamber

partial vacuum

In 1643, an Italian scientist, Evangelista Torricelli, made one of the first barometers, using water (legend has it he may even have used wine) as the liquid. A simple calculation would indicate that such a barometer would have been more than 10 m high.

$$1 \text{ atm} = 760 \text{ mm Hg}$$
$$= (13.6)(760 \text{ mm}) \text{ H}_2\text{O}$$
$$= 10.3 \text{ m H}_2\text{O}$$

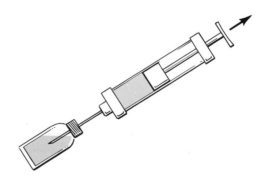

As the plunger in a hypodermic syringe is drawn upwards, a vacuum is created in the cylinder. Normal atmospheric pressure on the surface of the medication in the bottle pushes the liquid up into the syringe.

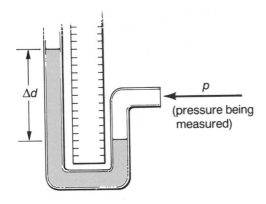

Δd

p

(pressure being measured)

Many devices, or gauges, have been invented to measure pressure. The simplest is the open-tube **manometer**, a u-shaped piece of glass tubing that is partially filled with a liquid such as water or mercury, as shown in the margin.

An unknown pressure may be determined by measuring the difference between the liquid level in the open side of the tube and the liquid level in the side exposed to the pressure being measured. For example, in a mercury open-manometer, if this difference in levels were 16 mm, then the gauge pressure being measured would be

$$p_{gauge} = \rho g \Delta d$$
$$= (13.6 \times 10^3 \text{ kg/m}^3)(9.8 \text{ N/kg})(1.6 \times 10^{-2} \text{ m})$$
$$= 2.1 \times 10^3 \text{ Pa}$$

Of course, the absolute pressure in this example is

$$p_{abs} = p_{atm} + p_{gauge}$$
$$= 1.013 \times 10^5 \text{ Pa} + 2.1 \times 10^3 \text{ Pa}$$
$$= 1.034 \times 10^5 \text{ Pa}$$

When measuring the pressure in common, everyday devices such as air pumps, pressure cookers, and oil pressure indicators on cars, we are measuring gauge pressure, not absolute pressure.

9.3 Pascal's Principle

In 1650, Blaise Pascal, a French mathematician, scientist, and philosopher, discovered one of the most important and useful properties of fluids, subsequently known as Pascal's Principle:

Pressure exerted on a contained fluid is transmitted undiminished throughout the fluid, acting in all directions and perpendicular to the walls of the container.

This important principle is involved in the operation of a large number of practical devices where the transmission of force is necessary. All modern automobiles are equipped with hydraulic brake systems similar to those depicted on the next page.

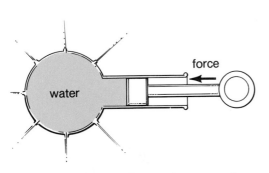

water

force

The simple device shown above may be used to demonstrate Pascal's Principle.

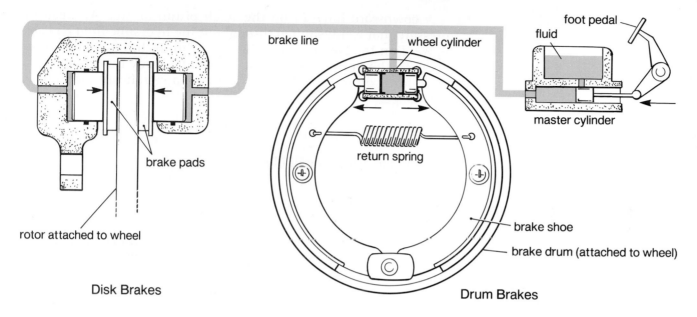

foot pedal

fluid

brake line

wheel cylinder

master cylinder

brake pads

return spring

rotor attached to wheel

brake shoe

brake drum (attached to wheel)

Disk Brakes

Drum Brakes

Depressing the brake pedal causes a force on the piston in the master brake cylinder and a consequent pressure on the brake fluid. This pressure is transmitted undiminished throughout the entire system of brake lines, and is thereby exerted on pistons in each of the wheel cylinders, pushing them outwards. In disk brakes, this forces the brake pads attached to a caliper against the rotor, and the resulting friction stops the wheel. In drum brakes, the wheel cylinder pistons exert an outward force on the brake shoes, pushing them against the rotating brake drums so that friction once again stops the wheel.

Another application of Pascal's Principle is the hydraulic lift, commonly used to lift heavy objects such as cars.

Why is it important that there be no air in a car's hydraulic brake system?

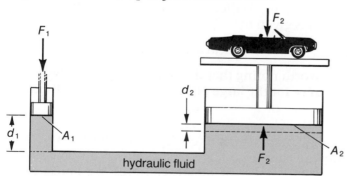

F_1

F_2

d_2

d_1

A_1

A_2

F_2

hydraulic fluid

A downward force F_1 on the small piston of area A_1 creates a pressure that is transmitted throughout the hydraulic fluid and acts upward on the larger piston. Since this piston has a much greater area, A_2, the upward force on it, F_2, can be many times the downward force on the small piston, creating a significant mechanical advantage.

$$A_2 \gg A_1$$

so that

$$F_2 \gg F_1$$

since

$$p_2 = p_1$$

A sample problem will illustrate.

Sample Problems

What downward force exerted on a small piston of radius 2.0 cm would lift a 2000 kg car, if the radius of the large piston is 12 cm?

To lift the car,

$$F_2 = mg$$
$$= (2000 \text{ kg})(9.8 \text{ N/kg})$$
$$= 1.96 \times 10^4 \text{ N}$$

According to Pascal's Principle,

$$p_1 = p_2$$
$$\frac{F_1}{A_1} = \frac{F_2}{A_2}$$

or

$$F_1 = \frac{A_1 F_2}{A_2}$$
$$= \frac{\pi(2.0 \text{ cm})^2(1.96 \times 10^4 \text{ N})}{\pi(12 \text{ cm})^2}$$
$$= 544 \text{ N, or } 5.4 \times 10^2 \text{ N}$$

The hydraulic lift is very similar to a first-class lever in its ability to multiply force. Its mechanical advantage is related to the ratio of the areas of its pistons, rather than the ratio of distances from the fulcrum, and is given by

$$\text{mechanical advantage} = \frac{F_2}{F_1} = \frac{A_2}{A_1}$$

It is also worth noting that the small piston must be pushed down a large distance for the large piston to go up a small distance. In fact,

$$\frac{d_1}{d_2} = \frac{A_2}{A_1}$$

A hydraulic press works like a hydraulic lift but the large piston pushes down. This large force pushes down on objects—stamping out parts from a sheet of metal, compressing books before their covers are attached, or force-fitting parts together and apart. Dump trucks, bulldozers, manufacturing robots, and industrial factories all use hydraulic devices that operate using Pascal's Principle.

The Syphon

We utilize some of the properties of fluids when we use a syphon. A syphon is a length of glass, rubber, or plastic tubing, bent so that its short arm may be immersed in a tank of liquid, as shown.

To start the syphon, it must first be filled with the liquid. Then the liquid will continue to flow so long as end E is kept below the level of liquid in the tank. There has always been conjecture about why syphons work as they do, but two theories have been proposed.

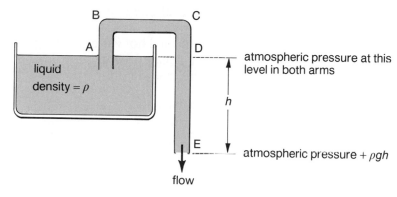

atmospheric pressure at this level in both arms

atmospheric pressure + ρgh

liquid density = ρ

flow

Atmospheric Pressure Theory

The pressures at A and D equal atmospheric pressure because these points are at the same level as the liquid's surface. If liquid did not flow, the pressure at E would be equal to atmospheric pressure plus the hydrostatic pressure ρgh, due to the liquid column DE. This excess pressure, ρgh, then causes liquid to flow from the tube at E, where the outside pressure is again atmospheric. Also, since the liquid must rise a distance AB, it follows that the syphon will not run if AB is greater than the barometric height for the liquid being syphoned.

Molecular Cohesion Theory

Experiments verify that pure liquids can be syphoned in a vacuum and, under certain circumstances, the syphon will run even when AB exceeds the appropriate barometric height. Atmospheric pressure does not seem to be essential. It seems that the flow of liquid occurs because the greater weight of column CE pulls down on the shorter column AB through the cohesive force between molecules of the liquid. This is very similar to the motion of a chain passing over a

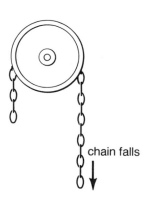

chain falls

frictionless pulley, which will always fall in the direction of the longer side.

Practice

(Unless otherwise specified, assume all pressures are gauge pressures.)

1. What is the atmospheric pressure in pascals on a day when a mercury column in a barometer is 750 mm high?

2. An open manometer containing water has a difference in level of 15 cm when connected to a tank of compressed gas. Find the excess pressure of the gas above normal atmospheric pressure.

3. The piston in a hydraulic automobile lift is 30 cm in diameter. What pressure is required to lift a car with a mass of 1200 kg?

4. A hydraulic punch press operates at a gauge pressure of 5.0 atm. What force is exerted on a piece of sheet metal if the output cylinder has a radius of 8.0 cm?

5. The expansion tank in an old-fashioned hot water heating system is open to the atmosphere, and is located 10 m above a pressure gauge on the furnace. What is the reading on the pressure gauge attached to the furnace?

6. A nurse pushes the plunger of a hypodermic syringe with a force of 4.0 N. If the internal radius of the cylinder is 0.80 cm, and the radius of the core of the needle is 0.20 mm, with what force is the vaccine ejected from the needle?

7. The maximum gauge pressure that the components of a hydraulic lift can withstand is 15 times normal atmospheric pressure. If the diameter of its output piston is 32 cm, what is the maximum mass that it can lift?

8. A cylindrical tank of radius 30 cm has a hole in its top to which is affixed a very long vertical tube, open at the top, with a tight seal at the joint. The tank is completely filled with water. Then water is slowly added to the tube until, at a height of 10 m above the water in the tank, the lid of the tank bursts. To what net force was the lid exposed just before it burst?

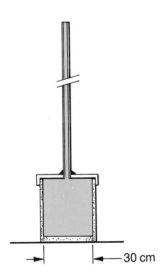

—| |←—30 cm

9.4 Buoyancy and Archimedes' Principle

Anyone who has ever tried to lift a rock from the bottom of a lake realizes that the rock seems to weigh much less while underwater than it does when it breaks the surface. The water helps overcome the downward force of gravity on the rock while it is submerged. This upward force on submerged objects is called the **buoyant force** and, for some objects, can even be sufficient to overcome completely the force of gravity and cause the object to float.

The buoyant force exists because fluids exert a pressure on submerged objects that increases with depth. A simple example will illustrate how we can calculate the value of the buoyant force on a submerged object.

Consider a block of iron, 1.0 m by 1.0 m by 1.0 m, situated underwater, as shown, with its top surface 1.0 m below the surface of the water.

The water pressure exerted downward on the top of the iron block is

$$p_1 = \rho g d_1$$
$$= (1.0 \times 10^3 \text{ kg/m}^3)(9.8 \text{ N/kg})(1.0 \text{ m})$$
$$= 9.8 \times 10^3 \text{ N/m}^2$$

so that the water's downward force on the top of the block is

$$F_1 = p_1 A$$
$$= (9.8 \times 10^3 \text{ N/m}^2)(1.0 \text{ m}^2)$$
$$= 9.8 \times 10^3 \text{ N}$$

A similar calculation would show that the water's upward force on the bottom of the iron block would be

$$F_2 = 1.96 \times 10^4 \text{ N}$$

Thus, the net upward force on the iron block due to the difference in water pressure on its top and bottom surface, and hence the buoyant force, is

$$F_b = F_2 - F_1$$
$$= 19.6 \times 10^3 \text{ N} - 9.8 \times 10^3 \text{ N}$$
$$= 9.8 \times 10^3 \text{ N}$$

The Greek philosopher Archimedes (287-212 B.C.) was intrigued by this buoyant force, and reasoned correctly that it had something to do with the liquid that was displaced by a submerged object. In our example the volume of water displaced by the iron block is

$$V = (1.0 \text{ m})(1.0 \text{ m})(1.0 \text{ m})$$
$$= 1.0 \text{ m}^3$$

and the mass of this displaced water is

$$m = \rho_w V$$
$$= (1.0 \times 10^3 \text{ kg/m}^3)(1.0 \text{ m}^3)$$
$$= 1.0 \times 10^3 \text{ kg}$$

The force of gravity on this displaced water is

$$F_g = mg$$
$$= (1.0 \times 10^3 \text{ kg})(9.8 \text{ N/kg})$$
$$= 9.8 \times 10^3 \text{ N}$$

Notice that the force of gravity on the displaced water equals the buoyant force on the cube of iron. We derived this result for a cube of iron immersed in water. Experiments verify, though, that it holds true for an object of any shape immersed, either wholly or partially,

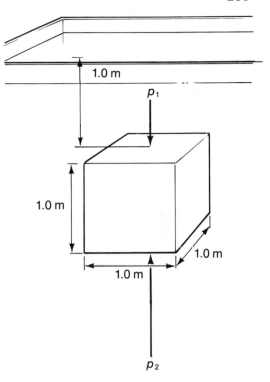

in any fluid. This was the basis of Archimedes' discovery, which has become known as **Archimedes' Principle**:

An object immersed in a fluid experiences a buoyant force that is equal in magnitude to the force of gravity on the displaced fluid.

Archimedes was acknowledged as the greatest scientist and mathematician of ancient Greece. When Hieron, King of Syracuse, became suspicious that his new crown was not made entirely of pure gold, he summoned Archimedes to make the determination without, of course, damaging the crown.

Perplexed at first, Archimedes stumbled upon the solution one day while taking a bath. Noting how the water level increased when he immersed himself, Archimedes submerged the crown and measured the increase in water level it caused. He repeated the same procedure using an equal weight of pure gold, and noted that the water level did not increase as much. The unscrupulous goldsmith had substituted some less dense, and less expensive, silver for the gold in the crown.

Legend has it that Archimedes was so excited by his discovery that he sprang from the bath and ran naked through the streets to the palace, shouting "Eureka!" meaning "I have found it!" Ever since, that exclamation has been regarded as an appropriate way to announce a startling discovery. By the way, crime didn't pay in ancient Syracuse, either, as the goldsmith was executed for his deceit.

Mathematically, the expression for the buoyant force is
$$F_b = mg$$
But
$$m = \rho V$$
Thus,

$$F_b = \rho V g$$

---

where F_b is the buoyant force acting, in newtons

ρ is the density of the fluid, in kilograms per cubic meter

V is the volume of fluid displaced, in cubic meters

g is the gravitational field strength, in newtons per kilogram

You will recall from Chapter 6 that the force of gravity on an object is often referred to as its "weight". Submerged objects "seem" to weigh less due to this buoyant force. Their "apparent weight" is given by
$$F_g \text{ (apparent)} = F_g - F_b$$

The following sample problems will illustrate how this principle is applied.

Sample Problems

1. An anchor of mass 100 kg and volume 4.0×10^{-2} m³ is resting on the bottom of a lake, with a rope of negligible mass attached to it. What force must be exerted on the rope to lift the anchor when it is (a) totally submerged, (b) halfway out of the water, and (c) completely above the water?

(a) The actual force of gravity acting on the anchor is always
$$F_g = mg$$
$$= (100 \text{ kg}) (9.8 \text{ N/kg})$$
$$= 9.8 \times 10^2 \text{ N}$$

In fact, to find the actual weight of the anchor, it must be weighed in a vacuum. Even the air displaced by the anchor exerts a very small buoyant force on it.

When totally submerged the buoyant force on the anchor is
$$F_b = \rho g V$$
$$= (1.0 \times 10^3 \text{ kg/m}^3) (9.8 \text{ N/kg}) (4.0 \times 10^{-2} \text{ m}^3)$$
$$= 3.9 \times 10^2 \text{ N}$$

Then, from the free body diagram, the force required to just lift the anchor is F_1 where

$$F_1 + F_b = F_g$$
$$F_1 = F_g - F_b$$
$$= 9.8 \times 10^2 \text{ N} - 3.9 \times 10^2 \text{ N}$$
$$= 5.9 \times 10^2 \text{ N}$$

(b) When the anchor is half submerged, the volume of water it displaces is $\frac{1}{2}(4.0 \times 10^{-2} \text{ m}^3)$, or $2.0 \times 10^{-2} \text{ m}^3$, so the buoyant force is

$$F_b = \rho g V$$
$$= (1.0 \times 10^3 \text{ kg/m}^3)(9.8 \text{ N/kg})(2.0 \times 10^{-2} \text{ m})$$
$$= 2.0 \times 10^2 \text{ N}$$

Then, the new force required to lift the anchor is

$$F_2 = F_g - F_b$$
$$= 9.8 \times 10^2 \text{ N} - 2.0 \times 10^2 \text{ N}$$
$$= 7.8 \times 10^2 \text{ N}$$

(c) There is no buoyant force when the anchor is above water, so the force necessary to lift it is

$$F_3 = F_g = 9.8 \times 10^2 \text{ N}$$

2. A sample of rock has a mass of 12.4 kg. When submerged in water, it has an "apparent mass" of 8.6 kg. What is the density of the rock sample?

The actual weight of the sample is

$$F_g = mg$$
$$= (12.4 \text{ kg})(9.8 \text{ N/kg})$$
$$= 122 \text{ N}$$

Its apparent weight when submerged in water is

$$F_g \text{ (apparent)} = m_a g$$
$$= (8.6 \text{ kg})(9.8 \text{ N/kg})$$
$$= 84 \text{ N}$$

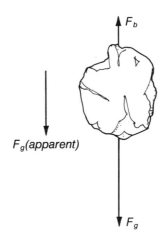

Therefore, the buoyant force on the rock sample is

$$F_b = F_g - F_g \text{ (apparent)}$$
$$= 122 \text{ N} - 84 \text{ N}$$
$$= 38 \text{ N}$$

Thus, the weight of water displaced by the submerged sample, according to Archimedes' Principle, is 38 N, the buoyant force. The mass of water displaced is

$$m_w = \frac{F_{g_w}}{g}$$
$$= \frac{38 \text{ N}}{9.8 \text{ N/kg}}$$
$$= 3.9 \text{ kg}$$

And, the volume of water displaced is

$$V_w = \frac{m_w}{\rho_w}$$

$$= \frac{3.9 \text{ kg}}{1.0 \times 10^3 \text{ kg/m}^3}$$

$$= 3.9 \times 10^{-3} \text{ m}^3$$

But this is also the volume of the rock sample, since it is totally submerged in the water.

For its density, then,

$$\rho_s = \frac{m_s}{V_s}$$

$$= \frac{12.4 \text{ kg}}{3.9 \times 10^{-3} \text{ m}^3}$$

$$= 3.2 \times 10^3 \text{ kg/m}^3$$

*P*ractice

1. A metal auto part has a volume of 150 cm³ and a mass of 1.35 kg.
   (a) What is the force of gravity on it?
   (b) What buoyant force will be exerted on it when fully immersed in water?
   (c) What is its apparent weight in water?
   (d) What is its apparent weight when immersed in kerosene, of relative density 0.800?
2. A plastic toy weighs 3.0 N in air and has an apparent weight of 1.4 N when immersed in water. Calculate
   (a) the buoyant force exerted on the toy by the water
   (b) the volume of water displaced by the immersed toy
   (c) the mass of the toy
   (d) the density of the plastic.
3. A young child can just lift a large stone from the bottom of a lake. The stone has a mass of 24 kg and its density is 2.5 x 10³ kg/m³.
   (a) What is the volume of the stone?
   (b) What is the buoyant force exerted on the stone by the water?
   (c) What is the force of gravity acting on the stone?
   (d) What lifting force does the child exert on the stone?
4. A plastic bobber on a fishing line has a volume of 16 cm³ and a relative density of 0.20.
   (a) What is the mass of the bobber?
   (b) What is the force of gravity on the bobber?
   (c) What buoyant force does the water exert on the bobber when it is fully submerged?
   (d) With what force must a fish pull down on the line in order to just submerge the bobber?

5. A piece of marble of mass 1.40 kg and relative density 2.80 is hung from a spring balance by a light thread and lowered into a beaker of water sitting on a level triple beam balance. Before the marble is immersed, the triple beam balance reads 5.75 kg. What are the readings on both the spring balance and the triple beam balance after the marble is immersed and the triple beam balance is again levelled?

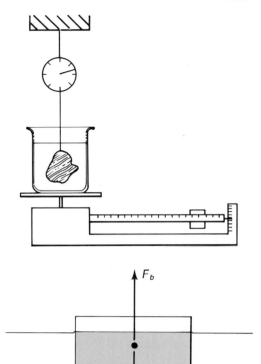

Flotation

When an object is floating, the buoyant force is equal to the force of gravity on the object, so that its "apparent weight" is zero. In general, the Principle of Flotation states:

A floating object displaces its own weight of the liquid in which it is floating.

The following sample problems will illustrate the use of this concept.

Liquid displaced, whose weight is equal to the weight of the floating object

Sample Problems

1. A barge has a mass of 4.8×10^5 kg and the area of its essentially flat bottom is 800 m². To what depth in fresh water will it sink when (a) empty, and (b) loaded with 20 cars of average mass 1000 kg? (Assume the sides of the barge are vertical.)

(a) When floating, the empty barge displaces 4.8×10^5 kg of water, which has a volume of

$$V_w = \frac{m_w}{\rho_w}$$
$$= \frac{4.8 \times 10^5 \text{ kg}}{1.0 \times 10^3 \text{ kg/m}^3}$$
$$= 4.8 \times 10^2 \text{ m}^3$$

The depth of water to which the barge must sink is

$$d = \frac{V_w}{A}$$
$$= \frac{4.8 \times 10^2 \text{ m}^3}{800 \text{ m}^2}$$
$$= 0.60 \text{ m}$$

(b) The new mass of the barge and its cars is

$$m_b = 4.8 \times 10^5 \text{ kg} + 20(1000 \text{ kg})$$
$$= 5.0 \times 10^5 \text{ kg}$$

and therefore, to float, it must now displace 5.0×10^5 kg of water, which has a volume given by

$$V_w = \frac{m_w}{\rho_w}$$

$$= \frac{5.0 \times 10^5 \text{ kg}}{1.0 \times 10^3 \text{ kg/m}^3}$$

$$= 5.0 \times 10^2 \text{ m}^3$$

The depth to which the barge now must sink is

$$d = \frac{V_w}{A}$$

$$= \frac{5.0 \times 10^2 \text{ m}^3}{800 \text{ m}^2}$$

$$= 0.625 \text{ m}$$

Notice that adding the 20 cars to the barge caused it to float only 2.5 cm lower in the water.

To solve this problem we must assume that the top surface of the block remains horizontal. In practice, the orientation of the floating cube is a very complex problem of stability, and it will not remain horizontal.

2. A cube of wood, of density 6.0×10^2 kg/m³, is 10 cm long on each side. (a) To what depth will it sink in water? (b) What is the density of a liquid in which it will sink with 8.0 cm immersed?

(a) For the wood cube,

$$m = \rho V$$

$$= (6.0 \times 10^2 \text{ kg/m}^3)(0.10 \text{ m})^3$$

$$= 0.60 \text{ kg}$$

Thus, when floating, the mass of water displaced by the cube is 0.60 kg.

For the displaced water

$$V = \frac{m}{\rho}$$

$$= \frac{0.60 \text{ kg}}{1.0 \times 10^3 \text{ kg/m}^3}$$

$$= 6.0 \times 10^{-4} \text{ m}^3$$

Then, for the depth to which the block sinks

$$d = \frac{V}{A}$$

$$= \frac{6.0 \times 10^{-4} \text{ m}^3}{(0.10 \text{ m})^2}$$

$$= 6.0 \times 10^{-2} \text{ m, or 6.0 cm}$$

(b) For the liquid displaced by the floating block,

$$V = lwd$$

$$= (0.10 \text{ m})^2 (0.080 \text{ m})$$

$$= 8.0 \times 10^{-4} \text{ m}^3$$

But the floating block and the liqud it displaces both have the same mass, 0.60 kg. Therefore, for the liquid's density

$$\rho = \frac{m}{V}$$
$$= \frac{0.60 \text{ kg}}{8.0 \times 10^{-4} \text{ m}^3}$$
$$= 7.5 \times 10^2 \text{ kg/m}^3$$

Hydrometers

Floating objects sink into a liquid until they have displaced an amount of liquid equal to their own weight. The depth to which they sink is, then, a measure of the density of the liquid in which they are floating, as Sample problem 2 indicated. Such a floating object, calibrated, may be used to measure the densities of liquids, and is called a **hydrometer.**

A practical hydrometer is usually a long, hollow glass tube weighted at one end so that it will float upright. When calibrated, a scale is marked on the hydrometer to show the density of the liquid at each particular depth to which it sinks, as shown.

Small hydrometers are used routinely in service stations to measure the densities of antifreeze mixtures and battery acid, thereby determining their concentrations. Antifreeze concentration indicates the temperature at which it will freeze, and battery acid concentration is a measure of the battery's state of charge.

Ships, Fish, and Submarines

Although a ship's hull is usually made of steel, which is considerably more dense than water, the ship floats. Because it is hollow, the hull displaces far more water than would be displaced by the steel alone. The "average density" of a ship, considering its hull, cargo, passengers, and all of the other things on board, including air, is still less than water, and so it floats. Some boats even have concrete hulls.

Fish neither float nor sink to the bottom. They usually remain suspended at a particular depth, but have the ability to rise or go deeper, as needed. To reach this equilibrium position, a fish must have a relative density of 1.0, exactly the same as water. They

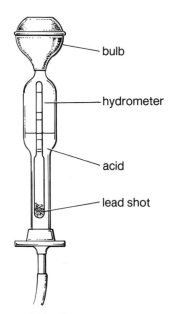

Battery acid hydrometer

The relative density of the sulfuric acid solution in a lead-acid storage battery is about 1.30 when fully charged, and about 1.15 when discharged.

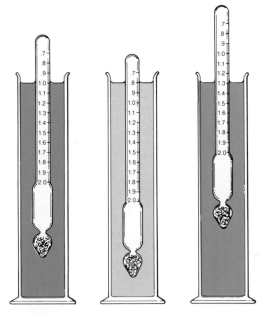

hydrometers

achieve this density by using a gas-filled sac, called a swim bladder, that reduces their density from about 1.08 to 1.00. When a fish contracts the swim bladder, its density increases slightly and it moves deeper in the water. When the bladder expands, density decreases, and the fish moves closer to the surface.

Large on-board water tanks allow submarines to control their depth in much the same way as swim bladders do for fish. To dive, a submarine takes water into the tanks, increasing its average density to a value greater than water's. To rise, compressed air is forced into the tanks to expel the water. This decreases the submarine's density to a value less than that of water, and it rises.

Lighter-than-Air Devices

Air exerts a buoyant force because it is a fluid. The air's buoyant force causes objects weighed in air to have an apparent weight that is slightly less than in a vacuum. For example, consider a small balloon filled with helium. As with all objects, gravity exerts a downward force on the balloon and its contents. However, helium is much less dense than air. The buoyant force of the air displaced by the helium-filled balloon is greater than the force of gravity acting on the balloon. As a result, there is a net force acting upwards on the balloon and it rises.

Lighter-than-air vehicles are based on this same Archimedean principle. Dirigibles, large hydrogen- or helium-filled airships, were popular in the 1930s. They transported hundreds of people in trans-Atlantic flights. You may have heard of the Hindenburg, the largest such airship, that crashed in flames near Lakehurst, New Jersey in 1937.

Hot-air ballooning is a sport that has increased in popularity. The air inside a large, fabric balloon expands when heated and becomes less dense that the colder air outside. This difference in density creates a buoyant force that is able to support the balloon, its gondola, and contents. Heating the air more causes the balloon to rise; allowing the air to cool causes the balloon to descend. The balloonist uses the ability of the balloon to rise and descend to maneuver it into air currents that cause it to move laterally. Because the balloon's lateral movement depends on the direction of the wind or air currents, it is very difficult to control and balloons have been known to land in some peculiar places.

ballast tanks

conning tower

keel

water

Surface   Diving trim   Submerged

Submarine diving

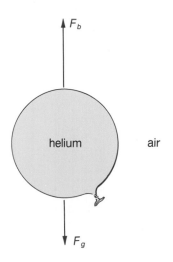

Practice

(Use the chart of densities on page 269 if necessary.)

1. A cube of oak with sides 15 cm long floats upright in water with 10.5 cm of its depth submerged. What is the density of oak?

2. When an iceberg floats in the ocean, what fraction of it is visible? (The relative density of ice is 0.92, and the relative density of sea water 1.03.)

3. A plastic duck floats half-immersed in water in the bathtub. What fraction of its volume would be immersed in a liquid of relative density 2.0?

4. A small rowboat with an aluminum hull and seats has a total mass of 80 kg.
   (a) What volume of aluminum is used in making the boat?
   (b) What is the buoyant force on this amount of aluminum when totally immersed in water?
   (c) What volume of styrofoam, of negligible mass, would have to be added to the rowboat so that it would stay afloat if it capsized and filled with water?

5. A rectangular piece of styrofoam of mass 3.0 kg floats with 5.0% of its volume under water. What is the maximum mass that the styrofoam can support without sinking?

6. A submarine of volume 4.67×10^3 m^3 and mass 4.39×10^6 kg is floating at the surface of sea water, of relative density 1.03.
   (a) What is the buoyant force on the submarine?
   (b) What volume of sea water does it displace?
   (c) What volume of sea water must its tanks take on to cause it to just submerge?

9.5 Bernoulli's Principle

To this point we have been studying the properties of fluids at rest, but we will now turn our attention to the behavior of fluids as they move. Liquids flowing through pipes, gases moving through ducts, and air moving in the form of wind are examples of moving fluids whose characteristics we will explore.

Let us begin by considering the steady flow of a fluid through a level tube, whose size changes as shown:

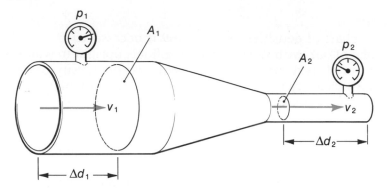

The larger tube has an area A_1, and the fluid at pressure p_1 is moving with a velocity v_1. The smaller tube has an area A_2 and the fluid at pressure p_2 is moving with a velocity v_2. In a given time, Δt, the fluid moves a distance Δd_1 in the large tube and Δd_2 in the small tube.

The volume of fluid moving through the large tube, in time Δt, is given by

$$\Delta V_1 = A_1 \Delta d_1$$

and the volume of fluid moving through the small tube in the same time is

$$\Delta V_2 = A_2 \Delta d_2$$

If the fluid flow is steady, and the fluid is incompressible, which is a good assumption for most liquids and even for some gases at constant pressure, then we can say that, in the same time

$$\Delta V_1 = \Delta V_2$$
$$A_1 \Delta d_1 = A_2 \Delta d_2$$

and dividing both sides of this equation by Δt, we have

$$\frac{A_1 \Delta d_1}{\Delta t} = \frac{A_2 \Delta d_2}{\Delta t}$$

But,
$$v_1 = \frac{\Delta d_1}{\Delta t} \text{ and } v_2 = \frac{\Delta d_2}{\Delta t}$$

so that

$$A_1 v_1 = A_2 v_2$$

This relationship is known as the **equation of continuity**, and is very useful in solving problems associated with steady fluid flow. It states that fluids move faster through smaller areas than they do through larger areas. An obvious example is a nozzle on a garden hose. With the nozzle wide open, water is ejected at the same speed as it moves through the hose. By constricting the opening, water comes out with a much greater velocity and, as a result, can be projected further.

Sample Problems

Water flows through a garden hose of internal diameter 1.5 cm at a speed of 2.0 m/s. With what speed does the water escape from the nozzle if the opening is reduced to a diameter of 0.50 cm?

For the hose,
$$A_1 = \pi r_1^2$$
$$= \pi(0.75 \text{ cm})^2$$
$$= 1.77 \text{ cm}^2$$

And for the nozzle,
$$A_2 = \pi r_2^2$$
$$= \pi(0.25 \text{ cm})^2$$
$$= 0.196 \text{ cm}^2$$

Therefore,
$$A_1 v_1 = A_2 v_2$$

so that
$$v_2 = \frac{A_1 v_1}{A_2}$$
$$= \frac{(1.77 \text{ cm}^2)(2.0 \text{ m/s})}{(0.196 \text{ cm}^2)}$$
$$= 18 \text{ m/s}$$

Practice

1. Hot air is supplied to a floor vent through a circular duct, of diameter 12 cm. Air leaves the hot air plenum from a furnace at a speed of 0.25 m/s in this duct, and is forced from the floor register at a speed of 0.90 m/s. If the hot air plenum has a square cross section, what are its dimensions?
2. A rectangular duct, of cross section 25 cm by 50 cm, carries fresh air to a room whose volume is 80 m³. With what speed must the air move through this duct, to replenish the room with fresh air every 5.0 min?

We learned previously that the pressure in a fluid at rest depends on depth. For a fluid in motion, its pressure changes as its speed changes. Measurements of fluid pressure at positions 1 and 2 in the tubes on page 292 reveal that the pressure p_1 is greater than p_2.

This relationship was discovered by Daniel Bernoulli, and its statement became known as Bernoulli's Principle:

For steady fluid flow, where the velocity of the fluid is high its pressure is low, and where the velocity is low the pressure is high.

This rather simple relationship explains the operation of a large number of useful and practical devices.

Daniel Bernoulli (1700-1782)
Daniel Bernoulli was a Swiss physicist born into a family of accomplished mathematicians. After a short stint teaching in St. Petersburg, Russia, he returned to Switzerland where his interest in fluids led to the statement of his now-famous Bernoulli's Principle.

To understand the behavior of gases under changing pressure and temperature, Bernoulli first assumed they were made up of a large number of small particles. He then applied the mathematics of probability and statistics to them. Over a century later, Maxwell and Boltzman expanded on this concept and added powerful support to the atomic theory.

Mathematically, Bernoulli's Principle may be expressed by the following equation, for the total energy of a fluid at a pressure p, of density ρ, moving with a velocity v, a distance h above a reference level of gravitational potential energy:

$$p + \frac{1}{2}\rho v^2 + \rho gh = \text{constant}$$

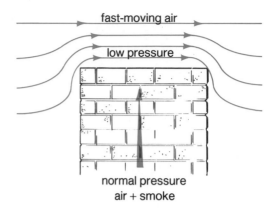

fast-moving air

low pressure

normal pressure
air + smoke

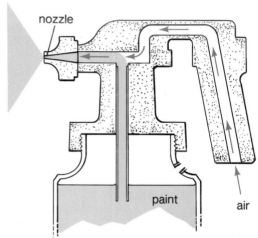

nozzle

paint

air

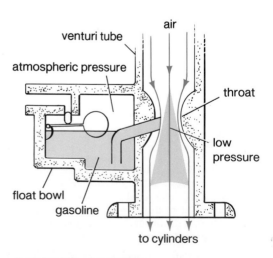

venturi tube

atmospheric pressure

air

throat

low
pressure

float bowl

gasoline

to cylinders

Automobile carburetor

9.6 *Applications:* Bernoulli's Principle

Chimneys

Hot air and smoke rise from any fire because of convection. A good chimney creates an updraught to draw smoke up the flue away from the fireplace, thus preventing smoke from entering the room. Air in the chimney flue is essentially at rest and at normal atmospheric pressure. Air, in the form of wind, is blocked by the chimney, and therefore moves quickly up, over the top of the chimney, and then back down, creating a low pressure region above the flue. This pressure difference causes the air and smoke in the flue to move upward out of the chimney and to be swept away by the wind.

Paint Sprayer

In a paint sprayer, fast-moving air from a compressor moves across the top of a vertical tube in a reservoir of paint, creating a low pressure area. The reservoir is open to the atmosphere, so normal atmospheric pressure pushes paint up the tube so that small droplets mix with the fast-moving air to form a fine spray.

Atomizers and spray cans use the same technique to mix fine drops of perfume, hair-spray, or household cleansers with the fast-moving air from a squeeze bulb, pump, or compressed gas propellant.

Carburetor

An automobile carburetor mixes gasoline droplets and air in much the same way, using a tube with a narrow constriction or throat, called a venturi.

Air is drawn into the venturi tube by the vacuum created by the engine. When the air passes through the throat, its velocity increases and its pressure drops. Normal atmospheric pressure on the surface of the gasoline in the float bowl forces gas into this air stream, where it mixes with the air before entering the cylinders for combustion.

Airplane Wings

Airplane wings and other air foils are constructed in such a shape that air passing over one surface has a greater distance to travel to maintain a steady flow, than does air passing over the other surface, as shown.

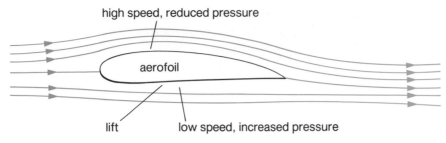

high speed, reduced pressure

aerofoil

lift   low speed, increased pressure

Consequently, the air that has to go further must move faster and, hence, be at a lower pressure. In the case of an airplane wing, this means that the downward pressure on the top of the wing is less than the upward pressure on the bottom, and the net result is an upward force, or lift, on the wing.

Formula I racing cars are often fitted with a rear wing, or spoiler, whose shape is opposite that of an airplane wing. In this case, the net force is down, pushing the fast-moving car against the road surface and increasing its traction.

Not only the rear wing spoilers, but the entire shape of modern racing cars is designed so that fast-moving air directed under the car creates a low pressure area, forcing the car down toward the road, increasing traction, and improving handling and acceleration.

Investigations

Investigation 9.1: Pressure in a Liquid

Problem:
How is the pressure in a liquid related to the liquid's depth and density?

Materials:
retort stand with two clamps
spring balance, calibrated in newtons, with thread
glass tube, 2 or 3 cm in diameter, with one end ground flat
metal plate, with hook, larger than diameter of glass tube
large beaker

Procedure:

Part A
1. As shown, clamp the glass tube firmly, in a vertical position over the beaker, flat end down.
2. With thread, suspend the flat metal plate from the spring balance, and measure its weight. Then clamp the spring balance so that the thread pulls up on the plate against the ground bottom of the tube with a force greater than the weight of the plate.

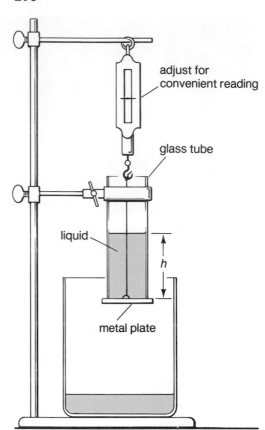

adjust for
convenient reading

glass tube

liquid

h

metal plate

3. Slowly add water to the glass tube and note the effect on the spring balance reading. Stop when water first begins to leak from the lower end of the tube, and record both the depth of the water and the reading on the spring balance.
4. Repeat 3 or 4 times using different initial spring balance readings, and record all of the data in a chart.
5. Measure the internal diameter of the glass tube.

Part B
6. Repeat the same procedure, but start with a large spring scale reading and fill the tube with a liquid of known density, to a specific depth.
7. Slowly lower the spring balance and note the effect on its readings. Stop when liquid first begins to leak, and record the spring balance reading.
8. Repeat 3 or 4 times using other liquids of known density to the same depth in the tube.

Calculations:

Part A
1. Calculate the cross-sectional area of the glass tube.
2. For each spring balance reading when leakage first occurred, calculate the force, F, of the water pushing down on the metal plate, using

F = spring balance reading – weight of metal plate

3. Divide each value of F by the cross-sectional area of the tube, to give the water pressure on the metal plate, p, when leakage first occurred.
4. Plot a graph of p versus d, the water depth, and comment on its shape.

Part B
5. Again, calculate the pressure on the metal plate when the liquid first begins to leak, in each case.
6. Using a reference, look up the densities of the various liquids and plot a graph of p versus ρ, liquid density. Comment on its shape.

Questions:
1. What is the relation between pressure and depth of a liquid?
2. What is the relation between pressure and density of a liquid?
3. What expression gives the joint relation between pressure, depth, and density of a liquid?
4. Why could you ignore the atmospheric pressure on the surface of the liquid in the tube?

CAUTION: For Investigations 9.1, 9.2, and 9.3 use vegetable oil ($\rho = 0.9$ kg/m³) and Karo syrup ($\rho = 1.4$ kg/m³). Avoid use of flammable solutions of alcohol.

Investigation 9.2: Buoyant Forces—Archimedes' Principle

Problem:
What is the buoyant force on an object immersed in a liquid?

Materials:
overflow can and beaker
spring balance with thread, calibrated in newtons
heavy object, such as a rock or metal solid
triple beam balance, calibrated in kilograms
three liquids of known density

Procedure:
1. Tie a thread to the heavy object and suspend it from the spring balance. Note its weight.
2. Fill the overflow can with water until it just starts to overflow. Find the mass of the dry beaker. When water has stopped dripping from the overflow can, place the dry beaker under its spout.
3. *Slowly* lower the heavy object into the overflow can, catching all of the displaced water in the beaker, and note the effect on the spring balance reading. When the object is completely submerged, record the final reading on the spring balance.
4. Find the mass of the beaker containing the displaced water.
5. Repeat the same procedure using two different liquids of known density.

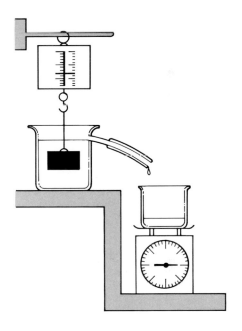

Calculations:
1. By subtraction, calculate the mass of liquid displaced by the submerged object, in each case. Determine the weight of the displaced liquid, in each case.
2. Also, calculate the buoyant force on the submerged object in each case, using
   F_b = actual weight of object − apparent weight of object
3. Enter all of the recorded and calculated data in a table, similar to the one shown.

Liquid	Weight of Object in		Buoyant force	Weight of:		
	air	liquid		beaker	beaker + liq	displaced liquid
	N	N	N	N	N	N
1						
2						
3						

Questions:
1. What is the relationship between buoyant force, the apparent loss in weight, and the weight of the liquid displaced, when an object is submerged?
2. How did the reading on the spring balance change as the object was being lowered into the liquid but before it was totally submerged?

Investigation 9.3: The Law of Flotation

Problem:
How much liquid does a floating object displace?

Materials:
large graduated cylinder
test tube with loop of thread attached
supply of metal shot
spring balance
three liquids of known density

Procedure:
1. Half fill the graduated cylinder with water and note the level. Attach a loop of thread to the test tube and place it in the graduated cylinder as shown.
2. Add metal shot to the tube, a little at a time, until the tube floats upright. Record the new water level in the graduated cylinder.
3. Remove the test tube from the graduated cylinder, dry it, and weigh it using the loop of thread to attach it to the spring balance. Do not remove the metal shot.
4. Repeat the same procedure several times, using different amounts of metal shot.
5. Repeat steps 1 to 4 for two other liquids of known density.

Calculations:
1. From the increase in liquid level in the graduated cylinder, determine the volume of liquid displaced by the floating test tube. Calculate the mass and weight of this volume.
2. Record all of the data and calculations in a chart similar to the one shown.

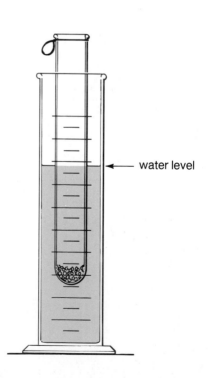

← water level

Liquid	Density	Weight of test tube and shot	Liquid displaced by test tube		
			Volume	Mass	Weight
	kg/m³	N	m³	kg	N
1					
2					

Questions:
1. What is the relationship between the weight of a floating object and the weight of the liquid it displaces?
2. Why would the same floating object sink to different depths in different liquids?
3. What practical device does the test tube and metal shot simulate? Describe how you might calibrate it.

Chapter Summary

1. Density is defined as the mass per unit volume of a substance, and is given by

$$\rho = \frac{m}{V}$$

   where density is expressed in kilograms per cubic meter or grams per cubic centimeter.
2. Relative density is the ratio of a substance's density to that of pure water at 4°C, and is a number with no units. The density of pure water at 4°C is 1.00×10^3 kg/m³.
3. Pressure is defined as the force acting perpendicular to a unit arca, and is given by

$$p = \frac{F}{A}$$

   where pressure is expressed in pascals (Pa). When a force of 1 N acts perpendicular to an area of 1 m², 1 Pa is the pressure. (1 Pa = 1 N/m²)
4. The pressure in a fluid at rest
   • is equal at equal depths in the fluid
   • acts equally in all directions
   • acts perpendicular to any surface the fluid contacts
   and is given by

$$p = \rho g d$$

   where ρ is the density of the liquid, d is the depth, and g is the gravitational force constant. This is in addition to any pressure exerted on the surface of the fluid.
5. Pressure due to the atmosphere acts on all objects and can be measured as the height of a column of liquid it will support, using a barometer.

$$\begin{aligned} \text{Normal atmospheric pressure} &= 760 \text{ mm Hg} \\ &= 101.3 \times 10^3 \text{ Pa} \\ &= 101.3 \text{ kPa} \end{aligned}$$

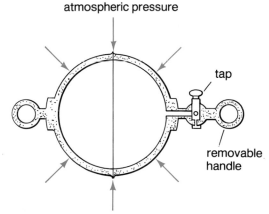
atmospheric pressure

tap

removable handle

This Magdeburg apparatus demonstrates the effects of atmospheric pressure. While the two hemispheres are held together, most of the air is extracted from between them using a vacuum pump. Then, because atmospheric pressure pushes them together, it is virtually impossible to pull them apart. Of course, once the tap is opened, the incoming air returns the internal pressure to normal and the hemispheres fall apart.

Everyday applications usually involve gauge pressures.

6. Gauge pressure is the difference between the actual pressure and the atmospheric pressure, and can be measured using an open-ended u-tube, called a manometer. Absolute pressure is the sum of gauge pressure and atmospheric pressure.

7. Pascal's principle states: "Pressure exerted on a contained fluid is transmitted throughout the fluid, undiminished, and in all directions, and acts perpendicular to the walls of its container." It explains the operation of hydraulic brakes, presses, and lifts, according to the relation

$$p = \frac{F_1}{A_1} = \frac{F_2}{A_2}$$

where $_1$ and $_2$ represent the input and output pistons.

8. A syphon is a flexible tube that can be used to transfer liquids from a higher to a lower level by first moving upward. Explanations are offered from an atmospheric pressure point of view and on a molecular cohesion basis.

9. Objects submerged in a fluid experience an upward buoyant force, F_b, equal to the weight of the fluid displaced, given by

$$F_b = \rho V g$$

where ρ is the density of the fluid , and V is the volume of the submerged object. This relation is known as Archimedes' Principle.

10. A floating object sinks into a liquid only until it has displaced its own weight of the liquid, so that the buoyant force is equal to the object's own weight, and the net force on the floating object is zero.

11. The density of a liquid may be measured by the depth to which a calibrated floating object sinks. Such a device is called a hydrometer and is used to measure the density of such liquids as antifreeze and battery acid.

12. When fluids move through confined areas, their velocity changes according to the relationship

$$A_1 v_1 = A_2 v_2$$

where A_1 and A_2 represent the cross-sectional areas of tubes through which the fluids move, and v_1 and v_2 represent their respective velocities. This equation of continuity implies that fluids move faster when they move through constricted areas.

13. Bernoulli's Principle states: "Where the velocity of a fluid is greater its pressure is less, and where the velocity is less its pressure is greater." This principle explains the operation of such devices as chimneys, atomizers, paint sprayers, carburetors, the lift on airplane wings, and the downward force on racing cars.

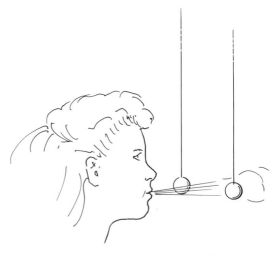

Suspend two ping-pong balls close together by light threads, as shown, and blow gently between them. Can you explain the unexpected result, using Bernoulli's Principle?

Chapter Review

Discussion

1. Give two reasons to explain why one substance might have a greater density than another substance, from a molecular point of view.
2. Explain how you can get a "paper cut" from the edge of a piece of paper, even though the paper exerts a relatively small force on your finger.
3. When measuring blood pressure, why is the pressure cuff always applied to the arm just at the level of the heart? What error in the reading would be introduced if the cuff were applied to the ankle of a person standing upright?
4. In preserving foods, Mason jars are boiled with their lids loosely attached. The lids are then screwed down tightly with metal rings while the jars cool. After cooling, the screw top rings are no longer needed. Explain.
5. How does the buoyant force on a scuba diver change as she moves from just beneath the surface of a lake to the bottom? How will the pressure on her body change? Why?
6. What would be the effect on a mercury barometer's reading of each of the following, considered separately?
   (a) The bore of the barometer tube was not uniform and got smaller near the top.
   (b) The air temperature increased noticeably while the atmospheric pressure remained the same.
   (c) The tube was tilted, so it was not exactly vertical.
   (d) Some air was introduced into the space above the mercury.
   (e) A reservoir twice the size of the previous one was used.
7. Draw a sketch of a u-tube manometer that is being used to measure the pressure of a partial vacuum.
8. A glass of water has a tight-fitting, rigid lid with a small hole in it. A glass straw is inserted into this hole and the joint around it is sealed tight. What will happen if you attempt to drink from the straw? Explain.
9. A man goes fishing in a canoe in a small, closed pond. He takes a heavy cast iron anchor from the bottom of the canoe and throws it overboard. Explain the effect on
   (a) the depth to which the canoe sinks in the water, and
   (b) the water level in the pond.
10. An ice cube is floating in a glass of water. After it is completely melted, what change would there be in the water level in the glass?

The heart pumps blood, under pressure, to all parts of the body. A measurement of blood pressure is an important indication of the state of a person's general health. The maximum blood pressure, when the heart is pumping, is called the systolic pressure, and the minimum pressure, when the heart is resting, is called the diastolic pressure. The doctor measures both of these pressures, in millimeters of mercury, and expresses them as the ratio of systolic to diastolic. Normal gauge blood pressure is about 120/80.

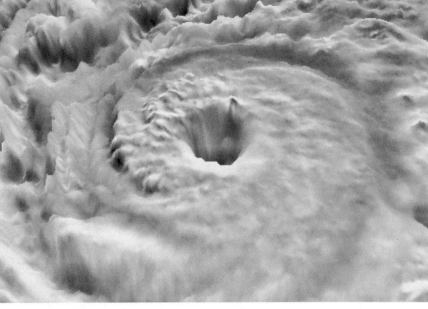

The eye of a hurricane

11. Why does a balloon filled with helium rise? Is there a lower limit on how much helium it must contain before it begins to rise? Explain.
12. What precaution would have to be taken to determine the "true mass" of an object? Explain.
13. During a severe hurricane or tornado, buildings often explode rather than collapse. Explain.
14. Explain why water from the bottom of a floating boat cannot be syphoned overboard.
15. Ask your teacher to show you a faucet with an aspirator in the lab. What do you feel when you place your finger over the opening on the side of the nozzle? Explain.
16. Write a 500-word report on a medical or industrial application of one of the properties of fluids studied in this chapter.

Problems

17. Calculate the mass of air in a room $14 \text{ m} \times 12 \text{ m} \times 3.5 \text{ m}$ if the density of air is 1.26 kg/m^3.
18. Calculate the hydrostatic pressure at a depth of 21 m in a fresh-water reservoir.
19. An open u-tube manometer contains alcohol of relative density 0.79 and shows a difference in level of 18 cm when connected to a supply of compressed gas. What is the gauge pressure of the gas?

Water towers provide high pressure water to millions of people for use in homes, industries, recreation, and fire-fighting.

Normal gauge water pressure from a household faucet is about 300 kPa.

20. One arm of a u-shaped tube open at both ends contains water, while the other arm contains motor oil of relative density 0.92. If the two liquids meet exactly at the bottom, and the level in the oil arm is 12.0 cm, what is the level in the water arm?

21. Theoretically, how high up a long straw could water be sucked, on a day when the atmospheric pressure was 102 kPa?

22. In a hydraulic brake system, the master cylinder has a diameter of 0.80 cm and the wheel cylinders have a diameter of 2.0 cm. If a force of 1.0×10^2 N is applied to the master cylinder by the brake pedal,
    (a) what pressure is transmitted by the brake fluid, in pascals?
    (b) what force does each wheel cylinder exert on its brake pad?

23. A hydraulic hoist has an output cylinder diameter of 30 cm, and an input cylinder diameter of 1.0 cm. If a force of 70 N is exerted on the input piston, what mass can be lifted? What is the mechanical advantage of this hoist?

24. A stone weighs 6.1 N in air, and its apparent weight when submerged in water is 4.1 N. What is its density?

25. The densities of air and helium are 1.29 kg/m³ and 0.178 kg/m³, respectively. What is the volume of a helium-filled balloon that experiences a "lift" of 8.90×10^4 N?

26. A nylon bushing, of mass 0.64 kg, sinks in gasoline, of relative density 0.68, and has an "apparent mass" of 0.090 kg when lifted below the surface. What is the density of the nylon?

27. A piece of wax of density 9.5×10^2 kg/m³ and mass 0.350 kg is anchored by a thread to a lead weight at the bottom of a beaker containing a salt solution, of density 1.06×10^3 kg/m³. If the wax is totally submerged, what is the tension in the thread?

28. A cylindrical hydrometer of mass 24 g and uniform cross-sectional area 0.80 cm² is floating vertically in water with 3.0 cm of its stem above the surface.
    (a) What is the length of the hydrometer?
    (b) What is the length of stem above the surface when it floats vertically in a liquid of relative density 1.2?

29. A geologist finds that a metal sample of mass 1.8 kg floats in mercury, of relative density 13.6, with 60% of its volume submerged. What is the density of the metal sample?

30. A ship of mass 1.20×10^6 kg is floating in sea water of relative density 1.03.
    (a) What volume of sea water does it displace?
    (b) If the ship sails into fresh water, what weight of cargo must be unloaded so that the same volume of water is displaced as before?

Hydraulic presses perform manufacturing functions that would be impossible manually. The use of hydraulics in industry, transportation, and on the farm has made life easier for many people and has given them more leisure time to enjoy.

Numerical Answers to Practice Problems

page 270
1. 3.9×10^2 m³
2. 5.5×10^3 kg/m³
3. (a) 3.2 kg (b) 9.7×10^2 kg/m³
4. 5.7×10^2 kg
5. 1.600

page 272
1. 1.4×10^4 N
2. 5.5×10^7 Pa
3. 1.23×10^4 Pa, 2.45×10^4 Pa
4. 1.5×10^{-2} m²

page 276
1. 8.0×10^3 Pa
2. 36 m
3. 2.9×10^6 N

page 282
1. 1.00×10^5 Pa
2. 1.5×10^3 Pa
3. 1.7×10^5 Pa
4. 1.0×10^4 Pa
5. 9.8×10^4 Pa
6. 2.5×10^{-3} N
7. 1.2×10^4 kg
8. 6.9×10^3 N

page 286
1. (a) 13.2 N   (b) 1.5 N
    (c) 11.7 N   (d) 12.0 N
2. (a) 1.6 N   (b) 1.6×10^{-4} m³
    (c) 0.31 kg   (d) 1.9×10^3 kg/m³
3. (a) 9.6×10^{-3} m³   (b) 94 N
    (c) 2.4×10^2 N   (d) 1.4×10^2 N
4. (a) 3.2×10^{-3} kg   (b) 3.1×10^{-2} N
    (c) 1.6×10^{-1} N   (d) 1.3×10^{-1} N
5. 8.8 N, 6.25 kg

page 291
1. 7.0×10^2 kg/m³
2. $\frac{1}{9}$
3. $\frac{1}{4}$
4. (a) 3.0×10^{-2} m³   (b) 2.9×10^2 N
    (c) 5.0×10^{-2} m³
5. 57 kg
6. (a) 4.30×10^7 N   (b) 4.26×10^3 m³
    (c) 4.08×10^2 m³

page 293
1. 20 cm × 20 cm
2. 2.1 m/s

31. A beaker of water is balanced on one side of an equal arm balance. A lead fishing sinker, of mass 50 g, is lowered by a thread and suspended, totally submerged, in the water. If the relative density of lead is 11.3, what mass must be added to or removed from the other arm to re-establish balance?

32. A certain brand of fishing line is advertised as "5 kg test line". What is the maximum mass of iron that can be suspended underwater by this fishing line without breaking it, if the relative density of iron is 7.6?

33. Air enters a carburetor through a tube of diameter 1.5 cm at a speed of 0.80 m/s. If the carburetor venturi reduces to a minimum diameter of 0.30 cm, what is the maximum velocity of the air-gas mixture moving through this throat? You may ignore the added volume of the gas.

34. A 4-cylinder 1200 cm³ car engine uses about 1200 cm³ of air (and gas mixture) every two revolutions. If the carburetor venturi has an inside diameter of 2.0 cm, calculate the average velocity of air flow through the venturi when the engine is idling at 800 rev/min.

Some careers that require an
understanding of the properties of fluids
studied in this chapter are:
medicine
deep-sea diving
robotics
fluid power technology
hydraulics
mechanical engineering
meteorology
aeronautics
transportation
auto mechanics
heating/air conditioning
hydrotherapist
naval architecture
oceanography

Meet a Meteorologist . . . Michael LePage

Michael works for a consulting engineering firm that specializes in microclimate studies. He is the only meteorologist on staff in a special laboratory where scale-models are used to study problems associated with wind, snow, air-borne pollutants, and the sun.

Q. Meteorologists are commonly known as weather forecasters but your work is somewhat different.
A. Yes, I'm not working strictly as a meteorologist but it's an important part of the work we do here.
Q. Describe the microclimate tests?
A. We use two main pieces of test equipment. One is a water flume, which is a long container filled with circulating water in which we place a model of a construction site. We drop sand into the water flume. When the water swirls in the same direction in which the wind swirls, the sand accumulates around the model buildings and on their roofs. This shows us exactly how snow would build up in a snowstorm. Designers of new buildings use this information to determine the strength of a roof. Also, the cost of snow removal is high and there are ways of positioning buildings so that snow doesn't accumulate as much.
The second main piece of equipment is the wind tunnel. At one end is a fan which can generate winds of up to 145 km/h. We place the model building, covered with tiny sensors, at one end of the tunnel. The sensors feed information to a computer that analyzes where the wind stress will come, what the wind will be like at the pedestrian level, and the wind speed of various locations.
Q. When did you first become interested in meteorology?
A. I was doing my Bachelor of Science degree in mathematics and took meteorology as an elective. I really enjoyed it and went on to get my Masters in meteorology.
Q. What does your job involve?
A. I spend most of the time at my desk preparing and writing reports. I meet with the clients who come to see their model being tested in the water flume and the wind tunnel. Sometimes I visit the site to take field measurements and get information for building the model. Much of our work requires travelling to different locations across the United States.
Q. What is the most interesting project you've worked on?
A. Recently we've been doing a series of tests for a domed stadium. We built a model of the stadium which was 60 cm tall, about 1/200th of the actual size. To test for drifting snow on the roof, we used ground walnut shells to simulate snow because they fall through the air at the same speed as snowflakes. In this way we can simulate snow loading on the roof in the wind tunnel. Computers are used to analyze the thousands of different readings. For the domed stadium we've also been doing an environmental impact study for the whole area. This involves testing vehicle emissions and pollutants emanating from smoke stacks in the area to determine air quality.
Q. What projects require extensive knowledge of meteorology?
A. One recent contract involved a roof collapse. Our firm was hired by the insurance company to determine whether the roof collapsed because of rain or wind. Their client was insured for one but not the other. I got weather maps and radar summaries, and recorded meteorology data from the area at the time of the event. I could then determine how much rain fell, where it fell, and where high winds occurred, and their maximum speed. I concluded that it was unlikely that the winds were high enough to cause the roof to collapse. Rain water was the culprit.
Q. What job opportunities are there for meteorologists?
A. Most meteorologists become forecasters, teachers or researchers at a university. Some specialize in aviation forecasting and work at airports. Many work in government environmental service branches. Then some, like me, do consulting work.

10

The Properties and Behavior of Waves

Chapter Objectives

- [ ] **Distinguish** *between objects vibrating in phase and out of phase.*

- [ ] **Relate** *frequency (or period) to wave speed and wavelength, using the Wave Equation.*

- [ ] **Predict** *how a given pulse will be reflected by the fixed end or the free end of a rope.*

- [ ] **Draw** *wave rays on wavefront sketches.*

- [ ] **Predict** *how a straight wave will be reflected by an obstacle, using the Laws of Reflection.*

- [ ] **Determine** *the resultant of two or more waves, using the Principle of Superposition.*

- [ ] **Determine** *the wavelength of interfering waves using a standing wave diagram.*

- [ ] **Relate** *frequency to wave speed and the dimensions of a standing wave pattern.*

- [ ] **Draw a diagram** *of the interference pattern between two point sources in phase.*

10.1 What Are Waves?

Energy can be transmitted from one place to another by a moving object, such as a baseball when thrown by a pitcher to a catcher. The kinetic energy given to the ball by the pitcher is transferred to the catcher. But this is not the only way to effect a transfer of energy. It can be brought about without any movement of matter from source to receiver—by means of a wave.

Imagine a cold winter morning. A car slides into the back of a line of cars that are stopped at an intersection. In the collisions that result, energy is passed down the line, from one car to the next. Such a travelling disturbance is called a wave.

When you push, pull, or shake a rope, you send waves down its length. When you shake a spiral "slinky" spring, your energy is transferred from coil to coil down the spring.

A water wave can travel hundreds of kilometers over the ocean, but the water just moves up and down as the wave passes. Energy is transferred from one water molecule to the next by the forces that hold the molecules together.

A **wave**, then, is a transfer of energy, in the form of a disturbance, usually through a material substance, or medium.

We live surrounded by waves. Some are visible, others are not. Water waves and the waves in a rope or spring we can see. Sound waves and radio waves we cannot. By observing the visible waves in ropes, springs, and water you can discover some characteristics that all waves, including invisible ones, have in common.

10.2 Vibrations

Most waves originate from objects that are vibrating so rapidly that they are difficult to observe with our unaided senses. For the purpose of observing the properties of vibrating objects, therefore, a slowly moving device such as a mass bouncing on a spring or, alternatively, a pendulum, is ideal. These are what we will use as our examples.

When an object repeats a pattern of motion—as a bouncing spring does—we say the object exhibits periodic motion. The vibration, or oscillation, of the object is repeated over and over with the same time interval each time.

When we describe the motion of a vibrating object, we call one complete oscillation a **cycle**. The number of cycles per second is called the **frequency** (*f*). The unit used to measure frequency is the **hertz** (Hz), named after a German scientist, Heinrich Hertz (1857-94), the discoverer of electromagnetic waves.

Another term used in describing vibrations is the **period** (*T*). Period is the time required for one cycle. Usually the second (s) is used for measuring the period, but for a longer period, like that of the rotation of the moon, the day (d) is used, or even the year (a).

Frequency and period are reciprocals. If the frequency is 60 Hz, the period is $\frac{1}{60}$ (or 0.017) s. If the period is 0.010 s, the frequency is 100 Hz.

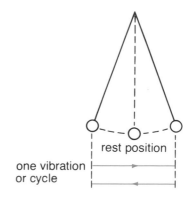

rest position

one vibration or cycle

$$\text{frequency} = \frac{\text{cycles}}{\text{time}} \qquad \text{period} = \frac{\text{time}}{\text{cycles}}$$

$$f = \frac{1}{T} \qquad T = \frac{1}{f}$$

$1 \text{ Hz} = 1 \text{ cycle/s}$

$\frac{1}{s} = s^{-1} = 1 \text{ Hz}$

Sample Problems

1. A pendulum completes 30 cycles in 15 s. Calculate its frequency and its period.

$$f = \frac{\text{cycles}}{\text{time}} = \frac{30 \text{ cycles}}{15 \text{ s}} = 2.0 \text{ Hz}$$

$$T = \frac{1}{f} = \frac{1}{2.0 \text{ Hz}} = 0.50 \text{ s}$$

2. What is the period of a pendulum that has a frequency of 10 Hz?

$$T = \frac{1}{f}$$

$$= \frac{1}{10 \text{ Hz}}$$

$$= 0.10 \text{ s}$$

Practice

1. A child on a swing completes 20 cycles in 25 s. Calculate the frequency and the period of the swing.
2. A metronome clicks 80 times in 20 s. What are its frequency and its period?
3. A stroboscope is flashing so that the time interval between flashes is $\frac{1}{80}$ s. Calculate the frequency of the strobe light's flashes.
4. Calculate the frequency and the period of a tuning fork that vibrates 24 000 times in 1.00 min.

Strobe photograph of an oscillating pendulum

As a pendulum swings, it repeats the same motion in equal time intervals. We say it exhibits periodic motion. Observing successive swings, we find that the distances reached by the pendulum on either side of the rest position are almost equal. In the same way a vertically bouncing mass on a spring exhibits periodic motion, and it too moves almost the same distance on either side of the rest position. This is a property of all objects oscillating with periodic motion.

The distance in either direction from the rest position to maximum displacement is called the **amplitude (A)** (see diagram).

The rest position is where the object will remain at rest. The object can move through its rest position.

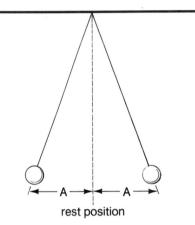

rest position

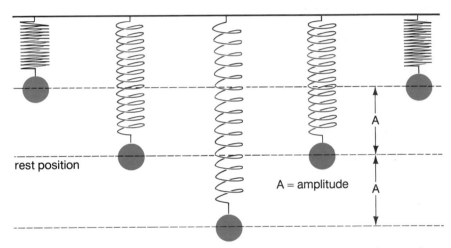

rest position

A = amplitude

Two identical pendulums are said to be vibrating **in phase** if, at any given moment, they have the same displacement from the rest position and are moving in the same direction.

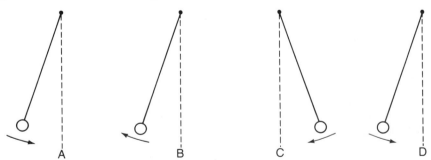

Pendulums A and D are in phase. B and C are not. B and D are not. Why?

The tines of a tuning fork do not vibrate in phase. When one tine moves to the right, the other moves to the left. The tines are said to be **out of phase**.

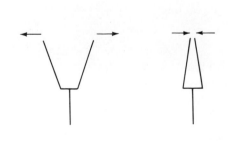

10.3 Wave Motion

A high wire artist kicks one end of the wire before starting to cross. She sees a small transverse movement dart along the wire and reflect back from the far end. The time taken for this round trip will tell her if the tension is correct. A football coach blows his whistle, creating fluctuations in the positions of air molecules and air pressure within it that make a shrill sound. Several children drop pebbles into a pond; the surface of the water oscillates up and down, and concentric ripples spread out in ever-expanding circles. Electrons shift energy levels at the surface of the sun, sending fluctuating electric and magnetic fields through a vacuum of space; eight minutes later they reach the surface of the Earth. These are all examples of wave transmission.

We should be quite clear about what is being transmitted. It is a disturbance from some normal value of the medium that is transmitted, not the medium itself. For the wire, it was a small sideways displacement from the normal equilibrium position. For the sound, it was a slight forward and backward motion of air molecules about their normal average position. In the water, the disturbance was a raising and lowering of the water level from equilibrium. The activity within the sunshine is a little harder to imagine, but here the disturbance is a fluctuating electromagnetic field where none normally exists.

Wave Terminology

The waves described above are examples of **periodic waves**, where the motions are repeated at regular time intervals. But a wave can also consist of a single disturbance called a **pulse**, or **shock wave**. Sometimes it is easier to observe a single pulse in a spring than to try to study a wave consisting of a series of pulses.

If you hold a piece of rope with your hand, and move your hand up and down, a wave will travel along the rope, away from you. Your hand, then, is the vibrating source of energy, and the rope is the material medium through which the energy is transferred. By moving your hand through one-half of a cycle, as illustrated, you can create what is called a **pulse**.

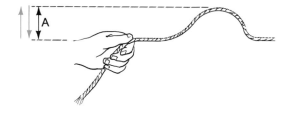

Chapter 10

When a water wave moves across an ocean or a lake, it moves at a uniform velocity. But the water itself remains in essentially the same position, merely moving up and down as the wave goes by. Similarly, when a rope is being vibrated at one end, the rope itself does not move in the direction of the wave motion: sections of the rope move back and forth or up and down as the wave travels along it.

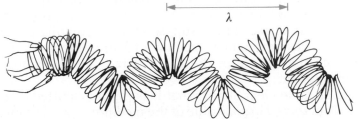

Pulses in a rope usually move too quickly to be properly observed, so we use a device such as a wave in a spiral spring, in which the speed of the pulse is relatively low.

Transverse wave in a coiled spring

Water waves and waves in a rope are examples of transverse waves. In a **transverse wave** the particles in the medium vibrate at right angles to the direction in which the wave travels. The high section of the wave is called a **crest** and the low section a **trough**. Since the crest lies above and the trough below the rest position (equilibrium), a crest is sometimes referred to as a **positive pulse** and a trough as a **negative pulse**.

Note, in the illustration below, that some of the pairs of particles on the wave are in phase, that is, they are moving in the same direction and are the same distance from the rest position. As can be seen, the distance between successive particles in phase is also one wavelength (λ).

In periodic waves, the lengths of successive crests and troughs are equal. The distance from the midpoint of one crest to the midpoint of the next, or from the midpoint of one trough to the midpoint of the

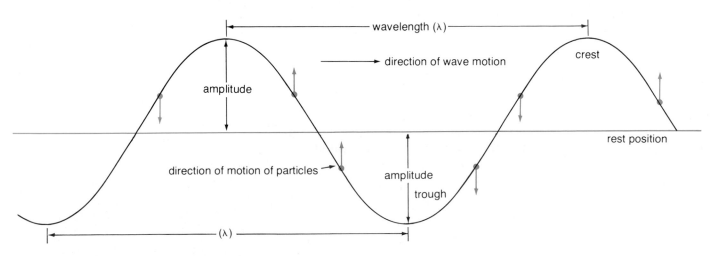

next is called the **wavelength** and is represented by the Greek letter λ (lambda). Note that in the illustration below, some of the pairs of particles on the waves are in phase; that is, they are moving in the same direction and are the same distance from the rest position. You can see that the distance between successive pairs of particles in phase is also one wavelength.

We have said that the amplitude of a wave is the distance from the rest position to maximum displacement. For a simple periodic wave, the amplitude is the same on either side of the rest position. As a wave travels through a medium, its amplitude usually decreases because some of its energy is being lost to friction. If no energy were required to overcome friction, there would be no decrease in amplitude and the wave would be what is called an ideal wave. As a rule, to make analysis easier, we will assume that the waves we are examining are ideal waves.

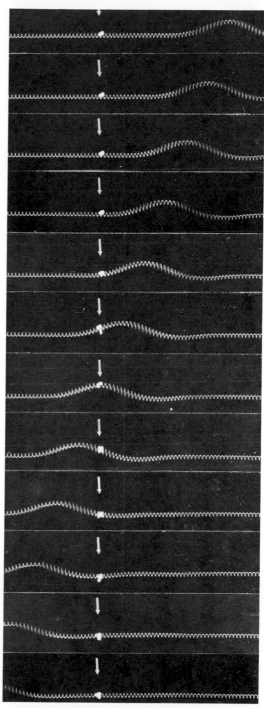

A crest moves through a spring from right to left.

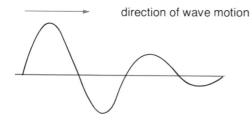 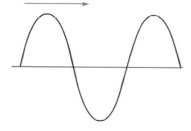

direction of wave motion

Most waves lose energy in the medium, resulting in a decrease in amplitude.

Ideal wave—no decrease in amplitude

In some types of waves the particles vibrate parallel to the direction of motion of the wave, and not at right angles to it. Such waves are called **longitudinal waves**. Longitudinal waves can be produced in "slinky" springs by moving one end of the spring back and forth in the direction of its length (see illustration on the next page).

The most common longitudinal waves are sound waves, where the molecules, usually air, are displaced back and forth in the direction of the wave motion. In a longitudinal wave, the regions where the particles are closer together than normal are called **compressions**, and the regions where they are farther apart are called **rarefactions**.

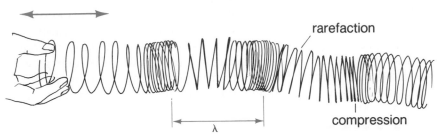

Longitudinal wave in a coiled spring

In transverse waves, one wavelength is the distance between the midpoints of successive crests or successive troughs. In longitudinal waves, one **wavelength** is the distance between the midpoints of successive compressions or rarefactions. The maximum displacement of the particles from the rest position is the **amplitude** of the longitudinal wave.

10.4 Transmission of Waves

If you hold a piece of rope with your hand, and move your hand up and down, a wave will travel along the rope, away from you. Your hand, then, is the vibrating source of energy, and the rope is the material medium through which the energy is transferred. By moving your hand through one-half of a cycle, as illustrated, you can create a crest, or positive pulse, along the rope. When you move your hand in the opposite direction, a trough is produced that also travels along the rope, right behind the crest. If the hand motion is continued, a series of crests and troughs moves along the rope at a uniform velocity. One cycle of the source produces one crest and one trough. The **frequency of the wave** is defined as the number of crests and troughs, or complete cycles, that pass a given point in the medium per unit of time (usually 1 s). The frequency of the wave is **exactly the same** as that of the source. It is the source alone that determines the frequency of the wave. Once the wave is produced, its frequency never changes, even if its speed and wavelength do. This behavior is characteristic of all waves.

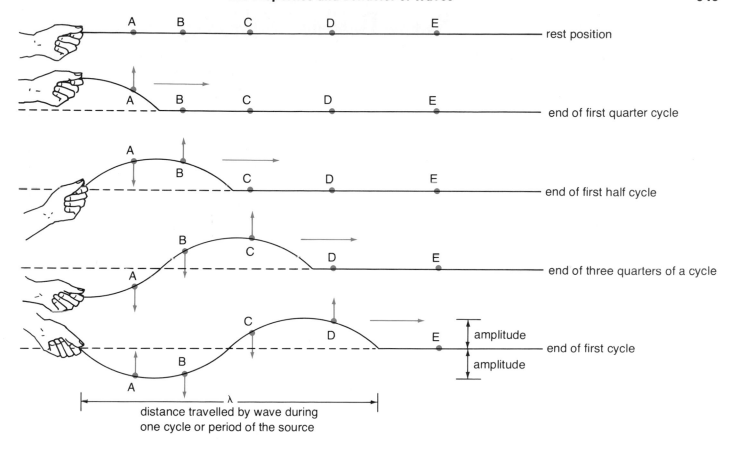

distance travelled by wave during
one cycle or period of the source

When a wave is generated in a spring or a rope, the wave travels a distance of one wavelength (λ) along the rope in the time required for one complete vibration of the source. Recall that this time is defined as the period (T) of the source.

Since
$$v = \frac{\Delta d}{\Delta t}$$

and
$$\Delta d = \lambda \text{ and } \Delta t = T$$

therefore
$$v = \frac{\lambda}{T}$$

But
$$\text{But } f = \frac{1}{T}$$

Therefore

$$v = f\lambda$$

This equation is known as the **Wave Equation**. It applies to all waves, visible and invisible.

Sample Problems

1. The wavelength of a water wave in a pond is 0.080 m. If the frequency of the wave is 2.5 Hz, what is its speed?

$$v = f\lambda$$
$$= (2.5 \text{ Hz}) (0.080 \text{ m})$$
$$= 0.20 \text{ m/s}$$

2. The wavelength in a water wave is 4.0 m, and the crest travels 9.0 m in 4.5 s. What is the frequency of the wave?

$$v = \frac{\Delta d}{\Delta t}$$
$$= \frac{9.0 \text{ m}}{4.5 \text{ s}}$$
$$= 2.0 \text{ m/s}$$
$$f = \frac{v}{\lambda}$$
$$= \frac{2.0 \text{ m/s}}{4.0 \text{ m}}$$
$$= 0.50 \text{ Hz}$$

3. The period of a sound wave from a piano is 1.18×10^{-3} s. If the speed of the wave in air is 3.4×10^2 m/s, what is its wavelength?

$$v = f\lambda$$
$$\text{or } v = \frac{\lambda}{T}$$

Therefore
$$\lambda = vT$$
$$= (3.4 \times 10^2 \text{ m/s})(1.18 \times 10^{-3} \text{ s})$$
$$= 0.40 \text{ m}$$

Practice

1. A source with a frequency of 20 Hz produces water waves that have a wavelength of 3.0 cm. What is the speed of the waves?
2. A wave in a rope travels at a speed of 2.5 m/s. If the wavelength is 1.3 m, what is the period of the wave?
3. Waves travel along a wire at a speed of 10 m/s. Find the frequency and the period of the source if the wavelength is 0.10 m.
4. A sound wave travels at 350 m/s. What is the wavelength of a sound with a frequency of 1.4×10^3 Hz?
5. A given crest of a water wave requires 5.2 s to travel between two points on a fishing pier located 19 m apart. It is noted in a series of waves that 20 crests pass the first point in 17 s. What is the wavelength of the waves?
6. An FM station broadcasts radio signals with a frequency of 92.6 MHz. If these radio waves travel at a speed of 3.00×10^8 m/s, what is their wavelength?

10.5 Transmission and Reflection

Water waves and waves in long springs travel at a uniform speed as long as the medium they are in does not change. But if, for example, two long springs that differ in stiffness are joined together, we find that the speed of a wave changes abruptly at the junction between the two springs. With a speed change there is a corresponding wavelength change. This wavelength change is predicted by the Wave Equation, $v = f\lambda$. Since the frequency of a wave remains constant once the wave is generated, the wavelength is directly proportional to the speed, that is, $\lambda \propto v$.

When a wave travels from a light rope into a heavy rope having the same tension, the wave slows down and the wavelength decreases. On the other hand, if the wave travels from a heavy rope to a light rope, both the speed and the wavelength increase. These properties are true of all waves. A change in medium results in changes both in the speed of the wave and in its wavelength. In a medium where the speed is constant, the relationship $v = f\lambda$ predicts that $\lambda \propto 1/f$. In other words, if the frequency of a wave increases, its wavelength decreases, a fact easily demonstrated when waves of different frequencies are generated in a rope or spring (see Investigation 10.2 on page 330).

One-dimensional waves such as those in a spring or rope behave in a special way when they are reflected. In the case of reflection from a rigid obstacle, usually referred to as **fixed-end reflection**, the pulse is inverted. A crest is reflected as a trough and a trough is reflected as a crest. On the other hand, if the reflection occurs from a **free end**, where the medium is free to move, there is no inversion— crests are reflected as crests and troughs as troughs. In both fixed-end and free-end reflection there is no change in the frequency or wavelength. Nor is there any change in the speed of the pulse, since the medium is the same.

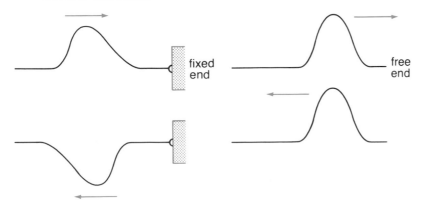

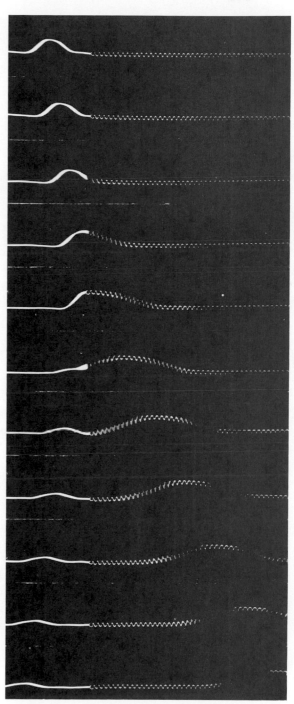

A pulse from a heavy spring (left) to a light spring (right)

On the other hand, when a wave travels into a different medium, its speed and wavelength change, as noted earlier. Also, at the boundary between the two media, some reflection occurs. This is called **partial reflection**, because some of the energy is transmitted into the new medium and some is reflected back into the original medium. This phenomenon is illustrated for a wave passing from a fast medium to a slow medium. Since the particles of the slower medium have greater inertia, this medium acts like a rigid obstacle, and the reflected wave is inverted. The transmitted wave is not inverted, however.

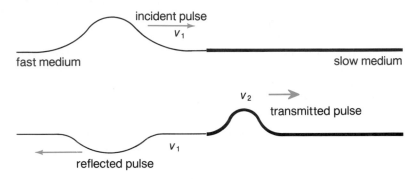

When a wave travels from a slow medium to a fast medium, the fast medium acts like a "free-end" reflection. No inversion occurs in either the reflected or transmitted wave, but there are changes in the wavelength and in the distance travelled by the transmitted wave, as illustrated below.

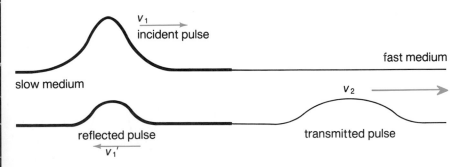

To summarize, then: when waves strike the boundary between two different media, partial reflection occurs. The phase of transmitted waves is unaffected in all partial reflections, but inversion of the reflected wave occurs when the wave passes from a fast medium to a slow medium.

A crest, moving right to left, is reflected from a rigid obstacle as a trough.

10.6 Waves in Two Dimensions

Waves in a stretched spring or in a rope illustrate some of the basic concepts of wave motion in one dimension. The behavior of waves in two dimensions may be studied by observing water waves in a ripple tank.

The ripple tank is a shallow, glass-bottomed tank on legs. Water is put in the tank to a depth of 2-3 cm. Light from a source above the tank passes through the water and illuminates a screen on the table below. The light is converged by wave crests and diverged by wave troughs, as illustrated, creating bright and dark areas on the screen.

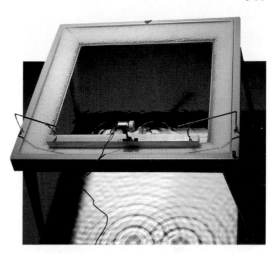

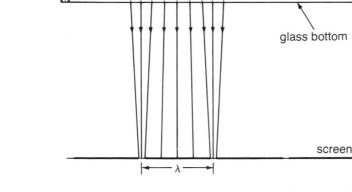

Bright lines occur on the screen where light rays converge.

The distance between successive bright areas caused by crests will be one wavelength (λ). Circular waves may be generated on the surface of the water by a point source, such as a finger or a drop of water from an eye-dropper. Straight waves may be produced by moving a dowel in the water.

Waves coming from a point source are circular, whereas waves from a linear source are straight. As a series of waves moves away from its source, the spacing between successive crests and troughs remains the same as long as the speed does not change. In other words, the wavelength does not change as long as the speed remains constant. When the speed decreases, as it does in shallow water, the wavelength also decreases.

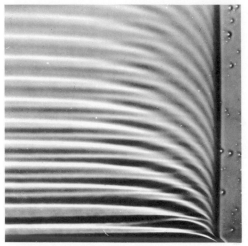

Waves travelling into shallow water, at the right, have a lower speed and a smaller wavelength.

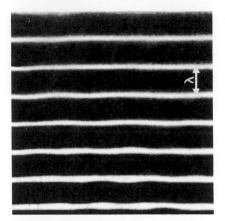

Periodic straight waves

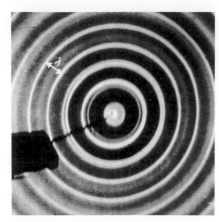

Periodic circular waves

When the frequency of a source is increased, the distance between successive crests becomes smaller. In other words, waves with a higher frequency have a shorter wavelength if their velocity remains constant.

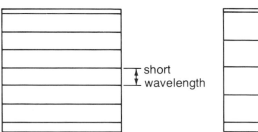

High-frequency waves

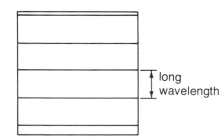

Low-frequency waves

Straight wavefront

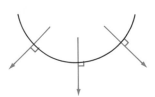

Circular wavefront

Although the wavelength and the speed of a wave may change as the wave moves through a medium, the frequency will not change. The frequency can be changed only at the source, and not by the medium.

The shape of a continuous crest or trough is called a **wavefront**. To determine the direction of motion, or transmission, of a wavefront, draw an arrow at right angles to the wavefront, as illustrated in the margin.

When waves run into a straight barrier, as illustrated below, they are reflected back along their original path.

If a wave hits a straight barrier obliquely, the wavefront is also reflected at an angle to the barrier. The angles formed by the incident wavefront and the barrier and by the reflected wavefront and the barrier are equal. These angles are called the **angle of incidence** and the **angle of reflection**, respectively.

Obliquely—"slanting, declining from the vertical or horizontal"

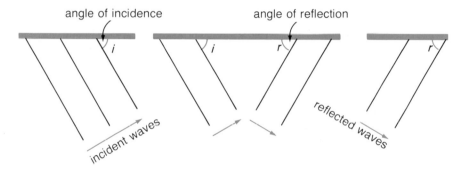

In neither case does the reflection produce any change in the wavelength or in the speed of the wave.

Sometimes we refer to **wave rays** instead of to wavefronts, in describing the behavior of waves. Wave rays are simply straight lines perpendicular to wavefronts indicating the direction of transmission.

When describing the reflection of waves using wave rays, the angles of incidence and reflection are measured relative to a straight line perpendicular to the barrier, called the **normal**. This line is constructed at the point where the incident wave ray strikes the reflecting surface. As may be seen from the geometrical analysis illustrated on the next page, the angle of incidence has the same value whether wavefronts or wave rays are used to measure it. In both cases the angle of incidence equals the angle of reflection. This is one of the laws of reflection.

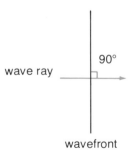

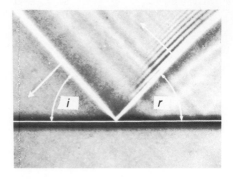

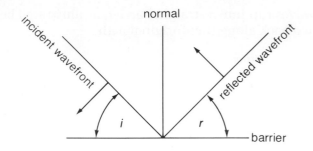

normal

incident wavefront

reflected wavefront

i r

barrier

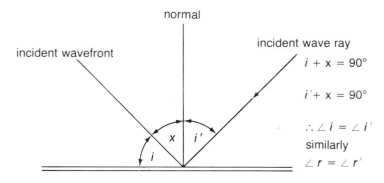

normal

incident wavefront   incident wave ray

$i + x = 90°$

$i' + x = 90°$

$\therefore \angle i = \angle i'$
similarly
$\angle r = \angle r'$

x i'

i

In the investigation (page 331) straight waves were reflected by a parabolic reflector to one point, called the **focal point**. This could have been predicted by means of the laws of reflection and wave rays.

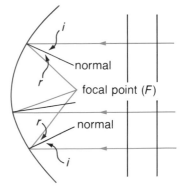

i

normal

r

focal point (F)

r

normal

i

parabolic reflector

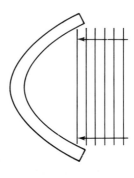

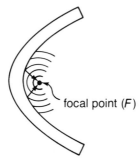

focal point (F)

10.7 Interference of Waves

Up to this point, we have been dealing with one wave at a time. What happens when two waves meet? Do they bounce off each other? Do they cancel each other out? When pulses travel in *opposite* directions in a spiral spring or rope, they pass through one another unaffected. This behavior is common to all types of waves. But continuous waves travelling out from a source may encounter other waves that either come from another source or are reflected waves from the same source. What happens, then, to certain particles in the medium when both waves continue to act on them at the same time?

When two or more waves act simultaneously on the same particles of a medium, whether in a simple rope or spring, or in water or air, we speak of **wave interference**. The resultant displacement of a given particle is equal to the sum of the displacements that would have been produced by each wave acting independently. This is called the **Principle of Superposition**. Note that the individual displacements may be positive (+) or negative (−). A plus or a minus sign must be included in each calculation of the resultant displacement.

In the example illustrated, pulses A and B are interfering, each making its own contribution to the resultant displacement of the particles in a medium. For example, point P in No. 3 is moved upward 8 mm by pulse A and up another 4 mm by pulse B for a total displacement of +12 mm. Other particles are moved varying distances from the rest position, each displacement being determined by the sum of the contributions of the two pulses. The solid lines represent the resultant displacement of all the particles at a given instant. The dotted lines represent the individual displacements of pulses A and B and are not seen when interference occurs. Only the resultant displacement is seen (solid line).

When pulses A and C interfere (next page), pulse A displaces the particles upward, whereas pulse C displaces them downward. Particle P is moved up 11 mm by pulse A and down 5 mm by pulse C, giving it a resultant displacement at one instant of +6 mm. The solid line indicates where other particles would be displaced by the interference of the two waves. Note that, in the areas of the medium where interference does not occur, the position of the particles in the medium (represented by the solid line) is that created by each individual wave.

Another statement of the Principle of Superposition is: "The resultant displacement of an individual particle is the algebraic sum of its separate displacements."

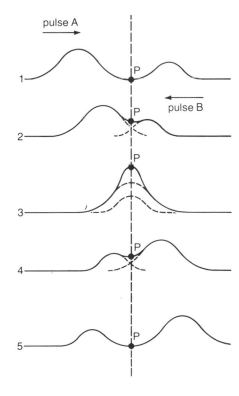

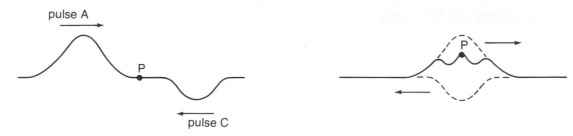

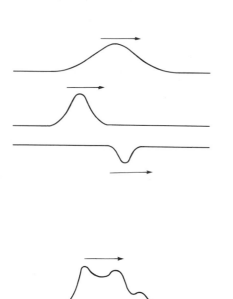

Three pulses and the resultant
displacement that is produced by
superposing them

When two or more waves interfere to produce a resultant displacement *greater* than the displacement that would be caused by either wave by itself, we call it **constructive interference**. When the resultant displacement is *smaller* than the displacement that would be caused by one wave by itself, we call it **destructive interference**.

The Principle of Superposition may be used to find the resultant displacement of any medium when two or more waves of different wavelengths interfere. In every case, the resultant is determined by an algebraic summing of all the individual wave displacements. These displacements may be added together electronically and the resultant displacement displayed on an oscilloscope, as illustrated. Once again, the resultant wave is the only one seen, not the individual interfering waves.

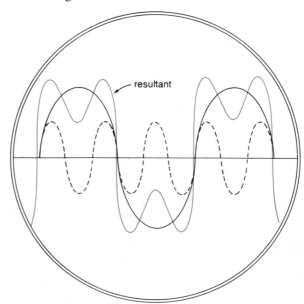

Resultant displacement as displayed on an oscillioscope. Note that only the solid blue line would be observed.

10.8 Standing Waves—A Special Case of Interference in a One-Dimensional Medium

The amplitude and the wavelength of interfering waves are often different. But if conditions are controlled so that the waves have the same amplitude and wavelength, yet travel in opposite directions, the resultant interference pattern is particularly interesting. It is referred to as a **standing wave interference pattern** or simply a standing wave. Whereas in most cases of interference the resultant displacement remains for only an instant, making it difficult to analyze the interference, standing wave interference remains relatively stationary. This makes it much easier to analyze and, therefore, a useful tool in the study of waves. Later, in Chapter 12, we will see its importance in the study of sound resonance.

When positive and negative pulses of equal amplitude and shape, travelling in opposite directions, interfere, there is a point that remains at rest throughout the interference of the pulses. This point is called a **node**, or **nodal point** (*N*). In the diagrams on the next page, two identical waves, A and B, are interfering. The resultant displacement caused by their interference produces areas of constructive and destructive interference. Note that the nodes are equidistant and that their spacing is equal to one-half of the wavelength of the interfering waves. Midway between the nodes are areas where double crests and double troughs occur. These areas are called **loops** or **antinodes**.

Standing waves may be produced by means of a single source. Reflected waves, for instance, will interfere with incident waves, producing standing waves. Since the incident waves and the reflected waves have the same source, and cross the same medium with little loss in energy, they have the same frequency, wavelength, and amplitude. The distance between nodal points may be altered by changing the frequency of the source. However, for a given length of rope or of any other medium, only certain wavelengths are capable of maintaining the standing wave interference pattern, because the reflecting ends must be nodal points.

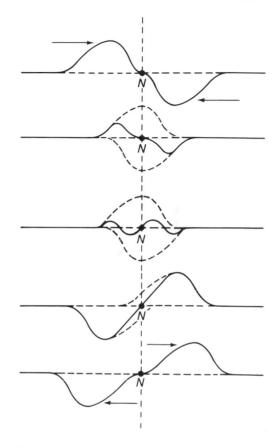

N = node point

This diagram shows a sequence of events as two identical waves travelling in opposite directions, A and B, interfere. Diagrams 1, 3, and 5 show the two identical waves interfering so that destructive interference occurs at every point in the medium. Thus, the resultant displacement line is horizontal. Diagrams 2 and 4 show the two waves interfering in such a way that there is constructive interference. The bottom diagram shows the resulting "standing wave interference pattern" created as the waves continually pass through one another. This is what would be seen by an observer (see next page).

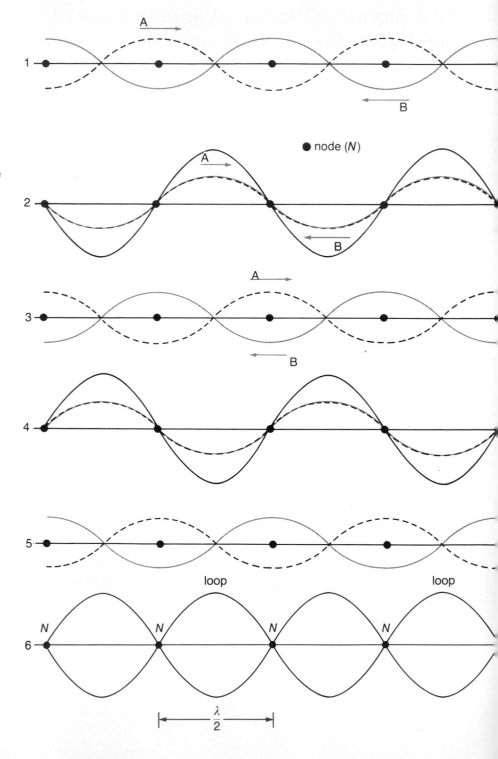

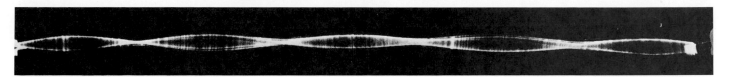

Standing waves in a vibrating string

Sample Problems

The distance between two successive nodes in a vibrating string is 10 cm. The frequency of the source is 30 Hz. What is the wavelength of the waves? What is their velocity?

The distance between successive nodes is $\frac{1}{2}\lambda$. Therefore the wavelength is 2(10 cm) = 20 cm.

$$v = f\lambda$$
$$= (30 \text{ Hz})(20 \text{ cm})$$
$$= 6.0 \times 10^2 \text{ cm/s}$$

Practice

1. A standing wave interference pattern is produced in a rope by a vibrator with a frequency of 28 Hz. If the wavelength of the waves is 20 cm, what is the distance between successive nodes?
2. The distance between the second and fifth nodes in a standing wave is 60 cm. What is the wavelength of the waves? What is the speed of the waves, if the source has a frequency of 25 Hz?

10.9 Interference of Water Waves

In a one-dimensional medium, such as a spring, successive regions of constructive or destructive interference may occur, sometimes producing fixed patterns of interference. What patterns of interference occur between two waves interfering in a two-dimensional medium—the ripple tank?

When two vibrating point sources are attached to the same generator, they have identical wavelengths and amplitudes. Also, they are in phase. As successive crests and troughs travel out from each source they interfere, sometimes crest on crest, sometimes trough on trough, and sometimes crest on trough. Thus, areas of constructive and destructive interference are produced. These areas move out from the sources in symmetrical patterns, producing nodal lines and areas of constructive inference.

A nodal line is a line joining a series of nodal points.

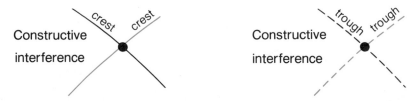

Constructive interference

Constructive interference

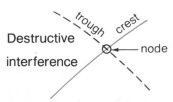

Destructive interference

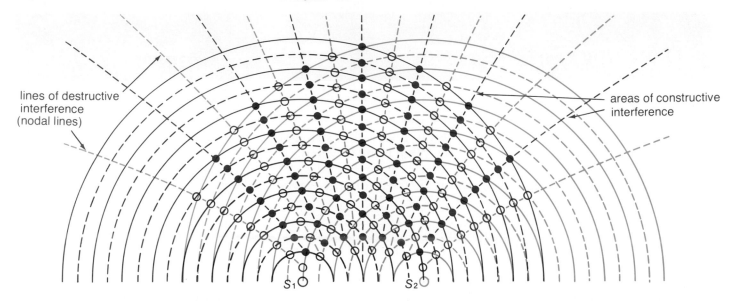

lines of destructive interference (nodal lines)

areas of constructive interference

The interference pattern between two identical point sources (S_1 and S_2), vibrating in phase, is a symmetrical pattern of nodal lines and areas of constructive interference in the shape of hyperbolae.

In the wave tank the nodal lines of destructive interference appear grey on the screen since the water is nearly level and the light is not refracted. (See Chapter 15 for more information about refraction.) Between the nodal lines are the regions of constructive interference. These appear as alternating bright areas (double crests) and dark areas (double troughs) on the screen.

Although the nodal lines appear to be straight when they move away from the sources, they are actually curved lines in a mathematical shape called a hyperbola. When the frequency of the sources is increased, the wavelength decreases, bringing the nodal lines closer together and increasing their number.

This **two-point-source interference pattern** is of great importance in the study of the interference of sound waves and light waves.

Having discovered many of the properties of waves, we can apply this knowledge in an investigation of the properties of sound, another wave phenomenon.

Investigations

Investigation 10.1: Analyzing the Motion of a Pendulum

Problem:
What is the relationship between the length and the frequency of a simple pendulum?

Materials:
apparatus as illustrated
stopwatch, protractor

Procedure:
1. Attach a simple pendulum to a rigid support, with the center of the bob about 100 cm below the pivot point. Measure the length of the pendulum from the pivot point to the center of the bob. Pull the bob aside about 20° and release it. Using a stopwatch, determine the length of time, in seconds, required for 10 cycles.
2. Decrease the length of the pendulum from 100 cm, in steps of approximately 20 cm, to a final length of about 20 cm. Determine the frequency of the pendulum for each length. Record your observations in a chart similar to that illustrated below.

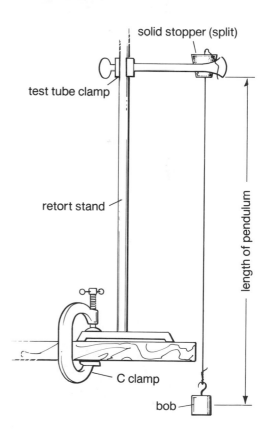

solid stopper (split)

test tube clamp

retort stand

length of pendulum

C clamp

bob

Length (cm)	Cycles	Time (s)	Frequency (Hz)	Period (s)
100				
80				
60				

3. Plot a graph of pendulum frequency (f) against pendulum length (L). Describe the graph obtained. What happens to the frequency of a pendulum as its length increases? What happens to the period of a pendulum as its length increases?
4. Adjust the pendulum length to the identical length used in your first observation. This time release the pendulum bob from approximately 10° so the pendulum vibrates with a smaller amplitude. Determine its frequency. Compare the frequency with that obtained when the pendulum oscillated with a larger amplitude, in step 1.

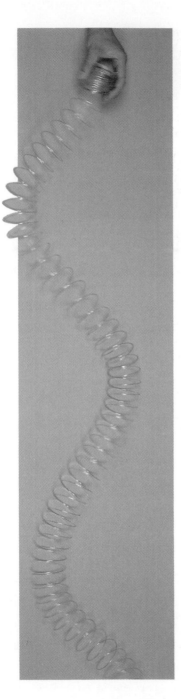

5. Replace the pendulum bob with one with a larger mass, making sure that the length of the pendulum remains the same (see diagram). Determine its frequency. Compare this frequency with that obtained in step 4.

Questions:
1. What effect does a change in the length have on the frequency and period of an oscillating pendulum?
2. For a pendulum with a fixed length, what is the effect on the frequency and period of an oscillating pendulum of
   (a) a change in amplitude?
   (b) a change in the mass of the bob?

Investigation 10.2: Transmission and Reflection of a One-Dimensional Transverse Wave

Problem:
How is a transverse wave in a coiled spring transmitted and reflected?

Materials:
long spiral spring

Procedure:
1. With the help of your partner, stretch the spring to a length of approximately 5 m on a smooth, clean floor. Your partner should hold one end of the spring rigid throughout this investigation.
2. Create a pulse at your end of the spring by moving your hand quickly from the rest position to one side and back to the rest position, at right angles to the length of the spring.
3. Describe the motion you observe of a point near the middle of the spring as the pulse passes.
4. Move your hand in such a way as to generate single pulses with different amplitudes. Does the amplitude of a pulse change as the pulse moves from one end of the spring to the other? Why?
5. Generate two pulses, one right after the other. Note how the distance between them changes as they move along the spring. What does this tell you about the speed of the pulses? Generate two more pulses, close together and one distinctly larger than the other. How does the amplitude of each pulse affect its speed?
6. Stretch the spring 2 m farther. How is the speed of each pulse affected by the change in the tension of the spring?

7. During the investigation, the pulses you generated at the free end of the spring were "reflected" from the fixed end. Compare the reflected pulses with the original pulses.
8. Suspend the spring vertically from a high point in the room so that it stretches close to, but does not touch, the floor. Avoid obstructions, since the spring must move freely along its whole length. (It may be necessary to bunch together some of the coils at the top.) Generate a transverse pulse at the top of the spring. Note whether the pulse is inverted when it is reflected from the "free" end of the spring. Compare the properties of fixed-end and free-end reflections.

Questions:
1. Describe what happens at a given point on the spring as the pulse passes.
2. Does the amplitude of the pulse change as the pulse moves from one end of the spring to the other?
3. Does the speed of the pulse vary as the pulse moves along the spring?
4. Is the speed of the pulse affected by changes in the amplitude?
5. Is the speed of the pulse affected by changes in the tension of the spring?
6. What change occurred in a pulse as it was reflected from the fixed end of the spring? from a free end?

Investigation 10.3: Longitudinal Waves

Problem:
How is a longitudinal wave transmitted through a spiral spring?

Materials:
spiral spring
masking tape

Procedure:
1. With the help of your partner, stretch the spring out to a length of approximately 3.0 m on a smooth, clean floor.
2. Attach masking-tape tabs at six equally spaced points along the spring.

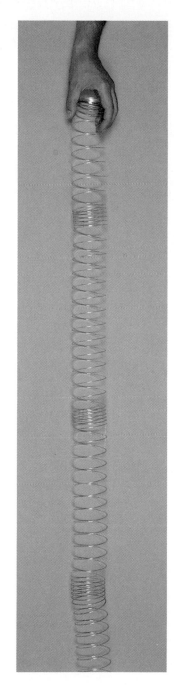

3. At one end of the spring, compress approximately 10 coils between your fingers.
4. Release the compressed coils and observe the motion of the masking-tape tabs as the pulse travels along the spring. Repeat this procedure a number of times, until the motion of the tabs is easily observed.
5. Place your hand in the coils at one end of the spring, and move your hand forward quickly. Note the motion of the tabs. Now, move your hand back quickly, and again note the motion of the tabs.
6. Move your hand back and forth quickly at a uniform frequency. Watch the series of pulses as it travels down the coil. Note the motion of the tabs.

Questions:
1. Describe how each section of the spring moved, relative to the direction of motion of the pulse along the spring.
2. What happened to the coils in the spring when your hand moved forward? (This is called a "compression".)
3. What happened to the spaces between the coils when your hand moved back? (This is called a "rarefaction".)
4. When you moved your hand back and forth at a uniform frequency, how did the spaces between successive compressions compare?
5. How many complete vibrations of your hand were required to produce one compression and one rarefaction?

Investigation 10.4: Water Waves—Transmission and Reflection

Problem:
How are circular and straight waves transmitted and reflected?

Materials:

ripple tank	wax blocks
light source	rubber hose
wooden or metal dowel	
screen dampers	

Procedure:

1. Put water in the tank to a depth of approximately 1 cm. Level the tank, to ensure that the depth of the water is uniform. (If necessary, place screen dampers at the perimeter of the tank to reduce reflection.)

2. Touch the surface of the water lightly at the center of the tank with your finger. What is the shape of the wave produced by such a point source? Make a sketch showing the wave and the source of the wave.

3. On your sketch, at four equally spaced points on the crest of the wave, draw arrows indicating the direction of wave motion. How can you tell, by the shape of the wave, that its speed is the same in all directions?

4. Generate a straight wave with the dowel by rocking it back and forth on the bottom of the tank. Does the wave remain straight as it travels across the tank? Does its speed change? In what direction does the wave move, relative to its crest? Draw a straight wave, showing the direction of its motion.

5. Generate continuous straight waves by rocking the dowel back and forth steadily. What happens to the wavelength if you reduce the frequency? Does the speed change? What do you predict will be the effect on the wavelength and on the speed of the waves if the frequency is increased?

6. Prop up the tank so that the water on one side is only 1 mm deep. Send straight waves from the deep end to the shallow end. In what way do the speed and the wavelength change as the waves move to the shallow end? Make a sketch illustrating any changes in wavelength.

7. Reduce the level in the tank to a depth of approximately 0.5 cm.

8. Form a straight barrier on one side of the tank, using the wax blocks sitting on edge on the bottom. Send straight waves towards the barrier so that their wavefronts are parallel to the barrier. How does the direction of transmission of the incoming, or incident, wavefronts compare with that of the reflected wavefronts? Does the speed or the wavelength of the waves change after they have been reflected? Make a diagram illustrating your observations.

9. Now arrange the barrier so that the waves strike it at an angle. How does the angle between incident wavefronts and the barrier compare with the angle between reflected wavefronts and the barrier? To help you judge the angles, align rulers or other straight objects with the wavefront images on the screen below. Make a diagram showing incident wavefronts and reflected wavefronts and their directions of transmission.

CAUTION: Keep the power cord away from any water. Your hands should be dry when handling the cord.

Adding a drop of liquid detergent to the water breaks down the surface tension in the water, making the shadows created by the barriers more distinct.

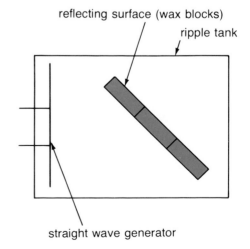

reflecting surface (wax blocks)

ripple tank

straight wave generator

10. Place some rubber tubing in the tank, allowing it to fill with water. Bend the tubing into the approximate shape of a parabola. With the dowel, generate straight waves towards the open side of the parabola. Observe how the wavefronts move before and after they strike the curved barrier. Record your observations in a sketch. Using your finger as a point source, generate circular waves that are reflected from the parabolic barrier as straight waves.

Questions:
1. What is the direction of the wave motion relative to the crest of a wave?
2. How does a decrease in the frequency of the source affect the wavelength of the waves? How is the wavelength affected if the frequency increases?
3. How is the speed of a wave affected by a change in frequency?
4. If the depth of the water decreases, what happens to the speed and the wavelength of a wave?
5. When a straight wave strikes a barrier so that its wavefront is parallel to the barrier, in what direction is the wave reflected?
6. When an incident wavefront strikes a barrier at an angle (that is, obliquely), how do the angles between the barrier and the incident and reflected wavefronts compare?
7. How are straight waves reflected by a parabolic reflector?

Investigation 10.5: Interference of Waves in a One-Dimensional Medium

Problem:
How do waves, moving in opposite directions, interfere in a one-dimensional medium?

Materials:
a spiral spring with tabs or a length of rubber tubing (or a wave machine)

Procedure:
1. Stretch the spiral spring or the rubber tubing between yourself and your partner. Or use the wave machine.
2. Simultaneously, generate positive pulses from both ends of the medium. Are the two pulses reflected off each other or do they pass through each other unaffected? Check your answer by simultaneously generating a positive pulse from one end and a negative pulse from the other.

A positive pulse = a crest. A negative pulse = a trough. See Section 10.3.

3. Noting a specific point near the middle of the medium, simultaneously generate positive pulses from both ends. How is the point affected when the two pulses act on it at the same time? What do you predict would happen if two negative pulses were used? Check your prediction.
4. Simultaneously generate a positive pulse from one end and a negative pulse from the other. How are certain points, located near the middle of the medium, affected when these two pulses act on them at the same time?

Questions:
1. How is a pulse affected when it passes through another pulse?
2. When two positive or two negative pulses act on the same particles at the same time, is the resultant displacement greater or smaller than it would be in the case of a single pulse acting alone?
3. When a positive and a negative pulse act simultaneously on a particle in a medium, is the resultant displacement greater or smaller than it would be in the case of either of the pulses acting alone?

Investigation 10.6: Standing Waves in a One-Dimensional Medium

Problem:
How are standing waves produced in a one-dimensional medium?

Materials:
a spiral spring or a length of rubber tubing (or a wave machine)

Procedure:
1. Simultaneously generate a series of waves of equal frequency and amplitude from each end of the medium (spring or tubing). Adjust the frequency until the medium maintains a fixed pattern. Compare the displacement of some particles in the medium with that of other particles. Draw a sketch illustrating the resultant displacement of the medium.
2. Change the frequency of the waves. How is the pattern affected when the frequency is increased? Decreased?
3. Fix one end of the medium rigidly. Generate a series of waves towards the fixed end. What is the effect on the medium when the incident waves interfere with the reflected waves? How is the pattern affected by changes in the frequency of the source? What is the resultant displacement, at all times, of the end of the medium (where the wave is reflected)?

Questions:

1. On your sketch of a standing wave interference pattern (step 1), indicate the points of constructive interference and destructive interference.
2. For complete destructive interference, what must be true of the wavelengths and amplitudes of the two waves?
3. Why is it easier to produce standing waves by the use of reflection than by means of two vibrating sources acting on the same medium?
4. In the standing wave interference pattern, what distance constitutes a wavelength?
5. Why is it easier to measure the wavelength of a wave using the standing wave interference pattern than it is to measure it directly?

Investigation 10.7: Interference of Water Waves in a Ripple Tank

CAUTION: Keep the power cord away from any water. Your hands should be dry when handling the cord.

Problem:
What patterns of interference are produced by identical water waves in a ripple tank?

Materials:
ripple tank
wax blocks
wave generator
straight wave source
two point sources

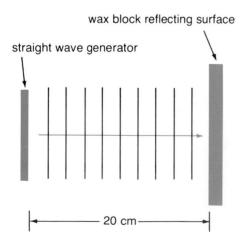

wax block reflecting surface

straight wave generator

|← 20 cm →|

Procedure:

1. Set up the ripple tank and put water in it to a depth of 1 cm.
2. Make a wave with one finger and then start a second wave some distance away. Observe the two waves. Repeat the procedure for various points in the tank. Do the two waves affect each other? Are they changed as a result of interference?
3. With the wax blocks, create a straight reflecting barrier approximately 20 cm from the straight wave generator and parallel to it.
4. Adjust the frequency of the wave generator so that a standing wave pattern is produced. Record your observations in a sketch, labelling one wavelength.
5. Increase the frequency of the source. What change occurs in the interference pattern?
6. Remove the wax blocks and the straight wave source and attach the point sources to the generator so that they are approximately 5 cm apart. Make sure that the two sources are in phase.

7. Adjust the generator to a frequency of approximately 10 Hz. Make a sketch of the interference pattern.
8. Increase the frequency of the generator gradually. Sketch the pattern at one higher frequency.

In the ripple tank, crests produce bright areas and troughs produce dark areas when illuminated from above. Undisturbed or flat water (nodal areas) appears semi-bright or grey.

Questions:

1. When two waves pass through each other, is either of them permanently changed? Was this true for one-dimensional interference?
2. What happened to the standing wave interference pattern when the frequency was increased? Why?
3. Describe in words the interference pattern between two point sources in phase.

Chapter Summary

1. A wave is a transfer of energy through a medium in the form of a disturbance. All waves originate from a vibrating source.
2. Frequency is the number of cycles per second. One cycle in one second is defined as one hertz (Hz).
3. The period is the time required for one cycle, and the unit in which the period is expressed is usually the second.
4. The frequency (f) and the period (T) are related by these equations:

$$f = \frac{1}{T} \text{ or } T = \frac{1}{f}$$

5. Particles or objects are said to be vibrating in phase if at any instant they have the same frequency, have the same displacement from their rest positions, and are moving in the same direction. If any one of these conditions is absent, the vibrating particles or objects are not in phase.
6. In a transverse wave, the particles of the medium move at right angles to the direction of the wave motion, while in a longitudinal wave, the particles in the medium vibrate parallel to the direction in which the wave is moving.
7. A transverse wave consists of alternate crests and troughs, whereas a longitudinal wave consists of alternate compressions and rarefactions.
8. One wavelength is the distance between equivalent points on successive crests or troughs, while in a longitudinal wave it is the distance between the midpoints of successive compressions or rarefactions.

9. The speed of a wave is unaffected by changes in the frequency or amplitude of the vibrating source.

10. If the frequency of a wave increases, the wavelength decreases provided that the medium does not change.

11. One vibration of the source produces one complete wavelength.

12. The frequency and the period of a wave are the same as those of the source, and they are not affected by changes in the speed of the wave.

13. An equation governing all waves is: $v = f\lambda$. It is called the Wave Equation.

14. Pulses reflected from a rigid obstacle (or a fixed end) are inverted. Pulses reflected from a free end are not inverted.

15. A wave ray is a straight line drawn at right angles to the wavefront, indicating the direction of the wave motion.

16. When waves are reflected from a solid obstacle, the angle of incidence is always equal to the angle of reflection. This is one of the laws of reflection and it holds for both curved and flat reflecting surfaces.

17. Waves can pass through each other in a medium without affecting one another. Only the medium is affected, momentarily.

18. The resultant displacement of a particle is the algebraic sum of the individual displacements contributed by each wave. This is called the Principle of Superposition.

19. If the resultant displacement is greater than that caused by either wave, alone, constructive interference is occurring. If it is less, destructive interference is occurring.

20. For total destructive interference to occur, with a resultant displacement of zero, the waves interfering must have identical frequencies, wavelengths, and amplitudes.

21. Nodal points, or nodes, are points in a medium that are continuously at rest, that is, the resultant displacement of the particles at these points is always zero. Points in a medium at which constructive interference always occurs are called loops.

22. A stationary interference pattern of successive nodes and loops in a medium is called a standing wave interference pattern.

23. The distance between successive nodes or loops in a standing wave interference pattern is one-half the wavelength of the interfering waves.

24. The interference pattern between two identical point sources, vibrating in phase, is a symmetrical pattern of alternating nodal lines and areas of constructive interference loops in the shape of hyperbolae.

Chapter Review

Discussion

1. One of the most important inventions in the history of science was the pendulum clock. Although it was first proposed by Galileo (1564-1642), it was Christian Huygens (1629-1695) who improved it so that it kept accurate time. Why does the pendulum keep accurate time? Why is it considered a landmark in the history of science?

2. A pulse is a wave of short duration. How could the driver of a diesel locomotive demonstrate a pulse in a train of freight cars?

3. How could you demonstrate a pulse, given six billiard balls and a flat billiard table?

4. You send a pulse down a string that is attached to a second string with unknown properties. The pulse returns to you inverted and with a smaller amplitude. Is the speed of the waves faster or slower in the second string? Explain your reasoning.

5. What happens when two billiard balls, rolling towards one another, collide head on? How does this differ from two waves or pulses that collide head on?

6. When a stone is dropped into water, the resulting ripples spread farther and farther out, getting smaller and smaller in amplitude until they disappear. Why does the amplitude eventually decrease to zero?

7. When standing waves are produced in a string, total destructive interference occurs at the nodes. What has happened to the wave energy?

Problems

8. A pendulum swings back and forth 20 times in 15 s. Calculate its period and its frequency.

9. A swimmer notices that 30 waves strike a breakwater in 1.00 min. What is the period of the waves in seconds?

10. Determine the frequency in each of the following.
    (a) a basketball player who scores 36 points in 24 min
    (b) a roadrunner who escapes from a coyote 27 times in a 9 min cartoon
    (c) a fan that turns 170 times in 15.0 s

11. Determine the period of each of the following.
    (a) the pulse from a human heartbeat that is heard 24 times in 15 s
    (b) a tuning fork that vibrates 2048 times in 8.0 s

    (c) the moon, which travels around the Earth six times in 163.8 d

12. Calculate the frequency of each of the following periods.
    (a) 5.0 s   (b) 0.80 s
    (c) 2.5×10^{-2} s   (d) 0.40 min

13. Calculate the period of each of the following frequencies.
    (a) 10 Hz   (b) 0.25 Hz
    (c) 500 kHz   (d) 3.5 Hz

14. The horizontal distance between the end points in the swing of a pendulum is 8.0 cm. What is the amplitude?

15. The tine of a tuning fork, when struck, has an amplitude of 0.13 cm. If the frequency of the fork is 200 Hz, what total distance will the tine travel in 1.00 min?

16. A cross section of a wave is shown below. Name the parts of the wave indicated by the letters on the diagram.

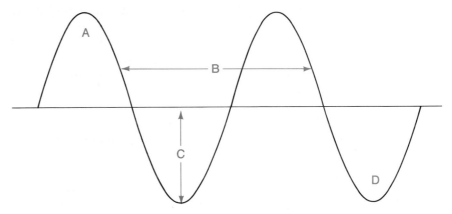

17. The diagram shows the profile of waves in a ripple tank.

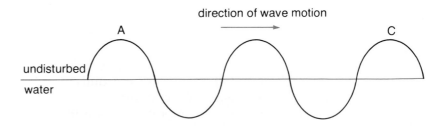

    (a) By measuring, find the wavelength and the amplitude of the waves.
    (b) If crest A takes 2.0 s to move to where crest C is now,
        (i)   what is the speed of the waves?
        (ii) what is the frequency of the waves?
        (iii) what is the frequency of the source?

18. The wavelength of a water wave is 8.0 m and its speed is 2.0 m/s. How many waves will pass a fixed point in the water in 1.0 min?

19.

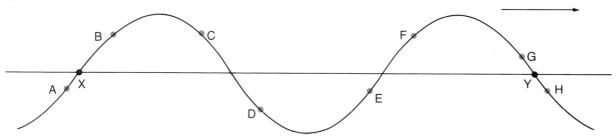

Examine this diagram of a wave and
(a) list all pairs of points that are in phase.
(b) determine the wavelength, in centimeters, by direct measurement.
(c) determine the speed of the waves, if they take 0.50 s to travel from X to Y.

20. Water waves with a wavelength of 6.0 m approach a lighthouse at 5.6 m/s.
(a) What is the frequency of the waves?
(b) What is their period?

21. 5.0 Hz waves move along a rope with a wavelength of 40 cm. What is their speed?

22. The distance between successive crests in a series of water waves is 5.0 m, and the crests travel 8.6 m in 5.0 s. Calculate the frequency of a block of wood bobbing up and down in the water.

23. Two people are fishing from small boats located 30 m apart. Waves pass through the water, and each person's boat bobs up and down 15 times in 1.0 min. At a time when one boat is on a crest, the other one is in a trough, and there is one crest between the two boats. What is the speed of the waves?

24. The wavelength of a water wave is 3.7 m and its period is 1.5 s. Calculate
(a) the speed of the wave.
(b) the time required for the wave to travel 100 m.
(c) the distance travelled by the wave in 1.00 min.

25. A water wave travels 60 cm in 2.0 s. If the wavelength is 5.0 cm, what is the frequency of the wave?

26. A boat at anchor is rocked by waves whose crests are 30 m apart and whose speed is 8.0 m/s. What is the interval of time between crests striking the boat?

27. What is the speed of a sound wave with a wavelength of 3.4 m and a frequency of 100 Hz?

28. The period of a sound wave emitted by a vibrating guitar string is 3.0×10^{-3} s. If the speed of the sound wave is 360 m/s, what is its wavelength?

29. A television station broadcasts with a frequency of 90 MHz. If the speed of the electromagnetic waves emitted by the station tower is 3.0×10^8 m/s, what is the wavelength of the waves?

30. The frequency assigned to an FM (frequency modulation) station is 102 MHz. What is the wavelength of the waves if they travel at 3.0×10^8 m/s?

31. Bats emit ultrasonic sound to help them locate obstacles. The waves have a frequency of 5.5×10^4 Hz. If they travel at 350 m/s, what is their wavelength?

32. What are the wavelengths in air of the lowest and the highest audible frequencies if the range of human hearing is 20 Hz to 20 kHz and the speed of sound is 342 m/s?

33. The diagram in the margin shows two pulses approaching one another. Sketch the appearance of the medium when the centers of the pulses coincide.

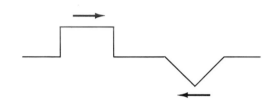

34. Two pulses move towards each other as illustrated. Sketch the resultant shape of the medium when the two pulses overlap.

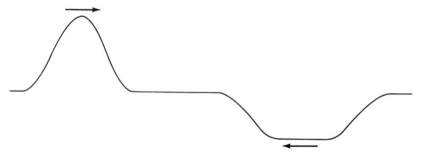

35. Trace the pulses illustrated into your notebook, and determine the resultant displacement of the particles of the medium at each instant, using the Principle of Superposition.

(a)

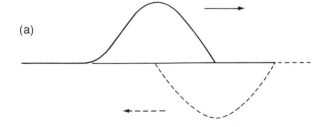

(b)

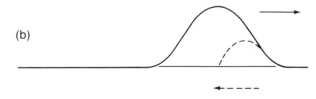

(c)

(d)

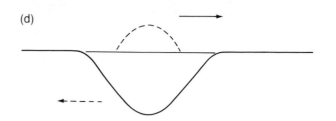

36. Points A, B, C, D, and E are marked on a stretched rope. Pulses X and Y, which have the same shape and size, are travelling through this rope at the same speed.
    (a) Which point(s) would have an instantaneous upward motion if both pulses were moving to the right?
    (b) Which point(s) would have an instantaneous downward motion if pulse X were moving to the right as pulse Y moved to the left?
    (c) Which point(s) would have no motion, provided the pulses were moving in opposite directions?

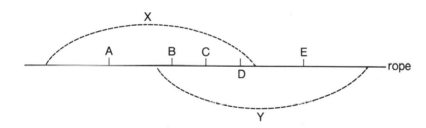

37. Trace the waves illustrated into your notebook and determine their resultant displacement.

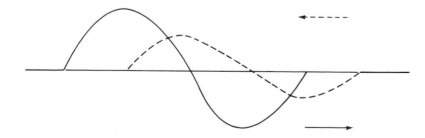

38.

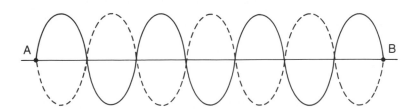

Using measurements taken directly from this diagram of a standing wave pattern, determine each of the following.
(a) the wavelength of the waves
(b) the speed of the waves, if they move between points A and B in 3.0 s
(c) the frequency of the waves

39. Calculate the wavelength if the distance between adjacent nodes in a vibrating medium is 4.0 cm.

40. Waves generated at point A are reflected at B to produce a standing wave as shown in the diagram. What is the wavelength of the travelling waves which produce this standing wave pattern?

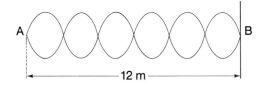

41. The distance between adjacent nodes in the standing wave pattern in a piece of string is 25.0 cm.
(a) What is the wavelength of the wave in the string?
(b) If the frequency of the vibration is 200 Hz, calculate the velocity of the wave.

42. Standing waves are produced in a string by sources at each end with a frequency of 10.0 Hz. The distance between the third node and the sixth node is 54 cm.
(a) What is the wavelength of the interfering waves?
(b) What is their speed?

43. Standing waves are produced in a string by two waves travelling in opposite directions at 6.0 m/s. The distance between the second node and the sixth node is 80 cm. Determine the wavelength and the frequency of the original waves.

44. In the middle of a page in your notebook, mark two points 4.0 cm apart. Using a compass, draw in circular wavefronts originating at the points with 2.0 cm wavelengths. Use solid lines for crests and dotted lines for troughs. Mark all the nodes and points of maximum constructive interference. Draw in the nodal lines.

45. A triangular pulse is created in medium A. The speeds of pulses in mediums A, B, and C are 1.0 cm/s, 2.0 cm/s, and 1.5 cm/s, respectively. Draw a diagram to show the nature and position of the reflected and transmitted pulses when the original pulse reaches the middle of medium C.

A   B   C

46. A light string is fastened to a heavy cord which in turn is fastened to a wall. The light string is 3.0 m long, and a pulse travels in it at a velocity of 2.0 m/s. The heavy cord is 0.50 m long, and the velocity of the pulse in it is 1.0 m/s. Discuss all the reflections and transmissions that occur up to 2.6 s after a short pulse is introduced at the end of the light string. Indicate the time at which each change occurs, noting any phase changes.

Numerical Answers to Practice Problems

page 309
1. 0.80 Hz, 1.3 s
2. 4.0 Hz, 0.25 s
3. 80 Hz
4. 400 Hz, 2.50×10^{-3} s

page 310
1. 0.60 m/s
2. 0.52 s
3. 1.0×10^2 Hz, 1.0×10^{-2} s
4. 0.25 m
5. 3.1 m
6. 3.2 m

page 327
1. 10 cm
2. 40 cm, 10 m/s

Earthquake Waves

There are about 400 earthquakes per day. Fortunately most are small. Minor earthquakes are primarily the result of volcanic activity, but they can also be caused by collapsing caves and mines, or by underground nuclear explosions. Major earthquakes result from the sudden releases of strain along fault lines, which are the boundaries between plates in the outer crust of the Earth. During an earthquake, shock waves radiate from its focus, the subterranean point of origin. The earthquake or seismic waves are most strongly felt at the epicenter, the point directly above the focus on the Earth's surface.

There are three types of seismic waves. The first and fastest is called the compression, primary, or P wave. It moves through the Earth's interior, compressing and expanding the rock in the direction of the wave's movement. Therefore it is a longitudinal wave. The second type is known as the shear, secondary, or S wave. It causes the Earth to vibrate at right angles to the direction the wave is travelling and thus is a transverse wave.

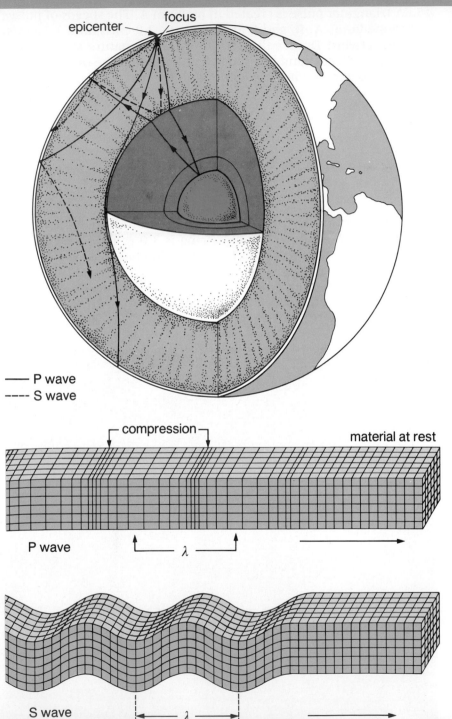

—— P wave
---- S wave

The slowest waves, which move along the Earth's surface, are called surface or L waves and are divided into two types. Rayleigh waves displace the ground vertically whereas Love waves move the ground from side to side. It is the surface waves that cause the havoc, death, and destruction inflicted by a major earthquake. Most of the damage, however, is not directly due to the earthquake waves themselves but to side effects such as landslides and floods in hilly areas and fire in urban areas. For example, during the 1923 earthquake in Japan, approximately 95% of the damage was caused by fire. Earthquakes that originate underwater displace large amounts of water, generating waves which, although barely noticeable in the open ocean, become tidal waves up to 60 m high near shore. These gigantic sea waves, also known as tsunamis, can cause massive damage in coastal regions.

The magnitude of an earthquake is determined by an instrument called a seismograph, which measures the maximum amplitude of a seismic wave. As illustrated, a cylinder supporting a chart paper is firmly anchored in the ground. A

A seismograph

pen attached to a spring-suspended mass traces a path on the chart paper as the cylinder slowly rotates. Because of its inertia, the mass maintains its relative position even if the earth moves, leaving a record of the seismic activity on the chart paper. The smallest perceptible tremor measures 2.5 on the Richter Scale, the scale used to measure the magnitude of earthquakes. The largest earthquakes register 8 or above. The scale is logarithmic. This means that an earthquake of magnitude 7 is approximately 32 times stronger than one of magnitude 6 and about 1000 times (32^2) stronger than one of 5.

11

The Production and Properties of Sound

Chapter Objectives

- ☐ **Relate** *the speed of sound to temperature.*

- ☐ **Define** *"Mach number."*

- ☐ **Relate** *the speed of sound to the wavelength and the frequency (or period).*

- ☐ **Give examples** *of sound intensity on the decibel scale.*

- ☐ **Describe** *the principal parts of the ear.*

- ☐ **Compare** *echoes and reverberations.*

- ☐ **Describe** *a method for determining the speed of sound in air, using echoes.*

- ☐ **Relate** *echo time to the speed of sound and the distance to a reflecting surface.*

- ☐ **Describe** *why reverberation time is important to the design of a concert hall.*

- ☐ **Describe** *why sound waves are diffracted and refracted in air.*

11.1 What Is Sound?

From our earliest years we are accustomed to a great variety of sounds: our mother's voice, a telephone ringing, a kitten purring, a piano being played, the blaring of a rock band, a siren, a jet engine roaring, a rifle shot. Some of these sounds are pleasant to the ear and some are not. They are all called **sounds** because they stimulate the auditory nerve in the human ear.

In the 18th century, the philosophers and scientists debated the question, "If a tree falls in the forest and no one is there to hear it, will there be sound?"

"Of course there will," said the scientists, "because the crash of the tree is a vibrating source that sends out sound waves through the ground and the air." To them, sound was the motion of the particles in a medium, caused by a vibrating object.

"Of course not," said the philosophers, "because no observer is present." To them, sound was a personal sensation, existing only in the mind of the observer.

This debate could never be resolved, because one group was defining sound objectively, in terms of its cause, and the other was defining it subjectively, in terms of its effects on the human ear and brain. In physics, we study the transmission of sound objectively, leaving the subjective interpretation of the effects of sound waves on the human ear and brain to the philosophers.

Every sound wave originates from a vibrating source. The average human is responsive to frequencies of between 20 Hz and 20 000 Hz (see table). Frequencies of less than 20 Hz are referred to as **infrasonic** and those of more than 20 000 Hz are called **ultrasonic**.

Subjectively—"dependent on an individual's point of view"
Objectively—"dependent on external evidence and not on thoughts or feelings"

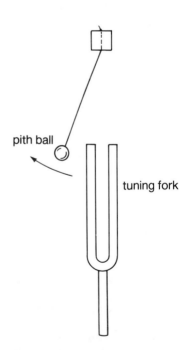

pith ball

tuning fork

The vibrating tuning fork causes the pith ball to be kicked aside.

Frequencies of Commonly Heard Sounds

Source	Frequency (Hz)	Source	Frequency (Hz)
Lowest piano note	27.50	Middle C of piano	261.63
Male speaking voice (average)	120	A above middle C	440.00
Female speaking voice (average)	250	Highest piano note	4186.01

Range of transmitted sound

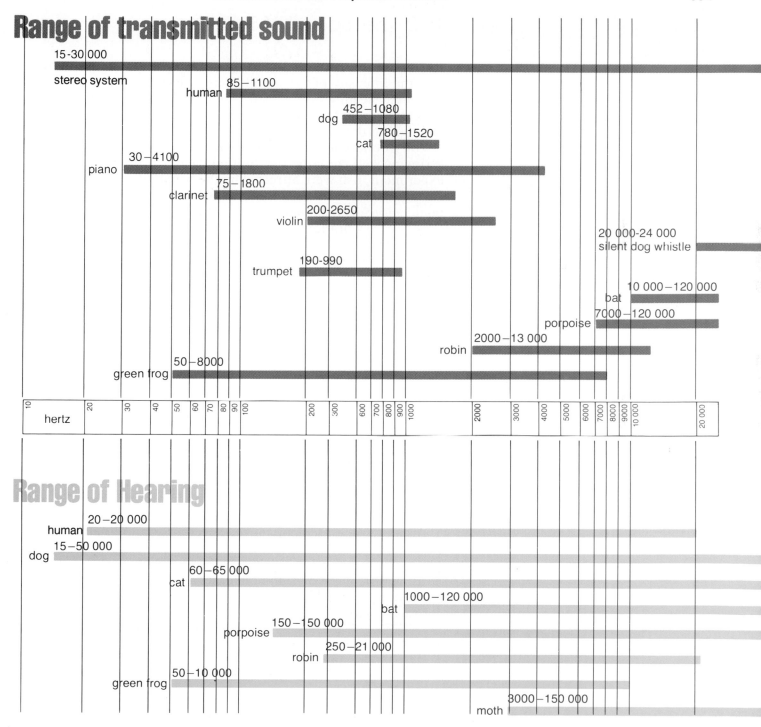

15-30 000
stereo system

85—1100
human

452—1080
dog

780—1520
cat

30—4100
piano

75—1800
clarinet

200-2650
violin

20 000-24 000
silent dog whistle

190-990
trumpet

10 000—120 000
bat

7000—120 000
porpoise

2000—13 000
robin

50—8000
green frog

hertz

Range of Hearing

20—20 000
human

15—50 000
dog

60—65 000
cat

1000—120 000
bat

150—150 000
porpoise

250—21 000
robin

50—10 000
green frog

3000—150 000
moth

11.2 The Speed of Sound

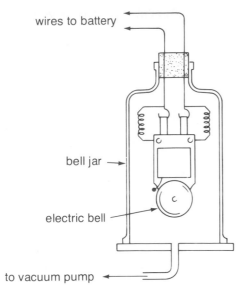

wires to battery

bell jar

electric bell

to vacuum pump

The speed of light was assumed to be great enough that the flash was seen instantaneously.

In 1654, Otto von Guericke, the inventor of the air pump, discovered that the intensity of the sound from a mechanical bell inside a jar decreased steadily as the air was removed from the jar. Today this effect is demonstrated by means of an electric bell in a bell jar from which air is drawn out by a vacuum pump.

Von Guericke learned from another experiment that the sound of a ringing bell could be transmitted clearly through water. In his experiment, fish were attracted by the sound of a bell in the water. An underwater swimmer sometimes hears an approaching motorboat before a swimmer on the surface does. Most of us have experienced vibrations in the ground from a passing truck or train. If you put your ear against a steel fence, you can hear the sound of a stone being tapped against it a considerable distance away.

These examples all point to the conclusion that sound needs a material medium for its transmission. It will not travel through a vacuum.

In the case of sound travelling along a metal fence, you may hear the same sound twice—first through the fence, then through the air. You hear it first through the fence because sound travels approximately 15 times faster in steel than it does in air. Experiments in water indicate that sound travels approximately four times faster in water than in air.

How fast does sound travel in air? The speed of sound in air was first accurately measured in 1738 by members of the French Academy. Cannons were set up on two hills approximately 29 km apart. By measuring the time interval between the flash of a cannon and the "boom", the speed of sound was calculated. Two cannons were used, and they were fired alternately, to minimize errors due to the wind and to delayed reactions in the observers.

Accurate measurements of the speed of sound in air have been made at various temperatures and air pressures. At normal atmospheric pressure and at 0°C, it is 332 m/s. If the air pressure remains constant, the speed of sound increases as the temperature increases. It has been found that the speed of sound in air changes by 0.6 m/s for each degree Celsius.

Speed of sound in air = (332 + 0.6 *T*) m/s
(at normal atmospheric pressure)

---

where *T* is the temperature in degrees Celsius.

Sample Problems

What is the speed of sound at (a) 20°C and (b) −20°C?

(a) $v = (332 + 0.6\ T)$ m/s
$\quad = [332 + 0.6\ (20)]$ m/s
$\quad = (332 + 12)$ m/s
$\quad = 344$ m/s

(b) $v = (332 + 0.6\ T)$ m/s
$\quad = [332 + 0.6(−20)]$ m/s
$\quad = (332 − 12)$ m/s
$\quad = 320$ m/s

Practice

1. What is the speed of sound in air when the temperature is (a) −10°C, (b) 24°C, and (c) 35°C?
2. How much time is required for sound to travel 1.4 km through air if the temperature is 30°C?

The speed of sound varies in different materials. In general, it is greater in solids and liquids than in gases, but there are some exceptions (see chart). For example, in lead and hydrogen sound has similar speeds at the same temperature. Some substances, such as earth and sea water, display a range of speeds for sound because other physical factors, and not just temperature, can affect the speed.

Speed of Sound in Various Media

Substance	Speed at 0°C (m/s)
carbon dioxide	258
oxygen	317
air	332
cork	500
lead	1200
alcohol	1241
hydrogen gas	1270
sea water*	1440-1500
fresh water	1500
pine wood	3320
copper	3560
marble	3810
maple wood	4110
steel	5050
aluminum	5104
earth	7000-13 000

*varies with depth, temperature, and salinity

11.3 Mach Number

High speeds for supersonic aircraft, such as the Concorde, are given in terms of **Mach number**, not kilometers per hour. The Mach number is the ratio of the speed of an object to the speed of sound.

$$\text{Mach number} = \frac{\text{speed of object}}{\text{speed of sound}}$$

The speed of sound at sea level and 0°C is 332 m/s, or approximately 1200 km/h. At an altitude of 10 km, it is approximately 1060 km/h. An aircraft flying at an altitude of 10 km with a speed of 1800 km/h has a Mach number of $\dfrac{1800 \text{ km/h}}{1060 \text{ km/h}}$, or 1.7.

Practice

1. What is the Mach number of an aircraft travelling at sea level at 0°C with a speed of (a) 1440 km/h, and (b) 900 km/h?
2. A military interceptor airplane can fly at Mach 2.0. What is its speed in kilometres per hour at sea level, and at 0°C?

11.4 The Transmission of Sound Waves

When a tuning fork is struck, it vibrates. As each tine moves out, it pushes air molecules out until they bump against their neighbours. This creates a steadily moving area of collision, called a **compression**. When the tine moves back it creates a region of emptiness, a **rarefaction**, into which the displaced air molecules rebound. This follows the compression outwards. In other words, sound travels out from its source as a longitudinal wave. As the tines move back and forth, rarefactions and compressions follow one another as the sound waves travel through the air away from the tuning fork (see illustration). The particles of air only vibrate. They do not move from the source to the receiver.

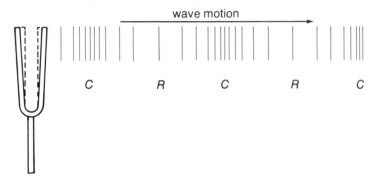

The diagram shows the propagation of sound waves in one direction only. Actually, the sound waves go out in all directions.

In sound waves, a compression is an area of higher than normal air pressure, and a rarefaction is an area of lower than normal air

schematic representation of the density of air molecules

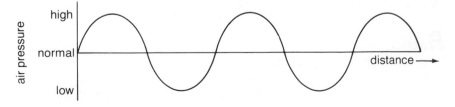

pressure. The graph illustrates these variations in pressure as a sound wave moves away from its source. Longitudinal waves are difficult to represent visually, and it is more helpful, at times, to use a graph of pressure variations.

As noted in the illustration in the margin, one wavelength is the distance between the midpoints of successive compressions or successive rarefactions. The amplitude of the sound wave describes the displacement of the air molecules from the rest position. In fact, all of the terms used to describe waves in the previous chapter are used to describe sound waves, although the term **pitch** is often substituted for frequency in musical references. The Wave Equation also holds as illustrated in the following example.

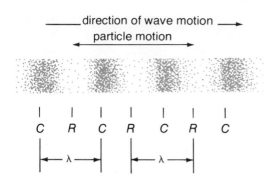

Sample Problems

The sound from a trumpet travels at a speed of 350 m/s in air. If the frequency of the note played is 300 Hz, what is the wavelength of the sound wave?
Given that v = 350 m/s, f = 300 Hz

$$\lambda = \frac{v}{f}$$
$$= \frac{350 \text{ m/s}}{300 \text{ Hz}}$$
$$= 1.17 \text{ m}$$

Practice

1. An organ pipe emits a note of 50 Hz. If the speed of sound in air is 350 m/s, what is the wavelength of the sound wave?
2. If a 260 Hz sound from a tuning fork has a wavelength of 1.30 m, at what speed does the sound travel?
3. A sound wave with a wavelength of 10 m travels at 350 m/s. What is its frequency?

11.5 The Intensity of Sound

Frequency, wavelength, and speed are all properties of sound that can be measured accurately.

Sound intensity, or loudness, is more difficult to measure because the amount of energy involved is small in comparison with other forms of energy and because the potential range of sound intensity is great.

The heat energy equivalent of the sound energy emitted over a 90 min period by a crowd of 50 000 at a football game is only enough to heat one cup of coffee! A stereo amplifier with a maximum power output of 50 W/channel has an actual sound output from the speakers of less than 2.5 W—more than enough to fill an auditorium with sound.

Sounds audible to humans can vary in intensity from the quietest whisper to a level that is painful to the ear—a difference of a factor of 10^{13}. The unit used to measure the intensity of sound is the **decibel** (dB), named after Alexander Graham Bell, the inventor of the telephone. On the decibel scale, 0 dB is fixed near the threshold of hearing, at a value of 0.000 000 000 001 W/m²(10^{-12} W/m²). The scale is not linear, with uniform gradations. A sound 10 times more intense than 0 dB is 10 dB, a sound 100 times more intense than 0 dB is 20 dB, a sound 1000 times more intense than 0 dB is 30 dB, and so on. The level of sound that is painful to the human ear (130 dB) is 10^{13} times more intense than the level at the threshold of hearing. The sound intensity levels for common sources are listed in a chart.

Alexander Graham Bell

Intensity is the average rate of energy flow per unit area across a surface perpendicular to the direction of propagation. That is,

$$\text{intensity} = \frac{\text{energy/time}}{\text{area}}$$

$$= \frac{\text{power}}{\text{area}}$$

or $\quad I = \dfrac{P}{4\pi R^2}$

where $4\pi R^2$ is the area of a sphere a distance R from the source.

intensity level (dB)

$$= 10 \log \frac{I_2}{I_1}$$

where I_1 is the initial intensity in W/m² and I_2 is the final intensity. For example, if $I_1 = 10^{-12}$ W/m² (threshold of hearing) and $I_2 = 1.0$ W/m² and we substitute in the above relationship,

$$dB = 10\log \frac{1}{10^{-12}}$$

$$= 10\log 10^{12}$$

$$= 120$$

We say there is an intensity difference of 120 dB between I_1 and I_2.

Sound Intensity Levels for Various Sources

Source	Intensity (dB)	Intensity (W/m²)
threshold of hearing	0	10^{-12}
normal breathing	10	10^{-11}
average whisper at 2 m	20	10^{-10}
empty theater	30	10^{-9}
residential area at night	40	10^{-8}
quiet restaurant	50	10^{-7}
two-person conversation	60	10^{-6}
busy street traffic	70	10^{-5}
vacuum cleaner	80	10^{-4}
at the foot of Niagara Falls loud stereo in average room passing subway train	90	10^{-3}
maximum level in concert hall—13th row	100	10^{-2}
pneumatic chisel	110	10^{-1}
maximum level of some rock groups	120	1
threshold of pain	130	10
military jet taking off	140	10^{2}
wind tunnel	150	10^{3}
space rocket instant perforation of the eardrum	160	10^{4}

The intensity of a sound received by the human ear depends on the power of the source and the distance between the source and the person. Like water waves, sound waves moving out from a point source spread their wave energy over an increasing area. Thus, the intensity of a sound decreases as the wave moves from the source to the receiver. The reading on the decibel scale also decreases as the distance increases. For example, a reading of 100 dB at 1 m becomes 60 dB at 100 m.

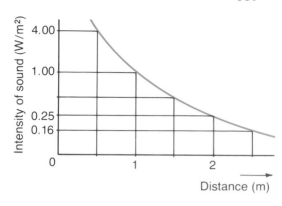

Graph of sound intensity versus distance

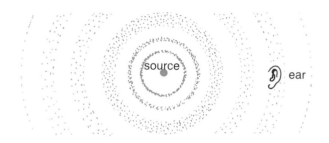

As a sound wave moves out from a source, its energy is spread more and more thinly.

11.6 The Human Ear

The human ear consists of three sections: the outer ear, the middle ear, and the inner ear. The outer ear consists of the external ear flap and a cylindrical canal (the meatus). The function of these two parts is to help the hearer identify the direction of the sound and to direct the sound to the eardrum. The **ear canal** is about 2 cm long, and so the eardrum is protected from direct injury. Although the hearing range of a healthy young adult is approximately 16 to 20 000 Hz, the structure of the ear canal amplifies frequencies between 2000 and 5500 Hz by a factor of nearly 10, emphasizing these frequencies.

The ear canal ends at the **eardrum**, which is constructed of a very tough, tightly stretched membrane less than 0.1 mm thick. The eardrum is forced into vibration by successive compressions and rarefactions coming down the ear canal. Compressions force the eardrum in and rarefactions cause it to move out, and the resultant vibration has the same frequency as the source of the sound waves.

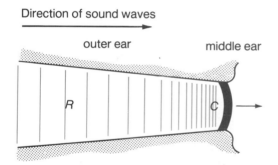

A rarefaction is actually an area of reduced atmospheric pressure. Thus, when a rarefaction approaches the external side of the eardrum, the higher atmospheric pressure in the middle ear causes the eardrum to move out.

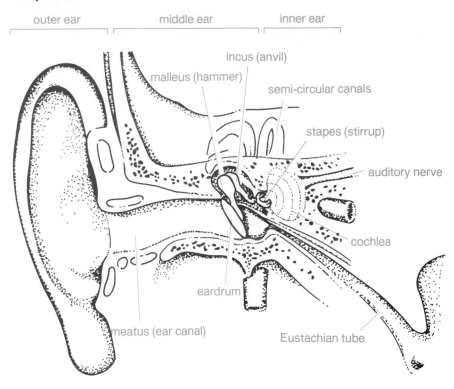

Even at the threshold of pain the eardrum vibrates with an amplitude of less than 10^{-10} m—a distance equivalent to the diameter of a hydrogen atom.

High sound levels make the use of ear-protection devices imperative.

Attached to the inside of the eardrum are three small interlocking bones: the **hammer** (malleus), the **anvil** (incus), and the **stirrup** (stapes). These bones constitute the middle ear and transmit the vibrations of the eardrum to the inner ear, mechanically amplifying them by a factor of three. The cavity containing the middle ear is filled with air and is connected to the mouth by the **Eustachian tube**. This tube is normally closed, but it opens during swallowing or yawning, equalizing the air pressure in the middle ear. If the Eustachian tube becomes blocked, because of a cold, for example, pressure equalization cannot take place, and the result is pressure in the middle ear which can be quite painful and can affect hearing.

The stirrup transmits the eardrum vibrations to the threshold of the inner ear. The vibrations set up pressure waves in the fluid that fills the inner ear's cochlea. The **cochlea** is a snail-shaped organ approximately 3.0 cm long, divided into two equal sections by a partition for most of its length. Waves are transmitted down one side of the cochlea, around the end of the partition, and back almost to the point of origin. As these waves move, they cause approximately 23 000 microscopic hairs to vibrate. Each hair is connected to a cell that converts the mechanical motion of the hair into an electrical signal, which is in turn transmitted to the brain by the auditory nerve. How these codified electrical signals are interpreted by the brain is a wondrous thing we know very little about.

In addition to the cochlea, the inner ear contains three hard, fluid-filled loops, called the semi-circular canals, which are situated more or less at right angles to each other. These act as miniature accelerometers, transmitting to the brain electrical signals necessary for balance.

Loud sounds do not as a rule harm the eardrum, although an exploding firecracker may cause it to burst. Such damage can be repaired, but permanent damage may be inflicted by intense sounds on the microscopic, hairlike cells in the inner ear. A particularly loud sound may rip away these delicate cells. A single blast of 150 dB or more can cause permanent damage to the ear, and levels of more than 90 dB over a prolonged period can produce the same effect. Persons employed in noisy places usually wear ear protectors as a precaution against this danger. Many cases of premature deafness are caused by prolonged exposure to loud sounds. Examples include rock musicians, music teachers, skeet shooters, factory workers, miners, construction workers, and young people listening to music at high levels. (A Walkman portable sound unit can produce 100 dB at the eardrum.)

The graph in the margin shows that all human beings suffer some loss of hearing as they grow older. The loss is significantly higher for those living in an industrial setting—whether or not they are employed in noisy occupations. Our increasingly noisy environment has penalties beyond mere annoyance, emphasizing the need for sound-pollution legislation.

The human ear is not equally sensitive to all frequencies. The graph on the next page describes the intensity level as a function of frequency for the human ear. The top curve represents the threshold of pain. Sounds with intensities above this curve can actually be felt and cause pain. Note that the threshold of pain does not vary much with frequency. The middle line represents the threshold of hearing for the majority of the population. Sounds below this line would be inaudible. Note that the ear is most sensitive to sounds with a frequency between 2000 Hz and 3000 Hz. A 1000 Hz sound can be heard at a level of 20 dB, whereas a 100 Hz sound must have an intensity of at least 50 dB to be audible. The dotted curve represents the hearing of a very good ear, usually less than 1% of the population. In general, only the young have such a low threshold of hearing.

The sound intensity levels of some rock bands exceed 110 dB.

Tests carried out on the Mabaan tribe in remote Sudanese villages in 1962 showed that the normal deterioration of their hearing was considerably less than the average North American's, and strikingly less than that of noise-exposed North American industrial workers.

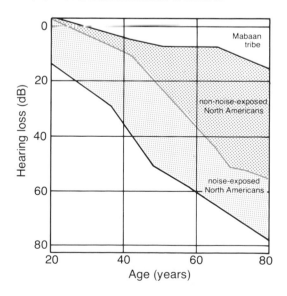

Note that although the threshold of
hearing is by definition 0 dB, it is not
0 dB for all frequencies for the human
ear. This occurs because the ear is not
equally sensitive at all frequencies, as the
graph of the threshold of hearing
illustrates.

Note that the frequency scale is
"logarithmic", in order to cover a wide
range of frequencies.

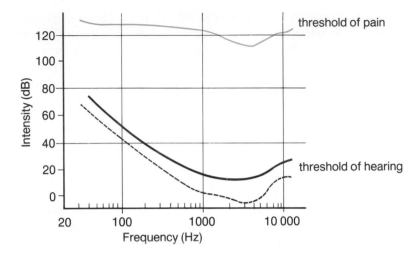

Sensitivity of the human ear as a function of frequency.

This variation in the sensitivity of the ear to both high and low frequencies is compensated for in many stereo and high fidelity systems. A "loudness" control circuit boosts the intensities of the low and high frequencies relative to the middle frequencies. The compensation is greatest at low volumes. As the volume level increases, the compensation decreases until there is little change at moderate volume levels.

11.7 The Reflection of Sound Waves

Sound waves radiating out from a source are reflected when they strike a rigid obstacle, the angle of reflection being equal to the angle of incidence. This can be demonstrated using two cardboard tubes inclined to one another and directed towards a flat surface, such as a blackboard or wall. A ticking watch placed near the end of one tube can be heard clearly by an ear at the end of the other tube only if the tubes are arranged so that the angle of incidence and the angle of reflection are equal.

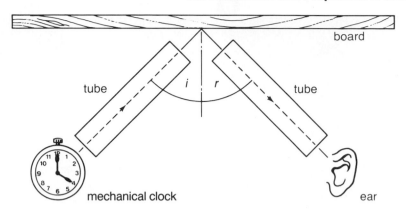

Sound waves may be clearly heard at the focus of the reflector.

Sound waves conform to the Laws of Reflection. Many science museums have excellent exhibits that demonstrate the reflection of sound waves. One type of exhibit involves a large reflector like the one shown in the photograph. A person standing at a distance from the reflector can whisper and still be heard clearly by a person standing at the focus of the reflector. The reflector collects the sound waves and focuses them into a small area, much the way a concave mirror can focus light waves. (Chapter 14 goes into detail about how curved mirrors work.)

Using the same laws of reflection, outdoor stages are designed to reflect the sound of a band or orchestra toward the audience. The performers are located near the focus of a hard concave reflector, which is often called a band shell because it looks like a large seashell. The Hollywood Bowl in California and the Hatch Shell on the Esplanade along the Charles River in Boston are two examples. In indoor concert halls, sometimes it is necessary to reflect sound from the ceiling. Large convex acrylic disks can be suspended from the ceiling to improve the acoustical properties of these buildings.

A microphone at the focal point of a concave reflector, called a **parabolic microphone,** is sometimes used to pick up remote sounds at a sports event or to record bird calls. (See the photo on the next page.)

Echoes are produced when sound is reflected by a hard surface, such as a wall or cliff. The echo can be heard by the human ear only if the time interval between the original sound and the reflected sound is greater than 0.1 s. For practical purposes, the distance between the observer and the reflecting surface must be greater than 17 m.

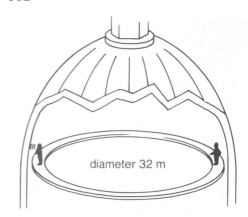

In the dome of St. Paul's Cathedral, London, whispers can be heard clearly 32 m away.

Parabolic microphones in use at a football game.

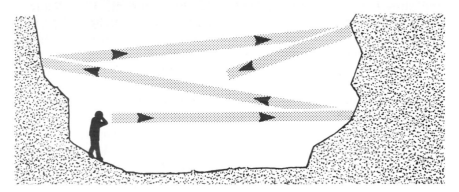

As the sound is reflected back and forth, the caller hears the echo of his or her call. The diagram shows only some of the sound waves. Actually, the waves are reflected all around the canyon, and only some of them return to the caller, making the echo less intense than the original call.

The **echo-sounder** is a device that uses the principles of sound reflection to measure the depth of the sea. A so-called "transducer" is placed in the bottom of a ship. It converts electrical energy into sound energy and sends out a series of equally spaced sound pulses with a frequency of approximately 30 kHz. The pulses are reflected from the sea bed back up to the ship where they are received by an underwater microphone, called a "hydrophone". The time interval between the emission of the signal and the reception of the echo is measured by a computer which then calculates the depth of the water and records it on a moving chart.

Similar equipment is used in the fishing industry to locate schools of fish. More sophisticated equipment of the same type is used by the armed forces to locate submarines. All such devices are called **sonar** (sound navigation and ranging) devices. Ultrasonic sonar devices are also used to detect flaws in railway tracks and pipelines, to determine the fat/lean ratio in live cattle and pigs, to diagnose brain damage, to detect breast cancer, and to monitor the growth of a human fetus in the womb.

A similar technique is used in **radar** (radio detection and ranging). A rotating transmitter sends out a series of high-frequency radio pulses that are reflected back as echoes from an object such as an airplane or a coastal cliff. The time interval between transmission of the signal and reception of the echo depends on the object's distance from the transmitter. The results are usually displayed on a cathode ray tube. It is important to note that radar employs very short radio waves that travel at the speed of light, not sound waves.

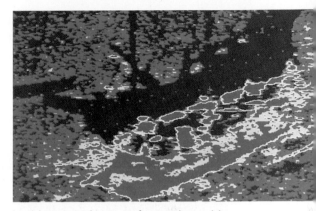

In this sonar image of a sunken ship, the ship is black. The colored area is the ship's sound shadow on the lake bottom.

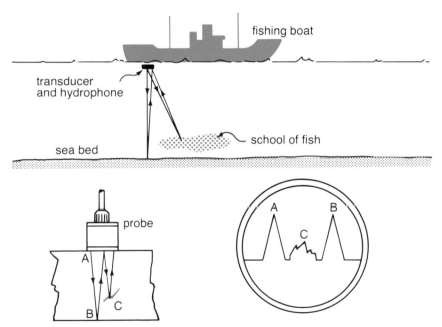

Echoes can be used to detect flaws in a metal casting.
A = pulse sent out by transducer
B = pulse reflected from bottom of metal
C = pulse reflected by a flaw in the metal

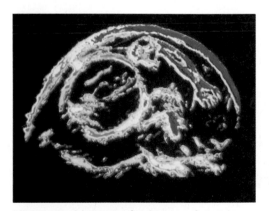

Ultrasound image of a human fetus in the womb

Sample Problems

A boy yells towards a cliff and hears his echo 3.0 s later. If the speed of sound is 340 m/s, how far away is the cliff?

$$\triangle d = v \triangle t$$
$$= (340 \text{ m/s}) (3.0 \text{ s})$$
$$= 1020 \text{ m}$$

Distance to the cliff
$$= \tfrac{1}{2}(1020 \text{ m})$$
$$= 510 \text{ m, or } 5.1 \times 10^2 \text{ m}$$

Practice

1. A student, 90 m from the foot of a cliff, claps her hands, and hears the echo 0.50 s later. Calculate the speed of sound in air.
2. A sonar device is used in a lake, and the interval between the production of a sound and the reception of the echo is found to be 0.40 s. The speed of sound in water is 1500 m/s. What is the depth of the water?

Technically speaking, reverberation time is the time taken for the sound intensity level, at the position of the listener, to fall 60 dB from the original intensity level.

11.8 Applications: Acoustics in Buildings

When the reflecting surface is less than 17 m away, the echo follows so closely behind the original sound that the original sound appears to be prolonged (Section 11.7). This effect is called **reverberation**. Reverberations are particularly noticeable in large, empty buildings such as cathedrals and concert halls, but they also occur when we shout in a road underpass or sing in the shower. A certain amount of reverberation may enhance the quality of sound. Excessive reverberation in a concert hall is undesirable because it interferes with the original sound, making speech and music indistinct.

The acoustics of a concert hall are the most important concern of the architect, and the most important property of a concert hall is its **reverberation time**. This is defined as the time required for sound of a standard intensity to die away and become inaudible. The reverberation time depends on the materials used on the walls, the height of the ceiling, the length of the hall, the type of music being played, and the presence or absence of an audience. In some halls the seats are designed so that when they are unoccupied they will absorb the same amount of sound as a seated person. Well designed halls for orchestral concerts tend to have a reverberation time of between 1 s and 2 s, and halls that are best for choral music have a reverberation time of 2 s to 5 s. Comparative absorption values of various construction materials are given in a chart. Notice that the absorption of sound by a given material varies with the frequency. By the careful choice of materials, a room can be made acoustically "dead", with a reverberation time near zero. Such rooms are called **anechoic**, and they are used for studying the performance of sound devices such as telephones, microphones, and loudspeakers.

Sound Absorption Coefficients for Various Substances

Substance	Frequency 512 Hz	Frequency 2048 Hz
cement	*0.025	0.035
brick	0.03	0.049
wood (pine)	0.06	0.10
carpet	0.02	0.27
fiberglass	0.99	0.86
acoustic tile	0.97	0.68
theater seats	1.6—3.0	—
seated audience	3.0—4.3	3.5—6.0

*To simplify the chart, units have not been supplied. Substances with larger coefficients have better sound absorption qualities, and hence shorter reverberation times.

11.9 Diffraction and Refraction of Sound Waves

A teacher in the hall can hear the sounds of the classroom through an open door, even though the students are out of sight and separated by a wall. Sounds travelling through an open window are easily heard outside, and even around the corner of a building. The "sound around the corner" effect is so familiar to us that we don't give it a second thought. Sound waves can travel around corners because of a property of waves called diffraction. **Diffraction** describes the ability of waves to move around an obstacle or through a small opening. Waves with relatively long wavelengths diffract more than those with short wavelengths. Lower frequency sound waves have relatively long wavelengths compared to the obstacles and openings they commonly encounter. They are diffracted, as illustrated on the next page. Higher frequency sounds have shorter wavelengths and diffract less. Thus, when sound travels from a loudspeaker, the bass notes travel easily into the next room while the treble notes do not. Test this out on your home stereo!

The Dallas Theater Center, designed by Frank Lloyd Wright

Equipment being tested in an anechoic chamber

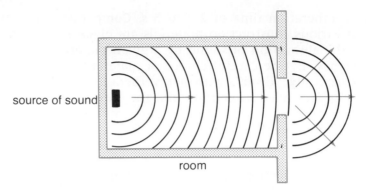

Sound waves are diffracted as they pass through a doorway from one room into the next.

The speed with which a sound travels through air can be affected by the temperature of the air. Sound waves travel faster in warm air then they do in cold air. If they move from air at one temperature to air at a different temperature, at an angle, they are refracted, as illustrated, in much the same manner as light rays. (See Chapter 15 for more information about refraction of light.)

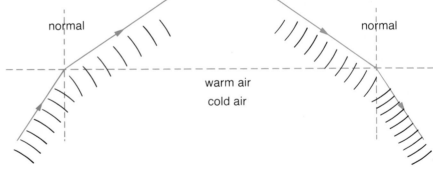

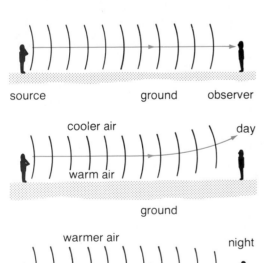

On a warm day, sound waves tend to be refracted upward from an observer, which decreases the intensity of the sound heard by the observer. On the other hand, at night, the cooler air near the surface of the Earth tends to refract sound waves towards the surface and so they travel a greater distance. This is particularly true on flat ground or on water. Watch what you say outdoors at night—you may be surprised at how far your voice carries!

Meet Cindy Martindale . . . Ultrasound Technologist

Cindy works in a radiology department of a hospital. She uses ultrasound to help doctors diagnose patients' conditions. She has been working in the clinic for about two years.

Q. What does an ultrasound technologist do?
A. I operate an ultrasound diagnostic unit. By placing a probe on the part of the patient's body requested by the patient's doctor, I create an image on a screen. The image is stored on film or videotape for analysis by the radiologist (a medical doctor specializing in radiology). While the examination is in progress I am responsible for the patient's safety and comfort.

Q. How does the unit work?
A. In simple terms, a probe sends out high frequency sound waves that interact with the various tissues and organs in the body. The reflected sound waves produce signals that go into a computer and are reproduced as an image on a screen.

Q. What part of the body do you usually examine?
A. Most of my time is spent making images of the abdomen for problems of the liver, gall bladder, pancreas, spleen, and reproductive organs. Sometimes we take images of the neck region when examining the thyroid gland.

Q. Do you do obstetric examinations?
A. Ultrasonics is a very important tool for examining the development of a fetus. X-rays utilize ionizing radiation that could harm the fetus, whereas sound waves are generally much safer for both the fetus and the mother.

Q. How do you keep up-to-date with all the changing technology in your field?
A. There is a professional association of ultrasonic technologists that periodically holds meetings, workshops, seminars, and conferences. As well, the equipment manufacturers run workshops. Mostly, I read journals that describe interesting cases and new techniques.

Q. You seem to enjoy your field of work. Why?
A. I love working with people and the whole job involves interacting with patients and fellow employees. The work is challenging because the technology is always advancing and we are continually learning new things. Every day is a different experience. I always get a thrill when I scan a mother and watch the miracle of life as a fetus develops. Ultrasonics is an expanding field and I highly recommend it as a career.

Q. What is an ultrasonic examination like for a patient?
A. The examination is very relaxing and painless—some patients even fall asleep! Usually the patient lies on a bed in a darkened room and I rub gelatin or oil on the part of the body to be scanned. Next the probe is rubbed gently over the body. When we are satisfied with the image it is stored. A typical examination requires about 15 minutes.

Q. Isn't ultrasound used for physiotherapy as well?
A. Yes, but the frequency of the waves is much higher. In this application, sound waves create heat to reduce pain and/or swelling. No image is created.

Q. How did you start your career?
A. I completed a two year course in the radiography (X-ray) program at college. The program ran for 11 months and involved clinical as well as classroom and laboratory work. Subjects included: chemistry, anatomy, pathology, physics, and biology. After working as an X-ray technologist for a short time I specialized in ultrasonics by taking a further 11 months training. Four months were spent in school. Clinical work occupied the remainder of the time.

Q. What courses are required in high school if one wishes to train for a career as an X-ray or ultrasound technologist?
A. Most colleges require that students take courses in mathematics, physics, and chemistry or biology to be accepted into a radiography course. Acceptance to an ultrasonics program usually requires two years prior education in a related field such as medicine, nursing or radiography.

Investigation

Investigation 11.1: Speed of Sound—Echo Method

Problem:
What is the speed of sound, as determined by the echo method?

Materials:
2 wooden blocks
stopwatch

Procedure:
1. Locate a high wall with clear space at least 100 m deep in front of it.
2. Clap two boards together and listen for the echo. Repeat until you have determined the approximate time interval between the original sound and the echo.
3. Now clap the boards after the echo so that the time between the previous clap and the echo is the same as the time between the echo and the next clap. In other words, clap the boards so that a regular rhythm is set up: clap...echo...clap...echo.
4. When you have achieved the correct timing, have your partner record, with the stopwatch, the number of seconds required for 20 or more clap intervals. (Remember to start counting with zero!)
5. Determine the average interval between claps. This interval is equal to the time taken for the sound to travel four times the distance between you and the wall.
6. Measure the distance to the wall in meters and the temperature of the air in °C.
7. Calculate the speed of sound in air.

Questions:
1. How does your value for the speed of sound in air compare with the accepted value? What was your percentage error?
2. Knowing the speed of sound, how might you determine the distance between your point of observation and a granite cliff some distance away?

Chapter Summary

1. The frequency limits of sound, for a normal human ear, are usually 20 Hz to 20 000 Hz.
2. Sound requires a material medium for its transmission.
3. The speed of sound waves in a medium is determined by the type of medium and the temperature of the medium.
4. Mach number is the ratio of the speed of an object to the speed of sound.
5. Sound travels as a longitudinal wave.
6. Sound intensity is measured in decibels (dB) or watts per square meter (W/m²), and 0 dB = 10^{-12} W/m².
7. The intensity of sound depends on the power of the source and the distance between the source and the receiver.
8. The human ear transforms sound waves into electrical impulses, which are transmitted to the brain for interpretation.
9. Hearing loss increases with age, and is accelerated by prolonged exposure to high-intensity sound.
10. Sound waves obey the Laws of Reflection.
11. Echoes may be used to determine the speed of sound in air and to locate objects in the same medium as the echo.
12. The types and locations of sound reflectors in a building determine its acoustical properties, including its reverberation time.
13. Sound waves are diffracted around corners and through small openings.
14. Sound waves are refracted because temperature variations in the air change the speed of sound.

Chapter Review

Discussion

1. Marchers in a parade sometimes find it difficult to keep in step with the band if it is some distance from them. Explain why.
2. Lightning can produce a sharp crack of thunder or a long rumble lasting a number of seconds, depending on the position of the observer in relation to the lightning discharge. The lightning could strike along a line towards the observer or perpendicular to that line. Using your knowledge of sound waves, explain why such variations in the sound of thunder occur.

3. How does a stethoscope transfer sounds from a patient's body to a doctor's ears?
4. How are sound waves used to map the bottoms of lakes and oceans?
5. Research and report on the laws and regulations regarding sound levels in the work place.
6. When eighty students in the concert band practise in the music room, the sound level could exceed 100 dB at times. One of the occupational hazards for music teachers is premature hearing loss. This can be reduced by the proper design and construction of the music room. List as many design features as you can for a "good" music room. Evaluate the music room in your school and make some suggestions for improvement, if necessary.
7. Investigate the laws related to sound pollution in your municipality and report back to class.

Problems

8. What is the speed of sound in air at each of the following temperatures?
   (a) 10°C   (b) 15°C   (c) −30°C
9. How long does it take sound to travel 20 km? (Assume the speed of sound is 340 m/s.)
10. A fan at a baseball game is 100 m from home plate. If the speed of sound is 350 m/s, how long after the batter actually hits the ball does the fan hear the crack? Assume that there is no wind.
11. A lightning flash is seen 10.0 s before the rumble of the thunder is heard. Find the distance to the lightning flash if the temperature is 20°C.
12. A man sets his watch at noon by the sound of a factory whistle 4.8 km away. If the temperature of the air is 20°C, how many seconds slow will his watch be?
13. 6.0 s after a girl sees the flash of a distant cannon, she hears the sound of the firing. How far away is the cannon, assuming there is no wind and that the temperature is 25°C?
14. A ship sends a sound signal simultaneously through the air and through the salt water to another ship 1000 m away. Using 336 m/s as the speed of sound in air and 1450 m/s as the speed of sound in salt water, calculate the time interval between the arrival of the two sounds at the second ship.
15. You are standing on a straight road and see lightning strike the ground ahead of you. 3.0 s later you hear the thunderclap. If the speed of sound is 330 m/s, how far will you have to walk to reach the point where the lightning struck?

16. A swimmer sees a parachutist hit the water and hears the impact twice, first through the water with one ear and then through the air with her other ear 1.0 s later. How far away did the impact occur? (Speed of sound in air = 340 m/s, speed of sound in water = 1.4×10^3 m/s)

17. What is the Mach number of a plane travelling at each of the following speeds at sea level in air with a temperature of 12°C?
    (a) 1020 m/s   (b) 170 m/s   (c) 1836 km/h

18. The tine of a vibrating tuning fork passes through its central position 600 times in 1.0 s. How many of each of the following has the prong made?
    (a) complete cycles
    (b) complete waves
    (c) compressions
    (d) rarefactions

19. Calculate the frequency of a sound wave if its speed and wavelength are
    (a) 340 m/s and 1.13 m.
    (b) 340 m/s and 69.5 cm.

20. Calculate the speed of a sound wave in air if its frequency and wavelengths are
    (a) 384 Hz and 90.0 cm.
    (b) 256 Hz and 1.32 m.
    (c) 1.50 kHz and 23.3 cm.

21. Find the wavelengths corresponding to each of the following frequencies, assuming that the speed of sound is 342 m/s.
    (a) 20 Hz   (b) 2.0×10^4 Hz

22. What is the wavelength in meters of sound waves with a frequency of 8000 Hz in (a) air, (b) water, (c) steel? (Use the values given in the table on page 353.)

23. A violin string is vibrating at a frequency of 440 Hz. How many vibrations does it make while its sounds travels 664 m through air at a temperature of 0°C?

24. The note A (440 Hz) is sounded by the oboe when the orchestra tunes up before a performance. How many vibrations does the oboe make before the sound reaches a person seated in the audience 40 m away? Assume the temperature in the concert hall is 20°C.

25. A vibrating 400 Hz tuning fork is placed in pure distilled water.
    (a) What are the frequency and the wavelength (in meters) of the sound waves produced within the water at 0°C?
    (b) What would be the frequency and the wavelength in the adjacent air, if the sound waves moved from the water into the air at 0°C?

26. The power of the sound emitted from an average conversation between two people is 10^{-6} W. How many two-people conversations would it take to keep a 60 W bulb glowing, assuming that all the sound energy could be converted into electrical energy?

27. A sound of 80 dB strikes an eardrum having an area of 4.0×10^{-5} m^2. How much energy is absorbed by the eardrum per second?

28. The specifications for a stereo tape cassette indicate that it has a signal-to-noise ratio of 60 dB. What is the ratio of the signal and the background intensity?

29. A student standing 99 m from a wall claps his hands and hears the echo 0.60 s later. Calculate the speed of sound in air.

30. A ship is travelling in a fog parallel to a dangerous, cliff-lined shore. The boat whistle is sounded and its echo is heard clearly 11.0 s later. If the air temperature is 10°C, how far is the ship from the cliff?

31. 3.5 s after a woman makes a sound, the echo returns from a nearby wall. How far is the woman from the wall, assuming that the speed of sound is 350 m/s?

32. A ship is 2030 m from an above-water reflecting surface. The temperature of the air and water is 0°C.
    (a) What is the time interval between the production of a sound wave and the reception of its echo, in air?
    (b) What would the interval be if the reflecting surface was under fresh water?

33. (a) A Navy ship patrolling the ocean receives its own sound signals back, by underwater reflection, 4.5 s after emitting them. The speed of sound in salt water is 1470 m/s. How far away is the reflecting surface, in meters?
    (b) Suppose the ship's sonar gives a distance readout in meters, using a computer program that assumes the ship is in salt water. If the ship was to enter fresh water, what would be the percent error in the readout?

34. A man drops a stone into a mine shaft 180 m deep. If the temperature is 20°C, how much time will elapse between the moment when the stone is dropped and the moment when the sound of the sound of the stone hitting the bottom of the mine shaft is heard?

35. Two observers, A and B, are located 1 km apart. Each has a gun and a stopwatch, and a wind is blowing directly from A to B. When the gun is fired by A, B hears the sound 2.96 s later. When the gun is fired by B, the sound is heard by A 3.04 s later. Calculate
    (a) the speed of sound travelling from A to B,
    (b) the speed of sound travelling from B to A, and
    (c) the speed of the wind.
    Note: All speeds are relative to the Earth.

36. A bat flying towards a stationary moth emits a sound wave that reflects back to the bat 0.01 s later. If the bat is flying toward the moth at 10 m/s, how far away is the moth when the bat receives the echo, assuming the speed of sound is 340 m/s?

37. A plane flying at Mach 2.0 bounces a radar signal off a mountain dead ahead. The echo returns in 10^{-5} s. Given that the radar signal travels at the speed of light (3.0×10^8 m/s) and the speed of sound is 350 m/s, how much time does the pilot have to react before impact?

Numerical Answers to Practice Problems

page 353
1. (a) 326 m/s (b) 346 m/s
    (c) 353 m/s
2. 4.0 s

page 353
1. (a) 1.2 (b) 0.75
2. 2.4×10^3 km/h

page 355
1. 7.0 m
2. 338 m/s
3. 35 Hz

page 364
1. 3.6×10^2 m/s
2. 3.0×10^2 m

The Interference of Sound Waves

Chapter Objectives

- **Diagram** *the areas of destructive interference surrounding a tuning fork.*

- **Calculate** *beat frequencies.*

- **Predict** *how changes in length, tension, diameter, and density will change the frequency of a vibrating string.*

- **Diagram** *the overtones of a vibrating string and* **calculate** *the corresponding frequencies.*

- **Explain** *how mechanical resonance occurs.*

- **Relate** *frequency, wavelength, and speed of sound to the length of an air column.*

- **Diagram** *constructive interference behind an object travelling faster than sound.*

- **Explain** *the Doppler Effect with a diagram.*

- **Relate** *the speed of a source to the source frequency, observed frequency, and speed of sound, using the Doppler equation.*

Introduction

It is quite common for two or more sound waves to travel through a medium at the same time. When two or more sound waves act on the same air molecules at the same time, interference occurs. In Chapter 10, the interference of transverse water waves was examined. It was found that water waves can interfere constructively or destructively.

Sound energy, travelling as a wave, should exhibit many of the properties of wave interference previously discussed. In this chapter we will investigate interference in sound waves and use this knowledge to examine some of its applications.

12.1 Interference of Identical Sound Waves

In Section 10.9, we examined the interference of two water waves, originating from two point sources in a ripple tank. Since the water waves were identical, a stationary interference pattern was produced, consisting of a symmetrical pattern of alternating nodal lines and regions of constructive interference. In this section we will examine the interference created by sound waves originating from two identical sources.

When a tuning fork vibrates, the tines are out of phase. A rarefaction is produced in the space between the tines, and at the same time a compression is produced on the outer side of each tine.

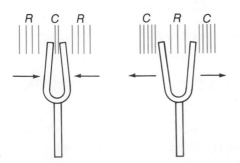

Stroboscopic photograph of a vibrating tuning fork

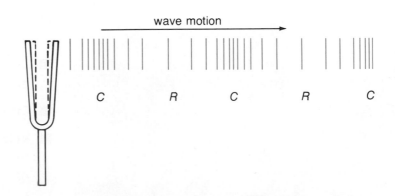

When the tines vibrate, a series of compressions and rarefactions is emitted from the outer sides of the tines and from the space between them, as illustrated. Since the tines are out of phase, the compressions and rarefactions interfere destructively, producing nodal lines that radiate out from the corners of the tines. In the area between the corners of the tines no interference occurs and a normal sound wave emanates from the tines. When the tuning fork is rotated near the ear, the relative sound intensity alternates between loud (normal sound intensity) and soft (destructive interference).

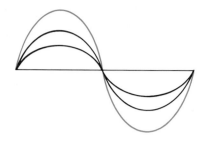

Constructive interference of sound waves (maximum intensity)

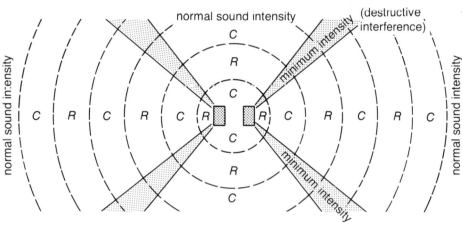

Top view of tuning fork, showing the areas of the destructive interference of sound waves

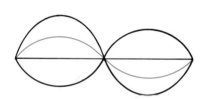

Sound is diminished.

The interference pattern between the two loudspeakers (see the illustration on the next page) is similar to the pattern that is observed in water waves, between two point sources. Areas of constructive and destructive interference are located symmetrically about the midpoint of the pattern, midway between the speakers. If the loudspeakers are in phase, there is an area of constructive interference (maximum sound intensity) at the midpoint. When the frequency is increased, the wavelength decreases. This produces more areas of destructive and constructive interference, as illustrated, but the symmetry of the interference pattern does not change. It is difficult to produce areas of total destructive interference, because sound waves are reflected from the walls and from other surfaces in the room.

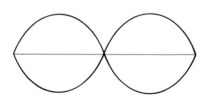

Total destructive interference of sound waves (minimum intensity)

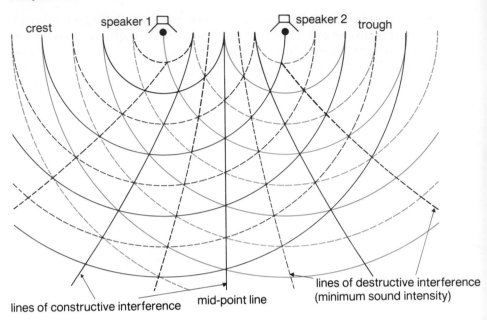

The interference of sound waves between two loudspeakers

William Herschel (1738-1822), a British astronomer, discovered the planet Uranus (in 1781) and the existence of double stars. He constructed the best telescopes of his day.

Interference in sound waves from a single source may be demonstrated with an apparatus called a **Herschel tube**. Sound waves from a source such as a tuning fork enter the tube, as illustrated, and split, travelling along two separate paths. If the paths are of the same length, the waves will meet on the other side in phase; that is, compression will meet compression, rarefaction will meet rarefaction, and the intensity will be at a maximum. If, on the other hand, the tube on one side is longer, the waves on that side will have to

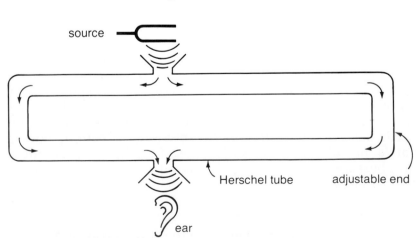

travel farther. At some point, compressions will emerge with rarefactions, and interfere destructively to produce a minimum sound intensity. Further extension of the tube on one side will reveal other positions in which constructive and destructive interference will occur.

In a large auditorium, sound waves are reflected by the walls and ceilings, producing reverberations (Section 11.8). The sound waves can also interfere with one another. In some areas, the audience will receive sound from more than one direction, resulting in interference that may decrease the intensity of the sound in those areas and produce "dead" spots in the auditorium.

Constructive interference will occur at points where the distances to the two sources is equal or differs by a whole number of wavelengths. At these points, the path difference is 0, λ, 2λ, 3λ, etc.

12.2 Beat Frequency

We have been examining the interference of sound waves with identical frequencies and wavelengths. Now we will consider the interference of sound waves with slightly different frequencies and wavelengths. If a tuning fork that has one tine "loaded" with plasticine is struck at the same time as an "unloaded" but otherwise identical tuning fork, the resulting sound will alternate between loud and soft, indicating alternating constructive and destructive interference. Such periodic changes in sound intensity are called **beats**.

The diagram on the next page shows two sources with slightly different frequencies. Thus, the wavelengths are not equal and the distances between successive compressions and rarefactions are dissimilar. At certain points, a compression from one source coincides with a rarefaction from the other, producing destructive interference and minimum sound intensity. When compression and compression coincide, constructive interference results, and maximum sound intensity occurs. The number of maximum intensity points that occur per second is called the **beat frequency**.

The diagram shows two beats being produced in 1 s. In other words, the beat frequency is two beats per second. The two sources have a frequency difference of 2 Hz. Thus, the difference in frequency between the two sources is equal to the beat frequency. For example, if a tuning fork of 436 Hz is sounded with a 440 Hz tuning fork, the beat frequency will be 4 Hz.

In practice, the human ear can only detect beat frequencies of less than 7 Hz.

$$\textbf{Beat frequency} = |f_1 - f_2|$$

---

where f_1 and f_2 are the frequencies of the two sources.

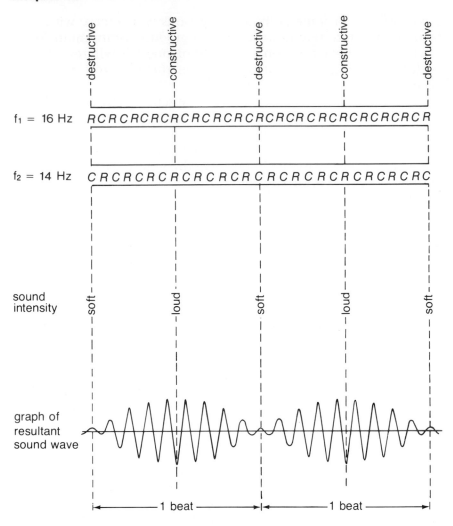

If the tension of the string increases, the frequency increases. If the tension decreases, the frequency decreases. See Section 12.3.

If the two sources have the same frequency (that is, if $f_1 = f_2$), no beats are heard. A piano-tuner makes use of this fact. She plays a note and at the same time sets in vibration a tuning fork or pitch pipe. If there are beats, the two frequencies are dissimilar and the tension in the piano string must be adjusted. Initially, the piano-tuner may have no idea whether the string's frequency is too high or too low. But she knows that the frequency of the beats will change when she adjusts the tension. If the frequency of the beats decreases when she tightens a string, she keeps on tightening it until no beats are audible. Then, the two vibrating sources have the same frequency and the string is "tuned". Once she has tuned seven notes using beat frequency, the piano-tuner adjusts all the other strings by tuning in perfect octaves and using her own sense of pitch.

Sample Problems

A tuning fork with a frequency of 256 Hz is sounded, together with a note played on a piano. Nine beats are heard in 3 s. What is the frequency of the piano note?

Beat frequency $= \dfrac{9 \text{ beats}}{3 \text{ s}} = 3$ Hz

Beat frequency $= |f_1 - f_2|$

$3 \text{ Hz} = |256 \text{ H}_2 - f_2|$

$f_2 = 253$ Hz or 259 Hz

Note that there are two possible answers. Without more information, there is no way of knowing which is correct.

Practice

1. A tuning fork with a frequency of 400 Hz is struck with a second fork, and 20 beats are counted in 5.0 s. What are the possible frequencies of the second fork?
2. A third fork with a frequency of 410 Hz is struck with the second fork in question 1, and 18 beats are counted in 3.0 s. What is the frequency of the second fork?

12.3 Vibrating Strings

Each string on a guitar has a separate, distinct frequency when set in vibration. The strings are tuned by turning pegs. This alters the tension, changing the frequency, or pitch. It is possible to have two strings of the same length and with the same tension, but with different frequencies. This can occur because the frequency is also affected by the diameter of the string and the material it is made of, which may be gut, steel, or aluminum. The pitch of a guitar string may, of course, also be altered by changing the effective length of the string. When you press a string against the neck of a guitar, the effective part of the string is shortened and the frequency thus increased. The pitch, or frequency, of a vibrating string, then, is determined by four factors—its length, its tension, its diameter, and the density of the material it is made of.

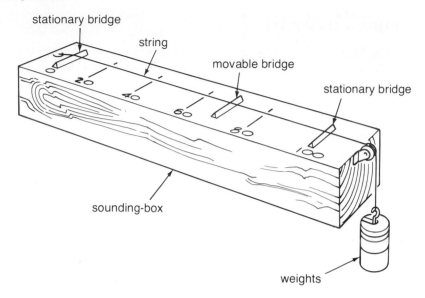

A sonometer can be used to investigate the relationship between the frequency of a stretched string and the tension of the string.

The exact dependence of the frequency of a vibrating string on each of these factors can be determined experimentally. The results are summarized below.

- The frequency increases when the length decreases. The frequency varies inversely with length. ($f \propto 1/L$) For example, if the length is halved, the frequency doubles.
- The frequency increases when the tension increases. The frequency varies directly as the square root of the tension. ($f \propto \sqrt{T}$) For example, if the tension increases by a factor of four, the frequency doubles.
- The frequency increases when the diameter decreases. The frequency varies inversely with the diameter. ($f \propto 1/d$) For example, if the diameter is halved, the frequency doubles.
- The frequency increases when the density decreases. The frequency varies inversely as the square root of the density. ($f \propto 1/\sqrt{\rho}$) For example, if the density decreases to one quarter of its former value, the frequency doubles.

All of these factors are taken into consideration when designing stringed musical instruments such as the guitar, violin, and piano. When constructing a piano, for example, it is theoretically possible to obtain the range of frequencies necessary (27 to 4096 Hz) by altering the length of the strings. But this would be absurd since, if

Alternate Expressions

$$\frac{f_1}{f_2} = \frac{L_2}{L_1}$$

$$\frac{f_1}{f_2} = \frac{\sqrt{T_1}}{\sqrt{T_2}}$$

$$\frac{f_1}{f_2} = \frac{d_2}{d_1}$$

$$\frac{f_1}{f_2} = \frac{\sqrt{\rho_1}}{\sqrt{\rho_2}}$$

Note: Do not confuse tension with period in the above expressions.

the shortest string were 1.0 m in length, the longest would be 150 m! This is avoided by winding wire around the bass strings, increasing both their diameter and density. To avoid having the treble strings too short, they are placed under greater tension. In a typical piano the total tension on the steel frame by the more than 200 strings is over 2.7×10^4 N, equivalent to the gravitational force on a mass of 2.7 t.

Sample Problems

1. The D string of a violin is 30.0 cm long and has a natural frequency of 288 Hz. Where must the violinist place his finger on the string to produce B (384 Hz)?

Given: $L_1 = 30.0$ cm, $f_2 = 288$ Hz, $f_1 = 384$ Hz

$$\frac{f_2}{f_1} = \frac{L_1}{L_2}$$

or

$$L_2 = \frac{f_1 L_1}{f_2}$$
$$= \frac{(288 \text{ Hz})(30.0 \text{ cm})}{384 \text{ Hz}}$$
$$= 22.5 \text{ cm}$$

Therefore, his finger should be placed 7.5 cm from the end of the string.

2. A piano string with a pitch of A (440 Hz) is under a tension of 140 N. What tension would be required to produce a high C (523 Hz)?

Given: $f_1 = 440$ Hz, $f_2 = 523$ Hz, $T_1 = 140$ N

$$\frac{f_2}{f_1} = \frac{\sqrt{T_2}}{\sqrt{T_1}}$$

or

$$T_2 = \left(\frac{f_2}{f_1}\right)^2 T_1$$
$$= \frac{(523 \text{ Hz})^2 (140 \text{ N})}{(440 \text{ Hz})^2}$$
$$= 198 \text{ N}$$

Practice

1. A 1.0 m string has a frequency of 220 Hz. If the string is shortened to 0.80 m, what will its frequency become?
2. A string under a tension of 150 N has a frequency of 256 Hz. What will its frequency become if the tension is increased to 300 N?

3. Two strings have the same diameter, length, and tension. One is made of brass (density = 8.70×10^3 kg/m) and the other is made of steel (density = 7.83×10^3 kg/m). If the frequency of the brass string is 440 Hz, what is the frequency of the steel string?
4. Two copper strings of equal length and tension have diameters of 0.80 mm and 1.0 mm respectively. If the frequency of the first is 200 Hz, what is the frequency of the second?

12.4 Modes of Vibration—Quality of Sound

In Section 10.8 we studied the interference of a standing wave pattern in a rope fixed at one end. A series of equally spaced loops (areas of constructive interference) and nodes (points of destructive interference) were formed as the waves interfered after being reflected from the fixed end. Note that, at the fixed end, a node always occurs—never a loop.

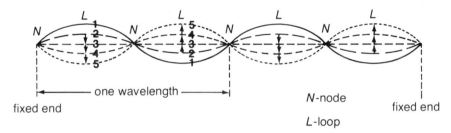

Motion of string in which there is a stationary wave

In a vibrating string stretched between two fixed points, nodes occur at both ends. Different frequencies may result, depending on how many loops and nodes are produced. In its simplest mode of vibration, the **fundamental mode**, the string vibrates in one segment, producing its lowest frequency or pitch, called the **fundamental frequency**, f_0. If the string vibrates in more than one segment, the resulting modes of vibration are called **overtones**. Since the string can only vibrate in certain patterns, always with nodes at each end, the frequencies of the overtones are simple (whole numbered) multiples of the fundamental frequency, called **harmonics**, such as $2f_0$, $3f_0$, $4f_0$, and so on.

This can be demonstrated with a sonometer. In this device, the string is touched at its exact centre with a feather, or lightly with a finger, and simultaneously stroked with a bow between the centre and the bridge. The string is able to vibrate in only two segments,

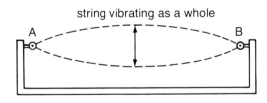

string vibrating as a whole

A string vibrating in its fundamental mode

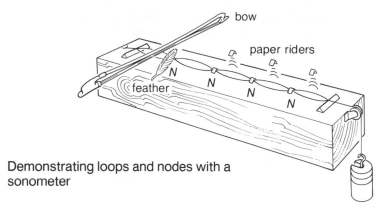

Demonstrating loops and nodes with a sonometer

producing the first overtone, which has twice the frequency of the fundamental. By adjusting the position of the feather or the bow, the string can be made to vibrate in three or more segments, which produces frequencies that are simple multiples of the fundamental frequency, as illustrated.

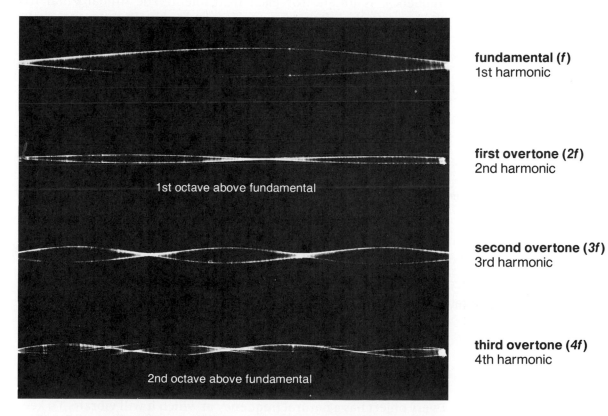

1st octave above fundamental

2nd octave above fundamental

fundamental (*f*)
1st harmonic

first overtone (*2f*)
2nd harmonic

second overtone (*3f*)
3rd harmonic

third overtone (*4f*)
4th harmonic

The strings of violins and other stringed instruments vibrate in a complex mixture of overtones superimposed on the fundamental.

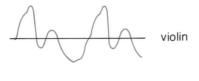

violin

clarinet

tuning fork

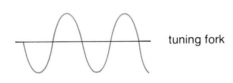

organ pipe

Oscilloscope tracings

Very few vibrating sources can produce a note free of overtones. An exception is the tuning fork, but even it has overtones when first struck. These disappear quickly, and because of this the tuning fork is valuable in studying sound and in tuning musical instruments.

The **quality** of a musical note depends on the number and relative intensity of the overtones it produces, along with the fundamental. It is the element of quality that enables us to distinguish between notes of the same frequency and intensity coming from different sources. We are able to distinguish easily between middle C on the piano, on the violin, and in the human voice.

The oscilloscope is an instrument used in the study of sound waves emitted from different sources. A tuning fork, struck lightly, produces a wave pattern that is symmetrical, because the fundamental is the only frequency present. If the tuning fork is struck sharply, it will produce overtones as well, and these will interfere with the fundamental.

Oscilloscope patterns show that the resultant wave, for a given frequency, is unique for each instrument. The fundamental frequency sets the pitch of a musical note, but in some cases the overtones may be more intense than the fundamental. The overtone frequency structures for various instruments are shown at left.

In the synthesizer the sound of a particular instrument, such as a piano, is simulated by electronically combining the specific overtone structure of the piano note with a fundamental to produce a musical note which nearly equals the sound of an actual piano. Using the same device, musical sounds can be produced which do not naturally exist. This is commonly referred to as electronic music.

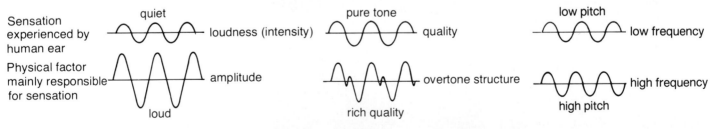

Oscilloscope patterns can be used to illustrate the three characteristics of musical sounds.

12.5 Mechanical Resonance

Every object has a natural frequency at which it will vibrate. To keep a child moving in a swing, we must push the child with the same frequency as the natural frequency of the swing. We use a similar technique to "rock" a car stuck in the snow. When a large truck passes your house, you may notice that the windows rattle.

These are all examples of a phenomenon called **resonance**, which is the response of an object that is free to vibrate to a periodic force with the same frequency as the natural frequency of the object. We call such resonance **mechanical** because there is physical contact between the periodic force and the vibrating object. It can be demonstrated with a series of pendulums suspended from a stretched string (see diagram).

When A is set in vibration, E begins to vibrate in time with it. B, C, and D may begin to vibrate, but they do not continue to vibrate, nor do they vibrate as much. When B is set in vibration, D begins to vibrate in sympathy, but A, C, and E vibrate spasmodically and only a little. The pairs A and E, and B and D, each have the same lengths and thus have the same natural frequencies. They are connected to the same support, so the energy of B (for example) is transferred along the supporting string to D, causing the latter to vibrate. This occurs only if D is free to vibrate. The periodic vibratory force exerted by one of the pendulums moves through the supporting string to all the other pendulums, but only the other one with the same natural frequency begins to vibrate in resonance.

Mechanical resonance must be taken into account in the designing of bridges, airplane propellers, helicopter rotor blades, turbines for steam generators and jet engines, plumbing systems, and many other types of equipment. A dangerous resonant condition may result if this is not done. The Tacoma suspension bridge in Washington state collapsed in 1940 when wind caused the bridge to vibrate. In 1841, a troop of British soldiers marched in step across a bridge, and the tramping feet created a periodic force that set the bridge in resonant vibration and the bridge collapsed.

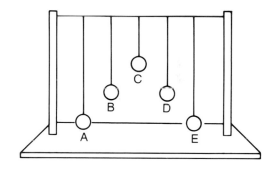

As a result of the collapse, British army regulations were changed, requiring soldiers to break step when crossing a bridge.

The Tacoma bridge vibrated in an overtone mode of two with three nodes.

Large amplitude oscillation of the Tacoma Narrows Bridge due to heavy gusty winds just prior to collapse (November 7, 1940)

Suspension systems for cars with radial tires must be designed so that the motion in the tires does not set up a resonant vibration in the suspension. Helicopter blades, propellers, and turbines must be expertly designed and balanced. If they are not, they may produce a resonant vibration when rotated at a certain speed, and the equipment to which they are attached may be destroyed.

12.6 Resonance in Air Columns

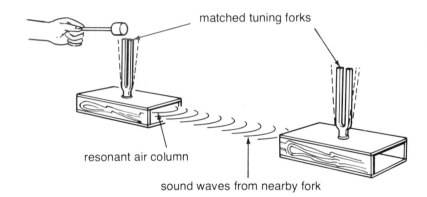

matched tuning forks

resonant air column

sound waves from nearby fork

Sound waves from one source can cause an identical source to vibrate in resonance. Suppose that two tuning forks of identical frequency, mounted on wooden boxes of identical length and open at one end, are placed about 1 m apart. When the first fork is struck and then silenced, a sound of the same frequency comes from the second fork even though it was not struck. Resonance has occurred because the forks have the same natural frequency. Energy has been transferred from one fork to the other by sound waves.

But why is the wooden box attached to the tuning fork? Why is it open at one end and why is the resonance box designed to be of a specific length?

If an air column is closed at one end and open at the other, it is referred to as a **closed air column**. When a vibrating tuning fork is held over the open end of such a column and the length of the column is increased, it is found that the loudness increases sharply at very specific lengths. If a different tuning fork is used, the same phenomenon is observed except the maxima occur at different lengths. To explain this behavior we must recall the behavior of standing waves (Section 10.8).

When a series of transverse waves was sent down a rope or spring towards a fixed end, it was reflected back, interfering with the incident waves. A node was always formed at the fixed end where the reflection occurred.

In a similar way, when longitudinal sound waves are emitted by a tuning fork, some of them travel down the closed air column. The end of the tube reflects the sound waves back, in the same way that the waves in a rope were reflected from the fixed end (Section 10.5). A node is thus formed at the bottom of the column, and, since the air is free to move at the top of the tube, a loop forms there.

When the resonance first occurs, the column is $\frac{1}{4}\lambda$ in length, since a single loop and node are formed. The next possible lengths with a node at one end and a loop at the other are $\frac{3}{4}\lambda$, $\frac{5}{4}\lambda$, and so on. Thus, the **resonant lengths** in a closed air column occur at $\frac{1}{4}\lambda$, $\frac{3}{4}\lambda$, $\frac{5}{4}\lambda$, $\frac{7}{4}\lambda$, and so on. The resonant length of the wooden box that is open at one end and attached to a tuning fork is $\frac{1}{4}\lambda$. For a 256 Hz tuning fork, $\frac{1}{4}\lambda$ would be approximately 34 cm at room temperature (20°C).

Sample Problems

The first resonant length of a closed air column occurs when the length is 18 cm. (a) What is the wavelength of the sound? (b) If the frequency of the source is 512 Hz, what is the speed of sound?

(a) first resonant length = $\frac{1}{4}\lambda$

$\frac{1}{4}\lambda = 18$ cm

$\lambda = 72$ cm

$\quad = 0.72$ m

(b) $v = f\lambda$

$\quad = (512 \text{ Hz})(0.72 \text{ m})$

$\quad = 3.7 \times 10^2 \text{ m/s}$

Practice

1. The first resonant length of a closed air column occurs when the length is 30 cm. What are the second and third resonant lengths?
2. The third resonant length of a closed air column is 75 cm. Determine the first and second resonant lengths.
3. What is the shortest air column, closed at one end, that will resonate at 440 Hz? The speed of sound is 352 m/s.

Resonance may also be produced in **open air columns** or pipes. If a standing wave interference pattern is created by reflection at a free end, a loop occurs at the free end. Since an open pipe is open at

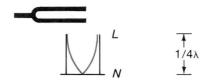

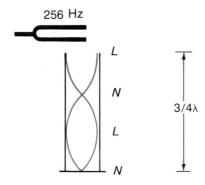

First resonant length

Second resonant length

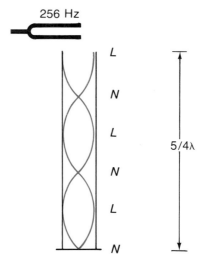

Third resonant length

Resonant lengths of a closed air column for a given frequency

The diagrams show the loops and nodes for the longitudinal displacement sound wave. For the pressure wave, they would be opposite, but the length is the same number of wavelengths.

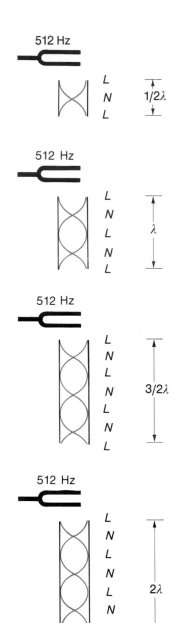

512 Hz

$1/2\lambda$

512 Hz

λ

512 Hz

$3/2\lambda$

512 Hz

2λ

Resonant lengths of an open air column with a sound of given frequency

both ends, loops are formed at both ends. The first length at which resonance occurs is $\frac{1}{2}\lambda$. Succeeding resonant lengths will occur at λ, $\frac{3}{2}\lambda$, 2λ, and so on, as illustrated.

Sample Problems

An organ pipe, 36 m long, open at both ends, produces a musical note at its fundamental frequency.
(a) What is the wavelength of the note produced?
(b) What is the frequency of the pipe, if the speed of sound in air is 346 m/s?
(a) Fundamental length $= \frac{1}{2}\lambda$
$$= 3.6 \text{ m}$$
$$\lambda = 7.2 \text{ m}$$
(b) $f = \dfrac{v}{\lambda}$
$$= \frac{346 \text{ m/s}}{7.2 \text{ m}}$$
$$= 48 \text{ Hz}$$

Practice

1. The second resonant length of an air column that is open at both ends is 48 cm. Determine the first and third resonant lengths.
2. An organ pipe, open at both ends, resonates at its first resonant length with a frequency of 128 Hz. What is the length of the pipe if the speed of sound is 346 m/s?

12:7 Applications: Musical Instruments

A musical note originates from a source vibrating in a uniform manner with one or more constant frequencies. **Music** is a combination of musical notes. (**Noise** is a combination of sounds characterized by vibrations that are constantly changing in frequency.)

Some combinations of musical notes of specific frequencies are pleasing to the ear. This effect is called **consonance**. Other combinations have a harsh effect that is called **dissonance**. The frequencies that are used for musical scales were chosen on the basis of experience and mathematical theory to provide the greatest possible number of pleasing combinations. The conventional musical scale and its frequencies are given in diagrams on the next page.

The eight-note scale illustrated is known as the **diatonic major scale**. There are various ways of representing it on paper. In scientific terms, the diatonic scale sets middle C at a frequency of 256 Hz, and high C at 512 Hz. Most tuning forks used in the laboratory are pitched to the scientific scale and thus are unsuitable for tuning musical instruments. To standardize musical pitch among instruments, a necessity in an orchestra or when playing in an ensemble, it has been agreed that the standard musical pitch will be based on the frequency 440 Hz (A). This is the note that is sounded by an oboist when the members of an orchestra are ready to tune their instruments in preparation for a performance.

When the base of a vibrating tuning fork is placed on a wooden table, the sound becomes louder and richer. The vibrating fork causes the wood to vibrate, giving the sound a greater intensity, and, since the wood produces overtones as well as the fundamental frequency of the fork, the quality of the sound is enhanced. Most stringed instruments, including the violin, illustrate the same principle.

The four strings of a violin are of equal length. They may be set in vibration by a bow, or plucked with a finger. Each string, besides vibrating along its whole length (producing the fundamental frequency), also vibrates in segments (producing an overtone frequency structure unique to the violin). This vibratory energy is transferred through the bridge that supports the strings to the post inside the violin. This sets the whole belly of the violin in motion, and the entire case together with the air it encloses vibrates in sympathy with the strings. Although some of the sound emitted by the violin comes directly from the strings, most of the sound waves originate from the body of the violin or from the air inside it. The quality of sound produced by violins varies greatly, being affected by the type of wood, the structure of the body, and even the quality of the varnish and glue.

All wind instruments use resonating air columns to produce their sounds. The origin of the sound may be air vibrating over an opening (organ, flute), or vibrating lips on a brass instrument (trumpet, trombone), or a vibrating reed (oboe, clarinet, organ). The resonating air column may be closed or open. Some columns are of fixed length, their resonant frequency being altered by the opening or closing of holes in the column (clarinet, recorder). Some instruments are played by altering the length of the air column (trumpet, trombone).

The mouth, the pharynx, and the larynx together constitute the vocal tract, which is a resonant chamber. The resonant frequencies are determined by the position of the articulators—the lips, the jaw, the tongue—and by the length of the vocal tract, which can be adjusted by the protrusion of the lips or the lowering of the larynx.

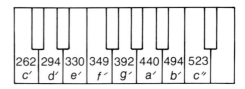

keyboard scale (musical)

staff notation

tonic sol-fa notation

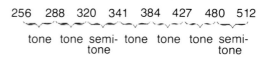

The vibrations of the strings are transmitted through the bridge and post and diffused throughout the violin. All surfaces and the air enclosed in the body of the violin vibrate, sending out separate sound waves that mingle with the original sounds from the strings.

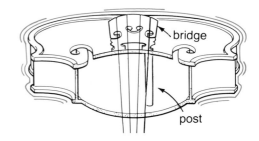

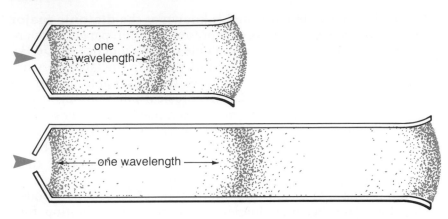

Changing the length of a pipe alters the frequency of the emitted sound
waves. The two pipes have the same number of waves. But since the
lower one is twice as long, its waves are twice as far apart, and so their
frequency is one-half that of the shorter pipe's waves.

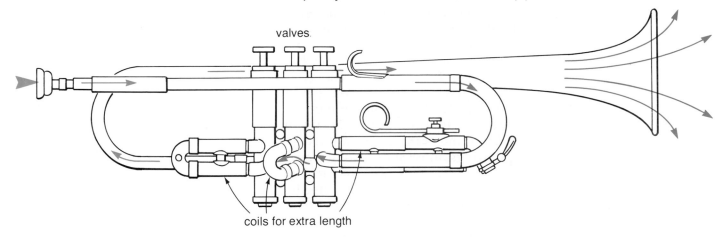

In a trumpet, the length of the air column is altered by opening and closing
valves. The sound is not affected by the trumpet's shape. The tubing is
coiled only for compactness.

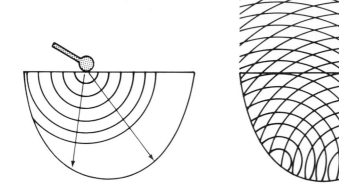

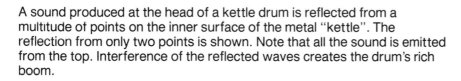

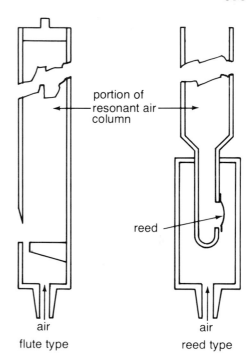

portion of
resonant air
column

reed

air
flute type

air
reed type

A sound produced at the head of a kettle drum is reflected from a multitude of points on the inner surface of the metal "kettle". The reflection from only two points is shown. Note that all the sound is emitted from the top. Interference of the reflected waves creates the drum's rich boom.

12.8 Sonic Booms

A static, or stationary, source radiates sound waves in concentric spheres. An airplane radiates spheres of sound waves from successive positions. Sphere 1 (in the diagram on the next page) was produced by a subsonic airplane at position 1, sphere 2 at position 2, and so on. Note that because the aircraft was moving, the wavefronts were farther apart behind it than they were in front of it.

When an airplane is flying at the speed of sound, the wavefronts in front of it pile up, producing an area of very dense air, or intense compression, called a **sound barrier**. Unless the aircraft has been designed to "cut" through this giant compression, it will be buffeted disastrously. In present-day supersonic aircraft, such as the Concorde, only slight vibration is noticed when the sound barrier is crossed.

At supersonic speeds, the spheres of sound waves are left behind the aircraft. These interfere with each other constructively, producing large compressions and rarefactions along the sides of an imaginary double cone extending behind the airplane from the front and the rear. This intense acoustic pressure wave sweeps along the ground in a swath whose width is approximately five times the altitude of the aircraft and is usually referred to as a **sonic boom**. The sonic boom is heard as two sharp cracks, like thunder or a muffled explosion.

For an airplane flying faster than the speed of sound at a height of 12 km, the sonic boom is produced for 30 km on either side of the flight path. Unless it comes from a supersonic aircraft at a low altitude, the sonic pressure wave is not strong enough to cause any damage on the ground, although the sudden noise may startle or frighten human beings and animals.

Most ecosystems, it is believed, can tolerate random sonic booms. Recurring booms over a long period, on the other hand, might upset them. Supersonic commercial aircraft, as a result, are restricted by many countries to subsonic speeds except over water.

The first supersonic flight was achieved on October 14, 1947, in California, by a Bell XS-1 rocket plane.

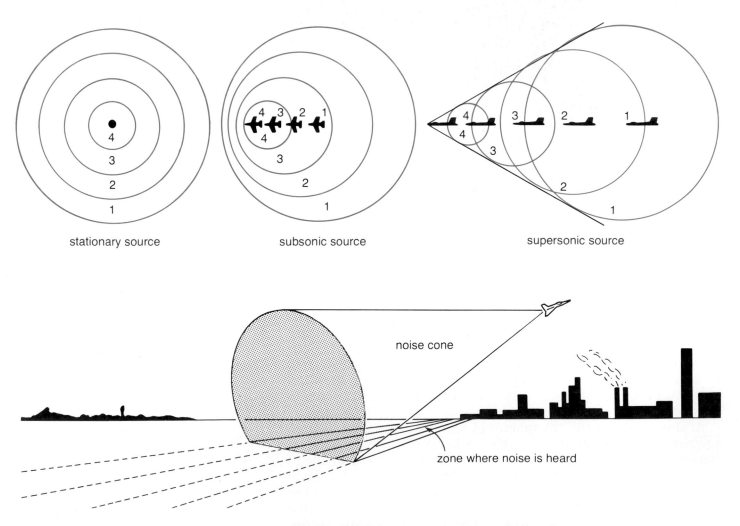

stationary source

subsonic source

supersonic source

noise cone

zone where noise is heard

Shock wave produced by a supersonic aircraft

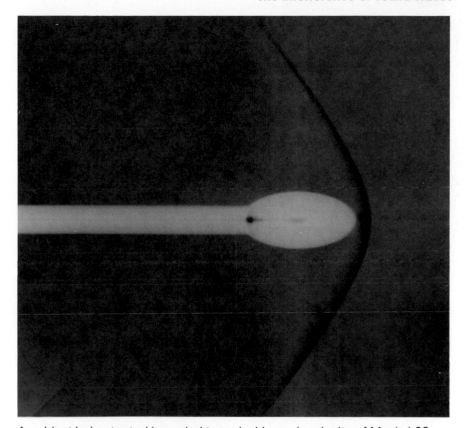

An object being tested in a wind tunnel with an air velocity of Mach 1.38

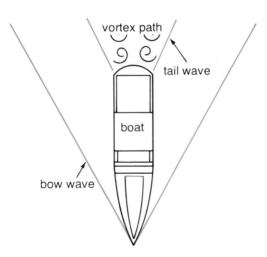

A motor boat moving through the water creates a pattern similar in shape to that of a sonic boom.

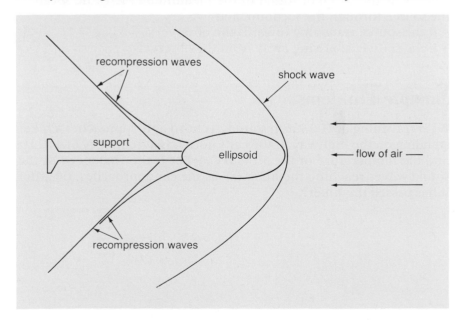

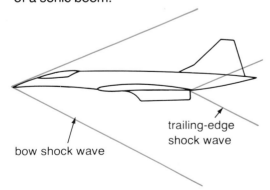

12.9 The Doppler Effect

Most of us have heard what is called the Doppler Effect at one time or another. As a fast-moving object such as a racing car or train passes by, a change in pitch, or frequency, is apparent. This effect is named after C. J. Doppler (1803-53), an Austrian physicist who was the first to explain the phenomenon.

The wavefronts in front of a moving car are relatively close together and those behind it relatively far apart. Observer C (in the diagram) will receive a larger number of compressions and rarefactions per second than observer A. Thus the pitch of the car's horn will seem relatively high to observer C and relatively low to observer A. For observer B, the pitch will rise when the car approaches him and drop as it moves away. For the driver, the pitch will not change.

The general principle of the **Doppler Effect** is that, when a source generating waves approaches an observer, the frequency of the source apparently increases, and when the source moves away from the observer the frequency apparently decreases.

It can be shown that the following relationship describes the effect on frequency when a source either moves toward or away from a stationary observer.

$$f_2 = f_1\left(\frac{v}{v \mp v_s}\right)$$

where v is the speed of sound in the medium and v_s is the speed of the source through the medium, and
− if the source is moving towards the observer
+ if the source is moving away from the observer

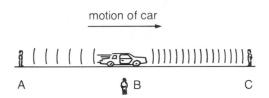

motion of car

A   B   C

Sample **P**roblems

A car travelling at 100 km/h sounds its horn as it approaches a hiker standing on the highway. If the car's horn has a frequency of 440 Hz and the temperature of the air is 0°C, what is the frequency of the sound waves reaching the hiker (a) as the car approaches, (b) after it has passed the hiker?

Given that $T = 0°C$, $v = 332$ m/s, and $v_s = 100$ km/h $= 27.8$ m/s

(a) $f_2 = f_1\left(\dfrac{v}{v - v_s}\right)$

$\qquad = 440 \text{ Hz}\left(\dfrac{332 \text{ m/s}}{332 \text{ m/s} - 27.8 \text{ m/s}}\right)$

$\qquad = 480 \text{ Hz}$

(b) $f_2 = f_1\left(\dfrac{v}{v + v_s}\right)$

$\qquad = 440 \text{ Hz}\left(\dfrac{332 \text{ m/s}}{332 \text{ m/s} + 27.8 \text{ m/s}}\right)$

$\qquad = 406 \text{ Hz}$

Although this phenomenon was first explained in relation to sound waves, it may be observed in any moving object that emits waves. The change in frequency and resulting change in wavelength is called the Doppler Shift. The Doppler Shift can be used to determine the speed of a star relative to the Earth.

Short-range radar devices, such as those used by the police, work on the Doppler Shift principle to determine the speed of a car. Radar waves from a transmitter in the police car are reflected by an approaching car and arrive back at a radar receiver in the police car with a slightly higher frequency. The original waves and the reflected waves are very close together in frequency, and beats are produced when the two are combined. The number of beats per second is directly related to the speed of the approaching car. This beat frequency is electronically translated into speed and displayed in the police car. Modern radar devices can even be used in moving police cars; they automatically correct this movement.

Investigations

Investigation 12.1: Interference in Sound Waves from a Tuning Fork and Two Loudspeakers

Problem:
What is the interference pattern produced in the region surrounding a tuning fork, and in the region between two identical loudspeakers?

Materials:
tuning fork
rubber hammer
audio signal generator
audio amplifier
two identical loudspeakers

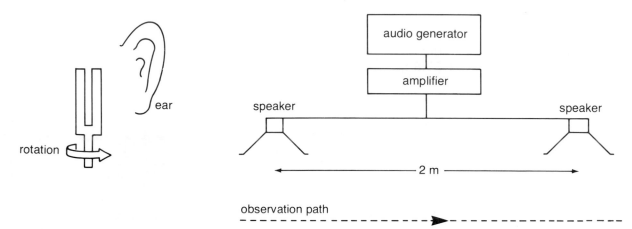

Procedure:
1. Strike the tuning fork sharply with the rubber hammer.
2. Place the vibrating tuning fork near your ear.
3. Rotate the tuning fork slowly, through one complete rotation, and note any variations in the intensity of the sound.
4. Ask your partner to note the positions of the tuning fork when the intensity of the sound is at its lowest and its highest levels.

   (Steps 5 to 8 are usually done as a class investigation.)
5. Set up the amplifier, generator, and speakers as illustrated, with the speakers approximately 2.0 m apart and raised about 1.0 m from the floor.
6. Adjust the frequency of the generator to approximately 500 Hz.
7. Walk along a path parallel to the plane of the speakers, and note any changes in the intensity of the sound.
8. Repeat this procedure for a higher frequency, e.g., 1200 Hz.

Questions:
1. What changes in intensity did you notice when the tuning fork was turned through one rotation?
2. In what specific areas near the tines was the sound intensity the greatest and the least?
3. What changes in intensity occurred when you walked from one speaker to the other?

4. What changes in the intensity pattern occurred when the speakers were adjusted to emit a sound of higher frequency?
5. What conditions of interference must have been necessary to produce the maximum intensity and the minimum intensity?

Investigation 12.2: Resonance in Closed Air Columns

Problem:
What lengths of a closed air column will resonate in response to a tuning fork of known frequency?

Materials:
80 cm of plastic pipe
large graduated cylinder
512 Hz and 1024 Hz tuning forks
meterstick
thermometer

CAUTION: Put on your safety goggles before beginning.

Procedure:
1. Place the plastic pipe in the graduated cylinder, as illustrated. Fill the graduated cylinder with water, as close to the top as possible.
2. Sound the tuning fork and hold it over the mouth of the plastic pipe. Have your partner move the pipe slowly out of the water, and listen for the first resonant point. At points of resonance the intensity of the sound originating from the tuning fork will increase dramatically. Ignore points of slightly increased intensity that are not of the same frequency as the tuning fork.
3. Using the meterstick, measure the length of the air column for the first point. Record your measurements in a chart, as illustrated.

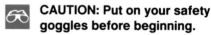

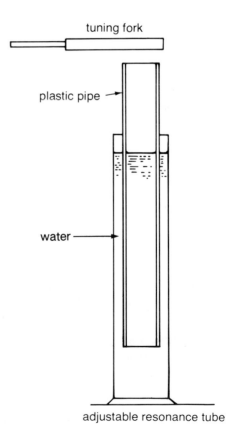

tuning fork

plastic pipe

water

adjustable resonance tube

Resonance point	Fork 1 ($f_1 = 512$ Hz)		Fork 2 ($f_2 = 1024$ Hz)	
	length in centimeters	length in wavelengths	length in centimeters	length in wavelengths
First				
Second				
Third				

4. Continue to raise the pipe, finding and measuring other resonant points.
5. Repeat the procedure with a tuning fork of higher frequency.
6. Record the air temperature in the room.

Chapter 12

Questions:

1. What is the speed of sound at the air temperature you recorded?
2. What is the wavelength of the sound wave emitted by each tuning fork used in the investigation?
3. What is the relationship between the length of the closed air column for the first resonant point you encountered and the wavelength of the tuning fork, for each fork?
4. What is the relationship between the length of the closed air column for the second resonant point you encountered and the wavelength of the tuning fork, for each fork?
5. As a general rule, what are the resonant lengths, expressed in wavelengths, for a closed air column?

Investigation 12.3: Speed of Sound in an Air Column Closed at One End

Problem:

It is your problem to design and implement a method to determine the speed of sound in an air column closed at one end.

Materials:

glass tube open at both ends
tall glass cylinder
water
retort stand
adjustable clamp
meterstick
tuning fork
rubber stopper or striking pad for tuning fork

CAUTION: **A glass tube may shatter if a vibrating tuning fork touches it.**

Investigation Design:

1. Write a clear statement of the problem under the heading of **Problem**.
2. Under the heading of **Procedure**, list in order the steps you would follow to solve the problem.

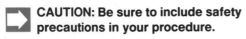 CAUTION: Be sure to include safety precautions in your procedure.

3. Draw a labelled diagram showing the proposed experimental set-up.
4. Submit your procedure to your teacher for approval before commencing with the investigation.

Investigation Report:
1. Perform the investigation by following the steps outlined in your procedure.
2. Under the heading of **Observations**, record the results of the investigation using charts where appropriate.
3. Under the heading of **Calculations**, show the relevant equation(s) and calculations used to determine the numerical solution to the problem.
4. Discuss the accuracy of your answer and identify possible sources of error.
5. Under the heading of **Conclusions**, provide an answer to the problem and comment on its validity.

Chapter Summary

1. The pattern of interference between two identical sound sources is similar to that produced in a ripple tank by two identical water-wave sources.
2. Beat frequency is the difference between the frequencies of two sources.
$$\text{Beat frequency} = |f_1 - f_2|$$

3. The frequency of a vibrating string is determined by its length, tension, diameter, and density.
4. A string may vibrate along its whole length in a single segment or in segments that are simple (whole-number) fractions of its length.
5. When an object vibrates in its simplest or fundamental mode of vibration it produces its lowest possible frequency, which is called the natural or fundamental frequency.
6. Frequencies of overtone modes are simple (whole-number) multiples of the fundamental frequency.
7. Mechanical resonance occurs when an object that is free to vibrate is acted on by a periodic force that has the same frequency as the object's natural frequency.
8. Resonance occurs in closed air columns whose lengths are $\frac{1}{4}\lambda$, $\frac{3}{4}\lambda$, $\frac{5}{4}\lambda$, and so on, of the original sound wave.
9. The resonant lengths of open air columns are $\frac{1}{2}\lambda$, λ, $\frac{3}{2}\lambda$, 2λ, and so on, of the original sound wave.
10. Music consists of notes with constant frequencies. Noise is sound with a constantly changing frequency.

11. Most musical instruments consist of a vibrating source and a structure to enhance the sound through mechanical and acoustical resonance.

12. A sonic boom is caused by the constructive interference of the sound waves that have been emitted behind an object that is exceeding the speed of sound.

13. The pitch of the sound emitted from an object approaching an observer appears to increase, and when the object is leaving the observer the pitch appears to decrease. This phenomenon is called the Doppler Effect.

Chapter Review

Discussion

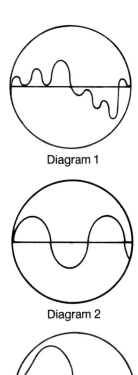

Diagram 1

Diagram 2

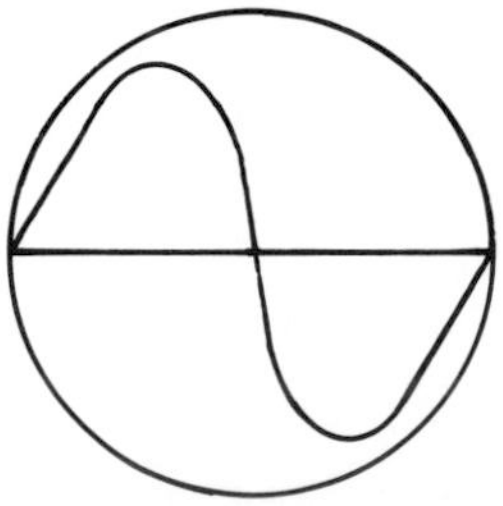

Diagram 3

1. Using *one* loudspeaker and a flat wall, you can get effects similar to those you might expect to obtain with *two* loudspeakers. Explain.

2. Why are the frets on the neck of a guitar spaced closer together as you move towards the bridge?

3. Why are some of the catgut strings on the bass violin wrapped with very fine wire?

4. Using the diagrams in the margin, choose the oscilloscope pattern which best displays the following:
   (a) the sound with the lowest pitch,
   (b) the sound with the greatest number of harmonics,
   (c) the sound with the shortest wavelength,
   (d) the loudest sound.

5. Write a brief (200-300 words) report on the Moog Synthesizer. As well as outlining the history of its development, briefly explain the physical principles of its operation.

6. Some music synthesizers operate with a personal computer. Write a brief report describing how this device can be effectively used by musical composers and arrangers.

7. Sound can be recorded digitally. Briefly explain the difference between analogue and digital sound recording.

8. When a heavy truck passes your house, certain dishes rattle. Explain.

9. When your car moves at a certain speed, there is an annoying rattle. If you speed up or slow down slightly, the rattle disappears. Explain.

10. Your car is stuck in ruts in the snow. How would you use the principle of resonance to free it?
11. Singers are reputed to be able to shatter delicate wine glasses by singing high, loud notes. Explain.
12. If you press the loud pedal on a piano and sing, a sound usually comes from the piano. Explain this phenomenon. Why might more than one piano string respond?
13. A steel guitar player produces a first overtone by plucking the string at the one-quarter point while gently holding the side of her finger at the midpoint of the string. Explain why this works. Where should the string be plucked and touched to produce the second and third overtones? (This can be demonstrated on the laboratory sonometer, or on any other stringed instrument such as the guitar or violin.)
14. Try the following on a piano.
    (a) Slowly depress middle C without sounding the note. (This raises the damper from the string and allows it to vibrate freely.) Strike the Cs below middle C one at a time and listen for any sound produced by middle C.
    (b) With middle C still free to vibrate, sound the following notes: C sharp below middle C, G above middle C, high C, C above high C.
       Explain your observations using your knowledge of resonance and overtones.
15. The voice of a person who has inhaled helium is high pitched and sounds funny. Why?
16. When you whistle through your lips how do you control the pitch of the whistle?
17. When you fill a "pop" bottle with water, you hear a rise in the pitch of the sound as it fills up. Explain.
18. How do you account for the noise you hear when you place a large sea shell to your ear?
19. You tune your woodwind instrument in the house at room temperature. When you go outside to play in the cold the pitch has changed. Will the pitch increase or decrease? Why?
20. A car muffler uses the principle of resonance to reduce engine exhaust noise. Its internal construction consists of a series of open tubes of different lengths. How might a tube be used to reduce the intensity of sounds with specific frequencies?
21. How many fundamental notes can be produced by a three-valve trumpet? Why?
22. Explain why sonic booms from high-flying aircraft are weaker than booms from low-flying aircraft.
23. The whistle of a diesel locomotive is sounded at a fixed frequency and with constant loudness, or intensity.

Vibrating in resonance with high intensity sound waves caused this glass to shatter.

(a) Compare the frequency and loudness of the sound heard by two observers, one 50 m away, and the other 1.0 km away.

(b) The first observer drives her car towards the whistle at a high speed. What changes in frequency and loudness will she notice?

24. You are travelling in a car near a speeding train. The train whistle blows, but you fail to hear the Doppler Effect. What conditions might prevent you from hearing it?

25. Music and the various forms of sound can provide numerous careers. List ten such careers.

Problems

26. You sound two tuning forks together. One has a frequency of 300 Hz, the other a frequency of 302 Hz. What do you hear?

27. A tuning fork with a frequency of 256 Hz is sounded at the same time as a second fork. 20 beats are heard in 4 s. What are the possible frequencies of the second fork?

28. Two sources with frequencies of 300 Hz and 306 Hz are sounded together. How many beats are heard in 4.0 s?

29. Two tuning forks are sounded together, producing three beats per second. If the first fork has a frequency of 300 Hz, what are the possible frequencies of the other fork?

30. Plasticine (which lowers the pitch) is added to one tine of the tuning fork of unknown frequency referred to in question 29. The number of beats decreases to one. What was the frequency of the unknown fork before plasticine was added to one of its tines? What are the possible new frequencies of the fork with plasticine?

31. Two nearly identical forks, one of which has a frequency of 384 Hz, produce seven beats per second when they vibrate at the same time. A small clamp is placed on the 384 Hz fork and then only five beats per second are heard. What is the frequency of the other fork?

32. A 400.0 Hz string produces 10 beats in 4.0 s when sounded at the same time as a tuning fork. When a little plasticine is placed on one tine of the tuning fork, the number of beats increases. What was the frequency of the fork before plasticine was added to it?

33. A source of sound is directed along a straight line perpendicular to a large brick wall. A girl walks along the line towards the wall, and notices that the intensity of the sound decreases to a minimum every 50 cm. What is the frequency of the sound? (Temperature of the air is 20°C.)

34. A stationary loudspeaker sends sound waves with a frequency

of 400 Hz towards a wall 10.0 m away. An observer walks along a line perpendicular to the wall and notes a series of points where the sound is loudest. If the speed of sound is 340 m/s, how far apart are the maxima?

35. A string 1.0 m long vibrates at the rate of 180 Hz. What will its frequency be if it is shortened to 50 cm? 60 cm?

36. A vibrating string has a frequency of 200 Hz. What will its frequency be if (a) its length is decreased to $\frac{1}{4}$ of its original length, or (b) its tension is quadrupled?

37. A string of given length and diameter and density is under a tension of 100 N and produces a sound of 200 Hz. How many vibrations per second will be produced if the tension is changed to (a) 900 N, (b) 25 N?

38. A string 80.0 cm long has a fundamental frequency of 300 Hz. If the length of the string is changed to 40.0 cm without changing the tension, what will the fundamental frequency become?

39. A string on a violin is 25.4 cm long and produces a fundamental frequency of 440 Hz. What must its length be shortened to, in order to produce a tone with a frequency of 523.3 Hz?

40. A 1.0 m string is under a tension of 1.0×10^2 N. The tension is increased to 1.5×10^2 N. If the new frequency is 400 Hz, what was the original frequency?

41. The frequency of one string 50 cm long with a diameter of 0.50 mm is 320 Hz. A second string under the same tension and made of the same material is 1.0 m long with a diameter of 0.25 mm. What is the frequency of the second string?

42. A string 0.50 m long is stretched under a tension of 2.0×10^2 N and its fundamental frequency is 400 Hz. If the length of the string is shortened to 0.35 m and the tension is increased to 4.0×10^2 N, what is the new fundamental frequency?

43. A string 1.0 m long produces a sound of 480 Hz. How many vibrations per second will be produced by segments of this string (a) 33.3 cm long, (b) 25 cm long, (c) 50 cm long, and (d) 10 cm long?

44. If the fundamental frequency produced by a guitar string is 400 Hz, what is the frequency of the second overtone?

45. A stretched string vibrates with a fundamental frequency of 200 Hz. What is the frequency of the third harmonic?

46. What is the beat frequency produced by the first overtones of two strings whose fundamental frequencies are 280 Hz and 282 Hz?

47. A tuning fork causes resonance in a closed pipe similar to the one used in Investigation 12.2. The difference between the length of the closed tube for the first resonance and the length for the second resonance is 54.0 cm. If the frequency of the fork is 320 Hz, what are the wavelength and speed of the sound waves?

48. A closed air column is 60.0 cm long. Calculate the frequency of forks that will cause resonance at (a) the first resonant length, (b) the second resonant length, and (c) the third resonant length (speed of sound = 344 m/s).

49. A closed tube 30.0 cm long resonates at its shortest resonant length with a tuning fork in a room where the air temperature is 25°C. Calculate:
    (a) the wavelength of the sound waves,
    (b) the frequency of the waves produced by the fork.

50. A pipe that is closed at one end can be made to resonate by a tuning fork at a length of 0.25 m. The next resonant length is 0.75 m. If the speed of sound is 338 m/s, calulate:
    (a) the wavelength of the sound emitted by the tuning fork,
    (b) the frequency of the fork.

51. A signalling whistle measures 5.0 cm from its opening to its closed end. Find the wavelength of the sound emitted and the frequency of the whistle if the speed of sound is 344 m/s.

52. Organ pipes, open at one end, resonate best when their length is $\frac{1}{4}\lambda$. Three pipes have lengths of 23.0 cm, 30.0 cm, and 38.0 cm.
    (a) Find the wavelength of the sound emitted by each pipe.
    (b) Find the frequency of each pipe, if the speed of sound is 341 m/s.

Organ pipes

53. A closed organ pipe has a fundamental frequency of 660 Hz when filled with air. What would its fundamental frequency be if it were filled with helium (speed of sound in helium at 20°C = 927 m/s)?

54. What is the length of an open air column that resonates at its first resonant length with a frequency of 560 Hz (speed of sound = 350 m/s)?

55. An open organ pipe has a fundamental frequency of 262 Hz at room temperature (20°C). What is the length of the pipe?

56. An organ pipe open at both ends is 1.23 m long. If the speed of sound is 340 m/s, what is its fundamental frequency?

57. The first resonant length of an open air column in resonance with a 512 Hz fork is 33.0 cm. Find the speed of sound.

58. A sports car sounds its horn (500 Hz) as it approaches a girl by the side of the road. She has perfect pitch and determines that the sound from the horn has a frequency of 520 Hz. If the speed of sound that day was 340 m/s, how fast was the sports car travelling?

59. You are standing at a railway crossing. A train approaching at 100 km/h sounds its whistle. If the frequency of the whistle is 400 Hz and temperature of the air is 20°C, what is the frequency you hear (a) when the train approaches you, (b) when the train has passed by?

60. How fast must a source of sound be moving if the observed frequency is 3% higher than the true frequency? (Assume the velocity of sound is 340 m/s.)

Numerical Answers to Practice Problems

page 381
1. 396 Hz, 404 Hz
2. 404 Hz

page 383
1. 275 Hz
2. 362 Hz
3. 463 Hz
4. 160 Hz

page 389
1. 90 cm, 150 cm
2. 15 cm, 45 cm
3. 20.0 cm

page 390
1. 24 cm, 72 cm
2. 1.35 m

13

Light Rays and Reflection

Introduction

We are all familiar with light—or think we are. Our eyes respond to light we receive from objects all around us. We see the sun, the moon, the stars, and the sky. We see the blue water, the brown earth, the green plant, and the red rose. Light from lasers serve in grocery checkout counters, concert light shows, CD players, and construction equipment. Many of us enjoy occupations and hobbies which utilize light, such as photography or filmmaking. Our very moods and emotions are affected by the shades and colors of light. But what is light—this mysterious phenomenon of infinitely varied color which moves at incredible speed from its source to our eye?

13.1 What Is Light?

The study of light probably began before the dawn of history. However, the earliest surviving records are from the ancient Greeks, dating back to the 5th and 6th century B.C. It is not surprising that light and vision were tied closely together in these early theories. For instance, philosophies attributed to Socrates and Plato theorized that light travelled from a person's eyes to the objects one saw. The followers of Pythagoras believed that light was made up of particles emitted from the objects, rather than from the eyes. With little modification, this particle model of light was the prevailing theory of many centuries.

While widely accepted, the particle theory was not without important challengers. The Greek philosopher Aristotle (4th century B.C.) put forth the theory that light moved as a wave, like ripples on the water. Much later, around 1500, Leonardo da Vinci noted similarities between the behavior of sound and light. He too attributed a wave nature to light.

In the 17th and 18th centuries, the particle-wave debate became more heated. Scientists were now able to test their theories with an increasing number of experiments. Most scientists accepted a theory put forth by Isaac Newton (1642–1727). Postulating that light moved as a stream of particles, Newton devised a theory which accounted for most of the known behaviors of light, including refraction, reflection, and color.

Refusing to accept Newton's theory, Dutch scientist Christian Huygens (1629–95) showed that a wave theory could also account for Newton's observations. In addition, the wave model explained

Interest in the wave-particle nature of light extended beyond the science community. Nineteenth-century artists, such as Georges Seurat, used a technique called pointillism. In the detail shown on the next page, you can see that Seurat painted with a multitude of tiny dots of color.

a small number of experiments which indicated that, like sound waves, light exhibited diffraction. However, the particle theory prevailed well into the 19th century, probably because of Newton's great reputation as a scientist.

In 1801, Thomas Young (1773–1829) provided the first clear evidence that light exhibited interference. Such behavior could not be accounted for by a particle model. There was no conceivable way in which particles could come together and cancel each other. A short time later the French physicist Augustin Fresnel (1788–1827) proposed a comprehensive mathematical wave theory. Supported by a number of detailed experiments, Fresnel's theory successfully accounted for all the observed behaviors of light. By the middle of the 19th century, opinion had swung towards support of the wave theory of light.

Possibly the most important development in the wave theory of light was the work of James Clerk Maxwell (1831–1879). Maxwell believed that light was a wave produced when electric forces accelerated charged particles within atoms. This kind of wave, and the energy it carried, was termed **electromagnetic radiation.** Experiments showed light to be a member of a very large family of similar radiating waves. Frequencies of these waves range from about 10^1 to 10^{25} Hz. Family members are often grouped by frequency and include radio waves, microwaves, light, ultraviolet rays, X-rays, and gamma rays. The entire range of electromagnetic radiation is called the **electromagnetic spectrum.** Visible light is the small portion of the electromagnetic spectrum at about 10^{15} Hz.

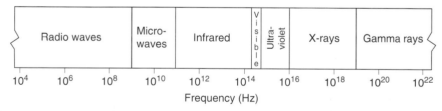

Radio waves	Micro-waves	Infrared	Visible	Ultra-violet	X-rays	Gamma rays

10^4 10^6 10^8 10^{10} 10^{12} 10^{14} 10^{16} 10^{18} 10^{20} 10^{22}

Frequency (Hz)

Maxwell's theories were extremely successful in explaining the behavior of light as well as predicting its speed. His theories became the basis for the development of radar, television, and many other modern forms of communication. Yet, the wave-particle controversy could not be laid to rest. Experiments performed in the 19th century uncovered behaviors which could only be explained with a particle theory.

Is there an answer to the question—*What is light?* Scientists now agree that neither a wave model nor a particle model alone can explain all the properties and behaviors of light. Present theory unifies the wave and particle natures of light as complementary properties in all electromagnetic radiation. Despite its complex nature,

Thomas Young (1773–1829) was an English scientist, physician, and linguist. During his life he was probably best known for his work as a physician. Although Young is remembered now for his experimental work in optics, he is equally noted as one of the first scholars to successfully decode Egyptian hieroglyphics.

most of the properties of light can be easily seen. In this and the next several chapters, we will examine the behaviors of light—including transmission, reflection, refraction, and dispersion.

13.2 The Speed of Light

When we turn on an electric light bulb, the light moves almost instantaneously from the bulb to our eye. We can see that light travels at a very high speed, but at what speed, exactly?

Galileo (1564–1642) made the first serious attempt to measure the speed of light. He instructed an assistant on a hilltop about a kilometer away to flash his lantern when he saw the flash of Galileo's lantern. By timing the interval between his flash and the assistant's flash he hoped to measure the speed of light. This experiment failed because the reaction time of the experimenters was much longer than the time the light took to make the round trip. Galileo recognized this fact and concluded that light moved too quickly to be measured by this technique.

Speculation about the movement of Jupiter's moons has added to our knowledge of the speed of light. Jupiter has at least sixteen moons, four of which are easily seen with a simple telescope. All of the moons move relatively quickly around Jupiter. One of them has a period of only 42.5 h. Although the accurate measurement of their periods had been made earlier, it was Olaus Roemer (1644–1710), a Danish astronomer, who attempted to predict the precise moment at which they would be eclipsed by Jupiter (as viewed from the Earth).

To his surprise, the eclipses came progressively earlier at the times of the year when the Earth approached Jupiter and progressively later when it was moving away from Jupiter. Roemer concluded, correctly, that light must travel at a finite speed, and that the eclipses were delayed because the light had to travel a greater distance when the Earth and Jupiter were farther apart. He calculated that when the Earth and Jupiter were farthest apart, it took 22 min, or 1320 s, for light to cross the diameter of the Earth's orbit.

A few years later, Christian Huygens, a Dutch mathematician and scientist, calculated the diameter of the Earth's orbit and, using Roemer's data, calculated the speed of light as follows:

$$AB = 3.0 \times 10^{11} \text{ m} \qquad v = \frac{\Delta d}{\Delta t}$$

$$\Delta t = 22 \text{ min} \qquad = \frac{3.00 \times 10^{11} \text{ m}}{1320 \text{ s}}$$

$$= 1320 \text{ s} \qquad = 2.3 \times 10^8 \text{ m/s}$$

Galileo Galilei, an Italian scientist, studied falling bodies, the strength of materials, astronomy, thermometry, time measurement, and basic mechanics. He was brought before the Inquisition for his support of the Copernican Theory of the solar system.

A composite of Jupiter and four of its moons.

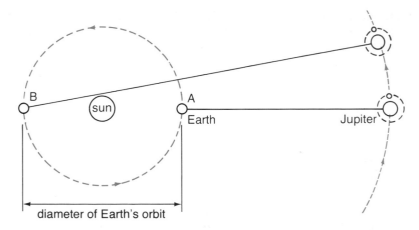

diameter of Earth's orbit

Modern telescopes and accurate timers have enabled scientists to determine that the time difference is 1.00×10^3 s; nevertheless, Huygens' calculation was astonishingly accurate considering the equipment he had. The value Roemer and Huygens gave for the speed of light was so great that their fellow scientists rejected it at first. The work of these two scientists was not accepted until after both were dead.

In 1905, Albert Michelson (1852–1931), an American scientist, made very accurate measurements of the speed of light. His work was recognized, and he was awarded the Nobel Prize for Physics in 1907. Michelson's method involved an ingenious arrangement of mirrors (see diagram below). Light from a very bright source was reflected from surface A, on an eight-sided, rotatable mirror, to a mirror located about 35 km away. The distant mirror reflected the light back to surface G where it was observed in a telescope. The octagonal mirror rotated, and there were only certain positions in

Albert Michelson

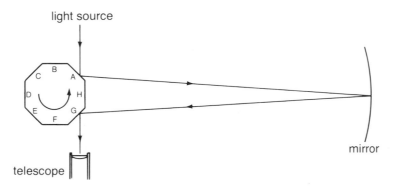

which it reflected light that could be seen in the telescope. These positions occurred every one-eighth of a rotation. If the mirror moved by this amount in the time interval taken by a light pulse making the round trip, then the telescope would detect the pulse reflected from face A via face F, in its new position.

For this to happen, the octagonal mirror had to rotate very quickly—approximately 32 000 times/min. The period of rotation of the mirror was accurately determined, and the time for the light to make the round trip was measured. The speed of light could then be calculated, using this time and the distance travelled by the light on its round trip.

In 1923, Michelson supervised the re-measurement of the speed of light with a long, evacuated tube in which light rays were repeatedly reflected for a total distance of over 16 km. Although he died before the final results were calculated, his experiment produced an even more accurate value for the speed of light.

Today we have very accurate measurements made with lasers. The currently accepted value for the speed of light in a vacuum is $c = 2.997\ 924\ 562 \pm 0.000\ 000\ 011 \times 10^8$ m/s. This value is usually rounded off to 3.00×10^8 m/s, except where greater accuracy is required. (The symbol "c" is used to represent the speed of light.)

Sample Problems

The average distance from the sun to the Earth is 1.5×10^8 km. How long (in minutes) does it take for sunlight to reach the Earth?

$$v = c = 3.00 \times 10^8 \text{ m/s}$$
$$\Delta d = 1.5 \times 10^8 \text{ km} = 1.5 \times 10^{11} \text{ m}$$
$$v = \frac{\Delta d}{\Delta t}$$
$$\Delta t = \frac{\Delta d}{v}$$
$$= \frac{1.5 \times 10^{11} \text{ m}}{3.00 \times 10^8 \text{ m/s}}$$
$$= 5.0 \times 10^2 \text{ s, or 8.3 min}$$

Practice

1. Light from the planet Uranus takes 242 min to reach the Earth. Calculate the distance from Uranus to the Earth.
2. A radar pulse travelling at the speed of light is sent to the moon, and after being reflected returns to the Earth. If the elasped time is 2.5 s, how far (in meters) is the moon from the radar transmitter?

13.3 The Transmission of Light

When the sun's light falls on a solid obstacle, a shadow is produced on the ground. The sharp edges of the shadow remind us that light travels in straight lines. This property of light is called **linear propagation**. This is a fairly obvious property, because we would be unable to line up the sights of a rifle with the target if this were not so. Later we will see that the rule has some exceptions, which occur when light passes through very small openings and past very small obstacles, but for most purposes we may assume that light travels in straight lines.

Sometimes, if there is dust in the air, we see "rays" of sunlight streaming into the room, or at sunset we may see the sun's rays breaking through the clouds. In everyday language, "ray" means a narrow stream of light energy, but in physics we give it a more precise meaning. A **ray**, in physics, is the path taken by light energy. It is usually represented by a solid line with an arrow indicating the direction of travel of the light energy. A **beam** of light is a stream of light rays, and it is represented by a number of rays. The rays may be converging, diverging, or parallel.

Imagine light as it spreads out from a small light source. The light moves outwards, carrying its energy in all directions. Consider, for instance, the light which passes through a small, square opening as shown below. Since light rays travel in straight lines, the light must spread out over a larger and larger surface area as it moves away. The amount of light energy that radiates per second per unit area is called **illumination.** The unit for illumination, E, is **lux.**

As seen in the drawing, the illumination of a light source drops off quickly with distance. Using similar triangles, the base of triangle COD is twice as large as AOB. Since the opening measures one

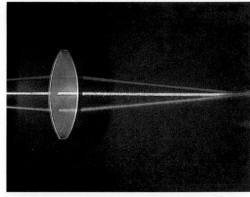

Converging beam

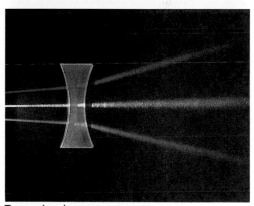

Diverging beam

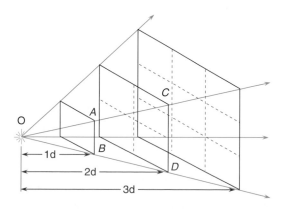

That light varies inversely with the square of the distance is known as the Inverse Square Law for Light. You studied a similar inverse square law for gravity in Chapter 5.

centimeter on each side, the surface covered by light at $2d$ is 2 cm on each side. The light energy spreads out over an area of 4 cm², four times larger than at the opening. At a distance of $3d$, the light spreads out over an area 9 cm², nine times larger than the opening. The area the light covers increases with the square of the distance from the light source. If the total energy moving away from the bulb is constant, then the energy which covers 1 cm² spreads out to cover 4 cm² and 9 cm². The energy per square centimeter would be one-fourth as great at $2d$ and one-ninth as great at $3d$. Illumination falls off with the square of the distance from the source.

$$E \propto \frac{1}{d^2} \text{ or } \frac{E_2}{E_1} = \frac{d_1^2}{d_2^2}$$

To achieve properly exposed pictures, photographers must have accurate information about available illumination. Some photographers use hand held light meters to measure the illumination that reaches the subject to be photographed. They then change the amount of available light or change camera settings to compensate for the amount of light available. Many newer cameras have built-in meters which automatically adjust camera settings for proper film exposure before a picture is taken.

Sample Problems

The illumination on a page is 20 lux. What will the illumination on the page be if it's moved 1.5 times farther from the light?

$$\frac{E_2}{E_1} = \frac{d_1^2}{d_2^2}$$

$$\frac{E_2}{20} = \frac{1}{(1.5)^2}$$

$$E_2 = \frac{20}{(1.5)^2}$$

$$E_2 = 8.8 \text{ lux}$$

Practice

A ceiling lamp that provides an illuminance of 25 lux on a table is lowered from 0.4 m to 0.2 m above the table. What is the new illumination on the table?

An early camera (*circa* 1835)

13.4 The Pinhole Camera

This device was originally called a "camera obscura" when it was invented in the 16th century. It consists of a light-proof box with a pinhole in one end and a screen of frosted glass or tracing paper at the other end. An image is formed on the screen by light travelling in straight lines from an object to the screen. It is easier to see the image on the screen if external light is excluded by shielding the outside of the box with a dark cloth or other covering.

Since light travels in straight lines, the rays of light from various parts of the object travel in straight lines through the pinhole and together form an inverted image on the screen. The image is usually smaller than the object. If a line is drawn through the pinhole and perpendicular to both the image and the object, it can be shown by similar triangles that

$$\frac{\text{height of image}}{\text{height of object}} = \frac{\text{distance of image from pinhole}}{\text{distance of object from pinhole}}$$

$$\frac{h_i}{h_o} = \frac{d_i}{d_o}$$

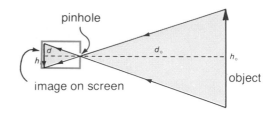

The formation of an image in a pinhole camera

This is called the **magnification equation**. The ratios $\frac{h_i}{h_o}$ and $\frac{d_i}{d_o}$ are called the **magnification** (M). For the magnification to be large, the object must be closer to the pinhole than the screen is. In most cases, the reverse is true and the image is smaller than the object.

$$M = \frac{d_i}{d_o} \qquad M = \frac{h_i}{h_o}$$

The magnification equation also applies to curved mirrors and lenses (see Sections 14.5 and 16.6). A sign convention is used with the magnification equation but this will be applied later and not used in this section.

An image that can be formed on a screen is called a **real image**. An image that cannot be formed on a screen is called a **virtual image**. The image formed in a pinhole camera is a real one.

In physics, the **characteristics of an image** are stated in terms of its orientation (erect or inverted), its size (larger, smaller, or the same size in comparison with the object), and its type (real or virtual). The characteristics of the image formed in a pinhole camera are: inverted, smaller, and real.

If the screen is replaced by a photographic plate, or film, pictures of stationary objects may be taken, provided that a long time exposure is used. Today, most photographs are taken with lens cameras. These admit more light than pinhole cameras, making shorter exposure times possible.

Sample Problems

Calculate the size of the image of a tree that is 8.0 m high and 80 m from a pinhole camera that is 20 cm long. What is its magnification? Given that: $h_o = 8.0$ m, $d_i = 20$ cm, and $d_o = 80$ m we can substitute in the magnification equation as follows.

$$\frac{h_i}{h_o} = \frac{d_i}{d_o}$$

$$\frac{h_i}{8.0\ m} = \frac{20\ cm}{80\ cm}$$

$$h_i = \left(\frac{0.20\ cm}{80\ m}\right)(8.0\ m)$$

$$= 0.020\ m,\ or\ 2.0\ cm$$

Note that the magnification does not have any units.

The magnification of the image is

$$M = \frac{h_i}{h_o}$$

$$= \frac{0.020\ m}{8.0\ m}$$

$$= 0.0025,\ or\ 2.5 \times 10^{-3}$$

*P*ractice

1. Calculate the distance from the pinhole to an object that is 3.5 m high, and whose image is 10 cm high in a pinhole camera 20 cm long.
2. Calculate the height of a building 300 m away from the pinhole that produces an image 3.0 cm high in a pinhole camera 5.0 cm long.
3. A 1.5 cm inverted image is produced on the screen of a camera when a picture is taken of an 80 m tall tree. What is the magnification?

13.5 Laws of Reflection

Light travels in a straight line until it strikes an object. If the object is **opaque**, like a piece of wood, the transmission is interrupted. If the object is **transparent**, like a piece of glass, light passes through.

Mirrors and highly polished opaque surfaces reflect light in predictable ways. The terms used by physicists when describing the reflection of light are as follows:

- The ray approaching the mirror is called the **incident ray**.
- The ray reflected by the mirror is called the **reflected ray**.
- The point where the incident ray strikes the mirror is called the **point of incidence**.
- The construction line drawn at right angles to the mirror at the point of incidence is called the **normal**.
- The angle between the incident ray and the normal is called the **angle of incidence**.

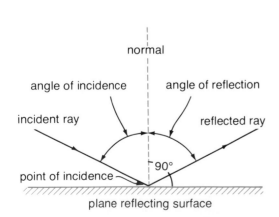

• The angle between the reflected ray and the normal is called the **angle of reflection**.

The angle of incidence equals the angle of reflection for any ray directed towards a plane mirror. This is true even when a ray strikes a plane mirror straight on, since the value of both angles is zero, and it holds without exception for all reflecting surfaces. Therefore, we can use the term "law" when describing this relationship between the angle of incidence and the angle of reflection. Also, the incident ray, the normal, and the reflected ray all lie in the same plane. This is another **law of reflection**.

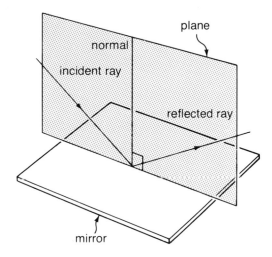

Laws of Reflection

• **The angle of incidence is equal to the angle of reflection.**
• **The incident ray, the reflected ray, and the normal all lie in the same plane.**

13.6 Images in a Plane Mirror

When you look into a plane mirror, your image appears to be located somewhere behind the mirror. But where? To find its position it is necessary to consider how the eye sees light rays coming from an object.

Although a lighted object gives off light in all directions, your eye only sees the particular diverging cone of rays that is coming towards it. If you go to the other side of the object, a different cone of rays will enter your eye.

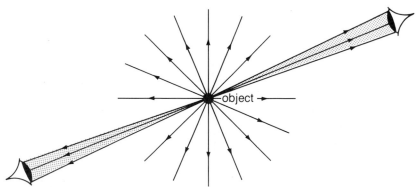

Although an object gives off light in all directions, the eye sees only a diverging cone of rays.

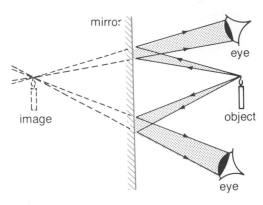

A plane mirror forms an image in this way.

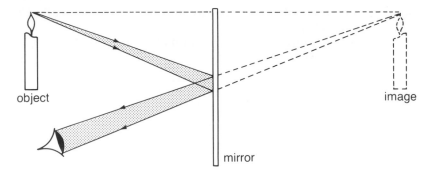

When you see an object in a plane mirror, the cone of rays is reflected by the mirror, as illustrated. Your eye cannot see that the light has been reflected and assumes that, since light travels in straight lines, the origin of the cone of light rays is behind the mirror.

We are familiar with the image in a plane mirror from our everyday experience with mirrors. When you look into a mirror, you see an image of your face, without any magnification, apparently located behind the mirror. If you move towards the mirror, your image will move closer to the mirror, so that the image is always the same distance from the mirror as the object. Unlike the image formed in the pinhole camera, which was formed on a screen and said to be real, the image we see in a plane mirror cannot be formed on a screen and is therefore described as virtual. The image in a plane mirror is produced at the point where the reflected rays, extended behind the mirror, appear to intersect.

When you look in a mirror and raise your right hand, the image appears to be a left hand coming up to meet your right hand. When printing is viewed in a plane mirror as shown below, the letters are reversed along the normal to the mirror. This is called **lateral inversion**.

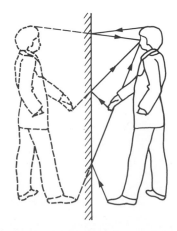

An image in a plane mirror is the same size as the object.

13 Light Rays and Reflection

13.1 What Is Light?

In summary, the characteristics of an image in a plane mirror are:
• It is the same size as the object.
• It is vertically erect.
• It is virtual.

Also, the image is reversed along the normal to the mirror and is located at the same perpendicular distance behind the mirror as the object is in front of it.

Sample Problems

Given an object located in front of a plane mirror, locate the image and show how the eye "sees" it.

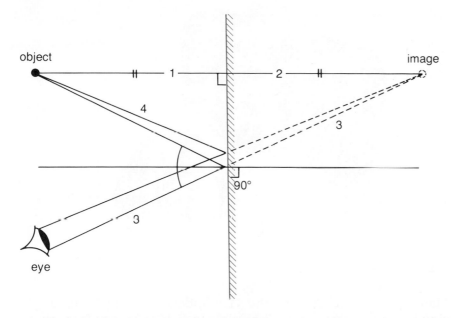

(Each step is indicated by number on the diagram.)
1. Draw a perpendicular from the object to the mirror.
2. Extend this line an equal distance behind the mirror to locate the image.
3. The eye considers that the light originates from a point source image behind the mirror. The light rays from a point source travel out in all directions, and they include a cone of rays travelling towards the eye.
4. Rays actually originate from the object, as illustrated. Note that the angle of incidence equals the angle of reflection.

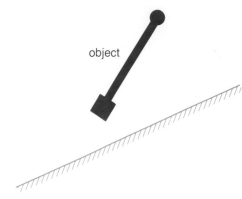

object

Practice 2.

Practice

1. A point object is located a perpendicular distance of 3.0 cm from a plane mirror.
   (a) Using a full-scale diagram, locate the virtual image.
   (b) Place an eye 2.0 cm to the left of the object. Using a ray diagram, show how the eye "sees" the image.
2. Trace this diagram into your notebook, and locate the image in the mirror.

13.7 Applications: Plane Mirrors

1. Plane Mirrors in Cameras

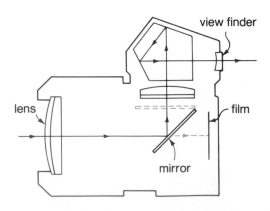

Plane mirrors are used in the viewfinders of many cameras. In simple cameras, they make it possible to view the scene from above the camera. In the single lens reflex (SLR) camera illustrated, the mirror is right behind the lens through which the picture is taken. It is hinged, and when the shutter is released, it flips out of the way to let the light strike the film. It automatically returns to its original position when the picture has been taken. The mirror that is used in this type of camera is called a **front surface mirror**, so called because the reflecting material (usually aluminum) is located on the front of the glass, not on the back as is usual with mirrors. Care must be taken when cleaning or handling this type of mirror because of the danger of damaging it by scratching.

2. The Periscope

A simple periscope consists of two plane mirrors facing each other, mounted at an angle of 45° to the horizontal and vertical planes. Because the light is reflected by two surfaces, the lateral inversion created by the first mirror is reversed by the second mirror, and the scene appears normal.

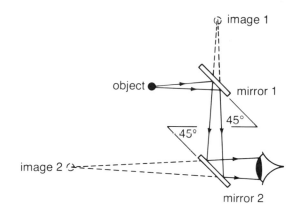

3. Diffuse Reflection

Mirrors, stainless steel, and sheets of glass are highly polished flat surfaces, unlike the surfaces of most objects, which are found to be highly irregular when viewed under a microscope. White paper and a painted ceiling are two good examples of irregular surfaces. When a parallel beam of light falls on such a surface, the individual rays have different angles of incidence, and are therefore reflected in different directions, rather than parallel to each other. This type of reflection is called **diffuse reflection**.

The electron micrograph of a crack in a laser disc reveals a smooth surface. The surface of paper, below, is more irregular.

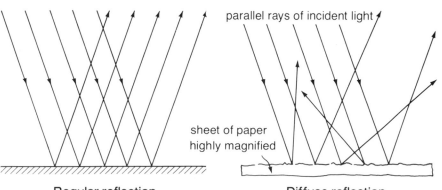

Regular reflection   Diffuse reflection

Chapter 13

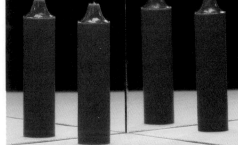

4. Images Formed by Two Mirrors at Right Angles

When two mirrors are mounted at right angles, not only are the two expected virtual images formed, but an extra image is produced as well. Some of the light that enters the eye has been reflected twice, producing a third image, as illustrated. Geometrically, the object and the three images lie at the corners of a rectangle whose center is at the intersection of the mirrors. If the angle between the mirrors is less than 90°, even more images are produced. Try it!

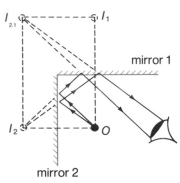

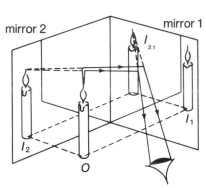

How your eye sees $I_{2.1}$ How your eye sees $I_{2.1}$

5. Reflection in Parallel Mirrors

Multiple images are formed by an object placed between two parallel mirrors. This effect is often seen in a barbershop or hairdressing salon where mirrors have been mounted on opposite walls.

The images are located on a straight line that passes through the object and is perpendicular to the mirrors. Each image appearing in one mirror acts as an object that produces another image in the other mirror. Thus, a series of virtual images is produced behind each mirror (see diagram). Since some of the light energy is absorbed by the mirrors at each reflection, the more distant images are fainter.

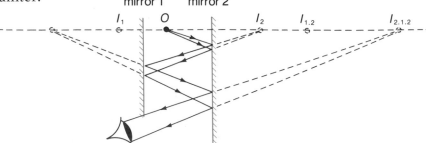

How the eye sees one of the many images in mirror 2.

The number of images (N) formed by two mirrors is predicted by the equation:
$N = \dfrac{360}{\theta} - 1$, where θ represents the angle between the mirrors. In the case of parallel mirrors, $\theta = 0$ and thus N approaches infinity.

6. The Kaleidoscope

A children's kaleidoscope consists of two long, narrow mirrors mounted along a tube at 60° angles to each other. At one end of the tube is a frosted glass plate that admits light. Small pieces of brightly coloured glass are placed between the mirrors. They act as objects which, because of multiple reflections, produce five images. The five images and the objects together form a symmetrical pattern in six sections. The number of different patterns is unlimited, since the pieces of glass are randomly rearranged as the tube is rotated.

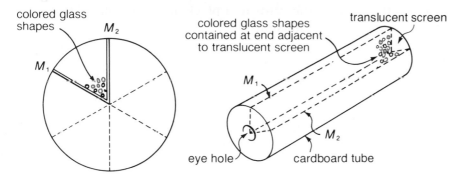

7. Arcade Shooting Gallery

Most shooting galleries use a large mirror placed so as to reflect a picture mounted horizontally below. This gives the impression of a long rifle range. The rifles usually shoot "light bullets", which are detected by light-sensitive targets. When light from a rifle strikes a target, a hit is recorded.

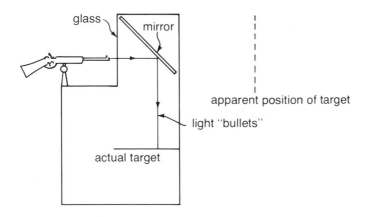

8. Theatrical Effects

A large sheet of plate glass can act as a mirror and at the same time allow objects on the stage behind it to be seen. An actor dressed as a ghost stands off stage. The area around him is painted and draped in a dull black, so that when a strong light is directed on him, the plate glass reflects some of it towards the audience, creating a virtual image of the actor. This illusion is complete when the objects behind the glass are seen at the same time, making the ghost appear to be transparent. The effect of a headless ghost may be created by covering the head of the actor in a black drape. Similar effects are used by magicians and illusionists.

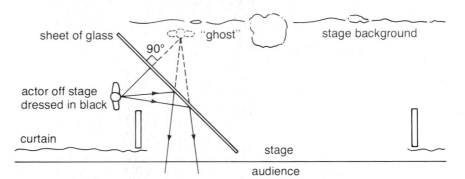

Overhead view of theatrical illusion.

9. Instruments

When a plane mirror is rotated by 10°, the angle of incidence increases by 10°. By the laws of reflection, the angle of reflection also increases by 10°. This means that a light ray is deflected by a total of 20°, which is twice the angle by which the mirror was rotated. Thus, a small rotation in a mirror causes a large movement in the reflected ray. This principle is used to magnify small movements of the hands of such devices as electrical meters.

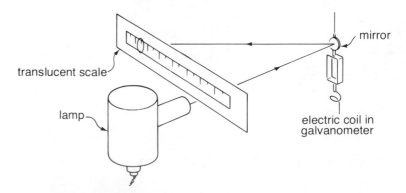

This device is sometimes called an optical lever.

10. See-through Mirrors

Most mirrors are made of a flat piece of glass on which a thin layer of a reflective material such as silver or aluminum has been deposited. Usually this layer is placed on the back of the glass that is to be a mirror and covered with an opaque, protective coating. The reflective layer is easily scratched and, in the case of silver, could be tarnished by certain gases in the atmosphere.

In "see-through" mirrors the protective coating is transparent and the reflective layer is so thin that some light passes through the glass. This allows an observer behind the mirror (and preferably in a darkened area) to see what is happening on the other side without being seen himself. Some sunglasses are constructed on the same principle.

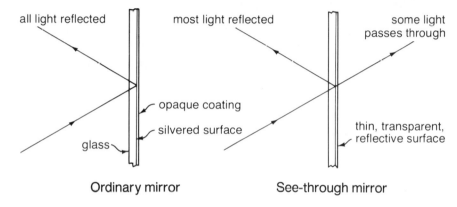

all light reflected

most light reflected

some light passes through

opaque coating

silvered surface

glass

thin, transparent, reflective surface

Ordinary mirror   See-through mirror

Very thin films are often used on the windows of skyscrapers for both aesthetic and efficiency reasons. This gives the windows a mirror effect in daytime. More importantly, it reduces the amount of air conditioning required in summer since less heat energy enters the building. In winter, the thin film also reduces the amount of heat lost from the windows by infrared radiation.

Investigations

Investigation 13.1: Images in a Pinhole Camera

Problem:
How is an image formed in a simple camera?

CAUTION: Put on your safety goggles and constrain long hair and clothing if you are using a candle.

Materials:
simple pinhole camera (no lens)
lighted object such as light bulb or lighted candle

Procedure:
1. Point your camera at the lighted source. This is the object.
2. Look at the image in your camera. Is it larger or smaller than the object? Is it erect or inverted, in comparison with the object?
3. Move the camera closer to the lighted object. Does the size of the image or its orientation change?

Questions:
1. From what part of the object does the light at the top of the image originate? From what parts of the object does the light at the middle and bottom of the image originate?
2. If you increase the distance of the camera from the object, what effect does this have on the size and orientation of the image? What is the effect of decreasing the distance?
3. Is the image's orientation erect or inverted throughout the experiment?
4. What type of image is formed in a camera?
5. What property of light, related to transmission, is demonstrated in the simple camera?

Investigation 13.2: Reflection in a Plane Mirror

Problem:
What laws govern the reflection of light in a plane mirror?

CAUTION: If the mirror breaks, do not touch or try to clean up the broken pieces. Notify your instructor.

Materials:
ray box (single slit)
plane mirror
mirror stand

Procedure:
1. Draw a diagram in your notebook like the one at the right, but larger.
2. Place the mirror on the line marked "plane mirror" so that the back of the mirror is on the line.
3. Direct single light rays, one at a time, along each line.
4. Draw in the reflected ray accurately, in each case.
5. Construct a normal at each point of incidence.
6. Measure the angles of incidence and reflection in each case, recording the values in a simple chart.

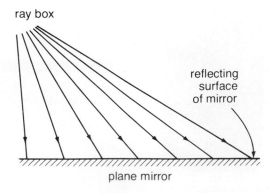

ray box

reflecting surface of mirror

plane mirror

Questions:
1. What is the relationship between the angle of incidence and the angle of reflection in each case?
2. At what angles of incidence do the incident ray and reflected ray travel along the same path?
3. If the angle of incidence is doubled, what happens to the angle of reflection? Why?

Investigation 13.3: Locating Images in a Plane Mirror

Problem:
What is the location of the image in a plane mirror?

Materials:
ray box (single slit)
plane mirror

CAUTION: If the mirror breaks, do not touch or try to clean up the broken pieces. Notify your instructor.

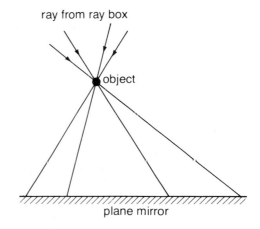

Procedure:
1. In your notebook draw a point object and mirror, as illustrated, but on a larger scale.
2. Draw in two cones of rays, so that they strike the mirror.
3. With the ray box, shine a ray of light down the outside of each cone. Draw in the reflected ray in each case.
4. Look into the mirror in such a way that you can see the light originating from the ray box. Where does the light appear to come from?
5. Using a piece of white paper as a screen, try to locate the image behind the mirror.
6. Look into the mirror. What are the orientation, the size, and the type of the image in the mirror?
7. Raise your right hand in front of the mirror. Which hand does the image in the mirror appear to be—the right or the left?
8. Tilt the mirror at an angle to the printing on this page. How does the image of the printing differ from the actual printing?
9. On your diagram, extend all the reflected rays behind the mirror until they meet. Use dotted lines.
10. Label the point of intersection of the extended rays. This is the location of the image.
11. Join the object and image with a dotted line.
12. Measure the angle this dotted line makes with the mirror.
13. Measure the distances along the dotted line, between the object and the mirror, and between the image and the mirror.

Questions:
1. In a plane mirror, where is the image?
2. Since the image cannot be put on a screen, what type of image is it that is formed behind a plane mirror?
3. What are the three characteristics of an image in a plane mirror?
4. Although the image in a plane mirror is not inverted vertically, relative to the object, it has been changed. How?
5. You are given the position of an object relative to a plane mirror. List the steps you would follow to locate the image behind the mirror.

Chapter Summary

1. The speed of light in a vacuum is constant, and has the value of 3.00×10^8 m/s.
2. Since, in most applications, light travels in straight lines, rays are used to represent the transmission of light from a source.
3. The amount of light energy that radiates per second over a surface area is called illumination (E).

$$E \propto \frac{1}{d^2}$$

4. A real image is one that can be formed on a screen.
5. A virtual image cannot be formed on a screen and is created by the apparent intersection of reflected light rays, when they are extended backwards, behind the reflecting surface.
6. The characteristics of an image are its size, orientation, and type.
7. An image formed in a simple pinhole camera is inverted, real, and smaller than the object.
8. The magnification equation is $\dfrac{h_i}{h_o} = \dfrac{d_i}{d_o}$.
9. A normal is a construction line drawn at right angles to a surface at a point of incidence.
10. The Laws of Reflection are: (1) the incident ray, the reflected ray, and the normal are all located in the same plane, and (2) the angle of incidence equals the angle of reflection.
11. The image in a plane mirror is the same size as the object, erect, and virtual. Such an image is located at the same perpendicular distance behind the mirror as the object is in front of it, and it is inverted along the normal. Parallel rays of light are reflected parallel to one another in regular reflection and non-parallel to one another in diffuse reflection.
12. Two or more mirrors produce multiple images.

Using Light for Distance Measurement

The fact that light travels in straight lines at a constant speed of 3.00×10^8 m/s (c) makes it valuable as a distance measuring tool. As discussed earlier in this chapter, the speed of light can be used to measure astronomical distances. But, to measure shorter distances, more elaborate equipment is necessary.

If a laser is aimed at a reflecting target, its distance from the laser can be determined by measuring the time interval taken by a returning pulse of light. Substituting into the equation $\Delta d = v \Delta t = c \Delta t$, the distance can be calculated. Since light could travel around the circumference of the Earth nearly 7.5 times in 1 s, the measurement of the time interval requires special techniques involving microelectronics. The laser, receiver and electronics can all be contained in a portable unit as shown in the photograph.

The retroreflector left on the moon

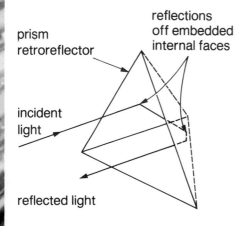

prism retroreflector

incident light

reflected light

reflections off embedded internal faces

Laser light is used because of its property called **coherence**. Simply put, laser light does not spread out very much as it moves away from its source, as is the case for most light. This means laser light will travel long distances as a narrow beam. To reflect the light from the target a transparent pyramid or corner reflector is often used. This reflector has identical triangular faces and is designed so that any beam entering the pyramid through its base is always reflected back in the same direction, regardless of the angle of entry (see diagram). Usually an array of these prisms is arranged on a flat support to increase the targeting area. (A similar design is used in bicycle reflectors.)

The principles of **lidar** (light detecting and ranging) are applied in devices used by engineers for surveying, to dig tunnels straight, or to check the alignment of aircraft wings. Astronomers have used lidar to measure the distance from the Earth to the moon to the nearest 5 cm. Geologists use lidar devices to measure accurately horizontal movement along a fault line

Laser beam directed at the moon from the McMath Solar Observatory

in earthquake research. Finally the military have been using it since the early 1960s for such things as distance ranging for artillery and for guiding cruise missiles above the ground at a constant low altitude.

Chapter Review

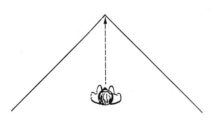

Discussion

1. Explain how a laser could be used to accurately measure distances on Earth. For example, the distance between fixed points on two mountains may be measured yearly to record any movement in the Earth's surface.
2. A photographer wants the same illumination on an object 6 m from the light source that was available at 2 m from the light source. How much stronger must the light source be?
3. A student walks towards a plane mirror at 1.0 m/s.
   (a) With what speed does her image approach the mirror?
   (b) With what relative speed do the student and her image approach each other?
   (c) If the student stands still and the mirror is moved towards her at 1.0 m/s, with what speed does the image move relative to the mirror?
4. Sometimes words on the fronts of trucks and buses are printed with the letters reversed. This makes the words difficult to read, which would normally be bad advertising. Why is this done?
5. Sometimes it is necessary to read printing on the back of an immovable object, using a mirror. What could you add to make the printing easy to read?

6. A boy with one black eye stands and looks at himself in the corner area of two vertical plane mirrors joined at right angles along a vertical line. A view of the situation as seen from above is shown. Which of the following does he see?
   (a) himself as others see him
   (b) a normal mirror image of himself
   (c) two black eyes
   (d) two normal eyes
   (e) two black eyes and two normal eyes
7. A playful physics student uses a grease pencil to print the word *Physics* on the outside surface of the rear window of the physics teacher's car. Sometime later the teacher glances into the inside rearview mirror while driving the car. What pattern is seen?
8. If you were to cut a lobster down the middle, you would find an eye on each side, a claw on each side, an antenna on each side, and so on. Each side would seem to be almost exactly like the other. In fact, they are not. If you were to fold the two parts together, the right claw would meet the left claw, not a right

claw. What type of image is the right half of the lobster, compared with the left half of the lobster? This phenomenon is called **plane symmetry**. List five other examples of plane symmetry found in nature.

9. A friend sits on a small table. You say, "The table is bending with your weight." Your friend disagrees. The bending is too slight to see, but you could prove that it did bend with the help of a small mirror, a ray box, and the white ceiling over your friend's head. Draw a sketch showing how you would place the light and the mirror relative to the table and the ceiling.

10. Explain why interior decorators sometimes use mirrors in small rooms.

11. Why is it easier to read a book printed on porous, matt-finished paper than one printed on shiny, smooth paper, under a bright light?

12. What is the magnification of a plane mirror?

Problems

13. In communicating with an automatic space station, radio signals travelling at the speed of light must travel a distance of 8.7×10^9 m each way. How long does it take for a radio signal to travel to the station and back?

14. A light-year is the distance light travels in one year. How far (in meters) does light travel in three years?

15. How much time would be required for a spaceship travelling at 3.0×10^5 m/s ($\frac{1}{1000}$ the speed of light) to reach the closest known star, Proxima Centauri, 4.3 light-years away? How long would it take for the spaceship that went to the moon (maximum speed 10 km/s)?

16. Periodically, a star explodes. If an explosion took place on a star 10 light-years away, when would the astronomers on Earth see it?

17. A pinhole camera 25 cm long is used to photograph a building 10 m high located 30 m from the camera. Calculate the height of the image on the film.

18. A pinhole camera 20.0 cm long is used to photograph a student 175 cm high. If the image is 10.0 cm high, how far from the camera is the student?

19. Determine the magnification in each of questions 17 and 18.

20. A large pinhole camera has a magnification of 0.050 for a tree located 5.0 m from the camera. What is the size of the image on the screen?

The distances of outer space are so great that they are usually not expressed in metric units, but rather in one of these units:
astronomical unit (AU) = 1.50×10^{11} m
light-year (ly) = 9.46×10^{15} m
parsec (pc) = 3.09×10^{16} m

21. What is the angle of incidence when there is an angle of 60°
    between the incident rays and the reflected rays?
22. The Laws of Reflection apply not only to light but also in
    mechanics. Transfer the diagram to your notebook and show

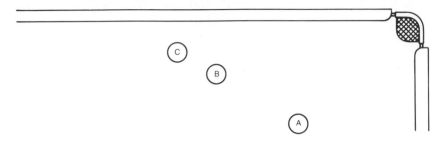

how to aim billiard ball A (with no spin) so that it will hit ball C
without hitting ball B.
23. In this diagram, which eye(s) would see the image in the
    mirror?

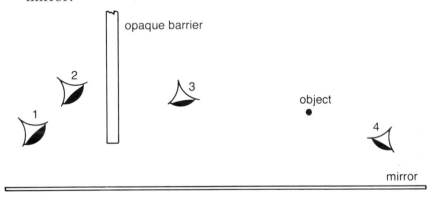

24. A ray of light falls on a plane mirror. The mirror is turned
    through 5°. The reflected ray is found to have turned through
    10°. Explain.
25. An object 4 cm high is located 15 cm in front of a plane mirror.
    What are the characteristics and the location of the image?
26. A student stands 3.0 m in front of a plane mirror.
    (a) How far behind the mirror is her virtual image?
    (b) If she steps forward 1.0 m, what distance will separate her
        from her virtual image?
27. A student sitting in an optician's chair views a chart located
    1.0 m behind his head by facing a mirror 2.5 m away from him.
    How far from him does the chart appear to be?
28. You can look into a mirror 10 cm wide and see reflected in the
    mirror the entire width of the room, which may be 5 m wide.
    Explain how this is possible.

29. A girl is 1.5 m tall and stands 2.4 m in front of a vertical mirror. For the mirror to be of minimum length, the light reflected from the girl's shoes should be reflected to the girl's eyes from the bottom of the mirror. If the girl's eyes are located a vertical distance of 12 cm from the top of her head, and she is able to see her entire body in the mirror, what will be:
    (a) the minimum length of the mirror?
    (b) the distance from the bottom of the mirror to the floor?

30. Trace the diagram at the left into your notebook.
    (a) Indicate the location of four of the virtual images formed by the two mirrors.
    (b) With separate ray diagrams, show how the eye "sees" each of the multiple images.

31. Light from a spotlight travels 60 m before falling on a concert stage. The illumination on the stage is 200 lux. When an enthusiastic concertgoer 10 m from the light stands up, the light temporarily illuminates him. What is the illumination on the concertgoer?

32. A light source placed 9.0 m from an object produces an illumination of 50 lux. If a second identical light source is to be used in addition to the first, how far from the object should it be placed in order to produce a total illumination of 200 lux?

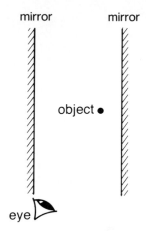

14

Curved Mirrors

Chapter Objectives

- **Identify** *the center of curvature, principal axis, radius of curvature, principal focus, focal plane, and focal length of a curved mirror.*

- **Explain** *how to determine focal length of a converging mirror, using a distant object.*

- **Determine** *the orientation and type of image formed by a curved mirror.*

- **Use a diagram** *to determine characteristics of images formed in curved mirrors.*

- **Explain,** *using a diagram, why a diverging mirror provides a wide field of view.*

- **State** *the orientation of an image, given the sign of the image height.*

- **Relate** *object distance, image distance, and focal length, using the mirror equation.*

- **Apply** *the magnification equation to curved mirrors.*

- **Illustrate** *spherical aberration.*

- **Describe** *how a converging mirror is used in a telescope, solar oven, or flashlight.*

14.1 Curved Reflectors

If you have ever been in the fun-house at an amusement park, you have seen your image distorted by a curved mirror. Similar distortions occur when you look into the bowl of a shiny spoon or at the chromed surfaces of an automobile. The images you see look peculiar because of the curved shape of the reflecting surfaces. They are created by light rays obeying the same laws of reflection that were discussed in Chapter 13.

A curved mirror may be thought of as a section of a hollow sphere. If the inside of the sphere is polished to reflect light, the resulting mirror has a **concave** shape and makes parallel light rays converge on each other. The shiny outside of a similar section has a **convex** surface that makes parallel light rays diverge. Hence the terms **converging mirror** and **diverging mirror**.

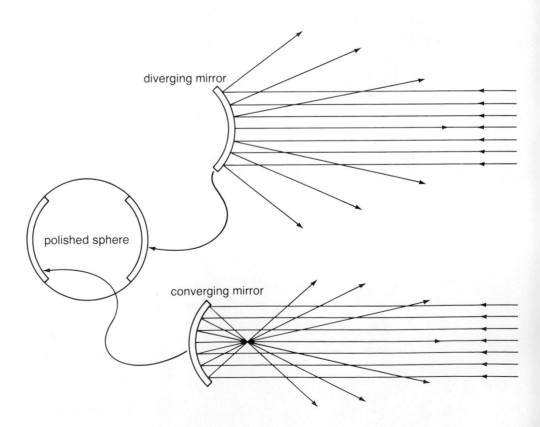

The center of a curved reflecting surface is called the **center of curvature** (C), and the **radius of curvature** is any straight line drawn from the center of curvature to the curved surface. The geometric center of a curved mirror is called the **vertex** (V), and the straight line passing through V and C is called the **principal axis.**

Most of the mirrors used are sections of spheres, shaped liked the watch glass used in chemistry. Because ray diagrams are difficult to draw in three dimensions, we will illustrate curved mirrors in two dimensions.

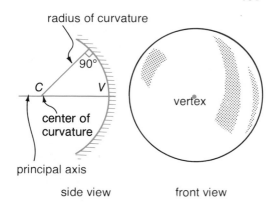

side view   front view

14.2 Reflection in a Converging Mirror

If a group of rays parallel to the principal axis strikes a converging mirror, the rays are all reflected to the same point on the principal axis, called the **principal focus** (F). Converging mirrors with a large radius of curvature and a relatively small surface area have their principal focus halfway between the vertex and the center of curvature. The distance along the principal axis between the principal focus and the vertex is called the **focal length** (f).

If several groups of parallel rays are reflected by a converging mirror, each group converges at a point. Each such point is a focus. When all the foci, including the principal focus, are joined, they form the **focal plane**, perpendicular to the principal axis. Thus, if a converging mirror is pointed at a distant object, the groups of rays coming from many different points on the object and reaching the mirror at slightly different angles converge at different points on the focal plane, producing a real image there. Closer objects form images located further from the mirror.

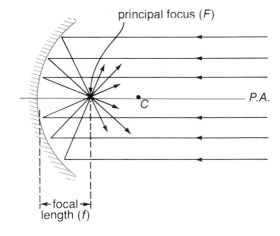

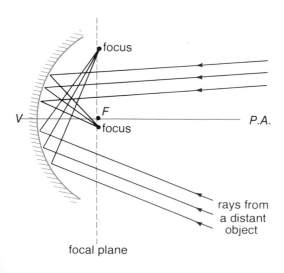

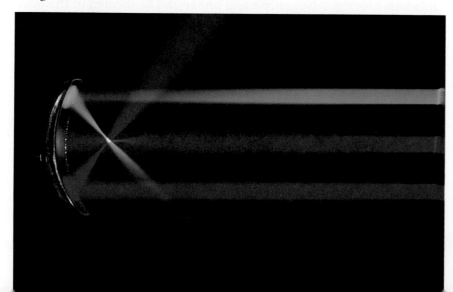

14.3 Images in a Converging Mirror

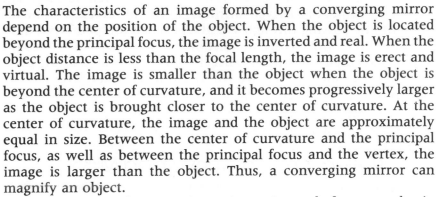

The characteristics of an image formed by a converging mirror depend on the position of the object. When the object is located beyond the principal focus, the image is inverted and real. When the object distance is less than the focal length, the image is erect and virtual. The image is smaller than the object when the object is beyond the center of curvature, and it becomes progressively larger as the object is brought closer to the center of curvature. At the center of curvature, the image and the object are approximately equal in size. Between the center of curvature and the principal focus, as well as between the principal focus and the vertex, the image is larger than the object. Thus, a converging mirror can magnify an object.

This property of converging mirrors is used, for example, in shaving mirrors, which have fairly large focal lengths, placing the user's face (the object) inside the focal point. Thus, the image is magnified, erect, and virtual. As the mirror is moved away from the face, the image becomes progressively larger and more distorted until, at the principal focus, no clear image can be seen. Beyond the principal focus, the image is inverted by the mirror. Try it yourself with a converging mirror (see Investigation 14.1).

The results that have just been described could have been predicted by means of ray diagrams, as will be explained in the next section.

A small object (O) in front of a mirror emits light in all directions. Only some of these rays are reflected from the curved mirror, always, of course, according to the Laws of Reflection. All of the reflected rays would intersect after reflection, forming an image of the small object. To find the location of the image in this way would be a laborious process. Also, only a real image can be located in this way.

To determine the position of an image (I) in a converging mirror it is necessary to use only two rays that intersect. But which two rays? In a converging mirror, any ray parallel to the principal axis is reflected through the principal focus (F). Conversely, any ray through F is reflected parallel to the principal axis. So we select two of the rays radiating out from the tip of the object—the one that passes through F and the one that is parallel to the principal axis.

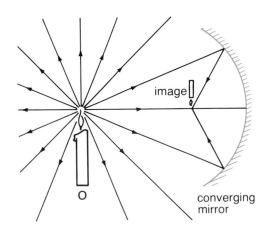

converging mirror

Another ray we can use is the one that goes through the center of curvature (C) from the tip of the object. Since it moves along a radius of curvature, it hits the mirror with an angle of incidence of $0°$. The reflected ray goes back along the same path as the incident ray, since the angle of reflection is $0°$. (Sometimes one or the other of the above rays does not hit the mirror.)

To locate the image in a converging mirror, then, we may use any two of the rays described in the following rules.

Rules for Rays in a Converging Mirror

1. A ray that is parallel to the principal axis is reflected through the principal focus.
2. A ray that passes through the principal focus is reflected parallel to the principal axis.
3. A ray that passes through the center of curvature is reflected back along the same path.

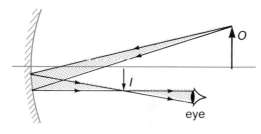

How the eye sees a real image in a converging mirror

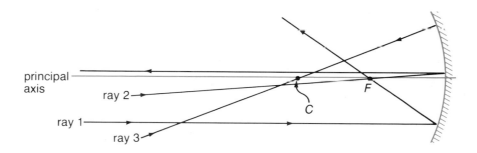

Using these three rays, let us consider how an image is formed for an object located between F and C in front of a converging mirror (diagram 1). Ray 1 is drawn parallel to the principal axis and is reflected through F. Ray 2 passes through F and is reflected parallel to the principal axis. Ray 3 passes through C and is reflected back along the same path. The point at which all three rays intersect is the image (I) location. Actually only two of these rays are required, but the third can act as a check.

The six diagrams show how the image is located. In each case the object (O) or the image (I) is represented by a vertical arrow. Note that if an object is on the principal axis and is perpendicular to it, the image is also perpendicular to the principal axis and has its base on it. Once the tip of the image is determined, the rest of the image is drawn in by dropping a perpendicular to the principal axis. Note also that only two rays are required to locate the tip of an image. The choice of rays is optional, but it is sometimes dictated by the location of the object. In diagram 2, for example, a ray through C does not hit the mirror.

1. Object between F and C

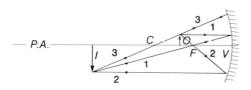

The image is: beyond C, real, inverted, larger than the object.

2. Object at C

   The image is:
   at C, real, inverted, the same size as the object.

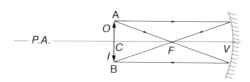

3. Object beyond C

The image is:
between C and F,
real, inverted, smaller than
the object.

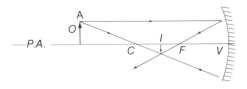

4. Object at F

No image is formed.

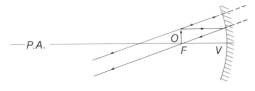

5. Object between F and V

The image is:
beyond the mirror,
virtual, erect, larger than
the object.

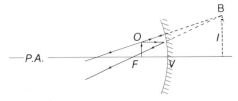

6. Object at a great distance

The image is:
at F, real, inverted, smaller than
the object.

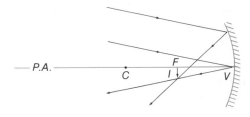

Real images are formed in diagrams 1, 2, and 3. It is important to note the difference between real and virtual images. A real image can be focused on a screen, but a virtual image cannot (Chapter 13). In ray diagrams, the tip of a real image is formed by the actual intersection of reflected rays, drawn as solid lines. The tip of a virtual image is located at the apparent intersection of reflected rays, when extended behind the mirror as dotted lines. The use of solid lines for objects, real rays, and real images, and the use of dotted lines for virtual images and construction lines are accepted conventions in ray optics.

In diagram 4, the rays from the tip of the object are reflected parallel to each other. No image is formed because neither the rays nor their extensions on the other side of the mirror intersect. Converging mirrors are used in this way in searchlights and in theater spotlights, since the reflected rays are all parallel and thus form a concentrated beam of light with little divergence.

In diagram 5, the reflected rays diverge from a point behind the mirror and do not intersect in front of the mirror. The image is located behind the mirror by extending the reflected rays backwards as dotted lines. The image formed is virtual, erect, and larger. This type of image is found in cosmetic and shaving mirrors, which magnify the object—your face.

In diagram 6, the rays are coming from a distant object. They intersect and form a real image on the focal plane of the converging mirror. Similar conditions exist when the image of a distant planet is formed by a reflecting telescope.

Each of the six ray diagrams predicts the location of the image in a converging mirror for various object distances. Compare these predicted images and their characteristics with the actual observations made in Investigation 14.1.

14.4 Images Formed by Diverging Mirrors

In a diverging mirror, the principal focus (F) and center of curvature (C) are virtual, since they are located behind the mirror. Rays directed towards the virtual principal focus are reflected parallel to the principal axis, and rays directed parallel to the principal axis are reflected in such a way that, when extended backwards, they go through the virtual principal focus. Rays directed towards the center of curvature are reflected back along the same path, since they follow a radius of curvature.

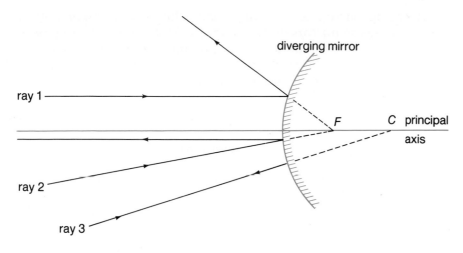

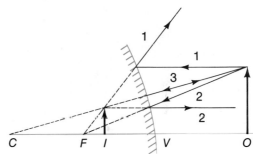

Image formed by a diverging mirror

The rules for rays in diverging mirrors are similar to the rules for rays in converging mirrors. The two sets may be combined to make a set of rules for all curved mirrors, as follows:

Rules for Rays in Curved Mirrors of Both Types

1. A ray that is parallel to the principal axis is reflected through (or as if it had gone through) the principal focus—real or virtual.
2. A ray passing through (or appearing to pass through) the principal focus is reflected parallel to the principal axis.
3. A ray passing through (or appearing to pass through) the center of curvature is reflected back along the same path.

Unlike the converging mirror, which produces real or virtual images depending on the location of the object, the diverging mirror produces only virtual images. These virtual images are all erect, smaller than the object, and located between the vertex and the principal focus.

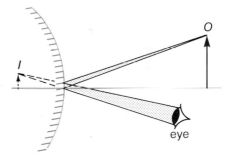

How the eye sees a virtual image in a diverging mirror

Diverging mirrors are useful because they give a wider field of view than plane mirrors of the same size. Unfortunately, all objects are not magnified by the same amount and the image is somewhat distorted. Diverging mirrors are used as rear-view mirrors on trucks and cars, and in stores to discourage shoplifting.

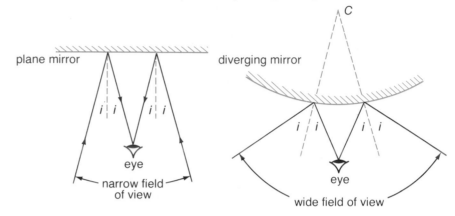

In a diverging mirror the images are all erect, smaller than the object, and virtual.

A truck mirror often combines a plane mirror and a diverging mirror.

A diverging mirror gives an expanded view and is commonly used in stores to monitor customers and discourage shoplifting.

14.5 Equations for Curved Mirrors

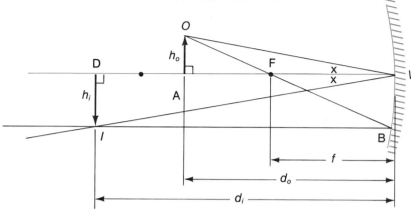

In the diagram, two rays are used to locate the image. The light ray OBI is the same as ray 2 in the previous section. The ray OVI, although it is not one of the convenient rays used in the previous section, also obeys the Laws of Reflection.

As a result, the triangles AOV and DIV are similar.

Therefore,
$$\frac{AO}{DI} = \frac{AV}{DV}$$

or
$$\frac{h_o}{h_i} = \frac{d_o}{d_i}$$

This is, of course, the magnification equation (Section 13.4) that holds for curved mirrors as well as pinhole cameras.

Using the other ray, OFB, the triangles FAO and FVB are similar. Therefore,
$$\frac{AO}{VB} = \frac{AF}{VF}$$

Since $AO = h_o$, $VB = h_i$, and $FV = f$,
$$\frac{h_o}{h_i} = \frac{d_o - f}{f}$$

but
$$\frac{h_o}{h_i} = \frac{d_o}{d_i}$$

Therefore
$$\frac{d_o}{d_i} = \frac{d_o - f}{f}$$

Dividing both sides by d_o, we obtain
$$\frac{d_o}{d_o d_i} = \frac{d_o - f}{d_o f}$$
$$\frac{1}{d_i} = \frac{1}{f} - \frac{1}{d_o}$$

In this derivation for small mirrors we will consider insignificant the very slight error introduced by the curvature VB.

Rearranging, we obtain

$$\frac{1}{d_o} + \frac{1}{d_i} = \frac{1}{f}$$

This is called the **mirror equation**. It is very useful, because it relates both image and object distances and the focal length. Note that if the object distance approaches infinity $(d_o \rightarrow \infty)$, $\frac{1}{d_o}$ approaches 0, making $d_i = f$. Thus the image is located on the focal plane, as discussed on page 439.

As we have seen, an image is sometimes formed in front of a curved spherical mirror and sometimes behind it. This makes it necessary to have a sign convention, so that we can distinguish between real and virtual images, and also get the correct answer when using the mirror equation.

Sign Convention

1. All distances are measured from the vertex of a curved mirror.
2. Distances of real objects and images are positive.
3. Distances of virtual objects and images are negative.
4. Object heights and image heights are positive when measured upward and negative when measured downward from the principal axis.

According to this convention, a converging mirror has a real principal focus and thus a positive focal length. A diverging mirror has a virtual principal focus and a negative focal length.

Using this convention for a real image formed by a converging mirror, h_o is positive and h_i is negative, whereas d_o and d_i are both positive. A negative sign must be added to the magnification equation so that it agrees with the sign convention.

To remember that the magnification is d_i over d_o and not the reverse, note that "i" occurs before "o" in the alphabet.

$$M = \frac{h_i}{h_o} = -\frac{d_i}{d_o}$$

The orientation of the image can be predicted, using the sign convention. The magnification is positive for an erect image and negative for an inverted image.

Sample Problems

1. An object is located 30.0 cm from a converging mirror with a radius of curvature of 10.0 cm.
   (a) At what distance from the mirror will the image be formed?
   (b) If the object is 4.0 cm tall, how tall is its image?

(a)

Since $R = 10.0$ cm, $f = \dfrac{R}{2} = 5.0$ cm.

$$\frac{1}{d_o} + \frac{1}{d_i} = \frac{1}{f}$$

$$\frac{1}{30.0 \text{ cm}} + \frac{1}{d_i} = \frac{1}{5.0 \text{ cm}}$$

$$d_i = 6.0 \text{ cm}$$

The positive value of d_i indicates that the image is real.

(b)

$$\frac{h_o}{h_i} = -\frac{d_o}{d_i}$$

$$h_i = -\left(\frac{d_i}{d_o}\right) h_o$$

$$= -\left(\frac{6.0 \text{ cm}}{30 \text{ cm}}\right) 4.0 \text{ cm}$$

$$= -0.80 \text{ cm}$$

Since h_i is negative, the image is inverted.

2. A diverging mirror with a focal length of -5.0 cm produces an image of an object located 15.0 cm from the mirror.
   (a) What is the distance of the image from the mirror?
   (b) What is the magnification?

Since it is a diverging mirror, the focal length is negative.

(a)

$$\frac{1}{d_o} + \frac{1}{d_i} = \frac{1}{f}$$

$$\frac{1}{15.0 \text{ cm}} + \frac{1}{d_i} = \frac{1}{-5.0 \text{ cm}}$$

$$d_i = -3.8 \text{ cm}$$

The image is virtual, since d_i is negative, and it is observed to be 3.8 cm behind the diverging mirror.

(b)

$$M = -\frac{d_i}{d_o}$$

$$= -\frac{-3.8 \text{ cm}}{15.0 \text{ cm}}$$

$$= 0.25$$

The magnification is positive, indicating that the image is erect.

The mirror equation can also be written as

$$\frac{1}{d_o} + \frac{1}{d_i} = \frac{2}{R} \left(\text{since } f = \frac{R}{2}\right)$$

where R is the radius of curvature.

When the mirror equation is applied for a plane mirror, the following results.
$R = \infty$ and $f = \infty$
Thus

$$\frac{1}{d_o} + \frac{1}{d_i} = \frac{1}{\infty} = 0$$

$$d_i = -d_o$$

and $M = 1$

Practice

1. Determine the image distance in each of the following.
   (a) A converging mirror has a focal length of 15 cm. The object is placed (i) 40 cm, and (ii) 10 cm from the mirror.
   (b) A diverging mirror has a focal length of −20 cm. An object is placed (i) 10 cm, and (ii) 30 cm from the mirror.
2. A candle 3.0 cm high is placed 30 cm from a converging mirror with a focal length of 20 cm.
   (a) By means of a scale diagram, locate the image and determine its height. State the characteristics of the image.
   (b) Using the mirror and magnification equations, determine the image position and its height. Compare your results with those obtained in part (a).
3. A converging mirror has a focal length of 20 cm. Where should an object be placed so that its virtual image will be twice as tall as the object?

Aberration: "failure of a mirror, refracting surface, or lens to produce an exact point-to-point correspondence between an object and its image" (*Webster's New Collegiate Dictionary*)

14.6 Spherical Aberration

In some curved mirrors, rays parallel to the principal axis, which strike the mirror near the edges, do not intersect at the principal focus. This defect is called **spherical aberration**. It may be avoided by designing mirrors in the shape of a parabola rather than a sphere. Such mirrors, called **parabolic mirrors**, are used where it is important that all light be reflected to a single focus, for example, in a solar oven or a telescope, or that all light reflected from one source be parallel, for example, in a searchlight or a car headlight.

Spherical aberration may occur in both large and small mirrors. As long as the mirror is small compared with the focal length, the amount of spherical aberration is negligible.

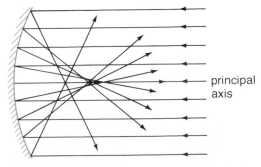

Failure of rays parallel to the principal axis to meet at a common focus is called spherical aberration.

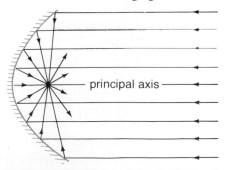

In a parabolic mirror, all rays parallel to the principal axis are reflected to the same focus.

Spherical aberration can also be eliminated by using an opaque shield in front of the mirror, blocking out the rays that would normally strike the edges of the mirror.

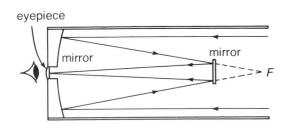

A dentist's examining room lamp. The light source is placed at the focal point of a spherical or parabolic mirror. The light rays of the reflected beam are parallel, thereby providing uniform illumination.

14.7 *Applications:* Curved Mirrors

1. Reflecting Telescopes

Parabolic mirrors are used in large telescopes to focus weak light from a distant star or planet onto the focal plane. The larger the diameter of the mirror, the stronger the concentration of light energy at the focus. This makes it possible for an astronomer to see distant stars whose light energy is so low that they cannot be seen without the assistance of a telescope. An eyepiece is used to magnify and focus the image.

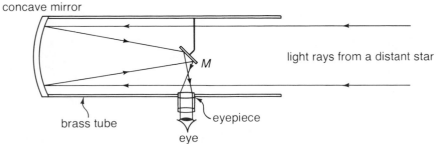

Newtonian focus

Cassegrain focus

Telescopes of the time had lenses that produced color distortions. Newton believed that these defects could not be corrected, and he designed the reflecting telescope. See Section 17.5.

The first telescope of this type was made by Isaac Newton in 1668. To make it convenient to see the image, Newton placed a plane mirror at 45° to the axis of the concave mirror, in front of the principal focus. This reflected the rays to one side, and the image could then be viewed through an eyepiece.

Newton's telescope had a mirror with a diameter of approximately 25 mm. Modern telescopes have mirrors with diameters ranging up to 6 m. The Hale telescope at the Palomar Observatory in California, once the largest in the world, has a diameter of 5.08 m. The largest single-mirror reflecting telescope in the world is located on Mount Semirodriki in the Caucasus Mountains of Russia. It has a diameter of 5.99 m and a total mass of 8.6×10^5 kg. Larger telescopes are now being made that use several mirrors to gather more light from faint stars and galaxies.

The mirrors for large telescopes are made of special glass coated with aluminum. They require a year or more of careful polishing to produce an accurate parabolic surface. In the largest telescopes, the astronomer can actually sit at the focal point, suspended above the mirror!

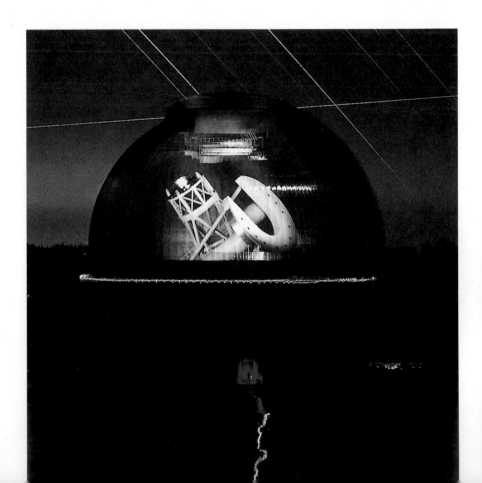

A long-exposure photograph of the 5.08-m Hale telescope at the Palomar Observatory in California

2. Solar Heaters and Furnaces

As sources of non-renewable energy become scarcer, ways of using the sun's energy become more important. A fundamental component of many systems is the concave reflector. The substance to be heated, usually water, is run through a tube at the focal point. The sun's energy is focused on this point, heating the water which is then stored or used to heat a building.

It is difficult to maintain high temperatures (of, say, 6000°C) for any length of time, partially because the container enclosing the furnace will melt or burn. But it is necessary to test some materials, for example, rocket components, at such temperatures. Solar furnaces provide the answer by concentrating the sun's energy on one point by means of a large concave reflector, thereby producing the high temperatures required. The largest solar furnace is located in the Pyrenees, in southern France. Many large flat mirrors are mounted so that they form a concave reflector. Smaller furnaces, to heat food, have been designed on the same principle.

Solar furnace used in research

The largest solar furnace in the world – in southern France

3. Fun-house Mirrors

Amusing effects can be produced by full-length, curved mirrors of both types. As noted in the following investigation, converging mirrors may produce larger or smaller images. The images in diverging mirrors are always smaller. The curved mirrors used in fun-houses are cylindrical, not spherical, and the combinations of converging and diverging mirrors produce amusing distortions.

Investigation

Investigation 14.1: Images Formed by a Converging Mirror

Problems:
1. What is the focal length of a converging mirror?
2. What are the characteristics and locations of the images formed by an object located at various positions in front of a converging mirror?
3. Is the mirror equation valid for this mirror?

Materials:
light source (candle or small, clear electric bulb)
optical bench
converging mirror
white paper screen

Procedure:
1. Hold the mirror in the darkest part of the room and point it at an object some distance away, such as a window frame or a house near the school.

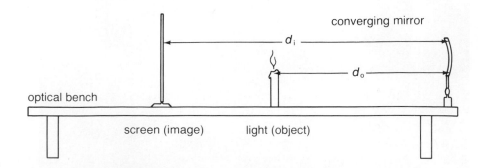

2. Move the cardboard screen back and forth until the object is clearly focused on the screen. Measure the distance between the mirror and the screen. This is the focal length of the mirror.
3. Using your measured value for the focal length, calculate the distances from the mirror of objects at the following object distances: $2.5\,f$, $2\,f$, $1.5\,f$, f, $0.5\,f$. Record your observations and calculations in your notebook, making a suitable chart.

Object distance: the distance from the vertex to the object
Image distance: the distance from the vertex to the image

Note that d_i is negative if the image is located behind the mirror and that

$$M = -\frac{d_i}{d_o}.$$

| Observa-tion | Object distance (d_o) | Image distance (d_i) | Characteristics | | | $\frac{1}{d_o}$ | $\frac{1}{d_i}$ | $\frac{1}{d_o} + \frac{1}{d_i}$ | Mag (M) |
			size	orien-tation	type				
1	$2.5\,f =$								
2	$2\,f =$								
3	$1.5\,f =$								
4	$f =$								
5	$0.5\,f =$								

4. Place the mirror at one end of the optical bench. It is more convenient to measure the distance of objects and images if the mirror is placed at the zero end of the scale.
5. Using chalk or masking tape, mark on the bench the object positions calculated in step 3.
6. Place the object at $2.5\,f$. Move the screen back and forth until the image is clearly in focus on the screen. Some tilting of the mirror may be necessary so that the light from the candle is not blocked by the screen. Record the image distance and the characteristics of the image.
7. Repeat step 6 for the other object distances. If an image is virtual, you should not record its distance.
8. Complete the columns $\frac{1}{d_o}$, $\frac{1}{d_i}$, and $\left(\frac{1}{d_o} + \frac{1}{d_i}\right)$ for the first three observations only.
9. Determine the value of the reciprocal of the focal length (f).
10. Calculate the magnification (M) for the first three observations only.

CAUTION: Put on your safety goggles and constrain long hair and cothing if you are using a candle.

If the image cannot be placed on a screen, it may be a virtual image. Look into the converging mirror, remembering where the images in plane mirrors are located.

Questions:
1. Describe how to find the focal length of a converging mirror.
2. As the object is moved closer to the mirror, what changes occur in the size of the image, the distance of the image, and the orientation of the image?
3. At what object distance was it difficult, if not impossible, to locate a clearly focused image?

4. Where would you place an object, relative to the principal focus, in order to form a real image? A virtual image?

5. How does the value of $\frac{1}{f}$ compare to $\left(\frac{1}{d_o} + \frac{1}{d_i}\right)$ in the first three observations?

Chapter Summary

1. The terms used with curved mirrors are: center of curvature, principal axis, vertex, radius of curvature, principal focus, focal plane, and focal length.

2. All rays parallel to each other and striking a converging mirror are reflected together at a point on the focal plane called the focal point. Rays parallel to the principal axis are reflected through the principal focus.

3. The focal length is the distance between the principal focus and the vertex, measured along the principal axis.

4. Rays from a distant object are considered to be very nearly parallel.

5. For objects located beyond the principal focus, the images in a converging mirror are all inverted and real. For objects located inside the principal focus, the images are all erect and virtual. The images are smaller for objects located beyond the center of curvature ($2f$) and larger for object distances of less than $2f$.

6. The three rays that may be used in drawing ray diagrams for curved mirrors are: (a) a ray parallel to the principal axis, which is reflected through (or as if it had gone through) the principal focus (real or virtual); (b) a ray passing through (or appearing to pass through) the principal focus, which is reflected parallel to the principal axis; and (c) a ray passing through (or appearing to pass through) the center of curvature, which is reflected back along the same path.

7. In ray diagrams, solid lines are used for objects and for real rays and images, and dotted lines are used for virtual rays and images, and for construction lines.

8. To locate the tip of an image in a curved mirror, using a ray diagram, at least two rays or their extensions must intersect on one side of the mirror or the other.

9. The equations that can be used for curved mirrors are $\frac{1}{d_i} + \frac{1}{d_o} = \frac{1}{f}$ and $M = \frac{h_i}{h_o} = -\frac{d_i}{d_o}$.

10. The sign convention used with the curved mirror and magnification equations are: real object and image distances are positive; virtual object and image distances are negative; up from the principal axis is positive, down is negative.
11. All the images formed in a diverging mirror are smaller than the object, erect, and virtual. They are all located between the vertex and the principal focus.
12. Spherical aberration occurs in curved mirrors when parallel rays do not all converge on the focal plane. One way to eliminate this is to change the shape of the mirror to a parabola.
13. Some uses of curved mirrors are: reflecting telescopes, solar heaters and furnaces, rear-view mirrors on cars and trucks, mirrors to discourage shoplifting, and fun-house mirrors.

Chapter Review

Discussion

1. A converging mirror reflects light from a distant object, causing it to focus 20 cm from the mirror. What is the radius of curvature of the mirror?
2. You are given a converging mirror, a lighted object, and a white screen. Explain how you would find the center of curvature.
3. When you look at the sun in a wavy lake, it appears distorted. Why?
4. According to the legend, the Roman fleet at Syracuse was burned when Archimedes focused the sun's rays using a large converging mirror. Was this practical?
5. Diverging mirrors are often used in stores to discourage shoplifting. Why are they useful in this application?
6. You are given some sheets of polished steel and told to design fun-house mirrors with each of the following groups of characteristics.
   (a) Every dimension of a person standing in front of the mirror is enlarged.
   (b) Every dimension is reduced.
   (c) All vertical dimensions are made larger, while horizontal dimensions remain the same (that is, the person appears taller and thinner).
   (d) The upper features are enlarged vertically and the lower features are reduced vertically, while the horizontal dimen-

sions remain the same (that is, the head appears very long and the legs short).

With sketches, indicate how you would bend the metal in each case.

7. Two students are doing the same laboratory investigation using identical converging mirrors with a focal length of 25 cm. Each places a candle in front of the mirror and creates an image three times larger. But when they compare notes, they find their object distances are different. How is this possible?

Problems

8. List in your notebook the names of the parts numbered 1 to 5 in this diagram.

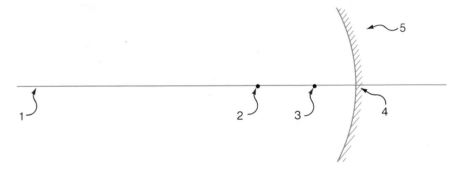

9. In each of these diagrams, an object and its image appear. Copy the diagrams into your notebook. Locate the center of curvature in each case.

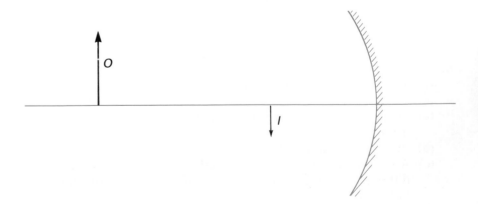

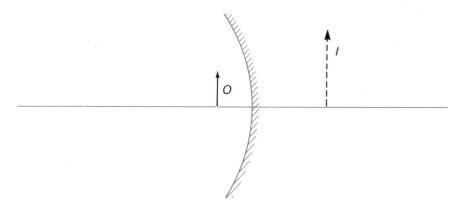

10. On each of these diagrams, the images formed by curved mirrors are indicated. Copy the diagrams into your notebook and, using ray diagrams, locate the objects.

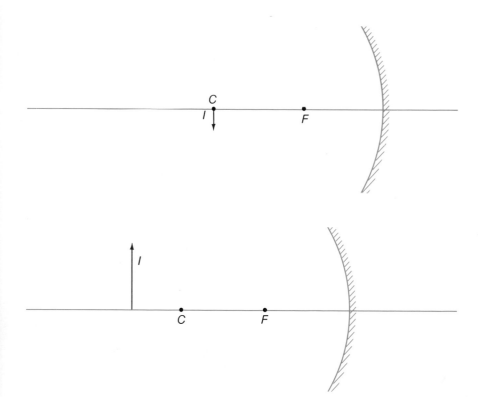

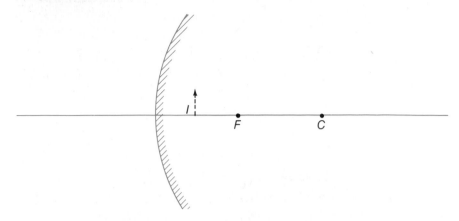

11. An object and its image, formed by a converging mirror, are indicated on each of these diagrams. Copy the diagrams into your notebook and, using ray diagrams, locate the principal focus of the mirror.

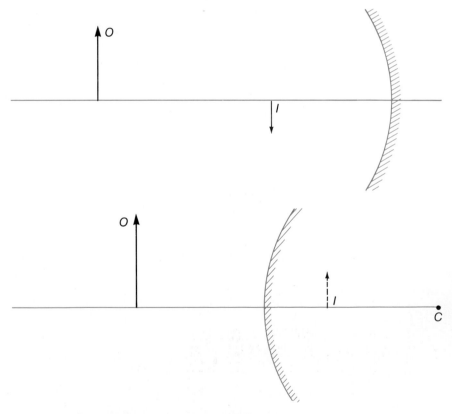

12. A candle 3 cm high is placed 30 cm from a converging mirror with a focal length of 20 cm. By means of a scale ray diagram,

locate the image, and determine its height. State the image's characteristics.

13. Use careful scale drawings to locate the images in each of the following cases. State the characteristics of each image.
    (a) A converging mirror has a focal length of 20 cm. An object is placed at (i) 10 cm, (ii) 30 cm, and (iii) 40 cm from the vertex of the mirror.
    (b) A diverging mirror has a focal length of 20 cm. An object is placed (i) 10 cm, and (ii) 30 cm from the vertex of the mirror.

14. A woman looks at herself in a magnifying converging mirror whose focal length is 20 cm. If her face is 10 cm from the mirror,
    (a) at what distance from the mirror is her image?
    (b) what is the magnification of her face?

15. A 2.0 cm high candle is placed 15 cm in front of a converging mirror with a focal length of 30 cm. How far "behind" the mirror does the candle appear, and how large is it?

16. A dentist holds a converging mirror with a focal length of 20 mm a distance of 15 mm from a tooth. What is the magnification of a filling in the tooth?

17. A trucker sees the image of a car passing her truck in her diverging rear-view mirror, whose focal length is −60 cm. If the car is 1.5 m high and 6.0 m away, what is the size and location of the image?

18. A spherical, polished metallic ball is used as a diverging mirror ($f = -20$ cm) over a birdbath. A bird, 25 cm tall, standing 50 cm away, looks directly at the mirror. What are the size and position of the bird's image?

19. When standing 2.0 m in front of an amusement park mirror, you notice that your image is three times taller. What is the radius of curvature of the mirror?

20. A child looks at his reflection in a spherical Christmas tree ornament 8.0 cm in diameter, and sees that the image of his face is reduced by one-half. How far is his face from the ornament?

21. A converging mirror has a focal length of 15 cm. Where would you place an object in order to produce an erect virtual image twice as tall as the object?

Numerical Answers to Practice Problems

page 448
1. 24 cm, −30 cm; −6.7 cm, −12 cm
2. $d_1 = 60$ cm, $h_1 = -6.0$ cm
3. 10 cm

Seeing The Edge Of The Universe

The ability of scientists and astronomers to see further into space has been limited by telescope technology. As discussed on page 448, large parabolic mirrors are used in reflecting telescopes. The larger the mirror, the more the light from distant stars and galaxies can be concentrated and the further one can see into space. But, there has been a size barrier since 1948 when the 5.08-m (200-in) Hale telescope was completed in California. Beyond this size, glass mirrors tend to sag and distort the images unacceptably, affected by their own weight and by expansion and contraction due to temperature change. In fact, the only larger single-mirror telescope constructed since that date, in the Soviet Union, is flawed and has limited use as a result.

One solution involves using several smaller mirrors together, simulating a single large one. Under construction by the University of California is the 10-m Keck Telescope, to be erected on Mount Mauna Kea in Hawaii. The primary mirror will be formed from 36 1.8-m hexagon mirrors, each individually controlled, forming a paraboloid surface 10 m in diameter. The mirrors will not be made of glass but of low-thermal-expansion ceramic material coated with a thin layer of aluminum. This telescope will be capable of seeing a single candle from the distance of the moon from the Earth, enabling astronomers to see objects 12 billion light years away.

Another alternative is to put a telescope in orbit above the Earth. All Earth-based telescopes have

The Keck telescope, with hexagon mirrors, under construction

some distortion and blurring caused by the Earth's atmosphere. The atmosphere also absorbs light from distant stars and galaxies, making it difficult to detect their faint light. The Hubble Space Telescope—launched on April 24, 1990, by the space shuttle *Discovery*—solves both of these difficulties because it is above the atmosphere. Unfortunately scientists discovered a flaw in the primary mirror of the telescope—a spherical aberration which causes images

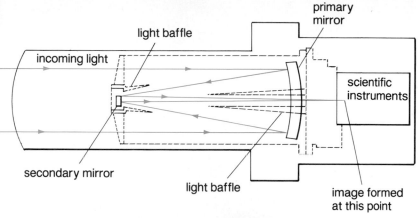

light baffle

primary mirror

incoming light

scientific instruments

secondary mirror

light baffle

image formed at this point

This schematic shows how starlight enters the open front end of the Hubble Space Telescope, is projected from the primary mirror to the secondary mirror, and is then directed to a focus inside the scientific instruments at rear. The light baffles preclude unwanted light, which may have been deflected off some part of the telescope, from reaching the image formed within the scientific instruments.

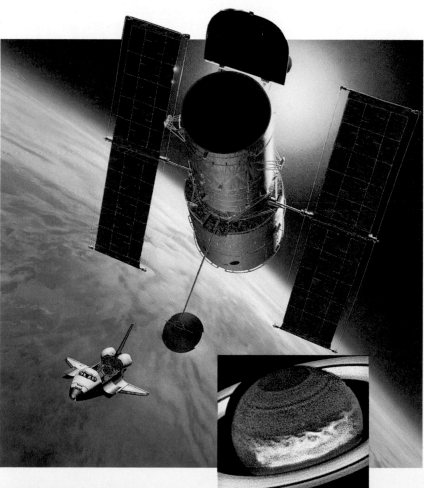

recorded by the telescope to be fuzzy. Astronomers found that computer processing could "clean" the images somewhat. Complete repair of the Hubble Telescope's optical system will require a space shuttle mission, currently planned for 1993.

Astronomers hope to make many discoveries with the Hubble Telescope, such as planets orbiting other stars. Some discoveries may have to wait until the telescope is fully repaired. But the Hubble Telescope has already surpassed ground-based telescopes in recording some exciting events. In 1990, the Hubble Telescope provided excellent views of a storm on Saturn that was larger than any storm ever observed in our solar system. The Hubble Telescope also recorded excellent images of the Orion nebula, a large gas cloud in which star formation is taking place. Once the Hubble Telescope is fixed, it should be able to investigate the farthest reaches of the universe, providing answers to the most challenging questions of astronomy and physics.

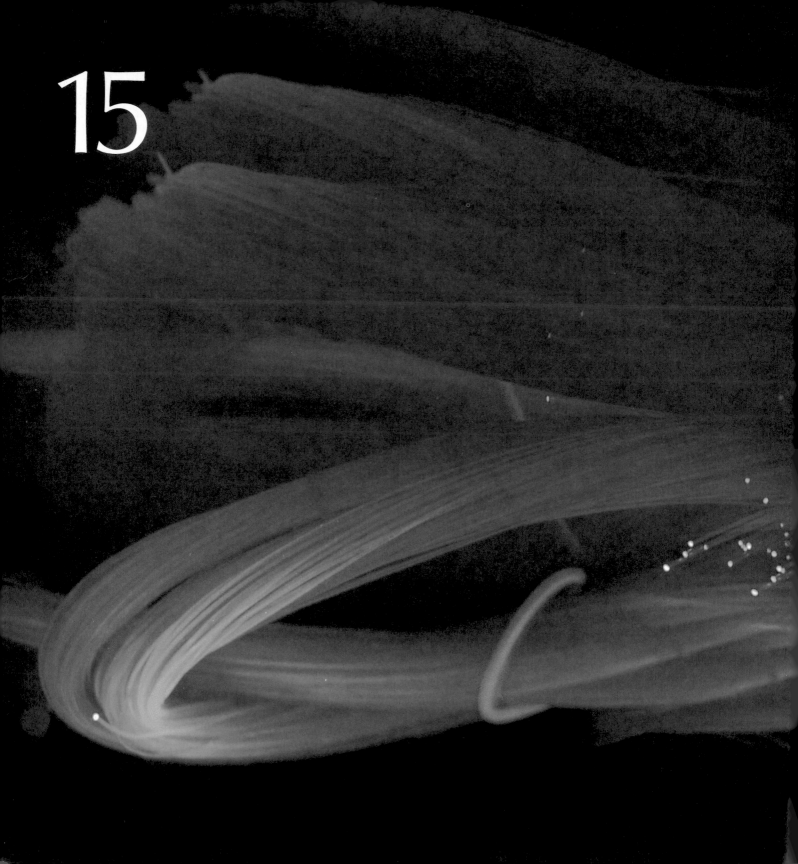

Refraction of Light

Chapter Objectives

- **Identify** *on a diagram the normal angle of incidence, and angle of refraction.*

- **Relate** *the speed of light in a medium and in air to the index of refraction.*

- **Define** *"index of refraction" in terms of the speed of light and Snell's Law.*

- **State** *the Laws of Refraction.*

- **Predict** *the direction in which a ray will be refracted, given the relative optical densities or the indices of refraction.*

- **Relate** *the index of refraction to the angle of incidence and the angle of refraction.*

- **Describe** *the conditions under which total internal reflection occurs and* **determine** *the critical angle.*

- **Explain** *everyday applications of refraction and total internal reflection.*

- **Explain,** *using a diagram, total internal reflection in an optical device.*

15.1 Refraction

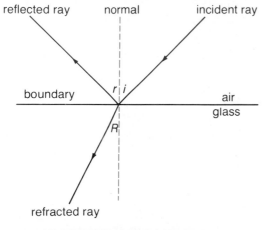

A straight stick appears bent when partially immersed in water; the sun appears oval rather than round when it is about to set; a stream may appear to be much shallower than you know it to be; the pavement shimmers on a hot summer's day. These are some of the effects caused by the **refraction**, or change in direction, of light as it passes at an angle from one medium into another.

When light passes at an angle from air to glass, it immediately changes direction. Also, at the boundary between the air and the glass, most of the light passes through the glass, but some is reflected according to the Laws of Reflection. This is called **partial reflection and partial refraction**. The diagram illustrates this phenomenon, and shows the angles used when describing refraction. The **angle of incidence** (*i* in the diagram) is the angle between the incident ray and the normal at the point of incidence. The **angle of refraction** (*R*) is the angle between the refracted ray and the normal.

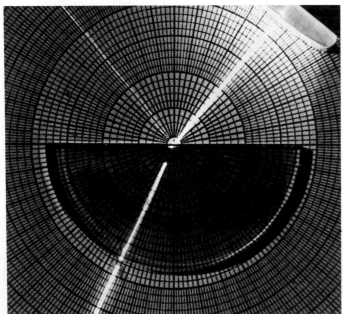

Light travelling obliquely from air into glass is bent towards the normal.

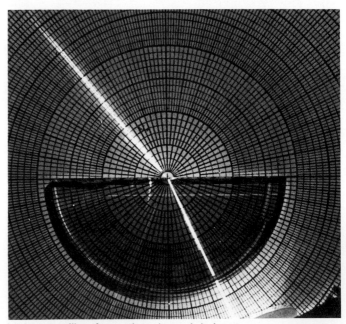

Light travelling from glass into air is bent away from the normal.

In both the photograph and the illustration, note that the ray of light is bent towards the normal when it passes from air into glass. This is always the case when light passes from one medium to another that is optically denser. The speed of light is reduced when it passes into an optically denser medium, as in the transition from air to glass. Thus, "optically denser" and "the speed of light is reduced" are synonymous when discussing the properties of a transparent medium.

If the light travels from one medium into a less optically dense medium where its speed is greater, the ray bends away from the normal. This is shown in the photograph for a ray of light travelling from glass to air.

By examining the three photographs on these two pages we can notice three additional properties of light. When the light passes from air into glass or from glass into air with an angle of incidence equal to zero, there is no refraction. This is illustrated in the photograph in the margin. Secondly, where the ray strikes the boundary between the air-glass interface at an angle, the incident ray and refracted ray are always on opposite sides of the normal and they are always in the same plane as the normal.

Finally, in all three photographs it is apparent that the ray box could have been placed on the opposite side of the glass and the light would have been refracted along exactly the same path. This illustrates the **Principle of the Reversibility of Light:** If a light ray is reversed, it travels back along its original path.

Rays travelling along the diameter of a circular piece of glass are not refracted at either boundary, since the angles of incidence are zero at each interface.

15.2 Index of Refraction

The speed of light in a vacuum (**c**) is $2.997\,924 \times 10^8$ m/s (see Section 13.2). In air, the speed of light is only about $0.000\,87 \times 10^8$ m/s less than in a vacuum. Thus the value 3.00×10^8 m/s can be used for air or a vacuum. In other transparent media, such as water or glass, the speed is significantly smaller. It was a French scientist, Jean Foucault, who, in 1862, devised a method for measuring the speed of light in both air and water. He found that light travels in water at approximately three-quarters the speed it travels in a vacuum, i.e., at $0.75\,c$. Other materials produce different values, but the speed is always smaller than the speed of light in a vacuum. The term "optically dense" is used when referring to a medium in which the speed of light decreases.

Indices of Refraction

Substance	Index of refraction (n)
vacuum	1.0000
air (0°C, 101 kPa)	1.0003
water	1.33
ethyl alcohol	1.36
quartz (fused)	1.46
glycerine	1.47
Lucite or Plexiglas	1.51
glass (crown)	1.52
sodium chloride	1.53
glass (crystal)	1.54
ruby	1.54
glass (flint)	1.65
zircon	1.92
diamond	2.42

Note: for yellow light, wavelength = 589 nm

The ratio of the speed of light in a vacuum (c) to the speed of light in a given material (v) is called the **index of refraction** (n) of that material. That is,

$$n = \frac{c}{v}$$

The indices for various materials are given in the table in the margin. n varies slightly with the color of the light, except in a vacuum. The values in the table are for a specific color of yellow light.

The higher the index of a given substance, the more the light is slowed down when it travels from a vacuum into the substance. Air, with an index of refraction of 1.0003, slows it down very little. Zircon, with an index of 1.92, slows it down considerably more.

Sample Problems

1. The speed of light in a liquid is 2.25×10^8 m/s.
   What is: (a) the refractive index of the liquid,
             (b) the liquid?

   (a) $c = 3.00 \times 10$ m/s, $v = 2.25 \times 10^8$ m/s

   $$n = \frac{c}{v}$$
   $$= \frac{3.00 \times 10^8 \text{ m/s}}{2.25 \times 10^8 \text{ m/s}}$$
   $$= 1.33$$

   (b) Using the table in the margin, the liquid is probably water.

2. Using the table in the margin, calculate the speed of light in Lucite.

   $$c = 3.00 \times 10^8 \text{ m/s} \qquad n = 1.51$$

   $$n = \frac{c}{v}$$

   Therefore $$v = \frac{c}{n}$$
   $$= \frac{3.00 \times 10^8 \text{ m/s}}{1.51}$$
   $$= 1.99 \times 10^8 \text{ m/s}$$

Practice

1. What is the index of refraction of a liquid in which the speed of light is 2.50×10^8 m/s?
2. The index of refraction of diamond is 2.42. What is the speed of light in diamond?
3. Zircon is often used as an imitation diamond in costume jewellery. Calculate how much the speed of light decreases when it passes from air into zircon.
4. Light travels from air into quartz. How long will it take to travel through a piece of quartz 1.00 m thick?

15.3 Laws of Refraction

Although the phenomenon of refraction had been known for centuries, it was not until 1621 that Willebrod Snell (1591-1626), (1591-1626), a Dutch mathematician, determined the exact relationship between the angle of incidence and the angle of refraction. This enabled scientists to predict the direction a ray of light would take in various media. **Snell's Law** says:

$$\frac{\sin i}{\sin R} = \text{constant}$$

This relationship tells us that for all angles of incidence greater than $0°$, the ratio $\sin i/\sin R$ gives the same value for a boundary between two transparent media. In the case of an air-glass interface, the value is approximately 1.5.

It has been found that the Snell's Law constant and the index of refraction (n) are one and the same thing. Consequently, the Snell's Law relationship may be rewritten as:

$$\frac{\sin i}{\sin R} = n$$

The **Laws of Refraction** may now be summarized:

- **The ratio of the sine of the angle of incidence to the sine of the angle of refraction is a constant (also known as Snell's Law).**
- **The incident ray and the refracted ray are on opposite sides of the normal at the point of incidence, and all three are in the same plane.**

Sometimes the index of refraction for light going from a vacuum into a substance is referred to as the *absolute refractive index*. The value of the index for light travelling from air into the substance is so close to the value of the absolute refractive index that we only distinguish between them in rare instances. In this text, when the term "index of refraction" is used, we are using the value of the absolute refractive index. When light travels between two materials with different indices of refraction, the ratio of their absolute indices of refraction is referred to as the relative index of refraction. For example, for light travelling from water into glass, the relative index of refraction is:

$$_w n_g = \frac{n_g}{n_w} = \frac{1.50}{1.33} = 1.13$$

For light travelling from glass into water, the relative index of refraction is:

$$_g n_w = \frac{n_w}{n_g} = \frac{1.33}{1.50} = 0.89$$

Snell's Law equation for light travelling from air to glass is

$$\frac{\sin i}{\sin R} = n, \text{ or } \frac{n}{1}$$

If the light travels from glass to air, the angle of incidence will be in the glass and the Snell's Law relation becomes altered to

$$\frac{\sin i}{\sin R} = \frac{1}{n}$$

Thus, if the Snell's Law ratio for air into glass is 1.5, the Snell's Law ratio for glass into air will be $1/1.5 = 0.67$. This fact is shown experimentally in Investigation 15.2.

Chapter 15

When light travels from one transparent medium into another, some reflection always occurs. This is partial reflection and partial refraction. The degrees of reflection and refraction that occur depend on the angle of incidence and the optical densities of the two media. This will be examined in Section 15.5.

Sample Problems

1. Illustrated is the path of a ray entering a medium (x) of unknown index of refraction. Calculate the index of refraction of medium x.

$$\frac{\sin i}{\sin R} = n$$

$$\frac{\sin 30°}{\sin 24°} = n$$

$$n = \frac{0.500}{0.407}$$

$$= 1.23$$

2. Light travels from air into water ($n_w = 1.33$). If the angle of incidence is 30°, what is the angle of refraction?

$$\frac{\sin i}{\sin R} = n$$

$$\frac{\sin 30°}{\sin R} = 1.33$$

$$\sin R = \frac{\sin 30°}{1.33}$$

$$= \frac{0.500}{1.33}$$

$$= 0.385$$

$$R = 22°$$

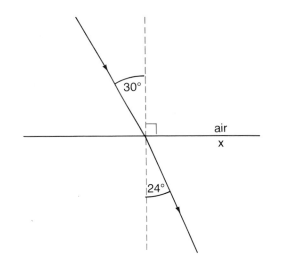

Practice

1. Light passes from air into diamond with an angle of incidence of 60°. What will be the angle of refraction?
2. A transparent substance has a refractive index of 1.30. What is the angle of incidence in air when the angle of refraction in the substance is 45°?
3. What is the index of refraction of a material if the angle of incidence in air is 50° and the angle of refraction in the material is 40°?

15.4 Snell's Law–A General Equation

For convenience when dealing with Snell's Law, we can use sub-scripts to denote particular angles and substances.

For example, if light travels from air into glass,

$$\frac{\sin i}{\sin R} = {}_an_g$$

where ${}_an_g$ is the refractive index for light travelling from air into glass.

Since ${}_an_g$ represents the ratio $\dfrac{n_g}{n_a}$, the above relationship can be rewritten as:

$$\frac{\sin i}{\sin R} = \frac{n_g}{n_a}$$

In developing a general equation for the refraction of light, we replace the angle of incidence (i) in the first medium with the symbol θ_1, and the angle of refraction in the second medium with the symbol θ_2. The index of refraction of the first medium, air, in our example, is replaced by the symbol n_1; and the index of the second medium, n_g, is replaced by the symbol n_2. Thus the above expression is rewritten as:

$$\text{or} \qquad \frac{\sin \theta_1}{\sin \theta_2} = \frac{n_2}{n_1}$$

$$\boldsymbol{n_1 \sin \theta_1 = n_2 \sin \theta_2}$$

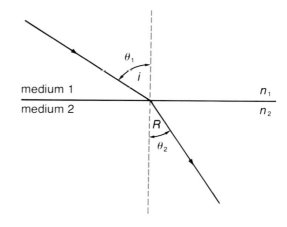

The subscripts denote the different media. It is customary to use subscript 1 for the incident medium and subscript 2 for the refracting medium. The general expression of Snell's Law may be used in solving any refraction problem.

Sample Problems

1. Light travels from crown glass (g) into air (a). The angle of refraction in air is 60°. What is the angle of incidence in glass?

$$n_g \sin \theta_g = n_a \sin \theta_a$$
$$1.52 \sin \theta_g = 1.00 \sin 60$$
$$\sin \theta_g = \frac{1.00(0.866)}{1.52}$$
$$= 0.570$$
$$\theta_g = 34.7°$$

2. Light travels from crown glass (g) into water (w). The angle of incidence in crown glass is 40°. What is the angle of refraction in water?

$$n_g \sin \theta_g = n_w \sin \theta_w$$
$$1.52 \sin 40° = 1.33 \sin \theta_w$$
$$(1.52)(0.643) = 1.33 \sin \theta_w$$
$$\sin \theta_w = \frac{(1.52)(0.643)}{1.33}$$
$$= 0.735$$
$$\theta_w = 47.3°$$

Practice

1. If the index of refraction for diamond is 2.42, what will be the angle of refraction in diamond for an angle of incidence, in water, of 60°?
2. A ray of light passes from water ($n_w = 1.33$) into carbon disulfide ($n_{cs_2} = 1.63$) with an angle of incidence of 30°. What is the angle of refraction in the carbon disulfide?
3. A diver shines her flashlight upward from beneath the water at an angle of 30° to the vertical. At what angle to the vertical does the beam of light emerge from the water?

15.5 Total Internal Reflection and the Critical Angle

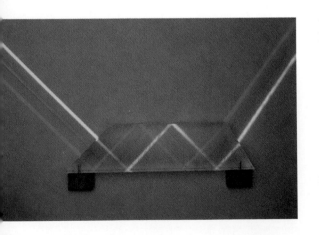

When light travels from one medium to another where its speed changes, some of the light is reflected and some is refracted. This property of light is referred to as partial reflection/partial refraction, as stated previously. In cases where the speed of the light increases, for example, from glass to air, the light is reflected to a greater extent than in cases where the speed decreases.

As the angle of incidence increases, the intensity of a reflected ray becomes progressively stronger and the intensity of a refracted ray progressively weaker. Also, as the angle of incidence increases, the angle of refraction increases, eventually reaching a maximum of 90°. Beyond this point, refraction ceases, and all the incident light is reflected, at the boundary, back into the optically denser medium. This phenomenon is called **total internal reflection**. It can only occur when light rays travel into a medium where the speed of the light increases and, hence, the angle of refraction is always greater than the angle of incidence.

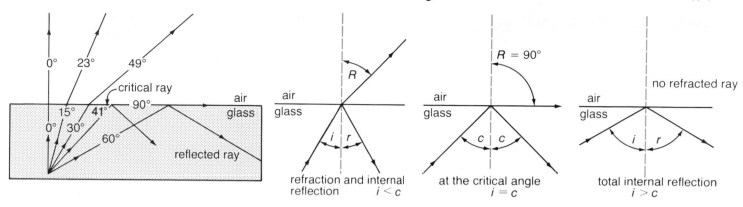

refraction and internal reflection $i < c$ at the critical angle $i = c$ total internal reflection $i > c$

What happens when light rays pass from glass into air

When the angle of refraction is 90°, the incident ray forms an angle of incidence that has a unique value for any two materials. This unique angle of incidence is called the "critical angle of incidence", or simply the **critical angle**. For light travelling from crown glass into air, the critical angle can be determined as follows:

$$n_g \sin \theta_g = n_a \sin \theta_a$$
$$1.52 \sin \theta_g = 1.00 \sin 90°$$
$$\sin \theta_g = \frac{(1.00)(1.00)}{1.52} = 0.658$$
$$\theta_g = 41°$$

For water, with an index of refraction of 1.33, the critical angle is approximately 49°. For zircon ($n_z = 1.92$) the critical angle is 31°. Substances with higher indices of refraction refract the light to a greater degree and thus have lower critical angles. The critical angle for diamond ($n_d = 2.42$), for example, is only 24.5°.

Total internal reflection has many applications. For example, if, when you swim underwater, you look up at the smooth surface, you will see the world compressed into a circle. This circle is defined by the critical angle of water, which is 49° (see diagram). Beyond this circle, the surface of the water reflects light from objects beneath it, and appears as a large mirror.

This phenomenon is difficult to see, because most water surfaces are not perfectly flat. Viewed at an angle, from underwater, the water's surface is a shimmering mirror.

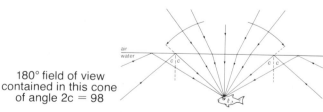

180° field of view contained in this cone of angle 2c = 98

A fish's-eye view of the world

Light rods used for telephone transmissions

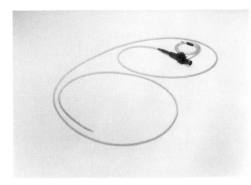

Fiberscope used by doctors to examine interior organs

Ordinary mirrors reflect less than 100% of the light they receive. Total internal reflection reflects almost 100% of the light, making the images brighter. This is important in such optical devices as binoculars and cameras, where total internal reflecting prisms are used extensively.

Another application of the phenomenon of total internal reflection is the "light rod", a product of the new technology of fiber optics. Light rods are made from very thin glass and plastic fibers, sometimes as small as 15 μm in diameter. These are so designed that the light undergoes total internal reflection every time it encounters an internal surface. Even if the fibers are bent or twisted, the critical angle is not usually exceeded, and the light energy is transmitted undiminished to the other end. A bundle of these tiny fibers is called a "light pipe".

Individual fibers are now replacing the thousands of wires that connect telephone substations, and may eventually be connected to each home. In this application, the telephone signal modulates (changes the intensity of) a small laser. The laser light is transmitted through a glass fiber, carrying with it many more telephone calls at one time, with much less loss in energy than would be the case with copper wire. It is possible to send information both ways, simultaneously, on the same fiber.

In medicine, fiber optics bundles are used to transmit pictures of internal organs. For example, a patient's stomach can be examined by inserting a flexible light pipe down her throat and into her stomach. Light sent down some of the fibers illuminates the stomach wall. Other fibers carry the reflected light back to a small television camera. The light transmitted through each fiber forms part of the picture of the stomach wall. This picture, which is a mosaic formed by all the fibers, is magnified and displayed on a television screen. The more fibers there are, and the smaller they are, the more detailed the picture. (A typical bundle has 5×10^4 fibers and a diameter of 3 mm.) Such inspections of the esophagus, stomach, bowel, and even the inside of the heart, allow safe examinations that would not normally be possible without surgery.

Practice

1. What is the critical angle in flint glass when light passes from flint glass into air?
2. If the index of refraction for water is 1.33, what is the critical angle for water?
3. The critical angle for a medium is 40.5°. What is the index of refraction of the medium?

15.6 Lateral Displacement and Deviation of Light Rays

When a light ray passes from air into glass and then back into air, it is refracted twice. If the two refracting surfaces are parallel, the **emergent ray** is parallel to the incident ray but it is no longer moving in the same path. Such sideways shifting of the path of a ray is called **lateral displacement**. The lateral displacement is greater for thick refracting materials than for thin ones, as illustrated on the following page.

If the surfaces of the refracting material are not parallel—as, for example, in a prism—an emergent ray will take a completely different path. Such a change in the direction of a ray is measured in degrees. The angle between the incident ray and the emergent ray is called the **angle of deviation**.

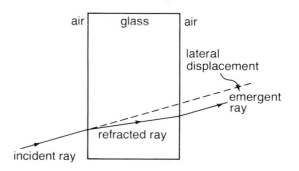

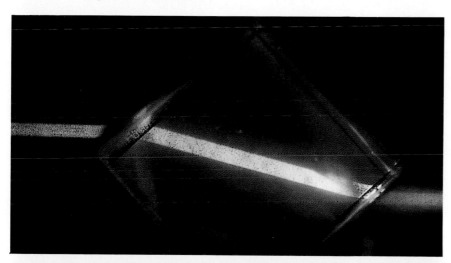

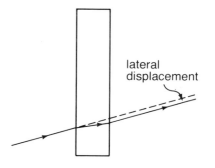

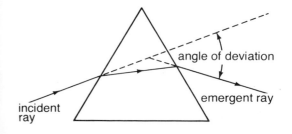

15.7 *A*pplications: Refraction

1. Apparent Bending of a Straight Stick in Water

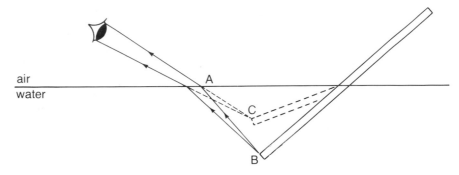

A stick appears bent in water.

Rays of light from the end of the stick, B, pass from water into air, bending away from the normal because they are entering a less dense medium. These rays enter the eye as illustrated, and appear to originate from a point, C, that is higher in the water than B. This is because the eye assumes that the light travelled in a straight line.

The same will be true of light rays coming from other points on the immersed section of the stick and so, viewed from above the surface of the water, the stick will appear to be bent. A similar distortion is produced when you look at stones at the bottom of a shallow stream. The stones appear to be closer to the surface than they really are, a fact that becomes very evident if you try to walk on them!

2. Atmospheric Refraction

The setting sun creates an optical illusion because the light from it is refracted in passing from the vacuum of outer space into the air surrounding the Earth. The density of the air increases as the light gets closer to Earth, so the refraction also increases, resulting in a curved path. To the observer, the sun's light appears to be coming from a higher point in the sky than it really is. In fact, when the observer sees the sun set, the light seen is coming from below the horizon. The sun has already set!

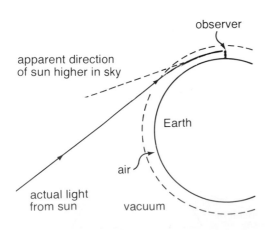

When the sun is very close to the horizon, the light from the lower part of it is refracted more than the light from the upper part. This gives the impression that the sun has a flattened bottom (see photograph). Thus, the sun appears to be oval, rather than round.

The sun and the moon appear larger when they are near the horizon. This illusion is not caused by atmospheric refraction. When the sun or the moon is close to the horizon, we are able to compare it with familiar objects such as trees and buildings, and it appears large in comparison with them. When the sun is high in the sky, there is nothing to compare its size with, and it appears to be smaller than it was near the horizon.

The Earth's atmosphere consists of flowing masses of air of varying density and temperature. Not surprisingly, then, the refractive index varies slightly from one region of the atmosphere

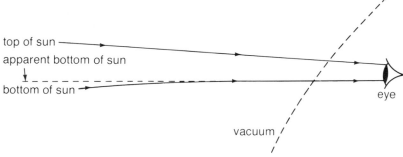

to another. When light from a star enters the atmosphere, it is refracted as it moves from one mass of air to another, and, since the variable masses of air are in motion, the star seems to twinkle.

Astronomers viewing stars must be aware of atmospheric refraction. Sightings near the horizon will be especially inaccurate since the starlight travels through more air.

Most large telescopes are located high on mountains, where there is less of the Earth's atmosphere between them and the stars, and where the air is more uniform in temperature. Many of the distortions of atmospheric refraction are thus avoided. Astronomers find that cold winter nights are usually best for celestial observations. Telescopes have been and will increasingly be placed in orbit above the Earth, to escape the effects of atmospheric refraction.

Shimmering Heat, and Mirages

Warm air has a slightly different index of refraction than cold air. When light passes through a stream of warm air, as it does above a stove or barbecue, it is refracted. This refraction is not uniform because the warm air rises irregularly, in gusts. The light from objects seen through the warm air is distorted by irregular refraction, and the objects appear to shimmer.

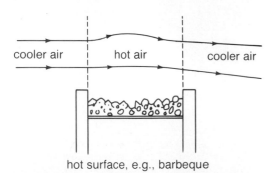

hot surface, e.g., barbeque

A mirage makes this road appear wet.

The same effect is observed over hot pavement in the summer. A similar phenomenon occurs when gasoline vapor rises from the car while we are filling the tank.

Mirages are most often associated with deserts, but they may occur over any hot, flat surface, such as a road on a summer day. What appears to be a sheet of water sometimes appears on the highway a short distance ahead of us, but we never reach it because it is an optical illusion. We are deceived because we associate reflections from ground level with pools or lakes and make the natural inference that the road is wet.

The word "mirage" comes from the French verb *se mirer*, to be reflected. As the light from the sky nears the Earth's surface, it is progressively refracted by successive layers of warmer air as shown, each with a lower index of refraction. Its angle of incidence to the boundaries of these layers thus gets bigger and bigger. Eventually, it is totally internally reflected upwards from one of the layers as shown. We are conditioned to think of light as always travelling in straight lines and so our eye sees a virtual image of the sky below the road. We assume that there must be a layer of water on the road because, in our experience, it is usually water and not air that causes reflection.

Sometimes mountains, telegraph poles, and other objects located beyond a hot, flat surface create a mirage.

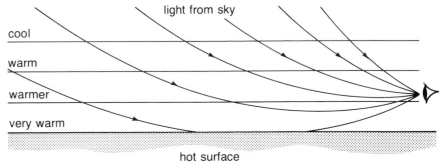

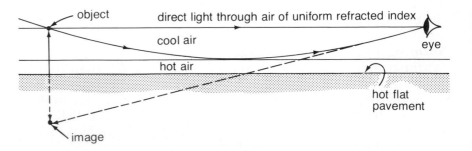

3. Total Internal Reflection

The life of an ordinary mirror is limited by the fact that the metallic undercoating tends to tarnish in air. Also, only 90% of the light energy is reflected by most metallic reflectors, the other 10% being absorbed by the reflective material. This problem may be remedied by using total internal reflection prisms, which reflect nearly all the light energy and have untarnishable reflective surfaces.

In a submarine periscope, two 45° right-angle glass prisms are mounted as illustrated. Light entering and leaving each prism is not refracted because the angle of incidence is 0°. Light rays striking the hypotenuse side of the prism at an angle of 45° are reflected, because the critical angle for ordinary glass is 42°.

Total reflection prisms are also used in combination with a series of lenses in binoculars, and they are sometimes used in projectors to change the orientation of the image from inverted to erect.

Plane mirrors, made by silvering the back of the glass, can produce extra images because of the reflection from the front surface of the glass and because of internal reflections in the glass. Ordinarily, these extra images are much weaker than the image formed by the silvered surface at the back, hence they go unnoticed. In optical instruments, extra images are a nuisance. For this reason, the plane mirrors in reflex cameras and the curved mirrors in telescopes are silvered on the front surface.

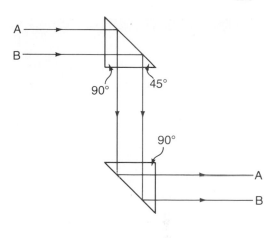

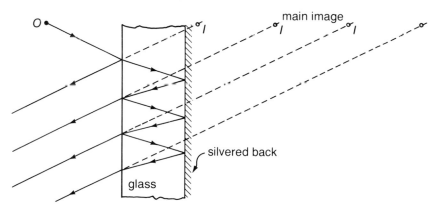

Multiple images are formed in a thick glass mirror.

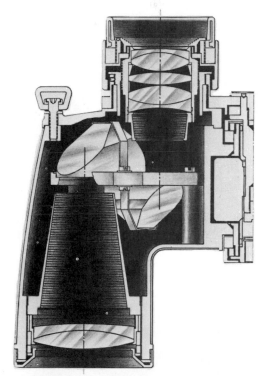

The sparkle of diamonds is partly a result of total internal reflection. Diamonds have a high index of refraction ($n_d = 2.42$) and thus a low critical angle (24.5°). When rays of light strike the top surface of a diamond, they either enter it or are reflected. Those that enter strike the lower surface of the diamond from the inside. However, only the rays that strike it at an incident angle less than 24.5° can

escape. The rest will be totally internally reflected. Even those that do strike at an angle less than 24.5° will be partially reflected back into the diamond if the surface is highly polished.

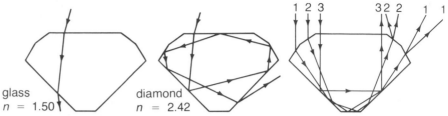

glass
$n = 1.50$

diamond
$n = 2.42$

Consequently, much of the light that enters a diamond undergoes multiple internal reflection before finally emerging. (In glass, much more of the light escapes through the lower side because the critical angle for glass is much higher, about 42°. Any ray that strikes the lower surface with an incident angle less than 42° can escape.)

It is the job of the person who cuts the diamond to angle the surfaces so that as much light as possible leaves the diamond through the top surface, not through the lower surface, and to polish the surfaces so that the internal reflection is as great as possible.

Investigations

Investigation 15.1: Refraction of Light—Air into Glass

Problem:
How is light refracted when it passes from air into an optically denser medium, like glass?

Materials:
ray box (single-slit)
semi-circular glass (or plastic) block
polar coordinate paper

Procedure:
1. Place the glass block on the polar coordinate paper, as illustrated. Note that the 0°–180° line acts as a normal and passes through the center of the flat surface.
2. Direct a single ray of light at the flat surface of the glass, along the normal. Make absolutely sure that the ray passes through the center of the flat surface. Measure the angle of refraction, and record it in your notebook in a chart, as illustrated.

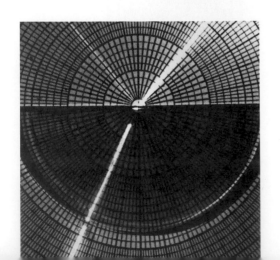

Observation	Angle of incidence (i)	Angle of refraction (R)	sin i	sin R	$\dfrac{\sin i}{\sin R}$
1	0°				
2	10°				
3	20°				
4	30°				

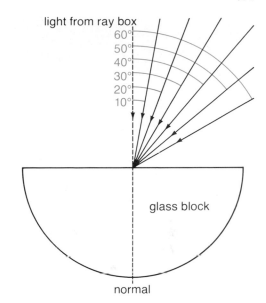

light from ray box

glass block

normal

3. Repeat the procedure for angles of incidence of 10°, 20°, 30°, 40°, 50°, and 60°, recording your observations in the chart.
4. Using a table of sines or a calculator, determine the values of the sines of the angles of incidence and refraction.
5. Calculate the ratio sin i/sin R for each pair of angles.

Questions:
1. When light travels from air into glass with an angle of incidence of 0°, that is, along the normal, what happens to it?
2. When light travels from air to glass at an angle of incidence greater than 0°, how is it bent, in relation to the normal?
3. Where are the incident and refracted rays located, in relation to the normal?
4. How does the angle of refraction compare with the angle of incidence in each case?
5. What do you note about the ratio sin i/sin R for all angles of incidence greater than 0°?
6. If light travels from glass into air, how will it bend in relation to the normal?

Investigation 15.2: Refraction of Light—Glass into Air

Problem:
How is light refracted when it passes from a medium such as glass into a medium that is less optically dense, such as air?

Materials:
ray box (single slit)
semi-circular glass (or plastic) block
polar coordinate paper

Procedure:
1. Place the glass block on the polar coordinate paper, as illustrated. Note that the 0°–180° line acts as a normal and that it goes through the center of the flat surface.

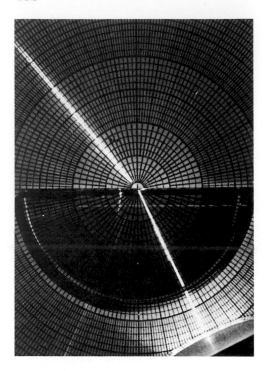

2. Direct a single ray of light at the curved surface of the glass, along the normal. Measure the angle of refraction in air.
3. Repeat the procedure for angles of incidence, in glass, of 10°, 20°, 30°, 40°, 50°, and 60°, recording your observations in a suitable chart (see illustration). Be sure to use the "comments" column for any additional observations.
4. Determine the values of the sines of the angles of incidence and refraction, and calculate the ratio sin i/sin R for each pair of angles.

	Angle of incidence	Angle of refraction	sin i	sin R	sin i/sin R	Comments
1	0°	0°	0	0	undefined	no refraction
2	10°					
3	20°					
4	30°					

Questions:

1. How was the light refracted when the angle of incidence was 0°?
2. When light travels from glass into air, at an angle other than 0°, how is it bent in relation to the normal?
3. Which angle is always the greater, the angle of incidence or the angle of refraction?
4. Where are the incident and refracted rays located in relation to the normal?
5. What is the value of the sin i/sin R ratio for glass-air interface?
6. What is the relationship between this value and the value determined in step 5 in the previous investigation?
7. Why is there no refraction at the curved surface in all cases?
8. What other phenomenon occurs increasingly as the angle of incidence increases?
9. Above approximately 45°, what happens to all the light once it reaches the boundary between the glass and the air?
10. At what angle of incidence is the angle of refraction 90°? Determine the answer experimentally and check your answer mathematically.

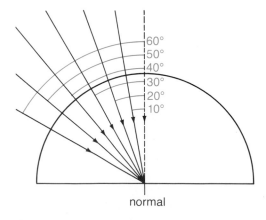

normal

Meet Blair Wong . . . Optician

Blair is a registered dispensing optician for a Massachusetts firm that specializes in eye exams, contact lens fittings, and the dispensing of eyewear. Part of his work involves training other opticians, apprentice opticians, and optometric technicians regarding the latest breakthroughs in eyewear and contact lens technology.

Q. What does an optician do?
A. The optician's job is to design and dispense eyewear—eyeglasses and contact lenses. The main goal is to ensure that a patient's eyewear has the best possible design and fit, based on his or her individual needs.

Q. How is an optician different from an optometrist or an ophthalmologist?
A. An optician dispenses eyewear based on a prescription from an optometrist. The optometrist is a person who is qualified to examine the eye for defects in vision and then prescribe lenses or exercises to correct the problem. An ophthalmologist is a physician who specializes in the structure, function, and diseases of the eye.

Q. When did you become interested in becoming an optician?
A. I first became interested in this field during my high school physics course. I had not been especially interested in physics until we covered a chapter on optics—the study of light and lenses. I found this topic fascinating and decided to learn more about it.

Q. How does one become an optician?
The requirements differ from state to state but generally there are two ways to become a registered dispensing optician. One way is to attend a school that offers an associate-degree program for opticians. A second way is to serve an apprenticeship with a trained, experienced optician. Once an individual has acquired the necessary background and training, he or she must take a national and a state examination. Upon successful completion of the exam, a person can apply for certification to dispense eyewear to patients in that state.

Q. What happens when you see a new client for the first time?
A. Each new patient can bring his or her existing eyewear or a prescription for new eyewear, or the patient can be scheduled for an examination by one of our optometrists. However, before we design any new eyewear, we need to gather information—such as the type of work the patient does, his or her reading habits, hobbies, and sports and recreational activities. Also, we need to know whether there is a medical condition that may affect the patient's vision. We find out too if the patient is interested in eyeglasses or contact

lenses. All of this information is used to create the best possible eyewear.

Q. How do you keep up with the latest technology in the optical field?
A. At my company we do research in our own on-site laboratories, attend conferences, and read professional journals. Some staff members have published articles in the journals. We make sure that our patients have access to the latest technology the optical field can offer.

Q. What are some of the recent breakthroughs in eyewear technology?
A. Many improvements have been made in eyewear. For example, the use of high-density plastics has allowed the creation of lenses that are lighter in weight than standard plastic lenses. Another advancement has been made in the design of bifocal lenses. In the past, a bifocal lens had a line across the center. The top of the lens served one function, and the bottom served another. Bifocal lenses can now be replaced with progressive lenses, which have no line. The correcting power changes gradually as the eye moves from the top to the bottom of the lens, offering patients a smoother transition from distance viewing to viewing something up close.

Q. What is the most interesting aspect of your work?
A. I enjoy the challenge of satisfying the needs of each patient to the best of my ability. It is important that each patient's eyewear be as comfortable and effective as possible. It is a rewarding feeling to help people look well, feel well, and see well.

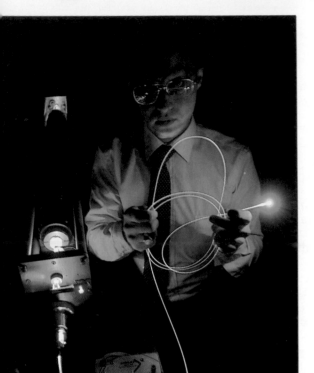

Chapter Summary

1. The terms used in describing light refraction are: incident ray, angle of incidence, normal, refracted ray, and angle of refraction.
2. When light enters a medium more optically dense than air, its speed decreases.
3. The index of refraction is the ratio of the speed of light in air to the speed of light in the medium.

$$n_m = \frac{v_{air}}{v_{medium}}$$

4. The Laws of Refraction are:
   (a) The ratio $\sin i / \sin R$ is a constant for a given medium, for all values of the angle of incidence except $0°$ (Snell's Law).
   (b) The incident ray and the refracted ray are on opposite sides of the normal, and all three are in the same plane.
5. (a) When a ray of light passes from one medium into another, denser, medium, it bends towards the normal ($\angle R < \angle i$).
   (b) When a ray of light passes from one medium into another, less dense, medium, it bends away from the normal ($\angle R > \angle i$).
   (c) When a ray of light passes from one medium into another of different optical density at right angles ($90°$) to the boundary, no refraction occurs ($\angle i = \angle R = 0°$).
6. The conditions for total internal reflection are:
   (a) The ray of light passes from one medium into another that is less dense.
   (b) The angle of incidence exceeds the critical angle.
7. When the angle of incidence is equal to the critical angle, the angle of refraction is $90°$.
8. The general mathematical relationship used with Snell's Law is $n_1 \sin \theta_1 = n_2 \sin \theta_2$, where 1 represents the incident medium and 2 represents the refracting medium.

Chapter Review

Discussion

1. Light travels from medium A to medium B. The angle of refraction is greater than the angle of incidence.
   (a) Which medium has the higher index of refraction?
   (b) In which medium does the light travel at a lower speed?

2. Using your knowledge of refraction and the table on page 466, describe how you would identify an unknown, clear substance.

3. The index of refraction for blue light in glass is slightly higher than that for red light in glass. What does this indicate about
   (a) the relative speeds of red light and blue light in glass, and
   (b) the angles of refraction for each color, for the same angle of incidence?

4. How could the index of refraction of salt water be used to find the concentration of a salt solution?

5. It is easy to see a drop of water on the print of a glossy magazine but it is difficult to see it on the white area of the same page. Explain why.

6. How does refraction lengthen a day at both sunrise and sunset?

7. Hot air rises over a heated stove element. The wall behind the stove appears to shimmer. Explain.

8. To successfully spear a fish, you must aim below the apparent position of the fish. Explain.

9. In which medium does light travel faster—one with a critical angle of 27° or one with a critical angle of 32°? Explain. (For both cases, air is the second medium.)

10. Is the critical angle for glass with an index of refraction of 1.53 greater or less than that for glass with an index of refraction of 1.60? Would your answer be different if the second medium were water instead of air?

11. Diamond has a critical angle of 24°. Crown glass has a critical angle of 42°. Why does a diamond sparkle more in bright light than a piece of crown glass does, even with the equivalent shape?

12. What observation illustrates the fact that diamond has a slightly different index of refraction for each of the various colors of the spectrum?

13. Total internal reflection is easily seen in an aquarium. Where does it occur—at the boundary between the water and the glass, or at the boundary between the glass and the air? Explain your answer.

14. A refractometer is a device used to measure the index of refraction of transparent materials. In one design the material to be evaluated is placed in contact with a glass plate of known refractive index. Using a ray box, the critical angle for internal reflection is measured.
    Describe the physical principles used in this instrument, using a diagram.

Problems

15.

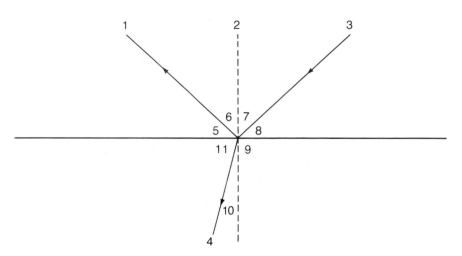

Relate each of the following terms to one of the numbers: angle of incidence, normal, refracted ray, angle of reflection, incident ray, angle of refraction, reflected ray.

16. Transfer the following diagrams into your notebook. Draw in the general direction of the refracted ray(s) in each case.

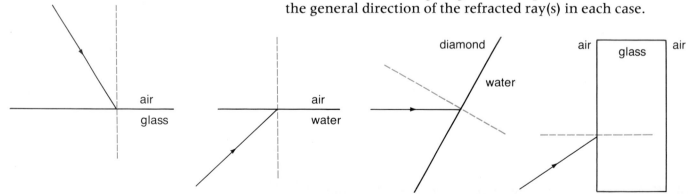

17. The speed of light in three different media is as follows:
(a) 2.25×10^8 m/s (b) 1.24×10^8 m/s (c) 1.95×10^8 m/s
Determine the index of refraction of each medium, and, using a table of indices of refraction (see Section 15.2), identify the medium in each case.

18. The speed of light in plastic is 2.0×10^8 m/s. What is the refractive index of plastic?

19. Given that the speed of light in air is 3.00×10^8 m/s, find the speed of light in each of the following:

(a) fused quartz ($n_q = 1.46$) (b) diamond ($n_d = 2.42$)
(c) flint glass ($n_g = 1.65$) (d) carbon disulphide ($n_{cs} = 1.63$)

20. The index of refraction of crown glass for violet light is 1.53, and for red light it is 1.51. Assuming that the velocity of light in a vacuum is 3.00×10^8 m/s, what are the speeds of violet light and red light in crown glass?

21. Using Snell's Law, determine the constant when the angle of incidence and the angle of refraction are:
(a) $50°$ and $30°$ (b) $30°$ and $18°$ (c) $60°$ and $38°$

22. (a) What is the index of refraction of a medium if the angle of incidence in air is $63°$ and the angle of refraction is $30°$?
(b) What is the angle of refraction in a medium if the angle of incidence in air is $48°$ and the index of refraction of the medium is 1.58?
(c) What is the angle of incidence in a medium in the case where the angle of refraction in air is $40°$ and the index of refraction of the medium is 1.58?

23. A ray of light passes from air into water ($n_w = 1.33$) at an angle of incidence of $50°$. What is the angle of refraction?

24. Light travels from air into water. If the angle of refraction is $30°$, what is the angle of incidence?

25. A ray of light in air strikes a block of quartz at an angle of incidence of $30°$. The angle of refraction is $20°$. What is the index of refraction of the quartz?

26. Prove, geometrically, that a ray of light entering a plate of glass always emerges in a direction parallel to the incident ray.

27. One ray of light in air strikes a diamond ($n_d = 2.42$) and another strikes a piece of fused quartz ($n_q = 1.46$), in each case at an angle of incidence of $40°$. What is the difference between the angles of refraction?

28. A ray of light strikes a block of polyethylene ($n_p = 1.50$) with angles of incidence of (a) $0°$, (b) $30°$, (c) $60°$. Determine the angle of refraction in each case.

29. An underwater swimmer looks up towards the surface of the water on a line of sight that makes an angle of $25°$ with a normal to the surface of the water. What is the angle of incidence in air for the light rays that enter the swimmer's eye?

30. A beam of light is directed on the flat surface of a block of fused quartz. Part of the beam is refracted with an angle of refraction of $30°$. What is the angle of reflection?

31. A coin lies on the bottom of a swimming pool under 1.2 m of water and 1.0 m from the edge of the pool, as illustrated. A flashlight beam is directed over the edge of the pool to illuminate the coin. At what angle relative to the pool wall must the flashlight be aimed?

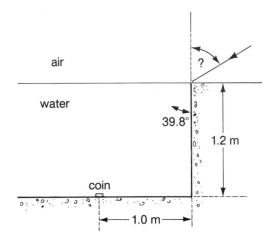

32. What is the critical angle for light rays passing from (a) crown glass ($n_g = 1.52$) into air, and (b) crown glass into water ($n_w = 1.33$)?

33. In each of the following questions, the second medium is air.
    (a) What is the critical angle if the index of refraction for a medium is 1.68?
    (b) What is the index of refraction of a medium if the critical angle is 40°?

34. (a) Is the critical angle for glass with an index of refraction of 1.53 greater or less than that for glass with an index of refraction of 1.60?
    (b) If the medium into which the light is passing is air, what is the critical angle for each type of glass in (a)?

35. From inside an aquarium, a ray of light is directed at the glass so that the angle of incidence, in water, is 30°.
    (a) Determine the angle of refraction when the ray emerges from the glass into the air.
    (b) If the angle of incidence in the water is 52°, at what angle will the rays emerge from the glass?

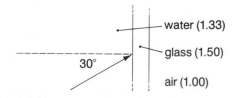

36. Several transparent liquids are carefully poured, one after another, into a glass container, as illustrated. Each liquid is immiscible (will not mix) with its neighbor. A ray of light, with an angle of incidence in the glass of 10°, is projected up through the liquids. What will be the angle of refraction in air?

CAUTION: Do not attempt to pour these liquids. Carbon disulfide is extremely flammable and poisonous; the vapor is potentially explosive.

air ($n = 1.00$)

oleic acid ($n = 1.43$)

water ($n = 1.33$)

carbon disulphide ($n = 1.46$)

glass ($n = 1.50$)

10°

Numerical Answers to
Practice Problems

page 467
1. 1.20
2. 1.24×10^8 m/s
3. 1.44×10^8 m/s
4. 4.88×10^{-9}s, or 4.88 ns

page 468
1. 21°
2. 67°
3. 1.19

page 470
1. 28°
2. 24°
3. 42°

page 472
1. 37.3°
2. 48.8°
3. 1.54

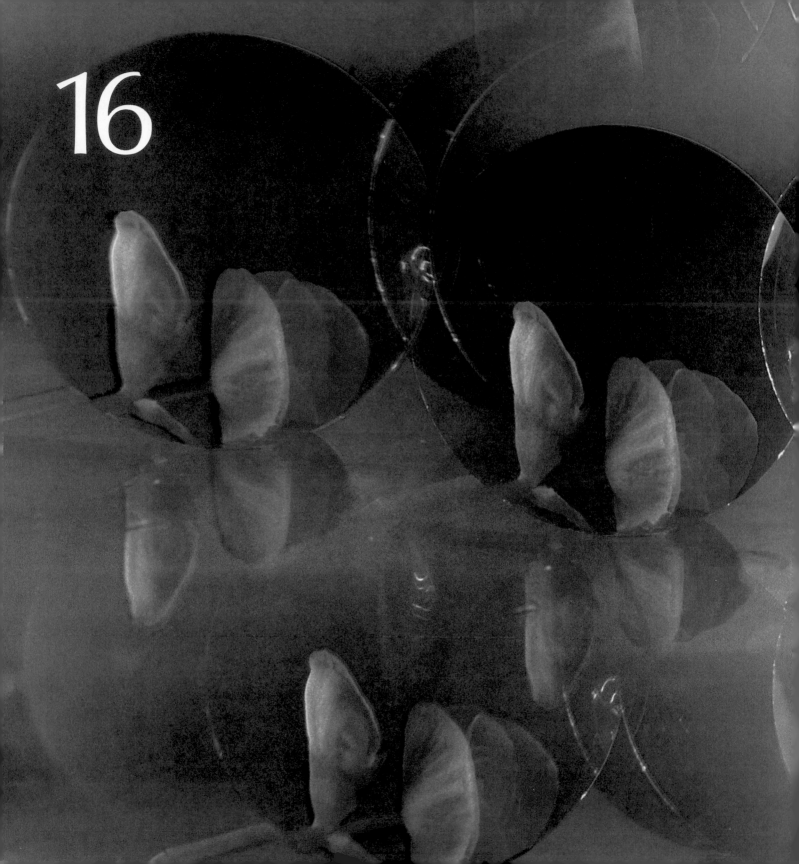

16

Lenses and Their Applications

Chapter Objectives

- **Identify** *the principal axis, optical center, focus, focal plane, and focal length of a lens.*

- **Diagram** *the position of an image formed by a lens and* **state** *the characteristics of the image.*

- **Relate** *object distance and image distance to focal length, using the lens equation for converging and diverging lenses.*

- **Apply** *the magnification equation to lenses.*

- **Identify** *the parts of a camera and the human eye, and* **describe** *their functions.*

- **Describe,** *using a diagram, nearsightedness, farsightedness, and astigmatism and* **state** *which type of lens corrects each.*

- **Illustrate** *how an image is formed in a magnifying glass, a projector, a refracting telescope, and a microscope.*

16.1 Lenses

Lenses are not a recent invention. They were first used by the Chinese and Greeks and later, in medieval times, by the Arabs. Lenses of many different types play an important part in our lives. They are used in cameras, telescopes, microscopes, and projectors, and they enable millions of people to read comfortably and to see clearly.

Lenses are of two types: **converging** and **diverging.** Converging lenses bring light rays together. Diverging lenses spread light rays apart. The two are easily distinguished by their shape. Converging lenses are thickest at the center whereas diverging lenses are thinnest at the center. Some common types of lenses are illustrated.

Converging lenses are also called convex lenses. Diverging lenses are also called concave lenses. Many lenses are constructed of both convex and concave surfaces. Eyeglasses are a good example. It is more instructive to name a lens by what it does to light than by its shape.

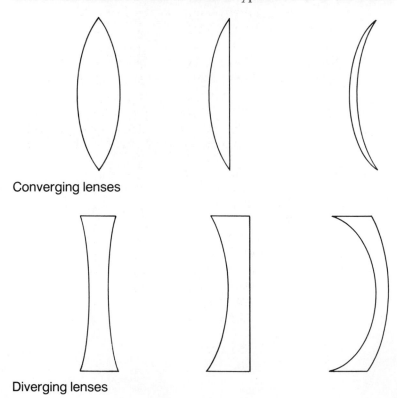

Converging lenses

Diverging lenses

16.2 Refraction in Lenses

When a ray of light travels obliquely from air into glass, it is refracted towards the normal; when it travels obliquely from glass into air, it is refracted away from the normal. In diagram (a) the shape of the glass causes the light to be refracted downwards. In diagram (b) the ray is refracted upwards. If the ray of light strikes the air-glass boundary straight on, no refraction occurs (diagram (c)).

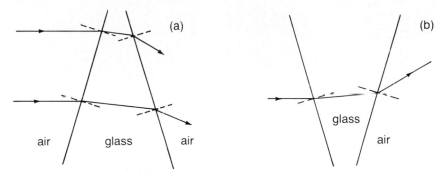

A lens is usually a circular piece of glass with uniformly curved surfaces that change the direction of light passing through. When a series of rays passes through a lens, each ray is refracted by a different amount at each surface. Rays striking the lens near the edge are bent the most, because the angles of incidence are greatest there. The least bending occurs at the center of the lens because the two surfaces are nearly parallel there. Parallel rays striking a converging lens are refracted together. A diverging lens spreads parallel rays out uniformly, as illustrated.

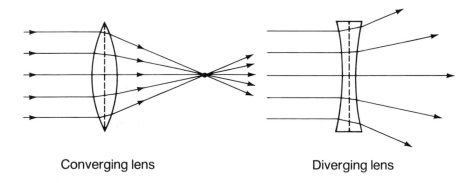

Converging lens   Diverging lens

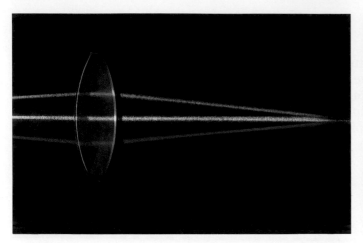
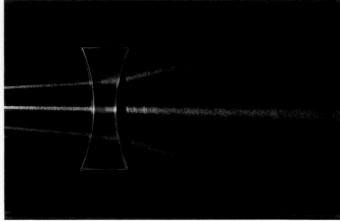

16.3 Images Formed by Converging Lenses

In all lenses, the geometric center is called the **optical center** (O). A line drawn through the optical center perpendicular to the surfaces of the lens is the **principal axis.** If a lens is thin, a group of rays parallel to the principal axis is refracted through a point on the principal axis called the **principal focus** (*F*). The **focal length** (*f*) is the distance between the principal focus and the optical center, measured along the principal axis.

Other groups of parallel rays, not aligned with the principal axis, also converge at focal points, but not on the principal axis. All focal points, including the principal focus, lie on the **focal plane**, perpendicular to the principal axis. When a converging lens refracts light from a distant object, the rays arriving at the lens are nearly parallel; thus, a real image is formed on a screen at a distance of one focal length from the lens.

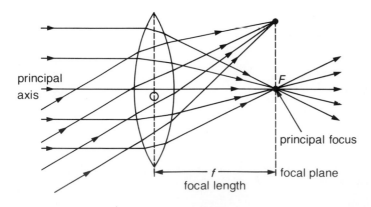

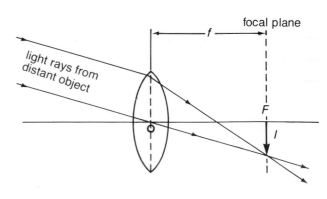

A lens may be turned around so that the light can pass through it from the opposite side. It is found that the focal length is the same on both sides, even if the curvature is different. To distinguish between them, the secondary principal focus is usually expressed as F'.

An object gives off light rays in all directions, but, for the purpose of locating its image, we are interested only in those rays that pass through the lens. Of these, as in the case of curved mirrors, three are particularly convenient for locating the tip of the image. The following are the three rays that may be used, although two are enough.

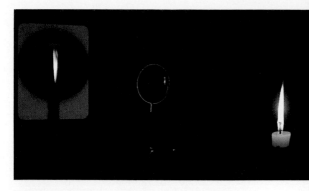

Forming the real image of the candle on the screen

Rules for Rays in a Converging Lens

1. A ray that is parallel to the principal axis is refracted through the principal focus (F).
2. A ray that passes through the secondary principal focus (F') is refracted parallel to the principal axis.
3. A ray that passes through the optical center goes straight through, without bending.

Any two of these rays may be used to locate the tip of the image.

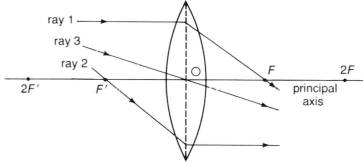

The non-refraction of the ray passing through the optical center may seem strange, since most rays passing through the optical center are laterally displaced. The explanation is that, in the thin lenses we are using, the lateral displacement of the ray is so small that we may assume that the ray is not refracted.

F represents the real principal focus, located on the side of the lens away from the object. The symbol F' represents the secondary principal focus, located on the same side of the lens as the object.

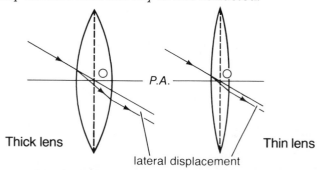

Thick lens   Thin lens

lateral displacement

In actual fact, this analysis only holds for small angles of incidence.

In the diagrams below, a construction line has been drawn through the optical center perpendicular to the principal axis. The actual path of the light ray is indicated by a solid line. For simplicity, when drawing ray diagrams in lenses, we may represent all the refraction of light as occurring along the construction line. The result is almost the same.

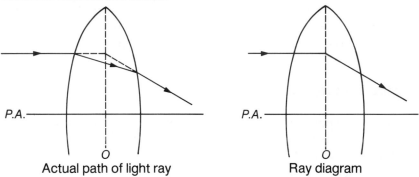

Actual path of light ray   Ray diagram

The rules for ray diagrams in converging lenses may be used as shown in the accompanying summary, to locate the images formed by a converging lens.

If an object is located more than $2f$ from the optical center (diagram 1 below), a ray parallel to the principal axis refracts through F; a ray through F' refracts parallel to the principal axis; and a ray through O passes straight through. The image is located where the three rays intersect.

As with converging mirrors, only two rays are required. The third ray acts as a check. Often one of these three rays fails to pass through the lens and cannot be used. As noted in diagram 1, the characteristics of the particular image are real, inverted, and smaller than the object. The image positions for other object locations are illustrated. Note that in diagram 4 no clear image is produced, because the rays do not intersect on either side of the lens. In diagram 5, the image is located on the same side of the lens as the object. It is virtual, erect, and larger.

1. Object beyond $2F'$.

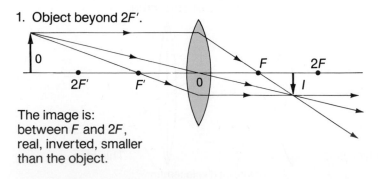

The image is:
between F and $2F$,
real, inverted, smaller
than the object.

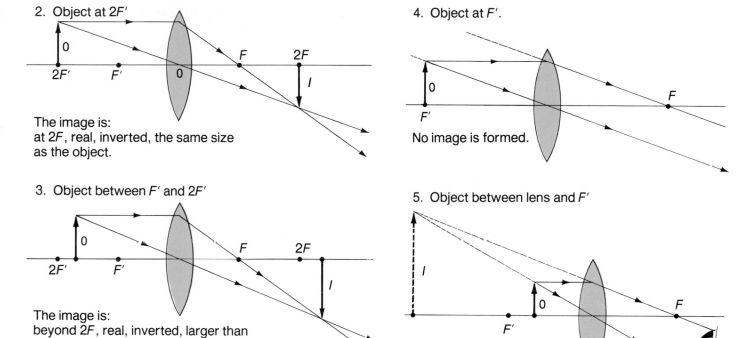

2. Object at 2F'

The image is:
at 2F, real, inverted, the same size
as the object.

4. Object at F'.

No image is formed.

3. Object between F' and 2F'

The image is:
beyond 2F, real, inverted, larger than
the object.

5. Object between lens and F'

The image is:
behind the object, virtual,
erect, larger than the object.

16.4 Images Formed by Diverging Lenses

In a diverging lens, parallel rays are refracted so that they radiate out
from a virtual focus, as illustrated.

   The rays we use to locate the position of the image in a diverging
lens are similar to those we used with converging lenses. As a result,
one set of rules is used for all lenses. The important difference is that
the principal focus in the converging lens is real, whereas in the
diverging lens it is virtual.

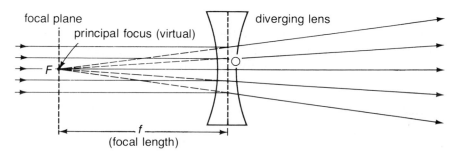

Rules for Rays in Curved Lenses of Both Types

1. A ray that is parallel to the principal axis is refracted so that it passes through (or appears to pass through) the principal focus (F).
2. A ray that passes through (or appears to pass through) the secondary principal focus (F') is refracted parallel to the principal axis.
3. A ray that passes through the optical center goes straight through, without bending.

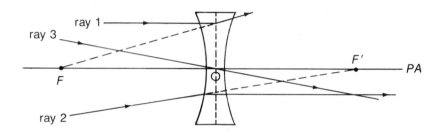

As with converging lenses, we assume, with ray diagrams in diverging lenses, that all refraction occurs at the construction line through the optical center. This makes the ray diagrams easier to draw.

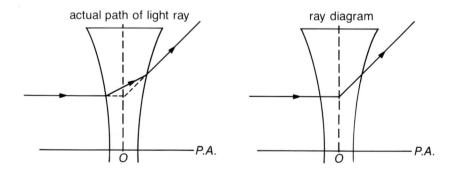

The only exception to this property occurs when the object is virtual.

The next diagram illustrates the formation of an image by a diverging lens. For all positions of the object, the image is virtual, erect, and smaller. Also, it is always located between the principal focus and the optical center.

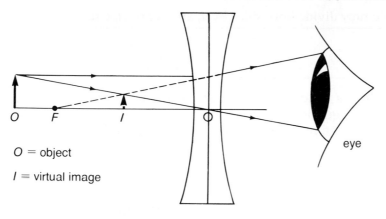

O = object

I = virtual image

The ray through the principal focus (F') is not usually used to find the image formed by a diverging lens.

16.5 The Thin Lens Equation

Just as we did for the curved mirrors, we can derive an equation for thin lenses, relating the image distance, the object distance, and the focal length.

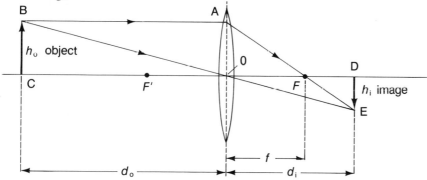

In the diagram, the triangles AOF and EDF are similar.

Therefore,
$$\frac{AO}{OF} = \frac{ED}{DF}$$

or
$$\frac{h_o}{f} = \frac{h_i}{d_i - f}$$

and
$$\frac{h_i}{h_o} = \frac{d_i - f}{f}$$

But
$$\frac{h_i}{h_o} = \frac{d_i}{d_o}$$
(because triangle BCO is similar to triangle EDO)

Therefore
$$\frac{d_i}{d_o} = \frac{d_i - f}{f}$$

We now divide both sides by d_i and rearrange to obtain

$$\frac{1}{d_o} + \frac{1}{d_i} = \frac{1}{f}$$

This is called the **lens equation**. It is exactly the same as the mirror equation. As was the case with the mirror equation, a sign convention must be used with the lens equation.

Sign Convention

1. All distances are measured from the optical center of the lens.
2. Distances of real objects and images are positive.
3. Distances of virtual objects and images are negative.
4. Object heights and image heights are positive when measured upward and negative when measured downward from the principal axis.

In this convention, a converging lens has a real principal focus and a positive focal length. A diverging lens has a virtual principal focus and a negative focal length.

As was the case for curved mirrors, the magnification is positive for an erect image and negative for an inverted image. The form of the magnification equation to be used is:

$$M = \frac{h_i}{h_o} = -\frac{d_i}{d_o}$$

Sample Problems

1. An object 8.0 cm high is 18 cm from a converging lens having a focal length of 10 cm.
   (a) How far is the image from the lens?
   (b) How tall is the image?
   Given that $h_o = 8.0$ cm, $d_o = 18$ cm, and $f = 10$ cm:

   (a) $$\frac{1}{d_o} + \frac{1}{d_i} = \frac{1}{f}$$

   $$\frac{1}{18 \text{ cm}} + \frac{1}{d_i} = \frac{1}{10 \text{ cm}}$$

   $$d_i = 22.5 \text{ cm}$$

   (b) $$\frac{h_i}{h_o} = -\frac{d_i}{d_o}$$

   $$h_i = -\left(\frac{d_i}{d_o}\right) h_o$$

   $$= -\left(\frac{22.5 \text{ cm}}{18 \text{ cm}}\right) (8.0 \text{ cm})$$

   $$= -10 \text{ cm}$$

   The image is real, since d_i is positive. The image is inverted, since h_i is negative.

2. A diverging lens has a focal length of −4.0 cm. If an object is placed 8.0 cm from the lens, how far from the lens is the image?
$d_o = 8.0$ cm, $f = -4.0$ cm   (since it is a diverging lens)

$$\frac{1}{d_o} + \frac{1}{d_i} = \frac{1}{f}$$

$$\frac{1}{8.0 \text{ cm}} + \frac{1}{d_i} = \frac{1}{-4.0 \text{ cm}}$$

$$d_i = -2.7 \text{ cm}$$

Since the image distance is negative, the image is virtual. It is located on the same side of the lens as the object.

3. Where must a postage stamp be placed in front of a magnifying glass (converging lens; $f = 10$ cm), if a virtual image is to be formed 25 cm in front of the lens? What is its magnification?
$f = 10$ cm, $d_i = -25$ cm   (since it is a virtual image, on the same side of the lens as the object)

$$\frac{1}{d_o} + \frac{1}{d_i} = \frac{1}{f}$$

$$\frac{1}{d_o} + \frac{1}{-25 \text{ cm}} = \frac{1}{10 \text{ cm}}$$

$$d_o = 7.1 \text{ cm}$$

The diagram for this problem would be similar to diagram 5 on page 495.

$$M = -\frac{d_i}{d_o}$$

$$= -\frac{-25 \text{ cm}}{7.1 \text{ cm}}$$

$$= 3.5$$

The image is erect, as indicated by a positive value for the magnification.

Practice

1. An object 8.0 cm high is placed 80 cm in front of a converging lens of focal length 25 cm.
   (a) By means of a scale ray diagram, locate the image and determine its height.
   (b) Using the lens and magnification equations, determine the image position and its height.
2. A lamp 10 cm high is placed 60 cm in front of a diverging lens of focal length −20 cm.
   (a) By means of a scale ray diagram, locate the image and determine its height.
   (b) Using the appropriate equations, calculate the image position and the height of the image.

3. A typical single lens reflex (SLR) camera has a converging lens with a focal length of 50.0 mm. What is the position and size of the image of a 25 cm candle located 1.0 m from the lens?

4. A converging lens with a focal length of 20 cm is used to create an image of the sun on a paper screen. How far from the lens must the paper be placed to produce a clear image?

5. The focal length of a slide projector's converging lens is 10.0 cm.
   (a) If a 35 mm slide is positioned 10.2 cm from the lens, how far away must the screen be placed to create a clear image?
   (b) If the height of a dog on the slide film is 12.5 mm, how tall will the dog's image on the screen be?
   (c) If the screen is then removed to a point 15 m from the lens, by how much will the separation between film and lens have to change from part (a)?

16.6 The Camera

A camera consists of a light-proof container using a lens or combination of lenses to form a real, inverted image on a light-sensitive **film**. The film provides a transparent base for a thin layer of silver bromide, or some other material, which changes chemically when exposed to light. A sharp image of the scene being photographed is focused on the film by varying the distance between the film and the lens, usually by means of a mechanical mount carrying the lens. The amount of light striking the film is very important. A **shutter** of variable speed and a diaphragm with a variable **aperture** (opening) control the quantity of light admitted through the lens.

Good quality microscopes, binoculars, and cameras may contain 6 to 10 thin lenses. A single lens camera is not made up of one lens but a series of lenses (see illustration).

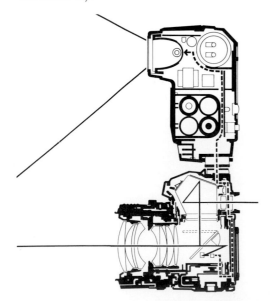

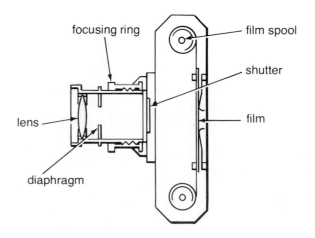

Normally, the shutter is closed. It opens for only a fraction of a second when the picture is being taken. The opening through which the light energy passes is calibrated in steps that progressively double the area of the opening. These steps are usually numbered $f/22$, $f/16$, $f/11$, $f/8$, $f/5.6$, $f/4$, etc. The smaller the **f-number** or **f-stop**, the greater the amount of light entering the lens. The smallest f-stop is the largest opening, and it is used to describe the "speed" of the lens. For example, a camera with a 1.9 lens has a lens with a maximum aperture of $f/1.9$.

Several combinations of shutter speed and f-stop allow the same amount of light to reach the film. For example, $f/16$ at $\frac{1}{250}$ s is equivalent to $f/11$ at $\frac{1}{500}$ s. A light meter calibrated in aperture/speed combinations is a convenient aid in determining the correct exposure of the film. Most light meters are electrically operated and incorporate a galvanometer connected to a needle. Many modern cameras perform this task automatically.

An iris diaphragm controls the amount of light that passes through a camera lens.

16.7 The Human Eye

The human eye is in many respects similar to a camera. The **cornea** and **lens** combine to focus the image on a thin, curved layer of light-sensitive cells called the **retina.** These cells respond to the various intensities and colors of the light that falls upon them, and they send electric signals along the **optic nerve** to the brain. The image on the retina is inverted and reversed, but the brain straightens this out and you "see" the image the right way up.

The image is focused on the retina by the lens. The lens is flexible

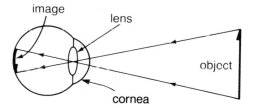

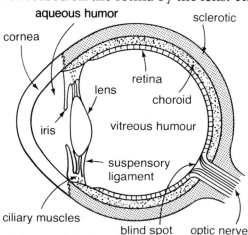

Main features of the human eye

The iris diaphragm changes the size of the pupil.

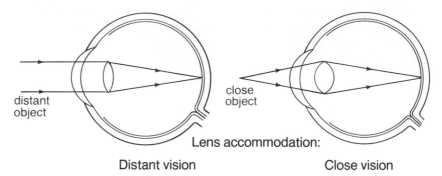

Lens accommodation:

Distant vision   Close vision

and its focal length can be altered by the pressure of the ring-shaped **ciliary muscles** surrounding it. The lens is thinner at the middle when the ciliary muscles are relaxed and thicker when they are contracted.

The process of changing the shape of the lens to make it possible to see nearby and faraway objects clearly is called **accommodation**. Accommodation occurs almost instantaneously, but the human eye can only focus on one object at a time. For example, when your eyes are focused on the print in a book, objects across the room are out of focus.

In front of the lens is a doughnut-shaped ring called the **iris diaphragm,** or, simply, the iris. The hole (aperture) in the center is known as the **pupil.** The size of the pupil is controlled by the iris, governing the amount of light entering the eye.

The eyeball itself is made up of a tough white wall called the **sclerotic.** Its front portion is transparent and forms the cornea. The shape of the eye is maintained by the pressure of colorless, transparent fluids in the eye. The liquid between the cornea and the lens is a water-like substance, the **aqueous humor.** The remainder of the eye is filled with a clear, jelly-like substance, the **vitreous humor.**

16.8 Defects in Vision and Their Correction

Farsightedness

Farsightedness, or **hypermetropia**, is a defect in the eye resulting in the inability to see nearby objects clearly. It usually occurs because the distance between the lens and the retina is too small, but it can occur if the cornea-lens combination is too weak to focus the image on the retina. This defect can be corrected by glasses or contact lenses that converge the rays of light so that the lens can focus the image clearly.

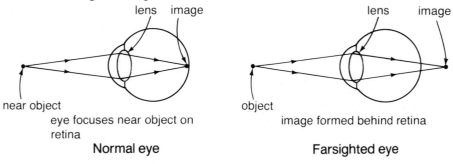 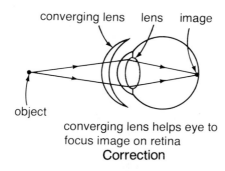

Normal eye — near object — eye focuses near object on retina

Farsighted eye — object — image formed behind retina

Correction — converging lens — lens — image — object — converging lens helps eye to focus image on retina

As a person grows older, the eye lenses lose some of their elasticity, resulting in a **loss in accommodation**. This kind of farsightedness is known as **presbyopia**. It, too, can be corrected by glasses with converging lenses. Distant vision is usually unaffected, so **bifocals** are used. These have converging lenses in the lower portion of each frame, convenient for reading and other close work for which the eyes are lowered.

Nearsightedness

In nearsightedness, or **myopia**, the distance between the lens and retina is too great or the cornea-lens combination is too strong. As a result, parallel light rays from distant objects are focused in front of the retina. Correction is accomplished by means of glasses or contact lenses with diverging lenses. These diverge the light rays so that the eye lens can focus the image clearly on the retina.

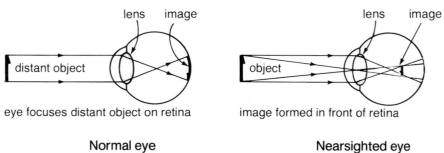 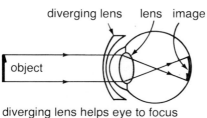

Normal eye — distant object — eye focuses distant object on retina

Nearsighted eye — object — image formed in front of retina

Correction — diverging lens — lens — image — object — diverging lens helps eye to focus image on retina

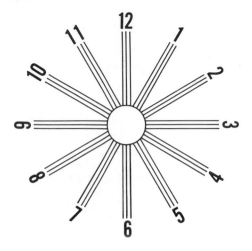

One test for astigmatism uses a wheel with numbered spokes. By noting which lines appear blurred to the patient, the oculist can determine what kind of astigmatism exists.

Astigmatism

Astigmatism occurs when either the cornea or the lens of the eye is not perfectly spherical. As a result, the eye has different focal points in different planes. The image may be clearly focused on the retina in the horizontal plane, for example, but in front of the retina in the vertical plane. Astigmatism is corrected by wearing glasses with lenses having different radii of curvature in different planes. They are commonly cylindrical lenses. Astigmatism is tested for by looking with one eye at the pattern in the margin. Since the astigmatic eye focuses rays in one plane at a shorter distance than another, sharply focused lines in the pattern will appear black, whereas those out of focus will appear blurred.

Diopters

The unit used by opticians to describe and prescribe lenses is the power (P) in diopters (d). The power of a lens is simply the inverse of the focal length of a lens in meters.

$$P \text{ (diopters)} = \frac{1}{f \text{ (meters)}}$$

For example, if your optometrist prescribes a corrective lens for farsightedness having a power of 2.5 d, he or she means a converging lens with a focal length of $f = 1/P = 1/2.5\ d = 0.40$ m = 40 cm. The greater the power of a lens, the shorter the focal length. Since the power is derived from the focal length, the sign convention for lenses is used. Thus a lens with a power of $-2.0\ d$ is a diverging lens with a focal length of 50 cm.

To "see" your blind spot, hold the book at arm's length, cover your left eye, and focus your right eye on the apple. By changing the distance between your eye and the book you can make the orange disappear as its image falls on the point of the retina where the optic nerve begins. The blind spot is outside the area of normal vision and is usually not noticed.

Cataracts

A cataract is an opaque, cloudy area that develops in the normally clear lens of the eye. If untreated, the cataract gradually blocks or distorts the light entering the eye, reducing vision progressively.

Cataracts are fairly common, occuring mostly in the elderly as a natural aging process. Other causes include: eye injuries or infections, diabetes, drugs, excessive exposure to ultraviolet, X-ray and gamma radiation. Some types of cataracts tend to be hereditary and thus run in families.

The lens of the eye is normally a clear, flexible, bloodless structure composed mainly of protein and water. Working with the cornea, it focuses light to form a sharp image on the retina. In order to function well, it requires a good supply of nutrients from the surrounding fluids. With a decrease in nutrient supply—as commonly occurs in aging—the lens loses its transparency and flexibility, causing cataracts.

In the initial stages little or no treatment is required, except eyeglasses. If cataracts spread to a point where they significantly interfere with sight, surgical removal of the lens is usually the only effective treatment. This is the most common of all eye operations and can be accomplished in one of two ways.

One surgical technique involves freezing the iris and removing the lens intact. In the second approach, a hollow needle is inserted into the lens. Its tip vibrates at a high frequency, fragmenting the cataract and removing it by suction through the hollow core of the needle.

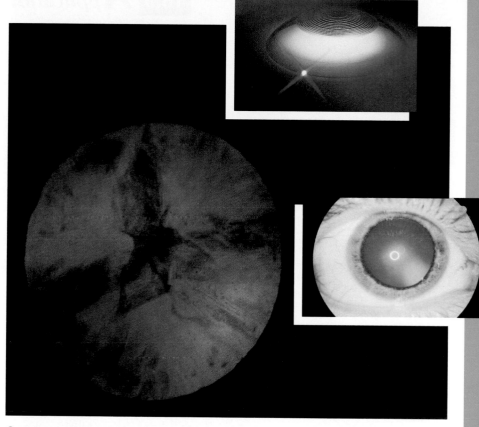

Severe cataracts prevent light from reaching the retina.
Top Inset: A multi-focus contact can replace bifocals for cataract patients.
Bottom inset: A clear healthy lens is backlit to show the reddish retina.

Removing the lens means the eye cannot focus an image on the retina. Traditionally, this has been corrected by glasses or contact lenses with high magnifications.

Many pilots and gunners during the Second World War received eye injuries from fragments of shattered plexiglass windscreens. Eye doctors noted that small pieces of this plastic could be left in the eye without causing infection or being rejected by the body as a foreign substance. After research with animals, a plastic lens was developed called an **intraocular lens implant**. This is inserted in the eye immediately after the damaged lens is removed. Once the eye has healed glasses are prescribed, but they are not nearly as strong as is the case with the traditional procedure. It should be noted that the implanted lens is not flexible and is not attached to the ciliary muscles. Thus it can not accommodate near and far objects. The patient usually wears bifocals or trifocals.

16.9 *A*pplications: Lenses

1. Projector

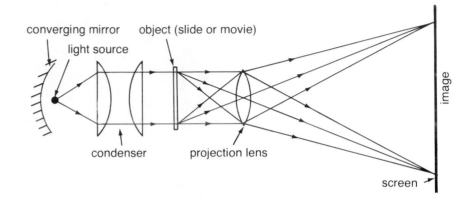

The diagram shows the arrangement of lenses and mirrors in a typical slide or movie projector. The source of light is usually a tungsten filament lamp, a carbon arc, or a quartz iodide lamp that produces the bright light necessary to illuminate a slide or movie. Two converging lenses refract the light so that the object to be projected is uniformly illuminated. The object is placed a distance of between one and two focal lengths in front of the projection lens so that a large real image is produced on the screen.

The image is inverted, so the slide or film must be inverted vertically and horizontally when placed in the projector. The projection lens is mounted in a sliding tube or geared mount so that it may be moved back and forth to focus the image on the screen.

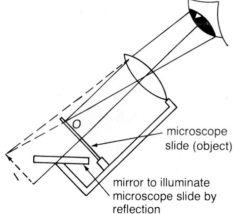

Simple microscope

2. Microscope

A simple microscope or magnifying glass consists of a single converging lens. The object to be magnified is placed inside the focal length. This produces a virtual, larger, and erect image.

A compound microscope uses two converging lenses of short focal length, arranged as illustrated. The **objective lens** produces, from the small object, an inverted, enlarged, real image I_1, which acts as the object for the second lens, called the **eyepiece**. Since the new object is located inside the focal length of the eyepiece, the eyepiece acts as a magnifying glass, producing a virtual, enlarged image (I_2)

of the real image (I_1). The focusing of the final image is achieved by mounting the eyepiece in a tube that can be adjusted up and down by means of a geared wheel.

In most compound microscopes, two or more objective lenses of different focal lengths are mounted on a rotating disk, called the nosepiece. Each has a different power of magnification. The limit of clear magnification for the compound microscope is about 900×.

The magnification of a compound microscope may be determined by multiplying the magnifying power of the eyepiece by that of the objective lens.

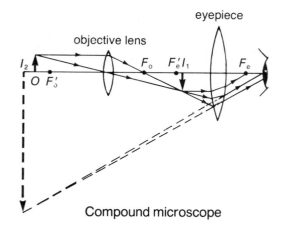

Compound microscope

3. Telescopes

The **astronomical telescope** is constructed from two converging lenses. The objective lens has a long focal length and the eyepiece has a short focal length. Since the telescope is used to view distant objects, the rays of light are nearly parallel when they enter the objective lens. The objective lens forms a real image (I) just inside the principal focus (F) of the eyepiece. The eyepiece acts as a magnifying glass, producing a virtual image of great magnification. The image is inverted, but for astronomical purposes this does not matter.

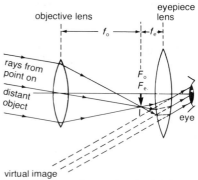

Astronomical telescope

The **terrestrial telescope** is similar in construction to the astronomical telescope, except for an additional converging lens located between the objective lens and the eyepiece. The purpose of this extra lens is to invert the image so that it has the same orientation as the object.

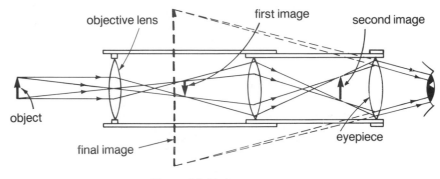

Terrestrial telescope

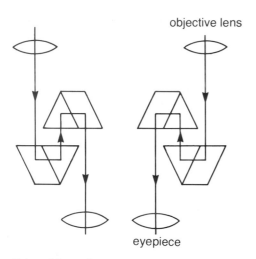

objective lens

eyepiece

Prism binoculars

Prism binoculars consist simply of two refracting telescopes mounted side by side, one for each eye. Between each pair of lenses is a pair of prisms. These invert the image to make it erect, and reduce the distance between the two lenses. Binoculars are much shorter than a telescope and thus easier to handle. Note that the distance the light travels between the two lenses in a telescope and between the two lenses on each side of a pair of binoculars is the same, although the telescope is longer.

Investigation

Investigation 16.1: Images Formed by a Converging Lens

Problems:
1. What are the characteristics and locations of the images formed by an object located at various positions in front of a converging lens?
2. Is the lens equation valid for this lens?

Materials:
optical bench
converging lens
light source
white paper screen

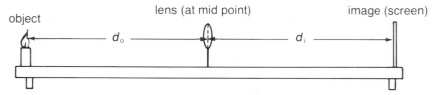

object   lens (at mid point)   image (screen)

d_o d_i

Procedure:

CAUTION: Put on your safety
goggles and constrain long hair
and clothing if you are using a candle.

1. Hold the lens in a dark part of the room so that light from a distant object passes through it and onto the screen. Move the screen back and forth until the image is clearly focused. Measure the distance between the lens and the screen. This distance is the focal length (f) of the lens.
2. Repeat step 1, this time turning the lens around so that the other side of it faces the screen. Compare the numerical values of the focal length, measured on both sides of the lens. How do the two focal lengths compare?
3. Using the value of the focal length obtained in step 1, calculate the following object distances: 2.5f, 2.0f, 1.5f, f, and 0.5f. Record the information in a chart in your notebook.

Observation	Object distance (d_o)	Image distance (d_i)	size	Characteristics orientation	type	$\dfrac{1}{d_o}$	$\dfrac{1}{d_i}$	$\dfrac{1}{d_o} + \dfrac{1}{d_i}$	Mag (M)
1	2.5$f =$								
2	2.0$f =$								
3	1.5$f =$								
4	$f =$								

4. Place the lens in the exact center of the optical bench.
5. Using chalk or masking tape, mark the object distances calculated in step 3 on the optical bench.
6. Place the object at 2.5 f. Move the screen back and forth until the image is focused clearly on the screen. Record the image distance and the characteristics of the image.
7. Repeat step 6 for the other object distances. Image distances for virtual images are not required.
8. Complete columns $\dfrac{1}{d_o}$, $\dfrac{1}{d_i}$ and $\left(\dfrac{1}{d_o} + \dfrac{1}{d_i}\right)$ for the first three observations only.

9. Determine the value of the reciprocal of the focal length (f).
10. Calculate the magnification (M) for the first three observations and enter the values in the chart.

Questions:
1. What was the focal length of your converging lens?
2. In the investigation, focal lengths were measured for both sides of the lens. How do the two focal lengths compare?
3. As the object moves closer to the lens, what regular changes occur in the size of the image? The distance of the image? The orientation of the image?
4. At what object distance was it difficult, if not impossible, to locate a clearly focused image?
5. Where would you place an object, in relation to the principal focus, to form a real image? To form a virtual image?
6. How does the value of $\dfrac{1}{f}$ relate to the value of $\left(\dfrac{1}{d_o} + \dfrac{1}{d_i}\right)$ for the first three observations?
7. Using ray diagrams, locate the image for each object position in the investigation. To fit the diagram on your page, use a focal length of 3.0 cm. An object 1.0 cm high is recommended.
8. Each of the diagrams drawn in question 7 represents the ray diagram for an application of the converging lens. Beside each diagram, place an appropriate label chosen from the following: "copy camera" (image is the same size and real), "hand magnifier" (image is larger and virtual), "slide projector" (image is larger and real), "35 mm camera" (image is smaller and real), "spotlight" (parallel light—there is no image).

Chapter Summary

1. The terms used with curved lenses are: optical center, principal axis, principal focus, focal length, and focal plane.
2. The focal length of a lens is the distance between the optical center and the principal focus, measured along the principal axis.
3. The rules for rays in curved lenses are:
   • A ray parallel to the principal axis is refracted so that it passes through (or appears to pass through) the principal focus (F).
   • A ray passing through (or appearing to pass through) the secondary principal focus (F') is refracted parallel to the principal axis.
   • A ray passing through the optical center does not bend.

4. To locate the image formed by a lens, using a ray diagram, at least two of the rays listed in the rules, or their extensions, must intersect on one side of the lens or the other.

5. For an object located beyond the focal length of a converging lens, the image is inverted and real. For an object located inside the focal length, the image is erect, virtual, and larger than the object.

6. The images formed in diverging lenses are always erect, smaller than the object, and virtual, and they are located between the principal focus and the optical center.

7. The equations used for lenses of both types are:
$$\frac{1}{d_i} + \frac{1}{d_o} = \frac{1}{f} \text{ and } M = \frac{h_i}{h_o} = -\frac{d_i}{d_o}.$$

8. The sign convention used with the lens and the magnification equations is: real objects and image distances are positive; virtual objects and image distances are negative; up is positive and down is negative.

9. The amount of light striking the film in a camera is controlled by the shutter and diaphragm. The smaller the f-stop setting, the larger the opening for light to enter the camera.

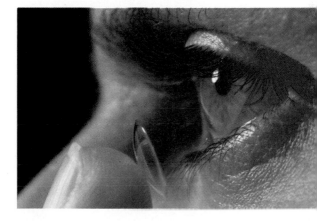

10. The primary parts of the human eye are: cornea, lens, retina, ciliary muscles, iris, diaphragm, pupil, aqueous and vitreous humors, optic nerve, and sclerotic.

11. Farsightedness is a defect in the eye in which the images of nearby objects cannot be focused on the retina. It is corrected by using a converging lens.

12. Nearsightedness is a defect in the eye preventing the images of distant objects from being focused on the retina. The correction is to use a diverging lens.

13. Converging lenses and combinations of converging lenses are used in such applications as magnifying glasses, spotlights, projectors, cameras, telescopes, binoculars, and microscopes.

*C*hapter *R*eview

Discussion

1. List ten occupations where the use of optical instruments involving the application of mirrors and lenses is important.

2. Write a brief report (200-300 words) on the latest techniques used to improve the vision for either a detached retina or glaucoma.

3. A converging lens is sometimes called a "burning glass". Does the sunlight burn because the lens magnifies? Where, relative to the lens, must the object to be burned be placed?

4. A lens can be formed by a bubble of air in water. Is such a lens a converging, or a diverging one? Use a diagram in your answer.

5. Explain briefly how contact lenses correct eye defects, and how they remain in the correct position for many hours.

6. Using one or two converging lenses, an optical bench, and a candle as an object, arrange the lens(es) and the candle to simulate the following optical instruments: a camera, a microscope, a photo copier, a refracting telescope.

7. Why do swimmers with normal eyesight see distant objects as blurry when swimming underwater? How do swimming goggles or a face mask correct this problem?

8. A converging lens of diamond and a lens of crown glass have the same shape. Which lens will have the larger focal length? Explain your answer.

9. A copy machine has a converging lens with a focal length of 40 cm. How far from the lens must documents be placed if the copies are to be exactly the same size as the original?

10. In cameras the f–number affects the depth of field (resolution) of a particular photograph. What is the relationship between the f–number and the resolution of the lens in a camera? Some research will be necessary to answer this question.

11. A properly exposed photograph was taken at $\frac{1}{100}$ s with an aperature of $f/8$. What lens opening would be required if the shutter speed is changed to (a) $\frac{1}{50}$ s, (b) $\frac{1}{200}$ s?

12. A person's vision in one eye is corrected using a lens with a power of 5.2 d. Is the eye nearsighted or farsighted?

13. To direct parallel light rays through the slide, the light source of a projector is located at the center of curvature of the converging mirror and at the principal focus of the converging lens in the condenser, as illustrated. Why?

CAUTION: Put on your safety goggles. Constrain long hair.

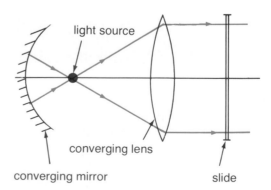

light source

converging lens

converging mirror

slide

Problems

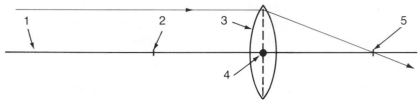

14. In your notebook, write the names of each of the numbered parts.
15. Each of the two diagrams below shows an object and the image formed by a converging lens. Copy the diagrams into your notebook and by means of ray diagrams locate the principal focus of each lens.

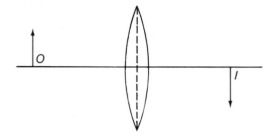

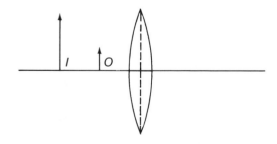

16. An object 8.0 cm high is placed 80 cm in front of a converging lens of focal length 25 cm. By means of a scale ray diagram locate the image and determine its height.

17. Use accurate scale drawings to locate the images in each of the following situations, and state whether the image is real or virtual, erect or inverted, and smaller, larger, or the same size.
    (a) A converging lens has a focal length of 20 cm. A 5.0 cm object is placed (i) 10 cm from the lens, (ii) 30 cm from the lens, and (iii) 40 cm from the lens.
    (b) A diverging lens has a focal length of 20 cm. A 5.0 cm object is placed (i) 10 cm from the lens, and (ii) 30 cm from the lens.
18. Using a scale ray diagram, locate the position of the image of a candle 10 cm high, placed 20 cm in front of a converging lens of focal length 25 cm.
19. Using a scale ray diagram, locate the image of an object 5.0 cm high that is 15 cm in front of a diverging lens of focal length 25 cm.
20. A lamp 10 cm high is placed 60 cm in front of a diverging lens of focal length 20 cm. By means of a scale ray diagram, locate the image and determine its height.
21. For questions 18, 19, and 20, check your answer using the lens equation.
22. A candle is placed 36 cm from a screen. Where between the candle and the screen should a converging lens with a focal length of 8.0 cm be placed to produce a sharp image on the screen?
23. An object 5.0 cm high is placed at the 20 cm mark on a meter stick optical bench. A converging lens with a focal length of 20 cm is mounted at the 50 cm mark. What are the position and size of the image?
24. A camera lens has a focal length of 6.0 cm and is located 7.0 cm from the film. How far from the lens is the object positioned if a clear image has been produced on the film?
25. A lens with a focal length of 20 cm is held 12 cm from a grasshopper 7.0 mm high. What is the size of the image of the grasshopper? State its position and type.
26. A projector is required to make a real image, 0.5 m tall, of a 5.0 cm object placed on a slide. Within the projector, the object is to be placed 10.0 cm from the lens. What must be the focal length of the lens?
27. A 3.0 cm flower is placed 40 cm from a lens with a focal length of 10 cm. What is the position, size, and type of image?
28. An amateur photographer takes a series of photographs of a lunar eclipse using a camera with a focal length of 6.0 cm. What will be the size of the moon's image on the film? (diameter of moon = 3.5×10^6 m, distance to the moon = 3.7×10^8 m)

29. A philatelist (stamp collector) uses a magnifying glass with a focal length of 10 cm. In order to examine a rare postage stamp, he holds the lens 4.0 cm from his eyes. If the distance for the most comfortable viewing of the image is 30 cm from his eyes, how far from the lens must the postage stamp be placed? What will the magnification be?

30. A lens has a focal length of +20 cm and a magnification of 4. How far apart are the object and the image?

31. (a) What is the focal length of a lens with a power of 7.5 d?
    (b) What is the power of a lens with a focal length of -15 cm?
    (c) Are the lenses converging or diverging? Justify your answers.

32. A book is placed 25 cm from an eyeglass lens with a power of 2.5 d. Where is the image formed?

33. A lens with a power of +5.0 d produces a clear image on a screen 2.0 m away. What is the magnification of the object?

34. In a compound microscope, the image is formed by two converging lenses. The real image, formed by the first lens (called the objective), is then used as the object by the second lens, called the eyepiece, to create a larger, virtual image. Use the following information to determine the position and size of the final image created by the two lenses: the object is 1.0 cm in height and is placed 2.5 cm from the objective lens ($f = 2.0$ cm); the eyepiece is 12 cm from the objective lens and has a focal length of 2.3 cm.

Numerical Answers to Practice Problems

page 499
1. (b) 36 cm, -3.6 cm
2. (b) -15 cm, 2.5 cm
3. 5.3 cm, -1.3 cm
4. 20 cm
5. (a) 5.10 m (b) -62.5 cm (c) 0.13 cm

17

Light and Color

Chapter Objectives

- **Describe,** *using a diagram, the dispersion of white light through a prism.*

- **Describe** *two methods of recomposing the colors of the spectrum to form white light.*

- **Predict** *the color seen by an observer, given the color of the incident light and the color of a transparent filter or reflecting surface.*

- **Describe** *how the Additive Theory of Color is applied in color television and on a stage or in a film studio.*

- **Distinguish** *among infrared radiation, ultraviolet radiation, and visible light.*

- **Describe,** *using a diagram, how dispersion and internal reflection occur in a single raindrop.*

- **Illustrate** *how chromatic aberration is produced by converging lenses.*

- **Describe** *how a spectrometer is used to identify an unknown compound.*

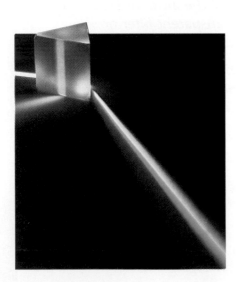

Had Newton never worked in optics, astronomy, dynamics, or celestial mechanics, he would still be considered one of the greatest scientists on the basis of his contribution to mathematics. Best known for his fundamental breakthrough in calculus, including the concepts and methods of differentiation and integration, he did significant work in other aspects of analysis, algebra, classical and analytical geometry, methods of finite difference, the classification of curves, and interpolation.

Chapter 17

17.1 Dispersion and Recomposition

It has been known at least since the days of the ancient Egyptians that fragments of clear, colorless glass and precious stones emit the colors of the rainbow when placed in the path of a beam of white light. It was not until 1666, however, that this phenomenon, called **dispersion**, was systematically investigated. The refracting telescope had recently been invented by a Dutch eyeglass maker named Lippershey, and Isaac Newton—then 23 years old—was starting to search for a technique for removing coloration from the images seen through telescopes.

In 1672, Newton described his experiments to the Royal Society in London. His theory that white light was made up of many colors was revolutionary, and it was greeted with skepticism. Indeed, Newton and another English physicist, Robert Hooke, became involved in a bitter debate, and Newton refused to publish his conclusions until after Hooke's death, 32 years later!

Newton used, as a source of light, a small round hole in one of his window shutters at Cambridge. A prism placed in a beam of sunlight coming through the hole produced an elongated patch of multicolored light on the opposite wall. Newton called this a spectrum and noted the colors—red, orange, yellow, green, blue, indigo, and violet.

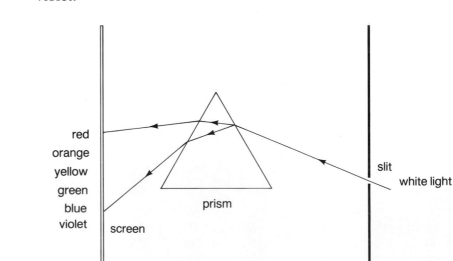

The notion of seven basic colors comes from ancient times, but today we refer to only six basic colors because most people are unable to see indigo as a distinct color. Actually, there is an infinite number of different colors, for each basic color of the spectrum merges gradually with the next.

The colors of the spectrum may be recombined, by means of a lens, to form white light, as shown in the diagram. This process, called **recomposition**, may also be achieved with a series of mirrors, as illustrated. Newton also demonstrated recomposition by painting the spectral colors on a disk and rotating the disk at a high speed. The rotating disk appeared white.

Recompositon using a Newton disk

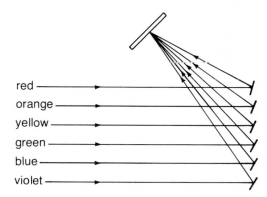

red
orange
yellow
green
blue
violet

Recombination of spectrum colors by mirrors

The Newton disk demonstration of recomposition usually appears off-white because of the difficulty of reproducing pure color with paint or ink.

The demonstration of recomposition with **Newton's Disk** is only possible because of the **persistence of vision**. The image of a color produced on the retina of the eye is retained for a fraction of a second. If the disk is rotated fast enough, the image of one color is still present on the retina when the image of the next color is formed. The brain sums up and blends together the rapidly changing colored images on the retina, producing the effect of a white image.

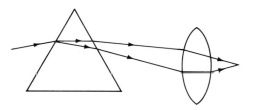

Recomposition using a lens

17.2 Color by Subtraction

If light energy is directed towards an object, some of the light is reflected and some is absorbed. And, when light energy is absorbed, it is usually converted into heat, causing the object to warm up.

Why is the Sun Red at Sunset?
Dust particles in the air scatter light from the sun and the sky. The tiny specks of dust scatter blue light more effectively than red light, letting more red light pass through to our eyes.

When the sun is high in the sky, it looks yellow-white because its rays are passing through a fairly clear atmosphere. But at sunset the sun turns a fiery red because at a lower angle the sun's light has more of the dusty atmosphere to pass through. The dustier the air, the more the sunlight is scattered and the more spectacular the sunset.

However, a natural phenomenon that sends huge quantities of dust into the air, such as a volcanic eruption or a forest fire, creates the opposite effect. When vast quantities of large dust particles are emitted into the atmosphere, they scatter the red light more than the blue, letting more of the blue light pass through to our eyes. When this happens the sun appears blue-white and the moon blue. This condition occurs very rarely, hence the expression "once in a blue moon".

When white light falls on an object, and all of it is reflected, the object appears white. If some colors are reflected while others are absorbed, the object appears to be colored, since the eye only receives the reflected color or colors. Thus, a leaf appears green under white light because it absorbs all the colors except green, which is reflected. Similarly, a rose appears red under white light because all the colors, except red, are absorbed. Although black is usually considered to be a color, in reality it is not. Black cannot be a color of light since it is the absence of any light at all. For example, in a dark room, all objects appear black since they do not radiate or reflect any light.

When white light shines on red glass, the glass looks red whether you see it by reflected light or by transmitted light, since the glass absorbs all colors except red. Red is both transmitted and reflected. Most transparent substances appear the same by transmitted light as they do by reflected light, but there are some exceptions. The oil used to lubricate automobile engines appears reddish by transmitted light and greenish by reflected light.

The dyes and pigments used in transparent filters and in paints are not pure. For instance, yellow coloring should, in theory, absorb all the colors of the spectrum except yellow. In fact, most colorings are not that selective, and the colors adjacent to yellow in the spectrum, that is, orange and green, are only partially absorbed. The transmitted yellow is not pure and is referred to as **compound yellow.** Most objects which appear yellow by reflected or transmitted light are compound yellow.

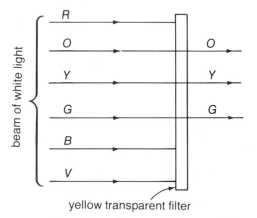

The subtractive primary colors are blue, yellow, and red.

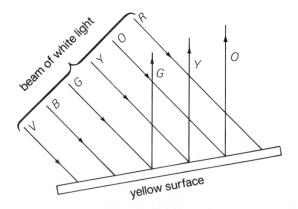

When several color filters are combined, various parts of white light are absorbed, depending on the filters used. When a yellow transparent filter followed by a red transparent filter is placed in front of a beam of white light, the yellow filter absorbs all colors except orange, yellow, and green, and the red filter absorbs all colors except red and orange. Thus, orange is the only color that is transmitted through the two-filter combination. Similarly, a combination of blue and yellow filters absorbs all colors except green. This technique of beginning with white light and absorbing or subtracting colors until the color left is the one desired is called color by subtraction, or the **Subtractive Theory of Color**.

In the mixing of paints, a similar process occurs. When blue paint and yellow paint are mixed, the result is green paint. This would not be possible if pure blue were mixed with pure yellow. In fact, the process depends on the fact that the paint pigments in common use are compound colors. Compound yellow contains pigments that reflect orange, yellow, and green light and absorb blue light. **Compound blue,** being impure, reflects green, blue, and violet light but absorbs red and yellow light. When the two paints are combined, the only color that is not absorbed by the blue and yellow pigment is green, which is reflected. The mixing of pigments or dyes and the use of transparent filters to obtain desired colors is a fairly complicated matter, and the explanations given here are simplified.

The color of the light illuminating an object will affect the color of the object. A red object will appear red under white light or red light, but it will appear black under green light. The explanation is that the red object reflects only red light. Green light contains no red light, so none of it is reflected. For example, the rose on the left appears red in white light. The same rose on the right appears black in green light.

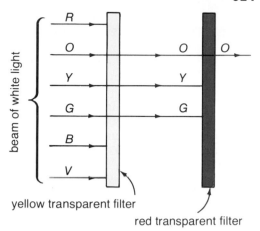

Most color printing is done by a four-color process. The colors used are cyan, yellow, magenta, and black.

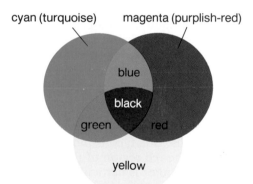

The subtractive method of color production. When the primary pigments (cyan, magenta, and yellow) are mixed, different colors are produced by subtractive absorption. When all the wavelengths of light in the visible spectrum are absorbed, the mixture appears black.

The Theory of Color Vision

We do not yet know all the details of how the human eye perceives color. The most acceptable theory of color vision was first proposed in the 19th century by Thomas Young, a British scientist, and Hermann Helmholtz, a German physicist and physiologist.

There are two types of light sensitive cells in the retina of the eye. They are classified by shape: rods and cones. There are approximately 125 million rod cells in a typical retina. The rod cells are not sensitive to color and send only monochrome images (black, white and shades of grey) to the brain. Rods are only sensitive to low-intensity light and are primarily used for night vision.

The cone cells, shorter and thicker than the rods, respond to higher-intensity light, such as daylight, and give color vision. According to the Young-Helmholtz theory, there are three types of cone cells. One type is most sensitive to the red region of the spectrum. Another is particulary sensitive to the green region and a third to the blue-violet. Each type of cone cell is responsive to a range of colors. The red-sensitive cones respond not only to red, but also to orange, yellow, and green. The green-sensitive cones respond to yellow and blue as well as green, and the blue-sensitive cones respond also to violet and green.

Colored light excites at least two sets of cone cells because of their overlapping sensitivity. For example, yellow light excites both the red- and green-sensitive cones. The shade of yellow would depend

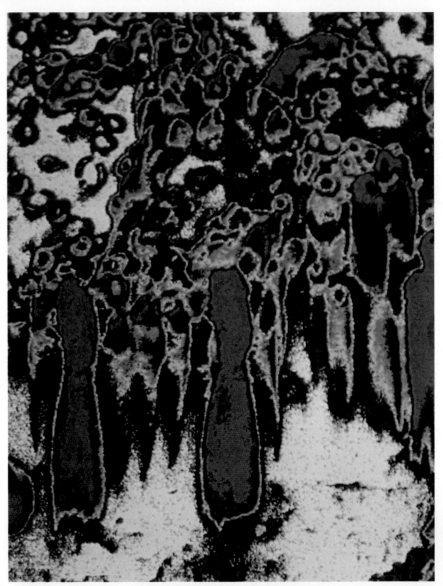

A photograph of the retina taken by an electron microscope

on the relative strength of the impulses received from each type of cone cell. In a similar way, the

perceived shade of blue would depend on the strength of the impulses from the green- and blue-

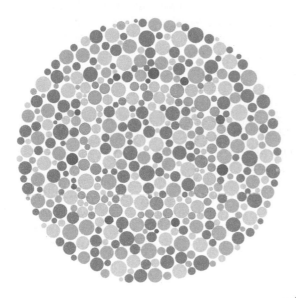

In this test for color blindness, if you cannot see the green square then you have a "green" deficiency.

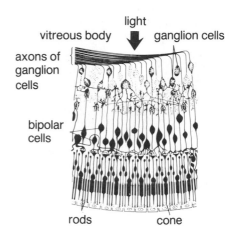

three-color theory, the evidence, as yet, is not conclusive. Also, the theory does not explain some details of color sensation. Nevertheless, it is a useful theory because it works in explaining most of the processes of color vision.

Color blindness is a popular, but incorrect, term describing an inability to distinguish between certain colors. Literal color blindness, or seeing things only in shades of gray, is very rare.

Most people who are color blind are unable to distinguish between red and green—most frequently in dim light and less frequently under normal lighting conditions.

Defects in color vision are almost always hereditary, and although they are passed on by the mother, they affect men more than women. There is no cure for color blindness but it rarely interferes with everyday life. It may be an impediment in some careers, however.

In this test, color-blind patients can trace either the red curve or the purple curve.

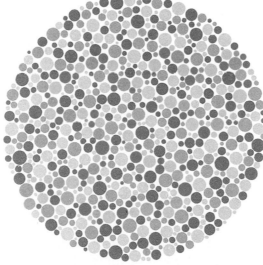

sensitive cones. If all three sets of retinal cones are equally stimulated, the resulting sensation is that of white light.

Although there is some experimental evidence to support the

17.3 Color by Addition

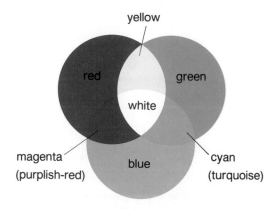

The additive method of color production. When light beams of the primary colors (red, green and blue) are projected on a white screen, their mixtures produce the colors indicated. By varying the intensities of the beams, most colors or hues can be produced by additive mixing.

If you examine the picture on a color television tube, you will find thousands of tiny dots or bars of color, each less than 1.0 mm in width. When the set is turned on, small dots of red, blue, and green light appear. No other colors are present. How is it possible for these small areas of color to combine to produce all the colors of the spectrum, as well as white light?

Red, blue, and green are called the **additive primary colors.** If three spotlights with red, blue, and green filters are directed on a screen so that they overlap, yellow is produced by the red and green lights, cyan by the green and blue, and magenta by the red and blue. Yellow, cyan, and magenta are called secondary colors. In the central region, where red, blue, and green overlap, white is produced. By varying the intensities of the colored lights, most of the colors of the spectrum can be produced. Creating a color by combining the additive primaries is called using the **Additive Theory of Color.** This technique is used in theaters and television studios. Banks of red, blue, and green lights are hung above the stage and any color can be produced by varying the intensities of the banks. As mentioned above, the technique is also used in color television (see Section 17.5, Part 4).

17.4 Infrared and Ultraviolet Radiation

If the light from the sun is directed through a prism, it can be shown that invisible radiation is produced beyond either end of the visible spectrum.

Just beyond the red end of the spectrum is a region occupied by a radiation called **infrared.** This was discovered in 1800 by the English astronomer William Herschel (1738–1822). He used a blackened thermometer bulb on the various regions of the spectrum and found a heating effect beyond the various red in the spectrum.

It has since been found that more than half of the energy coming from the sun is infrared radiation and that infrared radiation provides most of the heat energy requirement of the Earth. Infrared radiation can penetrate clouds, smoke, and haze. It is useful for photography at high altitudes, military reconnaissance, photography in the dark, "heat" photography of the human body to assist in the detection of cancer, and the locating of heat losses in a building. Infrared radiation also has a therapeutic effect when used on damaged muscles. Infrared heat lamps or radiators are also used to keep food warm in restaurants, dry paint in car body shops, and keep spectators warm in outdoor arenas.

The false-color thermograph detected infrared radiation escaping from the house.

The year after Herschel's discovery, Johann Ritter (1776–1810) placed certain salts in the region beyond the visible violet and found that they glowed, or were fluorescent, in the dark. Quinine sulfate, vaseline on paper, most white shirts, and natural white teeth are examples of other substances that are fluorescent under **ultraviolet** radiation.

Ultraviolet radiation is easily absorbed by clouds, smoke, and haze, but it has the ability to burn the outer layer of the skin, causing sunburn. It also has the beneficial effect of accelerating the manufacture of vitamin D in the skin. Ultraviolet radiation from sun

Ultraviolet radiation is commonly called "black light". Most ultraviolet radiation sources emit some visible violet light as well.

Suntan lotion is supposed to filter out some of the ultraviolet radiation that causes burning.

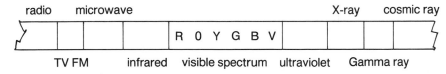

(diagram not to scale)

lamps must be treated with respect. Excessive exposure may produce a bad sunburn or cause destruction of areas in the retina, resulting in blind spots. Carbon arc lamps, mercury vapor lamps, and arc welders also emit ultraviolet radiation, as well as visible light, and thus should be used with care. Most of the ultraviolet radiation received by the Earth, from the sun, is absorbed by our atmosphere.

Freshly washed white shirts usually fluoresce under ultraviolet radiation, because there is a residue of detergent left in the cloth. To make a shirt "whiter than white", as television commercials claim, most manufacturers of detergents use chemicals (sometimes called "blueing" agents) that fluoresce under blue light as well as under ultraviolet radiation. The blueing adds fluorescence to the white light normally reflected by a white surface, and it appears "whiter".

17.5 *A*pplications: Color and Light

1. The Rainbow

A rainbow is the sun's spectrum produced by water droplets in the atmosphere. Light enters the spherical rain droplets where it is refracted, dispersed, and reflected internally. The violet and red rays intersect internally, as illustrated, emerging with the violet at the top, the red at the bottom, and the other colors of the spectrum in between. Looking at millions of drops, the observer sees the spectrum in an arc of a semi-circle with red on the outside and violet on the inside.

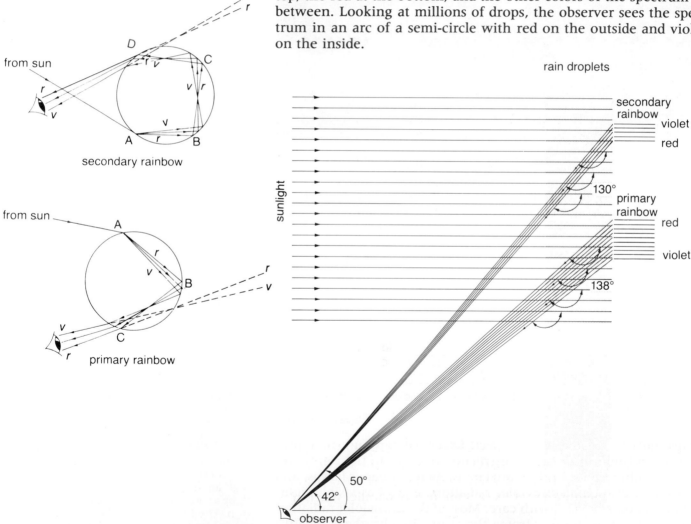

secondary rainbow

primary rainbow

rain droplets

The rainbow arc appears at specific points in the sky because only droplets of water that are located along that arc will reflect the spectrum at the correct angle into the eye of the observer. The angle is approximately 42° to the horizontal sunlight. Note that the sun must be shining over the shoulder of the observer. Rainbows can only occur when sunlight shines directly on a large region of water droplets, not water vapor.

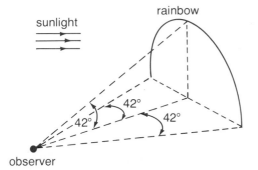

The refractive index is slightly different for each color of light. Thus the lens has a slightly different focal length for each color.

2. Chromatic Aberration

When white light passes through a lens, the lens disperses it into its components, forming the colors of the spectrum. This creates colored fringes around objects viewed through the lens, which can be annoying in optical instruments such as cameras and telescopes. (This was the problem that prompted Newton to investigate light and color.)

The defect, called **chromatic aberration,** is usually corrected by means of combinations of converging and diverging lenses made of glass with differing optical densities. The dispersion of one lens is corrected by that of the other. Cameras of good quality usually use two or more components to correct for the effects of dispersion. These combinations are called **achromatic lenses.**

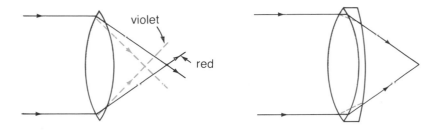

Chromatic aberration is due to the inability of a single lens to focus all colors at a single point. It is minimized by combining a converging lens with a weak diverging lens, constructed of a different type of glass.

3. The Spectrometer

A better way to produce a pure spectrum is to use a parallel beam of light in an instrument called a **spectrometer.** The source of light is placed at the principal focus of the first lens (in the **collimator**), which refracts the light so that its rays are nearly parallel when it is dispersed in the prism. This light then enters a **telescope** made up of two converging lenses, and the resulting spectrum is magnified

Note that the sky is bright inside the primary bow but dark between the secondary and primary bows.

by the eyepiece. In some instruments the eyepiece is replaced by photographic film on which the spectrum is recorded. Such a spectrometer is called a **spectrograph.**

The spectrum produced by a substance when it is heated to incandescence is called an **emission spectrum.** The emission spectra of solids and of liquids are continuous, one color merging into the next. An example is the spectrum produced by the hot filament of an incandescent lamp. The emission spectra of gases, usually heated by an electric spark, appear as a series of bright colored lines. Each element or compound has its own unique spectrum. Because of this property spectra can be used to identify the presence of an element or compound, even in a small sample of the substance.

The spectra of all known elements and compounds have been accurately recorded by scientists. These spectral "fingerprints" are used to identify elements, for example, hydrogen in distant stars. This is accomplished by directing light from the star into a spectrograph, which records the star's spectrum, and then comparing the star's spectrum with the known spectra of various substances.

The terms "continuous" and "line" are used to distinguish between the two main types of emission spectra.

Spectrometer

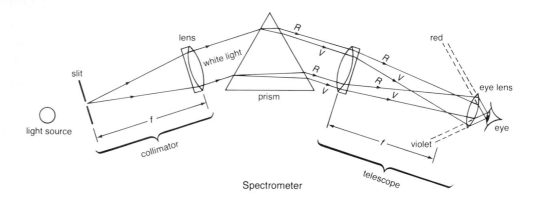

Spectrometer

The spectrum of white light

helium

4. Color Television

A color television receiver produces all the colors of the spectrum, using the Additive Theory of Color (see Section 17.3). On the back of the picture-tube screen is a thin coating of phosphor material. Phosphors are a group of chemicals that give off light when hit by fast-moving electrons (see Section 24.3). In black-and-white television, they give off white light and thus are called white phosphors. In color television there are over 600 000 small dots or bars of three types of phosphor—red, green, and blue. These are arranged in groups of three, each group having the three additive primaries. Three separate electron beams are directed at these groups, one for each color. When the red phosphors are hit, red light is given off. When the red and green phosphors are hit, yellow light appears. If all three are hit equally, white light results, and so on. Since the phosphor dots or bars are small and close together, only the resultant colors are seen, not the individual colored light producing them. The intensity and color of the picture is controlled by varying the energy of the three electron beams as they scan the screen.

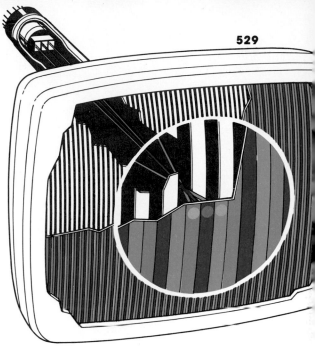

The additive theory is used in color television.

Investigations

Investigation 17.1: Dispersion in a Prism

Problems:
1. How is a ray of white light refracted by a prism?
2. What results when the colors of the spectrum are combined?

Materials:
ray box
triangular glass prism
white screen

Procedure:
1. Set up the apparatus as illustrated, putting the screen at least 50 cm away from the prism.
2. Rotate the prism until it produces maximum bending of the incident light. Adjust the screen so that the refracted light strikes it. Observe the pattern on the screen and record in a small

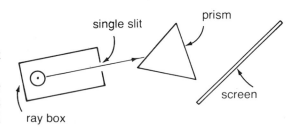

Newton's experiment with a prism

diagram both the pattern of the colors and the manner in which the pattern was formed by the prism.
3. Place a converging lens in the path of the beam of refracted light. Adjust the position of the lens in relation to the screen until the light rays converge at a single point on the screen. In a diagram, record the path taken by the light from the ray box to the screen.

Questions:
1. List the colors on the screen, in order, beginning with the color that was refracted the least. What is this band of many colors called? What is the name of the process of breaking down white light into its components?
2. What effect did the converging lens have on the band of colored rays?
3. What is white light composed of?

Investigation 17.2: Color by Subtraction

Problem:
What colors are present after white light has passed through various colored filters and filter combinations?

Materials:
clear showcase bulb
replica diffraction grating
set of colored filters

If the lamp is mounted in front of a black background, the spectral colors will be seen more easily. The spectrum will be repeated on either side of the lamp. The spectra closest to the lamp are the brightest and the easiest to see.

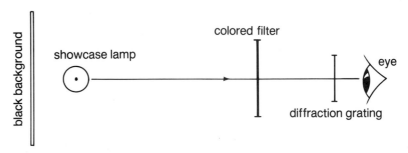

Procedure:
1. Set up the showcase lamp in a darkened room so that the filament is vertical.
2. View the white light through the diffraction grating, adjusting the axis of the grating so that spectra are formed to the right and left of the filament. List the colors you see.
3. Place a red filter between the lamp and the diffraction grating. List the colors you see.

4. Repeat step 3, using a blue, a green, and a yellow filter, in turn.
5. Place a red and a yellow filter together so that light passes through both before reaching the grating. What color(s) still pass through the two filters?
6. Repeat step 5, using filter combinations of yellow and blue, and red and green.

Questions:
1. "None of the filters used was pure, that is, allowed only one color to pass through it." Explain this statement, drawing on your observations.
2. Explain your observations for red-yellow, yellow-blue, and red-green, when each of these combinations was used to filter white light.
3. This method of producing a specific color from white light uses a concept called the Subtractive Theory of Color. Explain why this is an appropriate name for it.

Chapter Summary

1. Dispersion is the separation of white light into its component colors by a prism.
2. The colors of the spectrum, when recombined, form white light.
3. White objects tend to reflect light. Black objects tend to absorb light.
4. In the Subtractive Theory of Color, the colors of the spectrum, contained in white light, are subtracted by filters or dyes until the desired color remains.
5. The additive primary colors are red, blue, and green. Using the Additive Theory of Color, any other color of the spectrum can be produced by mixing additive primary colors together in the proper proportions.
6. Infrared and ultraviolet radiations are beyond the red and violet areas of the spectrum, respectively. Neither is visible to the human eye but both are important to life on Earth.
7. Rainbows are formed by the dispersion and internal reflection of the white light from the sun by water droplets in the atmosphere.
8. Dispersion causes chromatic aberration in lenses. This defect can be partially corrected by using two or more lenses of glasses with different optical densities.

9. Each element and compound emits a characteristic spectrum when heated to incandescence. The spectrometer and the spectrograph are devices used to analyze such spectra.
10. Color television makes use of the Additive Theory of Color.

Chapter Review

1. List five careers where the intense study of optics is a prerequisite.
2. When white light passes through a prism, the colors of the spectrum are produced on a screen. If a student views the spectral colors through a converging lens, he may see an image with the colors reversed. Explain why.
3. Why are nights brighter when there is snow on the ground?
4. A yellow filter is placed in front of a beam of red light. What color of light emerges from the filter? Explain your answers.
5. Blue sky viewed through a yellow filter looks green. What conclusion can you draw about the sky, and the filter that was used?
6. An American flag is illuminated by a blue light. What colors will its red, blue, and white parts appear to be? Explain your answer.
7. As the director of a school variety concert, how could you "dress" the students in black if all of them wore blue costumes?
8. Why is it against the law for a supermarket to put red lights over its meat display or to package bacon in red cellophane?
9. Yellow sodium vapor lamps are commonly used for street illumination. Skin and lips look different under these lights. Why?
10. A girl buys a dress in a store with fluorescent lighting, and finds when she gets home that the dress is a slightly different color than she thought it was. Can you suggest a possible explanation?
11. You can get very hot when sunbathing under glass, but you will not get a sunburn. Why?
12. Why must the eyes be covered or shielded when a person is getting a tan under a sun lamp?
13. The sun gives off ultraviolet radiation and infrared radiation as well as visible light. During a solar eclipse, the moon blocks out most of the visible light coming from the sun, creating a dark shadow at certain points on the Earth. An observer is standing in the eclipse shadow.

(a) What radiations will still be received by the observer?

(b) Since it is dark in the shadow, will the pupils of the observer's eyes be enlarged or contracted?

(c) Why is it dangerous to view the eclipse with the naked eye?

14. (a) In what direction will you see a rainbow when the sun is in the western sky?

(b) Can a rainbow be formed if the raindrops are located only between you and the sun? Explain your answer.

15. Why is there chromatic aberration in lenses but none in plane mirrors or curved mirrors?

16. Inexpensive children's telescopes, binoculars and microscopes usually produce images with colored edges. Explain why.

17. The focal length of a lens is determined using red light from a helium-neon laser. How will the focal length compare with that measured using the green light from an argon laser?

18. Sunlight is made up of most of the colors of the spectrum. Although it is refracted by the atmosphere, it is not dispersed as it travels through the air. What does this tell you about the relative speeds of the various colors of the spectrum in air?

19. How might spectrographic analysis provide evidence that a specific industry has disposed of chemicals in the city's sewer system?

A solar eclipse

18

Electrostatics

Chapter Objectives

- **Identify** the two types of electric charge, and **state** the Law of Electric Charges.

- **Summarize** a simple model of matter.

- **Describe** electric charges on an object in terms of an excess or deficit of electrons.

- **Distinguish** between a conductor and an insulator.

- **Identify** the charges on ebonite rubbed with fur and glass rubbed with silk.

- **Explain** separation of charge on a neutral conductor when a charge is brought near.

- **Describe** how a neutral object may be charged by contact and by induction.

- **Use** an electroscope to detect the presence of a charge and **identify** its type.

- **Describe** the electric fields around a single charged sphere, two charged spheres, and two charged parallel plates.

- **Explain** results of the Millikan experiment.

- **Relate** the unit of electric charge to the elementary charge.

18.1 Electrification

The existence of electrical forces has been known since the days of the early Greeks when scientists observed the ability of rubbed amber to attract small bits of dried straw. They called this phenomenon the "amber effect". The Greek word for amber is "elektron", and the effect soon became known as "electriks", or electricity.

Any material that behaved like amber after being rubbed was said to be electrified, or **electrically charged**. Materials that showed no amber effect were said to be **neutral**.

Systematic study of electricity began only during the Renaissance, when it was found that many substances like amber became electrified when rubbed. It was also observed that these substances fell into two categories. When two pieces of the same material were rubbed with a third material they always repelled each other. But when each was rubbed with a different material, they either attracted or repelled one another, depending on the materials.

There seemed to be two "electric states". Benjamin Franklin first identified these two states, and he gave them the names that we still use today—**positive charges** and **negative charges**. He concluded that all objects possess electricity and that a neutral object possesses what he called a "normal" amount. To charge an object positively, he thought, meant adding to the normal amount of electricity, whereas to charge an object negatively meant taking away from the normal amount.

Electric charges are rearranged when you rub a balloon with a wool cloth. After the objects acquire opposite charges, they attract each other.

For purposes of identification, he described as "negative" the charge that an ebonite rod acquires when rubbed with fur. Any other object that is repelled by a charged ebonite rod must likewise be charged negatively. Any charged object that is attracted to a charged ebonite rod, such as a glass rod rubbed with silk, must be charged positively.

Now we can state the **fundamental law of electric charges**:

Opposite electric charges attract each other.
Similar electric charges repel each other.
Charged objects attract some neutral objects.

The Law of Electric Charges

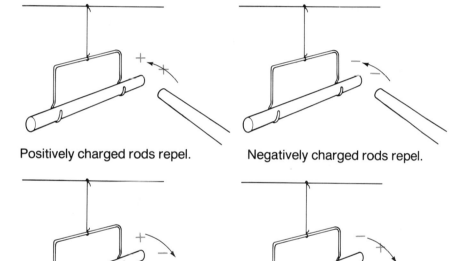

Positively charged rods repel.   Negatively charged rods repel.

Oppositely charged rods attract.

To understand fully how charged objects attract or repel and how a charged object can attract a neutral object, we need to understand the structure of matter. Scientists have developed a simple model of the structure of matter that we can use to explain these phenomena.

There are many common substances that behave like amber when rubbed, including:
orlon and other synthetic materials after they have been in a clothes dryer (static-cling)
plastic wrap and vinyl garbage bags
plastic foam packaging material
nylon stockings and wool rugs.
When such objects behave like amber they are said to be "charged".

18.2 Electrical Structure of Matter

Scientists have developed highly sophisticated and extremely accurate models of the structure of solids, liquids, and gases during the last 150 years. For a basic understanding of the electrical effects under consideration here, a rather simple model often used in the early part of this century will serve well enough.

The principal concepts embodied in this model may be summarized as follows:

1. All matter is composed of sub-microscopic particles, called **atoms**.
2. Electric charges are carried by particles within the atom that are called **electrons** and **protons**.
3. Protons are found in a small central region of the atom, called the **nucleus**. They are small, heavy particles, and each one carries a positive electric charge of a specific magnitude, called the **elementary charge**.
4. Electrons move in the space around this central nucleus. They are small, very light particles (each with only slightly more than $\frac{1}{2000}$ the mass of a proton), yet each of them carries a negative electric charge equal in magnitude to that of the proton.
5. Atoms are normally electrically neutral, because the number of positive protons in the nucleus is equal to the number of negative electrons moving around the nucleus.
6. **Neutrons** are small, heavy particles (each slightly heavier than a proton) found in the nucleus, and they carry no electric charge.
7. If an atom gains an extra electron, it is no longer neutral but has an excess of electrons and, hence, a net negative charge. Such an atom is called a **negative ion**.
8. If an atom loses an electron, it will have a deficit of electrons, and, hence, a net positive charge. Such an atom is called a **positive ion**.

Consider, first, the electrical effects in solids. The atoms of a solid are held tightly in place; their nuclei are not free to move about within the solid. Since these nuclei contain all of the protons, the amount of positive charge in a solid remains constant and fixed in position. However, it is possible for negative charges within a solid to move, for some of the electrons have the ability to move from atom to atom.

Objects that are charged negatively have an **excess of electrons**. Objects charged positively have a **deficit of electrons**. Both types always have their normal number of protons.

"Atom" comes from the Greek "atomos", which means, literally, "not able to be cut".

The nucleus of an atom occupies only about one part in 10^{12} of the volume of the atom. Except for the electrons and the nucleus, the atom consists of empty space.

The Principle of Conservation of Electric Charge states: "Whenever a quantity of positive charge is created in a closed system, an equal quantity of negative charge appears also."

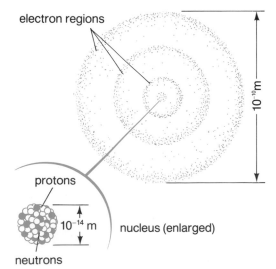

electron regions

10^{-10} m

protons

10^{-14} m

nucleus (enlarged)

neutrons

A visual depiction of this simple model of the atom

All electric charges in solids are due to an excess or deficit of electrons.

Most solids fall into one of two broad categories, as far as their electrical properties are concerned—**insulators** and **conductors**.

Conductors

A conductor is a solid in which electrons are able to move easily from one atom to another. Most metals are excellent conductors, the best being silver, copper, and aluminum. Some of the electrons in these conductors have been called "free electrons" because of their ability to move about.

Insulators

An insulator is a solid in which the electrons are not free to move easily from atom to atom. Plastic, cork, glass, wood, and rubber are all excellent insulators.

To determine whether a material is a conductor or an insulator, perform the following test:

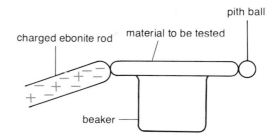

If the material is a good conductor, the pith ball will move away when contact is made with the charged ebonite rod.

18.3 Transfer of Electric Charge

Electric charges on solid objects are due to an excess or deficit of electrons (Section 18.2). The charging of an object, then, simply requires a transfer of electrons to or away from the object. If electrons are removed from an object, it will be charged positively; if electrons are added, it will be charged negatively.

Neutral and charged objects may be represented by sketches, with positive and negative signs marked on the objects, as follows:

A third class of materials, called semi-conductors, lies between these two. These important materials are used in transistors and computer microchips.

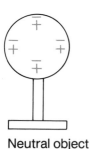

Neutral object

Negatively charged object

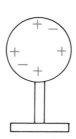

Positively charged object

Charging by Friction

In Section 18.1, you saw that some substances acquire an electric charge when rubbed with another substance. For example, an ebonite rod became negatively charged when rubbed with fur. We can explain this phenomenon with the help of the electrical structure of the atom, described in Section 18.2.

An atom holds onto its negative electrons by the force of electrical attraction of its positive nucleus. Some atoms exert stronger forces of attraction than others on their electrons. When ebonite and fur are rubbed together, some of the electrons from the atoms in the fur are "captured" by the atoms in the ebonite, which exert stronger forces of attraction on those electrons than do the atoms in the fur. Thus, after the rubbing, the ebonite has an excess of electrons and the fur has a deficit.

The same explanation may be applied to many other pairs of substances, such as glass and silk. The **electrostatic series** table includes many of the substances that can be charged by friction. If any two substances in the table are rubbed together, the substance that is higher in the table becomes negatively charged, while the other substance becomes positively charged. For example, an insulated brass rod becomes negatively charged when rubbed with paraffin wax, which becomes positively charged.

The rubbing action between two substances does not generate electric charge. It merely provides the very close contact necessary for electrons to transfer from one substance to the other.

The traditional method of obtaining negative and positive charges has been to use ebonite rods and glass rods, respectively. Recently, strips of vinylite and acetate, each rubbed with paper, have been used to produce negative and positive charges. Although they are easier to charge, because of their flimsiness they are more difficult to manipulate in the laboratory.

Electrostatic Series	
−	Hold on to
gold	electrons tightly
sulphur	
brass	
copper	
ebonite	
paraffin wax	
silk	
lead	
fur	
wool	
glass	
acetate	Hold on to
+	electrons loosely

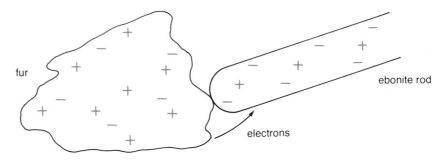

Transfer of electrons from fur to ebonite

Pith-ball Electroscope

An **electroscope** is a device that can be used to detect the presence of an electric charge and to determine the charge's "sign" (that is, whether it is positive or negative). A pith-ball electroscope is a light, metal-coated ball suspended on an insulating thread. If the ball is charged, it may be used to detect the presence of a charge on other objects brought near it. It will be repelled by a similarly charged object and attracted to an oppositely charged object or a neutral object.

Metal-leaf Electroscope

A metal-leaf electroscope consists of two thin metal leaves suspended from a metal rod in a glass container. A metal knob or plate is usually attached to the top of the metal rod. Since the central part of such an electroscope is made of a conducting material, any charge on it spreads out over the entire knob, rod, and leaves. Since the leaves are then charged similarly, they repel one another, thus indicating the presence of a charge. The farther apart they move, the greater the charges they are carrying.

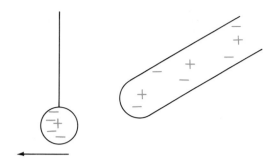

Repulsion of a negative pith ball by a charged ebonite rod

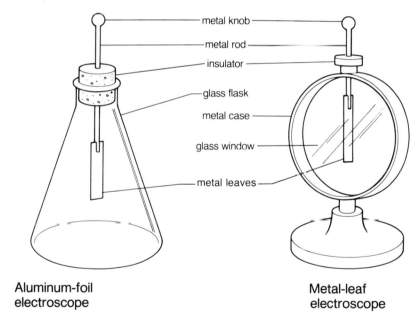

Aluminum-foil electroscope

Metal-leaf electroscope

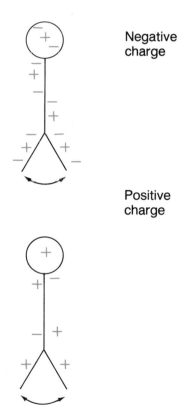

Negative charge

Positive charge

Similar net charges on a pair of leaves cause the leaves to move apart, thus indicating the presence of a charge on the electroscope.

Induced Charge Separation

The positive charges on a conductor are fixed and cannot move. The negative electrons are free to move from atom to atom. When a negatively charged ebonite rod is brought near to a neutral pith-ball or metal-leaf electroscope, some of the free electrons are repelled by the ebonite rod and move to the far side of the electroscope.

The separation of charge on the neutral pith-ball and on the neutral metal-leaf electroscope is caused by the presence of the negative ebonite rod. This separation is called an **induced charge separation**.

In physics, the word "induced" suggests something that is forced to happen without direct contact—something that would not happen spontaneously.

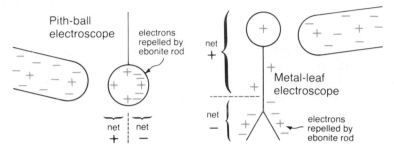

Induced charge separation caused by the presence of a charged ebonite rod

A charge separation will also result from the presence of a positively charged glass rod.

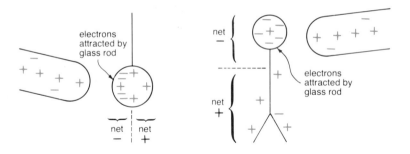

Induced charge separation caused by the presence of a charged glass rod

In both examples involving the pith-ball electroscope, the charge induced on the near side of the ball is opposite to the charge on the rod. As a result, the pith ball is attracted to the rod, whether the rod is charged negatively or positively. This is how a charged object can attract some neutral objects.

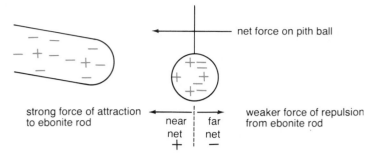

Attraction of a neutral pith ball by a charged ebonite rod

The strength of the electric forces depends on the distance between charges. As the distance increases, the magnitude of the force of attraction or repulsion decreases.

Charging by Contact

When a charged ebonite rod is touched to a neutral pith-ball electroscope, some of the excess electrons on the ebonite rod are repelled by their neighbors and move over onto the pith ball. The pith ball and the ebonite rod share the excess of electrons that the rod previously had. Both have negative charges. A similar sharing of electrons occurs when a charged ebonite rod touches the knob of a metal-leaf electroscope.

When a positively charged glass rod is used, some of the free electrons on the neutral pith-ball or metal-leaf electroscope are attracted to the glass rod, until the electroscope shares the deficit of electrons that the rod previously had. Both have positive charges.

An object that is charged by contact has the same charge as the charging rod.

To be precise, the relationship between electric force and distance is an inverse square law; doubling the distance between two small charges decreases the magnitude of the force by a factor of four.

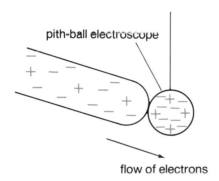

pith-ball electroscope

flow of electrons

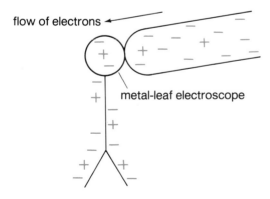

flow of electrons

metal-leaf electroscope

Charging by contact with a charged ebonite rod

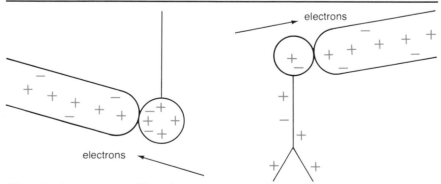

Charging by contact with a charged glass rod

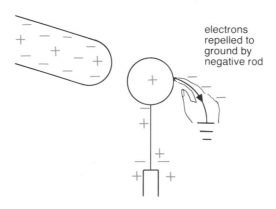

electrons
repelled to
ground by
negative rod

Grounded electroscope in the presence
of a negatively charged rod

Charging by Induction

A charged rod can induce a charge separation on a neutral conductor (page 542). When a charged ebonite rod is brought close to the knob of a neutral metal-leaf electroscope, free electrons on the electroscope will move as far away as possible from the negative rod. If the electroscope is touched, electrons are induced to flow out of the electroscope through the finger. When the finger is removed, the electroscope is left with a deficit of electrons, and hence with a positive charge.

A positively charged rod held near the knob of an electroscope induces electrons to move through the finger onto the electroscope. When the finger is removed the electroscope is left with an excess of electrons, and hence with a negative charge.

Notice that the leaves of the electroscope fall, indicating a neutral condition of the leaves while the finger is in position.

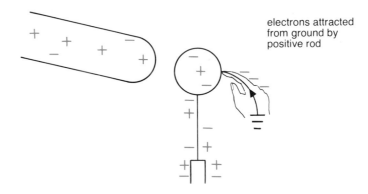

electrons attracted
from ground by
positive rod

Grounded electroscope in the presence of a positively charged rod

---

An object that is charged by induction has the opposite charge to that of the charging rod.

18.4 *A*pplications: Electric Discharge

Many of the everyday effects of electrostatics involve a charged object losing its charge and being neutralized. This is called **electric discharge**. Some common examples are discussed below.

1. Grounding

The Earth is a relatively good conductor, and, because of its size, it can receive or give up a large number of electrons without becoming appreciably charged. If a negatively charged conductor is connected to the Earth, surplus electrons on the object will drain off to the Earth until the object has discharged completely and is neutral. Similarly, a positively charged object connected to the Earth will attract electrons up from the Earth until the object is neutralized. Both of these situations are examples of discharge by **grounding**.

When a charged object is "grounded", it shares its charge with the Earth, each receiving a share proportional to its size. But the Earth is very much larger than any object on it, and the share retained by the object is so small as to be negligible. We simply assume that it has been completely discharged.

2. Atmospheric Discharge from the Surface of a Conductor

Because similar charges repel each other, the charge on a conductor spreads out over the entire surface. The distribution of charge over the surface of a sphere is uniform, but for other shapes the charge tends to be concentrated near any sharply contoured features. For example, the greatest concentration of charge occurs around sharp, pointed areas on a conductor's surface.

Charge distribution is uniform over surface of sphere.

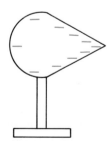

Charge distribution becomes more concentrated near sharp, pointed contours.

All air contains some positive and some negative ions. Moist, humid air contains many more of these ions. When ionized air comes into contact with the surface of a charged conductor, oppositely charged ions are attracted towards the conductor, and similarly charged ions are repelled. Electrons are easily transferred to and from highly charged areas of the conductor, and the conductor will discharge as a result.

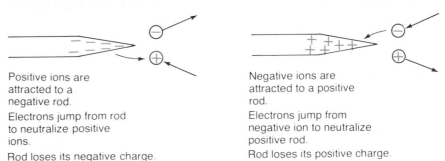

Positive ions are attracted to a negative rod.
Electrons jump from rod to neutralize positive ions.
Rod loses its negative charge.

Negative ions are attracted to a positive rod.
Electrons jump from negative ion to neutralize positive rod.
Rod loses its positive charge.

Discharge of highly concentrated point-charge distributions

3. Sparks and Arcing

When an object has an excess of electrons, the electrons exert strong forces of repulsion on each other and move as far away from each other as possible. If such a charged object approaches another conductor, some electrons may even jump across the gap of air between the two. This type of discharge is called a **spark**.

As electrons jump across the gap, a cracking sound is heard and a small flash of light is often seen. The electrons ionize the air and produce a great quantity of heat. This heat causes the air to expand rapidly and thereby to produce a compression wave that spreads out at the speed of sound and is heard as a cracking noise. The heat energy is also capable of causing the air molecules to produce light energy, which we see as a flash.

This type of spark will be familiar if you have ever walked around on a rug and then touched a metal doorknob.

Friction between rubber tires and the road causes vehicles to be electrically charged. Gasoline trucks used to drag a metal chain to allow this charge to drain off to ground. Otherwise, the heat created by a spark discharge might ignite flammable vapor from the truck and cause an explosion. More recent tires have carbon in the rubber that acts as a conductor so that static charges do not accumulate on the vehicle.

When a large number of electrons jump across a gap between two conductors, a tremendous amount of heat is generated. The temperatures produced can be sufficient to "weld" metals together. A device that welds metals by means of the heat generated by forming a large current across a gap in a conductor is called an "arc welder".

In hospital operating rooms, all personnel are required to wear special "conducting" boots, to eliminate the possibility that a spark caused by the build-up of static electricity will ignite the flammable gases present.

4. Lightning

By far the most awesome example of electric discharge is **lightning**. Rapid heating and the formation of large rain drops from smaller ones in the atmosphere cause clouds to become electrically charged. A charged cloud induces a strong opposite charge on the surface of the Earth directly beneath it. If the charge on the cloud increases beyond a certain point, a gigantic spark discharge occurs in the form of lightning. Surplus electrons from a negatively charged cloud may jump across the air gap to Earth; or electrons may jump from ground across the air gap to neutralize the deficit of electrons on a positively charged cloud. Lightning strokes may also travel between two oppositely charged clouds, or between two opposite charge centers in the same cloud. The pathway becomes ionized and guides the main charge flow.

The dangers presented by lightning are immense. The discharge takes the shortest path to Earth and therefore usually strikes the tallest conductor in the vicinity. For this reason, pointed lightning rods are attached to the tops of tall buildings and connected by good conductors to the Earth. When lightning strikes such a rod, electrons are conducted to or from the ground safely, with little or no danger to the building or its occupants.

Properties of a Lightning Stroke
Length—from 150 m to about 3 km
Duration—from 0.002 s to as much as 1.6 s
Width—from 1 cm to about 30 cm
Temperature—up to 30 000°C
Electricity—up to 200 C (coulombs) of charge transferred, with a power up to many billions of kilowatts

Lightning rods are not, as a rule, needed in cities. Tall buildings have sharp, pointed features that act as areas of high concentration of induced charge. As a result, lightning rarely strikes shorter objects in urban areas.

Lightning discharges

As a result of the high temperatures created in a lightning stroke, oxygen and nitrogen in the atmosphere combine chemically to produce nitrates. These nitrates fall to Earth with the rain and replenish our supply of natural fertilizer. Ozone, which protects the Earth from harmful cosmic radiation from outer space, is also produced from oxygen atoms in the atmosphere during lightning storms.

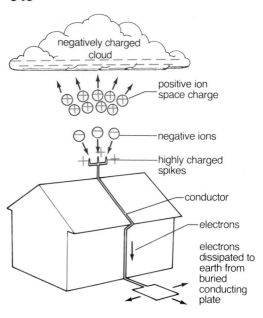

Protection of a building by a lightning rod

In addition, lightning rods can even prevent lightning from occurring in their vicinity. The atmosphere contains many positive and negative ions. A negatively charged cloud will induce a positive charge on the ground, and this positive charge will be concentrated in the pointed lightning rods. Negative ions in the air above the rod are attracted to it and give up their surplus electrons, which the rod conducts to the ground. Positive ions in the air are repelled by the lightning rod, and produce a region of positive charge in the atmosphere below the cloud. This space charge reduces the strong electrical force between the cloud and the Earth, and this is often sufficient to prevent lightning from occurring.

5. Electrostatic Generators

The photograph on the next page shows a student touching a large metal sphere. Notice that the student's hair is standing on end, a result of the electrostatic repulsion of similar electric charges on each strand. The student's body is receiving an electric charge by conduction from the metal sphere, which is part of an electrostatic charge generator known as a Van de Graaf generator.

The Van de Graaf generator was invented in 1931 by Robert Van de Graaf, an American physicist working at the Massachusetts Institute of Technology.

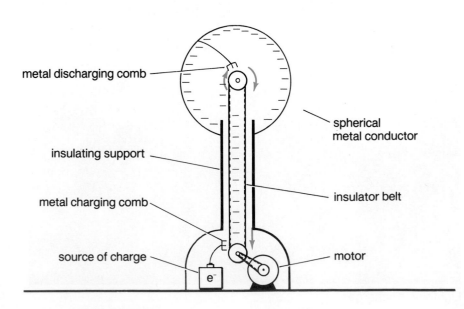

A source of electric charge at the bottom of the machine charges a metal comb that is adjacent to a moving belt. Because of the discharging effect of points, this charge is literally sprayed onto the belt. The belt, made of a special insulating material, carries the charge up to the center of a large metallic sphere, where a second metal comb, connected to the inside of the sphere, removes the charge. After a short interval of time, an extremely large amount of charge can build up on the outside surface of the hollow sphere. When a second grounded sphere is brought near, the charged sphere will discharge through the air between them in a bolt of artificial lightning. The Van de Graaf generator can produce both positive and negative charges, depending on the sign of the charge transferred to the moving belt by the source.

18.5 Electric Fields

Electric charges exert forces of attraction and repulsion on each other even when they are not in contact with each other. This kind of "action-at-a-distance" force is already familiar to you: the gravitational force existed between two masses, even though they were not touching. The gravitational force that one mass exerts on another was explained in terms of a gravitational field of force. When a mass was placed in the gravitational field of another mass, the first mass experienced a force of attraction towards the second mass.

The same kind of reasoning may be used to explain electrical forces. Every charged object creates an **electric field of force** in the space around it. Any other charged object in that field will experience a force of electrical attraction or repulsion.

The electric field may be represented by drawing a series of **field lines** around the charged object. Field lines show the direction of the electric force on a small positive test charge placed at each and every point in the field. For the sake of simplicity, field lines are drawn to show the path taken by this small positive test charge when allowed to move freely under the influence of the electric force. The strength of the electric field at any point is indicated by the relative distance between adjacent field lines. Closer lines mean a stronger field.

In Chapter 5, you were introduced to g, the gravitational field strength, measured in newtons per kilogram. The electrical field strength can also be measured; it is expressed in newtons per coulomb.

Consider, for example, what the electric field around a positively charged sphere might be like. If we place a positive test charge just to the right of the positively charged sphere, the force on it will be a repulsion, and it will move to the right.

If the positive test charge is then placed at other similar points around the sphere, and in each case a field line is drawn, the entire electric field will appear as shown at the left.

The relative distance between adjacent field lines at a given point is an indication of the strength of the electric field at that point. The electric field of a negatively charged sphere would be identical, except that the field lines would point in the opposite direction.

More complex electric fields may be created by using more than one charged object. In such cases, the positive test charge has more than one electric force acting on it. Being small, it moves in the direction of the resultant of these forces.

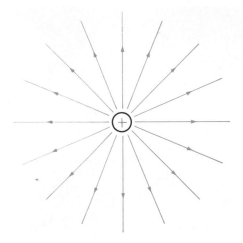

Electric field of a positively charged sphere

NOTE:
The electric field of two negative spheres close together is identical to this, except that the field lines point in the opposite direction.

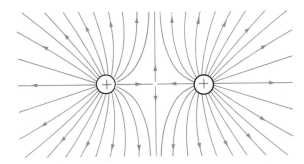

Electric field of two positively charged spheres close together

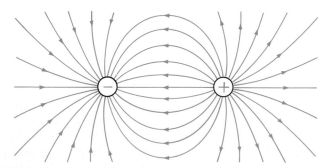

Electric field of two oppositely charged spheres close together

Electric field of two oppositely
charged parallel plates close together

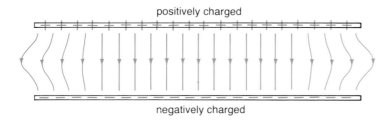

positively charged

negatively charged

Between the plates except near the edges, the field lines are
straight and equally spaced, representing an electric field with a
constant magnitude and direction. Such a field is called a **uniform
electric field**.

18.6 Measuring Electric Charge

For a quantitative study of electricity, we must be able to measure
the electric charge on an object. Electric charge is measured in units
called coulombs (C), after the French scientist Charles de Coulomb
(1736–1806). To give you an idea of the magnitude of a coulomb: 1 C
of electric charge is approximately the amount that would pass
through a 100 W light bulb in 1 s, operating at 100 V.

Early in the century, an American physicist, Robert Millikan
(1868-1953), devised and performed a series of experiments proving
that there does exist a smallest unit of electric charge; all other
electric charges are simple multiples of this smallest charge. He
reasoned that this elementary charge is the charge on a single
electron.

Millikan assumed that, when tiny oil drops are sprayed from an
atomizer, they become charged by friction—some acquiring an
excess of a few electrons while others have a deficit. Although there
was no way of knowing how many extra electrons there were on an
oil drop, or how many were missing, Millikan was able to devise a
technique for measuring the *total* amount of charge on each individual drop.

Oil drops were sprayed into the space between two parallel metal
plates. A light was shone on the oil drops, and they were observed
through a telescope. A battery was connected to the plates,
creating a uniform electric field in the space between the plates. As a
result, an upward electric force was exerted on those drops whose

Robert A. Millikan

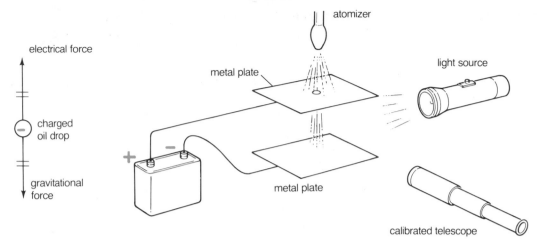

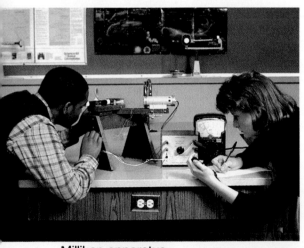

The speed of fall of the drop enabled Millikan to calculate its radius, and hence its mass.

Millikan apparatus

charge was the same sign as the lower plate's. By adjusting the amount of charge on the plates, it was possible to isolate a single oil drop and balance it so that the downward gravitational force and the upward electrical force were equal.

Then, using measurements of the "balancing field", and the speed with which the drop fell when the field was removed, Millikan was able to calculate the amount of electric charge on the oil drop, in coulombs.

By repeating this procedure many times, using the same oil drop with different amounts of charge on it, and using different oil drops, Millikan was able to compile a long list of values for the amount of charge on an oil drop. But how was he able to determine the value of the charge on an electron from this list of values for the total charge on a drop?

Millikan reasoned that the charge on each oil drop must be a whole-numbered multiple of some smallest amount of charge, the charge on a single electron.

Suppose that Millikan measured the charge on 12 oil drops and obtained these values:

3.2×10^{-19} C	16.0×10^{-19} C
17.6×10^{-19} C	6.4×10^{-19} C
8.0×10^{-19} C	12.8×10^{-19} C
11.2×10^{-19} C	4.8×10^{-19} C
1.6×10^{-19} C	9.6×10^{-19} C
19.2×10^{-19} C	14.4×10^{-19} C

Two observations must have been clearly evident to him from these typical values for the charge on an oil drop:

1. The smallest value for the charge on an oil drop is 1.6×10^{-19} C.
2. All the other values are whole-numbered multiples of 1.6×10^{-19} C.

Our list is much shorter than Millikan's was, but it illustrates how he reached his conclusion that electric charge always occurs in multiples of a smallest unit, the charge of an electron, which he called the elementary charge (e).

$$e = 1.60 \times 10^{-19} \text{ C}$$

We can see that if one electron has a charge of 1.60×10^{-19} C, then it must take $\dfrac{1}{1.60 \times 10^{-19}}$ or 6.24×10^{18} electrons to make up 1 C of charge. For the present, we will use this as the value of a coulomb:

$$1 \text{ C} = 6.24 \times 10^{18} \, e$$

Using this value for the coulomb, we can devise an equation to make an important calculation.

If a charged object has an excess or deficit of N electrons, each with a charge e (the elementary charge), then the total charge, Q, on the object, measured in coulombs, is given by:

$$Q = Ne$$

Sample Problems

1. Calculate the charge on a metal-leaf electroscope that has an excess of 5.0×10^{10} electrons.
$$Q = Ne$$
$$= (5.0 \times 10^{10})(1.6 \times 10^{-19} \text{ C})$$
$$= 8.0 \times 10^{-9} \text{ C}$$
and since the charge is due to an excess of electrons, it is negative.

2. How many electrons have been removed from a positively charged pith-ball electroscope if it has a charge of 7.5×10^{-11} C?
$$N = \frac{Q}{e}$$
$$= \frac{7.5 \times 10^{-11} \text{ C}}{1.6 \times 10^{-19} \text{ C}}$$
$$= 4.7 \times 10^{8} \text{ electrons}$$

Practice

1. In a lightning bolt, it is estimated that a charge of 20 C is transferred from a cloud to Earth. How many electrons make up the lightning bolt?

Millikan was awarded the Nobel Prize for Physics in 1923. Nobel Prizes for physics, chemistry, and other fields have been awarded almost annually since 1901, according to the terms of the will of Alfred Bernard Nobel (1833–96), the Swedish industrialist who invented dynamite. The awards are made by the Swedish Royal Academy of Sciences. Each prize has a cash value, which increases from year to year; in 1990 it was about $190,000.

Charles Augustin de Coulomb (1736–1806)
Coulomb was a French physicist who, after serving as a military engineer in the West Indies, returned to France to do research. There he devised a torsion balance that measured the amount of force acting on it by the resulting twist of its thin suspending fiber. Using this balance and pairs of small electrically charged spheres, he was able to show that the electric force between two charged spheres is directly proportional to the product of the magnitudes of the charges on the spheres and inversely proportional to the square of the distance between their centers. This famous relation, called Coulomb's Law, was of immense importance to our understanding of interatomic electric forces. In his honor, the unit of electric charge is called the coulomb.

2. A metal-leaf electroscope is given a negative charge of 1.2 μC by induction. How many electrons move through your finger when you touch the knob of the electroscope?
3. An ebonite rod with an excess of 6.4×10^8 electrons shares its charge equally with a pith ball when they touch. What is the charge on the pith ball, in coulombs?

Investigations

Investigation 18.1: Electric Charges and Forces

Problem:
What types of electric charges are there, and what effect do they have on each other?

Materials:

ebonite rods and fur	paper
glass rods and silk	sawdust
insulated rod hanger	iron filings
suspended pith ball	

Procedure:
1. Rub one of the ebonite rods vigorously with the fur and place it in the hanger, suspended by a thread. Then rub the other ebonite rod with fur and bring it near the suspended rod. What effect does the second rod have on the first?
2. Repeat the same procedure with the glass rods, rubbing them with the silk.
3. Suspend a glass rod rubbed with silk in the hanger and bring an ebonite rod rubbed with fur near it. What effect does the ebonite rod have on the glass rod?
4. Suspend the pith ball from a thread and touch it with your finger. Slowly bring a charged ebonite rod near to, but not touching, the pith ball, and note its effect. Describe what happens after the pith ball and the ebonite rod have touched.
5. Repeat the procedure using a charged glass rod.
6. Using first a charged glass rod and then an ebonite rod, approach each of the following in turn and note the results: small bits of paper, sawdust, iron filings, and a thin stream of water from a tap.

A ping-pong ball painted with metallic aluminum paint (or smeared with graphite) and suspended by a silk thread makes a good pith ball.

Questions:
1. How many different types of electric charge were you able to identify?
2. Give simple descriptions of the interaction between similarly charged objects and of the interaction between oppositely charged objects.
3. What happens when a charged rod is brought near some neutral objects? Does the same thing occur with all neutral objects? If the charged rod touches a neutral object, what happens?
4. What must be true about water droplets for them to behave as they do in the presence of a charged rod?

Investigation 18.2: Induced Charge Separation

Problem:
How can a charged object cause charges on a nearby neutral object to move?

Materials:

pith-ball electroscope   ebonite rod and fur
metal-leaf electroscope   glass rod and silk

Procedure:
1. Touch the pith ball with your finger to neutralize it. Rub the ebonite rod with the fur and bring it close to the pith ball. Observe the motion of the pith ball carefully. Do not let the rod touch the pith ball.
2. Repeat the procedure using the glass rod rubbed with silk.
3. Touch the knob of the metal-leaf electroscope to neutralize it. Charge an ebonite rod, and bring it close to, but not touching, the knob of the electroscope. Observe the motion of the metal leaves as the rod is brought near, and then as it is removed.
4. Repeat, using the glass rod rubbed with silk.

Questions:
1. If an ebonite rod acquires a negative charge when rubbed with fur, what charge does a glass rod acquire when rubbed with silk?
2. As the charged ebonite rod was brought near the pith-ball electroscope, which way did the pith ball begin to move? Why? Draw a sketch to show the pith ball, with the charged rod near it, and the effect of the rod on the positive and negative charges on the neutral pith ball.

Experiments with charged objects work best on cool dry days. Warm humid air contains many positive and negative ions. If such air comes into contact with a charged object, the ions in the air will neutralize the charged object by contact. Also, moisture gets on charged surfaces and creates discharge paths. If your electroscope seems to be "leaking" its charge, this may be due to the humidity of the surrounding air.

3. Which way does the pith ball move when the charged glass rod is brought close to it? Why? Draw another sketch showing the new distribution of charge on the neutral pith ball.
4. As each rod is brought near to the knob of the metal-leaf electroscope, what happens to the leaves? Why? Draw sketches to show the distribution of charge on the knob and leaves of the electroscope, in each case.
5. What happens to the leaves when the charged rods are removed? Why? What is the net charge on the electroscope?
6. Why does touching an object with your hand ensure that it is neutral? Be sure your explanation covers both cases: when the object has an excess of electrons, as well as when it has a deficit.
7. When a nearby charged object causes a change in the distribution of charge on a neutral object, this is called an induced charge separation. Is it possible to create an induced charge separation on an insulator? On a conductor? Explain your answers.

To understand fully how touching something will neutralize it, look back at Section 18.4 on grounding.

Investigation 18.3: Charging by Contact

Problem:
How can you charge an object by contact?

Materials:

pith-ball electroscope   ebonite rod and fur
metal-leaf electroscope   glass rod and silk

Procedure:
1. Neutralize the pith-ball electroscope by touching it with your finger. Charge an ebonite rod, and touch it to the pith ball. Then bring the rod close to the pith ball again, and observe the pith ball's motion.
2. Repeat the procedure using the glass rod rubbed with silk.
3. Neutralize the metal-leaf electroscope with your finger. Now touch the knob with the (charged) ebonite rod, and observe the motion of the leaves after the rod has been removed.
4. Repeat, using the glass rod rubbed with silk.
5. Charge the metal-leaf electroscope by touching the knob with the (charged) ebonite rod. Recharge the ebonite rod and bring it close to, but not touching, the knob. Notice the effect on the leaves. Now bring the (charged) glass rod close, and notice its effect on the leaves.
6. Repeat the same steps, but this time use the metal-leaf electroscope, charged by contact with the (charged) glass rod.

Just before contact is made between the charged ebonite rod and the neutral electroscope, a small spark composed of "over-anxious" electrons may be observed jumping from the rod to the electroscope.

Questions:

1. When the charged ebonite rod touched the pith ball, what charge did the pith ball acquire? How do you know? Which way did the electrons move? Illustrate your answers with sketches labelled "before contact", "during contact", and "after contact".
2. When the charged glass rod touched the pith ball, what charge did the pith ball acquire? Once again, draw sketches to illustrate your answers.
3. What charge did the metal-leaf electroscope acquire when it was touched with the charged ebonite rod? Draw a sketch representing the electroscope after the rod was removed.
4. What charge did the metal-leaf electroscope acquire when it was touched with the charged glass rod? Once again, draw a sketch representing the electroscope after the rod was removed.
5. When an object is charged by contact, what charge does it acquire, as compared with the charge on the rod?
6. When a rod of the same charge is brought close to the knob of a charged metal-leaf electroscope, what is the effect on the metal leaves? Draw a sketch that explains that effect.
7. When a rod of the opposite charge is brought close to the knob of a charged metal-leaf electroscope, what effect does this have on the metal leaves? Again, draw an explanatory sketch.

Investigation 18.4: Charging by Induction

Problem:
How can you charge an object by induction?

Materials:

pith-ball electroscope	glass rod and silk
metal-leaf electroscope	2 short metal rods
ebonite rod and fur	2 glass beakers (250 cm^3)

Procedure:
1. Place a short metal rod across the top of each of the two beakers and arrange the beakers so that the ends of the rods touch. Now bring the (charged) ebonite rod near the end of one of the rods, but not touching it. Separate the two rods by moving only the far beaker, taking care not to touch the metal rod. Finally, remove the ebonite rod from the vicinity. Test the metal rods, in turn, for a charge by bringing the (charged) pith-ball electroscope near them. Bring the rods into contact again, by touching only the beakers, and again test them for a charge while they are touching.

If a spark jumps from the ebonite rod to the metal rod, ground the metal rod, recharge the ebonite rod, and start over again. This time, do not bring the ebonite rod quite so close to the metal rod.

If the rod does accidentally touch the electroscope, touch the pith ball with your hand and start over again.

2. Neutralize the metal-leaf electroscope with your finger. Bring the (charged) ebonite rod near to, but not touching, the knob. Touch the knob with your finger, and observe the leaves. Remove your finger, and then remove the rod. Observe the motion of the leaves. Bring the rod near again, and observe its effect on the leaves.
3. Repeat the entire procedure, using the (charged) glass rod.

Questions

1. Why were the metal rods placed on glass beakers? What effect did the ebonite rod have on some electrons in the touching metal rods? Draw sketches to show the ebonite rod, the two metal rods touching, and the distribution of charge on the rods. When the rods were separated, what was the charge on each of them? What charge was on each rod after they were made to touch again? Explain your answers.
2. What would have been different about the resultant charge on each rod if a charged glass rod had been used instead of a charged ebonite rod? Illustrate your answer with a sketch.
3. Why did the leaves of the metal-leaf electroscope move apart when the charged ebonite rod was brought near? When you touched the knob with your finger, what was happening in your finger? Why were you told to remove your finger before removing the rod? Draw sketches to show what was happening before, during, and after contact with the knob by your finger.
4. Why did the leaves move apart when the charged glass rod was brought near? What was happening in your finger, this time, when it touched the knob? Again, illustrate your answers.
5. When an object is charged by induction, what charge does it acquire, compared with the charge on the rod?

Investigation 18.5: An Experiment Similar to Millikan's

Problem:
How can we determine the mass of an individual marble using a Millikan-like technique?

Materials:
a large number of small bags, each containing an unknown number of identical marbles
triple-beam balance

Procedure:
1. Without looking into the bags or in any other way trying to find out how many marbles each contains, measure the mass of each bag and record the values in a table.
2. Combine your results with those of your classmates and try to determine the value of the mass of one marble.

Questions:
1. Describe your method of determining the mass of a marble. For it to be valid, what must be true about the marbles?
2. Why must a large number of values be used, to get a reliable value for the mass of a marble? What error would you make if, by chance, all the bags you measured had an even number of marbles in them?
3. In what way do the results of the Millikan experiment resemble your results?

Chapter Summary

1. There are two types of electric charges, called negative and positive. Opposite charges attract, similar charges repel. Either type of charge will attract some neutral objects.
2. The simple electrical theory of matter states:
   (a) All matter is composed of atoms.
   (b) Electric charge, in the atom, is carried by protons and electrons.
   (c) Protons, in the nucleus, are small and heavy and carry a specific quantity of positive charge, called the elementary charge.
   (d) Electrons, moving around the nucleus, are small and light and carry an equal quantity of negative charge (the elementary charge).
   (e) In a neutral atom, the number of negative electrons is equal to the number of positive protons.
   (f) An atom with an excess of electrons is called a negative ion.
   (g) An atom with a deficit of electrons is called a positive ion.
3. All electric charges in solids are due to an excess (negative charge) or deficit (positive charge) of electrons.
4. Electrons in conductors are loosely held by their atoms and can move freely from atom to atom. Electrons in insulators are tightly held, and cannot move from atom to atom.

Benjamin Franklin tested his theory of electricity by means of a kite and a key on a damp conducting string during a lightning storm. He was lucky he wasn't electrocuted.

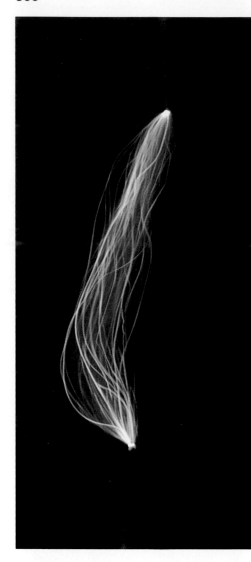

5. Some substances can be charged by rubbing them with another substance. An ebonite rod becomes negative and fur becomes positive when the two are rubbed together. Similarly, glass becomes positive and silk becomes negative when the two are rubbed together.

6. Electric charges may be detected by means of a pith-ball or metal-leaf electroscope.

7. A charged object brought close to a neutral conductor induces a separation of charge on the conductor.

8. Conductors may be charged by contact with another charged object. The charge thus acquired by the conductor is similar to the charge on the charged object.

9. Conductors may be charged by induction, by use of another charged object. The charge thus acquired by the conductor is opposite to the charge on the charged object.

10. The simple electrical theory of matter may be used to explain:
    (a) charging by both contact and induction
    (b) the distribution of charge on a conductor
    (c) the discharging effect of points
    (d) grounding
    (e) sparks and arcing
    (f) lightning

11. Charged objects create electric fields of force in their surrounding space. Field lines, drawn to depict the electric field, represent the force on a small positive test charge at any point in the field.

12. Electric charge is measured in coulombs (C). The charge, Q, on any object is given by

$$Q = Ne$$

where N represents the number of excess or deficit electrons, and e represents the elementary charge.

13. Robert Millikan, in the oil-drop experiments that made him famous, verified that an elementary charge does exist, and that it is the charge on an electron. He found its value to be

$$e = 1.60 \times 10^{-19} \text{ C}$$

Thus, 1 C is the charge on 6.24×10^{18} electrons.

The Photocopier

The office photocopier has become an important element in the communication of graphic information. The process used in most photocopiers is called **xerography**, and utilizes the simple laws of electrostatics from this chapter.

The heart of the copying process is an aluminum drum covered by a very thin (< 50 µm thick) coating of a photosensitive substance called selenium. A photo-sensitive material is one that gives off an electric charge when exposed to light. The process is started by **charging** the drum to a potential difference of about 700 V. It will retain this charge, distributed uniformly over its surface, as long as it remains in the dark.

When a document to be copied is placed face down on a glass plate, and the cover closed, bright light from a source within the copier is directed onto the original, then reflected from it through a lens and onto the charged selenium drum. In places where the original document is white, light is strongly reflected onto the selenium drum, causing it to discharge in these areas. Conversely, where the original is black, no light is reflected onto the drum, so that it remains charged in these areas. Thus, as a result of the **exposure** of the original to light, an electrical image of it is created on the drum; neutral where the original is white, charged where the original is black. As long as the drum is kept dark, this image will remain.

The electrical image on the drum is **developed** into a dry copy, using a substance called "toner". Except for its black colour, toner looks very much like baking flour. It consists of very tiny (about 0.005 mm diameter) plastic particles, coloured by adding lamp black. In the development process, toner particles are given an opposite charge to that on the selenium drum, and are then "cascaded", or dumped, over the rotating drum. As a result of their opposite charge, they are attracted to the charged areas of the drum. They do not adhere to the neutral areas, falling into a collecting bin for re-use. Thus, a toner-image of the original is created on the drum.

To create a permanent copy of this image, the toner must be **transferred** to paper. To do this, a sheet of paper is given a charge that is opposite to that of the toner particles. As the drum rolls across this paper, toner particles that adhere to the drum will be attracted, instead, to the paper, forming a black-and-white image.

If you rubbed a finger across the paper, at this stage, the toner would smudge terribly. To "fix" the image, heat in the form of radiant energy is allowed to fall on the paper, melting the plastic toner particles and bonding or **fusing** them to the paper to produce a fixed dry copy.

As a final step, the selenium drum must be **cleaned** of any excess toner. It is first charged with the same charge as the toner particles (thereby loosening any that adhere), and then brushed clean with a cotton or rayon material.

As can be seen, the photocopying process involves six distinct steps:

1. charging
2. exposure
3. development
4. transfer
5. fusing
6. cleaning

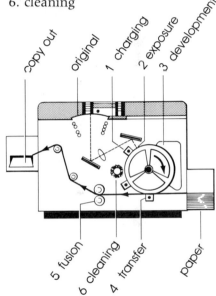

From an understanding of these processes, you can answer the following simple questions about how photocopiers work.

1. Why does the first copy take longer to make than subsequent multiple copies?
2. How are enlarged and reduced photocopies made?
3. Why are copies hot, and why do they often stick together after they are made?
4. Which substances in the process have to be replenished from time to time?

*C*hapter *R*eview

Discussion

1. If an ebonite rod is rubbed with fur, the rod becomes negatively charged. What is the source of this charge?
2. Two rods, one brass and the other plastic, have been charged by contact at one end while being supported by an insulator at the other end. Compare the distribution of electric charge on the two rods.
3. If the knob of a positively charged electroscope is approached slowly by a negatively charged rod, what happens to the leaves of the electroscope? Why?
4. Explain fully what happens when a positively charged rod touches the knob of a neutral metal-leaf electroscope.
5. A negatively charged rod is brought near a neutral metal sphere on an insulating stand. What type of charge would you expect to find on the side of the sphere nearest the rod? On the farthest side? Explain your answers. How would these results differ if the sphere were made of plastic?
6. The Empire State Building in New York City is probably struck by lightning more than any other structure in the surrounding area. Explain why this is so, and why damage seldom results.
7. (a) Why are metallic fibers used in the pile of some carpets?
   (b) Why is it dangerous to rub clothing with the hands while it is being cleaned with kerosene or naphtha?
8. (a) Define electrostatic induction.
   (b) Given a glass rod, silk, and two metal spheres mounted on insulated stands, describe how to charge the spheres oppositely by electrostatic induction.
9. Why, in winter, does a spark sometimes jump between a person's hand and a metal object he is about to touch? Why does this occur less frequently in the summer?
10. A neutral pith ball is lowered by a long insulated string between two metal plates on insulated stands, as shown. The plate on the left is connected to the negative terminal of an electrostatic generator, and the plate on the right is grounded.

    Predict the behavior of the pith ball and explain your prediction by drawing the diagrams in your notebook and showing the charge distribution on each object.

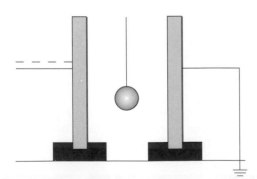

11. Copy these diagrams in your notebook and add + and − signs, representing electric charges, to the following sequence of diagrams:

(a) Three neutral metal spheres on insulating stands are touching.

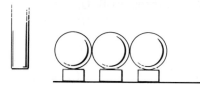

(b) A positive rod is brought near.

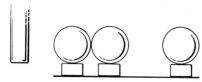

(c) The far sphere is moved, using the insulating stand.

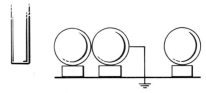

(d) The middle sphere is grounded.

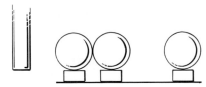

(e) The ground is removed.

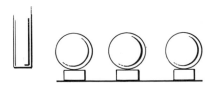

(f) The remaining spheres are separated, using the insulating stands.

(g) The positive rod is removed.

12. The following observations are made of the interactions between various combinations of four pith balls, A, B, C, and D. The force between C and D is a repulsion. A attracts both B and D. If A is attracted to an ebonite rod that has been rubbed with cat's fur, what are the charges on B, C, and D?

13. Four neutral metal spheres W, X, Y, and Z are located as shown:

A negatively charged plastic strip is inserted in the space between X and Y. While it is held there, sphere W is moved to the left away from X, and sphere Z is moved to the right away from Y. The charged plastic strip is then removed. What charge will be found on each of the spheres? Explain your answer by drawing a series of diagrams, similar to question 11.

Problems

14. (a) What is meant by "the elementary charge"? What is its accepted value?
    (b) What is the charge on a metal-leaf electroscope with a deficit of 5.0×10^{11} electrons?
15. (a) In 5.0 s, 3.0 C of electric charge pass through the filament of a light bulb. How many electrons move through the filament in this time?
    (b) How much charge does the Earth acquire if 2.5×10^{11} electrons leave a grounded metal-leaf electroscope?

Electrostatic Precipitators

One of the most disturbing consequences of our society's high degree of industrialization is the increasing level of pollution in our atmosphere. Most of the substances polluting our air are particulate by-products of industrial processes that enter the atmosphere in the form of fly-ash, dust, and fumes from smoke stacks. Although very expensive, the technology exists to remove most of these particulates from the flue gases before they leave the smoke stacks, using applications of electrostatics.

The operation of an industrial electrostatic precipitator utilizes a phenomenon known as **corona discharge.** Consider a cylindrical duct with a thin wire running down its center, as shown:

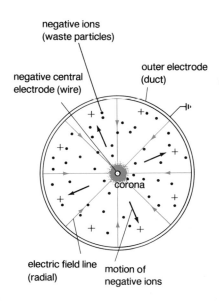

Corona discharge

When a negative charge is supplied to the central wire and the cylindrical duct is grounded, a radial electric field is established between the wire and duct, as shown. The field is stronger near the wire and becomes weaker closer to the cylindrical duct. When a very large negative charge is placed on the wire, the electric field near the wire can be so strong that the air near it becomes ionized. The result, as evidenced by a green glow around the wire, is known as corona discharge. Electrons created in the region of ionization move toward the outer electrode and attach themselves to waste particles in the flue gas moving through the duct. These waste product "ions" will now be attracted to the outer electrode, where they collect on the walls of the duct. If the waste particles are solids, the duct is vibrated periodically, shaking them loose to fall into a hopper. Liquid particles simply run down the walls of the duct and are collected for disposal. It is estimated that over 40 million metric tons of waste pollutants are removed from flue gases in this way annually in North America.

The solution to many air pollution problems is available, but unfortunately the cost of installation and maintenance of these devices is considerable. Because industry has been slow to adopt these measures voluntarily, many environmentalists want stricter anti-pollution legislation. Ultimately, these groups will need to compromise as they work out solutions to the problems of pollution.

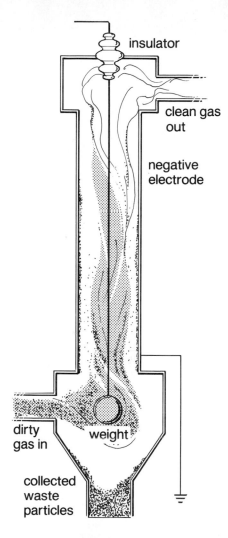

In this simplified diagram of an electrostatic precipitator, a single grounded duct carries the flue gases loaded with solid waste particles. The weighted central wire acts as a negative electrode to produce a corona discharge.

19

Current Electricity

Chapter Objectives

- **Define** "electric current" and **state** the unit of electric current and its equivalent.

- **Relate** electric current to charge and time.

- **Measure** the electric current past any point in a conductor, using an ammeter.

- **Define** "electric potential" and **state** its equivalent.

- **Relate** work done (or electrical energy) to charge and electric potential difference.

- **Measure** the electric potential difference between any two points in a conductor using a voltmeter.

- **Give examples** of devices that act as sources of electric potential, and **describe** the mechanism of each.

- **Give examples** of electric loads and **describe** how each uses electrical energy.

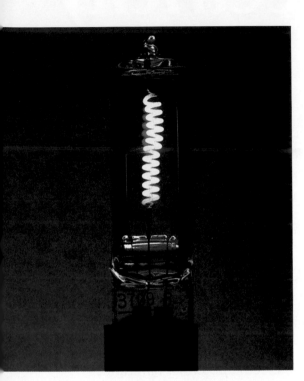

An electric current moving through this light bulb causes atoms in the filament to release energy in the form of heat and light.

When electrons flow through the conductor always in the same direction, they constitute a "direct current" (DC). When the electrons reverse their direction at regular, short intervals, they constitute an "alternating current" (AC). You will learn more about DC and AC in Chapter 23.

For a discussion of the direction of electric current, see page 588.

Introduction

When a conductor acquires an excess or a deficit of electrons, we say it has an electric charge. We know that, because of the forces of repulsion that act between like charges, this charge distributes itself over the surface of the conductor. For this to happen, electrons must be able to move. When electric charges move from one place to another, we say that they constitute an **electric current**. All electrical devices operate because of electric current through their components. Can we measure the amount of electric charge that is moving through a given component? Can we measure the rate at which it is moving? And what causes electrons to move in the first place?

These and many more related questions will be examined in this chapter.

19.1 Moving Electrons: Electric Current

Moving electric charges constitute an electric current. In metals, these moving charges are electrons. Electric current is defined as the amount of charge that moves past a given point in a conductor per second. For example, consider a cylindrical wire such as the one shown.

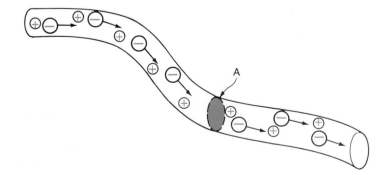

We may think of A as the cross-sectional area of the conductor. Then if a total charge of Q (in coulombs) flows through the area A in a time of t (in seconds), the electric current I through the wire is:

$$I = \frac{Q}{t}$$

Electric current is measured in units called **amperes** (A), after the French physicist André Marie Ampère (1775-1836). The definition of an ampere depends on a knowledge of the electromagnetic force acting between parallel conductors, but, in terms of the amount of the charge that is flowing and the time,

1 A is the electric current when 1 C of charge moves past a point in a conductor in 1 s.

$$1 \text{ A} = 1 \text{ C/s}$$

Sample Problems

1. Calculate the amount of current through an electric toaster if it takes 900 C of charge to toast two slices of bread in 1.5 min.

$$t = 1.5 \text{ min}$$
$$= 90 \text{ s}$$
$$I = \frac{Q}{t}$$
$$= \frac{900 \text{ C}}{90 \text{ s}}$$
$$= 10 \text{ A}$$

2. A light bulb with a current of 0.80 A is left burning for 20 min. How much electric charge passes through the filament of the bulb?

$$t = 20 \text{ min}$$
$$= 1.2 \times 10^3 \text{ s}$$
$$Q = It$$
$$= (0.80 \text{ A})(1.2 \times 10^3 \text{ s})$$
$$= 9.6 \times 10^2 \text{ C}$$

3. A gold-leaf electroscope with 1.25×10^{10} excess electrons is grounded and discharges completely in 0.50 s. Calculate the average current through the grounding wire.

$$I = \frac{Q}{t}$$
$$= \frac{Ne}{t}$$
$$= \frac{(1.25 \times 10^{10})(1.6 \times 10^{-19} \text{ C})}{0.50 \text{ s}}$$
$$= 4.0 \times 10^{-9} \text{ A}$$

André Marie Ampère (1775-1836)
Ampère was a professor of mathematics living in Paris when Oersted made his famous discovery that a wire carrying an electric current could deflect a magnetic needle. Ampère devised a left-hand rule relating the direction of electron flow and the direction of the N-pole of a magnetic compass. (See Section 22.2.) He showed and explained that two parallel current-carrying wires either attracted or repelled each other. To explain the magnetic properties of materials such as iron, Ampère proposed the existence of tiny electrical currents within the atom, long before the existence of the electron was even suggested. Although his contemporaries regarded his theories with skepticism, Ampère was honored by the naming of the unit of electric current, the ampere, after him.

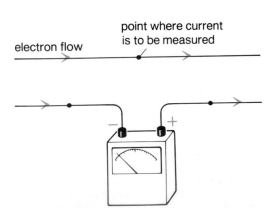

A multi-range DC ammeter

Practice

1. How much electric current is there when 12 C of charge pass a point in a conductor in 4.0 s?
2. What is the current through a light bulb when it takes 24 s for 18 C of charge to pass through its filament?
3. How much charge passes through the starting motor, if it takes 4.0 s to start a car and there is a current of 225 A during that time?
4. A small electric motor draws a current of 0.40 A. How long will it take for 8.0 C of charge to pass through it?
5. How many electrons pass through a light bulb in each second if the bulb has a current of 0.50 A through it?

Measuring Electric Current

The electric current through a conductor may be measured directly with an instrument called an **ammeter**.

To measure the current past a given point, the conductor must be temporarily broken at that point and the ammeter inserted into the conducting path, as illustrated.

All the current through the conductor must go through the ammeter. Also, the ammeter must be connected so that the electrons enter through its negative terminal and leave by its positive terminal. Can you imagine what would happen to the needle of the ammeter if you accidentally reversed the connections?

point where current
is to be measured

electron flow

Practice

1. Most ammeters are designed so that they can be used to measure more than one range of current values. In such ammeters, the range is determined by a dial on the case, or by a choice of terminals to be used for connecting the conductor to the ammeter. Numbers representing the various ranges of current are marked on the same scale.

   The choice of numbers, all printed on the same scale, is often confusing. A typical multi-range ammeter scale is illustrated with two sample needle positions.

   Copy the table into your notebook and determine the current reading indicated by each position of the needle for each of the six ranges of current.

Current range	0-5 mA	0-100 mA	0-250 mA	0-1 A	0-2.5 A	0-5 A
Current reading Needle position 1						
Current reading Needle position 2						

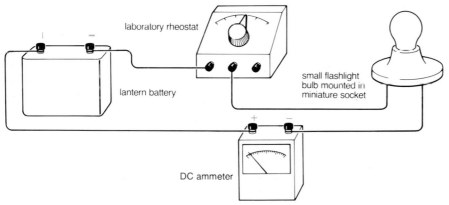

2. Using a 6 V battery, a rheostat to regulate current, an ammeter, some wires, and a small flashlight bulb, construct an apparatus similar to the one shown. Use the range of current that results in the greatest deflection of the needle without sending the needle off the scale.

laboratory rheostat

lantern battery

small flashlight bulb mounted in miniature socket

DC ammeter

Adjust the dial on the rheostat to five or six different positions, in turn, and for each position record the reading on the ammeter and give a brief description of the brightness of the bulb.

Whenever you are unsure which range to use on a multi-range meter, use the largest range first, and work down until there is a reasonable deflection of the needle.

Every electrical instrument has two terminals, each with a specified polarity—either positive (red) or negative (black). For an instrument to operate as intended, electrons must enter via the negative terminal and leave via the positive terminal.

19.2 Electric Potential

As you know, when electrons move through a conductor they constitute an electric current. You also know how to measure the amount of electric current. But the really significant question is: what causes the electrons to move through the conductor? What could be pushing or pulling them, causing them to move?

A useful analogy is provided by a ball sitting at rest on the surface of the Earth. The Earth is surrounded by a gravitational field of force pulling in on the ball. Work must be done on the ball to overcome this force and move the ball away from the Earth, thereby increasing its gravitational potential energy. If the ball is then released, the gravitational field will cause it to move back toward the Earth, converting its gravitational potential energy into other useful forms.

In physics, new situations are often explained by means of an analogy. An analogy may be thought of as a model that is familiar and easily understood and helps us to understand some similar phenomenon.

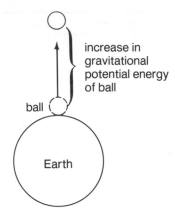

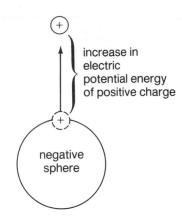

Allesandro Volta (1745-1827)

**Count Allesandro Volta
(1745-1827)**
After a childhood showing little promise
as a scholar, Volta forged ahead,
becoming professor of physics at the
high school in Como, Italy. His first
major contribution was the discovery of
the electrophorus, a device capable of
producing and storing a large electrical
charge. His reward was a professorship
at the University of Pavia and
membership in the Royal Society.

Volta's most significant achievement
was the invention of the first electric
battery using bowls of salt solution
connected by arcs of metal with copper
at one end and tin or zinc at the other.
For this invention Napoleon awarded
him the medal of the Legion of Honor
and made him a Count.

A small positive charge at rest next to a negatively charged sphere
is in a similar situation. The negative sphere is surrounded by an
electric field of force, pulling in on the positive charge. Again, work
must be done on the small positive charge to overcome this electric
force and pull it away from the negative sphere. In this case, the
small positive charge has an increase in electric potential energy as a
result. If released, the positive charge will move back toward the
negative sphere in much the same way that the ball moved back
toward the Earth, thereby losing electric potential energy. Charged
particles moving in the presence of an electric field and converting
electric potential energy into some other form of energy constitute
an electric current.

In the case of conduction through solids, it is electrons that are
moving in response to electric fields in the conductors. In fluids and
plasmas, both positive and negative ions move in response to electric
fields. There are many devices that are capable of providing charges
with electric potential energy (as we shall see in Section 19.3) by
doing work on them in the presence of an electric field. The amount
of work that is done on a given quantity of electric charge to move it
through an electric field is equal to the increase in electric potential
energy of the charge.

We define the *electric potential difference V* between two points A and B
this way:

$$V = \frac{W}{Q}$$

where W is the amount of work that must be done to move a small
positive charge Q from point A to point B (strictly speaking, this
gives the electric potential of point B with respect to point A).

1 V is the electric potential difference between two points if it takes 1 J of work per coulomb to move a positive charge from one point to the other.

$$1\ V = 1\ J/C$$

Because of the units in which it is measured, electric potential difference is often referred to as "voltage". A 12 V car battery is a battery that does 12 J of work on each coulomb of charge that flows through it.

As charges move from one point to another through a conductor, they lose energy. As a result, they experience a decrease in electric potential. This decrease is often referred to as an electric potential difference or, simply, a potential difference between the two points. "Electric potential difference" is the correct term and it should always be used in preference to "voltage".

The electrical energy lost or work done by a charge, Q, going through a potential difference, V, may be written:

$$E = QV$$

Since it is often easier to measure the current and the time during which it lasts, we can use the equation

$$Q = It$$

and, substituting in the first equation, we get

$$E = VIt$$

as an expression for the electrical energy lost by a current, I, through a potential difference, V, for a time, t.

In practice, there are many situations in which the term "voltage" is commonly used. Whenever you see "voltage", remember that it means the same as electric potential. Increases in electric potential are often referred to as "voltage rises", and decreases are called "voltage drops".

Sample Problems

1. A 12 V car battery supplies 1.0×10^3 C of charge to the starting motor. How much energy is used to start the car?

$$E = QV$$
$$= (1.0 \times 10^3\ C)(12\ V)$$
$$= 1.2 \times 10^4\ J$$

2. An electric toaster uses a current of 10 A for 125 s to make toast, while giving off 1.5×10^5 J of heat energy. What is the potential difference across the toaster?

$$V = \frac{E}{It}$$
$$= \frac{1.5 \times 10^5\ J}{(10\ A)(125\ s)}$$
$$= 1.2 \times 10^2\ V$$

Note that, in the equation $E = VIt$, when SI units are substituted for V, I, and t, the units of E are joules:

$$E = VIt$$
$$= (volt)\ (ampere)\ (second)$$
$$= \left(\frac{joule}{coulomb}\right) \left(\frac{coulomb}{second}\right) (second)$$
$$= joule$$

Electricity is used to operate and monitor such life-saving medical equipment as pacemakers, respirators, oxygen tents, and lung and kidney dialysis machines.

Electrical energy is sold to homes in units called kilowatt hours, not in joules. We can easily see that

$$1 \text{ kW} \cdot \text{h} = (1000 \text{ J/s})(3600 \text{ s})$$
$$= 3.6 \times 10^6 \text{ J}$$

A multi-range DC voltmeter

*P*ractice

1. What amount of energy does a toaster use to make toast if it has 800 C of charge passing through it with a potential difference of 120 V?
2. What is the potential difference across a refrigerator if 75 C of charge transfer 9.0×10^3 J of energy to the compressor motor?
3. An electric baseboard heater draws a current of 6.0 A and has a potential difference of 240 V. For how long must it remain on to use 2.2×10^5 J of electrical energy?
4. A flash of lightning transfers 1.5×10^9 J of electrical energy through a potential difference of 5.0×10^7 V between a cloud and the ground. Calculate the quantity of charge transferred in the lightning bolt.
5. Calculate the energy stored in a 9.0 V battery that can deliver a continuous current of 5.0 mA for 2.0×10^3 s.
6. If a charge of 0.30 C moves from one point to another in a conductor and, in doing so, releases 5.4 J of electrical energy, what is the potential difference between the two points?

Measuring Electric Potential Difference

The potential difference between any two points may be measured with an instrument called a **voltmeter**. To measure a potential difference with a voltmeter, the two terminals of the voltmeter are connected between the two points, as illustrated.

There must be a very small current through the voltmeter between the two points. Also, the voltmeter must be connected so that electrons enter through its negative terminal and leave by its positive terminal.

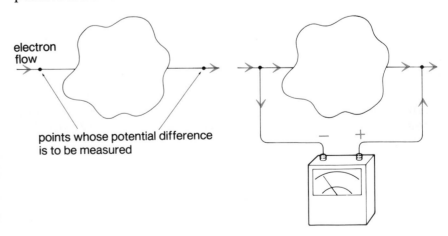

electron flow

points whose potential difference is to be measured

Practice

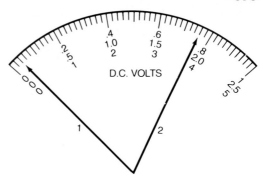

1. Most voltmeters may be used to measure several ranges of values of electric potential difference. A typical multi-range voltmeter scale is illustrated, with two sample needle positions. Copy the table into your notebook and determine the voltage reading indicated by each needle position for each of the seven ranges of electric potential.

Electric potential range	0-1 V	0-2.5 V	0-5 V	0-10 V	0-25 V	0-50 V	0-100 V
Electric potential reading Needle position 1							
Electric potential reading Needle position 2							

2. Using a 6 V battery, a voltmeter, some wires, a rheostat, and a small flashlight bulb, construct the apparatus illustrated. Use whatever voltmeter range produces the greatest deflection of the needle without going off the scale.

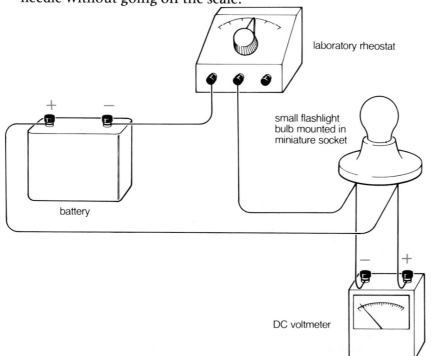

laboratory rheostat

small flashlight bulb mounted in miniature socket

battery

DC voltmeter

The electric potential difference that an energy source can maintain is often described by expressions such as "6 V battery" or "115 V supply". The "voltage rating" of some common sources of electric potential difference are:

single dry cell	1.5 V
lead-acid storage cell	2.0 V
automobile battery	12 V
normal household outlets	110 V-120 V
heavy-wiring household outlets	220 V-240 V
electric streetcar and bus supply	550 V
long-distance transmission lines	50 kV-750 kV

Adjust the dial on the rheostat to five or six different positions, in turn, and for each record the value of the potential difference across the light bulb, and give a brief description of the brightness of the bulb.

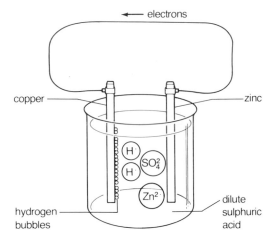

The voltaic cell

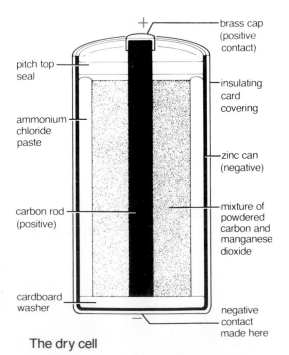

The dry cell

19.3 Producing Electric Potential Energy

As already shown, any device that is capable of separating electric charge (that is, removing electrons from their atoms) acts as a source of electric potential energy. At a time when meeting enormous demands for electrical energy is one of our foremost concerns, all possible sources of electric potential energy should be considered. What follows is a review of some of the better-known sources.

Electrochemical Cells

(a) The Voltaic Cell

When two strips of different metals are placed in a solution of an acid or base, a separation of electric charge occurs. The metal strips are called electrodes and the acid is called the electrolyte. The full explanation is quite complicated but essentially what is involved is the ability of the electrolyte to dissociate (break down) into positive and negative ions. These ions move freely about in the electrolyte and react chemically with each of the electrodes. The chemical reactions result in an excess of electrons being left behind on one of the electrodes while an equal deficit of electrons occurs on the other electrode. A common voltaic cell is made with copper and zinc electrodes and uses an electrolyte of dilute sulfuric acid; it will produce a potential difference of about 1.1 V. Although voltaic cells have great historical significance, they are no longer in common use.

(b) The Dry Cell

The operation of a dry cell is very similar to that of a voltaic cell. The electrodes used are usually of zinc and carbon and the electrolyte is a moist paste of ammonium chloride and several other materials. The dry cell has many advantages over the voltaic cell. It is almost unbreakable and easy to handle, and it can maintain a constant potential difference of about 1.5 V. Several dry cells may be connected together to produce even greater potential differences, and when this is done we call the resulting source of electric potential energy a battery of cells, or, simply, a battery.

(c) Secondary Cells

Both the voltaic cell and the dry cell will continue to separate charge and produce a potential difference only as long as there are ample quantities of each electrode and of the electrolyte. When one of these runs out, the cell will no longer operate, and we say it is "dead". The cell is now useless and must be discarded.

Many electrochemical cells in use today are called secondary or storage cells; they are cells in which the chemical reaction producing electrical potential energy is reversible. When the cell gets weak, electrical energy may be supplied to it to produce a chemical reaction that renews the cell's ability to separate charge. Automobiles and many types of portable appliances, such as razors and camera flash units, rely on secondary cells for their energy. When a secondary cell loses its ability to separate charge, it requires "charging". Energy is added during the charging process so that the battery can continue to separate charge.

"Rechargeable" Ni-Cad (nickel-cadmium) dry cells have become very popular for use in toys, portable radios, and tape players that are subject to extended use. When these batteries run down, they can be plugged into a 120 V outlet, using an adaptor, and in a period of hours be recharged for further use.

Electrical energy is convenient, clean, and relatively safe to use, but producing electrical energy by burning coal or utilizing nuclear fuel without adequate care may do irreparable harm to our environment. The use of coal, gas, and oil as fuels in some electrical power generating stations has contributed to the depletion of these scarce natural resources.

Electromagnetic Generators

If a conductor is moved through a magnetic field, the electrons in the conductor experience a force that causes an electric current. This process is called electromagnetic induction. The energy needed to move the conductor through the magnetic field is converted into electric potential energy.

Electric generators and the principles of electromagnetic induction will be discussed in detail in Chapter 23.

Piezoelectricity

Crystals of certain materials, such as quartz and Rochelle salt, react to mechanical forces exerted on them by producing a small electric potential difference. The potential difference produced depends on the amount of force applied to the crystal. This property and the reverse (that is, vibrations of the crystal caused by the application of an electric potential to it) are called the piezoelectric effect.

A phonograph needle connected to a piezoelectric crystal can convert vibrations produced by the grooves in a record into small

Generators in a hydroelectric power plant

Quartz crystal watches use the piezoelectric effect to keep time. A small potential difference applied to the quartz crystal by a dry cell causes the crystal to vibrate with a regular frequency.

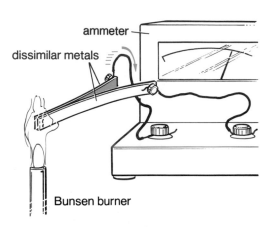

dissimilar metals

ammeter

Bunsen burner

Banks of solar cells on a geosynchronous communications satellite

pulses of electric potential capable of being amplified and reproduced as sound. Also, if the crystal is connected to a diaphragm and vibrated by incoming sound waves, it will produce small electrical impulses and will act like a microphone.

Thermoelectricity

A device called a thermocouple may be constructed by joining two wires of different metals at both ends to form a loop. If the two junctions are then exposed to different temperatures, an electric potential will be developed in the loop, and a flow of electrons will result. The potential difference produced depends on the difference in temperature between the ends of the loop. This device is useful as a thermometer for measuring temperatures over an extremely large range of values.

Photoelectricity

Light energy, too, may be used to do work on electric charge and produce an electric potential difference. When light of a sufficiently short wavelength is used to illuminate certain metals, the surface electrons of the metal absorb its energy and are then capable of overcoming the forces binding them to their atoms. This phenomenon, called the photoelectric effect, was first explained by Albert Einstein in 1905.

More recently, solar cells have been developed to utilize the energy of the sun. Thin wafers of special materials, called semiconductors, are treated to form a junction. When light from the sun falls on this junction, a small electric potential difference is produced. Each solar cell has an area of only a few square centimeters and produces a potential difference of less than 1 V, so it takes a large number of solar cells, connected together, to form a solar battery that will produce a large enough potential difference to be of practical value. Because of their lightness and reliability, solar cells have had extensive use as a power source on satellites and space probes.

19.4 *Applications:* Electrical Energy

Electric potential energy is used to operate an enormous range of gadgets, devices, and appliances, yet most of these make use of electrical energy for one of three basic purposes: to produce heat, to produce light, or to produce motion.

Heating Elements

Electrons enter a heating coil, or element, and immediately encounter opposition to their motion from the charges in the atoms that make up the heating element. Other electrons coming along behind them repel them forward. As all the electrons make their way through the heating element, they transfer much of their energy to the atoms of the heating element by "colliding" with them (although no contact takes place as we normally understand the word—the interaction takes place "at a distance" through electric repulsion and attraction). The atoms thus vibrate more rapidly. When this happens, an observer watching the heating element says that it is becoming hot. Since the electrons leaving the element have less electrical potential energy than they had when they entered, there is a potential difference across the element.

It is dangerous to have more current through a conductor than it can handle. Overheating may result, producing a danger of fire. As a precaution against such a mishap, a **fuse**, or **circuit-breaker**, is often included in the conducting path. These cheap, simple devices are designed to melt, or mechanically open, so that the conductor will break whenever the safe amount of current is exceeded.

For most conducting wires found in homes, 15 A fuses are used. This means that if the current through one of the wires exceeds 15 A, a fuse will "blow" and the current will stop. Thicker wires designed for higher currents may be fused at 20 A, 30 A, or even more. It is always unwise to use a larger fuse than the one specified, since doing so defeats the purpose of the fuse.

This chart shows wire gauges for copper conductors, and the proper fuse to use with each.

Wire gauge	Fuse required
14	15 A
12	20 A
10	30 A
8	50 A
6	70 A

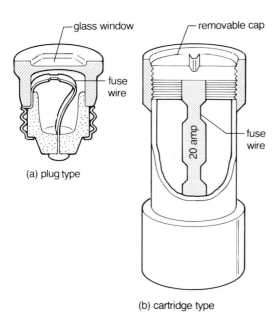

(a) plug type

(b) cartridge type

The tungsten filaments in incandescent light bulbs operate at temperatures in excess of 3000°C.

Light Bulbs

A similar situation occurs when electrons enter the filament of an incandescent light bulb. The electrons collide with atoms in the filament, thereby transferring some of their energy to the atoms. The atoms vibrate rapidly as they absorb this energy, and considerable heat is generated. At a sufficiently high temperature, the atoms release energy in the form of light. The greater the number of electrons going through the filament, the more energy its atoms will absorb, the higher the temperature will get, and, hence, the brighter the light produced will be.

Fluorescent lights are similar to neon lights. A phosphor coating is painted on the inside of the tube. The light tube is filled with mercury vapor which, when excited by the application of a potential difference, produces ultraviolet radiation. The ultraviolet radiation striking the phosphor coating produces white light.

   In the case of a neon light, the process is similar, except that the electrons are moving through a gas rather than through a solid filament. Electrons colliding with (neon) gas atoms transfer energy to the atoms internally; such a collision does not cause the atom as a whole to vibrate very much. As a result, the gas does not become very hot; instead, its atoms send most of the energy out again in the form of light.

Motors

When electrons enter a motor, they pass through a coil of wire and use their energy to create a magnetic field. This magnetic field interacts with other magnets in the motor, causing the coil to rotate. The coil will continue to rotate as long as electrons continue to flow through the magnetizing coil. We will study the operation of electric motors in greater detail in Chapter 23.

   We call devices that use electrical energy, **loads**, and devices that produce electrical energy for the circuit, **sources**. These electrical loads and sources take part in a transfer of energy that may occur in an electric circuit. In Chapter 20, we will consider the characteristics of electric circuits and their role in transferring electrical energy.

Chapter Summary

When appliances are plugged into outlets in the home, electrons flow first in one direction for a very short time and then in the other direction for the same time. This type of current is called "alternating current (AC)". You will learn more about AC in Chapter 23.

1. When electrons move through a conductor, they constitute an electric current, I. This is expressed as:

$$I = \frac{Q}{t}$$

   where Q is the charge moving past a point in a conductor (in coulombs) and t is the time (in seconds).
   I is measured in coulombs per second, or amperes, and $1 \text{ A} = 1 \text{ C/s}$.

2. Work must be done on electrons to separate them from their atoms, and hence they acquire electric potential energy. The electric potential difference V (in volts) between two points is expressed as $V = W/Q$, where W is the work (in joules) that must be done to move a small charge Q (in coulombs) from one point to the other. V is measured in joules per coulomb or volts, and $1 \text{ V} = 1 \text{ J/C}$.

3. The electric current through a conductor may be measured with an ammeter, and the potential difference between any two points in the conductor may be measured with a voltmeter.
4. Devices that do work by exerting forces on charges act as sources of electric potential. Some common examples are:
   (a) electrochemical cells, which use energy stored in chemicals to do work on charges,
   (b) electromagnetic generators, which use the force on a moving conductor in a magnetic field to do work on charges,
   (c) piezoelectric crystals, which convert tiny mechanical forces into electric potential,
   (d) thermoelectric junctions, which use a difference in temperature to do work on charges,
   (e) solar cells and photoelectric surfaces, which use the energy of light to produce an electric potential.
5. Devices that use the energy possessed by moving electrons are called loads. Some common examples are:
   (a) coils and elements, which use electrical energy to produce heat,
   (b) filaments in bulbs, which use electrical energy to produce light,
   (c) motors, which use electrical energy to produce motion.

A common use of a piezoelectric crystal is in the spark lighter for a gas barbecue. Turning a spring loaded dial causes the crystal to receive a sharp mechanical jolt. This jolt causes an electric potential difference to be produced between the crystal and the gas burner. If these are separated by a small gap, a spark will jump across the gap and ignite the gas in the burner.

Chapter Review

Discussion

1. (a) What is an electric current?
   (b) Write an equation that may be used to calculate the electric current in a conductor.
   (c) What unit is used to measure electric current?
2. List three types of energy that may be used to make electrons flow through a conductor, and name a device that employs each of those three types of energy to produce an electric current.
3. What is the basic difference between a primary cell and a secondary cell? To which category does a dry cell belong? A lead-acid storage battery?
4. Describe the significance of two points in a conductor that are at the same potential. How much work must be done to move an electron between the two points?

Sulfur emitted from coal burned to generate electricity combines with water vapor in the atmosphere to produce acid rain.

Many electrical generating stations create thermal pollution in surrounding lakes and rivers by discharging warm water.

Nuclear fuel used in many new generating stations produces dangerous radioactive wastes that must be disposed of with great care.

5. What is the most likely source of electrical energy for each of the following:
   (a) a cellular telephone
   (b) a digital watch
   (c) a car stereo
   (d) a home VCR
   (e) a ship-to-shore radio
   (f) a communications satellite
   (g) a phonograph cartridge
   (h) a thermometer used to measure the temperature of hot flue gases
6. Show that the unit for the product VIt is the same as the unit for energy.

Problems

7. How much charge is transferred by a current of 0.40 A in 15 min?
8. How long does it take for a current of 7.5 mA to transfer a charge of 15 C?
9. What is the potential difference between two points if 1 kJ of work is required to move 1 C of charge between the two points?
10. What is the energy of an electron accelerated through a potential difference of 1.0 MV?
11. What is the potential difference between two points when a charge of 80 C has 4.0×10^2 J of energy supplied to it as it moves between the points?
12. There is a current of 0.50 A through an incandescent lamp for 2.0 min, with a potential difference of 120 V. How much energy does the current transfer to the lamp?
13. There is a current of 2.0 A through a hair-blower that transfers 10 800 J of energy to the blower in 45 s. What is the potential difference across the hair-blower?
14. An electric toaster operating at a potential difference of 120 V uses 34 200 J of energy during the 30 s it is on. What is the current through the toaster?
15. An electric drill operates at a potential difference of 120 V and draws a current of 7.5 A. If it takes 50 s to drill a hole in a piece of steel, calculate the amount of electrical energy used by the drill in that time.
16. An electric motor is used to do the 9.6×10^3 J of work needed to lift a small load. If the motor draws a current of 2.0 A for 20 s, calculate the potential difference across the motor.

Effect of Electricity on the Human Body

	AC	DC
least current detected	1 mA	5 mA
threshold of muscular control	8 mA	70 mA
danger to life	25 mA	80 mA
ventricular fibrillation	100 mA	100 mA

17. In a lightning discharge, 30 C of charge move through a potential difference of 10^8 V in 2.0×10^{-2} s. Calculate:
    (a) the current represented by the lightning bolt,
    (b) the total energy released by the lightning bolt.
18. How much energy is gained by an electron accelerated through a potential difference of 3.0×10^4 V?
19. A 12 V automobile battery is rated by its manufacturer at 60 A·h. That is, it can deliver a current of 1.0 A continuously for a period of 60 h, or 60 A for 1.0 h, or any other equivalent combination, before needing to be recharged. Calculate:
    (a) how long the battery can deliver a current of 180 A,
    (b) the total charge the battery is able to deliver without recharging,
    (c) the total amount of electrical energy that is stored in the battery.
20. How much energy is required to dry your hair, if the hair dryer draws 12 A from a 110 V outlet for 6.0 min?

Numerical Answers to
Practice Problems
page 570
1. 3.0 A
2. 0.75 A
3. 9.0×10^2 C
4. 20 s
5. 3.1×10^{18}

page 574
1. 9.60×10^4 J
2. 1.2×10^2 J
3. 1.5×10^2 s
4. 30 c
5. 90 J
6. 18 V

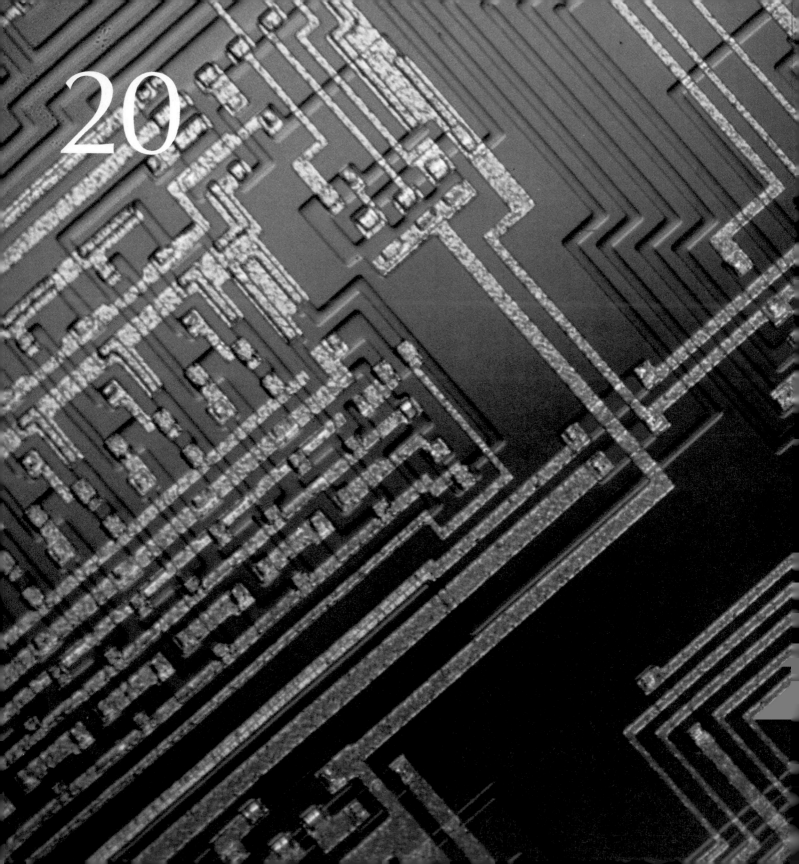

Electric Circuits

Chapter Objectives

- **Identify** the standard symbols used in electric circuit diagrams and **interpret** schematic diagrams for simple circuits.

- **Draw** simple series and parallel circuits and **describe** the current and electric potential relationships in each.

- **Relate** potential difference to current in simple circuits, using Kirchhoff's Laws.

- **Define** "resistance", using Ohm's Law.

- **Relate** potential difference to current and resistance.

- **Explain** four factors that affect the resistance of a cylindrical conductor.

- **Determine** the equivalent resistance of resistors connected in series or in parallel.

- **Analyze** simple series, parallel, and series-parallel circuits.

- **Relate** electric power to current, potential difference, and resistance.

- **Define** the kilowatt hour and **relate** power and time to energy.

20.1 Electric Circuits

Electrons move in the presence of an electric field to regions of lower electric potential. As a result of the work done on them, the electrons possess electric potential energy that they can use to produce heat, light, and motion as they pass through various loads which reduce their electric potential. To make it possible for electrons to do this, we connect sources of electric potential energy to electric loads by means of circuits, such as the one illustrated.

This micro-processor contains thousands of electrical circuits on a silicon chip the size of a match head.

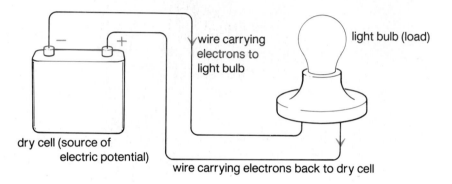

As electrons go through this simple circuit (see diagram) from the negative terminal of the dry cell, through the light bulb, and back to the positive terminal of the dry cell, they transfer the electric potential energy they acquired from the dry cell to the light bulb. In a sense, then, electrons act as carriers of energy from the source of electrical energy (the dry cell) to the user of electrical energy (the light bulb).

Electrons can only go through a circuit if it provides them with a complete path. Any break in the circuit will cause the electric current to cease. The circuit is then said to be an "open circuit".
If, by chance, two wires in a circuit touch, so that electrons can pass from one wire to the other and return to the positive terminal of the source without passing through the load, the circuit is said to be a "short circuit".

In the circuit diagrams in this chapter, a small dot (—•—) on a conductor will indicate a point in the circuit where a connection between two or more wires must be made. This will help you in wiring these circuits.

Circuit Symbols

The various paths from source to load and back may be very complicated and may contain many different types of electrical devices and connectors. To simplify descriptions of these paths, circuit diagrams are drawn using symbols, and showing exactly how each device is connected to other devices. The components of an electric circuit are called elements, and the symbols most commonly used in such **schematic diagrams** are displayed here.

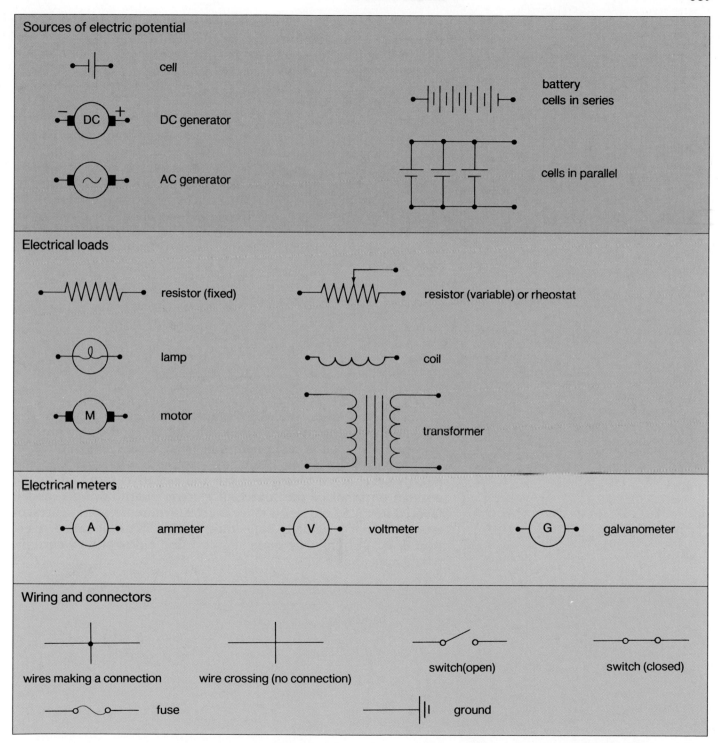

The Direction of the Electric Current

Early in the nineteenth century, Benjamin Franklin made the assumption that there were two electrical states: one with more than the normal amount of electricity, which he called a positive charge, and one with less than the normal amount of electricity, which he called a negative charge.

Electric current was defined as the rate of movement of electrically charged particles past a point, so it was only natural to assume that the charge moved from an area where there was an excess (positive charge) to an area where there was a deficit (negative charge). Thus, the direction of the electric current was defined as moving from the positive terminal to the negative terminal of the source of electric potential. This assumption about the direction of the electric current was called "conventional current". The circuit diagram below would correspond to the current direction, using this convention:

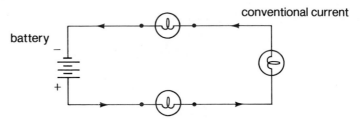

Much later, after the conventional current assumption had become firmly entrenched in scientific literature, the electron was discovered. It soon became clear that what actually constituted an electric current in a solid conductor (such as a wire) was a flow of negatively charged electrons from the negative terminal to the positive terminal of the source of electric potential. This model, favored by many physicists since it gives a more accurate representation of what is actually happening in the circuit, is called "electron flow" current. The same circuit, using electron flow current, would appear as:

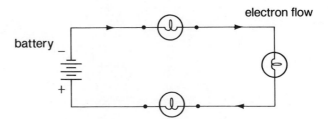

This text uses the electron flow current throughout. All calculations involved in the analysis of any electric circuit are unaffected by the approach used, and only a very few changes in thinking are required to translate from electron flow to conventional current. These changes are summarized here:

1. In all circuit diagrams, the direction of conventional current would be opposite to that of the electron flow current, indicated in this text by the arrows on the conductors.

2. Any references in the text to "electron flow through a conductor from negative to positive" would be equivalent to "conventional current through a conductor from positive to negative".

   It should be noted that the term "current" will be used to denote the magnitude of the rate of charge flow. For example, a current of ten amperes can refer to an electron flow rate of ten coulombs per second.

It should also be emphasized that the above comments refer only to the flow of electrically charged particles in solids. In liquids and gases the charged particles can flow in either direction, and sometimes simultaneously. It might help to realize that negative charge flowing north along a wire is electrically equivalent, in every way, to positive charge flowing south.

Series Circuits

One simple way of joining several loads together is to connect them in **series** to a source of electric potential. In this type of connection, the electrons have only one path to follow through the circuit, and as a result each electron must go through each load in turn; every electron that goes through a series circuit goes through each load in the circuit before returning to the source. Here is an example of a series circuit:

In a series circuit, a key word to remember is "and": electrons pass through one load *and* the next load, and so on, as they return to the positive terminal of the source. The current is exactly the same at any point in a series circuit; charge cannot pile up in the circuit.

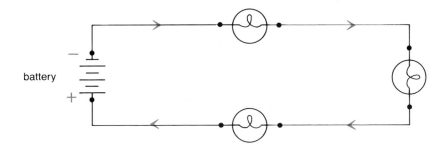

Parallel Circuits

In a parallel circuit, a key word to remember is "or": electrons pass through one load *or* the next load, and so on, as they return to the positive terminal of the source.

In a **parallel** circuit, the electrons have a choice of several paths through the circuit, and, as a result, may pass through any one of the several loads in the circuit. Every electron that goes through the parallel circuit goes through only one of the circuit's loads before returning to the source. This is how loads connected in parallel may appear:

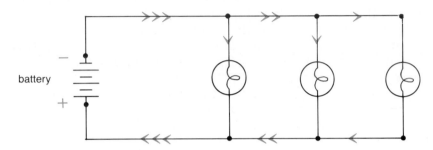

It is easy to get the impression that electrons "race" through a circuit from the negative terminal to the positive terminal of the source. In fact, they move relatively slowly, and it would take a long time for any one electron to make its way completely through any practical circuit. In a copper wire with a diameter of about 1 mm and an electric current of 1 A, the electrons are drifting through the conductor with a speed of approximately 10^{-2} cm/s. However, the current stops and starts at essentially the same time in all parts of the circuit.

Notice that in this circuit, there are three different paths through the circuit. Each electron will take only one of the three paths.

20.2 Kirchhoff's Laws for Electric Circuits

As electrons move through a circuit, they lose energy in the various loads they pass through, and they often have to part company and go different ways when they reach a junction of more than two wires. Two basic questions about how electric circuits operate are:
1. When electrons have several loads to pass through, what governs the amount of electric potential energy they will lose in each load?
2. When electrons have a choice of several possible paths to follow, what governs the number of electrons that will take each path?

An understanding of the operation of simple series and parallel circuits depends on the answers to these questions. Gustav Robert Kirchhoff (1824-1887), a German physicist, proposed that the answers could be found by applying two fundamental conservation laws to electric circuits:

Conservation of Energy: As electrons move through an electric circuit they gain energy in sources and lose energy in loads, but the total energy gained in one trip through a circuit is equal to the total energy lost.

Conservation of Charge: Electric charge is neither created nor lost in an electric circuit, nor does it accumulate at any point in the circuit.

By performing careful experiments similar to those at the end of the chapter, Kirchhoff was able to describe each of these conservation laws in terms of quantities easily measurable in electric circuits. They have since become known as **Kirchhoff's Voltage Law** (KVL) and **Kirchhoff's Current Law** (KCL).

Kirchhoff's Voltage Law
Around any complete path through an electric circuit, the sum of the increases in electric potential is equal to the sum of the decreases in electric potential.

Kirchhoff's Current Law
At any junction point in an electric circuit, the total electric current into the junction is equal to the total electric current out.

These relationships are invaluable in understanding the transfer of electrical energy in a circuit and will provide the basis for our examination of electric circuit analysis in this chapter.

G.R. Kirchhoff (center) and his colleagues, R.W. Bunsen and Sir H.E. Roscoe

Sample Problems

1. Calculate the potential difference, V_2, in this circuit:

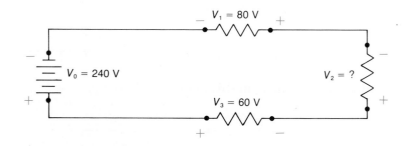

In a series circuit, each load carries all of the current and has part of the potential difference.

Applying KVL to the circuit,
$$V_0 = V_1 + V_2 + V_3$$
$$\therefore V_2 = V_0 - V_1 - V_3$$
$$= 240 \text{ V} - 80 \text{ V} - 60 \text{ V}$$
$$= 100 \text{ V}$$

2. Calculate the electric current, I_3, in this circuit:

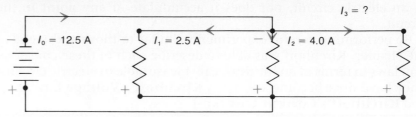

In a parallel circuit, each load has the entire potential difference but carries only part of the current.

Applying KCL to the circuit,

$$I_0 = I_1 + I_2 + I_3$$
$$\therefore I_3 = I_0 - I_1 - I_2$$
$$= 12.5 \text{ A} - 2.5 \text{ A} - 4.0 \text{ A}$$
$$= 6.0 \text{ A}$$

Practice

Loads connected in series have the same current; loads connected in parallel have the same potential difference.

1. Find V_0 in this circuit:

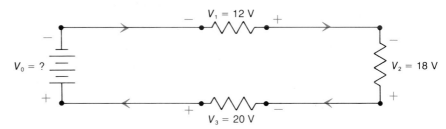

2. Find I_0 in this circuit:

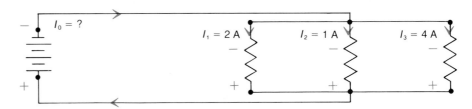

3. Find V_2, V_4, I_3, and I_4 in this circuit:

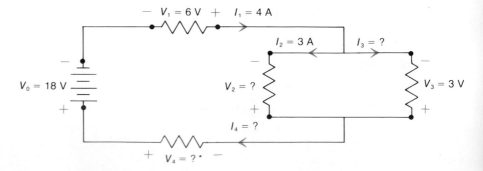

4. Find V_2, V_5, V_4, I_1, and I_4 in this circuit:

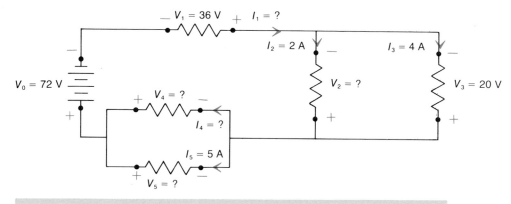

20.3 Resistance in Electric Circuits

When electrons pass through a device that uses their electrical energy, they experience an opposition, or **resistance**, to their flow, which results in a loss of energy. The energy they lose is given to the molecules and atoms of the conductor as they move through it. To measure the amount of resistance that a quantity of moving charge encounters, we compare the electric potential difference the charge experiences as it passes through a conductor with the amount of electric current.

The circuit shown below contains a resistance and a source of variable potential difference. The ammeter will indicate the current flowing through the resistance, while the voltmeter will indicate the potential difference across the resistance.

A resistor is actually a conductor, but one of limited capability. Electrons lose energy as they pass through a resistor, because they collide with its molecules and in doing so transfer energy to them. The filament of a light bulb and the heating element in a toaster are examples of resistors.

There are other types of devices as well as resistors that use electrical energy, but we will consider only resistors here.

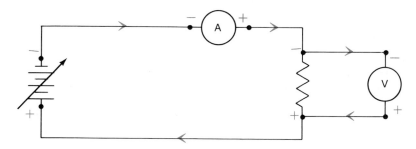

By varying the potential difference of the source, and making simultaneous measurements of current and potential difference, the following graph may be drawn:

Mathematically, this graph is of the form Y = *m*X, where *m* is the slope of the straight line.

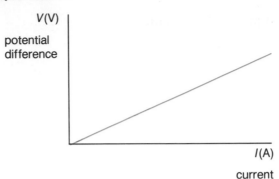

Not all resistances obey Ohm's Law: that is, $\frac{V}{I}$ is not a constant ratio; its value changes as V and I themselves change. A load that obeys Ohm's Law is called an "ohmic" resistance. Most metals are ohmic. Other substances are called "non-ohmic".

Ohm's Law

Georg Simon Ohm (1787-1854), a German physicist, found that, for a given conductor, the ratio $\frac{V}{I}$ is a constant. From this constant ratio, he formulated what we now call **Ohm's Law**:

The potential difference between any two points in a conductor varies directly as the current between the two points.

This relationship may be written as

$$\frac{V}{I} = \text{constant}$$

and, since the constant depends on the properties of the particular resistor being used, we give it the symbol R and call it the resistance. Thus, Ohm's Law may be written:

$$\frac{V}{I} = R$$

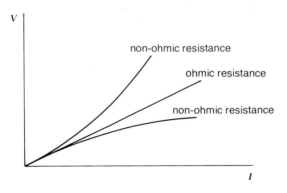

V is measured in volts, and I is measured in amperes, so R is measured in volts per ampere, and this new unit, the unit of electric resistance, is called the **ohm** (Ω).

Ω is the symbol for the letter omega in the Greek alphabet, corresponding to the letter "O" in the alphabet used in English writing.

1 Ω is the electric resistance of a conductor that has a current of 1 A through it when the potential difference across it is 1 V.

$$1\ \Omega = 1\ \text{V/A}$$

Sample Problems

1. Find the resistance of an electric light bulb if there is a current of 0.80 A when the potential difference across the bulb is 120 V.

$$R = \frac{V}{I}$$

$$= \frac{120 \text{ V}}{0.80 \text{ A}}$$

$$= 1.5 \times 10^2 \ \Omega$$

2. What is the potential difference across a toaster of resistance 13.7 Ω when the current through it is 8.75 A?

$$V = IR$$

$$= (8.75 \text{ A}) \ (13.7 \ \Omega)$$

$$= 120 \text{ V}$$

3. What is the current through an electric baseboard heater with a resistance of 38 Ω when the potential difference across it is 240 V?

$$I = \frac{V}{R}$$

$$= \frac{240 \text{ V}}{38 \ \Omega}$$

$$= 6.3 \text{ A}$$

Practice

1. A portable radio is connected to a 9.0 V battery and draws a current of 25 mA. What is the resistance of the radio?
2. An electric clothes dryer is connected to a 230 V source of electric potential. If it has a resistance of 9.2 Ω, calculate the current it draws.
3. A large tube in a television set has a resistance of 5.0×10^4 Ω and draws a current of 160 mA. What is the potential difference across the tube?
4. An electric toaster has a resistance of 12 Ω. What current will it draw from a 120 V supply?
5. What potential difference is required to produce a current of 8.0 A in a load having a resistance of 64 Ω?
6. An iron, designed for use at 120 V and 5.0 A, is connected to a source of 240 V. Calculate the current the iron will draw at the higher potential, and state what will happen to the iron.

Georg Simon Ohm (1787-1854)
Ohm was born in Bavaria, the son of a master mechanic who was interested in science and saw that his son received a proper scientific education. Ohm became a high school teacher but longed to work at the university. To secure a university post, he began to do research in the area of electrical conduction. After his discovery of Ohm's Law, he received so much public criticism that he was forced to resign even his high school position. His fellow scientists felt that his discoveries were based too much on theory and lacked the experimental proof to make them acceptable.

After years of living in poverty, he was finally recognized by the Royal Society, which conferred membership on him in 1842. He was also awarded a professorship at the University of Munich, where he spent the last five years of his life with his ambition realized.

Factors Affecting Resistance

At very low temperatures (within a few degrees of absolute zero) the electrical resistance of metals seems to disappear completely, and they become "superconductors". The field of low-temperature physics is called "cryogenics". Low-temperature electric power lines have been proposed as a way of transmitting electric power efficiently over great distances.

We have seen that the resistance of a given conductor is a constant regardless of the potential difference across it or the current through it. The value of its resistance depends on the following physical properties:

1. Length
The resistance of a conductor varies directly with its length; doubling the length of a conductor doubles the resistance. Stated mathematically, $R \propto L$.

2. Cross-sectional area
The resistance of a conductor varies inversely with its cross-sectional area; doubling the cross-sectional area halves the resistance. Stated mathematically, $R \propto \dfrac{I}{A}$.

3. Temperature
In most materials, an increase in temperature will cause an increase in resistance. This increase typically will range between 3% and 5% for each $10°C$ increase in temperature. However, for some materials, for example, glass and carbon, an increase in temperature will cause a decrease in resistance.

The fact that resistance varies with temperature complicates the manufacturing of electrical measuring instruments that will have to be exposed to a wide range of temperatures. Alloys have been developed whose resistance is little affected by temperature. Manganin, a mixture of manganese, nickel, and copper, has a change in resistance of less than 0.01% for each 1°C change in temperature. Semi-conductors have a resistance that decreases with increasing temperature.

4. Material
The atomic structure of a material has a marked effect on its resistance. Good conductors such as copper and aluminum have very low resistances, whereas poor conductors such as nichrome and mercury have higher resistances. Insulators such as glass and rubber have very high resistances. The resistance per unit of a material is called its *resistivity*. The unit of material used has a length of 1 m and a cross-sectional area of 1 m². The resistivity (ρ) of a material varies with its temperature. Stated mathematically, $R \propto \rho$.

Combining all of the factors that affect the resistance of a conductor, the following equation results:

$$R = \rho \, \frac{L}{A}$$

Resistivities (ρ) of Various Materials

	(in $\Omega \cdot m^2/m$ at $20°C$)
aluminum	2.6×10^{-8}
copper	1.7×10^{-8}
iron	10.0×10^{-8}
lead	22.0×10^{-8}
mercury	95.8×10^{-8}
nichrome	100.0×10^{-8}
platinum	10.0×10^{-8}
silver	1.5×10^{-8}
tungsten	5.5×10^{-8}

where R is the resistance, in ohms
    L is the length, in meters
    A is the cross-sectional area, in (meters)²
  and ρ is the resistivity in $\Omega \cdot m^2/m$

20.4 Resistance in Series and in Parallel

The currents through the various branches of an electric circuit, and the differences in electric potential between various points in the circuit, depend on three relationships:

- Kirchhoff's Voltage Law (KVL): Around any complete path through an electric circuit, the total increase in electric potential is equal to the total decrease in electric potential.
- Kirchhoff's Current Law (KCL): At any junction point in an electric circuit, the total current into the junction is equal to the total current out of the junction.
- Ohm's Law: The potential difference between any two points in an electric circuit is directly proportional to the electric current between the two points, and the resistance between the two points is given by

$$R = \frac{V}{I}$$

Most electric circuits used in homes, appliances, and automobiles contain more than one source of electric potential and many different types of loads connected together in complicated networks of conductors. No matter how complex it may be, a circuit can be "analyzed" completely using the three relationships stated above. To analyze an electric circuit means to determine, for each element in the circuit:

1. the current through it
2. the potential difference across it
3. the value of its resistance, if it is a load element

When there are several resistances in a circuit, the first step in the analysis of the circuit is often the calculation of the total resistance in it. The simplest situation occurs when all the resistances are connected either in series or in parallel.

Resistance in Series

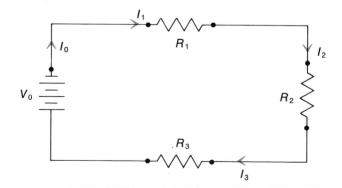
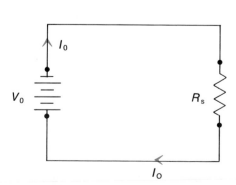

Adding resistance in series increases the total resistance in a circuit, thereby decreasing the current from the source.

The diagram on the previous page shows a circuit with one source of electric potential, V_0, and three resistances, R_1, R_2, and R_3, as indicated. We would like to find the value of the equivalent resistance of R_1, R_2, and R_3 connected in series. If we call this equivalent resistance R_s, the circuit would simply contain the source, V_0, and the resistance, R_s. The amount of current through the circuit from the source is I_0.

Applying Kirchhoff's Voltage Law to the circuit,

$$V_0 = V_1 + V_2 + V_3 \tag{1}$$

The "equivalent" resistance has the same current and potential difference as the resistances it replaces.

Applying Ohm's Law to each individual resistance,

$$V_1 = I_1 R_1 \quad V_2 = I_2 R_2 \quad V_3 = I_3 R_3 \quad \text{and } V_0 = I_0 R_s \tag{2}$$

Substituting equations from (2) into (1),

$$I_0 R_s = I_1 R_1 + I_2 R_2 + I_3 R_3$$

But, applying Kirchhoff's Current Law to the circuit,

$$I_0 = I_1 = I_2 = I_3$$

Therefore, as an expression for the equivalent resistance of R_1, R_2, and R_3, in series, we get

$$R_s = R_1 + R_2 + R_3$$

And if the number of resistances connected in series is n, the equivalent resistance will be given by

$$R_s = R_1 + R_2 + \ldots + R_n$$

Sample Problems

1. What is the equivalent resistance in a series circuit containing a 16 Ω light bulb, a 27 Ω heater, and a 12 Ω motor?

$$R_s = R_1 + R_2 + R_3$$
$$= 16 \ \Omega + 27 \ \Omega + 12 \ \Omega$$
$$= 55 \ \Omega$$

2. A string of eight lights connected in series has a resistance of 120 Ω. If the lights are identical, what is the resistance of each bulb?

$$R_s = R_1 + R_2 + \ldots + R_8$$
$$= 8 \ R_1 \text{ if all are identical}$$
$$120 \ \Omega = 8 \ R_1$$
$$R_1 = \frac{120 \ \Omega}{8} = 15 \ \Omega$$

Practice

1. Find the equivalent resistance in each of these cases.
   (a) 12 Ω, 25 Ω, and 42 Ω connected in series
   (b) three 30 Ω light bulbs and two 20 Ω heating elements connected in series
   (c) two strings of Christmas tree lights connected in series, if the first string has eight 4 Ω bulbs in series, and the second has twelve 3 Ω bulbs in series.
2. Find the value of the unknown resistance in each of these cases.
   (a) a 20 Ω, an 18 Ω, and an unknown resistor connected in series to give an equivalent resistance of 64 Ω
   (b) two identical unknown bulbs connected in series with a 50 Ω and a 64 Ω heater to produce an equivalent resistance of 150 Ω
   (c) each light in a series string of 24 identical bulbs with an equivalent resistance of 60 Ω

Resistance in Parallel

We can use the same approach to find the equivalent resistance of several resistances connected in parallel. If we call the equivalent resistance of R_1, R_2, and R_3 connected in parallel, R_p, then the circuit appears as shown.

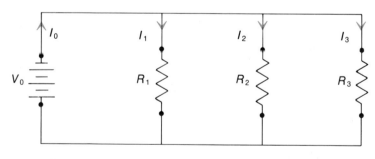 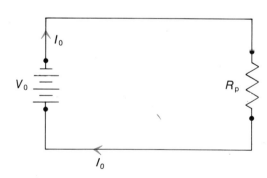

Applying Kirchhoff's Current Law to the circuit,
$$I_0 = I_1 + I_2 + I_3 \qquad (1)$$

Applying Ohm's Law to each individual resistance,
$$I_1 = \frac{V_1}{R_1} \quad I_2 = \frac{V_2}{R_2} \quad I_3 = \frac{V_3}{R_3} \quad \text{and} \quad I_0 = \frac{V_0}{R_p} \qquad (2)$$

Substituting equations from (2) into (1),
$$\frac{V_0}{R_p} = \frac{V_1}{R_1} + \frac{V_2}{R_2} + \frac{V_3}{R_3}$$

But, applying Kirchhoff's Voltage Law to the circuit,
$$V_0 = V_1 = V_2 = V_3$$
Therefore, as an expression for the equivalent resistance of R_1, R_2, and R_3, in parallel, we get

$$\frac{1}{R_p} = \frac{1}{R_1} + \frac{1}{R_2} + \frac{1}{R_3}$$

And, if the number of resistances connected in parallel is n, the equivalent resistance will be given by

$$\frac{1}{R_p} = \frac{1}{R_1} + \frac{1}{R_2} + \dots + \frac{1}{R_n}$$

Adding resistance in parallel decreases the total resistance in a circuit, thereby increasing the current from the source.

Equivalent resistance increases when resistors in parallel are removed from a circuit, much like a traffic jam that results when lanes close on the highway.

Sample Problems

1. Find the equivalent resistance when a 4 Ω bulb and an 8 Ω bulb are connected in parallel.

$$\frac{1}{R_p} = \frac{1}{R_1} + \frac{1}{R_2}$$

$$R_p = \frac{1}{\dfrac{1}{R_1} + \dfrac{1}{R_2}}$$

$$= \frac{1}{\dfrac{1}{8\ \Omega} + \dfrac{1}{4\ \Omega}}$$

$$= 2.7\ \Omega$$

2. What resistance would have to be added in parallel with a 40 Ω hair dryer to reduce the equivalent resistance to 8 Ω?

$$\frac{1}{R_p} = \frac{1}{R_1} + \frac{1}{R_2}$$

$$\frac{1}{R_2} = \frac{1}{R_p} - \frac{1}{R_1}$$

$$R_2 = \frac{1}{\dfrac{1}{R_p} - \dfrac{1}{R_1}}$$

$$= \frac{1}{\dfrac{1}{8\ \Omega} - \dfrac{1}{40\ \Omega}}$$

$$= 10\ \Omega$$

*P*ractice

1. Find the equivalent resistance in each of these cases.
   (a) 16 Ω and 8 Ω connected in parallel
   (b) 20 Ω, 10 Ω, and 5 Ω connected in parallel
2. Calculate the equivalent resistance of two, three, four, and five 60 Ω bulbs in parallel. What is the simple relationship for the equivalent resistance of n equal resistances in parallel?

20.5 Electric Circuit Analysis

With the information that has been presented so far about electricity, a complete analysis of any simple series or parallel electric circuit containing resistances is possible, provided that you know enough about the elements in the circuit. Because so many different electric circuits are possible, there can be no standard approach to the analyzing of a circuit. The steps to take in each case will depend on the information you have about the circuit, and what you want to find out.

Normally, the resistance of circuit wiring is negligible and can be overlooked when analyzing circuits. In circuits that cover great distances, however, this may not be the case.

*S*ample *P*roblems

1. Find: V_1, V_2, V_3
   I_0, I_1, I_2, I_3

   Applying Ohm's Law to the entire circuit,

   $$I_0 = \frac{V_0}{R_t} \quad \text{where } R_t \text{ is the total resistance in the circuit}$$

   But, since R_1, R_2, and R_3 are connected in series

   $$R_t = R_s = R_1 + R_2 + R_3$$
   $$= 6\,\Omega + 10\,\Omega + 8\,\Omega$$
   $$= 24\,\Omega$$

   Then

   $$I_0 = \frac{V_0}{R_s}$$
   $$= \frac{60\text{ V}}{24\,\Omega}$$
   $$= 2.5\text{ A}$$

   Using Kirchhoff's Current Law,
   $$I_0 = I_1 = I_2 = I_3 = 2.5\text{ A}$$

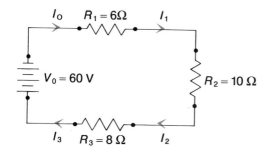

Then

$$V_1 = I_1 R_1 \qquad\qquad V_2 = I_2 R_2 \qquad\qquad V_3 = I_3 R_3$$
$$\quad = (2.5 \text{ A}) (6 \text{ }\Omega) \qquad\quad = (2.5 \text{ A}) (10 \text{ }\Omega) \qquad = (2.5 \text{ A}) (8 \text{ }\Omega)$$
$$\quad = 15 \text{ V} \qquad\qquad\quad = 25 \text{ V} \qquad\qquad = 20 \text{ V}$$

As a final check, we could apply Kirchhoff's Voltage Law to the circuit, so that

$$V_0 = V_1 + V_2 + V_3$$
$$= 15 \text{ V} + 25 \text{ V} + 20 \text{ V}$$
$$= 60 \text{ V}$$

which is, in fact, the value we were given for V_0.

2. Find: V_0, V_1, V_2, V_3
$$I_0$$
$$R_1, R_2$$

Using Kirchhoff's Current Law,

$$I_0 = I_1 + I_2 + I_3$$
$$= 2 \text{ A} + 4 \text{ A} + 6 \text{ A}$$
$$= 12 \text{ A}$$

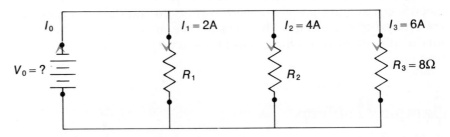

Applying Ohm's Law to R_3,

$$V_3 = I_3 R_3$$
$$= (6 \text{ A}) (8 \text{ }\Omega)$$
$$= 48 \text{ V}$$

But, using Kirchhoff's Voltage Law around each of the three branches in the circuit,

$$V_0 = V_1 = V_2 = V_3 = 48 \text{ V}$$

Then, using Ohm's Law once again,

$$R_2 = \frac{V_2}{I_2} \qquad\qquad R_1 = \frac{V_1}{I_1}$$
$$= \frac{48 \text{ V}}{4 \text{ A}} \qquad\qquad = \frac{48 \text{ V}}{2 \text{ A}}$$
$$= 12 \text{ }\Omega \qquad\qquad = 24 \text{ }\Omega$$

As a final check, we may calculate the equivalent resistance in the circuit, R_p, using

$$\frac{1}{R_p} = \frac{1}{R_1} + \frac{1}{R_2} + \frac{1}{R_3}$$

$$R_p = \frac{1}{\dfrac{1}{R_1} + \dfrac{1}{R_2} + \dfrac{1}{R_3}}$$

$$= \frac{1}{\dfrac{1}{24\ \Omega} + \dfrac{1}{12\ \Omega} + \dfrac{1}{8\ \Omega}}$$

$$= 4\ \Omega$$

and

$$I_0 = \frac{V_0}{R_p}$$

$$= \frac{48\ V}{4\ \Omega}$$

$$= 12\ A$$

3. Find: V_1, V_2, V_3
   I_1, I_2, I_3
   R_2

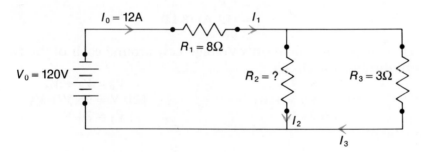

Using Kirchhoff's Current Law,

$$I_0 = I_1 = 12\ A$$

Applying Ohm's Law to the entire circuit

$$R_t = \frac{V_0}{I_0}$$

$$= \frac{120\ V}{12\ A}$$

$$= 10\ \Omega$$

If the parallel pair of resistors R_2 and R_3 are, for the moment, thought of as one single resistor, R_p, then R_1 and R_p are connected in series, and their total resistance is given by

$$R_t = R_1 + R_p$$
$$10\ \Omega = 8\ \Omega + R_p$$
$$R_p = 2\ \Omega$$

Then, using the relationship for the equivalent resistance in parallel,

$$\frac{1}{R_p} = \frac{1}{R_2} + \frac{1}{R_3}$$

$$\frac{1}{R_2} = \frac{1}{R_p} - \frac{1}{R_3}$$

$$R_2 = \cfrac{1}{\cfrac{1}{R_p} - \cfrac{1}{R_3}}$$

$$= \cfrac{1}{\cfrac{1}{2\ \Omega} - \cfrac{1}{3\ \Omega}}$$

$$= 6\ \Omega$$

Using Ohm's Law,

$$V_1 = I_1 R_1$$
$$= (12\ \text{A})\ (8\ \Omega)$$
$$= 96\ \text{V}$$

Then, applying Kirchhoff's Voltage Law around each of the two paths through the circuit,

$$V_0 = V_1 + V_2 \qquad\qquad\qquad V_0 = V_1 + V_3$$
$$120\ \text{V} = 96\ \text{V} + V_2 \qquad\qquad 120\ \text{V} = 96\ \text{V} + V_3$$
$$\therefore V_2 = 24\ \text{V} \qquad\qquad\qquad \therefore V_3 = 24\ \text{V}$$

and, finally,

$$I_2 = \frac{V_2}{R_2} \qquad\qquad\qquad I_3 = \frac{V_3}{R_3}$$

$$= \frac{24\ \text{V}}{6\ \Omega} \qquad\qquad\qquad = \frac{24\ \text{V}}{3\ \Omega}$$

$$= 4\ \text{A} \qquad\qquad\qquad = 8\ \text{A}$$

As a check, $I_0 = I_2 + I_3 = 4\ \text{A} + 8\ \text{A} = 12\ \text{A}$, as given.

Practice

1. In this circuit, find V_1, V_2, I_0, I_1, and R_2.

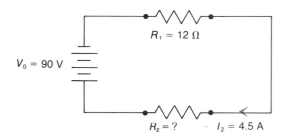

$R_1 = 12\ \Omega$

$V_0 = 90\ V$

$R_2 = ?$ $I_2 = 4.5\ A$

2. In this circuit, find V_0, V_1, I_2, R_1, and R_2.

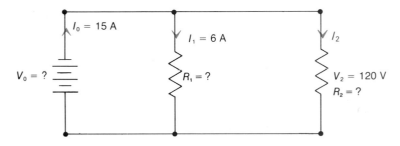

$I_0 = 15\ A$

$I_1 = 6\ A$

I_2

$V_0 = ?$

$R_1 = ?$

$V_2 = 120\ V$
$R_2 = ?$

3. In this circuit, find V_1, V_3, I_1, I_2, I_3, and R_3.

$R_3 = ?$

$V_0 = 120\ V$

$V_2 = 45\ V$
$R_2 = 30\ \Omega$

$R_1 = 10\ \Omega$

4. In this circuit, find V_0, V_1, V_2, V_3, I_0, I_1, and I_2.

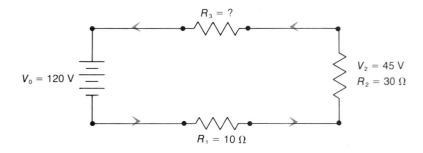

$V_0 = ?$ $R_1 = 60\ \Omega$ $R_2 = 60\ \Omega$ $R_3 = 30\ \Omega$

$I_3 = 6\ A$

5. In this circuit, find V_1, V_2, V_3, I_0, I_1, I_2, and I_3.

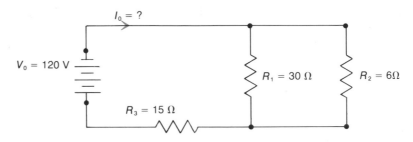

20.6 Power in Electric Circuits

When electrons move through a circuit, they dissipate the energy they receive from the source in the various loads they encounter. In Section 19.2, a formula for the amount of energy lost was developed: when there is a current, I, through a potential difference, V, for a time, t, the energy dissipated is given by

$$E = VIt$$

It is often more useful to know the rate at which a load uses energy. This quantity was defined in Section 7.2 in connection with mechanics, and it was called **power**. Power is the rate at which energy is used or supplied.

$$P = \frac{E}{t}$$

Substituting the expression above for electrical energy, we get

$$P = \frac{E}{t}$$
$$= \frac{VIt}{t}$$
$$= VI$$

as an expression for the electric power dissipated by a current, I, through a potential difference, V.

Note that potential difference is measured in volts (joules per coulomb) and current is measured in amperes (coulombs per second), and the unit of electric power is the product of the units of potential difference and current, namely,

$$\text{(volt) (ampere)} = \left(\frac{\text{joule}}{\text{coulomb}}\right) \left(\frac{\text{coulomb}}{\text{second}}\right)$$
$$= \frac{\text{joule}}{\text{second}}$$
$$= \textbf{watt}$$

So electric power is measured in watts—the same unit that was used to measure mechanical power.

If the load has a resistance, R, then its power may also be expressed, using Ohm's Law, as

$$P = VI$$

But, from Ohm's Law, $\quad I = \dfrac{V}{R}$ and $V = IR$

so we can write

$$P = VI$$
$$= (IR)I$$
$$= I^2R$$

as well as

$$P = VI$$
$$= V\left(\dfrac{V}{R}\right)$$
$$= \dfrac{V^2}{R}$$

Thus, to summarize, for a load with a current, I, potential difference, V, and resistance, R, the power is given by

$$\boldsymbol{P = VI}$$
$$\boldsymbol{P = I^2R}$$
$$\boldsymbol{P = \dfrac{V^2}{R}}$$

and, when proper units are used for I, V, and R, power will always be measured in watts.

The **power rating** of all electrical appliances is required by law to be indicated on a specification plate on the appliance, and some common values are shown in the table.

Sample Problems

1. What is the current drawn by a 100 W light bulb operating at a potential difference of 120 V?

$$P = IV$$
$$\therefore I = \dfrac{P}{V}$$
$$= \dfrac{100\ \text{W}}{120\ \text{V}}$$
$$= 0.830\ \text{A}$$

Appliance	Power rating	Current (with 120 V supply)
iron	1200 W	10 A
stove	6 to 10 kW	*
refrigerator	200 W	1.7 A
toaster	1000 W	8.3 A
microwave oven	600 W	5.0 A
vacuum cleaner	500 W	4.2 A

*Stoves operate at 240 V and draw currents in the range of 25 A to 40 A.

These power ratings refer to the electrical power used by the appliances, and not their power output which, due to their relative efficiencies, may be considerably lower.

2. What is the resistance of a 600 W microwave oven that draws a current of 5.0 A?

$$P = I^2 R$$

$$\therefore R = \frac{P}{I^2}$$

$$= \frac{600 \text{ W}}{(5.0 \text{ A})^2}$$

$$= 24 \ \Omega$$

3. What power is dissipated by an electric frying pan that has a resistance of 12 Ω and operates at a potential difference of 120 V?

$$P = \frac{V^2}{R}$$

$$= \frac{(120 \text{ V})^2}{12 \ \Omega}$$

$$= 1.2 \times 10^3 \text{ W, or } 1.2 \text{ kW}$$

*P*ractice

1. What is the potential difference across a 1250 W baseboard heater that draws 5.2 A?
2. If a 700 W toaster and an 1100 W iron are plugged into the same 120 V outlet in parallel, what total current will they draw?
3. What is the maximum power that may be used in a circuit with a potential difference of 120 V and a 20 A fuse?
4. A portable heater is plugged into a 120 V outlet and draws a current of 8.0 A for 10 min. Calculate each of the following.
   (a) the quantity of electric charge that flows through the heater
   (b) the energy consumed by the heater
   (c) the power dissipated by the heater

The Cost of Electricity

Electric appliances get their ability to do work by using energy supplied by your local electric power system, which bases its charges on the amount of electrical energy used in a given billing period.

The basic unit of energy, the joule, is a very small unit, and, for this reason, the electrical energy consumed is measured by means of a larger unit derived from the joule.

Energy used may be written as

$$E = Pt$$

Then, if power is measured in kilowatts (kW) and time is measured in hours (h), electrical energy may be measured in **kilowatt hours** (kW · h).

---

1 kW · h is the energy dissipated in 1 h by a load with a power of 1 kW.

It is often useful to calculate the relationship between the joule and the kilowatt hour, using the equation

$$E = Pt$$
$$= (1 \text{ kW}) (1 \text{ h})$$
$$= 1 \text{ kW} \cdot \text{h}$$
$$\text{or} = (1000 \text{ J/s}) (3600 \text{ s})$$
$$= 3.6 \times 10^6 \text{ J}$$

---

1 kW · h = 3.6 × 10⁶ J = 3.6 MJ

The power dissipated by each of several appliances operating simultaneously may be added to get an expression for the total power being used. When this power is multiplied by the time for which it is used, an expression for the total energy is arrived at. The utility company installs a meter on each house to make this measurement and to keep track of the amount of electrical energy used by the house. Then, by multiplying the number of kilowatt hours of energy used by the rate (price per kilowatt hour), the total cost of the electricity is calculated.

The rate charged for electric energy varies across the country. In some areas, the rate decreases as the amount of energy used increases. Some power companies charge a monthly fee and then a fixed rate per kilowatt hour. Others charge a different rate in the summer than in the winter. Utilities that depend on fossil fuels for generating electricity sometimes add a fuel charge that varies with the price of fossil fuels.

A meter reader servicing a domestic electrical meter

Some people think that the power companies encourage excessive use of energy by their rate structure: They feel that you would be more careful about using energy if the rate got higher the more you used.

Sample Problems

1. Calculate the cost of operating a 400 W spotlight for 2.0 h a day for 30 d at a rate of 8.0¢/kW · h.

$$E = Pt$$
$$= (0.400 \text{ kW}) (60 \text{ h})$$
$$= 24 \text{ kW} \cdot \text{h}$$
$$\text{Cost} = (24 \text{ kW} \cdot \text{h}) (8.0¢/\text{kW} \cdot \text{h})$$
$$= \$1.92$$

2. Find the cost of operating an oven for 3.0 h if it draws 15 A from a 240 V supply, at a rate of 10.0¢/kW · h.

$$P = IV$$
$$= (15 \text{ A}) (240 \text{ V})$$
$$= 3600 \text{ W}, \quad \text{or} \quad 3.6 \text{ kW}$$
$$E = Pt$$
$$= (3.6 \text{ kW}) (3.0 \text{ h})$$
$$= 10.8 \text{ kW} \cdot \text{h}$$
$$\text{Cost} = (10.8 \text{ kW} \cdot \text{h}) (10.0¢/\text{kW} \cdot \text{h})$$
$$= \$1.08$$

Practice

1. Find the cost of operating an electric toaster for 3.0 h if it draws 5.0 A from a 120 V outlet. Electric energy costs 7.7¢/kW · h.

2. What is the cost to a storekeeper of leaving a 40 W light burning near his safe over the weekend, for 60 h, if electricity costs 8.0¢/kW · h?

3. The blower motor on an oil furnace, rated at 250 W, comes on, for an average of 5.0 min at a time, a total of 48 times a day. What is the monthly (30 d) cost of operating the motor, if electricity costs 9.0¢/kW · h?

4. The following appliances were operated for a thirty day month, in a 120 V circuit: a coffee percolator of resistance 15 Ω for 0.50 h/d, a 250 W elecric drill for 2.0 h/d, and a toaster that draws 5.0 A for 15 min/d.
   Calculate the electric bill for the month at an average cost of 9.5¢/kW · h.

Electric Circuits in the Home

The distribution of electrical energy to the many devices and appliances in the typical home utilizes many of the concepts about electric circuits developed in this chapter.

Three wires lead into the home. One is called the **neutral conductor** and is maintained at the potential of the Earth since it is grounded, usually by being connected to the city plumbing system. The other two conductors are each maintained at an average potential difference of 120 V with respect to the neutral conductor. A voltmeter would measure a potential difference of 240 V between these two 120 V conductors.

The two ungrounded conductors pass through an electrical meter that is usually located outside the residence, where the total electrical energy supplied can be measured and recorded in kilowatt hours. From there, these two 120 V conductors pass through a main cut-off switch, and each is connected in series with a main fuse, or circuit breaker.

The three conductors are then connected to a distribution panel from which all of the branch circuits used in the home originate. A 120 V branch circuit is created by making connections to the neutral conductor and either of the 120 V conductors, through bus bars to which they are attached. A fuse or circuit breaker is connected in series with the ungrounded conductor in each branch circuit, to protect that circuit from drawing more current than its wires can safely conduct.

A typical distribution panel may

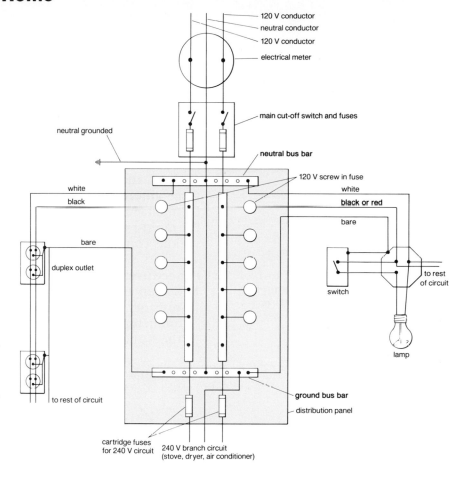

contain as many as twenty-four 120 V branch circuits. Each branch circuit contains outlets and light fixtures, connected in parallel, and switches connected in series with any of these devices to control them. The number of elements that may be safely connected in any branch circuit is determined by the gauge of wire used in the circuit, and is listed in the electrical code that applies to your municipality.

Special 240 V branch circuits may be created by connecting the

two 120 V conductors (thereby excluding the neutral). These higher voltage circuits are used for electric heating, clothes dryers, central air conditioning, and electric water heaters.

Even if you feel you understand how these electric circuits in your home operate, you should never attempt to make additions to, or repairs on an electric circuit without the assistance of a knowledgeable and licensed electrician.

Investigations

Investigation 20.1: Ohm's Law

Problem:

What is the relationship between the potential difference across a conductor and the electric current through it?

Materials:
rheostat and 6 V or 9 V battery
three different resistors (30 Ω to 100 Ω)
DC multi-range ammeter
DC multi-range voltmeter
various connecting wires

As a safety precaution, always "turn off" a circuit before making any changes or before connecting or disconnecting a meter.

Procedure:
1. Set up the circuit illustrated, using the largest of your three resistors. You will be told what range to use on the voltmeter and ammeter. Make sure the polarities of the meters are as shown by the + and − signs on the circuit diagrams.

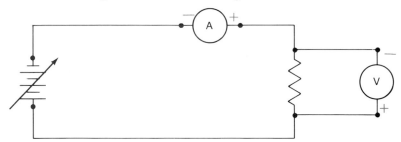

2. Adjust the power supply until the readings on both meters are the maximum ones. Record these readings and then turn the power supply down in five or six equal stages, each time recording the ammeter and voltmeter readings, until both meter readings reach zero.

Resistor	Potential difference (V)	Electric current (I)	$\dfrac{V}{I}$

3. Repeat the procedure for each of the other resistors, each time recording corresponding pairs of values for V and I. Record all the values in a table.

4. For each pair of values of V and I, calculate the ratio $\dfrac{V}{I}$ and record it in the table.

5. On one sheet of graph paper, plot graphs of V versus I for each resistor. Plot I on the horizontal axis, and label each graph.

Questions:

1. Notice that the ratio $\dfrac{V}{I}$ is constant for each resistor. By looking at your table, describe how the resistance of a resistor is determined.

2. Describe the shape of each graph of V versus I. What happens to the current through a resistor when the potential difference is increased? What mathematical relationship between V and I is represented by such a graph?

3. What is the only significant difference between the three graphs? Calculate the slope of each graph.

4. Compare the ratio $\dfrac{V}{I}$ to the slope of its graph for each resistor.

Investigation 20.2: Series Circuits

Problem:
What are the electric potential and electric current relationships in series circuits?

Materials:
6 V or 9 V battery
three different resistors (30 Ω to 100 Ω)
DC multi-range ammeter
DC multi-range voltmeter
various connecting wires

Procedure:
1. Set up the series circuit shown in the diagram. Points a to h are labelled for reference only and represent junction points in the circuit.

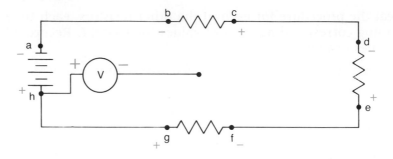

For example, if the voltmeter reading is 7.3 V at point d and 4.7 V at point e, then the potential difference across load de is (7.3 − 4.7) V, or 2.6 V.

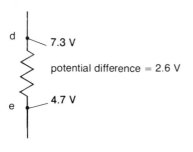

When this circuit is temporarily broken at point a, and an ammeter is inserted, the circuit should look like this:

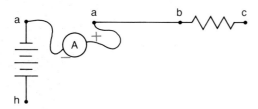

2. Connect the positive terminal of the voltmeter to point h, and then touch the negative terminal to each of the other labelled points in turn, noting and recording the reading of the voltmeter in each case. Calculate, by subtraction, the potential difference across the power source and across each load and conductor. Remove the voltmeter from the circuit.

Junction point	Electric potential	Conductor	Potential difference	Electric current
a		ab		
b		bc		
c		cd		
d		de		
e				
f				

3. Temporarily break the circuit at point a and insert an ammeter into the circuit at that point. Note and record the value of electric current past point a. Remove the ammeter, reconnect point a, and then repeat the procedure at each remaining point in the circuit, noting and recording the current in each case.

Questions:
1. How many different paths are there for an electron to take through the series circuit?
2. Calculate the sum of the decreases in electric potential along the path, and the sum of the electric potential increases. State the relationship between the two.
3. In a series circuit, how does the total current from the power source compare with the current through each individual resistance?

Investigation 20.3: Parallel Circuits

Problem:
What are the electric potential and electric current relationships in parallel circuits?

Materials:
6 V or 9 V battery
three different resistors (30 Ω to 100 Ω)
DC multi-range ammeter
DC multi-range voltmeter
various connecting wires

Procedure:
1. Set up the parallel circuit illustrated, using the same notation for junction points.

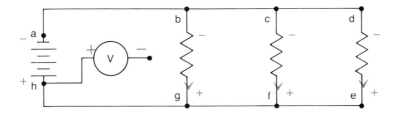

2. In the same way as before, by connecting the positive terminal of a voltmeter to point h, take readings of electric potential at each point, and then calculate by subtraction the potential difference across the source and across each load and conductor.

Junction point	Electric potential	Conductor	Potential difference	Electric current
a		ab		
b		bc		
c		cd		
d		de		
e				

3. By temporarily breaking the circuit at each point and inserting an ammeter, measure the current through each conductor in the circuit. Be sure when you break the circuit that you insert the ammeter into the conductor whose current you are trying to measure, and also that you reconnect the previous junction.

Questions:

1. How many different paths are there for an electron to take through the parallel circuit?
2. Calculate the sum of the electric currents in the three branches of the circuit, and compare with the current leaving the source. State the relationship between the two.
3. In a parallel circuit, how does the potential difference across each load compare with the potential difference across the power source?

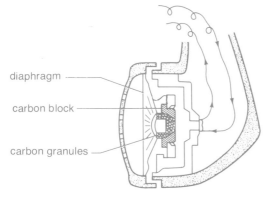

diaphragm

carbon block

carbon granules

The telephone mouthpiece (microphone), invented in 1876 and still in use today, utilizes a button of carbon granules with a potential difference across it as a detector of sound waves. Incoming sound waves hit the diaphragm, causing it to move in and compress the carbon granules. This has the effect of changing the electrical resistance of the carbon button, and the current flowing through it. This current is, then, an electrical copy of the sound-wave pattern hitting the diaphragm.

Chapter Summary

1. Loads and sources of electric potential are connected together in complete circuits by conductors. The network of conductors and circuit elements may be represented in a schematic diagram using standard symbols.
2. Circuit elements may be connected together in series (in which case all the electrons pass through each load in succession) or in parallel (in which case some of the electrons pass through one load and some through another).
3. In every electric circuit,
   (a) around any complete path, the total increase in electric potential and the total decrease in electric potential are equal.
   (b) at any junction point, the total electric current into the junction and the total electric current out of the junction are equal.
   These relationships are known as Kirchhoff's Laws.
4. Between any two points in a circuit containing resistances only, the ratio of potential difference to current is constant, and this constant is called the resistance. This relationship, known as Ohm's Law, may be represented as

$$\frac{V}{I} = R$$

where R, the resistance, is measured in volts per ampere, or ohms, and $1\ \Omega = 1$ V/A.

5. The resistance of a cylindrical conductor depends on its
   (a) length
   (b) cross-sectional area
   (c) temperature
   (d) molecular structure, or resistivity

6. The equivalent resistance of n resistances connected in series is given by
$$R_s = R_1 + R_2 + \ldots + R_n$$
and the equivalent resistance of n resistances connected in parallel is given by
$$\frac{1}{R_p} = \frac{1}{R_1} + \frac{1}{R_2} + \ldots + \frac{1}{R_n}$$

7. The power, or rate of energy dissipation, of an electrical device is given by
$$P = IV$$
$$P = I^2R$$
$$P = \frac{V^2}{R}$$
where P, the power, is measured in joules per second, or watts, and 1 W $= 1$ J/s.

8. Electrical energy may be measured as the product of power and time in units called kilowatt hours, and
$$1 \text{ kW} \cdot \text{h} = 3.6 \times 10^6 \text{ J}$$
The cost of electric energy may be calculated by multiplying the number of kilowatt hours consumed by the price per kilowatt hour.

*C*hapter *R*eview

Discussion

1. Describe the current and potential difference characteristics of a series circuit and of a parallel circuit.

2. Draw a schematic diagram of a circuit consisting of a power source and one resistor connected in series with a combination consisting of two resistors connected in parallel with each other. Include a fuse, a switch, a voltmeter, and an ammeter. The fuse should protect the whole circuit, the switch should

Almost everyone has experienced an electric shock and, fortunately, survived. The pain and danger of electric shock are due to electric currents that pass through parts of the body due to a potential difference applied to the body. Internal, moist flesh has a low electrical resistance. If the outer layers of skin are even slightly moist, they may also have a low resistance. In this case, current can penetrate to vital organs, and even low-voltage shocks can cause serious damage and may even be fatal. Every year, many people are killed by 120 V shocks when they are in a bathtub or swimming pool, or even standing in a puddle of water.

interrupt the whole circuit, the voltmeter should measure the potential difference across the series resistor, and the ammeter should measure the current through one of the parallel resistors.

3. Describe the effect on the rest of the circuit when one of three lamps in a circuit burns out, if the three lamps are connected (a) in series, and (b) in parallel. Explain your answers.

4. A battery is constructed by connecting several 1.5 V dry cells together. Draw the circuit symbol of such a battery, if it consists of (a) three cells connected in series, and (b) four cells connected in parallel. What is the potential difference of the battery in each case?

5. Draw a schematic diagram for a circuit that may be used to determine the resistance of an unknown resistor.

6. Describe what is meant by resistance and list four factors that affect the resistance of a conductor. Describe the effect of each factor on the resistance of a conductor.

7. When a car battery is "low", it cannot deliver sufficient current to the starting motor to cause it to turn over. A healthier battery from another vehicle is often used to "boost" or recharge the weak battery. Should this second battery be connected in series or parallel with the first one, and why? What terminals from each should be connected together?

8. What is the effect on the total resistance in a circuit, when an extra resistor is added (a) in series, and (b) in parallel?

9. State three equations for calculating the power dissipated in a resistor, and show that, when proper units are used in these equations, the unit that results for power is watts.

10. (a) What quantity is measured in kilowatt hours?
    (b) What values of electric potential are found in the home, and where are these different values used?

11. Draw a graph of potential difference versus current for two different resistances, and indicate which has the greater resistance, and why.

Problems

12. A voltmeter connected across the ends of a heating coil indicates a potential difference of 60 V when an ammeter shows a current through the coil of 3.0 A. What is the resistance of the coil?

13. A flashlight bulb has a resistance of 7.5 Ω and is connected to a dry cell with a potential difference of 3.0 V. What is the current through the bulb?

14. What is the potential difference across a motor with a resistance of 40 Ω if the motor draws a current of 6.0 A?

15. A string of eight Christmas tree lights connected in series to a 120 V source draws a current of 0.75 A. Find
    (a) the total resistance of the string of lights
    (b) the resistance of each light
    (c) the potential difference across each light

16. (a) What is the resistance of a toaster that draws a current of 6.0 A from a 120 V source?
    (b) What resistance would have to be added in series with the same toaster to reduce its current to 4.0 A?

17. Calculate the total resistance in each of these cases.
    (a) 10 Ω, 30 Ω, and 50 Ω in series
    (b) 6 Ω, 5 Ω, and 30 Ω in parallel
    (c) 9 Ω in series with a combination consisting of 4 Ω and 12 Ω connected in parallel with each other.

18. How many 160 Ω resistors must be connected in parallel to draw a current of 6.0 A from a 120 V source?

19. The potential difference across a heating coil is 6.0 V when the current through it is 3.0 A. What resistance must be added in series with the coil to reduce the current through it to 2.0 A?

20. A portable radio is designed to operate at a potential difference of 6.0 V and a current of 250 mA, but the only source available has a potential of 10.0 V. What resistance must be added in series with the radio to make it operate properly?

21. Examine these circuits and find the values indicated.
    (a) Find: R_2, R_3 and V_3

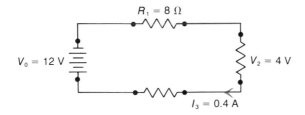

$R_1 = 8\ \Omega$

$V_0 = 12\ V$

$V_2 = 4\ V$

$I_3 = 0.4\ A$

    (b) Find: V_0, R_1, R_{total}

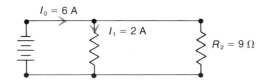

$I_0 = 6\ A$

$I_1 = 2\ A$

$R_2 = 9\ \Omega$

(c) Find: $R_3, I_1, I_2, I_4, I_5, I_6$

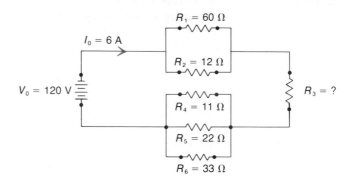

(d) Find: $I_1, R_1,$ and R_2

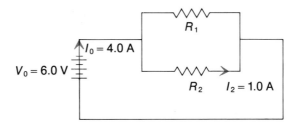

(e) Find: $I_0, I_1, I_2, I_3, I_4, V_1, V_2, V_3,$ and V_4

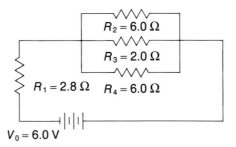

22. Calculate the electrical energy dissipated in 1.5 min when there is a current of 4.0 A through a potential difference of 60 V.

23. Calculate the power dissipated by each of the following loads.
    (a) a clothes dryer drawing 12.5 A from a 240 V source
    (b) a toaster that draws 12.0 A and has a resistance of 8.3 Ω
    (c) a 240 Ω heating pad plugged into a 120 V source

24. (a) What maximum power can be used on a 240 V circuit with a 15 A fuse?
    (b) How much more current can safely be drawn from a 120 V outlet fused at 20 A if an 800 W toaster and an 1180 W kettle are already operating in the circuit?
25. A 1.0 kW toaster, designed to operate at 120 V, is mistakenly connected to a source of 240 V.
    (a) What current is the toaster designed to draw?
    (b) What current will it draw when connected to 240 V?
    (c) What power will it use on 240 V, and what will be the likely result?
26. A refrigerator compressor draws 2.5 A from a 120 V source and operates for an average of 15 min out of each hour. Calculate the annual cost of operating the refrigerator if the average cost of electrical energy is 8.5¢/kW · h.
27. A battery charger draws 50 mA from a 120 V source while charging four batteries. If it takes 12 h to recharge the batteries, and the cost of the electrical energy is 8.0¢/kW · h, what is the cost of recharging the batteries?

Numerical Answers to
Practice Problems

page 592
1. 50 V
2. 7 A
3. 3 V, 9 V, 1 A, 4 A
4. 20 V, 16 V, 16 V, 6 A, 1 A

page 595
1. $3.6 \times 10^2 \ \Omega$
2. 25 A
3. 8.0×10^3 V
4. 10 A
5. 5.1×10^2 V
6. 10 A

page 599
1. (a) 79 Ω
   (b) 130 Ω
   (c) 68 Ω
2. (a) 26 Ω
   (b) 18 Ω
   (c) 2.5 Ω

page 600
1. (a) 5.3 Ω
   (b) 2.9 Ω
2. 30 Ω, 20 Ω, 15 Ω, 12 Ω, $\dfrac{R}{n}$

page 605
1. 54 V, 36 V, 4.5 A, 4.5 A, 8.0 Ω
2. 120 V, 120 V, 9 A, 20 Ω, 13.3 Ω
3. 15 V, 60 V, 1.5 A, 1.5 A, 1.5 A, 40 Ω
4. 180 V, 180 V, 180 V, 180 V, 3 A, 3 A, 12 A
5. 30 V, 30 V, 90 V, 6 A, 1 A, 5 A, 6 A

page 608
1. 2.4×10^2 V
2. 15.0 A
3. 2.4 kW
4. (a) 4.8×10^3 C
   (b) 5.8×10^5 J
   (c) 9.6×10^2 W

page 610
1. 14¢
2. 19¢
3. $2.70
4. $3.22

Magnetism

Chapter Objectives

☐ **State** *the Law of Magnetic Poles.*

☐ **Explain** *characteristics of a magnetic force field and* **draw** *simple magnetic fields.*

☐ **Describe** *Earth's magnetic field and* **define** *"north-seeking pole", "magnetic declination", and "magnetic inclination".*

☐ **List** *three ferromagnetic substances and* **state** *the conditions under which they may be induced to become magnetized.*

☐ **Describe** *the domain theory of magnetism and* **define** *"magnetic dipole", "magnetic domain", "alignment of domains", and "random orientation of domains".*

☐ **Explain** *demagnetization, magnetic induction, reverse magnetization, breaking a bar magnet, and magnetic saturation.*

21.1 Magnetism and Magnetic Forces

The iron oxide that makes up lodestone is also known as magnetite (Fe_2O_3).

Lodestone, showing magnetic attraction of iron nails

Even before 600 B.C., the Greeks had discovered that a certain type of iron ore, which later came to be known as lodestone, or magnetite, was capable of exerting forces of attraction on other small pieces of iron. Also, when pivoted and allowed to rotate freely, a piece of lodestone would come to rest in a north-south position. Because it had this property, lodestone was used widely in navigation. Chemically, lodestone consists mainly of iron oxide, a mineral that was first found near a place called Magnesia, in Greece. Hence the term **magnetism.**

Nowadays, lodestone is hardly ever used for its magnetic property. Artificial magnets are made from various alloys of iron, nickel, and cobalt, by a procedure that will be explained in Section 21.4.

When a magnet is dipped in iron filings, the filings are attracted to the magnet, and concentrations of them accumulate most noticeably at the opposite ends of the magnet. We call these areas of concentrated magnetic force **poles.** When a magnet is allowed to rotate freely, one of the poles tends to "seek" the northerly direction and it is called the **north-seeking pole** or more simply the **N-pole.** The other pole, which points in a southerly direction, is called the **south-seeking pole,** or the **S-pole.**

When the N-pole of one magnet is brought near the N-pole of another freely swinging magnet, a force of repulsion is observed. Similarly, two S-poles repel each other. On the other hand, N-poles and S-poles always attract each other. These observations lead to what is called the Law of Magnetic Poles:

Opposite magnetic poles attract. Similar magnetic poles repel.

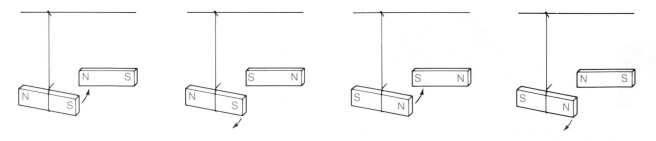

21.2 Magnetic Fields

When an N-pole and an S-pole are brought close to each other, they begin to attract even before they touch. This "action-at-a-distance" type of force is already familiar, from your examination of the gravitational force (Chapter 5) and the electric force (Chapter 18). The effect of those forces was described in terms of a "field of force" in the surrounding space. Similarly, we will consider the space around a magnet in which magnetic forces are exerted as a **magnetic field of force**.

To detect the presence of such a magnetic field, we need a delicate instrument that is affected by magnetic forces. Small filings of iron respond to magnetic forces, but their poles are not marked and so we cannot determine which way they are pointing. A more complete observation of the magnetic force at a given point in a magnetic field can be made by means of a small test compass with clearly marked poles.

A magnetic field may be represented by a series of lines around a magnet, representing the path the N-pole of a small test compass would take if it were allowed to move freely in the direction of the magnetic force. Then, at any point in the field, a magnetic field line indicates the direction in which the N-pole of the test compass would point. The photographs on the next page show the magnetic fields in the vicinity of a single bar magnet, and pairs of bar magnets close together.

When we talk about the poles of magnets, we usually leave out the word "seeking." The pole of a magnet marked "N" is the north-seeking pole—the pole that would point to the north pole of the Earth if allowed to swing freely. So, we should not think that the N-pole of a compass pointing towards the north pole of the Earth contradicts the law of magnetic attraction of unlike poles. The magnetic pole at the north end of our planet is really a south-seeking pole.

A single, isolated magnetic pole can never be produced, but it is often useful to imagine one.

A magnetically propelled monorail transit system

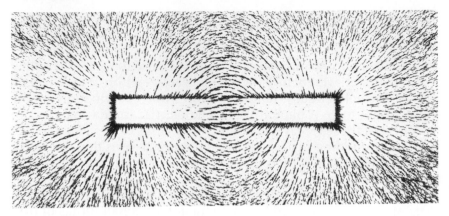

The magnetic field of a bar magnet

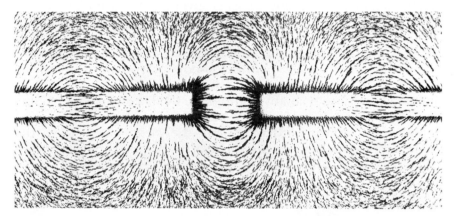

The magnetic field of a pair of opposite poles, close together

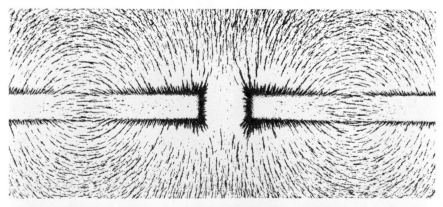

The magnetic field of a pair of similar poles, close together

21.3 Magnetic Field of the Earth

A small compass in the presence of a magnetic field will rotate until its N-pole points in the direction of the field. The early navigators used this discovery to find the direction of north. But what magnetic field was their compass reacting to? In the 16th century, William Gilbert (1540-1603), a distinguished physicist who was also physician to Queen Elizabeth I, stated that the Earth itself had a magnetic field and behaved as if it had a large bar magnet in its interior, inclined at a slight angle to its axis. The diagrams show the Earth, its magnetic field, and the bar magnet that was at one time believed to be responsible for this field.

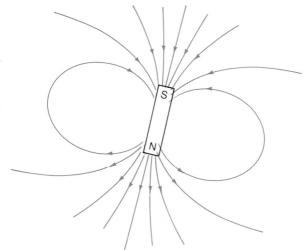

The magnetic field of an inclined bar magnet

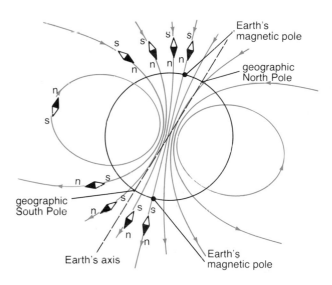

Magnetic Declination

A magnetic compass points towards the Earth's magnetic north pole, rather than towards its geographic north pole (that is, the northern end of the Earth's axis). The angle between the geographic north, or true north, and magnetic north varies from position to position on the Earth's surface and is called the **magnetic declination.** A navigator using a magnetic compass must know the angle of declination of her location before she can find the true north.

Apart from slight movements of the magnetic poles and a small decrease in field strength, the Earth's magnetic field has remained

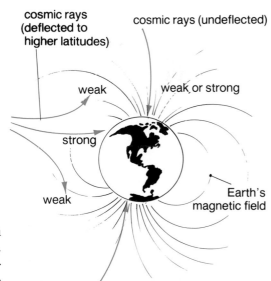

The Earth's magnetic field protects us by deflecting potentially harmful cosmic radiation from outer space. The weaker cosmic rays are shunted completely to one side, whereas the stronger ones are deflected to higher latitudes.

quite constant during the seven centuries since the magnetic compass came into use. But the magnetic field is slowly changing. On the map below, the solid lines connect places that have equal magnetic declination. The dashed lines connect places where the declination is changing at equal rates. Scientists have hypothesized that these changes occur because the Earth's magnetic field is slowly rotating about the Earth's axis, taking about 1000 years to make one rotation.

Geophysicists have investigated long-term changes in the Earth's magnetic field by studying the orientation of magnetic minerals in solidified volcanic rock. These crystallized minerals aligned themselves with the magnetic field of the Earth at the time of their solidification, and this can be determined precisely by using the ra-

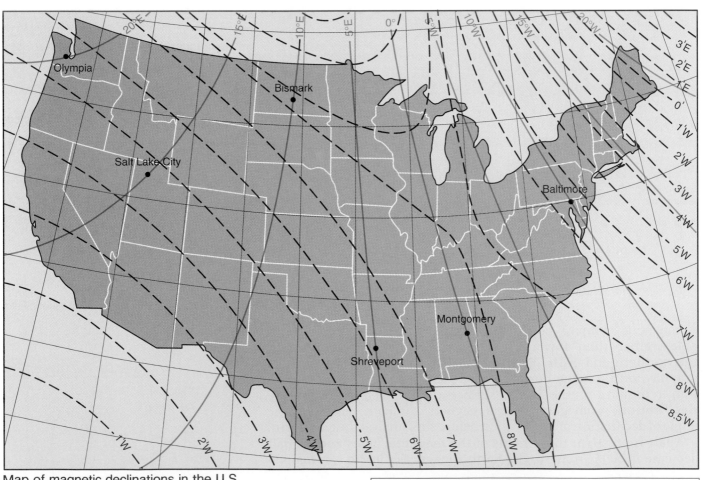

Map of magnetic declinations in the U.S.

——— Lines of equal magnetic declinations, in degrees.
- - - - Lines of equal annual change in magnetic declination, in minutes of arc per year.

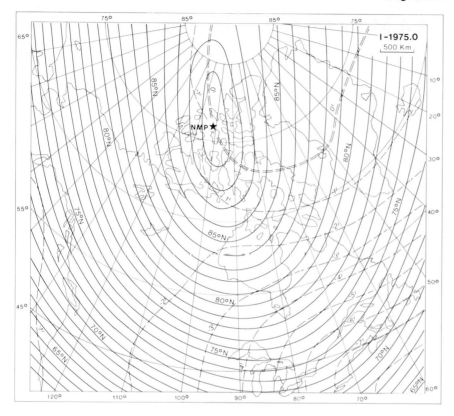

Magnetic inclinations near the North
Magnetic Pole

dioactive dating techniques described in Chapter 26. From these
data, geophysicists have determined that the Earth's magnetic field
has reversed polarity many times in the past.

Magnetic Inclination, or Dip

The magnetic field of the Earth is not just horizontal; it has a vertical
component as well. A magnetic compass gives only the direction of
its horizontal component. Also, the direction of the Earth's magnetic field lines varies over the Earth's surface.

The angle between the direction of the magnetic field at a given
position and a horizontal line is called the **magnetic inclination** or
"dip", and it may be measured with a dipping needle, which is a
magnetized compass needle pivoted about a horizontal axis exactly
at its center of gravity. If there were no magnetic field it would
remain in its original position. However, when aligned with a
magnetic compass pointing north, the N-pole of the dip needle will
point down towards the Earth (in the northern hemisphere), and the
angle of dip may be measured on the protractor provided.

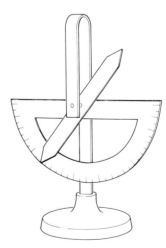

Magnetic dipping-needle

In sketches of magnetic fields, $\otimes$ represents a magnetic field line pointing into the page and $\odot$ represents a magnetic field line pointing out of the page.

21.4 Magnetic Materials: Induced Magnetism

Small pieces of iron stroked in one direction with lodestone become magnetized. Even bringing a piece of iron near a magnet causes it to be magnetized. Nickel and cobalt, and any alloy containing nickel, cobalt, or iron, behave in the same way. These substances are called **ferromagnetic,** and you can induce them to become magnetized by placing them in a magnetic field.

Atomic dipoles are lined up inside domains but domains are pointing in random directions.

Magnetic material in an unmagnetized state

Domain Theory of Magnetism

The atoms of ferromagnetic substances may be thought of as tiny magnets with an N-pole and an S-pole. These atomic magnets, or **dipoles,** interact with their nearest neighboring dipoles and a group of them line up with their magnetic axes in the same direction to form a **magnetic domain.** In an unmagnetized piece of iron there are millions of these domains, but they are pointing in random directions so that the piece of iron, as a whole, is not magnetized. The top diagram represents this unmagnetized condition. (The actual boundaries between magnetic domains are very irregular in shape and the domains are of varying size. These diagrams are greatly simplified for easier presentation.)

When a piece of unmagnetized iron is placed in a magnetic field (that is, near another magnet), the dipoles act like small compasses and rotate until they are aligned with the field. The piece of iron will then consist of a large number of dipoles pointing north and one end will become an N-pole, while the other end will become an S-pole. The next diagram shows the same piece of iron in the magnetized condition.

Atomic dipoles (not domains) turn so that all domains point in the direction of the magnetizing field.

Magnetic material in a fully magnetized state

Effects of the Domain Theory

(a) Magnetic Induction

A permanent magnet brought near an iron nail will cause the iron nail to temporarily become a magnet. The field of the permanent magnet causes the dipoles in the iron nail to align, momentarily. If a steel needle is stroked continuously in one direction with a permanent magnet, its dipoles will align and, due to the carbon atoms in the steel, will stay aligned for some time, making the needle act like a permanent magnet.

(b) Demagnetization

When a piece of iron becomes demagnetized, its aligned dipoles return to random directions. Dropping or heating an induced magnet will cause this to occur. Some materials, such as pure iron, revert to random alignment as soon as they are removed from the magnetizing field. Substances that become demagnetized spontaneously and instantly are called **soft ferromagnetic** materials. Iron may be alloyed with certain materials, such as aluminum and silicon, that have the effect of keeping the dipoles aligned even when the magnetizing field is removed. These alloys are used to make permanent magnets and are referred to as **hard ferromagnetic** materials.

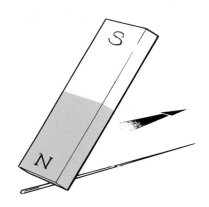

(c) Reverse Magnetization

The bar magnets used in classrooms are made of hard ferromagnetic alloys, and they remain magnetized for a long time. The letter N is stamped on that end of the magnet to which all the N-poles of the aligned domains point. If a bar magnet is placed in a strong enough magnetic field of opposite polarity, its domains can turn and point in the opposite direction. In that case, the N-pole of the magnet is at the end marked S. The magnet is reverse-magnetized.

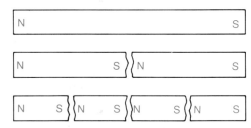

Effect of breaking a bar magnet

(d) Breaking a Bar Magnet

Breaking a bar magnet produces two pieces of iron whose dipole alignment is identical to the original piece. Both pieces will also be magnets, with N-poles and S-poles at opposite ends. Continued breaking will produce the same results, since the domains within the magnet remain aligned even when the magnet is broken.

(e) Magnetic Saturation

In most magnets, a large number of the dipoles are aligned in the same direction, but not all.

The strength of a bar magnet may be increased only up to a certain level. The peak will occur when as many as possible of its dipoles are aligned. The material is then said to have reached its **magnetic saturation**.

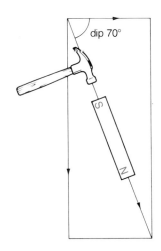

Magnetism by Earth induction

(f) Induced Magnetism by the Earth

If a piece of iron is held in the Earth's magnetic field and its atoms are agitated, either by heating or by mechanical vibration (that is, by hitting the iron with a hammer), alignment of its dipoles will result. This is most easily accomplished by holding the piece of iron

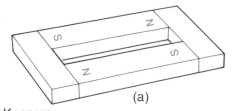

Keepers
(a) on bar magnets

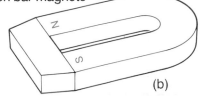

(b) on a horseshoe magnet

pointing north and at the local angle of inclination, while tapping it with a hammer.

Steel columns and beams used in building construction are invariably found to be magnetized. Steel hulls of ships and railroad tracks are also magnetized by the Earth's magnetic field.

(g) Keepers for Bar Magnets

In time, a bar magnet will become demagnetized as the poles at its ends begin to reverse the polarity of the atomic dipoles inside it. If bar magnets are stored in pairs with their opposite poles adjacent and with small pieces of soft iron (called "keepers") across the ends, demagnetization does not occur. The keepers themselves become strong induced magnets and form closed loops of magnetic dipoles, thus preventing demagnetizing poles from forming.

Investigation

Investigation 21.1 : Magnetic Fields

Problem:
What is the nature of the magnetic field in the region around a bar magnet, and in the region of a pair of bar magnets close together?

Materials:
two bar magnets
small plotting compass
iron filings
large sheets of blank paper

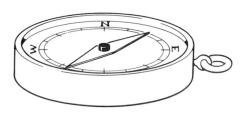

Plotting compass

Procedure:
1. First, check the compass and bar magnets to ensure that their polarity is correctly marked. (It is possible, as you have seen in Section 21.4, to reverse-magnetize a magnet.) Place the compass several meters away from any other magnets or metallic substances, and allow it to swing freely. If the compass has been correctly magnetized, one of its poles should point north when it comes to rest. Then, this N-pole should point towards the S-pole of each of the bar magnets when brought close to them. Make sure that the compass and the bar magnets are correctly magnetized before proceeding.
2. Place one of the bar magnets on a table at the center of a large sheet of paper, mark its outline with a pencil, and label the poles

on the outline. Make a small dot on the paper close to the S-pole of the magnet, and place the plotting compass on the paper so that it points directly towards this dot. Now, make a second dot exactly at the opposite end of the compass needle. Move the compass until the needle points directly towards the second dot, and make a third dot at the opposite end of the needle. Continue the procedure until the resulting line of dots either makes its way back to the magnet or runs off the edge of the sheet. Join the dots with a smooth line, and put arrows on the line pointing in the direction of the N-pole of the compass.

3. Repeat the same procedure, using other starting points near the S-pole of the magnet. Try to cover your paper with field lines.

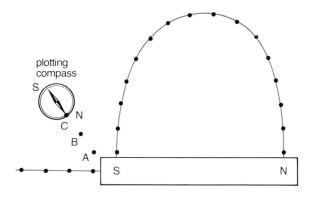

4. To get a more detailed impression of the magnetic field of a bar magnet, place the magnet *under* the same piece of paper, exactly where you drew the outline. Sprinkle iron filings gently over the entire surface of the paper, tap the paper several times, and note the relationship between the pattern of iron filings and the field lines you drew with the plotting compass. Draw a detailed sketch of the magnetic field thus revealed.

5. Under a fresh sheet of paper, place the two bar magnets in a straight line, with their opposite poles about 5 cm apart. After outlining the position of the poles on the sheet with a pencil, sprinkle iron filings on the paper and tap it gently. Draw a sketch of the magnetic field that is indicated by the position of the filings, using your compass to determine the direction of the magnetic field lines.

6. Repeat the same procedure, using two like poles, and sketch the magnetic field.

Questions:

1. From what area of the magnets do field lines seem to originate? To what region do they seem to return? Which field lines, if any,

leave the magnets but seem not to return? Why?

2. Do magnetic field lines ever cross each other? Could there be any magnetic lines of force in the regions of space between the field lines you have drawn? Check to see.

3. What do you notice about the spacing of the field lines as you move away from the poles? What does this spacing indicate about the strength of the magnetic field?

4. There is a theory of magnetism that states that every magnetic field line is a closed curve; but the field lines we have drawn seem to start at the N-pole and return at the S-pole. For the magnetic field you have plotted for the bar magnet, choose several field lines and sketch the portion of each line as you believe it would exist within the magnet.

Chapter Summary

1. Certain materials such as lodestone are capable of exerting magnetic forces and are called magnets. The forces are concentrated at opposite ends of a magnet, in areas called poles.

2. There are two characteristic poles of magnetic force, called north-seeking and south-seeking. The fundamental law of magnetic poles states:

Similar poles repel.

Opposite poles attract.

3. The region of magnetic force around a magnet is called a magnetic field and is represented by magnetic field lines that show the direction of the force on the N-pole of a small test compass at each point in the field.

4. The Earth has a magnetic field similar to that of a bar magnet, with its S-pole located near the geographic north pole of the Earth. Compasses point to this pole, called the magnetic north pole, and the angle between the magnetic north pole and the geographic north pole at any point on the Earth is called the magnetic declination.

5. The Earth's magnetic field has two components, the vertical and the horizontal, and the angle between the direction of the Earth's magnetic field (which varies) and a horizontal line pointing north is called the magnetic inclination, or dip.

6. Substances containing iron, nickel, or cobalt may be induced to become magnets by being placed in a magnetic field. They are called ferromagnetic materials.

The most up-to-date theory suggests that the Earth's magnetic field is due to the presence of swirling currents of molten magnetic iron in its interior. As this lava flows, the position of the north and south magnetic poles shifts, and the declination of any given point on the Earth's surface changes.

7. Induced magnetism may be explained by means of the theory of domains. Ferromagnetic materials are composed of a large number of tiny magnetic dipoles. Groups of aligned dipoles form magnetic domains that are normally oriented at random. In the presence of a magnetic field, the dipoles turn so that most domains are aligned to form a magnet.
8. The domain theory may be used to explain:
   (a) magnetic induction
   (b) demagnetization of a temporary magnet
   (c) reverse magnetization of a bar magnet
   (d) the breaking of a bar magnet into a large number of smaller magnets
   (e) magnetic saturation
   (f) magnetism induced by the Earth
   (g) keepers for bar magnets

Chapter Review

Discussion

1. What name is given to materials that are strongly attracted by a magnet? Name two such materials, other than iron and steel.
2. Describe how a screwdriver could be magnetized. What might happen if the screwdriver were heated or dropped? Explain your answer.

A magnetic compass

3. What name is given to the region in which a magnet influences other magnetic materials? How far does this region extend?
4. Describe two ways in which you could detect the presence of a magnetic field. Does any magnetic field exist in the spaces between the lines of iron filings around a magnet? Explain your answer.
5. Is the magnetic pole area in the northern hemisphere an N-pole or an S-pole? Explain.
6. Vertical retort-stand rods in laboratory classrooms are often found to be magnetized, and the polarity of such rods in the U.S. is opposite to the polarity of those in Australia. Explain this statement.
7. Given two apparently identical bars of steel, one a permanent magnet and the other unmagnetized, and without the help of any other equipment, describe a method for determining which bar is the magnet.
8. Describe what would happen to a magnetic compass and to a dipping needle if each were placed (a) at the magnetic north pole, and (b) at the equator.
9. Using the domain theory, explain the difference between soft iron and steel, and indicate which you would select for use as (a) a compass needle, and (b) keepers for a pair of bar magnets.

The Northern Lights

One of the most dramatic consequences of the Earth's magnetic field is the aurora borealis, or the Northern Lights (called the aurora australis, or the Southern Lights in the southern hemisphere.) The aurora is a vibrant curtain of light that enhances the sky on a circle about 15° from each magnetic pole. The lower edge of the aurora is usually at an altitude of about 100 km and aurorae are, generally, between 40 km and 100 km high. The upper edge of some aurorae have even been observed at altitudes of 800 km, evidence that significant accumulations of atmospheric gases exist at that altitude. Faint aurorae may appear white, but bright ones are most commonly yellow-green, with traces of red, blue, and violet.

Aurorae are caused by the solar wind, a stream of high-energy charged particles from the sun. Sometimes aurorae are visible from the middle latitudes, usually after solar magnetic storms, which increase the energy of the particles in the solar wind. When the solar wind encounters the Earth, most of the particles are deflected by the Earth's magnetic field. Near the poles, the particles enter the atmosphere undeflected because they come in parallel to the magnetic field lines. These high-energy particles collide with gas molecules in the atmosphere, raising the gas molecules to higher energy levels (see Section 25.5). The molecules then emit light as their energy level drops. By analyzing the spectra of light from

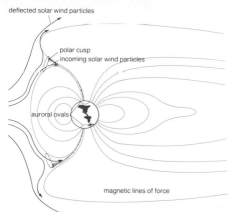

The aurora's cause

aurorae, scientists can identify the gases that are most abundant at these altitudes. Besides being beautiful, the aurora can be a powerful tool for research.

22

Electromagnetism

Chapter Objectives

- **State** *Oersted's basic principle of electro-magnetism.*

- **Describe** *the magnetic fields of straight conductors and coils and* **relate** *magnetic field direction to the direction of current.*

- **Explain** *the factors affecting the strength of the magnetic field of a coil.*

- **Define** *permeability and* **calculate** *the change in magnetic field strength using a core of known permeability.*

- **Describe** *the operation of a relay switch, a lifting electromagnet, and an electric bell.*

- **State** *the motor principle and* **explain** *the factors that affect the magnitude of the magnetic force on a conductor.*

- **Relate** *the direction of current and the direction of external magnetic field lines to the direction of the magnetic force on a conductor.*

- **Describe,** *using diagrams, the operation of a moving-coil speaker, a moving-coil galvanometer, and a DC motor.*

22.1 Electricity and Magnetism

In 1600, the English physician and scientist William Gilbert (1540-1603) published a volume entitled *De Magnete*, summarizing all that was then known about magnetism and static electricity. Gilbert, as well as many other scientists of his time and earlier, had noticed remarkable similarities between magnetism and static electricity. For example:

1. There are two types of electric charge: positive and negative; there are two types of magnetic poles: north-seeking and south-seeking.
2. Like charges and like poles repel each other; opposite charges and opposite poles attract each other.
3. Charged objects set up electric fields of force; magnetic objects set up magnetic fields of force.
4. Certain substances may be electrified by rubbing (ebonite rod with cat's fur); certain substances may be magnetized by rubbing (steel rod with lodestone).

These and other observations had led early scientists to believe that electricity and magnetism might be very closely related—might, in fact, be different aspects of the same phenomenon. Yet, by the end of the 18th century, no scientist had succeeded in showing that a strong magnet had any effect on a charged object, or vice versa. Accordingly, it was generally accepted around the beginning of the 19th century that, despite apparent similarities between electricity and magnetism, they were separate and distinct phenomena.

The principle of electromagnetism, discovered by Oersted, can be used to do work.

The discovery of the scientific principles of electromagnetism led to advances in technology that have revolutionized the twentieth century. They have had a profound effect on employment, home life, entertainment, industry, transportation, and communications.

22.2 Oersted's Discovery

In 1819, a Danish physicist, Hans Christian Oersted (1777-1851), made a discovery, while lecturing at the University of Copenhagen on electric circuits, that dramatically changed the course of science. Perhaps in an effort to demonstrate that electricity and magnetism were unrelated, he connected a battery to a long conducting wire and passed the wire above and parallel to a magnetic compass needle. Much to his surprise, when the switch was closed the needle of the compass rotated noticeably until it was at right angles to the wire. Thanks to a combination of luck and an open and alert mind, Oersted had discovered the **basic principle of electromagnetism**:

Whenever electrons move through a conductor, a magnetic field is created in the region around the conductor.

The Magnetic Field of a Straight Conductor

The region in which magnetic forces act, the magnetic field, may be represented by a series of magnetic field lines, whose shape is defined either by means of a plotting compass or by the use of iron filings (Chapter 21).

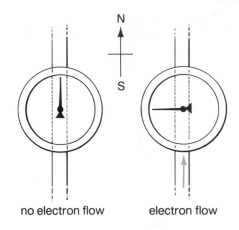

no electron flow   electron flow

Moving electrons create a magnetic field

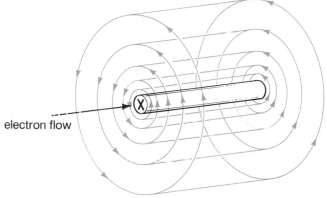

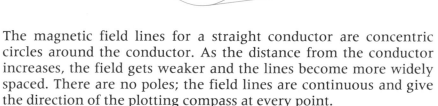

electron flow

The magnetic field lines for a straight conductor are concentric circles around the conductor. As the distance from the conductor increases, the field gets weaker and the lines become more widely spaced. There are no poles; the field lines are continuous and give the direction of the plotting compass at every point.

Reversing the direction of electron flow through the conductor would cause the field lines to point in the opposite direction, though their pattern would remain the same. An aid in remembering the relationship between the direction of the magnetic field lines and the direction of electron flow is the **left-hand rule for a conductor**:

By convention, ⊕ represents electron current flowing into the page and ⊙ represents electron current flowing out of the page. Also, the same convention may be adopted for depicting magnetic field lines into or out of the page.

The distinction between electron flow and conventional current directions, highlighted on page 588, has implications for electromagnetism as well.

All references to the various left-hand rules and the direction of electron flow could be read as "right-hand rule and the direction of the current". For example, the statement in bold type could be read as:

If a conductor is held in the *right hand* with the *right thumb* pointing in the direction of the *current*, then the curled fingers will point in the direction of the magnetic field lines.

Then the diagram would show the direction of the current from right to left through the straight conductor, in the direction of the thumb of a right hand holding it. However, even though the direction of the current is opposite, the right hand is used instead of the left, the magnetic field direction would still be the same.

If a conductor is held in the left hand with the left thumb pointing in the direction of electron flow, then the curled fingers will point in the direction of the magnetic field lines.

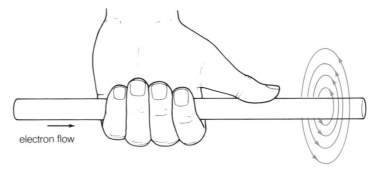

electron flow

The left-hand rule to determine the direction of the magnetic field about a conductor

*P*ractice

1. Three current-carrying conductors are illustrated, with their magnetic fields. Copy the diagrams into your notebook and indicate the direction of electron flow in each wire.

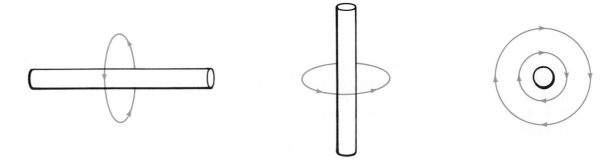

2. Three conductors are illustrated, with the direction of electron flow indicated. Copy the diagrams into your notebook and draw magnetic field lines around each, indicating polarities where applicable.

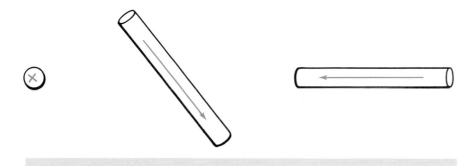

22.3 The Magnetic Field of a Coil or Solenoid

The magnetic field around a straight conductor may be intensified by bending the wire into a loop, as illustrated.

This loop may be thought of as a series of segments, each an arc of a circle, and each with its own magnetic field. The field inside the loop is the sum of the fields of each of the segments and is therefore strengthened. Notice that the field lines produced by the apparatus are no longer circles but become more like lopsided ovals.

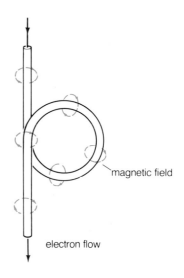

magnetic field

electron flow

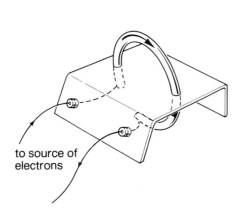

to source of electrons

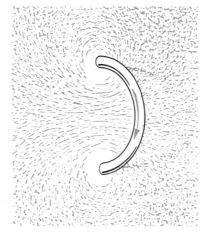

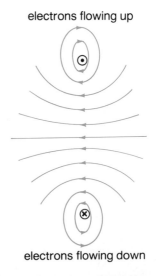

electrons flowing up

electrons flowing down

Another name for a coil is a solenoid. A solenoid may have an iron core that is moveable. When electrons flow through the coil, the magnetic field that is created causes the iron core to move into the coil's core. When the field is removed, a spring pulls the iron core out. This is a way that electro-magnetic energy may be transferred into mechanical energy.

The advantage of a magnetic field created by a current-carrying coil is that it has a constant magnitude and is confined to a well-defined space (the core of the coil).

The magnetic field may be further intensified by combining the effects of a large number of loops wound close together and forming a coil, or **solenoid**.

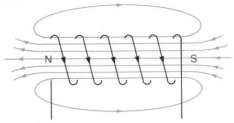

The field lines inside the coil are straight and almost equally spaced, and all point in the same direction. We call this a **uniform magnetic field**; the magnetic force is of the same strength and is acting in the same direction at all points in the field.

At both ends of the coil and on both sides, the magnetic field is quite weak, as the field lines begin to bend and spread out.

If the direction of electron flow through the coil is reversed, the direction of the field lines is also reversed, and the polarity of the magnetic field is reversed. To help you remember the relationship between the direction of electron flow through a coil and the direction of the coil's magnetic field, there is the **left-hand rule for a coil:**

If a coil is grasped in the left hand with the curled fingers representing the direction of electron flow, the thumb points in the direction of the magnetic field inside the coil.

Again, using conventional current, the direction of the magnetic field may be determined using the right-hand rule.

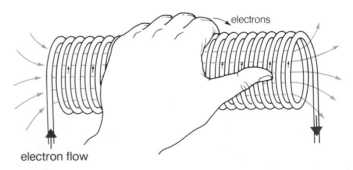
electrons

electron flow

The left-hand rule to determine the direction of the magnetic field of a coil

A great similarity is obvious between the magnetic fields of a coil and a bar magnet, as the diagrams indicate.

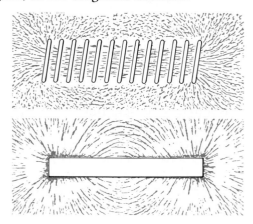

In some respects, the magnetic field of a coil resembles the electric field between two oppositely charged parallel plates. In both cases, the field lines are straight and evenly spaced.

The ends of a coil may be thought of as an N-pole and an S-pole, and the field within the core resembles the field in the interior of a bar magnet, with its ferromagnetic dipoles aligned so that they all point in the same direction.

The left-hand rule for a helix may also be stated this way: "If a coil is grasped in the left hand with the curled fingers representing the direction of electron flow, the thumb points towards the N-pole of the coil."

*P*ractice

Coils of wire wound on cardboard cylinders are illustrated. Copy the diagrams into your notebook, and on each diagram mark **(a)** the direction of electron flow, **(b)** the direction of the field lines at each end of the coil, and **(c)** the N-pole and S-pole of the coil.

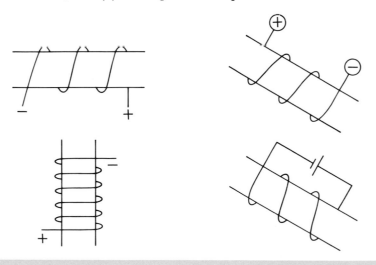

22.4 Factors Affecting the Magnetic Field of a Coil

A coil with electrons flowing through it has a magnetic field. It is very similar to a bar magnet. In fact, it is much more useful than a bar magnet. A bar magnet is able to pick up small pieces of iron but it cannot release them, and its strength cannot be varied. A coil, on the other hand, has a magnetic field that can be turned off and on and whose strength can be altered.

The strength of a magnetic field is related to the degree of concentration of its magnetic field lines. To increase the strength of the magnetic field in a coil, we must increase the number of magnetic field lines, or bring them closer together. The magnetic field strength in a coil depends on the following factors.

In SI, magnetic field strength is measured in units called tesla (T). 1 T is the magnetic field strength when a conductor 1 m long carrying a current of 1 A perpendicularly across the magnetic field experiences a force of 1 N.

$$1\ T = 1\ N/A \cdot m$$

Current in the Coil

Since the magnetic field in the core of a coil is created by the electrons flowing through the coil, the more current there is, the greater will be the concentration of magnetic field lines in the core. In fact, in an air core coil the magnetic field strength varies directly with the current in a coil: doubling the current doubles the magnetic field strength.

Number of Loops in the Coil

Each loop of wire produces its own magnetic field, and since the magnetic field of a coil is the resultant of the magnetic fields of all its loops, the more loops that are wound in the coil, the stronger will be its magnetic field. Magnetic field strength varies directly as the number of loops per unit length in a coil: doubling the number of loops in a given length of coil doubles the magnetic field strength.

A magnetic field strength of 1 T is quite strong. The greatest magnetic field strengths produced in laboratories are less than 100 T, whereas the magnetic field strength of classroom permanent magnets is about 10^{-1} T, and of the Earth about 10^{-5} T.

Type of Core Material

The material that makes up the core of a coil can greatly affect the coil's magnetic field strength. For example, if a cylinder of iron—rather than air—is used as the core for a coil, the coil's magnetic field strength may be several thousand times stronger than with air. An aluminum core will have almost no effect on the strength.

You saw in Chapter 21 how this occurs. The core material becomes an **induced magnet,** as its atomic dipoles align with the magnetic field of the coil. As a result, the magnetic field strength increases.

The factor by which a core material increases the magnetic field strength is called the material's **magnetic permeability** (μ). The permeability is the ratio of the magnetic field strength in a material to the magnetic field strength that would exist in the same region if the material were replaced by a vacuum:

$$\mu = \frac{\text{magnetic field strength in material}}{\text{magnetic field strength in vacuum}}$$

For example, a material with a permeability of 3 will make the field in a coil three times as strong as it would be in a vacuum.

Thus, the magnetic field strength of a coil varies directly as the permeability of its core material: doubling the permeability of the core doubles the magnetic field strength.

The effect of the iron core is limited, however, and reaches its maximum at a given value of field strength (called magnetic saturation).

μ is the Greek letter "mu" which corresponds to "m" in the English alphabet.

Ferromagnetism, Paramagnetism, and Diamagnetism

All materials that could be used as core materials may be divided into three groups according to their permeability.

Ferromagnetic materials become strong induced magnets when placed in a coil, and, as a result, have very high permeabilities. Iron, nickel, cobalt, and their alloys are ferromagnetic.

Paramagnetic substances magnetize very slightly when placed in a coil and increase the field strength by a barely measurable amount. As a result, they have permeabilities only slightly greater than 1. Oxygen and aluminum are paramagnetic.

Diamagnetic substances cause a very slight decrease in the magnetic field of a coil, and, as a result, their permeabilities are slightly less than 1. Copper, silver, and water are diamagnetic.

22.5 *Applications:* Electromagnetism

Applications of Oersted's discovery are many and varied. Many appliances, tools, vehicles, and pieces of machinery use a current-carrying coil to create a magnetic field. In almost every case, the magnetic field is used to cause another component to move by magnetic attraction. Such a device is called an **electromagnet**. A few examples will illustrate how electromagnets may be used.

Lifting Electromagnet

Large steel plates, girders, and pieces of scrap iron may be lifted and transported by means of a lifting electromagnet. A soft ferromagnetic core of high permeability is wound with a copper conductor. The ends of the coil are connected to a source of electric potential through a switch. Closing of the switch causes electrons to flow through the coil, and the soft iron core becomes a very strong induced magnet.

When the switch is opened and electrons stop flowing, the soft iron core becomes demagnetized instantaneously and releases its load. A U-shaped core is often used, with a coil wrapped around each leg. If the coils are wound in opposite directions, the legs become oppositely magnetized and the lifting ability of the magnet is doubled.

Electromagnetic Relay

A **relay** is a switch that turns an electric circuit on or off, and that is operated magnetically by a current flowing in a separate circuit. (See the diagram on the next page.) A pivoted bar of soft iron, called an **armature,** is held clear of the contact point by a light spring. No current flows through the left-hand circuit, and the lamp is off. When the switch is closed, current flows in the right-hand circuit, and the soft iron U-shaped core becomes magnetized. The magnetized core attracts the armature, pulling it to the right until it touches the contact point and completes the circuit. Current begins to flow in the left-hand circuit, and the lamp goes on.

When the switch is opened, electrons stop flowing, the core becomes demagnetized, and the armature is released. When the spring pulls the armature away from the contact point, current stops flowing in the left-hand circuit and the lamp goes off.

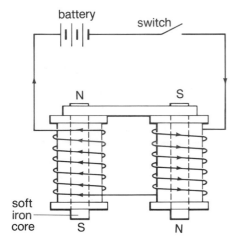

A lifting electromagnet

In a relay, the current in the electromagnet circuit can be very small (less than 1 mA) and still have the effect of controlling a very large (up to 10 A) current in the secondary circuit.

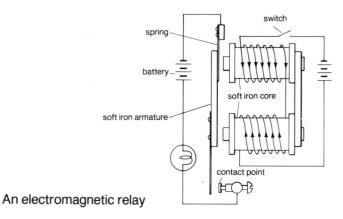

An electromagnetic relay

An electric doorbell

If the contact point were on the opposite side of the armature from the electromagnet, the relay would operate in reverse. The closing of the switch would then turn the left-hand circuit off, and vice versa.

Electric Bell

In an electric bell, a small hammer is attached to the armature. The armature is vibrated back and forth so that the hammer hits a gong repeatedly. The circuit that causes the armature to move is illustrated.

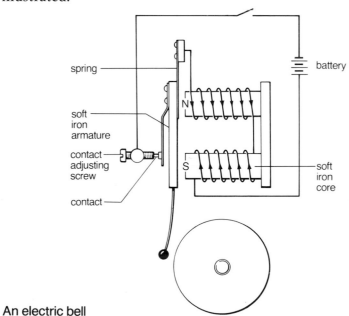

An electric bell

Logic circuits and computers could be built with electromagnetic relays but they would be very cumbersome and slow. Instead, solid state "gates" are used.

The circuit for the electric bell represents just a slight variation of the circuit for the electromagnetic relay.

There is only one circuit in the electric bell. It opens and closes as the armature makes and breaks contact with the adjusting screw.

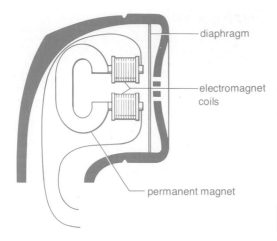

diaphragm

electromagnet coils

permanent magnet

The telephone earpiece also has an electromagnet in its circuit. A microphone at the transmitting end of the line produces a varying electric current with the same frequency as the sound wave it picks up. An identical varying current is supplied to the coils in the earpiece, producing an electromagnet of varying strength. This produces a corresponding variation in the force pulling on the diaphragm, causing it to vibrate and produce an exact copy of the sound wave that entered the microphone.

When the switch is closed, electrons flow and the soft iron cores become magnetized. The armature is attracted to the cores, causing the hammer to hit the gong; but at the same time it is pulled away from the contact, breaking the circuit. Since electrons no longer flow, the soft iron cores become demagnetized and release the armature. A spring pulls the armature back to re-establish contact, thereby completing the circuit, and the entire cycle begins again. Small sparks, evidence of electrons jumping across the gap, may be observed at the contact point as the circuit is alternately completed and broken.

Sample Problems

Calculate the effect on the strength of the magnetic field in a coil when each of the following separate changes is made.
(a) The current in the coil is increased from 2.0 A to 5.0 A.
(b) The number of loops in the coil is changed from 4000 to 1000.
(c) The core is changed from steel with a permeability of 3000 to iron with a permeability of 8000.

(a) Magnetic field strength varies directly with current.
$$\frac{\text{magnetic field after change}}{\text{magnetic field before change}} = \frac{5.0 \text{ A}}{2.0 \text{ A}}$$
$$= 2.5$$
Thus, the magnetic field strength is 2.5 times as great.
(b) Magnetic field strength varies directly with number of loops per unit length.
$$\frac{\text{magnetic field after change}}{\text{magnetic field before change}} = \frac{1000}{4000}$$
$$= 0.25$$
Thus, the magnetic field strength is 0.25 times as great.
(c) Magnetic field strength varies directly with permeability of core.
$$\frac{\text{magnetic field after change}}{\text{magnetic field before change}} = \frac{8000}{3000}$$
$$= 2.67$$
Thus, the magnetic field strength is 2.67 times as great.

*P*ractice

1. A coil with an iron core is used as an electromagnet. With 500 loops and a current of 1.5 A, it can exert a lifting force of 30 N. What force would it be able to lift, if the following changes were made?
   (a) The current was increased to 3.0 A.
   (b) The number of loops was increased to 750 without increasing the length of the coil.
   (c) Both of the above changes were made together.
2. An air-core electromagnet exerts a magnetic force of 0.50 N on a piece of iron. If the weight of the iron is 3.6×10^3 N, what is the permeability of a core material that could be used with the electromagnet so as to just support the piece of iron?
3. (a) A coil of 600 turns, wound using 90 m of copper wire, is connected to a 6.0 V battery and is just able to support the weight of a toy truck. If 200 turns are removed from the coil, but the wire is uncoiled and left in the circuit, what voltage would a battery need in order to support the truck?
   (b) If, in question 3 (a), the wire had been discarded when the 200 turns were removed from the coil, what voltage would then have been required to support the weight of the toy truck?

22.6 Conductor in a Magnetic Field—The Motor Principle

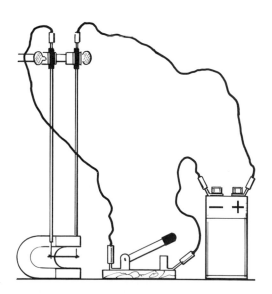

For centuries, scientists had been intrigued with the idea of constructing a device that would be capable of producing continuous motion by using some other form of energy. With Oersted's discovery of electromagnetism, the door was opened for the development of the electromagnetic **motor**. An Englishman, Michael Faraday (1791-1867), was able to devise such a motor as early as 1821.

By experimenting with current-carrying conductors in magnetic fields, Faraday was able to determine that a current-carrying conductor, placed in a magnetic field so that its moving electrons cut across the magnetic field lines, experiences a force. When placed parallel to the magnetic field lines, the conductor experiences no force. The force acts perpendicular both to the direction of electron flow and to the magnetic field lines. Reversing either the electron flow or the magnetic field causes the force to act in the opposite direction.

The next diagrams help to explain how the direction of this force is related to the magnetic field of the conductor and to the external magnetic field.

this uniform field   superposed on this field   produces this resultant field

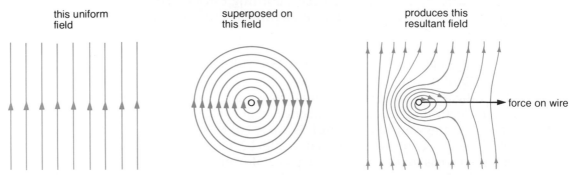

force on wire

The magnetic field pattern due to current in a straight wire at right angles to a uniform field

To the left of the conductor, the field lines point in the same direction and hence reinforce each other, producing a strong magnetic field. To the right, the fields are opposed and, as a result, tend to cancel each other, producing a weaker field. This difference in field strength, indicated by the spacing of the field lines, results in a force to the right on the conductor. If either the external field or the direction of the electron flow were reversed, the force would act in the opposite direction.

A more detailed investigation would show that the actual magnitude of the force depends on the magnitude of both the current and the magnetic field.

To summarize these effects, in what is called the **motor principle**:

A current-carrying conductor that cuts across external magnetic field lines experiences a force perpendicular to both the magnetic field and the direction of electron flow. The magnitude of this force depends on the magnitude of both the external field and the current, as well as the angle between the conductor and the magnetic field it cuts across.

The direction of the force on the conductor also depends on the direction of electron flow and the direction of the external magnetic field. It can be determined easily by using what is called the **left-hand rule for the motor principle**:

The magnitude of the force on a straight current-carrying conductor in a uniform magnetic field is:

$$F = BlI \sin \Theta$$

where B is the strength of the uniform magnetic field
l is the length of the conductor in the magnetic field
I is the current flowing through the conductor
Θ is the angle between the conductor and the magnetic field lines.

Once again, when using conventional current, the direction of the force on a conductor may be determined using the right-hand rule.

If the fingers of the left hand point in the direction of the external magnetic field, and the thumb represents the direction of electron flow, the force on the conductor will be in the direction in which the left palm faces.

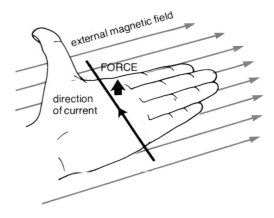

The motor principle is also used in the precise definition of the ampere. If two long wires are parallel to each other and electrons are flowing through each, the wires will experience a force of attraction or repulsion, depending on the directions of electron flow.

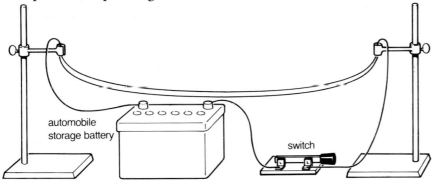

automobile storage battery

switch

The motor principle enables us to understand the SI definition of the coulomb, by providing a definition of the ampere:

1 C is the amount of electric charge flowing past a point in 1 s when the electric current is 1 A.

$$1\,C = 1\,A \cdot s$$

1 A is the current that, when flowing through each of two straight parallel wires placed 1 m apart in a vacuum, produces a force of 2×10^{-7} N between the wires for each 1 m of their length.

Currents in opposite directions—
wires forced apart

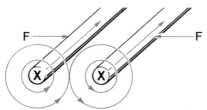

Currents in the same direction—
wires forced together

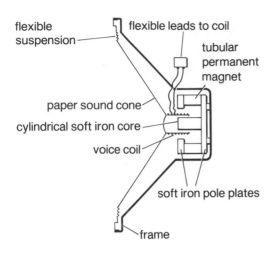

flexible suspension

flexible leads to coil

tubular permanent magnet

paper sound cone

cylindrical soft iron core

voice coil

soft iron pole plates

frame

A moving-coil loudspeaker

22.7 *Applications:* The Motor Principle

The force on a conductor in a magnetic field has a great range of practical uses. In each case, a conductor moves whenever electrons flow through it. Several common examples will help to illustrate this principle.

The Moving-Coil Loudspeaker

For a loudspeaker to be able to reproduce sound waves, it must vibrate back and forth rapidly in response to electrical signals from an amplifier. The diagram shows a cross section of a magnetically driven speaker.

Electrons pass through the voice coil, which is situated in a magnetic field. The field lines point radially between an inner cylindrical iron core and an outer tubular magnet. As a result, because the field is radial, electrons flowing through the coil are always moving at right angles to the field. The resulting force on the voice coil is parallel to the axis of the coil. The coil is attached to a large paper or plastic sound cone, so that, as it moves in response to this force, the cone also moves and sets the air vibrating. The suspension mechanism holding the vibrating coil returns it to its original position whenever no current is flowing through it.

The Moving-Coil Galvanometer

A **galvanometer** is a delicate device used to measure the magnitude and direction of small electric currents.

A rectangular coil of wire is wound on a light frame with a pointer attached, and pivoted in the jaws of a large horseshoe magnet. The front and back of the coil are parallel to the field of the magnet, while the sides are perpendicular to it. When electrons flow through the coil, there is no force on the front or back wires, since they are parallel to the magnetic field lines. There are opposite forces on the sides of the coil, because current is flowing perpendicular to the magnetic field but in opposite directions.

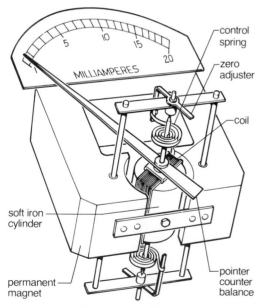

control spring

zero adjuster

coil

soft iron cylinder

permanent magnet

pointer counter balance

A moving-coil galvanometer

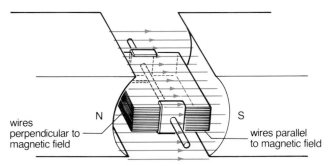

wires
perpendicular to —
magnetic field

N

S

wires parallel
to magnetic field

Relative directions of coil wires and magnetic field

A soft iron cylinder is fixed in the core of the coil to increase the strength of the magnetic field and, hence, the force on the conductor. The opposite forces on the sides of the coil cause the coil to rotate against the opposing force of the control springs until it comes to rest. The amount of rotation measured on the scale depends on the amount of current flowing through the coil; also, the direction of rotation depends on the direction of electron flow through the coil. If zero is marked at the center of the scale, the galvanometer will be able to measure current flowing in either direction. An amount of current that causes the pointer to move completely across the scale is called the **full-scale deflection current,** and it is usually just a few milliamperes. A galvanometer must be protected from any current greater than its full-scale deflection current.

The cylindrical soft iron core is fixed and does not rotate with the coil. Because of its large mass, it would decrease the sensitivity and speed of the coil's movement if it rotated also.

The Electric Motor

The explanation of the action of the moving-coil galvanometer showed that a current-carrying coil pivoted in a uniform magnetic field will begin to rotate. A closer examination of this rotation would reveal that the coil will only rotate until it is at right angles to the field, and then it will stop. For the coil to continue to rotate, the direction of the force on it would have to change every half rotation. This change could only be effected by changing the direction of the external magnetic field or of the current flowing through the coil. The diagram on the next page shows how it is possible to switch the direction of the current every half rotation.

A motor is a device that converts electric potential energy into mechanical kinetic energy.

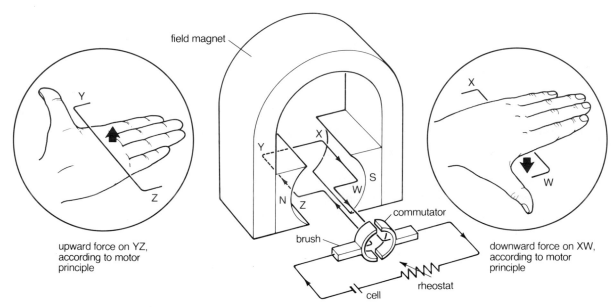

upward force on YZ, according to motor principle

field magnet

commutator

brush

cell   rheostat

downward force on XW, according to motor principle

A simplified electric motor

The ends of the coil are attached to a split copper ring, or **commutator**, that rotates with the coil. Continuous contact with the commutator is made by two stationary pieces of carbon, called **brushes**, which push gently against the rotating commutator. The brushes are connected to a battery. Electrons enter the coil through one brush and leave through the other.

When electrons flow through the circuit, side ZY of the coil experiences an upward force and side WX experiences a downward force, causing the coil to rotate in a clockwise direction, as illustrated. As the rotating coil reaches the vertical position, both brushes come opposite the gap between the commutator segments and no electrons flow. However, the inertia of the coil keeps it rotating until the brushes make contact again, this time each with the other half of the ring. This causes the direction of the electron flow through the coil to be reversed, and, hence, there is now a downward force on ZY causing it to continue rotating in a clockwise direction. This switching procedure is repeated every half cycle as long as electrons flow through the brushes. Reversing the polarity of either the magnet or the battery will cause the coil to rotate in the opposite direction.

The diagrams that follow show, schematically, the relative positions of the armature, coil, brushes, and commutator at four positions during one cycle of a DC motor, with an iron armature and an external source connected as shown:

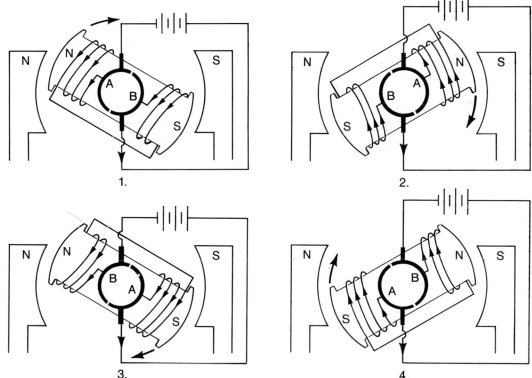

1.

2.

3.

4.

In diagram 1, electrons flow in through the top brush, into commutator segment A, and through the coils, eventually entering commutator segment B and leaving the motor through the bottom brush. End A of the armature becomes an N-pole, using the left hand rule, and is repelled by the N-pole of the field magnet, causing it to move away and rotate clockwise.

In diagram 2, tracing the path of electrons through the motor verifies that end A remains an N-pole and is, therefore, attracted toward the S-pole of the field magnet.

In diagram 3, a significant change occurs. The top brush is now in contact with commutator segment B. Electrons continue to flow down through the coils, leaving by commutator segment A and the bottom brush. End A of the armature now becomes an S-pole and is repelled by the S-pole of the field magnet, causing the clockwise motion to continue.

Again, tracing the flow of electrons through the motor in diagram 4 confirms that end A of the armature remains an S-pole and is attracted toward the N-pole of the field magnet, completing one full rotation of the motor.

The moving part of a motor is called the "rotor", and the stationary part is called the "stator".

The speed of rotation of a motor depends on:
1. the magnitude of the current flowing through it
2. the strength of its field magnet (stator)
3. the number of coils on its armature winding (rotor)
4. the permeability of its armature
5. the mechanical load connected to the shaft.

Can you go through the same reasoning but assume that the battery connections are reversed, so that electrons initially enter the motor through the lower brush?

This simple electric motor is not very powerful or efficient. To increase its power, a coil with a large number of windings around a soft iron core, called an **armature**, is used. The high permeability of the iron core and the large number of windings increases the magnetic field strength of the armature. These factors combine to produce a large force on the coil, causing it to rotate rapidly. In addition, a strong electromagnet is often used as the field magnet.

The rate of rotation of such a motor is easily controlled by varying the current in the coils, using a rheostat. Small motors controlled in this way are often used in battery-operated toys. Ripple tanks (see Chapter 10) use a small electric motor with an off-center axis to produce the vibrations necessary to create waves. Subway trains, trolley buses, streetcars, and diesel electric locomotives use large-scale motors based on similar principles.

When the field magnet is an electro-magnet, the field coils are sometimes connected in series with the armature coils (series-wound) and sometimes connected in parallel (shunt-wound). Series-wound motors produce a large turning force at low speeds, and are used where heavy loads have to be moved from rest, as they are in electric trains, buses, and streetcars. Shunt-wound motors will run at constant speed under varying loads, and as a result are used in many power tools where steady speeds are desirable.

Investigations

Investigation 22.1: Magnetic Field of a Straight Conductor

Problem:
What are the characteristics of the magnetic field around a straight conductor?

Materials:
battery (6 V or 9 V)
20 cm of bare 12-gauge copper wire
piece of stiff cardboard, 15 cm × 15 cm
four plotting compasses
iron filings
connecting wires with alligator clips

Procedure:
1. Push the short piece of bare copper wire through the middle of the cardboard square and support the cardboard in a horizontal position, as shown in the diagram on the next page.

2. Connect the upper end of the copper wire to either terminal of the battery, using a wire with an alligator clip. Connect another wire with a clip to the bottom of the copper wire, but do not connect it to the battery.

3. Lightly sprinkle iron filings on the piece of cardboard. Momentarily touch the loose wire to the other terminal of the battery, and tap the cardboard gently. Once the iron filings have assumed a pattern, disconnect the battery and sketch the pattern. Be sure to include the copper wire in your sketch. From the battery terminals used, determine whether electrons were moving up or down through the copper wire, and mark the direction on your sketch.

4. Place four plotting compasses on the cardboard, as shown in the diagram. Connect the battery and note the directions in which the compasses point. Add these directions to the sketch you drew of the iron filings.

5. Without moving the compasses, reverse the connections to the battery. Make another sketch. In which direction are electrons moving now?

Questions:
1. Describe the shape of the magnetic field lines produced by electrons flowing through a straight conductor.
2. What happens to the spacing and clarity of the field lines farther away from the conductor? What does this indicate about the magnetic field in these regions?
3. What effect does reversing the direction of the electron flow through the conductor have on the magnetic field?
4. Devise a simple rule for remembering the relationship between the direction of electron flow and the direction of the magnetic field lines.

Investigation 22.2: Magnetic Field of a Coil

Problem:
What are the characteristics of the magnetic field of a coil?

Materials:
battery (6 V or 9 V)
50 cm of bare 12-gauge copper wire
stiff cardboard and scissors
wooden dowel (about 15 cm long × 4 cm diameter)
iron filings
2 plotting compasses
connecting wires with alligator clips

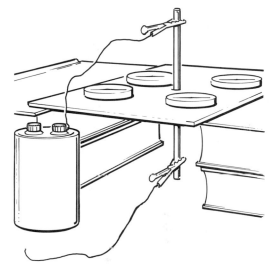

One of the wires from the conductor should be connected firmly to one of the terminals; the other wire should be touched momentarily to the other terminal. The resistance of the bare wire is very low. As a result, it draws a large current. This will cause the wire to get hot and the battery to discharge quickly if the terminals are connected for too long a time.

Procedure:

1. Make a coil by winding the bare copper wire around the dowel as many times as possible. Spread the loops out so that they are about 0.5 cm apart. Remove the dowel.
2. Using scissors, cut a piece of carboard to fit snugly into the core of the coil, as illustrated. Insert it into one end of the coil, and support the coil so that the cardboard is horizontal.
3. Connect one end of the coil to one of the terminals of the battery, using a wire with an alligator clip. Connect another wire with a clip to the other end of the coil, but do not connect it to the battery.

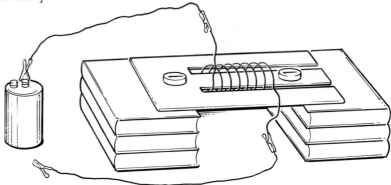

4. Lightly sprinkle iron filings on the cardboard, both inside and outside the coil. Momentarily touch the loose wire to the other terminal of the battery, and tap the cardboard gently. Once the iron filings have assumed a pattern, disconnect the battery and sketch the pattern including the coil. From the battery terminals you used, determine in which direction electrons were moving through the coil, and mark the direction on your sketch.
5. Place the compasses on the cardboard, one at each end of the coil. Reconnect the battery and note the directions in which the compasses point. Add these directions to your sketch of the iron filings.
6. Without moving the compasses, reverse the connections to the battery. Make another sketch. In which direction are electrons moving now?

Questions:

1. Describe the direction, shape and spacing of the magnetic field lines in the core of the coil.
2. What happens to these magnetic field lines at the ends of the coil?
3. Describe the magnetic field in the region to either side of the coil.
4. What effect does reversing the direction of electron flow through the coil have on the magnetic field?

5. Devise a simple rule for remembering the relationship between the direction of electron flow and the direction of the magnetic field lines.

Investigation 22.3: The Motor Principle

Problem:
Under what conditions does a conductor experience an electromagnetic force?

Materials:
pair of bar magnets
insulated wire (fine)
battery (6 V or 9 V)
5 cm length of bare 12-gauge copper wire
retort stand, clamp, and meterstick

The electron beam in a TV picture tube is deflected, or scanned, by means of electromagnetic coils.

Procedure:
1. Using the insulated wire, retort stand, clamp, meterstick, and bare copper wire, set up the apparatus as illustrated. Remove some insulation from the wire before attaching it to the bare copper wire.
2. Place the bar magnets so that the bare copper wire lies between opposite poles of the magnets, and parallel to a line joining them.

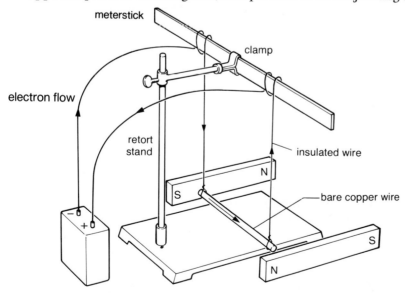

3. Connect the battery momentarily and note any effect this has on the conductor.

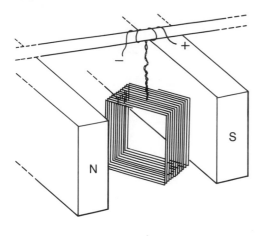

4. Rotate the magnets by 90°, so that the conductor now lies between the poles but perpendicular to the line joining them with one magnet above the conductor and one below it.
5. Reconnect the battery and observe any effect this has on the conductor.
6. Reverse the poles of the magnets. What effect does this have on the conductor? Reverse the connections to the battery. What effect does this have?
7. Wind the wire into a rectangular coil of 10 to 15 turns, as illustrated, and suspend the coil between the poles of the magnets. Connect the battery and notice the effect this has on the coil. Reverse the battery connections and repeat.

Questions:
1. What happens to a conductor when it is placed in a magnetic field so that it is
   (a) parallel to the magnetic field lines?
   (b) perpendicular to the magnetic field lines?
2. On what factors does the direction of the force on the conductor depend?
3. What factors do you predict would affect the magnitude of this force?
4. What happens to the rectangular coil when electrons flow through it? Do all four sides of the coil experience a force? Explain in terms of your answer to question 1.
5. What device does this simple coil and magnet simulate?

Investigation 22.4: Constructing a Simple DC Motor

Problem:
How can a simple DC motor be constructed?

Materials:
insulated wire
tape
pencil
2 common iron nails (about 7 cm long)
battery (6 V or 9 V)
block of wood
cardboard

Why not ask your teacher for a contest in class to see who can build the best motor out of everyday materials? The best motor would be the one that rotates the fastest. Of course everyone would have to use identical batteries!

Procedure:
1. Using something round and about 3 or 4 cm in diameter, make a coil consisting of about 20 turns of wire.

2. Remove the coil and tape the loops together on one side.
3. Split the coil windings in half, and position the coil straddling a sharp pencil, as shown in the diagram. When the coil is positioned so that the pencil will rotate like a well-balanced wheel on an axle, tape the coils on the side opposite that in 2.

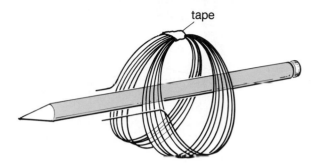

tape

4. Strip the insulation from the wires at the ends of the coil and position them along and on opposite sides of the pencil, as shown. Tape them in position with the bare wires exposed. This completes the armature for the motor.

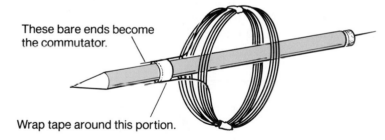

These bare ends become the commutator.

Wrap tape around this portion.

5. Tightly wrap a double layer of coils around each nail, leaving the bottom 1 cm free of windings, and ensuring that the ends of the wires are at the pointed end of the nails.
6. Obtain a small wooden block about the same length as the pencil used for the armature. Prepare two armature support brackets using pieces of cardboard cut to 10 cm × 5 cm.
7. Mount all of the items as shown in the diagram. The tops of the nails should be level with the pencil. A pin may be inserted in the eraser end of the pencil to act as a pivot. The windings on the nails have not been shown; they must be connected so the nails have the opposite polarity.

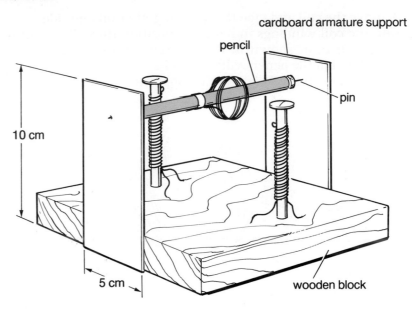

8. Complete the electrical connections as shown. When the battery
   is connected and the armature given a small push, the motor
   should continue to rotate. Minor adjustments to the alignment of
   the commutator or the balance of the armature may be necessary.

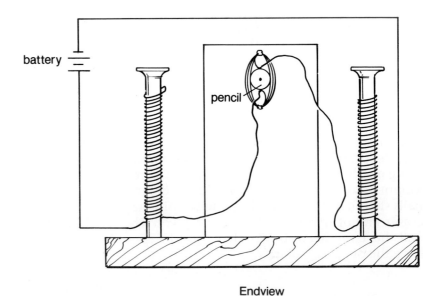

Endview

Superconductivity

As electrons flow through most conductors, they encounter resistance when they collide with other electrons and atoms. As a result, they lose energy and heat is generated. In 1911, the Dutch physicist Heike Kamerlingh Onnes made an important discovery. He found that a remarkable change occurs in the electrical properties of many metals when they are cooled to within a few degrees of absolute zero (O K, or $-273°C$). As the metal nears this frigid limit, it suddenly loses all its electrical resistance and becomes a superconductor. This allows the metal to carry an electric current without any loss of energy, and to generate immensely powerful magnetic fields. The first substance to exhibit superconductivity was mercury, at 4.2 K.

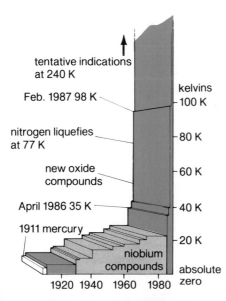

Highest known superconducting temperatures

Scientists have long recognized the enormous implications of superconductivity, but one stubborn obstacle has always stood in the way: the extreme difficulty and immense cost of reaching and maintaining the very low temperatures necessary for superconductivity to occur.

In April 1986, the scientific world was stunned by an amazing breakthrough. During the 1950s and 1960s, physicists had succeeded in producing superconductivity in various alloys containing niobium at temperatures as high as 23 K ($-250°C$). But there the progress stopped. In 1983, Karl Muller of the IBM Research Laboratory in Switzerland began looking for evidence of superconductivity in metallic oxides known as ceramics. (This was unusual since most ceramic materials are insulators at room temperatures.) In April 1986, after experimenting with various combinations of barium, lanthanum, copper, and oxygen, Muller and his associates revealed that superconductivity had occurred in these compounds at 35 K. This announcement set off feverish activity within the scientific community in an attempt to discover compounds that would superconduct at even higher temperatures.

Within a year the threshold of superconductivity had been pushed to 93 K in a compound containing yttrium in place of lanthanum. Week by week new compounds, all subtly different from their predecessors, were being discovered as even higher-temperature superconductors. Superconductivity-related

events, though not true superconduction, had been observed at the "balmy" temperature of 240 K ($-33°C$), and scientists are cautiously predicting room temperature superconductors will soon be discovered.

What are the implications of this astonishing technological advance? The transmission of electrical energy is a simple example. As much as 20% of the energy sent along high voltage transmission lines is lost in the form of heat generated by resistance. Transmission would be 100% efficient if superconducting cables were used, saving billions of dollars. Computers, medical resonance imaging equipment, magnetically levitated trains, and fusion energy generators will all be more powerful and less expensive because of superconductivity.

Chapter Summary

1. Oersted discovered the basic principle of electromagnetism, which is: Whenever electrons move through a conductor, a magnetic field is created in the region of the conductor.
2. The magnetic field of a straight conductor is a series of concentric circular field lines. The distance between these lines increases with the distance from the conductor. The direction of the field is given by the left-hand rule: If the left thumb gives the direction of electron flow, the curled left fingers give the direction of the magnetic field.
3. The magnetic field of a long coil or solenoid is a series of straight, equally spaced field lines in the core of the coil. The direction of the field is given by the left-hand rule: If the curled left fingers give the direction of the electron flow through the coil, the left thumb points in the direction of the magnetic field inside the coil.
4. The strength of the magnetic field of a coil depends on (a) the amount of current in the coil, (b) the number of loops per unit length in the coil, (c) the permeability of the core material.
5. Permeability refers to the ability of a material to change the magnetic field strength in a region of space, and is defined as
$$\mu = \frac{\text{magnetic field strength in material}}{\text{magnetic field strength in vacuum}}$$
6. The attraction of a ferromagnetic substance towards the core of a current-carrying coil may be used to explain the operation of (a) a lifting electromagnet, (b) a relay, and (c) an electric bell.
7. The motor principle states: A current-carrying conductor that cuts across external magnetic field lines experiences a force perpendicular to both the magnetic field and the current. The direction of the force is given by the left-hand rule: If the left fingers give the direction of the external magnetic field, and the left thumb gives the direction of the electron flow, the force is in the direction in which the palm faces.
8. The force on a conductor in a magnetic field may be used to explain the operation of (a) a moving-coil speaker, (b) a moving-coil galvanometer, and (c) a DC motor.

Chapter Review

Discussion

1. (a) State Oersted's basic principle of electromagnetism.
   (b) Sketch a top-down view of the magnetic field around the straight vertical wire shown in the photograph, using the directions of the compass needles. Explain why the field looks this way.
   (c) Sketch a top-down view of the magnetic field around the wire after the circuit is completed by connecting the wire to the battery terminal.

2. (a) Sketch the magnetic field of a current-carrying coil, showing the direction of the field lines in the core and marking the magnetic polarities of each end of the coil.
   (b) Draw a sketch of an experimental arrangement that could be used to magnetize a bar of iron so that it would have an S-pole at each end and an N-pole in the middle.
3. State the effect of each of the following changes, considered separately, on the strength of the magnetic field of a coil.
   (a) The current flowing through the coil is tripled.
   (b) The number of loops per unit length in the coil is halved.
   (c) The core material, with a permeability of 1000, is replaced by a material with a permeability of 4000.
   (d) All of the three previous changes are made together.

4. (a) Why is soft iron used rather than steel as a core material for the electromagnet in an electric bell?
   (b) Draw a sketch of an electromagnetic relay designed to turn a light bulb off when current flows through the control circuit.

5. Compare the magnetic field strength of two coils, one having 100 turns and carrying a current of 5.0 A, the other having 50 turns and carrying 20 A of current, if they both have the same length.

6. (a) What direction would a current-carrying coil assume if suspended freely in the Earth's magnetic field? Why?
   (b) Explain how to determine the direction of electron flow through a simple circuit, using a compass.
   (c) A compass needle is placed in its normal north-south direction above a horizontal conductor. In what direction must electrons move through the conductor in order for the compass needle not to move?

7. (a) State the motor principle and the left-hand rule for the direction of the force on a conductor in a magnetic field.
   (b) Make a fully labelled sketch of a simple DC motor, showing the field magnet polarity and the direction of electron flow required to make the coil rotate in a counter-clockwise direction.
   (c) A simple DC motor with two commutator segments is turned off, and the rotor comes to rest with the brushes touching the insulation between the segments. What will happen if the motor is turned on again? Why?
   (d) How could you restart the motor?

8. Sketch a moving-coil speaker, labelling the four key parts and explaining the role of each in converting pulses of electric current into vibrations that produce sound.

9. The diagram shows a rectangular coil of wire, WXYZ, between the poles of a magnet, and an axis about which it is free to rotate. Electrons flow through the coil in the direction shown.
   (a) Which side of the coil will start to move into the page?
   (b) In what position will the coil finally come to rest?

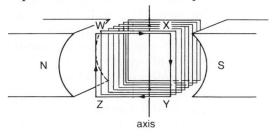

10. Using sketches of the magnetic fields around two parallel con-
    ductors, determine whether the conductors will attract or repel
    each other when electrons flow through them (a) in the same
    direction, and (b) in opposite directions.
11. Draw a sketch to show how a magnetic circuit-breaker might op-
    erate to limit the current flowing through a conductor to 20 A.
12. Most practical DC motors employ an electromagnet as the field
    magnet. Draw a sketch showing this electromagnet and the
    armature winding when the two are connected (a) in series, and
    (b) in parallel.
13. Copy each of the following diagrams in your notebook and add
    the requested information:
    (a) Show the direction of electron flow and the direction in
        which each of the compasses points.

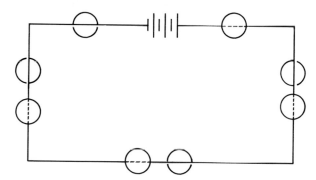

(b) Show the direction of electron flow and the direction in
    which each of the compasses points.

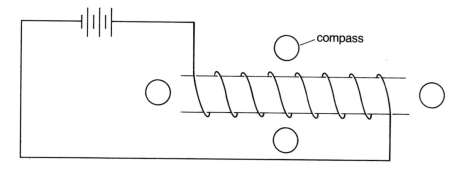

(c) Show the magnetic field of the magnet, the magnetic field of the wire, and the direction of the force on the wire.

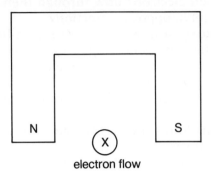

(d) Show the direction of electron flow through the wire.

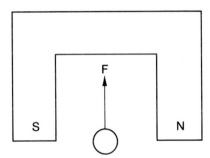

(e) Determine the polarity of the magnet.

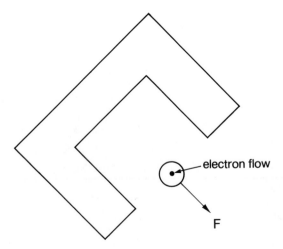

(f) Show the direction of electron flow through the brushes, commutator segments and coil, the polarity of the armature, and the direction of rotation of the motor.

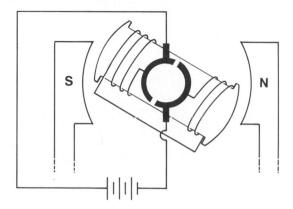

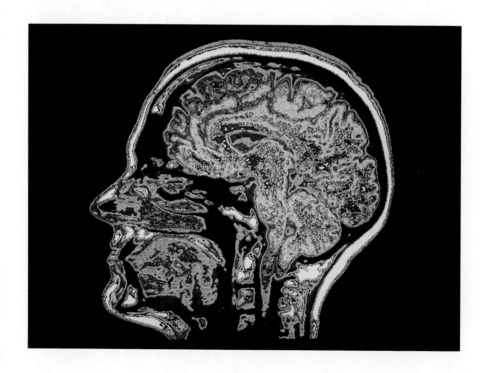

This photograph was produced using a technique called Magnetic Resonance Imaging (M.R.I.). The technique uses a strong magnetic field to align certain nuclei which then resonate in the presence of radiowaves to produce a faint signal.

23

Electromagnetic Induction

Chapter Objectives

- **State** *Faraday's Law and the conditions needed to induce current in a conductor.*

- **Explain** *the factors affecting the potential difference induced in a coil.*

- **Relate** *the induced electric current to the inducing magnetic field, using Lenz's Law.*

- **Describe** *how AC and DC generators work.*

- **Determine** *changes in the direction of induced current as a coil rotates.*

- **Analyze** *the induced current in DC and AC generators and* **graph** *the current.*

- **Explain** *why AC is used in large-scale electricity networks and the role of transformers in such a network.*

- **Explain** *how transformers change the electric potential and current and* **relate** *the number of turns in primary and secondary coils to the voltages and currents.*

23.1 The Electromagnetic Age

With the discovery of electromagnetism, a whole new technology was born. Mechanical devices using electromagnets began to appear, and motors were installed to do work previously done by human and animal effort. A new approach to manufacturing and industrialization was on the horizon, and it was certain to bring big changes in living standards.

However, the widespread introduction of electrical energy for heat, light, and machinery depended on the availability of a continuous source of electric potential. Until the early years of the 19th century, the only known source of continuous electric potential was the voltaic cell. It was during the 19th century that discoveries were made and techniques developed that led to the use of generators to supply the enormous appetite for electricity of our 20th-century society.

This chapter deals with the basic principles underlying the generation of electrical energy, as well as the techniques required for its distribution.

23.2 Faraday's Discovery

Shortly after Oersted had demonstrated, in 1819, the ability of moving electrons to create a magnetic field, his colleagues began investigating the feasibility of producing the reverse effect—a magnetic field causing electrons to move. Among those colleagues was Faraday, an experimental chemist-physicist of immense talent, who, in 1831, discovered the **basic principle of electromagnetic induction**.

Faraday made his discovery by experimenting with conductors in the vicinity of magnetic fields. His investigations involved three basic situations:

- moving a wire through the jaws of a horseshoe magnet
- plunging a bar magnet into and out of the core of a coil
- touching the iron core of a coil with a bar magnet and then removing the magnet.

**Michael Faraday
(1791 - 1867)**
Faraday, one of ten children in a poor laborer's family in Surrey, England, became a bookbinder's apprentice. This exposure to books kindled young Faraday's interest in science.

He attended a lecture at the Royal Society, given by Sir Humphrey Davy, and eventually persuaded Davy to take him on as an assistant. By learning on the job, Faraday became director of the lab in 1825, and in 1833 was appointed Professor of Chemistry at the Royal Institute.
In addition to his work in electromagnetism, Faraday made great contributions in the fields of organic chemistry, electrolysis, optics, and field theory.

In the first case, he found that electrons only flowed while the conductor was moving through the magnetic field. In the second case, electrons only began to flow when the bar magnet was moving into or out of the coil. And in the third example, electrons only moved through the coil when the iron cylinder was being magnetized or demagnetized.

He was able to combine these three conditions into one general statement, now known as Faraday's Law of Electromagnetic Induction:

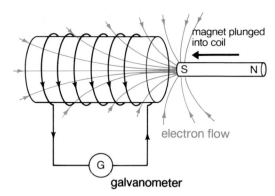

Whenever the magnetic field in the region of a conductor is moving, or changing in magnitude, electrons are induced to flow through the conductor.

Induction may be demonstrated with a device that Faraday constructed and used himself in his early studies of the induction effect. It consists of a doughnut-shaped ring of soft iron with two separate coils of wire wound around it, as illustrated.

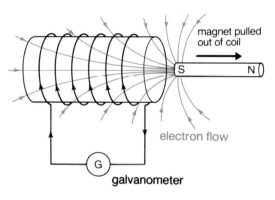

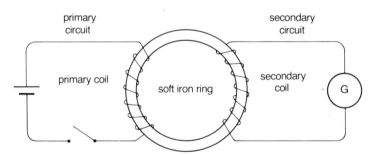

Faraday's iron ring

The primary coil is connected through a switch to a source of electric potential. The secondary coil is connected directly to a galvanometer. When the switch is closed, electrons begin to flow in the primary circuit, causing the entire iron ring to become magnetized. This sudden increase in magnetic field strength causes a current to be induced momentarily in the secondary coil. Once the current in the primary coil is steady and the magnetic field in the iron ring is established, the **induced current** no longer exists. If the switch is then opened, the iron ring becomes demagnetized and the consequent decreasing magnetic field strength once again induces a momentary current in the secondary coil, this time in the opposite direction.

It is important to note that there is no direct electrical connection between the conductors in the primary circuit and those in the secondary circuit. No electrons flow through the soft iron core from the primary circuit to the secondary circuit. Both coils are insulated from the core.

This effect is known as mutual induction and it occurs whenever a changing current in one coil induces a current in another coil near by. In fact, the two coils do not have to be coupled with an iron ring, which merely acts to strengthen an effect that would be present in any case. (We will examine the process of mutual induction more closely in Section 23.6, on transformers.)

23.3 The Magnitude of the Induced Electric Potential

A moving or changing magnetic field causes an electric current to flow through a conductor (if the conductor forms a complete circuit). In Investigation 23.1 at the end of this chapter, the magnitude of the induced current varied. Sometimes it was extremely small and occasionally it was quite large. There must have been something about the induction process that determined the magnitude of the induced current.

The simplest induction process to observe occurs when a bar magnet is plunged into the core of a coil that is connected to a galvanometer. By varying the speed with which the magnet is moved in and out of the coil, the number of turns on the coil, and the strength of the moving magnet, it is possible to conclude that the factors affecting the magnitude of the induced current are:

- **the number of turns on the induction coil**
- **the rate of change, or rate of motion, of the inducing magnetic field**
- **the strength of the inducing magnetic field**

In Chapter 20, in connection with Ohm's Law, we saw that the current through a circuit is proportional to the potential difference in the circuit, when the resistance remains constant. Thus, the three factors just listed are really factors affecting the magnitude of the induced potential difference in the coil. The induced current that results from this potential difference is then given by Ohm's Law as

$$I_{\text{induced}} = \frac{V_{\text{induced}}}{R}$$

Even when no galvanometer is connected to the induction coil, a magnet moving into its core will induce a potential difference in the coil. However, the circuit containing the coil must be complete before any induced current will exist.

23.4 The Direction of the Induced Current: Lenz's Law

When the N-pole of a bar magnet enters a coil, a galvanometer will indicate an induced current through the coil. When the N-pole is removed, the galvanometer will indicate a current in the opposite direction. Use of the S-pole of the bar magnet causes induced currents in directions opposite to the above. Evidently there is some simple relationship between the action of the inducing field and the direction of the induced current.

A few years after Faraday's discovery of induction, a German physicist working in Russia, Heinrich Lenz (1804-1865), succeeded in stating this relationship, which has since become known as Lenz's Law.

Lenz reasoned that when a current is induced through a conductor, the induced current itself sets up a magnetic field. This magnetic field, which we will call the **induced field**, then interacts with the **inducing field**, either attracting it or repelling it. In determining which of these interactions is the more likely one, it will help to consider an example.

If the N-pole of a bar magnet is inserted into the core of a coil, as illustrated, there will be an induced electron current through the coil. This current is either *up* or *down* across the front of the coil. There is no other path it can take.

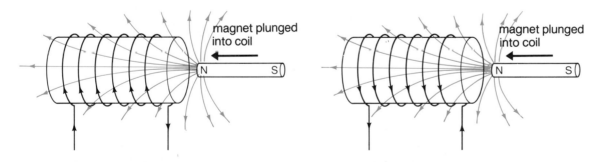

The two possible directions for the induced electron current, when an N-pole is plunged into a coil

Lenz began by assuming that the induced electron current is down, as in the sketch at the right. This current would produce an induced magnetic field in the coil, and, according to the left-hand rule, the right end of the coil would become an S-pole.

Mathematicians call this type of logic "indirect reasoning". If a problem has only two possible outcomes and you want to prove that one of them is true, you need only prove that the other cannot be true.

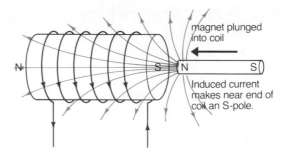

The S-pole would then attract the N-pole of the bar magnet, pulling it into the coil. It would no longer be necessary to move the N-pole of the inducing magnet into the coil; it would be attracted into the coil by the S-pole of the induced field.

Lenz reasoned that such a situation was impossible. The induction coil would have to be producing electrical energy (in the form of an induced current and potential difference) *by itself*, without using any other form of energy. The Law of Conservation of Energy does not permit such a process to occur; energy can only be converted from one form to another; it cannot be created or destroyed.

But where was the flaw? It must be in the original assumption about the direction of the induced current. The electrons, in the example being considered, must be moving *up* across the front of the coil rather than down, as assumed.

Heinrich F. Lenz
(1804 - 1865)
Lenz was a German physicist who was investigating electrical induction about the same time as Faraday. He made the generalization that the current induced by changing magnetic fields always produces effects that oppose the change. In 1833 he also reported his discovery of the manner in which electrical resistance varies with temperature.

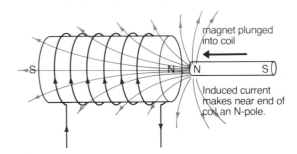

Three distinct phenomena are involved in the process of electromagnetic induction, and they must be clearly distinguished:
1. the action of the "inducing field"
2. the resulting "induced current and potential difference"
3. the magnetic field created by the induced current.

Then, the induced field has an N-pole at the right end, and this N-pole *opposes* the inward motion of the inducing magnet. That is, the inducing magnet must be pushed into the coil against the opposition of the induced field. The work done in moving the bar magnet into the coil against this opposing force is transformed into electrical energy in the induction coil.

In 1834, Lenz formulated this reasoning into a law for determining the direction of the induced current:

The electrons of an induced current flow in such a direction that the induced field they create opposes the action of the inducing field.

Sample Problems

1. Determine the direction of electron flow for the induced current in the case illustrated in the margin.

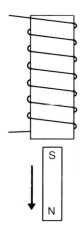

   The solution of this problem requires two steps in the reasoning process.

   (a) The lower end of the coil must become the N-pole of the induced field in order for it to *oppose* the removal of the S-pole of the inducing magnet (Lenz's Law).

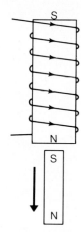

   (b) Applying the left-hand rule, we see that the electrons in the induced current must be flowing to the right, across the front of the coil.

2. Determine the pole of the induced field in the iron bar that is being inserted into the induction coil illustrated.

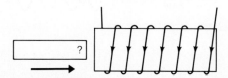

(a) Applying the left-hand rule, we see that the left end of the induction coil becomes an N-pole.

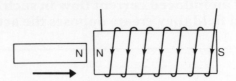

(b) According to Lenz's Law, the pole of the induced field in the iron bar that would be opposed by this N-pole as it enters the coil is an N-pole itself.

*P*ractice

1. Copy the following sketches into your notebook, and for each show
   (a) the polarity of the induced magnetic field
   (b) the direction of electron flow in the induced current

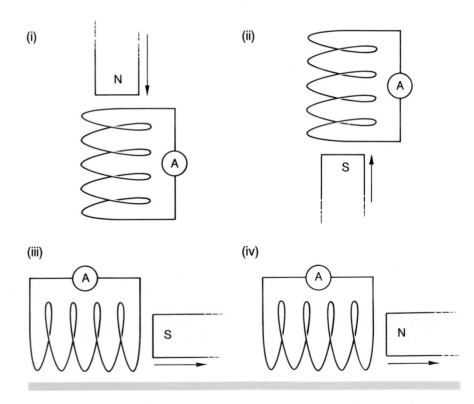

23.5 Electrical Generators: AC and DC

By the middle of the 19th century, the theoretical groundwork had been accomplished for the creation of a device that would be capable of producing a continuous electric current and electric potential difference by electromagnetic induction. As both Lenz and Faraday had discovered, the necessary device would have to provide for a magnetic field and a conductor to be in motion relative to each other, and for this motion to be sustained by some external force. The device which converts the mechanical energy of motion into electrical energy is called a **generator**.

Alternating Current (AC) Generator

The most convenient form of mechanical energy with which to drive a generator is rotation. This type of motion may be obtained from a windmill, a water-wheel, or a turbine driven by falling water or expanding steam. A coil of wire rotated by such motion in the jaws of a magnet would represent a very simple form of electric generator, as the sketch indicates.

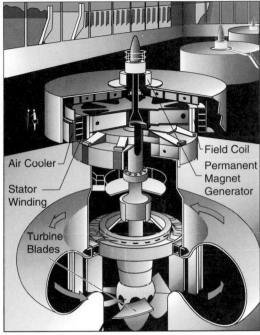

An industrial generator in a hydroelectric power plant

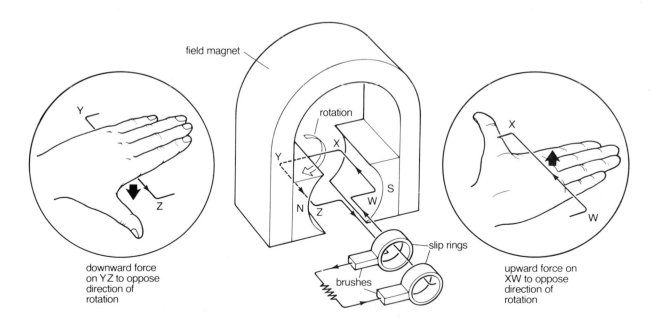

A simplified AC generator

The rectangular coil of wire WXYZ is rotated in the jaws of a permanent U-shaped magnet, known as a **field magnet**. Continuous connection to the spinning coil is achieved by the use of a pair of **slip rings** that rotate with the coil, and two carbon **contact brushes** that are in contact with the slip rings but remain stationary. Any load connected between the brushes becomes part of a complete circuit consisting of the load, the brushes, the slip rings, and the coil. As the coil rotates, its sides WX and ZY cut across the magnetic field lines of the field magnet, and an electric current is induced in the coil.

To determine the direction of this induced electron current as the coil rotates, we must apply Lenz's Law and the motor principle. As WX is rotated down, an upward magnetic force must be exerted on it to oppose this rotation, according to Lenz's Law. Using the motor principle, an upward magnetic force will be exerted on conductor WX if electrons are flowing from W to X. Similarly, electrons flowing from Y to Z will create a downward magnetic force on ZY to oppose the upward rotation. Thus, the induced electron current is in the direction WXYZ, leaving the generator through the first slip ring and brush.

After one-half of a rotation, the coil is again horizontal but with ZY on the right. Using the same reasoning as before, the induced electron current must be in the direction ZYXW. Notice that this is the reverse of the direction in the first half-cycle. A further rotation of one-half of a cycle returns the coil to its original position, and the entire process is repeated.

Such a generator in which the induced current changes its direction every half-cycle is known as an **alternating current (AC)** generator. A graph of electric current versus time for one rotation of the coil appears below, with a diagram showing the corresponding position of the coil at each instant.

Generators were originally called dynamos.

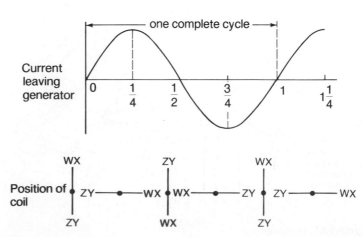

Notice that the current reaches its peak when the plane of the coil is horizontal and that it is momentarily zero when the plane of the coil is vertical. In the vertical position, WX and ZY are moving along magnetic field lines, not across them, and no current is induced. In the horizontal position, WX and ZY are cutting across the magnetic field at right angles, producing the maximum induced current.

The diagrams, below, show schematically the relative positions of the armature, coil, brushes, and slip rings at four positions during one cycle of an AC generator with an iron armature being driven in a clockwise direction by an external source of mechanical energy.

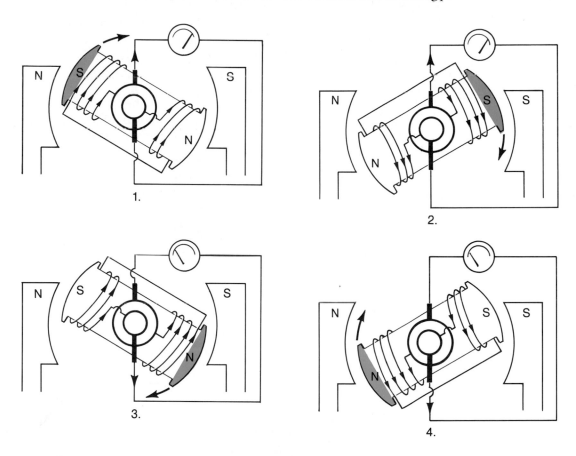

In diagram 1, the marked end of the armature is being rotated away from the N-pole of the field magnet. According to Lenz's Law its polarity must oppose this inducing action. Therefore, it becomes an S-pole, opposing its motion away from the N-pole of the field magnet. Then, using the left-hand rule, the induced current is up through the coils, into the outer slip ring, and leaves the generator through the upper brush, deflecting the galvanometer as shown.

In diagram 2, the marked end of the armature remains an S-pole, to oppose its motion toward the S-pole of the field magnet. By the left-hand rule, electrons flow down through the coils, into the outer slip ring, and again leave the generator by the upper brush, deflecting the galvanometer in the same direction.

In diagram 3, the marked end of the armature is being driven away from the S-pole of the field magnet and, to oppose this action, must become an N-pole. By the left-hand rule, electrons flow up through the coils, into the inner slip ring, and leave the generator by the lower brush, deflecting the galvanometer in the opposite direction.

In diagram 4, the marked end of the armature, to oppose its motion toward the N-pole of the field magnet, remains an N-pole. Electrons flow down through the coils, using the left-hand rule, into the inner slip ring, and leave the generator by the lower brush, deflecting the galvanometer in the same direction.

Notice that, in each complete rotation of the generator, the polarity of its armature (and hence the direction of the current through its coils) changes twice. The current leaving the generator alternates, in direction, twice each cycle.

Direct Current (DC) Generator

If the assembly of slip rings and brushes is replaced by a single split ring with two brushes, the simplified generator will appear as illustrated.

Friction between the rapidly spinning commutator and the stationary brushes causes wear. The brushes are made of graphite (carbon) for three reasons:
1. Graphite is a good conductor.
2. Graphite is fairly soft and will wear away due to friction, rather than cause the slip rings to wear. Contact brushes are designed to be easily replaced.
3. Graphite particles worn away by friction are a good lubricant. In practice, other materials are often used.

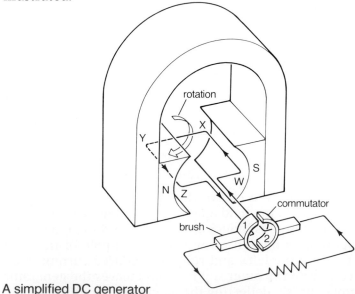

A simplified DC generator

This split ring, known as a "commutator", is designed to rotate with the coil in such a way that WX is always connected to segment 2 of the ring and ZY is always connected to segment 1. As before, the brushes remain stationary.

The internal action of this generator is identical to that of the AC generator. Electrons flow in the direction WXYZ for one half-cycle and then in the direction ZYXW for the other half-cycle. As before, the induced current changes direction when the plane of the coil passes the vertical position.

As the diagram shows, something else of significance also changes whenever the coil passes the vertical position: the contact brushes switch commutator segment connections.

The net result of these two simultaneous changes is that even though the electron current changes its direction through the coil every half-cycle, it always leaves the generator through the same contact brush, in this case the left one. This type of generator is called a **direct current (DC)** generator. A graph of electron current versus time appears below, with a diagram showing the position of the coil, the commutator segments, and the brushes at each instant.

The similarity between the AC generator and the DC generator is indicated by the fact that many classroom working models of the generator have both slip rings and a commutator. By altering the position of the brushes, both AC and DC generators can be demonstrated.

Current leaving generator

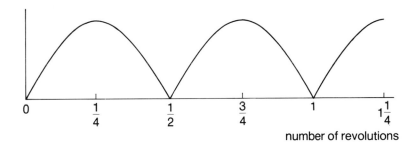

Position of coil

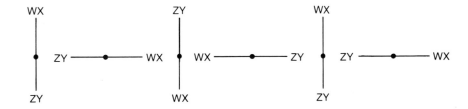

Relative positions of brushes and commutator

Notice that the changes in magnitude of the induced current are the same as those for the AC generator, increasing from zero when the coil is vertical to their maximum when the coil is horizontal. However, due to the switch in connections provided by the commutator, the electrons flow in the same direction during both halves of the cycle. Current in which the electrons always flow in the same direction is called direct current.

The diagrams below show, schematically, the relative positions of the armature, coil, brushes, and commutator segments at four positions during one cycle of a DC generator with an iron armature being driven in a clockwise direction by an external source of mechanical energy.

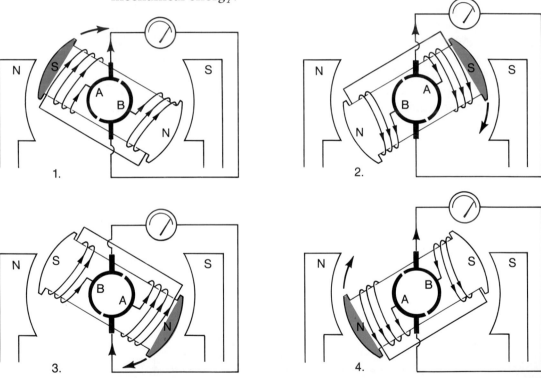

In diagram 1, the marked end of the armature is, again, an S-pole to oppose rotation away from the N-pole of the field magnet. Electrons flow up through the coil, into commutator disc A, and leave the generator by the upper brush, deflecting the galvanometer as shown.

In diagram 2, to oppose rotation toward the S-pole of the field magnet, the marked end of the armature remains an S-pole. Electrons flow down through the coil, into commutator disc A, and leave by the upper brush, deflecting the galvanometer in the same direction.

In diagram 3, the marked end of the armature must become an N-pole, to oppose rotation away from the S pole of the field magnet. Then, the electrons flow up through the coils, into commutator disc B, and leave the generator by the upper brush, deflecting the galvanometer in the same direction.

In diagram 4, the marked end of the armature remains an N-pole, to oppose its motion towards the N-pole of the field magnet. Electrons flow down through the coil, into commutator disc B, and leave the generator by the upper brush, deflecting the galvanometer in the same direction.

Notice that, in one complete rotation of the generator, the polarity of the armature changes twice. However, each time it changes, so does the connection between the commutator discs and the brushes. The net result is that electrons always leave the generator by the same brush and, hence, constitute a direct current.

Maximizing the Output from AC and DC Generators

Generators are designed to produce a maximum amount of electrical energy as efficiently as possible. This may be accomplished in several ways:
• by increasing the number of turns on the coil
• by winding the coil on a soft iron core, called an armature, to increase the strength of the inducing field
• by increasing the speed of rotation
• by increasing the strength of the field magnet

The strength of the field magnet is often increased by using an electromagnet rather than a permanent magnet. In fact, the current that is used to make the field magnet an electromagnet is often current that has been produced by the generator itself.

The simple DC generator that was described has a serious disadvantage, in that its current drops to zero every half-cycle between its peaks. This "ripple" can be very unsatisfactory when a steady source of direct current is required. A battery, for example, provides a direct current that remains constant in magnitude and direction.

This problem may be overcome by winding several separate coils on the armature, equally spaced from one another. Each coil requires its own pair of segments on a multi-segmented commutator. One coil, then, is always producing a maximum amount of current regardless of the position of the armature, and the net effect of the currents produced in all of the coils is a relatively "ripple free" current flowing through the contact brushes.

The commutator keeps switching from one coil to the next, as the armature rotates.

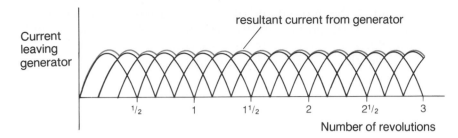

Current produced by a DC generator with three pairs of equally spaced commutator segments

23.6 The Victory of Alternating Current: The Transformer

AC generators and DC generators are equally easy to design and operate, and they produce electrical energy with equal efficiency. Yet all of our large-scale electrical energy supply systems are founded on AC generation. Why is this so?

Hydro-electric generating stations must be built where there is fast-moving or falling water. Fossil-fuel and nuclear stations are usually built near a large body of cooling water, and away from densely populated areas because of the pollution and radiation hazards. As a result, most of our electrical energy is generated far from the places where it is most needed. When electrical energy is transmitted, some of it is lost as heat in the line, so the problem of transmitting electrical energy over great distances has become a crucial one. A sample problem will help to explain what is involved.

Sample Problems

Calculate the percentage of electric power wasted as heat in a transmission line if 10 kW is transmitted along a cable with a total resistance of 1.0 Ω at an electric potential of 200 V.
The electric current in the line is

$$I = \frac{P}{V}$$
$$= \frac{10\ 000\ \text{W}}{200\ \text{V}}$$
$$= 50\ \text{A}$$

Transformers at a generating station increase voltage for efficient transmission.

The power dissipated as heat by this current is
$$P = I^2R$$
$$= (50 \text{ A})^2 \ (1.0 \ \Omega)$$
$$= 2500 \text{ W}$$
$$= 2.5 \text{ kW}$$

This represents a power loss of 25% in the transmission line, which is extremely inefficient.

Let us repeat the calculations, this time assuming that the 10 kW of electric power are transmitted at a higher electric potential, say 2000 V.

The current in the line is
$$I = \frac{P}{V}$$
$$= \frac{10\ 000 \text{ W}}{2000 \text{ V}}$$
$$= 5.0 \text{ A}$$

The power dissipated by this current is
$$P = I^2R$$
$$= (5.0 \text{ A})^2(1.0 \ \Omega)$$
$$= 25 \text{ W}$$

This represents a power loss of 0.25%, which is negligible.

Clearly, it is possible to transmit electrical energy efficiently if the energy is transmitted at a high potential and a low current. Such high voltages require special insulation to prevent arcing, but this problem has been effectively solved.

Most large electric generators produce electric potentials of about 10 kV. For efficient transmission, voltages much higher than that are needed. Then, after the electrical energy has been transmitted, it must be delivered at low voltages for most practical uses. What is needed is a device capable of changing the electric potential—increasing it for transmission and then reducing it for practical use, after transmission.

A simple device that is capable of changing electric potentials is the **transformer**, the structure of which is illustrated.

The transmission of power is also more economical at low currents, since thinner, less expensive wires can be used in the transmission cables. The very high voltages used in long-distance transmission lines require better insulation on the cables, but this problem has been effectively overcome.

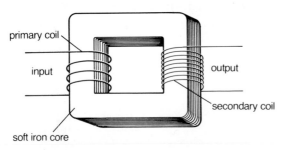

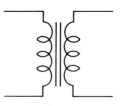

A schematic diagram of an iron core transformer.

Faraday's ring was, of course, just a simple form of transformer.

This transformer consists of a core of soft iron wound with two separate coils of wire. Current supplied to one of the coils (the **primary coil**) induces a current in the other coil (the **secondary coil**) due to mutual induction between the two coils. By varying the number of windings on the primary and secondary coils, the electric potential supplied to the primary coil may be increased or decreased.

The ability of a transformer to change the electric potential supplied to it depends on the ratio between the number of turns on its primary and secondary coils. A transformer with more windings on the secondary coil increases the voltage and is known as a **step-up transformer**. Conversely, a transformer with fewer windings on the secondary coil decreases the voltage and is known as a **step-down transformer**. In fact, the ratio of voltages is the same as the ratio of turns, and this equivalence may be expressed mathematically as:

$$V_1 : V_2 = N_1 : N_2$$
$$\text{or}$$

The terms "step-up" and "step-down" can lead to confusion, because a transformer that increases the voltage decreases the current, and vice versa. Remember that these terms refer to the effect the transformer has on the electric potential.

$$\frac{V_1}{V_2} = \frac{N_1}{N_2}$$

where N_1 is the number of primary windings
N_2 is the number of secondary windings
V_1 is the electric potential applied to the primary
V_2 is the electric potential induced in the secondary

Most transformers are designed so that as little energy as possible is wasted. The following measures are important in the designing of transformers.

1. Copper coils of low resistance are used to avoid power loss by heating (I^2R losses in the coils).
2. A core of high-permeability, soft, ferromagnetic material is used to decrease the energy required to change the magnetic field in the core.
3. The core is given a shape and a size that will ensure a large amount of mutual induction between the two coils.

In a well-designed transformer, power losses are reduced to a level that is negligible. We call such a transformer **ideal**, and we can assume that it is 100% efficient.

power output = power input
(secondary)   (primary)
$$P_2 = P_1$$
then
$$I_2 V_2 = I_1 V_1$$
and

$$\frac{V_1}{V_2} = \frac{I_2}{I_1}$$

---

where I_1 is the current in the primary coil

I_2 is the current in the secondary coil

These two equations enable us to solve a variety of mathematical problems arising from the use of transformers to change the values of the electric potentials in circuits.

Most practical transformers have efficiencies in the 96-98% range. This means that $P_2 = 0.96\ P_1$ for a transformer that is 96% efficient.

Sample Problems

A transformer is designed to operate a 12 V door chime from a 120 V supply. If the transformer has 800 turns on the primary coil and the door chime draws 1.5 A of current from the transformer, find (a) the number of turns on the secondary coil, and (b) the current supplied to the primary coil.

For a transformer,
$$\frac{N_2}{N_1} = \frac{V_2}{V_1}$$
then
$$\frac{N_2}{800} = \frac{12\ V}{120\ V}$$
$$N_2 = \frac{12\ V}{120\ V}\ (800)$$
$$= 80\ \text{turns}$$

Assuming that the transformer is "ideal",
$$\frac{I_1}{I_2} = \frac{V_2}{V_1}$$
then
$$\frac{I_1}{1.5\ A} = \frac{12\ V}{120\ V}$$
$$I_1 = \frac{12\ V}{120\ V}\ (1.5\ A)$$
$$= 0.15\ A$$

Practice

Assume that all transformers are ideal.

1. A transformer has 60 primary turns and 300 secondary turns. It is designed to supply a compressor motor requiring a current of 2.0 A at a potential difference of 5.5×10^2 V. What are the current and potential difference in the primary coil?
2. A transformer that is used to supply power to a toy train is plugged into a 1.2×10^2 V outlet and has various connections on its secondary coil to provide potential differences of 16 V, 12 V, 8.0 V, and 6.0 V to the train. If the primary coil has 1320 turns, how many turns must there be on the secondary coil at the position of each of the various connections?
3. A mercury vapor lamp operates at 3.0×10^2 V and has a resistance of 40 Ω. A transformer supplies the energy required, from a 1.2×10^2 V power line. Calculate (a) the power used by the transformer, (b) the primary current, and (c) the ratio of primary turns to secondary turns in the transformer.

A voltage and a current can also be induced in a secondary coil by a pulsating DC current in the primary coil. This is the basis of operation of the induction coil in an automobile with conventional ignition, where the high voltage necessary to fire the spark plugs is produced. Pulses of direct current are supplied to the primary coil of the induction coil by the opening and closing action of the ignition points. The high voltages induced in the secondary coil by this changing current are supplied to the spark plugs at the proper time and in the proper firing order by the action of the rotor in the distributor. The spark actually occurs when the ignition points open, causing a rapid decrease in primary current.

We have not yet considered how a transformer operates. The explanation involves most of the basic principles of electromagnetism and electromagnetic induction.

- The current and potential in the secondary coil occur as a result of electromagnetic induction. The secondary coil is an induction coil.
- For induction to occur in the secondary coil, the magnetic field in the core of the transformer must be changing in strength and/or direction (Faraday's Law of Electromagnetic Induction).
- Since this magnetic field is created by the current in the primary coil, the primary current must also be changing in magnitude and/or direction. The primary coil acts as a variable strength electromagnet.

If a source of alternating current is connected to the primary coil, then an alternating magnetic field is created in the iron core. This field increases in strength as the current increases, decreases in strength as the current decreases, and changes in direction as the current changes direction.

The field's maximum strength depends on the number of windings in the primary coil (as well as on the magnitude of the primary current and the permeability of the core). This continuously alternating magnetic field induces an alternating current and potential difference in the secondary coil. The maximum potential difference that can be induced in the coil depends on the number of windings on the secondary coil (as well as on the strength and rate of change of the inducing field).

If a source of "ripple-free" current (for example, a DC source such as a battery) were connected to the primary coil, then the core would become magnetized but the direction and magnitude of the magnetic field in the core would remain constant. Thus, no induction would occur in the secondary coil. Transformers do not operate on DC.

We are now in a position to state why AC is used, rather than DC, for the large scale distribution of electric power.

- Electrical energy is much more efficiently transmitted at high voltages.
- These high voltages can be achieved by the use of transformers, which may also reduce the voltage to a usable level after transmission.
- Transformers operate on AC.

Transformers are also used in radio and TV circuits, where they operate at frequencies in the range 20 Hz to 20 MHz. At these high frequencies, air cores are used rather than iron, since the magnetic dipoles in the iron would not be able to respond to such rapid changes in the direction of the magnetic field.

23.7 Distribution of Electrical Energy

The distribution of the vast amounts of generated electrical energy through a complex network of transmission lines and transformers to the millions of homes, schools, hospitals, and industries that are dependent on it presents an immense challenge. The distances and terrain over which the energy must be transmitted are often formidable.

The guiding principle in the operation of a transmission system is to increase the voltage to a high level at the generator and keep it at the highest safe level throughout the network.

Almost all electrical devices in North America operate on 60 Hz AC power, at a potential of 120 V (some use 60 Hz at 240 V or more). Large generators at the many power stations produce AC electric power of this frequency. This means that the direction is reversed 60 times every second, so that electrons travel in one direction for $\frac{1}{120}$ s and then in the opposite direction for the same length of time. In fact, there is a very short period once every $\frac{1}{120}$ s when the electron is reversing its direction and no current flows. Many years ago, electric power was generated at 25 Hz, and, at that frequency, a faint flicker was observable in fluorescent light tubes as the current stopped momentarily every $\frac{1}{50}$ s.

High-voltage transmission lines

A transformer substation

A step-down transformer

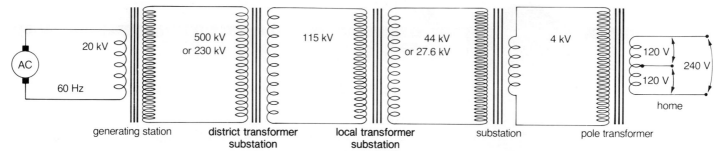

Steps in a typical electric power distribution network from generating station to the home.

In modern power distribution systems, electricity is generated at a potential of up to 20 kV and is immediately stepped up to 230 kV, or 500 kV, or even 765 kV by transformers near the generating stations. This very-high-voltage power is then sent (with relatively little loss) along transmission lines whose rows of towers are a familiar sight in the countryside.

Large district transformer stations are located along the transmission lines near cities, large towns, and industrial complexes. At these stations the power is stepped down to 115kV, and it is transmitted at that potential to local transformer substations. The local transformer substation found in each small town or municipality further reduces the potential to either 44 kV or 27.6 kV. From there, the power is distributed to transformer substations in each neighborhood where it is further stepped down to about 4 kV. Wires carry this power along residential streets to the last transformer in the chain, the pole transformer, reducing the potential to 240 V. In some modern subdivisions with underground wiring, pole transformers have been replaced by underground transformers to be found under the lawns of every fourth or fifth house.

Three wires lead from the pole transformer into each residence—one from each end of the secondary coil, and one from its center. In this way, both 240 V and 120 V potentials are made available for use in the home. (See Chapter 20.)

There is no complete conducting path from the generator to the home. The farthest along the distribution network electrons from your home can get is into the secondary coil of your nearest pole transformer. Even so, in AC, any given electron moves only a very short distance in the $\frac{1}{120}$ s before it reverses direction.

Investigations

Investigation 23.1:   Electromagnetic Induction

Problem:
How can electrons be induced to flow through a conductor by using a magnetic field?

Materials:
horseshoe magnet
bar magnet
conducting wires
coil with a hollow core
galvanometer or milliammeter
cylinder of soft iron to fit core of coil

Even the most sensitive of galvanometers will only deflect slightly, and you will need to look very closely to see just when it deflects.

Procedure:
1. Connect the ends of a long piece of wire to the terminals of the galvanometer. Place the wire in the space between the poles of the horseshoe magnet and note any effect this has on the galvanometer. Remove the wire from between the poles of the magnet and again note whether any electrons flow. Move the wire back and forth and then up and down between the poles of the magnet. Try to determine exactly when electrons flow and when they do not.
2. Connect the ends of the coil to the galvanometer. Plunge a bar magnet into the core of the coil. Allow it to remain there for a few seconds and then remove it. Note the effect of each of these actions on the galvanometer. Repeat the procedure, using the opposite pole of the bar magnet.
3. Place the iron cylinder in the core of the coil and then touch it with the bar magnet. Note the effect this has on the galvanometer. Remove the magnet and once again observe the galvanometer. Repeat the procedure with the opposite pole of the magnet.

Questions:
1. Describe three ways to make electrons flow through a conductor using a magnetic field.
2. Do the electrons in an induced current always flow through the conductor in the same direction? What determines their direction?
3. Oersted showed that moving electrons cause a magnetic field. Make a similar statement about the cause of an induced current.

Investigation 23.2: Factors Affecting Induction

Problem:
What factors affect the magnitude of the induced current in a coil?

Materials:
pair of bar magnets
two similar solenoids, of 300 turns and 600 turns
galvanometer (center-zeroed)
connecting wires

Procedure:
1. Connect the two coils and the galvanometer in series, as illustrated.

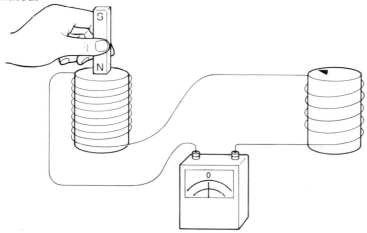

2. Using one of the bar magnets, insert its N-pole very slowly into the core of the 600-turn coil and measure the induced current. Repeat the procedure, this time moving the magnet more quickly into the coil. Follow the same procedure for a third time, moving the magnet as quickly as possible, and once again measure the induced current.
3. Insert the N-pole of the bar magnet steadily into the core of the 300-turn coil, measuring the induced current. Repeat this procedure moving the magnet at the same speed, this time using the 600-turn coil.
4. Holding the two bar magnets tightly together so that their N-poles are together, plunge the pair into the core of the 600-turn coil and measure the induced current. Repeat the procedure using a single bar magnet, and move the magnet at the same speed as you did when using the pair of magnets. Repeat again, using two magnets held side by side with opposite poles together and moving at the same speed.

Questions:

1. List the three factors that affect the magnitude of the induced current in a coil.
2. What set of conditions would lead to the maximum value of induced current?
3. When a single bar magnet is inserted into the core of a 300-turn coil at a speed of 10 m/s, the induced current is measured and found to be 12 mA. What would the value of the induced current become if each of the following were used?
   (a) a magnet three times as strong
   (b) a 900-turn coil of the same resistance
   (c) a speed of 5 m/s for the magnet
   (d) all the changes above, at once

Investigation 23.3: Transformers

CAUTION: Due to the danger of electric shock in this investigation, your teacher will do the procedure as a demonstration. Students should NOT perform the investigation. Observe the results of each part of the demonstration and record the data. Then answer the investigation questions.

Problem:
How are the input and output voltages in a transformer related to the number of windings on the primary and secondary coils?

Materials:
lab transformer set (iron core and several coils with different numbers of turns)
variac (AC variable voltage power source)
two AC multi-range voltmeters
6 V or 12 V battery
DC voltmeter
nichrome wire or long finishing nail

Procedure:
1. Set up the transformer as shown on the next page, using the coil with the fewest turns as the primary and the coil with the next fewest turns as the secondary.
2. Turn on the variac, and increase the voltage applied to the primary coil from zero to a maximum in several steps. Note both the primary voltage and the secondary voltage at each step.

Transformer cores are usually made not from a solid piece of soft iron but from many thin sheets of iron insulated from each other and attached together, much like plywood. This has the effect of reducing power losses in the core due to the presence of "eddy currents" that flow in the iron.

 CAUTION: Do not plug in variac until everything is set up.

 CAUTION: The wiring connections inside a variac may provide a fatal electric shock to a user. Improperly touching the wires or connection points on the laboratory transformer set can also provide a fatal shock.

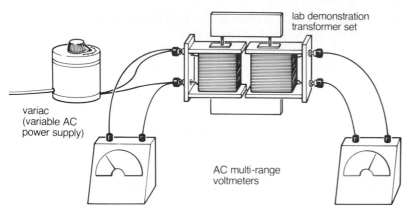

lab demonstration
transformer set

variac
(variable AC
power supply)

AC multi-range
voltmeters

3. With the primary voltage at a moderate value, substitute each of the remaining coils for the secondary coil, noting the secondary voltage each time. **CAUTION:** Unplug the variac each time before changing coils.

4. Repeat the entire procedure, starting with the coil with the most turns as the primary.

5. Record all your data in a chart as illustrated.

6. Connect the ends of the primary coil to the terminals of the battery, and connect the DC voltmeter across the secondary coil. Note the reading on the voltmeter. Bring a nail or a small compass near the iron core of the transformer and determine whether the core is magnetized.

7. (a) Using the coil with the most turns as the primary, and the coil with the fewest turns as the secondary, connect a piece of nichrome wire or a nail across the terminals of the secondary coil.

  (b) Connect the variac to the primary coil and increase it gradually to the maximum, observing the wire or nail connected to the secondary coil.

  (c) Remove the secondary coil and in its place use a hollow dish-shaped ring of metal with a wooden handle. Fill the ring with water, adjust the variac to maximum level, and, holding the ring by its wooden handle, observe the water.

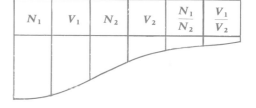

N_1	V_1	N_2	V_2	$\dfrac{N_1}{N_2}$	$\dfrac{V_1}{V_2}$

Questions:

1. What conditions led to a secondary voltage that was greater than the primary voltage? Less than the primary voltage?

2. What relationship exists between the ratio of windings and the ratio of voltages of the two coils? Express this relationship mathematically.

3. What happened to the wire or the nail during the demonstration? Why? What happened to the water?
4. During the investigation you may have noticed some humming and vibration. If you heard such sounds what do you think caused them?
5. What was the reading on the DC voltmeter connected across the secondary coil when the battery was connected to the primary? Was the iron core magnetized in that case? Explain why no potential difference is induced in the secondary coil when the primary coil is connected to a DC source.

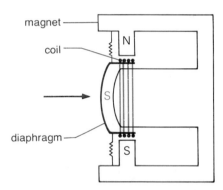

A new dynamic transducer has been developed to serve both as a transmitter (microphone) and as a receiver (speaker) in telephone sets. A small coil is attached to a light diaphragm in the field of a permanent magnet. Incoming sound waves vibrate the diaphragm, inducing a current to flow through the coil. Similarly, current supplied to the coil causes the diaphragm to vibrate and produce sound waves. This type of transducer will eventually replace the carbon-button microphone and electromagnetic speaker described in Chapters 20 and 22.

Chapter Summary

1. The basic principle of electromagnetic induction, discovered by Faraday, states: "Whenever the magnetic field in the region of a conductor is changing in magnitude or direction, electrons are induced to flow through the conductor."
2. The magnitude of the electric potential difference induced in a coil depends on:
   (a) the number of turns on the induction coil,
   (b) the rate of change of the inducing magnetic field,
   (c) the strength of the inducing magnetic field.
3. The direction of an induced current is given by Lenz's Law, which states: "The electrons in an induced current flow in such a direction that the magnetic field they create opposes the action of the inducing field."
4. Mechanical energy may be converted into electrical energy by means of a generator. A coil of wire is rotated in a uniform magnetic field in such a way that an electric current is continuously being induced in the coil.
5. The magnitude of the electric potential produced by a generator depends on:
   (a) the speed of rotation of the coil,
   (b) the strength of the field magnet,
   (c) the number of turns on the coil.
   The direction of the current induced in the coil at any point in the rotation is determined by Lenz's Law. The direction of the current in the coil is reversed every half-cycle, when the axis of the coil is parallel to the field lines.
6. If connection is made to the rotating coil by two slip rings and

brushes, the current leaving the generator changes direction every half-cycle, and it is called alternating current. If connection is made to the rotating coil by a single split ring (commutator) and two brushes, the current leaves the generator in the same direction throughout the entire cycle, and it is called direct current.

7. Alternating current forms the basis of modern large-scale electrical energy transmission and distribution networks. Electrical energy is transmitted with much greater efficiency at high voltages, and these high voltages are achieved by the use of transformers, which operate on AC.

8. A transformer can increase or decrease the electric potential, depending on the relative number of turns on its primary and secondary coils. For an ideal transformer

$$\frac{V_1}{V_2} = \frac{N_1}{N_2}$$

$$\frac{V_1}{V_2} = \frac{I_2}{I_1}$$

9. For efficient transmission of electrical energy, the potential is increased at the generator to a very high value, and then progressively decreased after transmission. Transformers are used at the various stages of the distribution network until the potential is reduced to a value of 240 V and 120 V, ready for use in the home.

Chapter Review

Discussion

1. (a) Explain what is meant by electromagnetic induction, and describe how an electric current or potential difference may be induced in a conductor.
   (b) State three factors that affect the magnitude of the potential difference induced in a coil.
   (c) Where does the electrical energy of the induced current and potential difference come from? What other form of energy is used up?

2. Two identical coils are placed side by side, as shown on the next page, and one is connected to a battery through a knife switch, while the other is connected to a galvanometer.

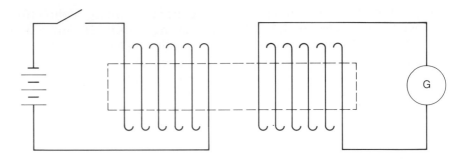

(a) Describe the effect on the other coil of opening and closing the knife switch.

(b) Would the same effect occur if one of the coils had been rotated by 90°, putting it at right angles to the other coil?

(c) How would the insertion of a bar of iron into the two coils, as shown by the dotted line, change the effect of opening and closing the switch?

3. (a) State Lenz's Law for the direction of an induced current.

(b) In this diagram, a straight conductor is lifted through the magnetic field shown. Determine the direction of the induced current in the wire.

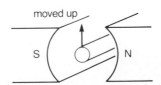

(c) Determine the direction of the current induced in the coil illustrated, by moving the magnet to the right.

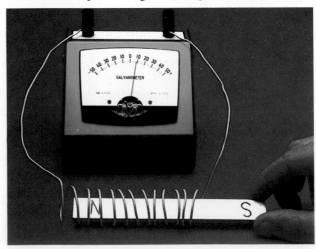

4. (a) What is the major structural difference between an AC generator and a DC generator?
   (b) How does the current flowing through the armature coil of a DC generator differ from the current flowing through the armature coil of an AC generator?
   (c) In comparison with the number of separate armature coils in a DC generator, how many segments should the generator's commutator have?
5. (a) Sketch a simple AC generator, labelling four key parts and describing the function of each.
   (b) Show how Lenz's Law and the motor principle may be used together to determine the direction of the induced current at any point in the rotation.
   (c) What features in the design of a practical form of AC generator have an effect on the potential difference the generator will produce?
   (d) Draw a graph of induced potential difference versus time for a model AC generator, rotating three times per second and producing a peak potential difference of 2.5 V. Label the time axis at each point where the graph crosses it.
6. What are the advantages of using high-voltage AC when transmitting electric power over long distances?
7. Draw a sketch of a transformer, labelling three main parts. State the function of each part, and show which laws of electromagnetism and electromagnetic induction govern its operation.
8. List 10 careers where a knowledge of electromagnetism and electromagnetic induction are necessary.

Problems

9. A bar magnet inserted completely into a coil of 500 turns produces an induced potential difference of 1.5 V. Determine the potential difference induced when each of the following changes is made, considered separately.
   (a) A 250-turn coil is used.
   (b) The bar magnet is moved twice as quickly.
   (c) Three identical magnets of the same polarity and strength are inserted at once, side by side.
   (d) All three of the above changes are made together.
10. A step-up transformer is designed to operate from a 12 V AC supply and to deliver energy at 240 V. If the secondary winding is connected to a 60 W, 240 V lamp, determine (a) the turns ratio of the transformer, and (b) the primary current.

Numerical Answers to
Practice Problems

page 690
1. 10 A, 1.1×10^2 V
2. 176, 132, 88, 66 turns
3. 2.2 kW, 19 A, 2:5

11. The transformer used to operate a model electric train has 1125 turns on its primary coil and 75 turns on its secondary. If it is plugged into a 120 V circuit, what potential difference does the model train receive?

12. A magnet induces a current of 8.0 mA in a 500-turn coil connected to a galvanometer. The total resistance of the coil and galvanometer is 100 Ω. The coil is then replaced by a 1500-turn coil, making the total resistance in the circuit 150 Ω. What current would then be induced by the same magnet moving at the same speed?

13. A generating station develops 15 000 kW of electric power. Assuming 100 per cent efficiency of transmission, calculate the current flowing through a 500 000 V transmission line leading from the generating station.

Magnetic Recording of Information

Magnetic recording of information plays a central role in modern communications and data processing, from the instant replay of televised sports events to the memory storage in home computers. The basic principle is straightforward: the information to be recorded, whether it is sound, video images, or digital data, is transformed into an electric current. When this current flows through an electromagnet, it causes a magnetizable surface (tape or disk) to be magnetized and a permanent record is created. If the magnetized surface moves past an electromagnet, a current is induced in the electromagnet that may be converted back into sound, a video image, or data for a computer.

Magnetic recording of data is quite different from other forms of communication and information storage. It can not be directly interpreted by humans, unlike books, pictures, and musical scores. Because the information is stored in the organized arrangement of particles on a magnetic surface, it must be read by a machine before it can be changed into a form that is comprehensible to the human eye or ear. In fact, because of magnetic recording of data, two or more machines can communicate effectively with each other without the intervention of a human being.

Although the principle of magnetic recording is relatively simple, the technology required to make it work is complex. The magnetic surface has to be manufactured with great care, the recording and playback electromagnets must be machined to very close tolerances, and the speed at which the magnetic surface moves must be accurately controlled.

The Recording Process

Let's consider the recording process on an audio cassette, where a strip of magnetic tape about 0.6 cm wide is moved past the recording electromagnet, called a "head", at a speed of about 5 cm/s. The iron core in the recording head is readily magnetized when there is a current in the coil, and loses its magnetism just as readily when the current stops. The shape of the head is such that its N and S poles are separated by a very small gap. The magnetic field created in this gap takes a looping path, creating what is called a "fringe field". The diagram shows how this field interacts with the magnetic tape.

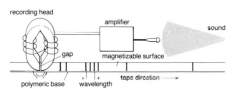

The tape consists of a thin plastic base coated with an even thinner layer of magnetic iron oxide particles in a polymer binder. As the tape moves past the gap in the recording head, the fringe field goes through the tape, thereby aligning the dipoles in its magnetic oxide coating. When the current stops there is no fringe field and, hence, no magnetization of the tape. Thus the tape becomes a magnetic copy of the current in the recording head, in both intensity and frequency.

The Playback Process

The tape carries a record of the original information in the orderly orientation of its magnetic particles. As it passes the playback head (which is identical to the recording head and, in many devices, is the same head as was used for recording) the moving magnetic field induces an electric current in the playback coil that is an exact copy of the information stored on the tape. This electric signal may then be amplified and reconverted into sound by a speaker. The diagram shows this process.

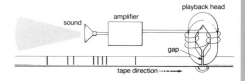

This same principle applies to the recording of data on audio tapes, video tapes, and floppy or hard disks. The regions of magnetization can be very small so that many "tracks" can be recorded on each surface. For example, on a double-density, double-sided $3\frac{1}{2}''$ floppy disk, there may be as many as 135 tracks per inch, making a total of 472 recording tracks. The disks are rotated quickly in a disk drive until the sector where information is to be stored or retrieved is located. The head that records information on a disk is called the "write head", and the head that retrieves the information is called the "read head". A typical floppy disk used with a home computer can store up to 6 million individual pieces of information, equivalent to 300 pages of single-spaced typewriting.

24

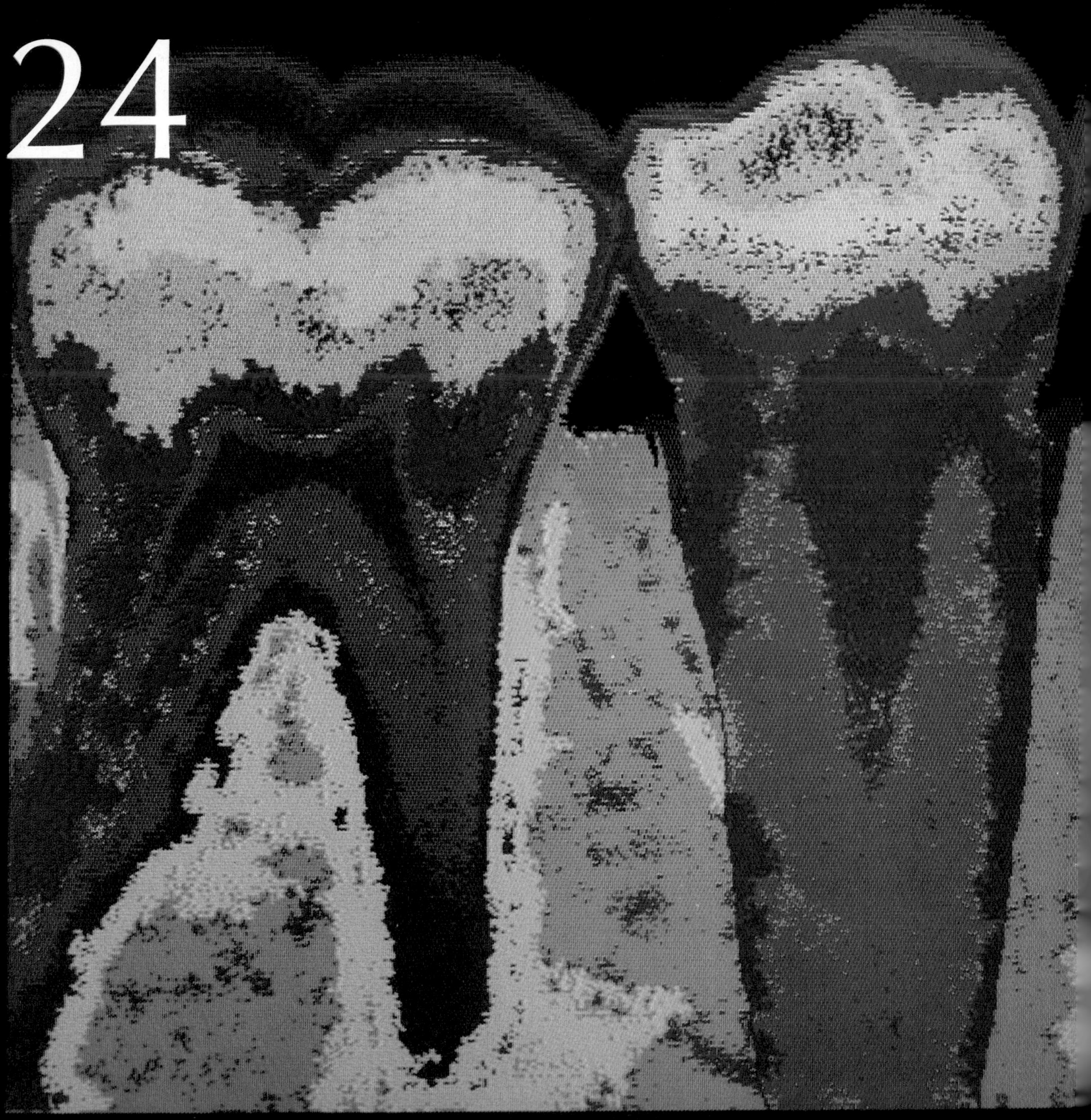

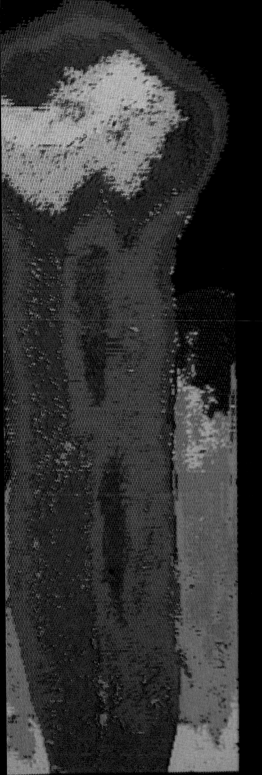

Investigating New Rays

Chapter Objectives

☐ **Describe** how electric discharge changes in a gas-discharge tube as it is evacuated.

☐ **Describe** experiments that were done to show that cathode rays move in straight lines, have mass, are deflected by magnetic fields, and have a negative charge.

☐ **Explain** what is meant by "thermionic emission" and the "Edison effect".

☐ **Explain** how the cathode ray tube is used in television, radar, and an oscilloscope.

☐ **State** five properties of X-rays and **describe** their industrial and medical applications.

☐ **Compare and contrast** alpha particles, beta particles, and gamma rays.

☐ **State** beneficial and harmful effects of X-rays and gamma rays on living tissue.

☐ **Describe** how four different types of radioactivity detectors function.

Introduction

In 1808, an English chemist, John Dalton, proposed that matter was composed of tiny particles called atoms. Every pure substance, according to his theory, was made up of a single type of atom, or combination of different atoms, called molecules. For over 90 years, atoms were considered to be the smallest particles of matter, and thus indivisible. (Dalton called them the "ultimate" particles of matter.)

In the second half of the 19th century, experiments were carried out which showed that the atom *was* divisible and that particles even more elementary than the atom existed. Many new kinds of particles were discovered, along with new forces that held them together, and powerful new sources of energy were revealed.

Analyzing the paths of subatomic particles emitted from a radioactive source

24.1 Cathode Rays

The fact that a noisy succession of sparks from an induction coil changes to a quiet, luminous discharge when the surrounding air pressure is reduced was known as early as 1750. But it was not until the middle of the 19th century, with the invention of more efficient vacuum pumps, that scientists were able to investigate this phenomenon more thoroughly.

The earliest investigations were made by Heinrich Geissler in Bonn, Germany. He had invented a new pump that produced extremely low pressures. He was also an expert glass-blower, and by skillfully shaping tubes in a variety of patterns, and using different gases and types of glass, he produced colorful displays of electric discharges. Geissler's work led to 40 years of intensive investigation, climaxed by the discovery of the electron.

A tube that allows an electric current to pass through a gas at low pressure is called a **gas-discharge tube**. A simple gas-discharge tube is illustrated. The two metal plates marked + and −, sealed in the ends of the tube, are called **electrodes**. The positive electrode is called the **anode** and the negative electrode is called the **cathode**.

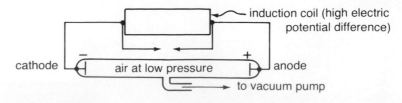

Gas-discharge tube

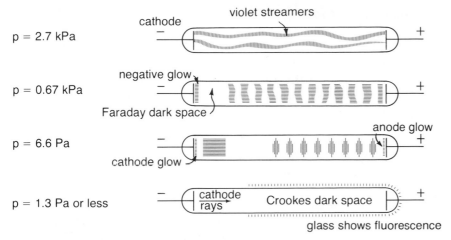

Electric discharge through air at low pressures

Note that atmospheric pressure is 100 kPa at sea level.

The electrodes are connected to a source of high electric potential (usually an induction coil producing more than 10 000 V). The tube is connected to a vacuum pump through a side tube.

Shortly after the pump is turned on, the discharge ceases across the induction coil, and the electrodes are joined by one or more violet streamers. As the pressure is further reduced, an intense pink discharge gradually fills the space between the electrodes. This discharge then begins to break up into two parts. A pink glow appears near the anode and a bluish glow near the cathode, separated by a dark, or clear, area called the **Faraday dark space.** As the tube is evacuated still further, the dark space expands and the color at the electrodes fades until the dark space fills the tube and only a faint green or violet glow surrounds the anode. At this stage the sides of the tube fluoresce, usually in green. The dark space between the electrodes at this stage is called the **Crookes dark space.**

The color of the discharge is orange-red if the tube contains neon gas instead of air. Such tubes are used in advertising signs.

Scientific interest centered on what was happening in the Crookes dark space. Various tubes were constructed and the pressure was reduced until the space between the electrodes was completely occupied by the Crookes dark space.

The early researchers decided that the colored glow in a gas discharge tube originated at the cathode. Therefore, they named this discharge the **cathode ray** and called the tube a **cathode ray tube.** Some of the investigations that were done to determine the properties of cathode rays are described next.

A Maltese cross tube

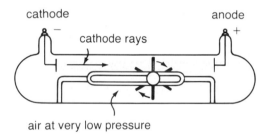

Paddle-wheel discharge tube

Maltese Cross Tube

In 1859, Julius Plücker, a German physicist, made a special tube in which the anode was an aluminum Maltese cross. The cross formed a distinct shadow in the fluorescent glow on the end of the tube, indicating that cathode rays travel in a straight line from the cathode to the anode.

Paddle-wheel Discharge Tube

In 1879, the English physicist William Crookes reported the results of his many experiments with cathode rays. In one tube he had placed a small paddle wheel, free to rotate, between the cathode and the anode. When cathode rays struck the blades of the paddle wheel, the wheel began to rotate as if it had been struck by a beam of tiny particles. This experiment showed that cathode rays might be composed of moving particles.

Cathode Rays in a Magnetic Field

In another tube Crookes showed that cathode rays are deflected by a magnetic field. It can be demonstrated that a force acts on moving electric charges in a magnetic field at right angles both to the magnetic field and to the direction of motion of the charge. Crookes found that cathode rays, when passing through a magnetic field, are deflected in exactly the same way (see illustration). On the basis of this experiment, Crookes proposed that cathode rays are a stream of negative particles, moving from the cathode to the anode.

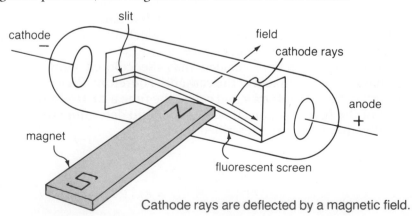

Cathode rays are deflected by a magnetic field.

Cathode Rays in an Electric Field

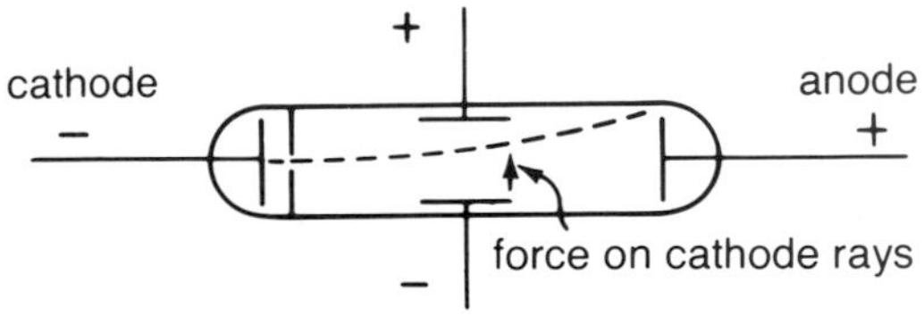

In 1890, Arthur Schuster, a professor of physics at Manchester University, sent a beam of cathode rays between two oppositely charged plates. The rays were repelled by the negative plate and attracted to the positive plate—another indication that cathode rays might be beams of small, negatively charged particles.

Cathode Rays Carry a Negative Charge

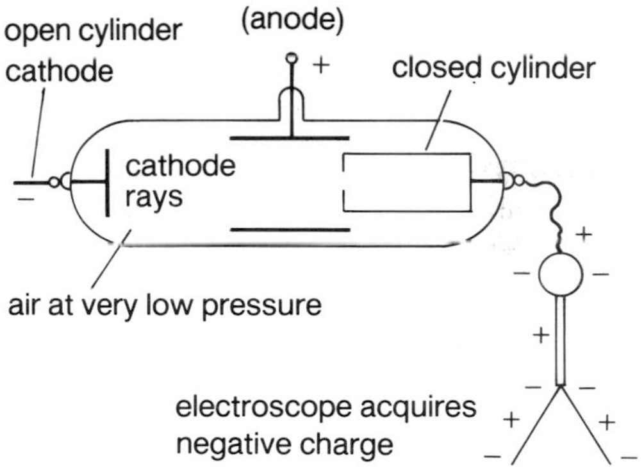

How Perrin demonstrated that cathode rays convey negative charge.

Jean Perrin, a physicist at the University of Paris, designed a tube to test Crookes's hypothesis. In his tube, the anode was a hollow aluminum cylinder, open at both ends. Near the end of the cylinder and insulated from it was a closed cylinder with a small opening at one end, as illustrated. Some cathode rays shot past the anode and into the closed cylinder. A charge quickly built up on the closed cylinder, indicated by the divergence of the leaves of a metal-leaf electroscope connected to it. The charge on the electroscope was checked in the usual way with a negative ebonite rod. This showed that cathode rays are negatively charged.

J. J. Thomson's Tube

In 1897, J.J. Thomson of Cambridge University repeated many of the earlier experiments and added one of his own—an attempt to measure the mass and charge of the particles in cathode rays.

Thomson's tube contained two charged plates to deflect the cathode rays in one direction, and two current-carrying coils placed so that their magnetic field would deflect the rays in the opposite direction. The electric and magnetic fields were adjusted to balance

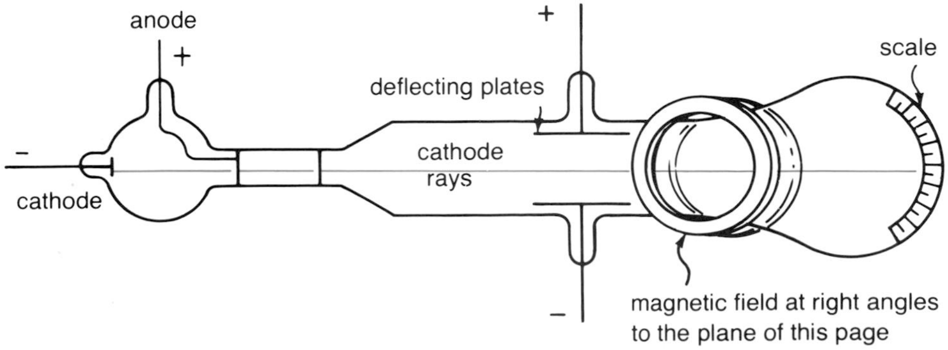

The magnetic coils are shown here displaced to the right. Actually, they overlap the deflecting plates.

24.6 Radioactivity

Photograph of radioactive substances

ele

cat

hea

N
u

Fluorescence is produced in some substances when they are exposed to the radiations from cathode ray tubes and X-ray tubes. It is also produced by a number of substances when exposed to sunlight. Early investigators suspected that the reverse might be true—some phosphorescent chemicals might emit weak X-rays when exposed to sunlight. But which ones?

In 1896, Henri Becquerel, a French physicist, carried out a number of experiments with phosphorescent crystals of different chemical compounds, placing them on top of photographic plates that had been wrapped in black paper, and putting the plates in the sunlight so that the chemicals would fluoresce. He then developed all the photographic plates to see whether there was any sign of X-rays having penetrated the black paper.

On Wednesday, February 26, Becquerel was preparing to perform the investigation with still another compound—this one containing uranium. He had already placed a sample of the compound on a photographic plate when he realized that the weather was too cloudy for the experiment. He placed the uranium compound and the photographic plate in a drawer to wait for better weather. By Sunday the sun had still not appeared. Expecting to find only a feeble image, Becquerel developed the plate he had stored away earlier in the week. To his surprise, it was strongly exposed. His explanation was that uranium compounds emit radiation that can expose photographic plates even when these are not exposed to sunlight. Becquerel had discovered **radioactivity**. Like many great discoveries, the observation was an "accident", but the scientist realized its significance. Soon others joined Becquerel in the search for more radioactive substances, and for an explanation of the nature of the radiation produced by them.

A few months later, Marie Curie, a young chemistry student in Paris, chose the new field of radioactivity for her graduate thesis, a subject that also interested her husband, Pierre, a physicist. In her investigation of uranium compounds, she found that the amount of radiation depended only on the amount of uranium present in the compounds, not on the nature or amount of the other elements in the compounds, nor on the shape or temperature of the compounds. This was a most important discovery, for it showed that the radioactivity of an element is determined by something inside the atoms which is unchanged by any external factors, even by the elements with which it is combined in a compound.

Marie Curie's experiments with uranium compounds led her to examine the ores from which uranium is obtained—pitchblende and chalcolite. To her surprise, she found that the ores were more radioactive than pure uranium. This suggested to her that other more radioactive substances were present in the ores, and she set out to find them.

She ground up pitchblende 20 kg at a time in a large iron pot, dissolved it, filtered it, crystallized it, collected it, redissolved it—over and over again until she was left with a minute quantity of a new element 300 times more radioactive than uranium. She named it **polonium**, after Poland, where she was born. Then she noticed that the residue from this separation was also highly radioactive.

In December 1898, after working together on the project for six months, Marie and Pierre Curie announced the discovery of another new radioactive element, also found in pitchblende, that was 900 times as radioactive as uranium. They named it **radium**.

In 1903, Becquerel and the Curies were awarded the Nobel Prize for physics jointly for their investigation of radioactivity. In 1911, Marie Curie was awarded a second Nobel Prize for her discovery of radium and polonium. She was the first woman to win a Nobel Prize and the only person ever to win two Nobel Prizes for science.

Radium was soon found to be effective in the treatment of cancer because it killed cancerous cells. Within a few years, hospitals around the world were using radiation therapy. At the same time, the dangers of the radiation were becoming painfully apparent. The hands of Pierre and Marie had been burned by exposure to radioactivity. They both complained of continuous fatigue, and were generally in poor health—the first signs of radiation sickness. Neither would believe that radiation could do any long-term damage. To prove this, in one of his experiments Pierre strapped a sample of radium to his arm. Within a few hours it produced a large burn. He felt he had proved his point when the burn healed.

We do not know how much effect radiation had on Pierre Curie, for in 1906 he was killed by a horse-drawn wagon. We do know that when Marie died she showed all the symptoms of radiation sickness, though she had lived for 30 years after her massive exposure. Others were not so fortunate. In the 20 years following Marie's experiments, more than 100 people died from exposure to radioactive radiation.

Both Becquerel and the Curies had noticed that some of the radioactive radiation could be deflected by a magnetic field. Some emitted radiations were deflected in the same way as cathode rays and thus were negative, while others were deflected in the opposite direction and thus were positive. At about the same time, Pierre Villard discovered a third and more penetrating radiation that was unaffected by magnetic or electric fields.

Marie Curie in her laboratory

Other radioactive elements discovered in pitchblende were actinium (1899), radon gas (1900), and protactinium (1917).

Cloud Chamber

The cloud chamber is a container supersaturated with alcohol vapor or water vapor. As a charged particle travels through the chamber, it knocks electric charges off any air molecules it happens to hit. These charged particles attract nearby vapor molecules, forming tiny drops of liquid that are seen as a small vapor trail in the chamber. The appearance of cloud chamber tracks varies according to the particle concerned. Cloud chamber tracks for alpha, beta, and gamma radiations are illustrated.

Particle "tracks" in a cloud chamber

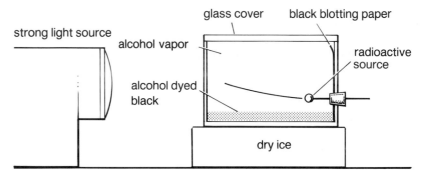

Cloud chamber

Appearance of cloud chamber tracks

Bubble Chamber

A bubble chamber makes use of a liquid, typically liquid hydrogen, which is kept close to its boiling point. When a charged particle passes through the liquid, bubbles of vapor form along the path of the particle. Usually a strong magnetic field is applied across the bubble chamber, causing the particles to move in curved paths. By noting the direction of the curvature, the charge of the particle can be determined. By measuring the radius of curvature, the mass and speed of the particle can be calculated. This type of detector is used in high energy particle research where physicists investigate the basic structure of matter.

A hydrogen bubble chamber

Particle tracks in a bubble chamber

Scintillation Detectors

William Crookes noted that, when an alpha particle strikes a thin layer of zinc sulphide, a flash of light, or **scintillation**, is created at the point of contact. By mounting a screen coated with zinc sulphide at one end of a brass tube and attaching a magnifying glass at the other end, Crookes created an alpha particle detector. He named it the **spinthariscope**. Although this device is not much used today, it was very useful for the purpose of counting alpha particles when the structure of the atom was being investigated, as we will see in the next chapter.

Modern scintillation counters use electronic means to convert minute flashes of light into measurable electrical currents. A solid phosphorescent material such as sodium iodide is cemented to the top of the photomultiplier tube. Inside the tube is a photo-cathode which emits an electron when struck by a pulse of light. Every time a radioactive particle enters the sodium iodide, an electron is subse-

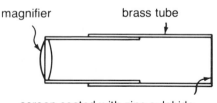

screen coated with zinc sulphide

Crookes spinthariscope

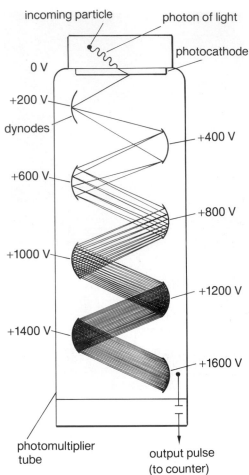

incoming particle

photon of light

photocathode

0 V

+200 V

dynodes

+400 V

+600 V

+800 V

+1000 V

+1200 V

+1400 V

+1600 V

photomultiplier
tube

output pulse
(to counter)

Scintillation counter with a
photomultiplier tube

The original unit for radioactivity was the curie. One curie represents 3.7×10^{10} disintegrations per second. Note the relationship with the becquerel.

1 g of radium releases about 25 J/h of energy.

quently emitted from the photocathode. This electron is accelerated toward the first positive electrode, called a **dynode**. This electron strikes the surface of the dynode with sufficient energy that it causes 2 to 5 electrons to be emitted from the first dynode and the multiplication process begins. Most photomultipiers have more than 10 dynodes and produce a multiplication factor of 10^6 or more. The electrical output of the photomultiplier is sent to an electronic counter which displays the number of particles/s entering the phosphor. Scintillation counters such as this can detect all three types of radioactive emissions.

Semiconductor Devices

A relatively recent innovation is the use of semiconductor materials as detectors. As discussed briefly in section 18.3, semiconductors are materials that are neither good conductors nor good insulators. When an electrical potential difference is applied across the material, a particle passing through the material causes ionization briefly modifying the electrical characteristics of the device. The resulting electrical pulse can be counted electronically in the same manner that was used in the scintillation counters and Geiger-Müller tubes.

24.8 Units Of Radioactivity

The unit used to measure radioactivity is the **becquerel (Bq)**. The level of radiation is 1 Bq when one particle is emitted per second from a radioactive source. That is,

---

1 Bq = 1 emission/s

Thus, the radioactivity of 8.6 Bq is the same as 8.6 emissions/s, or 516 emissions/min. For most radioactive sources, the becquerel is too small a unit. For example, one gram of radium has a radioactivity of 3.7×10^{10} Bq. As a result, the kilobecquerel (kBq) and megabecquerel (MBq) are often used. The radioactivity of radium would more likely be expressed as 3.7×10^4 MBq or 37 GBq.

Investigation

Investigation 24.1: Detecting Radiation

Problems:
1. How can radiation be detected?
2. What factors influence the detection of radiation?

Materials:
Geiger-Müller tube with ratemeter
radioactive sources (beta and gamma)
strips of thick paper, glass, aluminum, and lead

Caution: Even when working with low-level radioactive sources, care must be taken that sources are kept away from your body except for short periods of time.

Investigation
1. Move all radioactive sources several meters away from the tube. Turn on the ratemeter at high amplification. Place the tube in the position it will occupy for the remainder of the investigation, and observe the activity rate, if any. This will provide a measure of the background radiation present near the tube.
2. Move the beta source towards the tube until a full-scale deflection is obtained. Measure the distance to the tube from the source (d). Move the beta source away from the tube in steps of about $\frac{1}{4}d$, and record the activity in your notebook, in a table such as the following one.

Distance	$d =$	$1.25d =$	$1.50d =$	$1.75d =$	$2.00d =$
Rate					

Plot a graph of activity rate versus distance.

3. Move the beta source back to the position of full-scale deflection. Place strips of thick paper, one at a time, between the source and the tube. Record any difference in rate. Repeat this procedure using strips of glass, then aluminum, then lead. Plot graphs of activity rate versus the number of strips of each material used. Put all graphs on the same sheet of graph paper.
4. Repeat the entire experiment using the gamma source.

CAUTION: Put on your safety goggles and plastic gloves.

CAUTION: Handle the Geiger Müller tube with care; it is fragile. Do not touch after it has been turned on.

CAUTION: Wash your hands after the investigation.

Questions:

1. What factors can influence the measured activity rate of a radio-active source?
2. What could cause the background radiation observed?
3. If the distance of a source from a tube is doubled, what should happen to the measured activity rate? Try to find a relationship between rate and distance from your graphs. (Hint: Plot rate versus $1/d^2$)
4. List in order of effectiveness the materials used to absorb beta radiation. Does this order also hold true for gamma radiation?
5. Which type of radiation is more penetrating? Suggest a reason for your answer.
6. What thickness of each type of material would be needed to shield all radiation from the beta source effectively? Use your graphs to assist your predictions.
7. Answer question 6 for the gamma source.

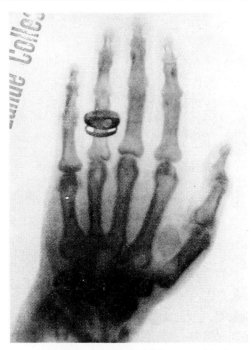

An early X-ray taken by Röntgen. Notice the ring on the patient's hand.

The important difference between X-rays and gamma rays is the source of energy. The origin of X-rays is the electron structure of the atom. The nucleus is the origin of gamma radiation.

Chapter Summary

1. Electric currents can flow through gas-discharge tubes, producing a variety of color effects, provided that the gas pressure is low.
2. Cathode rays consist of tiny, negatively charged particles called electrons moving at a high speed from the cathode of a gas-discharge tube to the anode. They travel in straight lines, have energy, and are deflected by magnetic and electric fields.
3. In the process called thermionic emission, electrons are emitted from a hot surface located within a partial vacuum.
4. In vacuum tubes, electric current can be controlled, rectified, and amplified by the use of additional electrodes.
5. A modern cathode ray tube consists of a heated cathode, a control electrode, an anode, focusing electrodes, deflecting magnetic or electric fields, and a screen coated with phosphor.
6. Cathode ray tubes are used in television receivers, radar equipment, and oscilloscopes.
7. X-rays are produced by the collision of high-energy electrons with an anode.
8. X-rays are electromagnetic radiations with short wavelengths which travel in straight lines at the speed of light, have high penetrating ability, have no charge, expose photographic film, and make fluorescent screens glow.

9. X-rays can be used in medical diagnosis, for the treatment of cancer, and for the detection of defects in manufactured products.
10. X-rays and gamma radiation can kill or change the genetic structure of human cells; they must therefore be used with great caution.
11. Radioactive emissions consist of alpha and beta particles and gamma rays.
12. Alpha particles are positively charged helium nuclei with relatively low kinetic energies and low penetrating ability. Beta particles are fast-moving electrons with high kinetic energy and high penetrating ability. Gamma radiation is an electromagnetic radiation with a very short wavelength, high energy, and an extremely high penetrating ability.
13. The becquerel (Bq) is the unit of radioactivity, and it represents particle emission at the rate of one particle per second.
14. Radioactivity can be detected by means of photographic plates, fluorescent screens, scintillation counters, cloud chambers, bubble chambers, Geiger-Müller tubes, and semiconductor devices.

Properties of the Radiation from Radioactive Substances

Radiation	Relative mass	Charge	Penetrating power	Nature
α	7300	+2	poor	charged helium atoms
β	1	−1	medium	fast electrons
γ	0	0	excellent	electromagnetic waves with a short wavelength

Chapter Review

1. Describe the observation that shows each of the following properties of cathode rays.
   (a) They travel from cathode to anode.
   (b) They travel in straight lines.
   (c) They have energy.
   (d) They are negatively charged.
2. The arrow in this diagram represents a stream of electrons moving in the plane of the paper from left to right. How would the electrons be deflected, relative to the paper, in each of the following cases?
   (a) A is negatively charged.
   (b) B is positively charged.
   (c) A is an S-pole and B is an N-pole.
3. When a thin beam of cathode rays is sent through a magnetic field, the beam is deflected to one side but remains a thin beam. What would happen if:
   (a) the beam consisted of negative particles, all with the same mass, but with various amounts of charge?

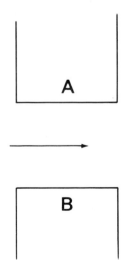

Question 2

     (b) the beam consisted of negative particles, all with the same charge, but with various masses?

     (c) the beam consisted of negative particles whose charge was proportional to their mass? (A particle with three times the mass would have three times the charge.)

4. Does Thomson's experiment prove that all electrons have the same mass and the same charge? Explain your answer.

5. Using a diagram of a simple vacuum diode, explain how a current flows through the tube.

6. What would be the effect of each of the following on the beam of electrons in a cathode ray tube and on the dot of light on the screen?

     (a) A hotter filament is used.

     (b) The anode voltage is increased.

     (c) The control electrode is made more negative.

7. The cathode ray tube is used in radar. It is also used in sonar (section 11.7) particularly in military ships and submarines. Briefly compare the two applications, stating the similarities and the differences.

8. What properties of X-rays enable them to make X-ray photographs?

9. Explain why it is dangerous to X-ray a human fetus.

10. X-rays can be used to destroy cancer cells. Why are there often side effects such as loss of hair, dizziness, and lack of energy?

11. How might X-rays be used to check welds in a gas pipeline?

12. What is the difference between X-rays and γ-rays?

13. If α-rays and β-rays with the same speed were passed through a magnetic field,

     (a) which particles would have the greater force acting on them?

     (b) which particles would undergo the greater deflection? Explain your answers.

14. Most airport security systems use X-ray machines to view luggage as it is checked before loading it onto an airplane.

     (a) Most photographic film passes through without damage. Why?

     (b) High-speed film must be protected. How?

15. Determine the activity of the sources with the following:

     (a) 100 000 emissions in 1 s

     (b) 4.8×10^6 emissions in 30 s

     (c) 3.2×10^3 particles in 1.2 min

16. A patient undergoing diagnostic tests for a kidney disease is injected with radioactive iodine which has an activity of 7.0 MBq. How many emissions come from the kidneys in 2.0 min, assuming the iodine is concentrated in the kidneys?

Physics—a Career

Why Study Physics?

Many students find that they enjoy the challenge and application of physics, and so may consider it as a career. Others may choose to pursue a career in a field related to physics, such as engineering, geology, oceanography, computer electronics, archaeology, or patent law. In both cases, the study of physics at secondary school, college or university will be a prerequisite.

What Do Physicists Do?

Men and women physicists are engaged in a variety of activities in industry, in research at university, government, and private laboratories, and in education. In research, physicists design and perform experiments to test and modify available theories and, as well, deduce ways of putting the principles involved to practical use. Other

Physicists often use computers.

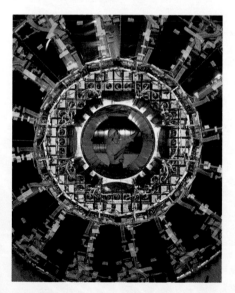

A technician repairs one of the particle detectors at CERN.

researchers, more interested in the mathematical aspects of physical theories, derive equations and develop mathematical models used to better understand the physical world. Many physicists are concerned with the application of physics to the needs of society. Some of them are teachers at secondary, college, and university levels. Finally, some physicists are administrators in government, universities and high-technology industries, where research and development are of paramount importance.

Careers in Physics

Physics Specialities
Astronomy
Astrophysics
Meteorology
Geophysics
Acoustics
Electronics
Solid-State Physics
Spectroscopy
Particle Physics
Nuclear Physics
Computer Technology
Plasma Physics
Optics and Laser Physics
Biophysics
Low Temperature Physics
Teaching Physics
Medical Physics

Engineering Specialities
Civil
Mechanical
Electrical
Geological
Industrial
Metallurgical
Aeronautical
Maritime
Chemical
Systems Design

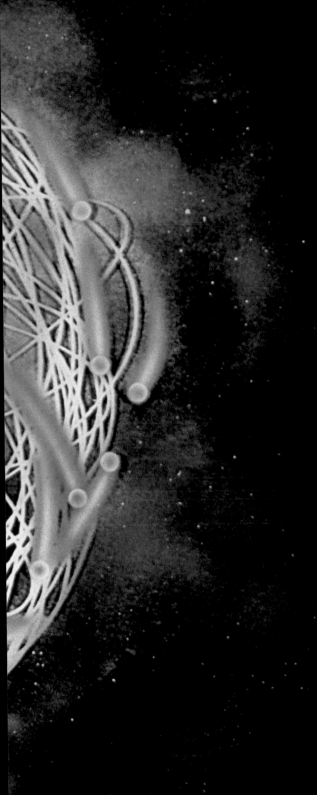

Investigating the Atom

Chapter Objectives

- **Describe** *Dalton's, Thompson's, Rutherford's, and Bohr's atomic models.*

- **Describe** *Mendeleev's reasoning in arranging the periodic table and* **explain** *Moseley's changes to the table.*

- **Explain** *the problem with orbiting electrons in Rutherford's model.*

- **Define** *"allowed orbit", "quantum number", "electron shell", "ground state", and "excited state".*

- **Determine** *both the energy and the radius of the allowed orbits for hydrogen atoms.*

- **State** *the numbers of neutrons, protons, and electrons for the first 18 elements.*

- **Define** *"isotope" and* **give examples.**

- **Explain** *how atoms absorb and reemit energy and* **describe** *emission spectra.*

- **Describe** *how substances emit laser light.*

Researchers at IBM manipulated individual atoms on the surface of a solid to make this photograph, produced on a scanning tunnelling microscope.

25.1 Early Ideas about the Atom

As early as 400 B.C., the Greek philosopher Democritus proposed that all matter was composed of tiny, indivisible particles called atoms. His theory was based more on philosophical reasoning than on any direct experimental evidence. Experimental evidence of the existence of atoms was not found until much later, early in the 19th century, by an English scientist, John Dalton (1766-1844). Even then, Dalton's atomic theory was based more on its usefulness in explaining observed natural phenomena than on experimental evidence. The evolution of the modern atomic theory from Dalton's theory is an outstanding example of the development of a scientific model.

Dalton's Atomic Theory

Dalton's theory, published in 1810, was the first systematic approach to the development of a model of matter. It made the following basic statements about the structure of matter:
- All matter consists of very small, indivisible, indestructible particles called atoms.
- All atoms of a given element are identical.
- Each element's atomic mass is unique, that is, different from the mass of any other element's atoms.
- Atoms combine together, in simple whole-number ratios, to form compounds. The smallest unit of a compound is a molecule.
- Atoms are neither created nor destroyed during a chemical reaction.

Dalton's model of the atom is sometimes called "the billiard-ball model of the atom": the atom has no internal or external features; it exists merely as an indivisible chunk of matter.

Dalton's billiard-ball atom

The Periodic Table

Dalton's atomic theory stated that all matter consists of atoms and combinations of atoms, or molecules. In the 60 years that followed, chemists were able to figure out which substances were **elements**, composed of a single kind of atom, and which were **compounds**, composed of molecules. In addition, they were able to figure out the relative masses of the various kinds of atoms. They knew, for example, that the hydrogen atom is the lightest, and assigned it an atomic mass of 1. The carbon atom was found to be 12 times as heavy, giving it an atomic mass of 12.

As early as 1869, a Russian chemist, Dmitri Mendeleev (1834-1907), began searching for some fundamental laws regarding the structure of atoms with similar chemical and physical properties. He arranged the 63 known atoms in ascending order of atomic mass, grouping elements with similar chemical and physical properties in separate vertical columns.

The real genius of Mendeleev's work lies in the fact that his table contained several "holes"—blank spaces where elements appeared to be missing. He reasoned that the spaces represented elements that had not yet been discovered. He even went so far as to predict some of their properties, should they be found. To date, all of the first 105 spaces in this table, called the **Periodic Table of the Elements,** have been filled (see Appendix E).

With a few modifications, Dalton's theory stands unchanged after more than 150 years. It has been altered and amended, as must all good scientific models, to account for new experimental discoveries. Perhaps the most significant change that it has undergone concerns the divisibility of the atom. Towards the end of the 19th century, scientists using research tools and techniques not available to Dalton made discoveries that could not be explained by the concept of a tiny, solid, indivisible and indestructible atom.

Thomson's Atomic Model

In Chapter 24, you became familiar with the properties of cathode rays. It was Crookes who first deduced that cathode rays consist of negatively charged particles, and his deduction was supported by Arthur Schuster and J.J. Thomson.

In fact, Thomson was able to measure the ratio of mass-to-charge for these particles, using a tube that could deflect the beam both electrically and magnetically. He estimated the speed of the particles to be about 3×10^7 m/s and their mass to be about $\frac{1}{1800}$ of the mass of a hydrogen ion. He called them electrons. He was able to show that electrons have identical properties regardless of the electrode material or the gas in the discharge tube. As a result, he suspected that they must be a fundamental particle found in all atoms. By investigating the properties of cathode rays, he had made a discovery that would be the starting point for a whole new way of looking at the structure and nature of matter. (See also Section 24.1.)

Today, atomic masses are measured in units called "unified atomic mass units" (u).

$$1 \text{ u} = 1.660\ 44 \times 10^{-27} \text{ kg}$$

The mass of an atom of carbon-12 was chosen arbitrarily as exactly 12 u. The masses of all other atoms are expressed in unified atomic mass units relative to carbon-12.

The first 92 elements (with a few exceptions) occur naturally. Some of the 105 elements that are known today have been under observation only for short periods in the laboratory. Artificially created, they existed for only a few micro-seconds and then changed into other substances. Still, scientists were able to recognize properties that make these substances unique. Elements 104 and 105 were unnamed for a long time, but they are now called Kurchatovium and Hahnium, respectively.

The mass of an electron is 9.11×10^{-31} kg.

sphere of uniformly distributed positive charge

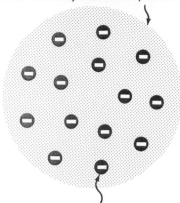

negatively charged electrons
embedded throughout

Thomson's raisin-bun atom

A device for detecting and measuring
radioactive emissions, the Geiger
counter, was named after Hans Geiger,
whose work led to its development.

Gold foils were used by Rutherford
because gold is relatively dense and acts
as a good scattering center for alpha
particles. Also, gold can be rolled thin
enough that most alpha particles will
pass through the foil and be deflected
only by a single nucleus, if at all. Even
so, the gold foils used in this experiment were about 400 atoms thick.

Thomson devised a model of the atom based on his findings, and it was widely accepted about the turn of the century. In this model, the atom was represented as a sphere of positive charge with negative electrons embedded in it, much like raisins in a bun. Thomson knew that atoms are neutral, so he believed that there were just enough negative electrons in his model to balance the positive charge throughout the remainder of the atom. As we will see, Thomson's model was not able to stand up for long.

25.2 The Discovery of the Nucleus: Rutherford's Experiment

In 1911, two German physics students, H. Geiger and E. Marsden, working under Ernest Rutherford at the University of Manchester, performed a series of experiments that led to a greater understanding of the internal structure of the atom.

A beam of alpha particles from a radon source was shot at a thin sheet of gold foil, less than 10^{-4} cm thick. When an alpha particle strikes a screen coated with zinc sulfide, a tiny flash of light (called a scintillation) is produced at the point where the alpha particle hits the screen. A zinc sulfide screen and microscope detector were mounted so that they could be moved to any position around the gold foil. (See also Section 24.6.)

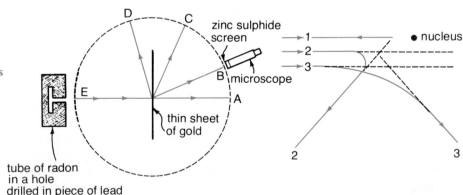

Apparatus used by Geiger and
Marsden to measure scattering
angles of alpha particles

The paths of three alpha particles
as they approach the positive
gold nucleus closely enough to
be scattered

Geiger and Marsden spent months laboriously recording the numbers of alpha particles that were scattered at each angle by the gold foil. Their results may be summarized as follows:

- Most of the alpha particles were detected at point A, having passed through the gold foil without being noticeably deflected.
- Some alpha particles were detected at points B and C; furthermore, on rare occasions, alpha particles that had been deflected by more than 90° were detected at points D and even E.

In 1911, Ernest Rutherford (1871-1937), director of the laboratory at the University of Manchester and a supervisor of Geiger and Marsden, suggested the following explanation of their results:

- The positive alpha particles were scattered by the force of electric repulsion between themselves and the positive charges within the gold atoms.
- Since few alpha particles were noticeably scattered, the positive charge of the atom must be concentrated within a very small region of space. (Rutherford called this space the **nucleus**.) Only alpha particles that passed very close to the nucleus were scattered.
- The electrons were in orbit in the empty space around the nucleus of the atom, held by the force of electric attraction of the positive nucleus.

This explanation was immediately accepted, and it formed the basis of Rutherford's "nuclear atom" model, sometimes called the solar–system atom, with the electrons in orbit around the nucleus, just as the planets are in orbit around the sun. Rutherford's calculations showed that the nucleus has a diameter of about 10^{-14} m compared with an atomic diameter of about 10^{-10} m. Thus, the volume of an atom is about 10^{12} times the volume of its nucleus. Since the remainder of the atom is essentially empty space, it is easy to understand why a large majority of the alpha particles in the Rutherford gold-foil experiment passed through the foil without being scattered by the nucleus.

The actual structure of the nucleus was not immediately apparent to Rutherford. He did know that the hydrogen nucleus has the smallest charge of any known nucleus, and that all the other nuclei have charges that are whole-numbered multiples of this smallest charge. He also realized that the positive charge on the hydrogen nucleus is equal in magnitude to the negative charge on an electron. In 1920, he gave the hydrogen nucleus its name—he called it the **proton**. Other nuclei with greater amounts of positive charge must contain more protons, he said. For example, an oxygen nucleus, with a positive charge eight times that of a hydrogen nucleus, must contain eight protons. By the same reasoning, the oxygen nucleus might be expected to have a mass eight times that of the hydrogen nucleus. However, accurate measurements showed that

This is the same electrostatic force that was discussed in Chapter 18. The smaller the distance between the alpha particle and the nucleus, the greater the force of electrostatic repulsion.

If the atom and the nucleus are thought of as spheres whose volume is given by the equation $V = \frac{4}{3}\pi r^3$, then

$$\frac{\text{volume of atom}}{\text{volume of nucleus}} = \frac{\frac{4}{3}\pi(10^{-10})^3}{\frac{4}{3}\pi(10^{-14})^3}$$

$$= \frac{10^{-30}}{10^{-42}}$$

$$= 10^{12}$$

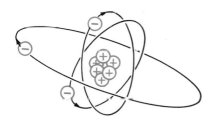

Rutherford's solar-system atom

Some modern theories visualize electrons as cloud-like distributions of negative electric charge, more concentrated in some places than in others.

To calculate the approximate density of a nucleus with a mass of 10^{-27} kg and a volume of 10^{-41} m³:

$$D = \frac{M}{V}$$

$$= \frac{10^{-27} \text{ kg}}{10^{-41} \text{ m}^3}$$

$$= 10^{14} \text{ kg/m}^3$$

This is about the same density as some stars.

the mass of the oxygen nucleus is not eight but 16 times the mass of the hydrogen nucleus. Rutherford and his collegues were, at first, perplexed by this problem, but later they proposed the existence of another particle in the nucleus, a particle with a mass approximately equal to that of a proton but with no electrical charge. These particles were called **neutrons**, and their existence was verified experimentally by the English physicist James Chadwick in 1932 (see Section 26.5).

With this new knowledge, it became possible to represent the structure of every known element in terms of the number of protons and neutrons in its nucleus, and the number of electrons in orbit around its nucleus. The number of protons in an atom's nucleus is called the **atomic number**. Since atoms are electrically neutral, and since the amount of positive charge on a proton is equal to the amount of negative charge on an electron, the atomic number is also the number of electrons orbiting the atom's nucleus. The total number of particles in the nucleus (protons and neutrons) is called the **atomic mass number**. Symbolically, then, the structure of any atom may be written as:

$$^A_Z X$$　　where A is the atomic mass number
　　　　　　　Z is the atomic number
　　　　　　　X is the atomic symbol

Such an atom is composed of Z protons, (A—Z) neutrons, and Z electrons.

25.3 The Bohr Model of the Atom

There was one major problem with Rutherford's "planetary model" of the atom. He reasoned that an atom's electrons must be moving around the nucleus in orbits, just as the planets move around the sun. If electrons were stationary, they would be attracted towards the positive nucleus, and the atom would collapse. In 1864, James Clerk Maxwell (1831-1879) had predicted that whenever an electric charge accelerated (changed its speed and/or its direction), it should give off energy in the form of an electromagnetic wave. In fact, Heinrich Hertz (1857-1894) succeeded in producing and detecting these waves in 1887. As a result, electrons in orbit around a nucleus should be giving off energy continuously, as they change direction. As they lose energy, an atom's electrons should quickly spiral in towards the nucleus, eventually colliding with it and being captured by it. Atoms should spontaneously collapse. Why, then, are they stable—why don't they continuously give off energy and collapse?

Niels Bohr (1885-1962)

In 1913, Niels Bohr (1885-1962), a Danish physicist working in Rutherford's laboratory, became interested in this problem. Based on the extensive research of others using hydrogen atoms, he published the following conclusions:

• Within an atom, there are certain **allowed orbits** around the nucleus, in which electrons can move indefinitely without giving off energy.

• Each of these allowed orbits represents a definite amount of electron energy. For an electron to occupy any one of the allowed orbits, it must possess the energy allowed for that orbit.

• The orbit with the least energy is found closest to the nucleus. Each orbit is assigned a **quantum number**, n, where $n = 1, 2, 3\ldots$(i.e., "$n = 1$" refers to the lowest energy orbit, "$n = 2$" refers to the second lowest energy orbit, etc.)

• Only a specific number of electrons can occupy each of the allowed orbits. Under normal conditions, all of an atom's electrons occupy orbits with the lowest allowed amounts of energy.

Bohr was able to determine both the energy and the radius of the allowed orbits for hydrogen atoms, in terms of the quantum number. He found that:

$$E_n = -\frac{13.6}{n^2}\ \text{eV}$$

$$r_n = 5.3 \times 10^{-11}\ n^2\text{m}$$

where E_n is the energy of an electron in the nth allowed orbit, in electronvolts

r_n is the radius of the nth allowed orbit, in meters

NOTE: The energies of electrons wthin atoms are usually measured in units called **electronvolts** (eV).

1 eV is the energy of an electron accelerated from rest by a potential difference of 1 V.

1 eV = 1.6×10^{-19} J

Thus, Bohr was able to draw scale diagrams of both the allowed orbits for the hydrogen atom, and also the allowed energy levels for an electron in a hydrogen atom.

Bohr assigned an energy value of 0 to an electron that was just able to escape from an atom. All electrons held within an atom's orbits, then, have a negative value of energy. Also, the difference between the energy at one energy level and the energy at the next level decreases as the quantum number increases. In fact, at very large values of n the levels become difficult to distinguish and seem to merge into a continuum. We will study the significance of these levels in Section 25.5.

The Bohr concept of allowed orbits and distinct energy levels for

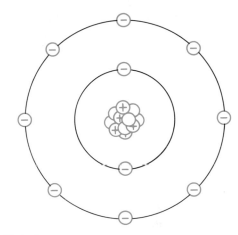

Bohr's atom

The amount of energy required to remove an electron completely from an atom is called the ionization energy, E_I. For a hydrogen atom, this energy is 13.6 eV.

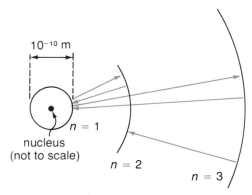

The first, second, and third Bohr orbits for the hydrogen atom

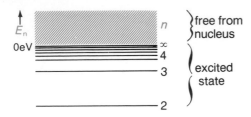

The Bohr energy-level diagram for the hydrogen atom

"Energy level" and "electron shell" are used interchangeably in references to Bohr's allowed orbits for electrons.

After element 18 (argon), the distribution of electrons in shells appears to become quite complicated. Even so, all the electrons in an atom are found in the lowest energy orbits available to them. If you are interested in this problem, try to find a periodic table that includes electron-shell distributions.

The name "isotope" was coined in 1913 by Frederick Soddy (1877-1956), an English chemist who was associated with Rutherford at McGill University. He was awarded a Nobel Prize for Chemistry in 1921.

electrons may also be applied to atoms that are more complicated in their structure than the hydrogen atom. Recent theories of atomic structure have almost abandoned any notion of electrons as particles moving around a nucleus in allowed orbits; nevertheless, the Bohr model is still useful in explaining many atomic phenomena and has not been discarded entirely.

Rutherford and Bohr were both aware of Mendeleev's periodic table, but their ideas concerning atomic structure and electrons in allowed orbits contradicted the order of some elements in the table. The table as we know it today represents the work of H.G. Moseley, a colleague of Rutherford, who arranged the elements in order of the number of protons in their nuclei, rather than their atomic masses. Each successive element in the table has one more proton and one more electron than its predecessor. The number of neutrons in the nucleus increases also, but not in such a regular fashion.

Bohr's theory suggested the existence of allowed orbits for the electrons, each orbit, or **electron shell**, being characterized by a specific amount of electron energy. The number of electrons that can occupy an electron shell with quantum number n was found to be $2n^2$.

As mentioned previously, a normal atom's elecrons will always be found in the available allowed orbits with the least energy.

The table on page 741 shows the first 18 atoms in the periodic table, with their atomic numbers, atomic masses, and electron orbit structures. The electron shells are named K, L, M, N, O, P, etc.

Each atom of a given substance has the same number of protons in its nucleus, but the number of neutrons may vary. Atoms of a substance that have different numbers of neutrons are called different **isotopes** of that substance. Hydrogen, for example, has three isotopes (see diagram on page 741).

Most of the elements in the periodic table have several isotopes, found in nature in varying proportions. In most cases, the average atomic mass of the various isotopes is used in the periodic table. In the chart on the next page, the atomic mass number for each element is that of its most abundant isotope. The known isotopes of all the elements are given in Appendix F.

Sample Problems

Determine the number of protons, electrons, and neutrons in the isotope of chlorine that has an atomic mass number of 37, often written as chlorine-37.

From the periodic table, the atomic number of chlorine is 17. Therefore, its chemical designation is

$$^{37}_{17}Cl$$

And, the number of protons $= Z = 17$
the number of electrons $= Z = 17$
the number of neutrons $= A - Z$
$= 37 - 17$
$= 20$

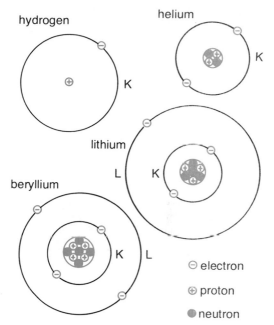

Element	Chemical symbol	Atomic number	Atomic mass number	#p	#n	#e	Distribution of electrons in Bohr orbits					
							K	L	M	N	O	P
							2	8	18	32	50	72
hydrogen	H	1	1	1	0	1	1					
helium	He	2	4	2	2	2	2					
lithium	Li	3	7	3	4	3	2	1				
beryllium	Be	4	9	4	5	4	2	2				
boron	B	5	11	5	6	5	2	3				
carbon	C	6	12	6	6	6	2	4				
nitrogen	N	7	14	7	7	7	2	5				
oxygen	O	8	16	8	8	8	2	6				
fluorine	F	9	19	9	10	9	2	7				
neon	Ne	10	20	10	10	10	2	8				
sodium	Na	11	23	11	12	11	2	8	1			
magnesium	Mg	12	24	12	12	12	2	8	2			
aluminum	Al	13	27	13	14	13	2	8	3			
silicon	Si	14	28	14	14	14	2	8	4			
phosphorus	P	15	31	15	16	15	2	8	5			
sulphur	S	16	32	16	16	16	2	8	6			
chlorine	Cl	17	35	17	18	17	2	8	7			
argon	Ar	18	40	18	22	18	2	8	8			

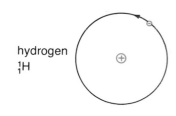

Rutherford-Bohr atom models

*P*ractice

By referring to the periodic table in Appendix O, write the chemical designation for each of the following isotopes, and state the number of protons, electrons, and neutrons in each.
(a) carbon-12
(b) copper-65
(c) magnesium-25
(d) nickel-60
(e) uranium-238

The isotopes of hydrogen

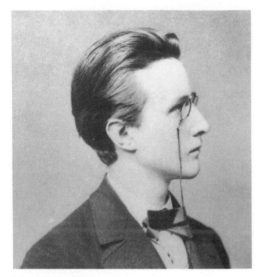

Max Planck

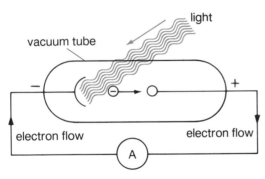

Electrons emitted by the illuminated surface move across the gap in the vacuum tube and form an electric current through the circuit that may be measured with a sensitive ammeter.

25.4 Another Look at the Nature of Light

At about the same time that Rutherford and Bohr were refining their models of atomic structure, other scientists were beginning to take a new interest in the nature of light. You may recall that certain properties of light can be explained by assuming that light behaves like a wave. As a result, the wave model of light enjoyed widespread popularity during the 18th and 19th centuries.

Towards the end of the 19th century, the German physicist Max Planck (1858-1947) undertook a study of the radiation emitted by very hot objects. The precise nature of his findings need not concern us, but their general significance is important: the wave theory of light did not fully account for the observed properties of the radiation emitted by hot objects. The wave theory of light, which had been so successful for so long, was seen to have serious deficiences.

At about the same time, a slightly different and equally puzzling phenomenon was observed by Wilhelm Hallwachs, another German physicist. He noticed that the energy of light can cause electrons to be emitted from atoms near the surface of some materials. Apparently, electrons could gain sufficient energy from light to "escape" from their atom and become totally free of the material itself. This phenomenon is called the **photoelectric effect** and it may be demonstrated by means of the apparatus shown.

Two startling facts were discovered through the use of this apparatus:
- For low-frequency light (i.e., long wavelengths), no electrons were emitted regardless of the intensity of the light.
- For frequencies higher than a certain value (i.e., shorter wavelengths), electrons were emitted even when the weakest intensities of light were used. Also, the number of electrons emitted appeared to depend only on the intensity of the light.

Planck and his colleagues were quite puzzled at first by this result. Light was believed to be wavelike. Hence, electrons could be expected to be emitted as soon as the light wave had transferred enough energy to any electron to free it from its atom. The amount of energy in a wave depended on its amplitude, so electrons should have been emitted almost immediately when a strong beam was used, and after a short build-up time when a weaker beam was used. Yet it seemed that it was the frequency, not the intensity, of the light that determined whether electrons were emitted from the illuminated surface.

In 1905, the German–born physicist Albert Einstein (1879-1955), living in Switzerland, was able to suggest an explanation that was consistent with Planck's other discoveries about the nature of radiation from hot objects. Einstein proposed that light energy was not transferred continuously and evenly, as the energy of a wave would be, but in small packages, or bundles, much like a stream of microscopic bullets. This approach, suggesting that the energy of light comes in small, discrete packages, is called the **quantum theory**, each "package" of energy being called a **quantum**. Einstein coined the term **photons** to describe these tiny particle-like quanta of light energy.

To explain the photoelectric effect, Einstein assumed that the energy of a photon depends on the frequency of the light—the higher the frequency, the more energy the photon possesses. As a result, in low-frequency light, even though an immense number of photons may have been striking the illuminated surface, no single photon possessed enough energy to free an electron, so that no electrons were emitted. Higher-frequency light consisted of photons whose energy, if absorbed by an electron, would be sufficient to cause the electron to be emitted.

The most important aspect of Einstein's explanation has to do with the relationship between a photon's energy and the frequency of light.

- **The energy of a photon varies directly with its frequency (the higher the frequency of a photon, the greater its energy).**
- **Each photon's energy corresponds to a specific frequency of light.**

25.5 Atoms and Light

Solids heated to a very high temperature give off light with a wide range of frequencies. Gases at low pressure also give off light when an electric current is passed through them or when they are heated. However, the light emitted by gases is not at all like the light given off by solids. Rather than emitting a continuous range of frequencies, each gas gives off its own distinct set of frequencies. The set of frequencies given off by a substance is called its **emission spectrum**. By observing the emission spectrum of a mixture of gases, it is possible to identify the gases present in the mixture.

The reason why a gas emits only its own special set of frequencies remained a mystery for many years. It took a combination of the Bohr-Rutherford model of the atom and Einstein's and Planck's quantum theory of light to provide the explanation. According to

If a negatively charged metal-leaf electroscope is connected to a clean sheet of zinc and irradiated with ultraviolet radiation, electrons emitted from the zinc photoelectrically will cause it to lose its charge. If at first it is neutral, the plate will become positive as electrons are emitted.

Einstein devised the equation $E = hf$, where E represents the energy of a photon, f represents its frequency, and h is a proportionality constant that Planck found to have a value of $6.63 \times 10^{-34}\ J \cdot s$.

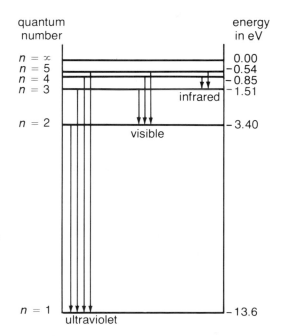

Energy-level diagram for hydrogen

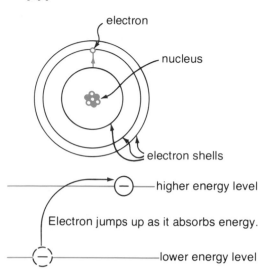

electron

nucleus

electron shells

higher energy level

Electron jumps up as it absorbs energy.

lower energy level

An electron absorbs energy when it jumps to a higher energy level.

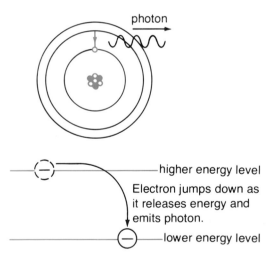

photon

higher energy level

Electron jumps down as it releases energy and emits photon.

lower energy level

An electron emits a photon when it jumps to a lower energy level.

Bohr, electrons in a given atom can only have certain specific values of energy that correspond to the allowed orbits, or electron shells, that they must occupy within the atom. Under normal conditions, all of an atom's electrons occupy the lowest energy levels available to them, and the atom is in its **ground state**. However, when an electric current is passed through a gas, or it is heated, some electrons can absorb energy and jump up into higher-energy levels. When such a transition occurs, the atom is said to be in an **excited state**, since it possesses more energy than it does when it is in the ground state. This type of transition may be depicted on an energy-level diagram, as shown in the margin.

An electron in an excited state is unstable, since there is a vacant, lower-energy level available to it. After a very short time (about 10^{-9} s) in the excited state, the electron will spontaneously jump down to one of the lower-energy levels, and will release its excess energy in the form of a photon of light. This transition may also be depicted on an energy-level diagram.

The energy of the emitted photon will be equal to the difference between the higher and lower energy levels, as follows:

$$E_{\text{photon}} = E_{\text{higher}} - E_{\text{lower}}$$

This difference in energy would result in the production of a photon with a specific frequency.

The spectrum of frequencies emitted by an atom represents all of the possible transitions for that atom between excited states and lower energy levels. For example, a hydrogen atom with one electron is in its ground state when this electron is in the K-shell ($n = 1$). If the electron absorbs energy and jumps into any other shell, then it must de-excite by one or more downward transitions until it is once again in the K-shell. Each of these downward transitions results in the emission of a photon; this is illustrated by the energy-level diagram for hydrogen on the previous page. Each arrow on the diagram represents a possible downward electron jump producing a photon with a definite frequency.

The emission spectrum for hydrogen shows the many colors of light whose photons have frequencies in the visible range, corresponding to downward transitions to the $n = 2$ energy level. Transitions to a lower energy level can occur in one step or in a series of steps.

25.6 *A*pplications: Lasers

Ever since Planck and Einstein first proposed the quantum theory, physicists have been intrigued with the idea of producing an intense beam of visible light photons powerful enough to burn holes through solids in milliseconds. The idea was pursued seriously in industrial research laboratories in the United States, Japan, Russia, and England during the late 1950s. The breakthrough came on July 7, 1960, when Dr. Theodore Maiman, a research physicist at Hughes Aircraft Company in California, built the world's first laser. Within months, the scientific community began to work feverishly on the development of this new technology. By 1965, most of the key concepts in laser technology had been discovered, and the emphasis of research turned to applications of the new phenomenon.

Laser is an acronym for **l**ight **a**mplification by the **s**timulated **e**mission of **r**adiation. Some substances or combinations of substances have excited states that are **metastable**; that is, electrons can jump up into these excited energy levels and stay there for a short time without jumping immediately back down into available lower-energy levels. Ruby crystals, calcium fluoride crystals, carbon dioxide gas, and a mixture of helium gas and neon gas are examples of substances with metastable excited states.

When many atoms or molecules are in a metastable condition (called a **population inversion**), the excited electrons may be stimulated to jump down to a lower level by the presence of another photon whose energy is exactly equal to the energy of the photon created by the downward transition.

An amplification of the light intensity is produced because the emitted photon is created "in phase" with the stimulating photon, so that they interfere constructively to produce a maximum intensity. Each of the two photons can then stimulate the emission of yet another identical photon, and a chain reaction occurs. The final result is a beam of photons, all with the same energy (frequency and wavelength) and all travelling in phase, producing a fine but very intense beam of light.

Lasers are used extensively today in communications, navigation, medicine, industry, and scientific research. A laser beam can make precise measurements to an accuracy of millionths of a centimeter—about $\frac{1}{250}$ the diameter of a human hair. A laser rangefinder (Section 14.2) has been used to measure the distance between the Earth and the moon to within 15 cm, and to map the contours of the bottoms and rims of the moon's craters. The applications of laser technology to medicine are multiplying rapidly. They range from the "welding" of a detached retina painlessly in 10^{-3} s to the treatment of certain types of skin malignancies. In industry, lasers are being used to weld

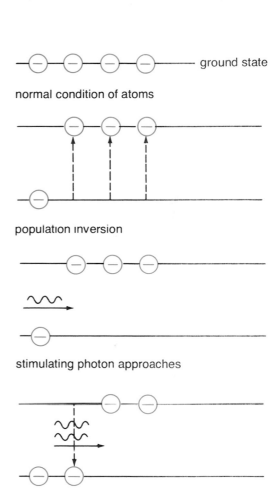

upper level

ground state

normal condition of atoms

population inversion

stimulating photon approaches

stimulated emission occurs

stimulated emission
chain reaction

Steps in the action of a laser

Scientists are at a loss to explain exactly why "stimulated emission" occurs. For some reason, the mere presence of a photon with just the right amount of energy is sufficient to cause an electron in a metastable state to jump down, or "lase".

dissimilar materials together, with temperatures in excess of 18 000°C, and to cut and shape tough and brittle metals instantly. In quality control applications, they are used to check the size, shape, and texture of manufactured parts with extreme precision. They are even used to read unified product identification codes at supermarket checkouts.

Chapter Summary

1. John Dalton proposed that matter consists of tiny indivisible particles, called atoms. Atoms of a given element are identical, and atoms of different elements have different masses. Dalton pictured the atom as a solid chunk of matter, with no internal or external features.
2. Mendeleev arranged all known elements into the periodic table, in order of increasing atomic mass, grouping atoms with similar chemical properties into vertical columns.
3. In Thomson's model, the atom was thought of as a uniform sphere of positive charge, with negative electrons distributed through it, much like raisins in a bun.
4. Ernest Rutherford, using data from the scattering of alpha particles by a thin gold foil, proposed a model of the atom in which most of the mass is concentrated in a very small central region called the nucleus. The remainder of the atom is empty space, except for the negative electrons that are in orbit around the nucleus.
5. Bohr proposed the existence of certain "allowed orbits" in which electrons can move without radiating energy in the form of electromagnetic waves. Each orbit has a specific amount of electron energy, and is assigned a quantum number $n = 1, 2, 3. \ldots$ The orbit closest to the nucleus contains electrons with the least energy.
6. For a hydrogen atom, the energy and radius of the nth orbit are

$$E_n = -\frac{13.6}{n^2} \text{ eV}$$

and
$$r_n = n^2 \times 5.3 \times 10^{-11} \text{ m}$$

7. Moseley reordered Mendeleev's periodic table by arranging the elements according to the number of protons in the nucleus. The symbol for an atom is:

   $^A_Z X$ where X is the atomic symbol

                   Z is the atomic number

                   A is the atomic mass number

   also Z = number of protons in the nucleus

         Z = number of orbiting electrons

         A = number of particles (protons + neutrons) in the nucleus

8. Light energy comes in small packages called quanta, or photons, and the energy of a photon varies directly with its frequency: the higher the frequency of a photon, the greater its energy.

9. Electrons within atoms can absorb energy and jump from their ground state into higher-energy, excited states. After a very short time, an electron will jump down to a lower available energy level, giving off its excess energy by creating a photon. All of the different photons given off by the atoms of a substance form that substance's emission spectrum.

10. Substances with metastable excited states can become lasers. A photon with just the right amount of energy can stimulate an electron in a metastable state to jump down and create an identical photon in phase with the stimulating photon. This process repeats itself in a chain reaction to produce a very intense beam of in-phase light.

Chapter Review

1. By giving a brief description of each of their models of the atom, show how the model was changed during the time of Dalton, Thomson, Rutherford, and Bohr.

2. What was the major difference between Mendeleev's periodic table and Moseley's?

3. (a) In the Rutherford gold foil experiment, what type of force causes alpha particles to be scattered by a gold nucleus?

   (b) Why are some alpha particles scattered at greater angles than others? What is the largest possible scattering angle for an alpha particle?

   (c) What type of "hit" between an alpha particle and a gold nucleus would cause the alpha particle to be scattered the maximum amount?

4. (a) Distinguish between the atomic number and the atomic mass number of an element.

   (b) What is meant by the term "isotopes of an element"? What do the isotopes of an element have in common, and how do they differ?

   (c) Write the proper chemical designation for each of the following isotopes, and indicate the number of protons, electrons, and neutrons in each atom.
      (i)   tritium   (iv) polonium-210
      (ii) carbon-14   (v)   lead-207
      (iii) lithium-7

5. (a) What defect was there, according to Maxwell's laws of electromagnetism, in Rutherford's model of the atom, with electrons moving in orbits around the nucleus?

   (b) Describe Bohr's assumption about the nature of electrons within atoms that solved this apparent problem.

6. (a) Using the equations from Section 25.3, calculate the radius and energy of the first five allowed orbits for the hydrogen atom.

   (b) What is the difference in energy between an electron in the L-shell and an electron in the K-shell of a hydrogen atom?

   (c) What is the ionization energy for hydrogen; that is, how much energy is required to completely remove an electron in the ground state from the atom? Hint: As an electron occupies an orbit with a higher quantum number, it is closer to being removed from the atom.

7. An electron in a hydrogen atom absorbs energy and jumps up into the N-shell ($n = 4$). Draw an energy-level diagram showing the electron in this excited state, and indicate on the diagram all of the various ways it could return to the ground state. State the number of different photons emitted during each of the possible downward transitions.

8. (a) What is a photon?
   (b) How did Einstein's and Planck's concept of light differ from the accepted theory at the turn of the twentieth century?
   (c) What does the energy of a photon depend on?

9. Arrange the following electromagnetic radiations in order of increasing photon energy: radio waves, infrared light, microwaves, visible light, gamma rays, ultraviolet light, X-rays.

10. (a) What is the "emission spectrum" of a substance?
    (b) Describe the way in which a substance such as mercury vapor, with an electric current passing through it, can give off light.

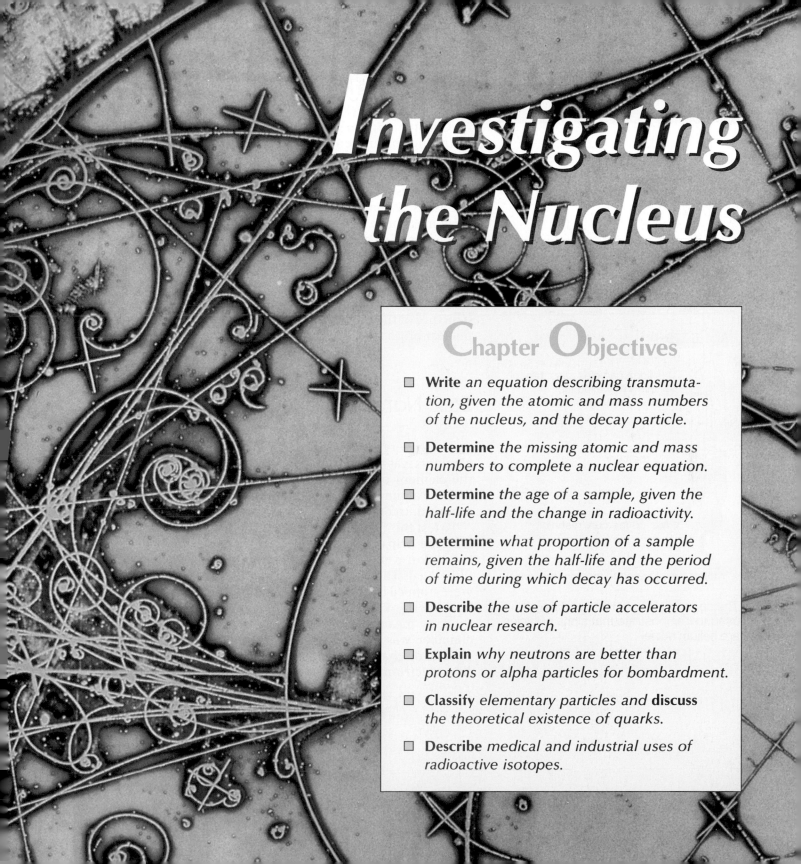

Investigating the Nucleus

Chapter Objectives

☐ **Write** an equation describing transmutation, given the atomic and mass numbers of the nucleus, and the decay particle.

☐ **Determine** the missing atomic and mass numbers to complete a nuclear equation.

☐ **Determine** the age of a sample, given the half-life and the change in radioactivity.

☐ **Determine** what proportion of a sample remains, given the half-life and the period of time during which decay has occurred.

☐ **Describe** the use of particle accelerators in nuclear research.

☐ **Explain** why neutrons are better than protons or alpha particles for bombardment.

☐ **Classify** elementary particles and **discuss** the theoretical existence of quarks.

☐ **Describe** medical and industrial uses of radioactive isotopes.

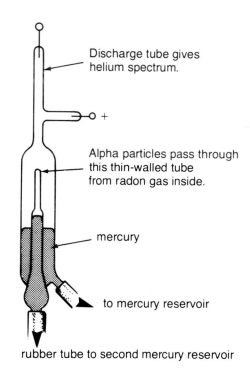

Discharge tube gives helium spectrum.

+

Alpha particles pass through this thin-walled tube from radon gas inside.

mercury

to mercury reservoir

rubber tube to second mercury reservoir

The apparatus Rutherford and Royds used to demonstrate that alpha particles are helium nuclei

26.1 What's in the Nucleus?

In Chapter 25, we learned through Rutherford's alpha particle scattering experiment that the positively charged nucleus has a diameter of approximately 10^{-14} m and occupies only a tiny fraction of the volume of an atom. Nevertheless, the nucleus contains nearly all the mass of the atom. These discoveries raise a number of questions. What is the internal structure of the nucleus? Is it one large mass or is it made up of a number of particles? How can the properties of so small an object be investigated?

The origin of the alpha and beta particles emitted by a radioactive substance puzzled scientists for many years. Finally, they concluded that these emissions must come from the atomic nucleus. Thus, the study of radioactivity became the key to an understanding of the structure of the nucleus, and this is where we will begin our study of nuclear physics.

26.2 Natural Transmutations

One discovery that was made by scientists working with radioactive elements was that helium gas was usually present, either enclosed in the element or as a product of radioactivity. Rutherford proposed that the alpha particle was a helium atom with its orbiting electrons removed. In other words, it was a helium nucleus.

To test this hypothesis, Rutherford devised an experiment in 1909 with the help of a student, T.D. Royds. Alpha particles from radioactive radon were passed through an inner thin-walled glass tube, as illustrated. The particles entered the evacuated outer chamber but were stopped by the thicker glass in the outer tube, trapped like mice in Rutherford's "mouse trap". The apparatus was left for a week and then, by means of mercury, the gas that had collected in the outer chamber was compressed into the upper part of the tube and an electric discharge was passed through it. When the resulting emission spectrum was analyzed, helium gas was detected, proving that the trapped alpha particles were helium nuclei, as Rutherford had hypothesized. Even more important, the experiment showed that the radon nucleus had spontaneously split, throwing off a small fragment (an alpha particle) and leaving behind a larger fragment— a different nucleus with different chemical properties (polonium).

$$\text{radon} \longrightarrow \text{polonium} + \text{helium}$$

The natural change of radon into polonium is an example of a **transmutation**—the process of changing one element into another. If a transmutation is accompanied by the emission of an alpha particle, it is called **alpha decay**. If a beta particle is emitted, it is called **beta decay**. The word "decay" is used because an atom with a large mass is changing, or decaying, into particles with smaller masses.

Alpha Decay

The alpha decay of radon will serve to illustrate the general properties of alpha decay. The equation for the alpha decay of radon is stated as follows:

$$^{222}_{86}\text{Rn} \longrightarrow \,^{218}_{84}\text{Po} + \,^{4}_{2}\text{He}$$
$$(\alpha \text{ particle})$$

The alpha particle is represented as $^{4}_{2}\text{He}$ since it is a helium nucleus. Note that the atomic number of the radon nucleus decreases by two, since two protons are lost, and that the mass number decreases by four, since two neutrons as well as the two protons are lost. The arrow in a nuclear equation indicates the direction of the transmutation and also may be thought of as an equals sign. The sum of the atomic numbers on the right side equals the atomic number on the left side, and the sum of the mass numbers on the right equals the mass number on the left.

In general, for alpha decay:

The rules for alpha and beta decay were first stated by Rutherford and Soddy on the basis of their study of radioactive decay at McGill University in Montreal, in the period 1899-1906.

$^{A}_{Z}\text{X}$	$\longrightarrow$	$^{A-4}_{Z-2}\text{Y}$	$+$	$^{4}_{2}\text{He}$
parent nucleus	$\longrightarrow$	**daughter nucleus**	$+$	α **particle (helium nucleus)**

Actually, a neutron breaks up into a proton, an electron, and a third massless particle called a neutrino. See Sections 26.7 and 26.8 for further details.

Beta Decay

When a beta particle is emitted by a radioactive element, the atomic number of the nucleus increases by one, but the mass number remains the same. For example, in the beta decay of sodium-24,

$$^{24}_{11}\text{Na} \longrightarrow \, ^{24}_{12}\text{Mg} + \, ^{0}_{-1}\text{e}$$

Beta particles are electrons with a high speed, and are represented as $^{0}_{-1}\text{e}$ since they have a charge of -1 but negligible mass (when compared with the nucleus).

This reaction appears to be impossible. After all, the electron is negative. How can it be emitted from a positively charged nucleus? The explanation lies in the fact that a neutron breaks up into a proton and an electron (beta particle). The production of a proton, which remains in the nucleus, accounts for the fact that the atomic number increases by one though the mass number remains constant. (The total number of particles in the nucleus remains the same.)

What has been described here is the more common type of beta decay where electrons are emitted. This is called β^- decay. Certain artificially created radio-isotopes decay, emitting positive electrons, also called positrons. See Section 26.8 for further detail.

In general, for beta decay:

$$^{A}_{Z}\text{X} \longrightarrow \, ^{A}_{Z+1}\text{Y} + \, ^{0}_{-1}\text{e}$$

| parent | daughter | β particle |
| nucleus | nucleus | (electron) |

Gamma Radiation

Usually accompanying alpha and beta decay is gamma radiation, which consists of photons, not particles, that have no mass or electric charge. Gamma rays, by themselves, produce no changes in the atomic number or the atomic mass of the nucleus. Gamma rays are represented by the symbol $^{0}_{0}\gamma$.

$$^{A}_{Z}\text{X} \longrightarrow \, ^{A}_{Z}\text{X} + \, ^{0}_{0}\gamma$$

Alpha decay and beta decay may be illustrated by a series of naturally occurring transmutations called the uranium-lead **decay series**. The nuclear equations for the first five of these transmutations are:

α-decay	$^{238}_{92}\text{U}$	$\longrightarrow$	$^{234}_{90}\text{Th}$	$+$	$^{4}_{2}\text{He}$	$+$	$^{0}_{0}\gamma$
β-decay	$^{234}_{90}\text{Th}$	$\longrightarrow$	$^{234}_{91}\text{Pa}$	$+$	$^{0}_{-1}\text{e}$	$+$	$^{0}_{0}\gamma$
β-decay	$^{234}_{91}\text{Pa}$	$\longrightarrow$	$^{234}_{92}\text{U}$	$+$	$^{0}_{-1}\text{e}$	$+$	$^{0}_{0}\gamma$
α-decay	$^{234}_{92}\text{U}$	$\longrightarrow$	$^{230}_{90}\text{Th}$	$+$	$^{4}_{2}\text{He}$	$+$	$^{0}_{0}\gamma$
α-decay	$^{230}_{90}\text{Th}$	$\longrightarrow$	$^{226}_{88}\text{Ra}$	$+$	$^{4}_{2}\text{He}$	$+$	$^{0}_{0}\gamma$

The gamma ray symbol has been written into each of these equations as a reminder that gamma radiation often accompanies alpha decay and beta decay. It is usually omitted, the primary concern being the particles created in the transmutation.

Decay series may also be shown by a graph of atomic number versus mass number, as illustrated.

When a radioactive isotope undergoes decay, the resulting isotope is often radioactive as well. The series of nuclear reactions required to produce a stable, non-radioactive isotope is referred to as a nuclear decay series.

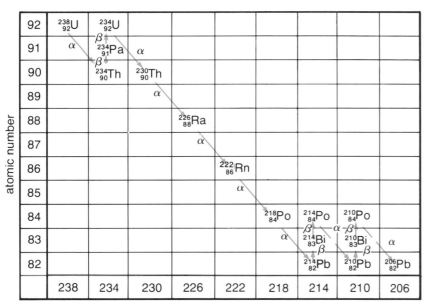

The decay chart for uranium-238

A chart that shows all of the decay products of a radioisotope is referred to as nuclide chart. In nuclear physics, nuclide charts are more useful than the periodic table. The last isotope in a nuclide chart is usually stable. This is illustrated in the chart for uranium-238 where lead-206 is not radioactive, and thus stable.

Sample Problem

Give the value of x and y in each of the following equations.

(a) $^{212}_{82}\text{Pb} \longrightarrow \; ^{212}_{x}\text{Bi} + \; ^{0}_{-1}\text{e}$

(b) $^{210}_{84}\text{Po} \longrightarrow \; ^{y}_{x}\text{Pb} + \; ^{4}_{2}\text{He}$

(c) $^{227}_{89}\text{Ac} \longrightarrow \; ^{227}_{90}\text{Th} + x$

(a) $x = 83$ (atomic numbers on right must add algebraically to 82)

(b) $x = 82$, $y = 206$ (mass numbers on right must add up to 210, atomic numbers must add up to 84)

(c) $x = \; ^{0}_{-1}\text{e}$ (for atomic numbers on right to add up to 89 and mass numbers to 227, the unknown particle must be a β particle)

Practice

Give the value of x and y in each of the following equations.

(a) $^{212}_{x}\text{Pb} \longrightarrow {}^{212}_{83}\text{Bi} + y$

(b) $^{214}_{83}\text{Bi} \longrightarrow {}^{x}_{y}\text{Po} + {}^{0}_{-1}\text{e}$

(c) $^{x}_{y}\text{Ra} \longrightarrow {}^{222}_{86}\text{Rn} + {}^{4}_{2}\text{He}$

(d) $^{215}_{84}\text{Po} \longrightarrow {}^{211}_{82}\text{Pb} + x$

(e) $^{3}_{1}\text{H} \longrightarrow x + {}^{0}_{0}\gamma$

26.3 Decay Rate and Half-life

As we have just seen, **radioisotopes** (radioactive isotopes) disintegrate spontaneously into different elements. These disintegrations are unaffected by changes in temperature or pressure, or by the other factors that normally affect the rate of chemical reactions. The rate at which a radioisotope of a given element disintegrates is specific to that element and is completely independent of everything else, even what compound may have formed.

The rate of decay is measured by a scale of time called the **half-life**. A half-life is the time required for one-half of the atoms in any sample of a radioisotope to decay. For example, thorium-234 has a half-life of 24 d. This means that if we start with a 100 g sample of thorium-234, after 24 d 50 g will have changed into other atoms and 50 g of thorium-234 will remain. After another 24 d, one-half of what remained will have disintegrated, leaving 25 g of thorium-234, and so on.

The term "half-life" was first used by Rutherford.

$^{234}_{90}$Th has a half-life of 24 days.

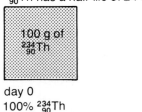

day 0
100% $^{234}_{90}$Th

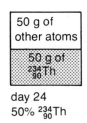

day 24
50% $^{234}_{90}$Th

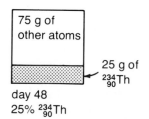

day 48
25% $^{234}_{90}$Th

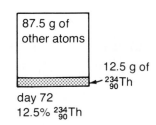

day 72
12.5% $^{234}_{90}$Th

Decay of thorium -234

The half-lives of radioisotopes vary from element to element. Some elements have very short half-lives, such as radon-226 (4 d) and polonium-214 (1.64×10^{-4} s). Others have long half-lives, such as strontium-90 (28.8 a), plutonium-239 (2.44×10^4 a), and uranium-238 (4.5×10^9 a).

Half-Lives of Common Radioactive Isotopes

Radioisotope	Symbol	Decay	Half-life
beryllium-8	$^{8}_{4}\text{Be}$	α	2×10^{-16} s
polonium-214	$^{214}_{84}\text{Po}$	α	1.64×10^{-4} s
oxygen-10	$^{19}_{8}\text{O}$	β	29 s
magnesium-29	$^{29}_{12}\text{Mg}$	β	9.5 min
lead-212	$^{212}_{82}\text{Pb}$	β	10.6 h
iodine-131	$^{131}_{90}\text{I}$	β	8.04 d
argon-39	$^{39}_{18}\text{Ar}$	β	5.26 a
cobalt-60	$^{60}_{27}\text{Co}$	β	5.3 a
strontium-90	$^{90}_{38}\text{Sr}$	β	28.8 a
radium-226	$^{226}_{88}\text{Ra}$	α	1.62×10^3 a
americium-243	$^{243}_{95}\text{Am}$	α	7.37×10^3 a
plutonium-239	$^{239}_{94}\text{Pu}$	α	2.44×10^4 a
uranium-235	$^{235}_{72}\text{U}$	α	7.04×10^8 a
uranium-238	$^{238}_{92}\text{U}$	α	4.45×10^9 a

The level of radioactivity emitted by an isotope may be measured by means of a device such as a Geiger counter. The reading will be in becquerels (Bq), the unit of radioactivity equivalent to one emission per second.

The level of radioactivity emitted by a sample of a substance is proportional to the mass of the sample. A 100 g sample of thorium-234 will have twice the radioactivity of a 50 g sample, four times that of a 25 g sample, and so on. Thus the graph of radioactivity versus time is similar to the graph of the percentage of the sample present versus the time elapsed. The graphs on the next page illustrate this. If the half-life of a radioisotope is known, the age of a sample of it may be determined if the original amount is known. Knowledge of the decay rate of certain isotopes has important applications in archaeology and geology.

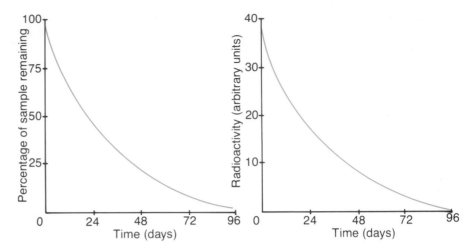

Decay curves for thorium

The following equations are used when doing calculations involving radioactive decay.

$$\lambda T_{\frac{1}{2}} = 0.693$$

where λ = the decay constant
$T_{\frac{1}{2}}$ = half-life

$$N_t = N_0 e^{-\lambda t}$$

where N_0 = the number of atoms at $t = 0$
N_1 = the number of atoms at time t
e = 2.718
λ = the decay constant

The two equations are used together. Usually the decay constant (λ) is known or can be calculated using the second relationship. For example, if radium-226 has a decay constant (λ) of 1.36×10^{-11} disintegrations per second, then:

$(1.36 \times 10^{-11})T_{\frac{1}{2}} = 0.693$

$$T_{\frac{1}{2}} = \frac{0.693}{1.36 \times 10^{-11}}$$

$$= 5.10 \times 10^{10} \text{ s or } 1620 \text{ years}$$

Sample Problem

A sample of radioactive iodine ($^{131}_{53}$I) emits beta particles at the rate of 250 MBq. What will be the activity after 16 d?

As seen in the chart on page 757, $^{131}_{53}$I has a half-life of 8 d. After 16 d, the sample will have gone through two half-lives and the activity will be one-quarter ($\frac{1}{2} \times \frac{1}{2}$) as great. Therefore, the activity of the source will be

$$250 \text{ MBq} \times \tfrac{1}{4} = 62.5 \text{ MBq, or } 6.25 \times 10^7 \text{ Bq}$$

Practice

1. The half-life of $^{90}_{38}$Sr is 28 a. If 60 g of $^{90}_{38}$Sr is currently in a sample of soil, estimate the amount of $^{90}_{38}$Sr in the sample 84 a later.
2. Tritium ($^3_1$H), a by-product of some nuclear power reactors, has a half-life of 12.3 a. How much time is required for its radioactivity to reach one-quarter of its original level?
3. The radioactivity of a sample is found to have decreased to one-sixteenth of its original level in 116 s. What is its half-life? Using the chart on page 757, determine which is the most likely radioactive isotope.

26.4 *A* pplications: Radioactive Dating

Carbon has two isotopes—carbon-12 (non-radioactive) and carbon-14 (radioactive). Carbon-14 is created in the upper atmosphere as a result of the collision of high-energy particles, coming from the sun, with air molecules. The resulting interactions change nitrogen atoms into the radioisotope carbon-14.

Both carbon isotopes can combine chemically with oxygen to form carbon dioxide gas. Carbon dioxide is taken in by green plants and eventually, via the food chain, both carbon-12 and carbon-14 are found in all living things. Once a living thing dies, the amount of carbon-14 begins to decrease because the carbon-14 decays, whereas the amount of carbon-12 remains constant.

The half-life of carbon-14 is known to be 5730 ± 30 a. If a 1 g sample of a living tree produces a radioactivity reading of 0.30 Bq, then a 1 g sample of a piece of wood with a radioactivity reading of 0.15 Bq must be from a tree that died approximately 5700 a ago. Carbon dating can be used to estimate the age of archaeological samples up to 50 000 a old.

The ratio of $^{14}C/^{12}C$ atoms in living trees is approximately $1.3 \times 10^{-12} : 1$.

Carbon dating assumes that there has been a constant rate of carbon-14 production in the atmosphere for the past 100 000 a.

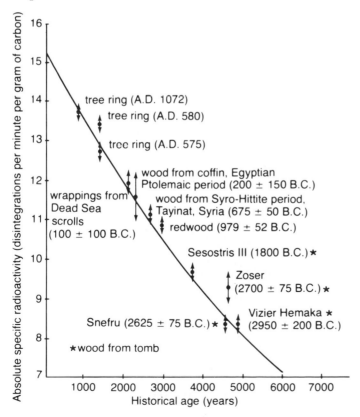

The graph shows samples from objects of known age, dated by the carbon-14 method. The curve is based on an assay of modern wood and laboratory measurement of the half-life of carbon-14. The individual points show the specific radioactivities of the various samples, from which their ages were estimated.

Radiocarbon dating is possible because plant and animal life absorb radioactive carbon-14. When an organism dies, the carbon-14 that disintegrates at a rate determined by the carbon-14 half-life of 5730 a is not replaced. At any stage, the amount of carbon-14 that is left in a specimen indicates its age.

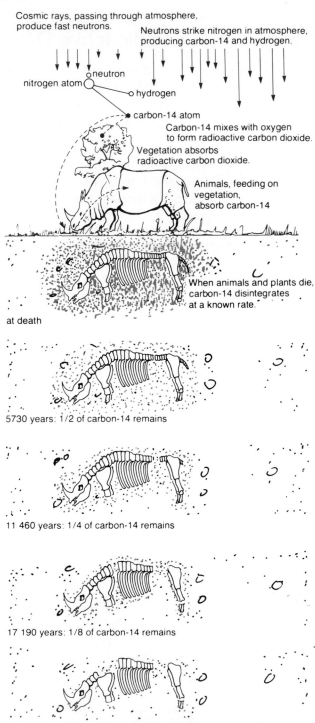

Cosmic rays, passing through atmosphere, produce fast neutrons.

Neutrons strike nitrogen in atmosphere, producing carbon-14 and hydrogen.

nitrogen atom ◯ o neutron

o hydrogen

● carbon-14 atom

Carbon-14 mixes with oxygen to form radioactive carbon dioxide.

Vegetation absorbs radioactive carbon dioxide.

Animals, feeding on vegetation, absorb carbon-14

When animals and plants die, carbon-14 disintegrates at a known rate.

at death

5730 years: 1/2 of carbon-14 remains

11 460 years: 1/4 of carbon-14 remains

17 190 years: 1/8 of carbon-14 remains

70 000 years: almost no carbon-14 remains

Another use of radioactive dating is in geology. Uranium-238, with a half-life of 4.6×10^9 a, disintegrates to lead-206. By determining the ratio of the two atoms present in a uranium sample, the age of the sample can be estimated. For instance, if a sample is half uranium-238 and half lead-206, then it is approximately 4.6×10^9 a old.

The oldest rocks on Earth, discovered in Tanzania, are estimated to be 3.6×10^9 a old. Rock formations in the Sudbury region of Ontario have been estimated to be almost as old. Recent radioactive dating of meteor fragments and Apollo 11 moon samples gives estimates of 4.5×10^9 a. Measurements such as these provide an approximation of the age of the Earth, since the radioisotopes of uranium were probably created when the Earth was formed.

Dating process	Material tested	Potential range: a	Half-life: a
carbon-14	wood charcoal shell	70 000	5 730
protactinium-231	deep sea sediment	120 000	32 000
thorium-230	deep sea sediment coral shell	400 000	75 000
uranium-234	coral	1 000 000	250 000
chlorine-36	igneous and volcanic rocks	500 000	300 000
beryllium-10	deep sea sediment	800 000	2 500 000
helium-4	coral shell	—	4.5 billion
potassium-40 argon-40	volcanic ash lava	—	1.3 billion

26.5 Chadwick's Discovery of the Neutron

Frédéric Joliot-Curie took his wife's name when they were married. Irène was the daughter of Marie Curie. The Joliot-Curies were awarded the Nobel Prize for Chemistry in 1935.

The neutron is a basic particle in the nucleus of all atoms except the hydrogen atom (see Chapter 25). Its existence had been predicted earlier by Rutherford and others, but it was James Chadwick (1891–1974) who proved that it existed. In 1930, the German physicists W. Bothe and H. Becker had found that beryllium, when bombarded with alpha particles, produced high-energy emissions that penetrated several centimeters of lead but had no detectable charge. Frédéric (1900–1958) and Irène (1897–1956) Joliot-Curie, working in France, found that these emissions caused protons to be emitted from compounds containing hydrogen, such as paraffin. In England, in 1932, Chadwick set up an experiment to identify the unknown emissions. In his apparatus, alpha particles struck a beryllium target, producing the emissions, which in turn struck a paraffin block, causing protons to be emitted into an ionization chamber.

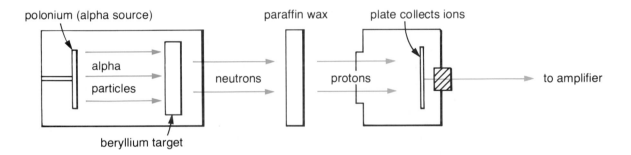

The apparatus Chadwick used to discover the neutron

James Chadwick (1891-1974), an English physicist, won the Nobel Prize for Physics in 1935 for his discovery of the neutron.

Using the cloud chamber, Chadwick calculated the energy of the individual protons. Recognizing that this energy had come from the collision between the unknown particles and the protons, and that energy was conserved in the collision, he calculated the mass of the unknown particle. Its mass was virtually the same as that of the proton. It was, indeed, the neutron whose existence Rutherford had predicted 13 years earlier.

26.6 Neutron Transmutation

The discovery of the neutron and the techniques necessary to isolate neutrons provided physicists with another important tool. Up to that point, the particles used in research into the structure of the nucleus had been the proton and the alpha particle. Both of these particles have positive charges, making it possible for them to be accelerated to a high value of kinetic energy, and steered in strong magnetic and electric fields.

The nuclei of all atoms are also positive. Thus, alpha particles and protons are repelled when they encounter a nucleus. Since the neutron is uncharged, it can approach the nucleus very closely, unaffected by its positive charge. A neutron is represented as $_0^1n$.

One of the first recorded neutron transmutations was that of lithium-6 into tritium and an alpha particle.

$$_3^6Li + {}_0^1n \longrightarrow {}_1^3H + {}_2^4He$$
$$\text{(neutron)} \quad \text{(tritium)} \quad \text{(helium nucleus)}$$

Uranium is the heaviest naturally occurring element. If it is bombarded with neutrons, even heavier elements are created. These elements do not occur naturally. The first element to be identified in this way was neptunium, named after the planet Neptune. It decays quickly to form another new element called plutonium, named after the planet Pluto. The nuclear reactions are as follows:

$$_{92}^{238}U + {}_0^1n \longrightarrow {}_{92}^{239}U$$
$$_{92}^{239}U \longrightarrow {}_{93}^{239}Np + {}_{-1}^0e \quad (\beta \text{ decay})$$

Neptunium decays to form plutonium.

$$_{93}^{239}Np \longrightarrow {}_{94}^{239}Pu + {}_{-1}^0e \quad (\beta \text{ decay})$$

Other elements have been produced, all radioactive, extending the periodic table to 105. These manufactured elements are referred to as the **transuranic elements** and they include neptunium, plutonium, mendelevium, curium, berkelium, californium, einsteinium, nobelium, and lawrencium. Note that most of the elements are named after the scientists and the research institutions that were involved in particle physics.

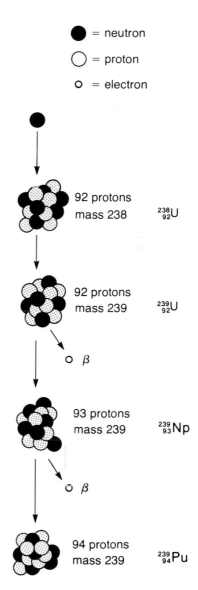

= neutron

= proton

= electron

92 protons
mass 238 $_{92}^{238}U$

92 protons
mass 239 $_{92}^{239}U$

β

93 protons
mass 239 $_{93}^{239}Np$

β

94 protons
mass 239 $_{94}^{239}Pu$

A neutron enters the nucleus of $_{92}^{238}U$, which then becomes $_{92}^{239}U$. This nucleus is unstable. It converts a neutron to a proton and an electron (β), ejects the electron, and becomes neptunium, $_{93}^{239}Np$. The neptunium soon emits an electron and becomes plutonium, $_{94}^{239}Pu$, with a half-life of 24 400 years.

In other words, neutrons decay inside the nucleus. But if neutrons decay inside the nucleus, do individual neutrons in a free state break down and change into protons? In the 1950s, when large quantities of free neutrons were available in atomic reactors, it was found that neutron decay does occur (the half-life is 12 min).

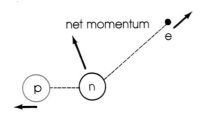

net momentum

Momentum not conserved

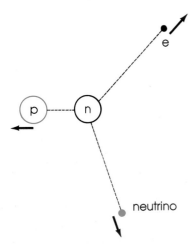

e

neutrino

Momentum conserved by the addition of a neutrino

26.7 The Neutrino

Careful experimentation around the turn of the century indicated that beta particles emitted during beta decay had less energy than predicted. In 1931, Wolfgang Pauli (of Exclusion Principle fame) suggested an explanation. He proposed that if the beta particle did not carry off all the available energy, the remainder might be given to a second particle. But what would the properties of this mysterious second particle be?

To begin with, we should recall that when beta particles are produced, a neutron in the nucleus is converted to a proton. We can symbolize the neutron as $_0^1n$, the proton as $_{+1}^1p$, and the electron as $_{-1}^0e$. The reaction had been written as follows before Pauli's particle was predicted:

$$_0^1n \longrightarrow {_{+1}^1p} + {_{-1}^0e}$$

When a neutron breaks down into a proton and an electron, the loss in mass is equivalent to approximately one-half the mass of an electron. In fact, Pauli's particle must have been considerably lighter, since the emitted electron usually gets most of the energy and sometimes all of it. As physicists recalculated their estimates of the mass of Pauli's particle, it became clear that it, like the proton, was a massless particle—it had a rest mass of zero.

Pauli's particle thus emerged as a neutral, massless particle. Enrico Fermi, the great Italian physicist, suggested that this particle be called the **neutrino,** which in Italian means "little neutral one". The name has been used ever since. The neutrino is usually given the symbol v, which is the Greek letter "nu". Now the equation for neutron decay can be written:

$$_0^1n \longrightarrow {_{+1}^1p} + {_{-1}^0e} + v$$

When a neutron is at rest, its momentum is zero. When it breaks down, the emitted electron will have momentum, as will the recoiling proton. According to the Law of Conservation of Momentum, the electron should shoot off in one direction and the proton in exactly the opposite direction. But the proton should have a much lower velocity, because of its greater mass, very much like a bullet and a gun when the gun is fired. This is not what happens. The electron and proton are both emitted at an angle, which means that the electron-proton system has momentum after the breakdown. Momentum is apparently created out of nothing, which the Law of Conservation of Momentum does not permit. However, if a neutrino is formed and comes off in a direction that will make the net momentum of the system zero, the Law of Conservation of Momentum is upheld.

26.8 The Positron and Antiparticles

In 1927, Paul Dirac, an English physicist predicted that an electron should exist in two different forms, both exactly the same except that one would be positive and the other negative. While studying cosmic rays, an American physicist, Carl Anderson, found particles which had the same properties as electrons except that they curved in the opposite direction in a magnetic field. Anderson had found Dirac's positively charged electron, which he called the **positron.**

The electron and the positron are usually called the negative electron and positive electron, respectively, and are represented by the symbols e⁻ and e⁺. The positron is called an **antielectron**, because it is exactly the same as the electron except that its charge is "anti", or opposite. These opposite particles, the electron and the positron, are referred to as **antiparticles**. It is now the practice to represent an antiparticle by the symbol of the particle, with a horizontal line above it. The symbol for a positron is $\overline{e}$.

In 1934, it was found that certain artificially created radioactive atomic nuclei produced positrons when they decayed. The first such nucleus was discovered by Frédéric and Irène Joliot-Curie. When bombarding aluminum atoms with alpha particles, they found that the radioactive product, phosphorus-30, emitted positrons spontaneously as it decayed to silicon-30, as follows:

$$^{30}_{15}P \longrightarrow {}^{30}_{14}Si + {}^{0}_{+1}\overline{e}$$

In the reaction, the electric charge is conserved (14 + 1 = 15) and the mass number, or number of particles in the nucleus, remains constant at 30. On the other hand, the atomic number of the lighter nucleus, silicon-30 (+ 14), is one less than that of phosphorus-30 (+ 15), indicating that the silicon-30 nucleus contains one proton less. For this to occur, a proton must have been converted into a neutron when the positron was emitted, reducing the atomic number by 1 and leaving the mass number unchanged. This is exactly the reverse of normal beta decay (β⁻ decay), where a neutron is converted into a proton when an electron is emitted. β⁺ **decay** is the process in which the emitted particle is a positron.

In β⁻ decay the massless neutrino is emitted. In β⁺ decay, the neutrino's antiparticle is emitted, the **antineutrino** $\overline{v}$.

Examples of nuclear equations for each type of decay are:

β⁻ decay

$$^{14}_{6}C \longrightarrow {}^{14}_{7}N + {}^{0}_{-1}e + v$$
$$\qquad\qquad\quad \text{electron} \quad \text{neutrino}$$

β⁺ decay

$$^{15}_{8}O \longrightarrow {}^{15}_{7}N + {}^{0}_{+1}\overline{e} + \overline{v}$$
$$\qquad\qquad\quad \text{positron} \quad \text{antineutrino}$$

Cosmic rays are an intensely energetic form of radiation bombarding earth from outer space.

Irène Joliot-Curie (1897–1956) was the daughter of Pierre and Marie Curie. After World War I, she went to work in her mother's laboratory, where she met and later married Frédéric Joliot (1900–1958), a researcher interested in fundamental atomic and nuclear processes. In 1933 Irène and Frédéric Joliot-Curie determined the conditions necessary for the formation of electrons and positrons. A year later, they demonstrated that artificial isotopes could be produced by alpha particle bombardment. This discovery paved the way for the production of artificial radioactive elements. For their work, they shared the Nobel Prize for Chemistry in 1935.

The Joliot-Curies continued their research work during World War II, as well as taking part in the French resistance. After the war they were active in the French Atomic Energy Commission. Irène Joliot-Curie died in 1956 of leukemia, the same disease that had taken her mother's life. In both cases, the leukemia is considered to have resulted directly from their lifelong work with radioactive materials, without the benefit of adequate safety precautions.

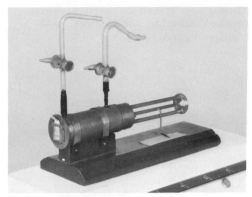

Rutherford's apparatus

26.9 Artificial Transmutation

Transmutation, the process by which one element is changed into another, was the alchemists' dream. The first artificial transmutation occurred when Rutherford and his colleagues investigated the effect of "firing" alpha particles into various gases.

Rutherford used an evacuated metal tube containing a radioactive alpha particle source and a zinc sulphide screen, as illustrated.

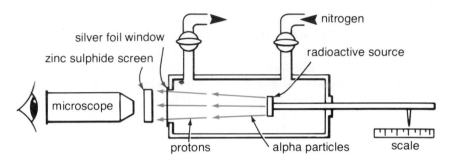

Rutherford's experiment to show that alpha-particle bombardment can disintegrate nitrogen nuclei

Any particles that passed through the silver foil window and struck the zinc sulphide screen gave off scintillations (flashes of light), which were observed through the microscope. Rutherford increased the distance of the source of alpha particles from the screen, until the scintillations stopped, indicating that the particles did not have enough energy to reach the screen. When he introduced nitrogen gas into the tube, scintillations again appeared on the screen. The particles hitting the screen were protons that had been knocked out of the nitrogen nuclei by alpha particles, causing the nitrogen nuclei to become oxygen nuclei. The nuclear reaction is written as follows:

$$^{14}_{7}\text{N} + {}^{4}_{2}\text{He} \longrightarrow {}^{18}_{9}\text{F} \longrightarrow {}^{17}_{8}\text{O} + {}^{1}_{1}\text{H}$$
$$(\alpha \text{ particle}) \qquad\qquad (\text{proton})$$

${}^{4}_{2}\text{He}$

α particle

${}^{14}_{7}\text{N}$

${}^{18}_{9}\text{F}$

proton ${}^{1}_{1}\text{H}$

${}^{17}_{8}\text{O}$

This was an exciting discovery. For the first time one substance had been changed to another artificially. Rutherford and his colleague, James Chadwick, succeeded in producing other transmutations, and they discovered that, aside from the new element, something of even greater value was produced—energy. The collision of the alpha particle with a nucleus released part of the energy stored in the nucleus.

Many more studies were made using alpha-particle sources, but their scope was limited by the low energy of the alpha particles and the inability to control the particles adequately.

In 1932, in Cambridge, J.D. Cockcroft and E.T.S. Walton produced nuclear disintegrations by means of artificially accelerated protons, using the apparatus shown. Transformers were used to produce a 400 000 V potential difference to accelerate the protons to extremely high speeds (800 km/s). When a proton struck the lithium it formed an unstable beryllium nucleus which then disintegrated into two helium nuclei. This nuclear reaction is represented as follows:

$$\underset{\text{(proton)}}{\overset{7}{_3}\text{Li} + {^1_1}\text{H}} \longrightarrow \underset{\text{(unstable)}}{{^8_4}\text{Be}} \longrightarrow \underset{\substack{\text{(alpha} \\ \text{particle)}}}{{^4_2}\text{He}} + \underset{\substack{\text{(alpha} \\ \text{particle)}}}{{^4_2}\text{He}} + \text{energy}$$

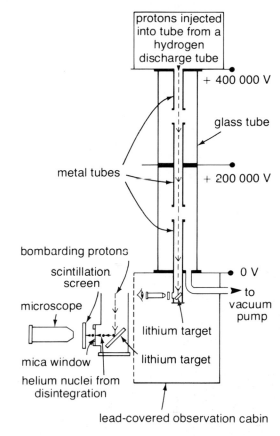

The Cockcroft-Walton proton accelerator

In the United States, E.O. Lawrence, R.J. Van de Graaf, and others developed devices to accelerate charged particles. Some of these devices are illustrated. Although modern **accelerators** are much more complex and powerful than those of the 1930s, the basic method of obtaining information about the nature of nuclei remains the same—observation of the collision between a projectile and a target nucleus. In the collision the original particles may be scattered with or without the production of radiation, and new products may be formed. The radiations and products are then studied by means of a variety of detection systems, including the cloud chamber and the mass spectrometer.

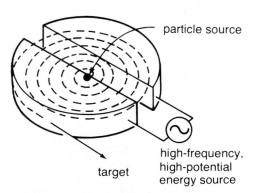

In the cyclotron, a field between two hollow semicircles accelerates the particles, which are kept in an outward spiral by a magnetic field perpendicular to their motion.

High-energy accelerators, sometimes called "atom smashers", are usually rated in terms of the energy of the accelerated particles, measured in electronvolts (1 eV = 1.6×10^{-19} J). The electronvolt is so small that the units used are the kiloelectronvolt (keV), the megaelectronvolt (MeV), the gigaelectronvolt (GeV), and the teraelectronvolt (TeV).

1 GeV = 10^9 eV
1 TeV = 10^{12} eV

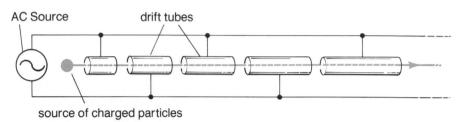

Schematic diagram of a linear accelerator. Charged particles accelerate as they are attracted by the alternately charged drift tubes.

Inside a linear accelerator

The Stanford linear accelerator is 3.0 km long.

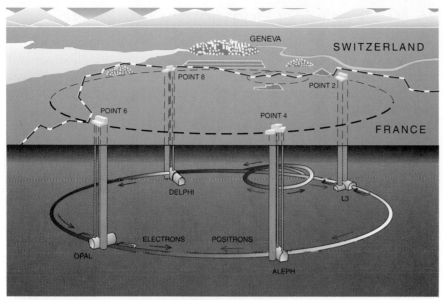

The CERN particle collider in Switzerland.

When a moving particle strikes a fixed target, most of the energy is lost to heat and deformation. On the other hand, if the two particles are moving in opposite directions and collide, then all the energy is available for the interaction. At CERN (European Council for Nuclear Research) in Geneva a second ring adjacent to the first stores accelerated particles so they can be used to collide with accelerated particles in the first ring.

The Fermi National Accelerator has a circumference of 6.3 km.

The Fermi Accelerator Laboratory at Batavia, Illinois has a circumference of 6.3 km. Buried in a circular tunnel are two superconducting accelerators. Beams of particles are accelerated in opposite directions. When they collide, some of them interact with energies in excess of 1 TeV (10^{12} eV). It is obvious that research on these scales is extremely expensive.

26.10 Classifying Elementary Particles

By the early part of this century, the discovery of the electron and the basic subatomic structure of the atom indicated that the electron, proton, and neutron were the elementary particles. By the mid 1930s, the photon, positron, and neutrino were also considered to be elementary. Since that time, hundreds of additional elementary particles have been discovered and are still being discovered. The question arises then, What particles are elementary? As more subatomic particles were discovered, it was found that they could be classified into three basic groups:

- The **photon** is in a category of its own, because it is only involved in electromagnetic interactions and has no rest mass.
- **Leptons** are particles that are involved solely with the weak nuclear force. An example of a lepton is the electron.
- **Hadrons** are particles that interact via the strong nuclear force. They include the neutron, the proton, and other particles with larger rest masses. Hadrons are further divided into the **mesons,** the **baryons,** and the **hyperons**.

Hadrons are nucleons, the name given to particles located in the nucleus of an atom.

The chart below shows the classification of elementary particles.

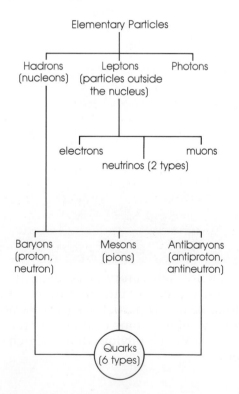

26.11 Quarks—The Stuff of Matter

As more and more particles were discovered in the 1960s and 1970s, it was found that the new particles were all hadrons. It became apparent that the four leptons were truly elementary particles, since they did not appear to break down into smaller particles. On the other hand, hadrons did.

In the late 1960s, using high-energy proton beams to probe nucleons, physicists noted that the nucleons appeared to have three separate centers of charge inside them. In the proton, these would combine to form a single quantum of charge. In the neutron, the charge centers would combine to balance out and create a net charge of zero. It was concluded that instead of being the fundamental particles of matter, the nucleons were made up of even smaller elementary particles.

At the same time, theoretical work was being done at the California Institute of Technology by American physicist Murray Gell-Mann (1929–   ). He was attempting to derive a possible general substructure of particles by listing all known particles. He saw a pattern, and proposed that hadrons were made up of six sub-particles, which he called **quarks.** He proposed the existence of three quarks and three **antiquarks.** The word "quark" did not have a special meaning, it simply appeared in the novel *Finnegans Wake* by James Joyce. (In fact, all the names that follow were casually and whimsically given. They have no connection with the properties of the subatomic particles. This practice is confusing, and can lead to misunderstanding if one is not careful.) Gell-Mann divided his three quarks into **flavors,** which he called **up, down,** and **sideways,** abbreviated **u, d,** and **s.** Later it became apparent that sideways had to do with **strangeness,** but the abbreviation remained the same.

Sheldon Glashow, a Danish-American physicist (1932–   ) predicted the existence of a fourth quark, called **charm** (symbolized by the letter "c"). Theoretical physicists had proposed a fifth and sixth quark and had given them names—**top** and **bottom** in America, and **truth** and **beauty** in Europe. Evidence for these quarks was found in 1984, using the large colliding beam accelerator at CERN, Switzerland.

In the 1970s and early 1980s, scientists found that the fundamental particles are the quarks and the leptons. Of the former fundamental triad—proton, neutron, and electron—only the electron survives as fundamental.

Sheldon Glashow

26.12 Writing Nuclear Reactions

In the equations we use to describe nuclear reactions, the sums of the mass numbers on each side are equal and so are the sums of the atomic numbers. Applying this rule to alpha decay, we note (Section 26.2) that the mass numbers of polonium and helium, 218 and 4, add up to the mass number of the radon, 222. Similarly, the atomic numbers of polonium and helium, 84 and 2, add up to that of radon, 86.

$$^{222}_{86}Rn \longrightarrow {}^{218}_{84}Po + {}^{4}_{2}He$$

When a deuterium nucleus collides with a magnesium nucleus, the two join momentarily but then quickly disintegrate into an alpha particle and a sodium nucleus. This nuclear reaction is written as:

$$^{26}_{12}Mg + {}^{2}_{1}H \longrightarrow {}^{4}_{2}He + {}^{24}_{11}Na$$

Note that the sum of the mass numbers on the right (4 + 24) equals the sum of those on the left (26 + 2), and that the sum of the atomic numbers on the right (2 + 11) equals the sum of those on the left (12 + 1).

Sample Problems

1. Write in the missing atomic numbers and mass numbers.
   (a) $^{27}_{13}Al + {}^{4}_{2}He \longrightarrow {}^{?}_{?}P$
   (b) $^{1}_{0}n + {}^{238}_{92}U \longrightarrow {}^{?}_{?}Np + {}^{0}_{-1}e$
   In part (a), the mass numbers add up to 31 (27 + 4) and the atomic numbers add up to 15 (13 + 2). Thus, the isotope is $^{34}_{15}P$. In part (b), the mass numbers of the isotopes on the left side of the equation add up to 239 and the atomic numbers of the isotopes add up to 92. Thus, the isotope of neptunium has a mass number of 239 and an atomic number of 93 (the sum of 93 and −1 is 92). The answer is expressed as $^{239}_{93}Np$.
2. Identify the unknown isotope in each of these nuclear reactions.
   (a) $^{1}_{0}n + {}^{14}_{7}N \longrightarrow {}^{14}_{6}C + ?$
   (b) $? \longrightarrow {}^{208}_{82}Pb + {}^{4}_{2}He$
   In part (a), the atomic number and mass number of the unknown isotope are both 1. Therefore it is the isotope of hydrogen, $^{1}_{1}H$. In part (b), the mass number of the unknown isotope is 212 and the atomic number is 84. Referring to Appendix E, we find that the element with an atomic number of 84 is polonium. Thus, the unknown isotope is $^{212}_{84}Po$.

Practice

Write in the missing information for the following nuclear reactions.

(a) $^{239}_{93}\text{Np} \longrightarrow ^{?}_{?}\text{Pu} + ^{0}_{-1}\text{e}$

(b) $^{15}_{7}\text{N} + ^{1}_{1}\text{H} \longrightarrow ^{12}_{6}\text{C} + ?$

(c) $^{2}_{1}\text{H} + ^{2}_{1}\text{H} \longrightarrow ^{3}_{?}\text{He} + ^{1}_{0}\text{n}$

(d) $^{1}_{0}\text{n} + ^{19}_{9}\text{F} \longrightarrow ^{?}_{?}\text{Ne} + ^{0}_{-1}\text{e}$

(e) $^{9}_{4}\text{Be} + ^{4}_{2}\text{He} \longrightarrow ? + ^{1}_{0}\text{n}$

(f) $^{212}_{83}\text{Bi} \longrightarrow ? + ^{0}_{-1}\text{e}$

(g) $^{14}_{7}\text{N} + ^{4}_{2}\text{He} \longrightarrow ? + ^{4}_{2}\text{He} + ^{1}_{1}\text{H}$

26.13 *Applications:* Artificial Radioisotopes

The nuclear structure of lighter elements can be changed by neutron bombardment. This is accomplished by placing the element near a source of high-energy neutrons, usually a nuclear power reactor. Many of the isotopes produced have a wide variety of practical applications.

Medical Therapy

Cobalt when bombarded by neutrons is transmuted into radioactive cobalt-60, as follows:

$$^{59}_{27}\text{Co} + ^{1}_{0}\text{n} \longrightarrow ^{60}_{27}\text{Co}$$

Cobalt-60 decays, emitting beta particles and high-energy gamma radiation. This gamma radiation is much more powerful than the highest energy X-rays. X-rays can control cancer by killing cancerous cells. Cobalt radiation serves the same purpose, using much simpler equipment. The cobalt-60 apparatus is commonly called the cobalt bomb. A photograph of the cobalt bomb appears in the margin.

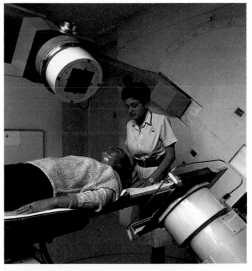

Cobalt bomb being used to treat cancer patient

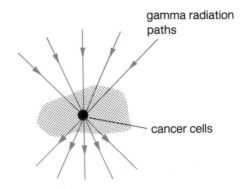

gamma radiation paths

cancer cells

By changing the angle at which the gamma rays strike the cancer, the exposure to surrounding tissue can be reduced.

Using the colbalt bomb, the patient is placed on a horizontal table and moved under a lead "window". Behind the window is a cobalt-60 source. When the window is opened, gamma radiation is emitted in a narrow beam. By manually changing the angle at which the beam strikes the cancerous tissue, the radiation can be concentrated in a small area, reducing damage to surrounding healthy cells (see illustration). Unfortunately, repeated treatments are necessary to kill all of the cancer cells. The death of healthy cells usually results in side effects such as hair loss, surface burns, and gastrointestinal distress.

In some cancer treatments it is more advantageous to encapsulate small quantities of a radioisotope and implant them in the body adjacent to the cancerous tissue. Because of their long half-lives, cobalt and radium capsules have to be removed after treatment. But if a radioisotope has a relatively short half-life, the activity reaches a low enough level that the capsules may be left permanently in the body (see photograph).

Radioisotopes are commonly used in medical research and for diagnostic purposes as tracers. To be used as a tracer the element or compound is first made radioactive by neutron bombardment. When introduced into the body its passage can be detected by a Geiger or scintillation counter. For example, the radioisotope sodium-24 is soluble in blood. Small quantities of sodium-24 are injected into the human body in blood circulation studies or to measure the level of kidney function. Another common use is to measure the activity of the thyroid gland in hormone production by monitoring its intake of radioactive iodine ($^{131}_{53}$I). The chart on the next page lists some of the radioisotopes and their uses. Tracers are also used in other biological studies. The radiograph in the margin on page 775 illustrates the distribution of radioactive sulphur in a fern frond.

In this X-ray photograph of a human lung, we can see small pieces of the radioisotope chromium-51. They were implanted to kill cancer cells, but because of their short half-life, they can be left there permanently.

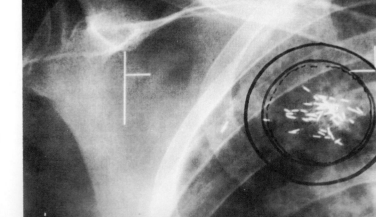

Some Applications of Radioisotopes

Isotope	Half-life	Principal Uses
cobalt-60	5.3 a	sterilization, food irradiation, waste treatment, cancer treatment, industrial radiography, gauging devices
iodine-131	8 d	thyroid imaging and therapy, leak detection
iodine-123	13 h	thyroid imaging, brain and heart studies
iodine-125	60 d	clinical tests
xenon-133	5 d	lung scanning
thallium-201	73 h	cardiac imaging
technetium-99	6 h	diagnostic tracer
calcium-45	165 d	metabolism studies, concrete testing
cesium-137	30 a	cancer therapy, radiography
phosphorus-32	14.3 d	chronic leukemia therapy, testing tread wear on tires
sodium-24	15 h	blood circulation, leak testing
iron-59	45.6 d	iron uptake studies of the spleen, wear and lubrication testing
gold-198	2.7 d	diagnostic tracer

Radiograph of a fern

Industrial Applications

Industry also makes good use of radioisotopes. Small quantities of radioactive substances can be added to machinery parts, such as gears, or to automobile piston rings as illustrated. The rate of wear can be calculated by measuring the radioactivity of the lubricating oil which contains the worn metal. Radioactive tracers can also be used to determine the flow rate in pipes, to detect leaks, and in corrosion studies. Using a strong source of gamma radiation, a radiograph can be produced similar to the photographs created by X-rays. One important use is in pipeline construction. Each welded joint is covered on the outside with strips of covered photographic film. A remotely controlled cart called a "pig" is rolled down the inside of the pipe and stops under each joint. The pig contains a radioactive source whose gamma rays expose the film, recording the location of any defects in the weld. Even large scale radiographs are possible, as illustrated by the jet turbine seen on the next page.

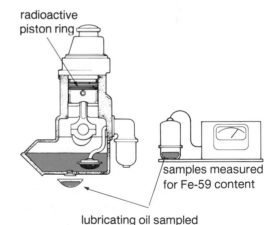

radioactive piston ring

samples measured for Fe-59 content

lubricating oil sampled

To study the wear in piston rings, radioactive iron-59 is implanted in the rings. As the metal wears off it is deposited in the lubricating oil. By measuring the radioactivity of the oil, as little as 3×10^{-4} g can be detected.

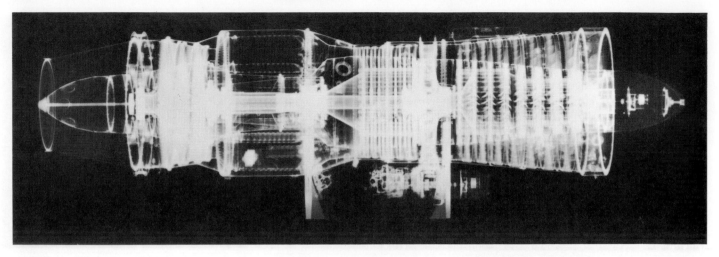

Radiograph of a jet turbine created by a gamma emitter

A common industrial use of radiation is for thickness gauging, particularly for continuous manufacturing processes involving sheet metal, paper, and plastic films. The amount of radiation passing through a material depends on its thickness. Variations in thickness are detected by a radioactive detector which signals a computer. The computer in turn is programmed to adjust the pressure accordingly, maintaining a uniform thickness in the material.

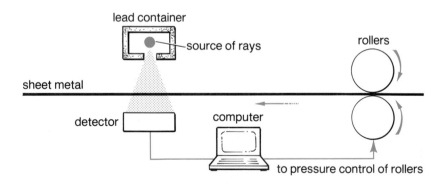

A gamma ray gauge measures the thickness of sheet metal to an accuracy of ±0.25%.

Sterilization and Food Preservation

For a number of years, disposable medical supplies such as bandages, rubber gloves, and syringes, and certain consumer products like sanitary napkins and baby soothers have been sterilized by exposing them to high levels of gamma radiation. Gamma rays can kill any living organism, including moulds and bacteria, thus sterilizing the medical supplies. This is done without any damage to the medical supplies. In fact, sterilization occurs after the products are sealed in their packages and put in a shipping container.

Gamma radiation can be used to perform four distinctive roles in the processing of food. Depending on the amount of radiation applied and the type of food exposed, gamma radiation can:

- slow down the ripening process of some fruits and inhibit the sprouting of potatoes and onions
- preserve food by destroying the micro-organisms that cause normal spoilage
- kill parasites and deadly micro-organisms, such as salmonellac, which may be found in food
- sterilize or kill the adults, larvae, and eggs of insects

These properties mean that foods such as spices, poultry, fish, meats, and some fresh fruit and vegetables can be stored for much longer periods of time without the use of chemical preservatives. For example, untreated poultry can be stored safely for only three days under refrigeration. Irradiated poultry can be stored up to three weeks under the same conditions. Strawberries can be stored up to ten days longer than normal. It must be noted that irradiation is not suitable for all foods, and it cannot be used to make an inferior product better. Also, the level of radiation must be controlled, since excessive radiation may affect the quality of the food.

Irradiated food can be stored for long periods of time without spoiling.

This automatic irradiator processes palletized goods. There is some concern that irradiated food does not provide the same vitamin content as non-irradiated food.

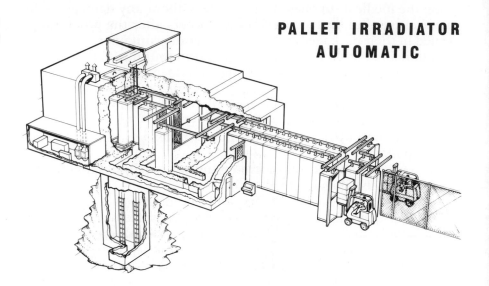

PALLET IRRADIATOR
AUTOMATIC

Irradiated food has been used by astronauts in space, and is being sold in some countries in Europe and Asia. It shows great promise for the long-term storage of basic food stuffs in the Third World where spoilage while in storage prevents badly needed food from reaching starving millions. To date, scientific research has shown that gamma radiation neither produces undesirable compounds nor makes the irradiated food radioactive. This is because the food is irradiated with gamma rays, not neutrons. One reason that its introduction into the North American market has been slow is psychological. People are wary of buying food labelled "Preserved by Gamma Radiation" because they do not understand the scientific process involved, and they have a fear of all radiation. Also, some believe that further scientific research must be done to prove conclusively that the process is completely safe.

Meet Kathy Allen . . . Nuclear Medicine Technologist

Kathy works as a registered technologist in the nuclear medicine department of a hospital. She performs a variety of tests, using small tracer amounts of radioactive materials. These tests help physicians reach a diagnosis and evaluate a patient's progress.

Q. When did you become interested in a science-related career?
A. I took several different science courses in high school. At one time, I had thoughts of becoming a nurse; however, a friend steered me toward a school for X-ray technology.

Q. Can you describe the X-ray technology program at your school?
A. The first 6 months involved intensive classroom study in all areas of science—biology, chemistry, and physics. The next 18 months involved clinical work, for which I travelled from one hospital to another, learning about different equipment and techniques. One of my last stops was in a clinic for nuclear medicine. I knew right away that this was the career for me.

Q. Was any additional training required?
A. I entered a 1-year program to become a qualified nuclear medicine technologist. Today several university hospitals offer 4-year programs in nuclear medicine.

Q. What is the most interesting aspect of your work?
A. I find it exciting that today's technology allows you to visualize the internal structures of the human body. By using small amounts of radioisotopes and various tagging agents, you are able to study each organ in the body and provide physicians with very accurate, up-to-date information.

Q. What types of equipment are used in your job?
A. The main tools are highly computerized imaging cameras that are used to study internal organs. EKG equipment is also used to perform tests on heart function. There are even Geiger counters to monitor the levels of radioactivity in the department.

Q. How are the imaging cameras different from X-ray equipment?
A. The two processes are quite different. An X-ray machine sends X-rays through the body onto a metal plate, and special film picks up the image. Imaging cameras read radioactive material that has been injected into the body. The camera's computer provides an image of the organ being studied.

Q. Are there any hazardous materials used in your work?
A. Several different radioisotopes are used, such as technetium, gallium, indium, and iodine. Each of these materials has a long half-life and can be dangerous at certain levels. Personnel are required to wear radiation badges and rings to monitor the levels of radiation. The hospital also employs a physicist, who keeps track of the radiation levels of everyone in the department. A great deal of attention is given to protecting the staff from the dangers of radioactivity.

Q. What is your work routine like?
A. The department has 5 technologists who rotate weekly through 5 different rooms. Two rooms are used for heart scans. The 3rd room is used for bone and liver scans. The 4th room is used for thyroid patients. The 5th room is reserved for hospital emergencies.

Q. What do you like best about your work?
A. I enjoy the contact with people. When some people walk into the department for the first time and see the word *nuclear,* they become a little nervous and sometimes scared. I enjoy putting them at ease and explaining the wonderful technology in the department. Usually their fear turns into amazement.

Q. What advice would you have for someone who is interested in a career such as yours?
A. I strongly advise that they speak directly to someone who is working in the field. Perhaps they should visit a hospital and get a first hand look at the job. Then they should visit a school that offers specific training programs in the field. Currently there are plenty of career opportunities for qualified individuals.

*I*nvestigation

Investigation 26.1: Half-life of a Radioisotope

Problem:
What is the half-life of the radioisotope barium-137m?

Materials:
cesium-137/barium-137 minigenerator
eluant (0.04 N hydrochloric acid) and squeeze bottle
scintillation or Geiger-Müller counter
10 mL beaker

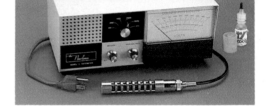

Background:
The cesium-137/barium-137 minigenerator contains a minute quantity of cesium-137 which has a half-life of 30 a. It decays by beta emission to form barium-137m, which in turn decays to barium-137. It is the later transition whose half-life we will measure. Barium-137m is soluble in a weak solution of hydrochloric acid (eluant). When the eluant is passed through the minigenerator, some of the barium-137m is dissolved. This process is called elution, and the procedure is referred to as "milking the cow" (minigenerator). The eluant is placed in a beaker and its radioactivity measured.

Procedure:
1. Allow the radiation counter to warm up and stabilize.
2. Remove all objects from the immediate area of the detector, and record the background count for a period of 3.0 min. Determine the background count in counts/min.
3. Elute the minigenerator with approximately 3 mL of eluant, carefully collecting it in the beaker. Place the beaker next to the detector. Do not move it for the duration of the investigation.
4. Using a chart, record the number of counts as follows. Measure the activity during one minute. Wait one minute and record the activity for the third minute. Repeat this procedure for six readings.
5. Correct the recorded activities by subtracting the background count.
6. Plot a graph of corrected activity versus time. The plotted points should be placed halfway through the first, third, fifth, etc., minute.
7. To make analysis easier, replot the graph on semi-log graph paper. Draw the best straight line through the points.

 CAUTION: Even when working with low-level radioactive sources, care must be taken that sources are kept away from your body except for short periods of time.

 CAUTION: Put on safety goggles and plastic gloves.

CAUTION: Handle the radiation counter with care; it is fragile. Do not touch after it has been turned on.

8. On the second graph take any two points where the activity has decreased by one-half. Read off the half-life from the time axis. Repeat for two more sets of readings and find the average value for the half-life.

9. Return the eluant to the container provided by your teacher, including any water used to rinse the beaker.

CAUTION: Wash your hands after the investigation.

Questions:

1. The accepted value for the half-life of barium-137m is 2.6 min. Calculate your experimental error.

2. If 15 000 counts/min was thc initial radioactivity of a sample of barium-137m, what will be the activity 624 s later? Express your answer in Bq.

3. The cesium-137/barium-137 generator is rated at 33.3 TBq. What is thc activity in emissions/s?

4. In step 6 you plotted the points half-way through each time interval. Explain why this is necessary.

Chapter Summary

1. An alpha particle is a helium atom with its orbiting electrons missing, that is, a helium nucleus. A beta particle is an electron.

2. Transmutation is the process by which one element is changed into another. If an alpha particle or a beta particle is emitted in the transmutation, this is called a decay.

3. In alpha decay, the atomic number of the parent nucleus decreases by two and the mass number decreases by four.

4. In beta decay, the atomic number of the parent nucleus increases by one and the mass number remains the same. A beta particle is an electron.

5. Gamma radiation always accompanies alpha and beta decay. Gamma radiation by itself produces no change in the atomic number or mass number of the parent.

6. In a nuclear equation, the sums of the mass numbers on each side of the equation are equal, as are the sums of the atomic numbers.

7. A half-life is the time required for one-half of the atoms in a sample of a radioactive isotope to decay into new atoms.

8. If the half-life of a radioactive isotope, the level of radioactivity, and the original activity are known, the age of the material can be determined.

9. The neutron, discovered by Chadwick, has no charge and its mass is almost the same as that of a proton.

10. The bombarding of heavy nuclei with neutrons can produce elements that do not occur naturally.
11. The neutrino is a neutral, massless particle emitted during beta decay.
12. An electron exists in two forms, one postive and one negative. A positively charged electron is a position, or antielectron.
13. Rutherford produced the first artificial transmutation, changing nitrogen into oxygen by alpha particle bombardment.
14. Particle accelerators are used to investigate the nucleus by bombarding nuclei with high-energy positive particles and analyzing the particles from the resulting collision.
15. Elementary particles are divided into three basic groupings: the photon, the leptons, and the hadrons.
16. The existence of six subparticles called quarks has been proposed.
17. Radioactive isotopes produced by neutron bombardment have many practical uses in industry and medicine.

Chapter Review

Photograph showing the transmutation of nitrogen

Discussion

1. Describe the change that occurs in the nucleus of a radioactive isotope when it undergoes transmutation by emitting (a) an alpha particle and (b) a beta particle. Write an equation, using symbols, giving an example of each type of decay.
2. Why are neutrons much better projectiles than alpha particles when they are used to produce nuclear reactions?
3. Why are there so few naturally occurring radioisotopes?
4. If the level of radioactivity of 10 g of two radioactive isotopes, one with a short half-life, and the other with a long half-life, were measured (a) shortly after the samples were obtained and (b) a long time after the samples were obtained, which isotope would have a higher level of radioactivity?
5. The accuracy of the carbon-14 method of dating has come under question in recent years. It has been found that cosmic radiation levels at the Earth's surface have not been constant but have varied because of shifts in the position of the Earth's magnetic field. Why would these changes affect the accuracy of carbon-14 dating?
6. Why is it difficult to detect a neutrino?

7. Write a short biography (200-300 words) of one of the following scientists who contributed to the discoveries and application of radioactivity: Wilhelm Röntgen, Antoine Becquerel, Marie Curie, Pierre Curie, Frédéric Joliot-Curie, Irène Joliot-Curie, Hans Geiger, Ernest Rutherford, William Crookes, Harold Gray, John Cockcroft, Ernest Lawrence, R. Van de Graaf.

8. After doing some research, write an essay (200-300 words) on one of the following topics:
   - a medical use for a radioisotope
   - an industrial use for a radioisotope not discussed in the text
   - a comparison of the types of ionizing radiation and the biological effects they can produce
   - the consequences of a whole body radiation overdose
   - procedures for irradiating a particular food for a longer storage life
   - radioisotopes and related equipment

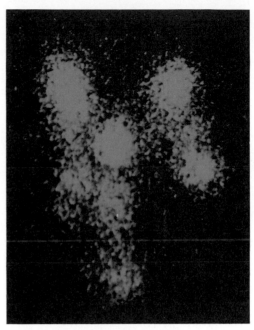

Radioactive iodine was used to make this image of a healthy thyroid gland.

Problems

9. In each of the following equations, either alpha decay or beta decay occurs. Determine the nature of the emitted particle in each case.

   (a) $^{222}_{86}Rn \longrightarrow ^{218}_{84}Po + ?$ (e) $^{141}_{57}La \longrightarrow ^{141}_{58}Ce + ?$

   (b) $^{238}_{92}U \longrightarrow ^{234}_{90}Th + ?$ (f) $^{141}_{56}Ba \longrightarrow ^{141}_{57}La + ?$

   (c) $^{35}_{17}Cl \longrightarrow ^{35}_{18}Ar + ?$ (g) $^{212}_{82}Pb \longrightarrow ^{212}_{83}Bi + ?$

   (d) $^{226}_{88}Ra \longrightarrow ^{222}_{86}Rn + ?$ (h) $^{215}_{84}Po \longrightarrow ^{211}_{82}Pb + ?$

10. Radium-226 decays to polonium-84 as follows:

$$^{226}_{88}Ra \xrightarrow{(a)} ^{222}_{86}Rn \xrightarrow{(b)} ^{218}_{84}Po \xrightarrow{(c)} ^{214}_{82}Pb \xrightarrow{(d)} ^{214}_{83}Bi \xrightarrow{(e)} ^{214}_{84}Po$$

   What kind of particle is emitted in each of the transmutations, labelled (a) to (e)?

11. A proton strikes a sodium-20 nucleus and an alpha particle is emitted. What is the mass number and atomic number of the residual nucleus? Write an equation for the nuclear reaction.

12. The half-life of a certain radioactive isotope is 20 h. How much of an original 320 g sample will remain the same radioactive isotope after (a) 40 h? (b) 80 h? (c) 5 d?

13. An experiment was performed to determine the half-life of technetium-99. The activity was measured over a 24 h period and the results are recorded below.

Time (h)	0	3	6	9	12	15	18	21	24
Activity (kBq)	17.0	12.2	8.9	6.5	4.5	3.2	2.3	1.5	1.1

  (a) Plot a graph of activity versus time.
  (b) Using the graph, determine the half-life of technetium-99.
  (c) Predict the activities for the following times:
      (i) 7 h,   (ii) 19 h,   (iii) 26 h.

14. Charcoal taken from the ruins of an early Viking settlement near St. Anthony, Newfoundland, is being used to carbon-date the settlement. A reading of 14 emissions/min $\cdot$ g^{-1} is recorded. Using the graph on page 759, determine the approximate age of the settlement.

15. Strontium-82 has a half-life of 25.0 d. If you begin with a sample having a mass of 140 g, in how many days will you have only 17.5 g of strontium-82 left?

16. The average natural radioactivity of 1 m^3 of radon gas is 10 emissions per second, or 10 Bq. If the half-life of radon gas is 4 d, how long will it take for 1 m^3 sample of radon gas to reach an average radioactivity of 2.5 Bq?

17. Following are some equations of artificial transmutations produced by particle bombardment. The particles produced are protons, deuterium nuclei, or neutrons. Using the periodic table (Appendix E), if necessary, determine the other product in each case.

  (a) $^{27}_{13}\text{Al} + ^{4}_{2}\text{He} \longrightarrow ?\ + ^{1}_{1}\text{H}$
  (b) $^{12}_{6}\text{C} + ^{2}_{1}\text{H} \longrightarrow ^{1}_{1}\text{H} + ?$
  (c) $^{9}_{4}\text{Be} + ^{1}_{1}\text{H} \longrightarrow ?\ + ^{2}_{1}\text{H}$
  (d) $^{14}_{7}\text{N} + ^{1}_{0}\text{n} \longrightarrow ^{14}_{6}\text{C} + ?$
  (e) $^{1}_{1}\text{H} + ^{1}_{0}\text{n} \longrightarrow ?$
  (f) $^{23}_{11}\text{Na} + ^{2}_{1}\text{H} \longrightarrow ^{1}_{1}\text{H} + ?$
  (g) $^{14}_{7}\text{N} + ^{4}_{2}\text{He} \longrightarrow ?\ + ^{1}_{1}\text{H}$

18. Indicate which of the following transmutations contain errors and in each case state why.
    (a) $^{141}_{58}Ce \longrightarrow ^{141}_{59}Pr + ^{0}_{-1}e$
    (b) $^{27}_{13}Al + ^{2}_{1}H \longrightarrow ^{27}_{14}Si$
    (c) $^{107}_{47}Ag + ^{1}_{0}n \longrightarrow ^{108}_{47}Ag$
    (d) $^{16}_{8}O + ^{1}_{1}H \longrightarrow ^{19}_{9}F$
    (e) $^{226}_{88}Ra \longrightarrow ^{230}_{90}Th + ^{4}_{2}He$

19. Determine the missing atomic numbers and/or mass numbers in each of the following nuclear transmutations.
    (a) $^{141}_{58}Ce \longrightarrow ^{?}_{59}Pr + ^{0}_{-1}e$
    (b) $^{214}_{82}Pb \longrightarrow ^{?}_{83}Bi + ^{0}_{-1}e$
    (c) $^{238}_{92}U \longrightarrow ^{?}_{90}Th + ^{4}_{2}He$
    (d) $^{215}_{84}Po \longrightarrow ^{211}_{?}Pb + ^{4}_{2}He$
    (e) $^{?}_{?}Pb \longrightarrow ^{212}_{83}Bi + ^{0}_{-1}e$
    (f) $^{238}_{92}U \longrightarrow ^{?}_{?}Th + ^{4}_{2}He$
    (g) $^{227}_{89}Ac \longrightarrow ^{?}_{?}Th + ^{0}_{-1}e$
    (h) $^{116}_{49}In \longrightarrow ^{?}_{?}In + ^{0}_{0}\gamma$

Radioactive uranium-235 has a half-life of 704 million years.

27

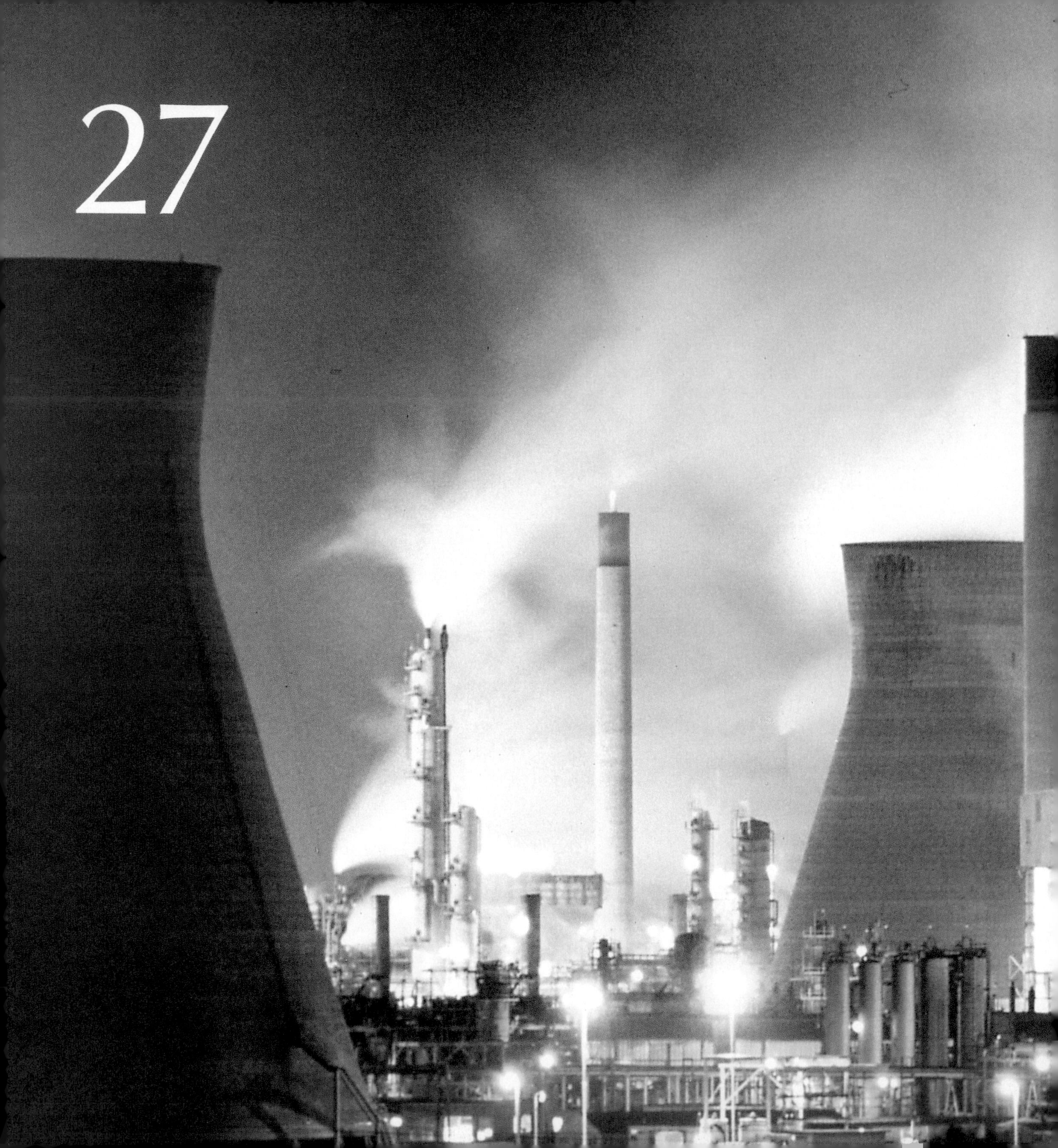

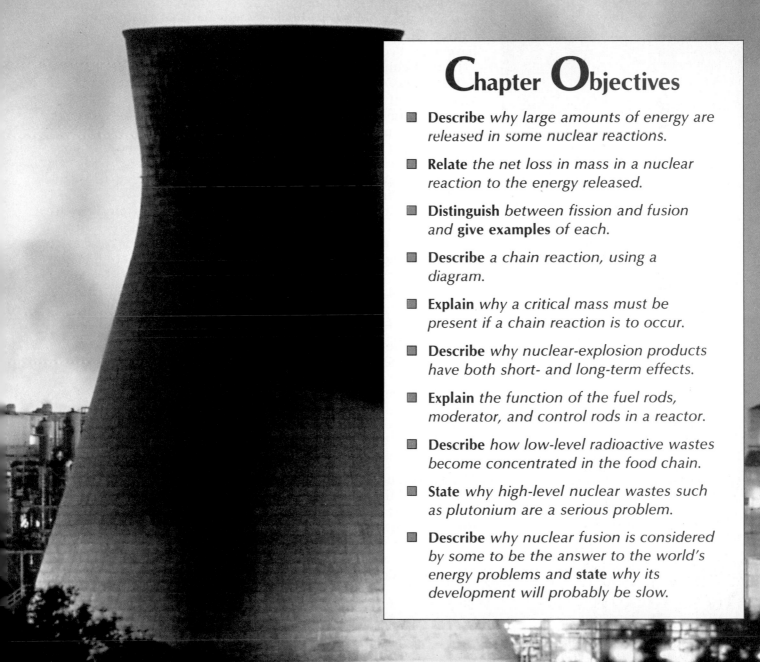

Nuclear Energy

Chapter Objectives

- **Describe** *why large amounts of energy are released in some nuclear reactions.*

- **Relate** *the net loss in mass in a nuclear reaction to the energy released.*

- **Distinguish** *between fission and fusion and* **give examples** *of each.*

- **Describe** *a chain reaction, using a diagram.*

- **Explain** *why a critical mass must be present if a chain reaction is to occur.*

- **Describe** *why nuclear-explosion products have both short- and long-term effects.*

- **Explain** *the function of the fuel rods, moderator, and control rods in a reactor.*

- **Describe** *how low-level radioactive wastes become concentrated in the food chain.*

- **State** *why high-level nuclear wastes such as plutonium are a serious problem.*

- **Describe** *why nuclear fusion is considered by some to be the answer to the world's energy problems and* **state** *why its development will probably be slow.*

27.1 Mass-Energy Relationships in Nuclear Reactions

Albert Einstein (1879-1955)

When a transmutation occurs, the total atomic number and the total atomic mass number of all the particles involved in the reaction do not change. It appears that both mass and electric charge are conserved. There is another aspect of a nuclear reaction that we have not yet considered—that of the conservation of energy.

In all chemical reactions, energy is either liberated or absorbed. For example, the burning of gasoline liberates energy, and the separation of water into hydrogen and oxygen by electrolysis absorbs energy. Nuclear reactions can also liberate or absorb energy, but we are primarily interested in those that liberate energy, because when that happens the quantity liberated can be enormous. So much energy can be released, in fact, that the Law of Conservation of Energy appears to be violated. Where does all this extra energy come from?

In 1905, Albert Einstein published his **Theory of Relativity**. In this important document, he suggested that mass is another form of energy—that a decrease in mass of a system might show up as an increase in the energy of the system. His equation relating energy and mass was:

$$E = mc^2$$

where E is the energy liberated, in joules

m is the mass that disappears, in kilograms

c is the speed of light, in metres per second

In 1932 Cockcroft and Walton, using their accelerator (see Section 26.9), bombarded lithium with protons, creating two alpha particles for each proton.

$$_1^1\text{H} + {}_3^7\text{Li} \longrightarrow {}_2^4\text{He} + {}_2^4\text{He}$$

The mass of the two alpha particles was found to be slightly less than the mass of the proton and the lithium nucleus together. It was found that the kinetic energy of the two alpha particles far exceeded the initial kinetic energy of the proton. Careful calculations showed that the extra energy possessed by the alpha particles exactly corresponded to the loss in mass, in accordance with Einstein's equation. The Law of Conservation of Energy, as it had been known before

Law of Conservation of Energy—see Section 7.

Einstein, had been violated: energy appeared to have been created. In fact, energy had not been created, but mass had been converted into energy.

Since 1932, hundreds of similar nuclear experiments have been devised to check Einstein's mass-energy relationship, and in each case it was found to be valid. The energy, because it usually originates in the conversion of nuclear mass into energy, is called **nuclear energy**. To provide some concept of the magnitude of the energy involved, we can calculate the amount of energy liberated if 1.0 kg of mass were completely transformed into energy.

$$E = mc^2$$
$$= (1.0 \text{ kg}) (3.0 \times 10^8 \text{ m/s})^2$$
$$= 9.0 \times 10^{16} \text{ J}$$

Nuclear fission and **nuclear fusion** are two types of nuclear reactions in which the amount of energy released is very large. The nature of these reactions and how they can be utilized for the benefit of our world are the topics of this chapter.

Nuclear energy is actually nuclear *potential* energy, since it is energy stored up in the nucleus.

According to the estimate in Chapter 7, the average energy consumption in the U.S. is 900 MJ/person/day. 9.0×10^{16} J would supply the energy needs for the entire U.S. for about 10 hours.

Sample Problems

A nuclear reaction produces 9.0×10^{11} J of heat energy because of the conversion of mass into energy. What mass was converted?

$$E = mc^2$$
$$m = \frac{E}{c^2}$$
$$= \frac{9.0 \times 10^{11} \text{ J}}{(3.0 \times 10^8 \text{ m/s})^2}$$
$$= 1.0 \times 10^{-5} \text{ kg, or } 10 \ \mu\text{kg}$$

Practice

1. The loss in mass in a fission reaction is 0.010 g. How much energy will have been produced?

2. Two hundred atoms of uranium-235 split. If each atom releases 3.2×10^{-8} J when fission occurs, what nuclear mass was converted into energy?

3. The nuclear equation for the fusion of two isotopes of hydrogen is shown. Written below each isotope is its mass in a unit called the atomic mass unit (amu). If 1 amu $= 1.66 \times 10^{-27}$ kg, calculate the nuclear energy released in the reaction by comparing the total mass before and after the reaction.

$$\underset{(2.014\ 10 \text{ amu})}{^2_1\text{H}} \quad + \quad \underset{(2.014\ 10 \text{ amu})}{^2_1\text{H}} \quad \longrightarrow \quad \underset{(3.016\ 03 \text{ amu})}{^3_1\text{He}} \quad + \quad \underset{(1.000\ 867 \text{ amu})}{^1_0\text{n}}$$

27.2 Nuclear Fission

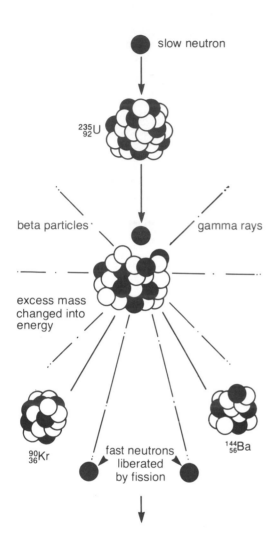

slow neutron

$^{235}_{92}U$

beta particles

gamma rays

excess mass changed into energy

$^{90}_{36}Kr$

fast neutrons liberated by fission

$^{144}_{56}Ba$

Otto Hahn (1879-1968), a German physical chemist, received the Nobel Prize for Chemistry in 1944 for the discovery of fission. In his later years he actively opposed the use of nuclear weapons.

With the help of the mass-energy relationship and the earlier measurements of atomic mass, it was determined that, if heavier atoms such as those of uranium were split into lighter atoms, nuclear energy would be released. This splitting or **fission** of the heavy nucleus cannot be done with a charged particle such as an alpha particle, which would be repelled by the high positive charge on the nucleus of the heavier atom. It was Chadwick's discovery of the neutron that made fission possible, since a neutron, with no electric charge, can approach a positive nucleus more closely in a collision than a positive proton or an alpha particle can.

In 1934, Enrico Fermi, an Italian physicist doing research in Germany, was attempting to produce transuranic elements, using neutron bombardment. It is probable that he achieved the first fission reaction but was not aware of having done so because he could not separate, and thus identify, the fission products. By 1939, two German chemists, Otto Hahn and Fritz Strassmann, managed to separate the products of fission chemically, and they discovered that a uranium nucleus had been split into two pieces—a barium nucleus and a krypton nucleus.

$$^{235}_{92}U + ^{1}_{0}n \longrightarrow ^{144}_{56}Ba + ^{90}_{36}Kr + 2^{1}_{0}n + energy$$

A week later, two Austrian physicists working in Denmark, Lise Meitner and Otto Frisch, obtained a similar result. Frisch coined the expression "nuclear fission", having noted that the process is similar to what occurs when a living cell divides into two equal parts in the biological process called fission. The importance of fission is that it is accompanied by the release of approximately 10 times as much energy as occurs in a normal nuclear disintegration, and more than a million times as much as occurs in any chemical reaction.

Subsequent research showed not only that a large amount of energy was released but also that two or three neutrons were emitted. These neutrons can each cause fission in another uranium nucleus with which they might happen to collide. When fission occurs in a second uranium nucleus, it too will emit two or three neutrons and release energy. As this process continues, more and more uranium nuclei undergo fission, releasing larger and larger numbers of neutrons as well as large amounts of energy. This is called a nuclear **chain reaction**.

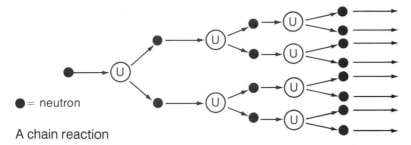

● = neutron

A chain reaction

Natural uranium is composed of 99.3% uranium-238, 0.7% uranium-235, and traces of uranium-234. Uranium-235 is the only fissionable isotope of uranium. Since the nucleus is very small in comparison with the atom, the chance of a neutron colliding with a uranium-235 nucleus is very small. To increase the likelihood of this happening, the number of uranium-235 atoms must be increased. The process of increasing the proportion of uranium-235 isotopes in natural uranium is called **enrichment**.

If too few of the uranium-235 isotopes are present, neutrons will escape from the surface of the mass and hence will not collide with other nuclei. Also, some of the neutrons will be absorbed by impurities. To sustain a chain reaction, the amount of uranium-235 must be increased until the number of neutrons produced exceeds the number lost from the surface and to impurities. This amount of uranium-235 is called the **critical mass**. When a critical mass is present, the chain reaction proceeds without any outside assistance, and we say that the fissionable material has "gone critical".

The probability of a collision between a neutron and a uranium-235 nucleus is also increased if the ejected neutrons are slowed down. The substances used to slow down neutrons are called **moderators**. Atoms with low atomic mass such as graphite, ordinary water, heavy water, and beryllium are excellent moderators since they slow neutrons down without absorbing them.

The neutrons are slowed down from approximately 4×10^6 m/s to 2×10^3 m/s.

The rate of a chain reaction is controlled by inserting substances that absorb neutrons, such as boron or cadmium, into the enriched uranium. These substances are made into **control rods**. The chain reaction is controlled by varying the amount of control substance present (by moving the rods in and out). If enough neutrons are absorbed by the rods, the reaction will stop altogether.

In a **nuclear bomb**, there are no control rods and the chain reaction continues unchecked. In a fraction of a second, enormous amounts of energy, fast-moving neutrons, and gamma radiation are released. The same energy that is released violently in the exploding of a nuclear bomb can be controlled and transformed into useful heat energy. This is accomplished by means of a device known as a **nuclear reactor**.

The first nuclear reactors were called "piles" because they consisted of piles of graphite blocks. The use of this term helped to disguise the reactors' true nature during the Second World War.

27.3 The First Reactor and the First Atomic Bombs

The first graphite reactor

Enrico Fermi (1901-1954)—second from the right

The concept of a controlled nuclear reaction was known both in Germany and in the United States by 1939, but the first nuclear reactor was not built until 1942. Albert Einstein, Enrico Fermi, Leo Szilard, and many other prominent European physicists moved to the United States because of the political climate in Europe in the 1930s and the disruptions of World War II. Through the influence of Einstein and others on President Roosevelt, financial assistance was given to nuclear research programs. The vast financial and physical resources of North America and the talents of European, American, British, and Canadian scientists were harnessed under a very secret program, code-named the Manhattan Project.

Fermi was one of the leaders in this project. He and his team constructed the first reactor in a squash court at the University of Chicago, in December 1942. It had taken three years of concentrated effort to obtain the necessary quantity of uranium-235. The reactor consisted of a pile of graphite blocks which acted as a moderator. Lumps of uranium were inserted into holes in the graphite. To control the reaction, neutron-absorbing cadmium strips were inserted into the pile.

The neutron and radiation levels were monitored as the reactor was constructed of layer upon layer of graphite. When the 57th layer was added, the neutron intensity level increased dramatically. The first chain reaction was occurring. Quickly, cadmium strips were inserted into the pile to shut down the reaction before heat and radiation could reach dangerous levels. The theory originating with the work of Einstein in 1905 had been verified experimentally, on a large scale!

The Manhattan Project continued. The chain reaction had been achieved, and its destructive use to help defeat Germany and Japan was of immediate importance. In a large plant at Oak Ridge, Tennessee, sufficient quantities of uranium were enriched for two nuclear bombs (commonly called atomic bombs); and enough fissionable plutonium-239 for a third bomb was extracted from nuclear reactors similar to the one designed by Fermi. One of the uranium-235 bombs was tested successfully in the desert in New Mexico on July 16, 1945. The other uranium bomb and the plutonium bomb were dropped on Hiroshima on August 6, and on Nagasaki on August 8, respectively. Thousands of people were killed and the two cities were levelled by the combination of heat, shock waves, gamma radiation, and high-energy neutrons. Many who survived

The ruins of Hiroshima—1946

were to die later of cancer caused by exposure to gamma radiation and by the absorption of radioisotopes into their bodies. The nuclear explosions in the summer of 1945 inaugurated a new era in world history.

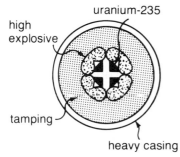

A cross section of a nuclear fission bomb. When the pieces of $^{235}_{92}U$ are forced together by the explosive charges, they have a mass exceeding the critical mass and are said to be "supercritical". Failure of one explosive charge will disable the bomb, since it can no longer sustain a chain reaction.

The chain reaction was first conceived in 1934 by Leo Szilard (1898-1964), a Hungarian-American physicist. Szilard, when he realized that the atomic bomb was to be used on the Japanese, proposed that it should be tested before an international audience so that the Japanese would recognize its power and (he predicted) surrender.

"Little Boy", the bomb dropped on Hiroshima

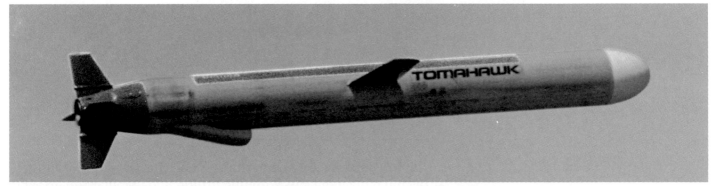

A modern cruise missile, designed to carry an atomic bomb

water molecule (H₂0)

heavy water
molecule (D₂0)

Ordinary, or "light", water molecules consist of an oxygen atom and two hydrogen atoms. In heavy water molecules, the central oxygen atom is linked to two deuterium atoms. The proportion of heavy water found in ordinary water is one part in 7000. It is very expensive to separate the two.

27.4 Nuclear Power Reactors

The Chain Reaction

Most nuclear power reactors use uranium-235 as their fuel. The fissionable uranium-235 atoms represent less than 1% of the atoms in natural uranium. (The other 99% are nearly all uranium-238 atoms, which do not fission.) When a uranium-235 atom undergoes fission, a chain reaction is unlikely since most of the free neutrons produced are absorbed by uranium-238 atoms, producing radioactive plutonium-239. The remainder are travelling too fast to cause other uranium-235 atoms to fission. A fast neutron's speed is not reduced when it collides with heavy atoms, such as the abundant uranium-238. But if the neutron collides with an atom or molecule with a relatively small mass, like a water molecule, some of its kinetic energy is absorbed. A series of collisions with other water molecules slows down the neutron sufficiently that fission is likely to occur. As mentioned previously, substances that slow down neutrons are called moderators.

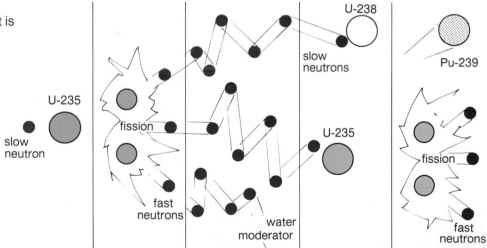

Ordinary water is a good moderator, but it often absorbs neutrons, removing them from the chain reaction. Graphite or heavy water is very effective as a moderator, since each slows down the neutrons but rarely absorb them. Heavy water is composed of an isotope of hydrogen called deuterium. (Deuterium is an isotope of hydrogen having a nucleus with one proton and one neutron, as seen in the illustration in the margin.)

Once the chain reaction begins there could be too many neutrons available, leading to too many fissions. The resulting release of energy might be so great that the reactor could literally melt down. To control the rate of the fission reactions, control rods, usually made of cadmium, are inserted into the reactor. The cadmium absorbs neutrons, slowing down or completely shutting down the chain reaction, depending on how far the control rods are inserted.

A Simplified Nuclear Power Reactor

We will now put the above concepts together to create a simplified reactor that produces energy.

The fission reaction occurs inside uranium fuel bundles like the ones pictured in the margin. The fuel bundles are located in a reactor core which is enclosed in a containment building. The thick concrete walls of the building shield the environment from the radiation produced in the core. In this simplified reactor, water functions as a moderator, slowing down the neutrons. The water also acts as a coolant, carrying the heat out of the reactor core.

A fuel bundle contains uranium pellets sealed in airtight metal sheaths. Most of the radioactive fission products are formed within the fuel and cannot escape unless the fuel becomes severely overheated.

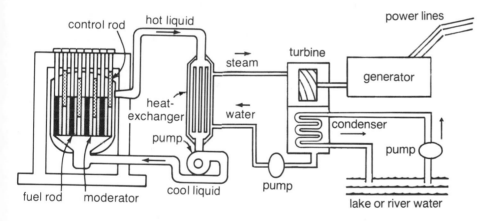

The basic parts of a fission nuclear power reactor

To start fission, the control rods are raised. The reaction begins when one of the uranium-235 atoms undergoes a relatively rare spontaneous fission. The neutrons released are slowed down by the moderator which surrounds the fuel bundles, and the slow neutrons can trigger new fissions. Thus each fission causes one or more fissions and a chain reaction is produced. Its rate can be adjusted or stopped completely using the control rods.

The kinetic energy of the fission products and the neutrons causes the temperature of the fuel and the moderator to increase, which in turn raises the temperature of the moderator surrounding the fuel. Even when the temperature of the moderator reaches extremely high values, the moderator does not boil since it is contained in a vessel at a very high pressure. We say the water has become superheated.

The superheated water is pumped to a heat exchanger. There the heat is used to convert water in a separate container into steam. The expanding steam turns a turbine connected to a generator, producing electricity.

Not all the energy created by the nuclear reaction goes to producing electricity. A significant amount is carried away as waste heat in a further cooling process. In many cases the heat is pumped into an adjacent body of water, such as a lake or river. In some cases it is discharged into the atmosphere by a cooling tower.

Commercial nuclear power reactors are more complex than the simplified one we have described. However, the basic process going on inside them is similar. The variations in design are associated with the different types of moderators and fuels used. Commercial reactors in the United States use ordinary water as the moderator, British and Russian reactors use graphite, and Canadian reactors use heavy water (D_2O). While Canadian reactors use natural uranium oxide, most other reactors are fuelled by "enriched" uranium. Enriched uranium fuel has been processed to increase the concentration of U-235 atoms from the usual level of 1% to between 2 and 3%.

Research reactors are similar in structure to power reactors, except that they do not generate large quantities of heat. They are used as sources of neutrons for bombardment experiments and for making artificial radioactive isotopes.

Light Water Reactor

In American commercial reactors, neutrons emitted in the fission reaction are slowed down by water, which also acts as the coolant. There are two basic versions of light water reactors. In the boiling water reactor, heat from the nuclear reactions boils the moderator-coolant in the reactor itself. The steam is then piped directly to the turbine. In a pressurized water reactor, the moderator-coolant is kept at very high pressure. The high pressure allows the moderator-coolant to become very hot (over 300°C) without boiling. The hot moderator-coolant is pumped to a boiler, where the coolant releases heat to boil lower pressure water. The steam produced in the boiler is then used to run the turbine. One safety advantage of the pressurized water reactor is that the coolant-moderator from the reactor does not flow through the turbine. This greatly reduces

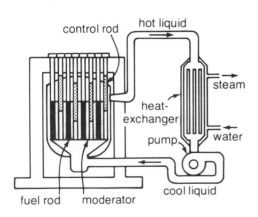

Pressurized water reactor

the possibility of leakage of radioactive materials from the reactor. About two-thirds of the commercial reactors presently operating in the United States are pressurized water reactors. The remainder are boiling water reactors.

Heavy Water Reactor

Canadian reactors use heavy water as a combined moderator and coolant. The hot moderator-coolant is pumped to a boiler. In the boiler, heat is used to convert ordinary water into steam, which in turn drives a turbine. An advantage of the Canadian reactors is that they can be refuelled without being shut down. This contributes to an efficient use of fuel.

The Gas-Cooled Reactor

Britain has developed a reactor that uses graphite as a moderator and carbon dioxide or helium gas, under pressure, as a coolant. The hot gas is passed to a boiler, where steam is created to drive a turbine.

Cooling towers are used in some reactors to condense the steam

Graphite Moderated Water-Cooled Reactor

The first working reactor used graphite as a moderator. Graphite is still the moderator used in the majority of Soviet reactors. Cooled with water, the reactors are capable of large power outputs. Like heavy water reactors, they do not have to be shut down while refuelling. However, they are much more susceptible to a runaway chain reaction than either light water or heavy water reactors.

The Fast Breeder Reactor

"Fast" refers to the speed of the neutrons in the reactor. Each time a neutron causes an atom to split, two or three neutrons are ejected. Only one is required to continue the chain reaction. In this type of reactor, the surplus neutrons are absorbed by fertile atoms, such as uranium-238, which are held in a blanket surrounding the core of uranium-235. The atoms in the blanket are changed into fissionable atoms such as plutonium-239 and uranium-233.

$^{239}_{94}$Pu is produced by neutron
bombardment.
See Section 26.6.

Although nuclear power reactors and
atomic bombs both use uranium as fuel,
there is a vast difference between them.
Atomic bombs use almost pure,
fissionable plutoniun-239 or
uranium-235 which must be compacted
rapidly and precisely to explode (see
page 727). The fuel in an atomic reactor
is too dilute and too dispersed to sustain
a nuclear explosion. Thus, a nuclear
reactor cannot explode like an atomic
bomb. The risk in a nuclear plant is
primarily from the release of
radioactivity.

The reactor is designed in such a way that the quantity of fissionable by-products "manufactured" exceeds the quantity of uranium-235 used as fuel. The fissionable by-products can themselves be used as fuel in the same reactor. So the fast breeder reactor "breeds" more fuel than it uses, and could therefore be used to extend the usefulness of nuclear fuel. "Conventional" reactors use only about 1% of the uranium mined to produce power. With fast breeder reactors, about 50% of the uranium could be used. Unfortunately fast breeder reactors are technically complex, and elaborate measures are required to separate the fissionable products from the other atoms. Their most serious disadvantage is that they produce quantities of fissionable products such as plutonium—substances that are deadly radioactive and can be used to make atomic bombs. For these reasons funds for the research and development of breeder reactors have been closely controlled.

27.5 Safety and Nuclear Power Reactors

When generating power from any source, it is not really a question of absolute safety, it is a question of the relative level of risk. There is some risk in every form of power generation. But what one seeks to do when designing a system is to minimize the risks. Also, one must make the very hard decision as to what is an acceptable level of risk.

For a nuclear reactor the biggest risk is that a number of the systems that cool the reactor core could fail. If that happens, overheating occurs, the core quickly reaches a temperature of over 5000°C, and it melts. This is referred to as the "China Syndrome" because the molten core could burn down through the concrete foundation of the reactor building and into the earth. This would have catastrophic effects, since highly radioactive material would be released into the environment.

While the probability of this happening is low, it is not low enough to be out of the question. In the past thirty years partial core melting has occurred on a number of occasions. The most famous have been the Three Mile Island incident in the United States where there was no direct loss of life, and the Chernobyl reactor fire, near Kiev, Russia, where over 30 workers were killed and a city of over 200 000 had to be evacuated. In both cases, mainly through human error, there was a breakdown in the core cooling system.

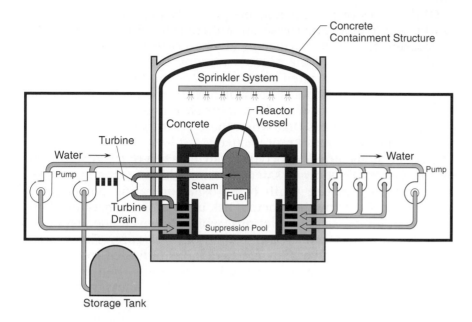

To isolate radioactive materials from the environment, commercial reactors are housed in special airtight containment buildings, airtight shells of steel and reinforced concrete. The entire plant is protected by several automatic monitoring systems with backup safety systems in case primary systems fail. For example, in a pressurized water reactor, the control rods are suspended above the reactor core by electromagnets. If the power fails, the rods fall into the core, stopping the chain reaction. (The same control rods are used to control the power output of the reactor.)

Even after fission stops, a reactor is extremely hot. With insufficient cooling, the fuel can still overheat. The excessive heat can cause a reactor meltdown or a rupture of the moderator-cooling system. If the reactor cooling system breaks outside the reactor, the release water quickly changes to steam, creating pressure in the containment building. If the pressure is not relieved, the reactor building might rupture, releasing the steam and its contents into the environment.

In the United States, reactor containment buildings have large auxiliary coolant systems. In an emergency, the water can be quickly released and circulated throughout the reactor. Containment buildings are also equipped with pools of water and sprinkler systems that condense the released steam, reducing steam pressure.

The Chernobyl reactor after the accident

Of the types of nuclear reactors presently in service around the world, water moderated reactors are considered to be the safest. Comparing the reactor accidents at Chernobyl and Three Mile Island illustrates one of the primary reasons.

In a graphite moderated reactor, such as the Chernobyl reactor, water coolant tends to absorb neutrons. In the event of a loss or overheating of the water coolant, more slow neutrons are available for fission. This means that when these reactors operate at higher power levels, the core is more active.

The Chernobyl accident occurred during a test of the reactor. Operators disconnected some safety systems which resulted in the reactor dropping to one tenth of its usual operating power level. While trying to bring the reactor back up to power, operators committed additional safety violations, which removed adequate control rods and left insufficient coolant in the core. The reactor quickly surged in power. Soviet calculations indicated that reactor power may have increased by 1000 times in less than 4 seconds. The tremendous energy release melted the fuel and destroyed the reactor container and cooling system. The resulting steam pressure and explosion blew flaming pieces of the core and hot graphite out of the building. A total meltdown of the reactor core was averted, but a significant amount of radioactive material escaped. Both short-term and long-term health consequences are still being evaluated.

Light water reactors are safer because the reactor becomes less active if the water level in the reactor core drops. As the amount of water in the core decreases, the remaining water boils more rapidly. With less water in the core, the number of moderating collisions between neutrons and water molecules decreases and the rate of fission slows down. An extreme loss of the water eliminates so many slow neutrons that fission stops and the reactor automatically shuts down. Unlike the Chernobyl reactor, a huge power surge could not occur.

In the Three Mile Island accident, the light water reactor did shut down, but due to operational errors, the reactor overheated. A partial meltdown of the reactor core occurred, and large amounts of radioactive material escaped into the containment structure. Steam pressure built up, but the containment building withstood the increased pressure. However, some radioactive gases did escape.

For a nuclear accident to occur, a number of systems must fail. Increased safety standards and additional training can decrease human error. The level of risk is low, but what constitutes an acceptable risk level is still being debated. As future fuel demands grow, all methods of energy production will have to be carefully evaluated.

27.6 By-products of Nuclear Power

The by-products of nuclear reactions may be categorized as: **high-level radioactive wastes, low-level radioactive wastes,** and **thermal discharges.**

High-level Radioactive Wastes

Most of these wastes come from the fission process. When the uranium-235 is fissioned, radioactive barium and krypton and other fission products are produced. The neutrons that are emitted transform the uranium-238, which is also present in the fuel rod, into radioactive plutonium, americium, and other products. Most of these products have long half-lives. They are known as high-level wastes because, gram for gram, they emit radiations with an intensity many billions times greater than the radiation of natural uranium oxide. The "spent" fuels rods are stored temporarily (that is, for a few years) under 4.0 m of water in tanks, usually inside the plants where they were used.

High-level wastes contain components that have a wide range of decay periods. Some will decay to 0.1% of their initial level within 300 years. Plutonium, which takes approximately 250 000 years to decay to this level, is lethally radioactive. Even a very small amount taken into the lungs by a human being can result in death. So it is imperative that high-level wastes such as plutonium be safely and securely stored.

Several methods for the **intermediate storage** (approximately 25 years) of high-level wastes have been proposed. In one method, concrete silos would be constructed above the ground. Each silo would hold several hundred bundles of spent fuel rods. In another arrangement, "farms" of water-filled pools similar to those at reactor sites would be used. Intermediate storage is required to allow time for the concentration of radioactivity to decrease to levels low enough that **permanent storage** can be effected.

The problem of long-term storage of high-level wastes has yet to be resolved. The fact that the wastes must be stored safely for a period of over 100 000 years makes the solution difficult, to say the least. Suggestions have included burying the wastes deep in salt mines. At present there are no permanent storage sites in the U.S. A pilot project to bury high-level waste in a salt formation beneath the desert surface in New Mexico has been delayed indefinitely.

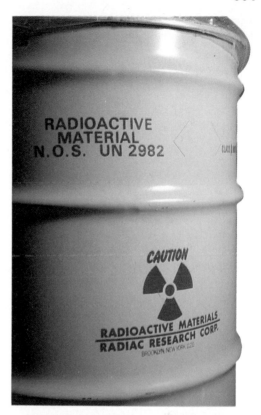

Underwater storage of spent fuel rods

Transporting spent fuel rods

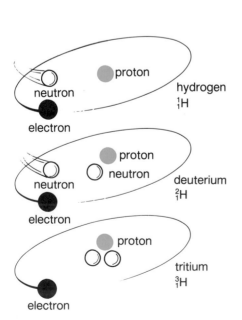

Proposed design for a permanent storage site

U.S. reserves of natural uranium will last only 30 years at the current rate of usage. The era of nuclear power would be greatly extended if the spent fuel were processed into plutonium fuel. However, such large-scale reprocessing would entail considerable risks. There would be the possibility of radioactive contamination of the environment, the problem of disposing of the dangerous wastes of reprocessing, and the possibility of theft by terrorists or criminals who could use the plutonium to make bombs.

The extensive use of nuclear fission as a source of electric power may be limited by the hazards this would present, unless management and control procedures are developed that are acceptable to all concerned.

Low-level Radioactive Wastes

A small amount of low-level radioactive material may be released in the form of fission products and activation products. **Fission products** are the lighter atoms, such as krypton-85, that are produced in the fission process. These substances are formed inside the fuel bundles, but they could escape from the reactor through small

Deuterium nucleus absorbs neutron and becomes tritium.

defects in the fuel coverings. **Activation products** result from neutrons in the reactor bombarding materials such as air, coolant metal in the plumbing system, and suspended particles in the coolant. An example is tritium, which is produced in all reactors containing water. In heavy water reactors, tritium is produced in greater quantities because neutrons are captured by the deuterium in the heavy water moderator.

Elaborate precautions are necessary for detecting and containing any radiation leak in a nuclear power plant. The whole plant is equipped with detectors, and workers are checked daily for excessive levels of radiation. Despite all precautions, there is a slight increase in the annual radiation count in the area of a nuclear power station.

Most solid and liquid low-level wastes are disposed of by being buried in soil beds that are able to trap radioactive components and prevent them from being carried into nearby rivers and streams. These disposal sites must be carefully monitored, and perpetually reserved for the burial of low-level radioactive wastes.

Low-level wastes can become concentrated in the food chain, as illustrated in the margin. They must be treated seriously and controlled because they are potentially harmful to all living things.

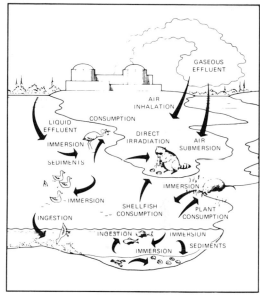

Generalized exposure pathways for organisms other than humans

Thermal Discharges

Both fossil fuel (coal, gas, oil) generating plants and nuclear plants require large quantities of cooling water to condense the steam back into water after it has done its job in the turbines. A nuclear plant requires approximately 50% more cooling water than a fossil-fuel plant of similar capacity. Usually, the cooling water is drawn from a river, lake, or ocean. The used warmer water is then discharged back into the same body of water. If the capacity of the available body of water is inadequate, the water must be cooled in a specially built tower or pond and used over and over again.

In large bodies of cold water such as the Great Lakes, the effects of discharging hot water are minimal, though it does cause some changes in the distribution of species and populations of fish, algae, and bottom-living organisms. In smaller bodies of water such as rivers, drastic biological changes can occur, including the excessive formation of algae and the depletion of oxygen in the water.

In an energy-short world, new ways are being investigated for using the waste hot water. It could provide heating for industries and homes near nuclear power plants, it could be distributed through pipes in the soil to increase crop yields, or it could be used to heat greenhouses.

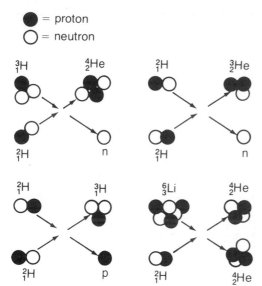

● = proton
○ = neutron

^3_1H ^4_2He ^2_1H ^3_2He

^2_1H n ^2_1H n

^2_1H ^3_1H ^6_3Li ^4_2He

^2_1H p ^2_1H ^4_2He

27.7 Nuclear Fusion

Fusion is the process by which light elements combine to produce heavier ones. Nuclei must be joined together, but all nuclei have positive charges and thus repel each other. For nuclei to fuse, they must be brought so close together that the stronger nuclear forces of attraction can overcome the electric repulsion. This can only occur when the two nuclei are no more than approximately 10^{-15} m apart.

In order for nuclei to come within 10^{-15} m of each other, the repulsion between their protons must be overcome. This can occur only if the atoms containing the nuclei are moving towards each other fast enough. If the atoms of a material are to move fast enough for their nuclei to fuse when they collide, the temperature of the material must be very high indeed. This reaction is the primary source of the world's energy. It has been taking place on the sun for at least 5.0×10^9 years. At 1 000 000°C, 1 g of deuterium can undergo fusion and release enough energy to supply the electrical needs of an average North American home for nearly 40 years.

A typical fusion reaction is:

$$^2_1H + {^2_1H} \longrightarrow {^3_2He} + {^1_0n} + energy$$

This and three other possible fusion reactions are illustrated in the margin.

Accurate measurements of atomic mass have shown that the mass of products is less than the mass of the reactants. Just as in the fission reaction, it is the amount of the loss in mass that is converted into energy. (See Practice problem 3, page 789.)

The first manufactured use of the energy of nuclear fusion was in the fusion bomb, popularly called the thermonuclear or hydrogen bomb. It was devised by a team led by the American physicist Edward Teller (1908-) and exploded in 1952. After a series of fission bombs had been exploded it was discovered that the temperatures created exceeded 10^8°C, high enough to sustain the fusion reaction. The structure of a fusion bomb is illustrated in the margin on the next page. When the fission bomb explodes, billions of high-speed neutrons are released. Some of these combine with lithium-6 nuclei to form tritium (^3_1H). The tritium, in turn, fuses with deuterium nuclei (^2_1H) releasing vast quantities of nuclear energy as follows:

$$^6_3Li + {^1_0n} \longrightarrow \underset{(tritium)}{^3_1H} + \underset{(\alpha\ particle)}{^4_2He}$$

$$\underset{(tritium)}{^3_1H} + \underset{(deuterium)}{^2_1H} \longrightarrow \underset{(\alpha\ particle)}{^4_2He} + {^1_0n} + energy$$

Tritium, a slightly radioactive isotope of hydrogen, is a by-product of nuclear fission and can be separated by the electrolysis of heavy water. More than 80% of the tritium sold for commercial purposes is used to power self-contained light sources. The remainder is used in medical and laboratory investigations as a low-level tracer for drugs and chemicals. Unfortunately, tritium is also used in the manufacture of nuclear weapons, so that exporting it requires caution.

The advantages of fusion power are that the fuel is cheap and easy to obtain (probably deuterium from water), and the by-products are harmless (primarily helium nuclei and a few neutrons). With these advantages, fusion power would seem to be the answer to the world's energy needs. However, human-made fusion has so far been accomplished only in the fusion bomb.

Various methods have been used in an attempt to create the necessary high temperatures and to use the resulting energy constructively. In one such method, hydrogen atoms are first ionized, to rid them of their electrons, and then compressed by strong electrical and magnetic fields to raise their temperature to the point at which fusion can occur. Several such methods have produced fusion reactions, but only for a fraction of a second.

Another technique involves the use of high-temperature lasers focused on tiny pellets of frozen deuterium. To be useful as a source of energy, the fusion process must liberate more energy than it consumes. The break-even point has not yet been achieved, and past experience with fission reactors suggests that fusion power will not be commercially viable before the end of the century.

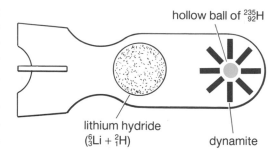

hollow ball of $^{235}_{92}H$

lithium hydride ($^{6}_{3}Li + ^{2}_{1}H$)

dynamite

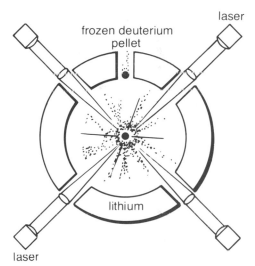

frozen deuterium pellet

laser

lithium

laser

A proposed method of achieving fusion, by firing a frozen deuterium pellet into an evacuated reaction chamber. At the center of the chamber, the pellet undergoes violent compression from lasers, causing the production of heat and neutrons. A blanket of lithium surrounds the chamber, recovers the heat, and breeds tritium.

The Tokamak Fusion Test Reactor at Princeton University

27.8 Nuclear Energy—an Answer or a Challenge?

Our principal sources of electrical energy, now and in the immediate future, are hydroelectric stations and thermal stations using fossil fuels or uranium. Conservation measures and supplementary sources of energy, such as solar energy, will probably affect the demand for electric power, but we will continue to rely heavily on the sources we are using now.

In the next decades the percentage of energy supplied by nuclear reactors will remain constant. In the more distant future, a new generation of nuclear reactors may be developed that will exploit the plutonium in the "waste" products of today's reactors. The exploitation of the fusion reaction is almost as elusive as it was 10 years ago, and most knowledgeable scientists and engineers say that it could be another 20 years before a commercially viable system is developed. So it appears that we must tolerate the presence of nuclear power stations in our society, at least for the next few decades.

When the word "nuclear" is used, many people think of bombs, usually because they do not understand the difference between a controlled and an uncontrolled neutron chain reaction. Ignorance has bred fear. Knowledge should breed respect and concern. The background knowledge you now have should enable you to contribute, as a responsible citizen, to the resolution of some of the issues society must face in the next decades.

Among the issues that affect the future of nuclear power are the risk of a system failure in a core cooling system, the risk of rupture in the moderator lines, the disposal of radioactive wastes, the siting of nuclear power plants, the sale of nuclear power plants to other countries, and the processing of high-level wastes. These issues are the concern of all citizens, and should not be left to business and government experts. Whenever the products of science and technology affect the well-being of future generations and the quality of life on this planet, it is time for citizens to get involved.

Chapter Summary

1. In some nuclear reactions, large quantities of energy are liberated since a small part of the nuclear mass of the reactants has been converted into energy according to the equation $E = mc^2$.

2. In nuclear fission, a heavier element splits into lighter elements, accompanied by a release of energy.

3. Transuranic elements are elements that do not occur naturally but are produced by the nuclear bombardment of heavy elements.

4. In a chain reaction, each fission is responsible for producing, on the average, one other fission, and the reaction can only continue as long as a sufficient quantity of fissionable material, called the critical mass, is present.

5. The chain reaction of uranium-235 in a reactor can only continue as long as the speed of the neutrons is slowed down by a moderator.

6. A chain reaction is controlled by the insertion among the fissionable materials of substances that absorb neutrons.

7. Fission bombs utilize enriched uranium or plutonium for the chain reaction.

8. The three primary components of every nuclear reactor are a fissionable fuel, a moderator, and control rods.

9. The heat produced by the fission reaction in a nuclear power reactor is converted into electric power by means of steam turbines that turn electric generators.

10. Commercial nuclear power reactors in the United States use enriched uranium as a fuel and ordinary water as a moderator. Reactors can also use graphite or heavy water as moderators.

11. The heat energy from the core of a nuclear reactor is usually transmitted by heavy water, ordinary water, or a gas.

12. Breeder reactors are constructed so that they produce more fissionable material than they use as fuel.

13. Because ordinary water absorbs neutrons, light water reactors have a much lower chance of a meltdown than graphite moderated reactors.

14. The by-products of nuclear power reactors include low-level and high-level radioactive wastes and heat.

15. Even low-level radioactive wastes tend to concentrate in the food chain, and thus can be dangerous to all living things.

16. Nuclear fusion is the process by which light elements combine to produce heavier ones as the nuclei join together, at high temperatures.

Chapter Review

Discussion

1. (a) What are two important isotopes of uranium?
   (b) One is fissionable and the other produces a transuranic element. Explain.
2. Why do chain reactions not normally occur in natural deposits of uranium? There has been one exception. Where, when, and how did it occur?
3. Nuclear bombs are defused by making it impossible for the pieces of fissionable material to come together to form a critical mass. Why does this make the chain reaction impossible?
4. Which is more likely to sustain a chain reaction—a block of porous uranium in air or one in water? Why?
5. Why are light water reactors considered to be
   (a) safer than graphite moderated power reactors?
   (b) more expensive to operate than heavy water power reactors?
6. What factors must be considered when siting a nuclear power reactor?
7. Two of the radioisotopes released from the damaged reactor at Chernobyl were isotopes of iodine and cesium. Why did these two substances cause radiation illness in those exposed?
8. Until recently, radioactive wastes were encased in concrete and dumped in the ocean. Explain why this method of disposal was discontinued.
9. Why does the burying of radioactive wastes deep in the ground protect this generation of human beings? Discuss why this may or may not be a satisfactory long-term solution.
10. A public hearing has been called concerning the location of a low-level nuclear waste disposal site in your area. You are asked to prepare arguments both for and against the proposal. List your arguments in point form.
11. In the late 1950s a United States bomber crashed in southern Spain, and the material from nuclear devices on board was distributed in the ocean and on the nearby beaches. Why were large quantities of the sand and earth trucked away before the area was considered safe?
12. Any country having a nuclear reactor has the capability of producing enough fissionable material to construct a bomb.
    (a) Explain why this is so.
    (b) What types of reactors would be most efficient producers of excess fissionable products?

13. Why does fusion require such a high temperature before it can begin?

14. Why is it impossible to sustain a fusion reaction in a normal container?

15. Although officially no nation has produced a neutron bomb, it is technically feasible. Why would such a bomb be attractive to military planners?

16. Astro-physicists speculate that stars are created when vast clouds of hydrogen come together because of mutual gravitational attraction, collapsing into denser and denser mass. Eventually fusion begins. Why?

17. Stars such as our sun undergo a series of fusion reactions between birth and death. After doing some research, describe the processes involved in 200 words or less.

18. When a fission bomb explodes, radioactive isotopes are produced on the Earth and in the atmosphere. The fusion reaction in a hydrogen bomb produces no radioactive isotopes. Why is there still radioactive "fallout"?

19. There are "clean" and "dirty" atomic and nuclear bombs. What is the difference between each type in terms of: (a) their construction, (b) the fallout products?

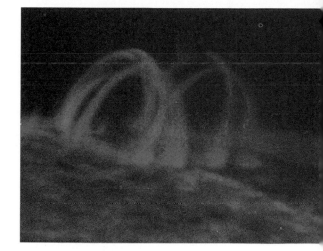

20. Write an essay (200-300 words) on one of the following topics:
    —The Connection Between Nuclear Energy and Nuclear Weaponry
    —How We Would Cope If Nuclear Power Reactors Were Banned
    —Is Nuclear Power an Acceptable Risk?
    —Fusion–The Energy Cure for the Future?
    —The Economic Realities of Nuclear Power
    —Decommissioning Nuclear Reactors

21. Write a short biography of one of the following scientists who contributed to the development of nuclear energy: Albert Einstein, Enrico Fermi, Lise Meitner, Otto Hahn, Ernest Lawrence, Robert Oppenheimer, Edward Teller.

22. Many of the scientists mentioned in the past four chapters were awarded Nobel Prizes for Physics or Chemistry. Find a listing of the prize winners for the period 1901–1990, and record the name and the discovery of each scientist whose contribution involved radioactivity or nuclear physics.

Problems

23. Each of the following represents the loss in mass produced by a fission reaction. In each case, calculate the energy released by the conversion of mass into energy.
    (a) 2.0 kg   (b) 40 g   (c) 0.1 mg

24. Predict the loss in mass that will occur in each case when the following quantities of energy are given off, because of the conversion of mass into energy in nuclear reactions.
    (a) 9.0×10^{16} J (b) 4.5×10^{14} J

25. The energy output of the sun is approximately 4.0×10^{26} J/s. If all this energy results from mass-energy conversion in the fusion process, calculate the rate at which the sun is losing mass.

26. The energy released by the fission of one atom of uranium-235 is 3.2×10^{-8} J. The energy released by the atomic bomb dropped at Hiroshima was estimated to be the equivalent of 18 140 t of dynamite or 8.0×10^{13} J.
    (a) How many atoms of uranium-235 underwent fission?
    (b) What mass of uranium-235 was converted into energy?

27. Find the quantity of nuclear energy liberated in each of the following nuclear reactions:

    (a) $^{235}_{92}\text{U}$ + ^1_0n $\longrightarrow$ $^{140}_{54}\text{Xe}$
          (235.043 925)   (1.008 67)   (139.921 61)

                                        + $^{94}_{38}\text{Sr}$ + (^1_0n)
                                            (93.9153 67)   (1.008 67) amu

    (b) ^3_2He + ^3_2He $\longrightarrow$ ^4_2He + $2(^1_1\text{H})$
          (3.016 03)   (3.016 03)   (4.002 60)   2(1.008 67) amu
          (1 amu = 1.66×10^{-27} kg)

Meet a Technical Supervisor in a Nuclear Power Plant . . .
Gay Wyn Quance

Gay Wyn works as a supervisor in the Emergency Preparedness Section of a nuclear power plant. She has been in the field of nuclear energy since 1978.

Q. What did you study in college?
A. I majored in chemistry and geology, earning an Honors Bachelor of Science degree.
Q. Were you always interested in science?
A. Yes, and my family encouraged my interest. At school I was fortunate to have instructors who encouraged me to pursue a science-related career.
Q. Have you always been involved in the safety aspect of nuclear energy?
A. Yes, in different areas. I've been involved in the commissioning of reactor shutdown systems for many years.

Q. What does commissioning involve?
A. The purpose of commissioning is to ensure that systems will operate as required when necessary. We put all systems through rigorous paces before starting up the reactor. It's like learning to drive in the parking lot before going on the highway.
Q. What are you working on now?
A. I'm working in the Emergency Preparedness Field. I work on programs that ensure that we are prepared for any incident involving a nuclear hazard (anything involving radiation).
Q. How are you prepared?
A. We have full plans to handle all conceivable accidents. Each plan is tested in exercises that realistically simulate an accident. The mock 'accidents' give people a chance to perform the tasks assigned to them under these conditions.
Q. Have you been involved in any large-scale emergency tests?
A. Yes. The purpose of these exercises is to simulate a real accident at the station so that all emergency response organizations within the area would be required to respond to the full extent of their responsibilities.
Q. This must be an enormous undertaking. What does it involve?
A. There are over 30 people involved in the design and more than 60 people evaluating the exercise.
Q. Did the people involved know it was a drill?
A. Yes. But we created a number of realistic incidents so that even though people knew it was a drill, they performed as if it were really happening.

Q. What were the results of the exercise?
A. The evaluation team determined that we're doing a very good job. It showed that we have an effective emergency response capability.
Q. Is the shutdown system good enough to prevent an accident like the one at Chernobyl?
A. U.S. reactors are completely different from the Chernobyl reactor. We believe we have an excellent shutdown capability which takes less than a second to shut down the reactor.
Q. How much do you use science skills in your everyday work?
A. I always use the organized thought processes that we learn when we study science and math. Equations are not just symbols and numbers, but relationships to be applied to a particular problem. Certain areas of my job are very technical. For instance, I do a radiation dose projection model which is an important part of the emergency response program.
Q. Do you need to know about computers, too?
A. Oh yes. I work with computers when I use large amounts of data or sophisticated mathematical models.
Q. What should students do if they're interested in a career in the field of nuclear energy?
A. They should contact people in the industry to find out where the jobs in nuclear energy will be in the future. Most people in the field are always willing to talk to young people.

Appendix A

Prefixes of the Metric System

Factor	Prefix	Symbol
10^{12}	tera	T
10^{9}	giga	G
10^{6}	mega	M
10^{3}	kilo	k
10^{2}	hecto	h
10	deka	da
10^{-1}	deci	d
10^{-2}	centi	c
10^{-3}	milli	m
10^{-6}	micro	μ
10^{-9}	nano	n
10^{-12}	pico	p
10^{-15}	femto	f
10^{-18}	atto	a

Some Examples

1.000 km (one kilometer)	= 1000 m
1 cm (one centimeter)	= 0.01 m
1.0 MJ (one megajoule)	$= 1.0 \times 10^{6}$ J
1.0 mA (one milliampere)	$= 1.0 \times 10^{-3}$ A
1.0 μV (one microvolt)	$= 1.0 \times 10^{-6}$ V
1.0 GHz (one gigahertz)	$= 1.0 \times 10^{9}$ Hz
1.0 pF (one picofarad)	$= 1.0 \times 10^{-12}$ F
1.0 Ta (one terayear)	$= 1.0 \times 10^{12}$ a

Appendix B

Selected Physical Quantities and Measurement Units

Physical quantity	Quantity symbol	Measurement unit	Unit symbol	Equivalent Unit
		Fundamental Units		
length	l	meter	m	m
mass	m	kilogram	kg	kg
time	t	second	s	s
electric charge	Q	coulomb	C	C
temperature	T	kelvin	K	K
		Derived Units		
area	A	square meter	m^2	m^2
volume	V	cubic meter	m^3	m^3
velocity	$\vec{v}$	meter per second	m/s	m/s
acceleration	$\vec{a}$	meter per second per second	m/s^2	m/s^2
force	$\vec{F}$	newton	N	$kg \cdot m/s^2$
work	W	joule	J	$kg \cdot m^2/s^2$
energy	E	joule	J	$kg \cdot m^2/s^2$
power	P	watt	W	$km \cdot m^2/s^3$
heat energy	E_H	joule	J	$kg \cdot m^2/s^2$
density	D	kilogram per cubic meter	kg/m^3	
pressure	p	pascal	Pa	$km/s^2/m$
frequency	f	hertz	Hz	s^{-1}
electric potential	V	volt	V	$kg \cdot m^2/C \cdot s^2$
electric current	I	ampere	A	C/s
electric resistance	R	ohm	Ω	$kg \cdot m^2/C^2 \cdot s$

Appendix C

Appendix D

Physical Constants

Constant	Symbol	Accepted value
velocity of light	c	3.00×10^8 m/s
gravitational constant	G	6.67×10^{-11} N·m²/kg²
rest mass of electron	m_e	9.11×10^{-31} kg
rest mass of proton	m_p	1.67×10^{-27} kg
rest mass of neutron	m_n	1.67×10^{-27} kg
charge on an electron	e	1.60×10^{-19} C
Planck's constant	h	6.63×10^{-34} J·s
Coulomb's constant	k	9.0×10^9 N·m²/C²
mean radius of Earth		6.38×10^6 m
mean radius of Earth's orbit		1.49×10^{11} m
mean radius of moon		1.74×10^6 m
mean radius of moon's orbit		3.84×10^8 m
length of year		3.16×10^7 s

Table of Natural Trigonometric Functions

Angle	Sine	Cosine	Tangent	Angle	Sine	Cosine	Tangent
1°	.0175	.9998	.0175	46°	.7193	.6947	1.0355
2°	.0349	.9994	.0349	47°	.7314	.6820	1.0724
3°	.0523	.9986	.0524	48°	.7431	.6691	1.1106
4°	.0698	.9976	.0699	49°	.7547	.6561	1.1504
5°	.0872	.9962	.0875	50°	.7660	.6428	1.1918
6°	.1045	.9945	.1051	51°	.7771	.6293	1.2349
7°	.1219	.9925	.1228	52°	.7880	.6157	1.2799
8°	.1392	.9903	.1405	53°	.7986	.6018	1.3270
9°	.1564	.9877	.1584	54°	.8090	.5878	1.3764
10°	.1736	.9848	.1763	55°	.8192	.5736	1.4281
11°	.1908	.9816	.1944	56°	.8290	.5592	1.4826
12°	.2079	.9781	.2126	57°	.8387	.5446	1.5399
13°	.2250	.9744	.2309	58°	.8480	.5299	1.6003
14°	.2419	.9703	.2493	59°	.8572	.5150	1.6643
15°	.2588	.9659	.2679	60°	.8660	.5000	1.7321
16°	.2756	.9613	.2867	61°	.8746	.4848	1.8040
17°	.2924	.9563	.3057	62°	.8829	.4695	1.8807
18°	.3090	.9511	.3249	63°	.8910	.4540	1.9626
19°	.3256	.9455	.3443	64°	.8988	.4384	2.0503
20°	.3420	.9397	.3640	65°	.9063	.4226	2.1445
21°	.3584	.9336	.3839	66°	.9135	.4067	2.2460
22°	.3746	.9272	.4040	67°	.9205	.3907	2.3559
23°	.3907	.9205	.4245	68°	.9272	.3746	2.4751
24°	.4067	.9135	.4452	69°	.9336	.3584	2.6051
25°	.4226	.9063	.4663	70°	.9397	.3420	2.7475
26°	.4384	.8988	.4877	71°	.9455	.3256	2.9042
27°	.4540	.8910	.5095	72°	.9511	.3090	3.0777
28°	.4695	.8829	.5317	73°	.9563	.2924	3.2709
29°	.4848	.8746	.5543	74°	.9613	.2756	3.4874
30°	.5000	.8660	.5774	75°	.9659	.2588	3.7321
31°	.5150	.8572	.6009	76°	.9703	.2419	4.0108
32°	.5299	.8480	.6249	77°	.9744	.2250	4.3315
33°	.5446	.8387	.6494	78°	.9781	.2079	4.7046
34°	.5592	.8290	.6745	79°	.9816	.1908	5.1446
35°	.5736	.8192	.7002	80°	.9848	.1736	5.6713
36°	.5878	.8090	.7265	81°	.9877	.1564	6.3138
37°	.6018	.7986	.7536	82°	.9903	.1392	7.1154
38°	.6157	.7880	.7813	83°	.9925	.1219	8.1443
39°	.6293	.7771	.8098	84°	.9945	.1045	9.5144
40°	.6428	.7660	.8391	85°	.9962	.0872	11.4301
41°	.6561	.7547	.8693	86°	.9976	.0698	14.3007
42°	.6691	.7431	.9004	87°	.9986	.0523	19.0811
43°	.6820	.7314	.9325	88°	.9994	.0349	28.6363
44°	.6947	.7193	.9657	89°	.9998	.0175	57.2900
45°	.7071	.7071	1.0000	90°	1.0000	.0000	

Appendix E

Periodic Table of the Elements

1 H 1.0079																1 H 1.0079	2 He 4.00260
3 Li 6.941	4 Be 9.01218											5 B 10.81	6 C 12.011	7 N 14.0067	8 O 15.9994	9 F 18.99840	10 Ne 20.179
11 Na 22.98977	12 Mg 24.305											13 Al 26.98154	14 Si 28.086	15 P 30.97376	16 S 32.06	17 Cl 35.453	18 Ar 39.948
19 K 39.098	20 Ca 40.08	21 Sc 44.9559	22 Ti 47.90	23 V 50.9414	24 Cr 51.996	25 Mn 54.9380	26 Fe 55.847	27 Co 58.9332	28 Ni 58.70	29 Cu 63.546	30 Zn 65.38	31 Ga 69.72	32 Ge 72.59	33 As 74.9216	34 Se 78.96	35 Br 79.904	36 Kr 83.80
37 Rb 85.4678	38 Sr 87.62	39 Y 88.9059	40 Zr 91.22	41 Nb 92.9064	42 Mo 95.94	43 Tc 98.9062	44 Ru 101.07	45 Rh 102.9055	46 Pd 106.4	47 Ag 107.868	48 Cd 112.40	49 In 114.82	50 Sn 118.69	51 Sb 121.75	52 Te 127.60	53 I 126.9045	54 Xe 131.30
55 Cs 132.9054	56 Ba 137.34	57 *La 138.9055	72 Hf 178.49	73 Ta 180.9479	74 W 183.85	75 Re 186.207	76 Os 190.2	77 Ir 192.22	78 Pt 195.09	79 Au 196.9665	80 Hg 200.59	81 Tl 204.37	82 Pb 207.2	83 Bi 208.9804	84 Po (210)	85 At (210)	86 Rn (222)
87 Fr (223)	88 Ra 226.0254	89 †Ac (227)	104 (260)	105 (260)													

*Lanthanoid Series

58 Ce 140.12	59 Pr 140.9077	60 Nd 144.24	61 Pm (147)	62 Sm 150.4	63 Eu 151.96	64 Gd 157.25	65 Tb 158.9254	66 Dy 162.50	67 Ho 164.9304	68 Er 167.26	69 Tm 168.9342	70 Yb 173.04	71 Lu 174.97

†Actinoid Series

90 Th 232.0381	91 Pa 231.0359	92 U 238.029	93 Np 237.0482	94 Pu (244)	95 Am (243)	96 Cm (247)	97 Bk (247)	98 Cf (251)	99 Es (254)	100 Fm (257)	101 Md (258)	102 No (255)	103 Lr (256)

Atomic masses corrected to conform
to the 1973 values of the Commission on
Atomic Weights.

14 Si 28.086	Atomic number
	Atomic symbol
	Average atomic mass

Appendix F

Table of Isotopes

Element	Symbol	Atomic number	Mass numbers of naturally occurring isotopes
Actinium	Ac	89	**227***, 228*
Aluminum	Al	13	27
Americium	Am	95	(243)
Antimony	Sb	51	**121**, 123
Argon	Ar	18	36, 38, 40
Arsenic	As	33	75
Astatine	At	85	210*, 215*, 216*, 218*
Barium	Ba	56	130, 132, 134, 135, 136, 137, **138**
Berkelium	Bk	97	(247)
Beryllium	Be	4	9
Bismuth	Bi	83	**209**, 210*, 211*, 212*, 214*
Boron	B	5	10, **11**
Bromine	Br	35	79, 81
Cadmium	Cd	48	106, 108, 110, 111, 112, 113, **114**, 116
Calcium	Ca	20	**40**, 42, 43, 44, 46, 48
Californium	Cf	98	(249)
Carbon	C	6	**12**, 13, 14
Cerium	Ce	58	136, 138, **140**, 142
Cesium	Cs	55	133
Chlorine	Cl	17	**35**, 37
Chromium	Cr	24	50, **52**, 53, 54
Cobalt	Co	27	59
Copper	Cu	29	**63**, 65
Curium	Cm	96	(248)
Dysprosium	Dy	66	156, 158, 160, 161, 162, 163, **164**
Einsteinium	Es	99	(254)
Erbium	Er	68	162, 164, **166**, 167, 168, 170
Europium	Eu	63	151, **153**
Fermium	Fm	100	(253)
Fluorine	F	9	19
Francium	Fr	87	223*
Gadolinium	Gd	64	152, 154, 155, 156, 157, **158**, 160
Gallium	Ga	31	**69**, 71
Germanium	Ge	32	70, 72, 73, **74**, 76
Gold	Au	79	197
Hafnium	Hf	72	174, 176, 177, 178, 179, **180**
Helium	He	2	3, **4**
Holmium	Ho	67	165
Hydrogen	H	1	**1**, 2
Indium	In	49	113, **115**

Element	Symbol	Atomic number	Mass numbers of naturally occurring isotopes
Iodine	I	53	127
Iridium	Ir	77	191, **193**
Iron	Fe	26	54, **56**, 57, 58
Krypton	Kr	36	78, 80, 82, 83, **84**, 86
Lanthanum	La	57	138*, **139**
Lawrencium	Lw	103	(257)
Lead	Pb	82	204, 206, 207, **208**, 210*, 211*, 212*, 214*
Lithium	Li	3	6, **7**
Lutetium	Lu	71	**175**, 176*
Magnesium	Mg	12	**24**, 25, 26
Manganese	Mn	25	55
Mendelevium	Md	101	(256)
Mercury	Hg	80	196, 198, 199, **200**, 201, 202, 204
Molybdenum	Mo	42	92, 94, 95, 96, 97, **98**, 100
Neodymium	Nd	60	**142**, 143, 144*, 145, 146, 148, 150
Neon	Ne	10	**20**, 21, 22
Neptunium	Np	93	(237)
Nickel	Ni	28	**58**, 60, 61, 62, 64
Niobium	Nb	41	93
Nitrogen	N	7	**14**, 15
Nobelium	No	102	(253)
Osmium	Os	76	184, 186, 187, 188, 189, 190, **192**
Oxygen	O	8	**16**, 17, 18
Palladium	Pd	46	102, 104, 105, **106**, 108, 110
Phosphorus	P	15	31
Platinum	Pt	78	190*, 192, 194, **195**, 196, 198
Plutonium	Pu	94	(242)
Polonium	Po	84	**210***, 211*, 212*, 214*, 215*, 216*, 218*
Potassium	K	19	**39**, 40*, 41
Praseodymium	Pr	59	141
Promethium	Pm	61	(147)
Protactinium	Pa	91	**231***, 234*
Radium	Ra	88	223*, 224*, **226***, 228*
Radon	Rn	86	219*, 220*, **222**
Rhenium	Re	75	185, **187***
Rhodium	Rh	45	103
Rubidium	Rb	37	**85**, 87*
Ruthenium	Ru	44	96, 98, 99, 100, 101, **102**, 104
Samarium	Sm	62	144, 147*, 148, 149, 150, **152**, 154
Scandium	Sc	21	45
Selenium	Se	34	74, 76, 77, 78, **80**, 82
Silicon	Si	14	**28**, 29, 30
Silver	Ag	47	**107**, 109
Sodium	Na	11	23
Strontium	Sr	38	84, 86, 87, **88**
Sulfur	S	16	**32**, 33, 34, 36

Element	Symbol	Atomic number	Mass numbers of naturally occurring isotopes
Tantalum	Ta	73	180, **181**
Technetium	Tc	43	(99)
Tellurium	Te	52	120, 122, 123, 124, 125, 126, 128, **130**
Terbium	Tb	65	159
Thallium	Tl	81	203, **205**, 206*, 207*, 208*, 210*
Thorium	Th	90	227*, 228*, 230*, 231*, **232***, 234*
Thulium	Tm	69	169
Tin	Sn	50	112, 114, 115, 116, 117, 118, 119, **120**, 122, 124
Titanium	Ti	22	46, 47, **48**, 49, 50
Tungsten	W	74	180*, 182, 183, **184**, 186
Uranium	U	92	234*, 235*, **238***
Vanadium	V	23	50, **51**
Xenon	Xe	54	124, 126, 128, 129, 130, 131, **132**, 134, 136
Ytterbium	Yb	70	168, 170, 171, 172, 173, **174**, 176
Yttrium	Y	39	89
Zinc	Zn	30	**64**, 66, 67, 68, 70
Zirconium	Ar	40	**90**, 91, 92, 94, 96

NOTES: Isotopes marked with an asterisk are naturally occurring radioactive isotopes. Most are members of one of the natural radioactive decay series, and some are present only in extremely small amounts. For elements with no naturally occurring isotope, the atomic mass number of the longest half-life artificial isotope is given in parentheses. For elements with more than one naturally occurring isotope, the most abundant one is indicated in bold type.

Appendix G

Scientific Notation—the Accuracy of Measured Quantities

In physics we measure many different physical quantities. No measured quantity is ever exact. There is always some error or uncertainty. The size of the error is determined both by the measuring device used and by the skill of the person using it. For example, if two students are measuring the frequency of a pendulum, one with an electronic stopwatch accurate to 0.001 s, and the other with a wristwatch accurate to the nearest 0.5 s, their margins of error will differ because one measuring device is more accurate than the other. On the other hand, if both students are using the same electronic stopwatch, their measurements will probably again be different, because their reaction times will be different and one is more skillful or takes more care than the other.

The way in which a measured quantity is written down indicates not just the quantity but also its degree of accuracy. For example, if we measure the length of a desk and state it to be 1.638 m, we are indicating by the three measured digits to the right of the decimal point that we used a ruler that is accurate to the nearest 0.001 of a meter. Digits that are obviously the result of careful measurement are called significant digits, or significant figures. The degree of accuracy of a measurement is shown by the number of significant digits it has.

While all non-zero digits are considered to be significant, it is not always easy to determine the number of significant digits when zeros occur in the measurement. For example, the distance from the Earth to the moon is commonly stated as 382 000 km. This number, as stated, is *probably* accurate only to the nearest 1000 km and thus has three significant digits (i.e., the 3, the 8, and the 2). The zeros merely indicate the position of the decimal point. Similarly, 0.000 536 cm contains only three significant digits.

However, zeros are sometimes significant. In each of the following cases there are four significant digits: 20.64 cm and 46.20 cm. In the second case, the zero indicates that the measurement is more accurate than 46.2 cm. Zeros after a decimal should not be added indiscriminately to a measured quantity, since each additional zero indicates a greater degree of accuracy.

Sometimes the nature of the measured quantity indicates the correct number of significant digits. For example, if a watch is used to measure 200 s, we know, since the watch has a sweep second hand, that the zeros are significant. Or, if a distance of 500 km is measured on a car's odometer, we can be fairly certain that the distance measured is accurate to the nearest kilometer, and thus to three significant digits. But if no information is available, we must assume that the zeros are there only to place the decimal and are not significant. For example, 46 000 has only two significant digits.

A person with a wristwatch might reasonably be expected to measure time intervals to the nearest second.

$$1 \text{ s} = 0.017 \text{ min}$$
$$= 0.000\ 28 \text{ h}$$

Therefore, that person can measure such time intervals as these:

26 s
304 s
3.00 min
146.42 min
7.0006 h

A person with an ordinary stopwatch (0.1 s) can do better, and electronic stopwatches are accurate to 0.01 s.

$$0.01 \text{ s} = 0.000\ 17 \text{ min}$$
$$= 0.000\ 002\ 8 \text{ h}$$

This means that a person with an electronic stopwatch can measure time intervals such as these:

11.23 s
4.0002 min
3.000 008 h

When we count objects, the number is exact. The degree of accuracy and the number of significant digits are not involved. For example, if we count the students in a class and get 32, we know that 32.2 or 31.9 are not possible answers. Only a whole-number answer is possible. Other examples of exact numbers are days in a month, swings of a pendulum, ticks from a recording timer, vibrations of a spring, electrons in an atom, and pennies in a dime.

Scientific Notation, or Standard Form

Trailing zeros in whole numbers can be confusing. For example, we said that 382 000 km, the distance to the moon, was *probably* accurate only to three significant digits, because when we give the number of kilometers as "382 000" we imply that we cannot be any more precise than that—presumably because we have no knowledge of the accuracy of the instruments and techniques that were used in making this measurement. In fact, the reading may be correct to the nearest 10 km rather than just the nearest 1000 km, but we cannot record that information by means of common notation. Unless we know differently, all trailing zeros in a whole number must be considered as place holders.

This problem is resolved by using what is called scientific notation, or standard form, which enables us to express very large and very small quantities in a form that is easily understood and conveys the number of significant digits. In scientific notation, the number is expressed by writing the correct number of significant digits with one non-zero digit to the left of the decimal point, and then multiplying the number by the appropriate power of 10 (positive or negative). Thus, if 382 000 km is accurate to the nearest 10 km, there are five significant digits, and the measurement should be expressed as 3.8200×10^5 km.

The number of electrons in a coulomb of charge is 6 242 000 000 000 000 000. This measurement is accurate only to four significant figures, but the degree of accuracy is not evident in the form in which it is recorded. In scientific notation it would be expressed as 6.242×10^{18}, which makes the number of significant digits quite clear. The mass of a proton is 0.000 000 000 000 000 000 000 001 672 kg. This measurement is known to be accurate to four significant digits, which is evident from the way it is written. But the form of the number is very inconvenient, and it is expressed in scientific notation as 1.672×10^{-27} kg.

Summary

- All counted quantities are exact.
- All measured quantities have some degree of error.
- All non-zero digits are significant; e.g., 259.67 has five significant digits.
- All zeros between non-zero digits and trailing zeros to the right of a decimal point are significant; e.g., 606 and 7.00 both have three significant digits.
- In whole numbers, all trailing zeros (those to the right of the last non-zero digit) are not considered to be significant unless, by inspection of the measured quantity, the number of significant digits can be assessed; e.g., 350 km on the odometer of a car would be assessed to have three significant digits.

- In decimal fractions smaller than 1, leading zeros (to the left of the first non-zero digit) are not significant; e.g., 0.003 68 has only three significant digits.
- In scientific notation, the number is expressed by writing the correct number of significant digits with one non-zero digit to the left of the decimal point, and then multiplying the number by the appropriate power of 10 (positive or negative).

Sample Problems

1. How many significant digits are there in each of the following measured quantities?
   (a) 47.2 m   (3)
   (b) 401.6 kg   (4)
   (c) 0.000 067 s   (2)
   (d) 6.00 cm   (3)
   (e) 46.03 m   (4)
   (f) 0.000 000 000 68 m   (2)
   (g) 0.07 m   (1)
2. Express each of the following numbers in scientific notation with the correct number of significant digits.
   *(a) 76 (7.6×10^1)
   (b) 0.60 (6.0×10^{-1})
   (c) 435 (4.35×10^2)
   (d) 5230 (four significant digits) (5.230×10^3)
   (e) 2 999 900 (five significant digits) (2.9999×10^6)
   (f) 0.000 16 (1.6×10^{-4})
   (g) 0.000 000 000 32 (3.2×10^{-10})
   (h) 760 (two significant figures) (7.6×10^2)

   *Scientific notation is optional for numbers between 1 and 100, except where the zeros preceding the decimal point create some uncertainty.

Practice

1. State the number of significant digits in each of the following.
   (a) 908   (b) 7.60   (c) 0.0050   (d) 0.010   (e) 760
   (f) 0.000 000 000 69   (g) 6.743
2. Express each of the following in scientific notation.
   (a) 6807   (b) 0.000 053
   (c) 5200 (two significant digits)
   (d) 39 879 280 000 (seven significant digits)
   (e) 0.000 000 000 813   (f) 0.070 40
   (g) 40 000 000 000 (one significant digit)
   (h) 0.80   (i) 68
3. Express each of the following in common notation.
   (a) 7×10^1 (b) 5.2×10^3 (c) 8.3×10^9
   (d) 10.1×10^{-2} (e) 6.3868×10^3 (f) 4.086×10^{-3}
   (g) 6.3×10^2

Calculations Involving Measured Quantities

Often in physics a measured quantity is combined mathematically with another measured quantity, using such operations as addition, subtraction, multiplication, division, or square root. It is important that the mathematical operations do not themselves appear to express accuracy that is not based on direct measurement. As a general rule, the results of the mathematical operations can be no more accurate than the *least* accurate direct measurement used in the calculation.

Addition and Subtraction

Suppose we have three measurements of length that are to be added together, e.g., 6.6 m, 18.74 m, and 0.766 m. Since the least precise measurement is 6.6 m (it is accurate to only the nearest 0.1 m), the sum cannot be expressed any more accurately than to the nearest 0.1 m. Thus the sum of 26.106 m has to be rounded off to 26.1 m. A similar procedure is followed in subtraction.

$$\begin{array}{r} 6.6 \text{ m} \\ 18.74 \text{ m} \\ \underline{0.766 \text{ m}} \\ 26.106 \text{ m} \end{array}$$

or 26.1 m

In rounding off to the correct number of significant digits, if the digit to be dropped is greater than 5, the next digit to the left is increased by 1. If the digit to be dropped is less than 5, the preceding digit remains the same. If the digit to be dropped is 5, the preceding digit is usually increased.

Rounding off is of particular importance when electronic calculators are being used. Even the simplest calculation may generate eight digits. It is important to understand when and how to round off, and to know the correct number of significant digits to use when rounding off.

Multiplication and Division

The area of a rectangle whose dimensions are given as 14.25 cm and 6.43 cm is (by multiplication) 91.6275 cm^2. The product appears to be much more accurate than the two measurements, though this obviously could not be so.

In any measured quantity, the last digit is the least reliable, and any calculation that involves this least reliable digit will itself be unreliable.

If we examine the multiplication of these two numbers, we note that the digits 6275 in the product were obtained by calculations involving the last digit in each number. The degree of unreliability increases from left to right, so that the 6 is not as unreliable as the 2 and so on. Since for all measured quantities the last digit involves some degree of unreliability, the product may reasonably be rounded off and expressed as 91.6 cm².

$$
\begin{array}{r}
14.25 \\
6.43 \\
\hline
42\ 75 \\
570\ 0 \\
8550 \\
\hline
91.6275
\end{array}
$$

In general, the product of two or more measured quantities is only as accurate as the factor that has the fewest significant digits, regardless of the decimal point. This rule also holds for division, squaring, and square root.

In this case, 14.25 (four significant digits) times 6.43 (three significant digits) gives a product of 91.6 (three significant digits).

Sometimes a calculation is easier to perform if scientific notation is used. In the answer to the expression $7\ 640 \times \dfrac{0.006\ 50}{0.054}$, for example, there may be some difficulty in placing the decimal point correctly. If the numbers are expressed in scientific notation and the powers of 10 are moved to the right, the mathematical operations will be easier to perform and there should be no difficulty in determining the proper position of the decimal point.

$$
\begin{aligned}
\frac{7\ 640 \times 0.006\ 50}{0.054} &= \frac{(7.64 \times 10^3)(6.50 \times 10^{-3})}{5.4 \times 10^{-2}} \\
&= \frac{(7.64)(6.50)}{(5.4)} \times \frac{(10^3)(10^{-3})}{10^{-2}} \\
&= 9.1963 \times 10^2 \\
&= 9.2 \times 10^2
\end{aligned}
$$
(correct to two significant digits)

Summary

- When adding or subtracting measured quantities, the answer should be expressed to the same number of decimal places as the *least* precise quantity used in the calculation.

- When multiplying, dividing, or finding the square root of measured quantities, the answer should have the same number of significant digits as the *least* precise quantity used in the calculation.

Sample Problems

1. What is the sum of 15.35 g + 236.4 g + 0.645 g?
   15.35 g + 236.4 g + 0.645 g = 252.395 g, or 252.4 g
   Since the least precise measurement is 236.4 g, the answer can only be precise to 0.1 of a gram, or one decimal place. Thus the answer is rounded off to 252.4 g.
2. Perform the following operations to the correct number of significant digits.
   (a) 87.63 m − 54.1 m = 33.53 m, or 33.5 m (correct to one decimal place)
   (b) 65.6 × 0.62 = 40.672, or 41 (correct to two significant digits)
   (c) 452.6 ÷ 37.2 = 12.167, or 12.2 (correct to three significant digits)
   (d) 4.9 ÷ 2.2 = 2.227, or 2.2 (correct to two significant digits)

Practice

1. Perform the following mathematical operations, expressing the answers to the correct number of significant digits.
   (a) 463.66 + 29.2 + 0.17   (b) 426.66 − 39.2
   (c) (2.6)(42.2)   (d) (65)(0.041)(325)
   (e) (0.0060)(26)(55.1)   (f) $\dfrac{650}{4.0}$
   (g) $\dfrac{0.452}{0.012}$ (h) $\dfrac{(5.21)(0.45)}{0.0060}$
   (i) 3.5^2 (j) $\sqrt{4.9}$
2. Simplify each of the following, using scientific notation where appropriate.
   (a) $10^2 \times 10^1$ (b) $10^4 \times 10^2$ (c) $10^{-2} \times 10^5$
   (d) $10^{-6} \times 10^2$ (e) $10^2 \div 10^5$ (f) $10^4 \div 10^7$
   (g) $10^{-6} \div 10^2$ (h) $10^{-6} \div 10^{-7}$
   (i) $(1.4 \times 10^2)(3 \times 10^1)$
   (j) $(3.5 \times 10^4)(2.0 \times 10^{-3})$
   (k) $(5.0 \times 10^{-5})(4.00 \times 10^{-3})$

(l) $\dfrac{5.0 \times 10^7}{3.0 \times 10^3}$ (m) $\dfrac{6.63 \times 10^{-34}}{4.8 \times 10^{-9}}$

(n) $\dfrac{(5.0 \times 10^6)(7.0 \times 10^{-4})}{2.00 \times 10^{-5}}$ (o) $\dfrac{(6.63 \times 10^{-34})(3.00 \times 10^8)}{5.98 \times 10^{-9}}$

(p) $\dfrac{(0.534)(6.2 \times 10^{-3})}{4.0 \times 10^1}$ (q) $\dfrac{(360)(5.0 \times 10^{-4})}{0.000\ 30}$

(r) $\dfrac{(6.67 \times 10^{-11})(5.98 \times 10^{24})(50)}{(7.0 \times 10^7)^2}$

3. If a gold atom is considered to be a cube with sides 2.5×10^{-9} m, how many gold atoms could stack on top of one another in gold foil with a thickness of 1.0×10^{-7} m?

4. On the average, 1.0 kg of aluminum consists of 2.2×10^{25} atoms. How many atoms would there be in a block of aluminum 10 cm by 1.2 cm by 15.6 cm, if the density of aluminum is 2.7 g/cm^3, or 2.7×10^3 kg/m^3.

Appendix H

Rapid Estimation—Orders of Magnitude

It is often useful to be able to estimate the value of a quantity. This may be because you want to check a calculation quickly, to determine whether the decimal is properly placed or whether the numbers were entered properly in an electronic calculator. When an exact solution is not needed and/or an accurate calculation would take more time than it is worth, a rapid estimation will do.

To make an "order of magnitude" estimate, all numbers are rounded off to one significant digit plus its power of 10. After the calculation has been made, only one significant digit is retained. Some examples will illustrate how a rapid estimation is made.

Sample Problems

1. Estimate the number of seconds in a year.
   number of seconds
   $$= (\text{seconds/hour})(\text{hours/day})(\text{days/year})$$
   $$= (3600\ \text{s/h})(24.00\ \text{h/d})(365.25\ \text{d/a})$$
   $$\approx (4 \times 10^3)(2 \times 10)(4 \times 10^2)$$
   $$\approx 3 \times 10^7\ \text{s}$$

The comparable answer to four significant figures is 3.156×10^7 s.

2. Estimate the volume of water in a round reservoir approximately 1 km in diameter, if the average depth of the water is 14 m.
   $$\text{volume of water} = \pi r^2 h$$
   $$\approx (3)(5 \times 10^2\ \text{m})^2(1 \times 10\ \text{m})$$
   $$\approx 75 \times 10^5$$
   $$\approx 8 \times 10^6\ \text{m}^3$$
   $$\approx 1 \times 10^7\ \text{m}^3$$

3. Approximately how many ping-pong balls with a radius of 1.8 cm could you put in a classroom whose dimensions are 18 m × 11 m × 4 m?
   $$\text{volume of room} = (18\ \text{m})(11\ \text{m})(4\ \text{m})$$
   $$\approx (2 \times 10)(1 \times 10)(4)$$
   $$\approx 8 \times 10^2\ \text{m}^3$$
   $$\approx 8 \times 10^8\ \text{cm}^3$$
   $$\text{volume of one ping-pong ball} = \frac{4}{3}\pi r^3$$
   $$\approx \frac{4}{3}(3)(2\ \text{cm})^3$$
   $$\approx 3 \times 10\ \text{cm}^3$$

The estimated number of balls is $\dfrac{8 \times 10^8\ \text{cm}^3}{3 \times 10\ \text{cm}^3} \approx 3 \times 10^7$.

Practice

1. Estimate the number of minutes in a human lifetime of 80 years.
2. Estimate the area of the lower continental United States in square kilometers, without using a calculator.
3. The speed of light is 3.00×10^8 m/s. How many meters are there in a light year?
4. A gold atom is approximately 2.5×10^{-10} m in "diameter". Estimate the number of atoms in a cubic centimeter of gold. Assume that the gold atoms line up in rows.
5. How many cups of water are required to fill a typical bathtub?

Appendix I

Expressing Error in Measurement

Observations and experiments constitute the basis of all natural science. But all observations and experiments involving numerical results are the result of measurements that contain some degree of error. From a practical standpoint, it is important to be able to estimate both the errors incurred in making measurements and the errors resulting from what is done with those measurements, because it is only then that we can safely use the conclusions drawn from the observations.

No matter how small the divisions on a measuring scale, there is a limit to the accuracy of any measurement made with it. Every measurement made on every scale has some unavoidable possibility of error, usually assumed to be one-half of the smallest division marked on the scale. The accuracy of calculations involving measured quantities is often indicated by a statement of the **possible error**.

Possible error can best be explained by an example. Using a metric ruler calibrated in centimeters and millimeters, you are asked to measure the length of a block of wood to the nearest millimeter. You do so and obtain the result of, say, 126 mm. Assuming that you read the numbers on the ruler correctly, the maximum possible error in your measurement is 0.5 mm. The possible error in the measurement would be indicated by 126 ± 0.5 mm.

Absolute error is the difference between the measured or observed value and the accepted value. The equation for absolute error is

absolute error = measured value − accepted value

Relative error is expressed as a percentage, and is usually called **percentage error**. It is calculated as follows:

$$\text{percentage error} = \frac{\text{absolute error}}{\text{accepted value}} \times 100\%$$

Sometimes, in an investigation, a calculation of a known value is being determined. For example, in an investigation to measure the acceleration due to gravity (see Section 4.5), the experimenter calculates a value of 9.5 m/s². Since the accepted value at the Earth's surface is known to be 9.8 m/s², the percentage error is calculated as follows:

$$\begin{aligned} \text{percentage error} &= \frac{\text{absolute error}}{\text{accepted value}} \times 100\% \\ &= \frac{\text{measured value} - \text{accepted value}}{\text{accepted value}} \times 100\% \\ &= \frac{9.5 \text{ m/s}^2 - 9.8 \text{ m/s}^2}{9.8 \text{ m/s}^2} \times 100\% \\ &= -3.1\% \end{aligned}$$

The negative sign indicates that the measured value was less than the accepted value. A positive sign would indicate that the measured value was greater than the accepted value.

Sometimes, if two values of the same quantity are measured, it is useful to compare the precision of these values by calculating the percentage difference between them, as follows:

$$\begin{aligned} \text{percentage} \\ \text{difference} \end{aligned} = \frac{\text{difference in measurements}}{\text{average measurement}} \times 100\%$$

For example, if two measurements of the acceleration due to gravity are 9.6 m/s² and 9.2 m/s², their percentage difference is calculated as follows:

$$\begin{aligned} \text{percentage difference} &= \frac{0.4 \text{ m/s}^2}{9.4 \text{ m/s}^2} \times 100\% \\ &= 4.3\% \end{aligned}$$

*P*ractice

1. A student measures the acceleration due to gravity and finds it to be 9.72 m/s². What is his percentage error, if the accepted value is 9.81 m/s²?
2. You estimate that the maximum possible error of an equal-arm balance is 0.01 g. What is the possible percentage error when you use this balance to measure each of the following masses?
   (a) 700 g (b) 20 g (c) 3 kg (d) 1.0 g
3. When measuring the index of refraction for water (see Section 15.2), a student's measurements produce values of 1.36 and 1.28. If the accepted value is 1.33, what is
   (a) the percentage difference for the measured values?
   (b) the percentage error for each value?

Appendix J

Graphing Scientific Data

You may have drawn *x-y* graphs in your mathematics class. Most of the graphs used in this book are different in that they involve experimental data. The following guidelines are to assist you in drawing a graph based on experimental data.

Speed-time graph for ball rolling down a slope

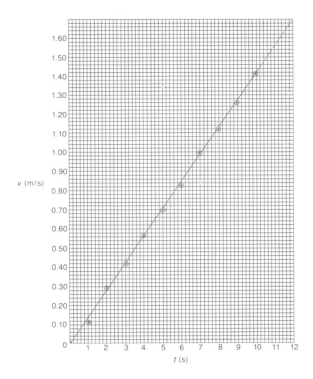

Step 1—Choosing the Axes

Determine which of the physical quantities is the **dependent variable** and which is the **independent variable**. The independent variable is the one whose values the experimenter chooses. In the graph illustrated, time is the independent variable since the experimenter chooses at which times to measure the speed of the ball. The independent variable is plotted on the horizontal axis and the dependent variable on the vertical axis. Usually the title of the graph indicates how the axes are to be labelled. For example, in the graph of A versus B, the values of A are plotted vertically, those of B horizontally.

Step 2—Scaling the Axes

When choosing scales, spread the measured values across the graph paper as widely as possible. The scales chosen must be easy to read and must have equal divisions. Each division must represent a small whole number of units of the variable being plotted, such as 1, 2, 5, 10, or some simple multiple of these. For example, the maximum measured reading for speed in the accompanying graph is 1.40 m/s.

The graph paper has 17 vertical divisions that could be used to plot speed. If we divided the number of divisions (17) into the maximum value to be plotted (1.40 m/s) we would obtain $\frac{1.40}{17}$, or 0.0823 m/s per division. The plotted values of speed would then take up the entire axis, but the numbers on the divisions would be very awkward. To simplify, we round up 0.0823 m/s to 0.1 m/s, thereby using only 14 divisions and having three left over.

Similarly, if the number of divisions in the horizontal scale (12) is divided into the maximum value to be plotted (5 s), we get $\frac{5}{12}$, or 0.417 s per division. We round 0.417 s up to 0.5 s, thereby using 10 divisions and having two left over. To summarize, choose the correct scale for an axis by dividing the maximum number of divisions on the axis into the maximum value to be plotted, and round the result up to the nearest 1, 2, 5, 10, or some simple multiple of these values.

Most of the graphs used in this book have an origin of zero, that is (0,0). It is not necessary to label every line on each axis, any more than it is necessary to label every division on a ruler. Each axis is labelled with the symbol for what is being plotted and the unit.

Step 3—Plotting the Data

Find each data point and mark it with a small dot *in pencil*. Around each dot draw a small circle not exceeding two small scale divisions in diameter. With a well-sharpened pencil, lightly draw in the smooth curve that best joins the small circles. Do not try to force your line to go through all dots, since experimental error will cause some points to be slightly off the smooth curve. If the points seem to lie on a straight line, use a ruler, preferably a transparent one, so that you can see all the points while selecting the best line. You have used pencil to mark your points and draw your smooth curve so that you can easily make changes, if necessary. Once you are satisfied with the curve you have chosen, draw it in, in ink.

Sometimes a point obviously has no experimental error, so the line must go through it. In the example we have used, (0,0) is such a point because the speed will be zero when $t = 0$.

Step 4—Choosing a Title

Every graph should be given a title. In this case, "Speed-time graph for a ball rolling down a slope" is the title. The title may be placed at the top of the page, or in a box in a clear area on the graph.

Step 5—Using the Graph

The graphing of data serves at least four functions:
1. It permits easy **interpolation** (finding values between measured points) and **extrapolation** (finding values beyond measured points). If a graph is extended, a dotted line is used.
2. The scatter of the points off the smooth curve gives an indication of the errors in the measured data.
3. Where a point falls far off the smooth curve, this suggests that a serious error may have been made and that the data for that point should be remeasured. Alternatively, it may indicate that there is another variable that has not been taken into consideration in the investigation.
4. We can deduce from the slope of the graph the mathematical relationship between the variables. For example, if the graph is a straight line through the origin, the relationship is of the form $y = mx$ (y is directly proportional to x). In some cases, the experimental values will not result in a straight line.

Numerical Answers to Problems in Appendices

Appendix G

Practice (page 818)

1. (a) 3
   (b) 3
   (c) 2
   (d) 2
   (e) 2
   (f) 2
   (g) 4
2. (a) 6.807×10^3
   (b) 5.3×10^{-5}
   (c) 5.2×10^3
   (d) $3.987\,928 \times 10^{10}$
   (e) 8.13×10^{-10}
   (f) 7.040×10^{-2}
   (g) 4×10^{10}
   (h) 8.0×10^{-1}
   (i) 6.8×10
3. (a) 70
   (b) 5200
   (c) 8 300 000 000
   (d) 0.101
   (e) 638 680
   (f) 0.004 086

Practice (page 819)

1. (a) 493.0
   (b) 387.5
   (c) 1.1×10^2
   (d) 8.7×10^2
   (e) 8.6
   (f) 1.6×10^2
   (g) 38
   (h) 3.9×10^3
   (i) 12
   (j) 2.2
2. (a) 10^3
   (b) 10^6
   (c) 10^3
   (d) 10^{-4}
   (e) 10^{-3}
   (f) 10^{-3}
   (g) 10^{-8}
   (h) 10^1
   (i) 4×10^3
   (j) 7.0×10^1, or 70
   (k) 2.0×10^{-7}
   (l) 1.7×10^4
   (m) 1.4×10^{-25}
   (n) 1.8×10^8
   (o) 3.33×10^{-17}
   (p) 8.3×10^{-5}
   (q) 6.0×10^2
   (r) 4.1
3. 4.0×10^2 atoms
4. 1.1×10^{25} atoms

Appendix H

Practice (page 820)

1. 4×10^7 min
2. 7×10^6 km²
3. 1×10^{16} m
4. 3×10^{22}
5. 1×10^3

Appendix I

Practice (page 821)

1. −0.92%
2. (a) 0.001%
   (b) 0.05%
   (c) 0.0003%
   (d) 1.0 g
3. (a) 6.1%
   (b) +2.3%, −3.8%

Numerical Answers to
Review Problems

Chapter 1

Simple Motion

10. 3 min
11. 497 s
12. 10.1 m/s, 9.24 m/s, 7.86 m/s
13. 26.7 km/s
14. 720 s
15. 2.2×10^4 m
16. 28 m
17. 0.36 s
18. (a) 10 km[S]
    (b) 10 km[S]
    (c) 2.4 km/h[S]
    (d) 54 km
    (e) 13 km/h
19. (a) 4.0 m/s
    (b) 0.15 m/s
    (c) −63 m/s
    (d) 5 m/s
20. A 2.0 m/s
    B 0
    C −2.5 m/s
    D 0
    E 4.4 m/s
21. (a) 98 km
    (b) 62 km[S]
    (c) (i) 2.4×10^2 km/h[S]
        (ii) 1.4×10^2 km/h[N]
        (iii) 1.3×10^2 km/h[S]
    (d) 2.1×10^2 km/h
22. (a) 40 km
    (b) 0.1 h
    (c) 80 km/h, 100 km/h
    (d) 0
    (e) 80 km
24. (a) 5.0 km/h
    (b) 10 km/h
    (c) 0
    (d) 6.4 km/h
    (e) 5.2 km/h
    (f) 5.8 km/h
25. (b) 7.5 s at 75 m
    (c) 40 m
26. (a) 360 m/s
    (b) 1.09×10^3 m/s

(c) 3.30×10^3 m/s
(d) 3.38×10^3 m/s
27. 24 min
28. 1.2 min
29. (a) 1.0 km
    (b) 15 min
    (c) 3.5 km

Chapter 2

Velocity and Acceleration

9. 15 m/s²
10. −4.5 m/s²
11. 2.9 m/s², 2.6 m/s², 2.8 m/s²
14. (a) (i) 4.0 m/s (ii) 6.0 m/s
        (iii) 3.1 m/s (iv) 2.0 m/s
    (b) (i) 0 (ii) 1.0 m/s²
        (iii) −0.67 m/s² (iv) 0.75 m/s²
    (c) (i) 16 m (ii) 50 m (iii) 64 m
15. (a) 4.0 m/s²
    (b) 300 m, 200 m
    (c) 100 m
    (d) 20 s
16. 7.2×10^3 m/s
17. 11 s
18. 40 m/s
19. 4.0 s
20. (a) 11.2 m/s
    (b) 5.60 m/s
    (c) 44.8 m
21. (a) 0.50 m/s
    (b) 1.0 m/s
    (c) 0.25 m/s²
22. 375 m
23. (a) 7.45 m/s
    (b) 31.3 m
24. (a) 60 m
    (b) 70 m
    (c) 10 m
25. 3.0
26. (a) 0.01 s
    (b) -2.4×10^3 m/s
27. (a) 6.0 m/s, 0, −6.0 m/s
    (b) 16 m, 25 m, 16 m
28. (a) 1.6 m/s²[down]

(b) 4.8 m
(c) 5.0 s
29. (a) 3.9×10^{13} m/s²
    (b) 6.4×10^{-6} s
30. (a) 60 m
    (b) 50 m
    (c) 5.0 m/s
    (d) 2 s
31. (a) 0.50 m/s²
    (b) 22 s
    (c) 1.7 m/s²
    (d) 28 s, 50 s
    (e) 0 s

Chapter 3

Vectors

8. 104 km[N]
9. 20 km[S]
10. 50 km/h[E]
11. (a) 2.0 m/s[E]
    (b) 0.5 m/s[W]
    (c) 3.0 m/s[W]
    (d) 5.5 m/s[W]
    (e) 8.0 m/s[W]
12. (a) 2.0 m/s[S]
    (b) 2.0 m/s[N]
13. (a) 3.6 m/s[N34°E]
    (b) 2.2 m/s[N]
    (c) 5.6 min, 7.6 min
    (d) 670 m
14. 26 km/h[E]
15. (a) [E30°S]
    (b) 17 km/h
16. (a) 349 km/h
    (b) [N4.1°E]
17. (a) 102 km/h
    (b) [E11°S]
18. (a) 330 km/h[E], 270 km/h[W]
    (b) 55 min, 67 min
    (c) 120 min
19. (a) 7.0 m/s[up]
    (b) 1.0 m/s[up]
    (c) 2.0 m/s[down]

20. 40 km[S30°W]
21. 14 km/h[E45°S]
22. (a) 50 km/h, 87 km/h, 150 km/h, 87 km/h
    (b) [N], [W30°N], [S], [E30°N]
    (c) 120 min, 69 min, 40 min, 69 min
    (d) 58 min
23. (a) 10 m/s[E], 10 m/s[W], 10 m/s[down], 10 m/s[up]
    (b) 20 m/s[E], 0, 14 m/s[E45°down], 14 m/s[E45°up]
24. 75 m
25. 1.3×10^{-2} cm/s²
26. 3.8×10^5 km

Chapter 4

Bodies in Free Fall

5. (a) −20 m/s
   (b) −59 m/s
6. (a) −20 m
   (b) -1.8×10^2 m
7. (a) −28 m/s, −36 m
   (b) −67 m/s, -2.2×10^2 m
8. 1.5 s
9. (a) 9.4 s
   (b) −93.1 m/s or −3.4 km/h
10. 100 : 1
11. (a) −10 tem/ces²
    (b) −20 tem/ces
    (c) −3.2 m/s²
12. (a) −44 m
    (b) 24 m
13. (a) 2.5 s
    (b) −25 m/s
14.

t(s)	v(m/s)	d(m)
0	29.4	0
1	19.6	24.5
2	9.8	39.2
3	0	44.1
4	−9.8	39.2
5	−19.6	24.5
6	−29.4	0

15. (a) −28 m
    (b) −14 m/s
    (c) 1.0 s
    (d) −24 m/s
16. (a) 2.0 s
    (b) 5.0 s

Chapter 5

Forces

12. (a) 735 N
    (b) 4.45 N
    (c) 1.96×10^4 N
13. (a) 0.25 N
    (b) 1.00×10^3 N
    (c) 1.2×10^{-4} N
14. (a) 0.10 kg
    (b) 10.2 kg
    (c) 6.3 kg
    (d) 4.54×10^6 kg
15. (a) 3.3 N/kg
    (b) 57 kg, 8.1 N/kg
    (c) 57 kg, 1500 N
16. (a) 50 kg
    (b) 490 N
    (c) 50 kg
17. (a) 150 N
    (b) 24.0 N
    (c) 6.00 N
    (d) 1.50 N
18. (a) 3.20×10^3 N
    (b) 7.20×10^3 N
    (c) 8.00×10^4 N
    (d) 1.28×10^4 N
19. 5.0 m/s²
20. 3.9×10^3 N
21. 5.3×10^2 N
22. (a) 2.3×10^5 N
    (b) 2.3×10^5 m/s²
23. 2.0×10^3 N/m
24. 22 cm
25. (a) 196 N
    (b) 0.153
    (c) 210 N
26. 0.26
27. (a) 98 N
    (b) 2.0×10^2 N
    (c) 4.9×10^2 N
28. (a) 61 N
    (b) 37 N
    (c) 0.49 N
29. (a) 40 N[E]
    (b) 11.0 N[N]
    (c) 0
    (d) 99 N [S 45°W]
30. 224 N[N63°E]

Chapter 6

Newton's Laws of Motion

18. (a) 2.0 N
    (b) 4.0 N
19. (a) 20 m/s²
    (b) 10 m/s²
20. 0.250 m/s²
21. (a) 6.0 m/s², 4.0 m/s²
    (b) 0.60 m/s, 0.40 m/s
22. (a) 3.7×10^3 N
    (b) 1.9×10^3 N
23. (a) 5.0 m/s²[E]
    (b) 2.5 s
    (c) 15.6 m
24. (a) −8.0 m/s²
    (b) 3.1 s
    (c) 39 m
25. 3.0 m/s²
26. 60 m/s
27. 1.6×10^4 N[S]
28. 5.0 s
29. 18 N[up]
30. 45 m/s
31. (a) 2.86×10^7 N
    (b) 4.8×10^6 N[up]
    (c) 1.6 m/s²
32. 10.2 m/s², 53.0 m/s²
33. 590 N in each case
34. 17 m/s
35. (a) 3.6×10^4 kg · m/s
    (b) 3.6×10^4 N · s
36. (a) 3.6 N · s
    (b) 80 m/s
37. 2.3×10^3 N
38. 0.13 kg/s
39. 11 m/s
40. 0.13 kg
41. (a) 0.10 m/s
    (b) 0.20 m/s

Chapter 7

Work, Power, and Energy

16. 0.12 J
17. 0.12 J
18. 1.8 J
19. 47 m
20. 1.3×10^3 J
21. 2.00 N
22. (a) 2.25×10^5 J
    (b) 2.25×10^5 J

23. 0

24. 5.8×10^4 J

25. 500 W

26. 300 s

27. (a) 1.3×10^6 J
    (b) 3.9×10^5 J

28. (a) 3.1×10^2 J
    (b) 12 W
    (c) 5.0 N

29. 0.204 m/s

30. (a) 2.78 m/s²
    (b) 139 m
    (c) 5.80×10^5 J
    (d) 5.80×10^4 W

31. (a) 2.35×10^4 W
    (b) 2.94×10^4 W

32. (a) 1.50×10^3 J
    (b) 7.5×10^3 J
    (c) 1.50×10^4 J

33. -9.80×10^8 J

34. (a) 235 J
    (b) 35.3 J
    (c) 45.1 J
    (d) 0
    (e) −49.0 J

35. (a) 7.8×10^{10} m³
    7.8×10^{13} kg
    (b) 1.53×10^{15} J
    (c) 3.5×10^{10} W

36. (a) 9.0 J
    (b) 81 J

37. (a) 2.0 m/s
    (b) 20 m/s
    (c) 85 m/s

38. (a) 0.20 m
    (b) 20.4 m
    (c) 367 m

39. (a) 7.5×10^2 J
    (b) 3.0×10^3 J
    (c) 2.3×10^3 J

40. (a) 98.0 J
    (b) 563 J
    (c) 661 J
    (d) 661 J
    (e) 269 J
    (f) 392 J
    (g) 661 J

41. (a) 8.8×10^3 J
    (b) 14 m/s
    (c) 12 m/s

42. (a) 63 m
    (b) 58 m
    (c) 35 m/s

43. (a) 4.0 m/s
    (b) 5.3 m/s

44. (a) 91%

45. (a) 2.4 m
    (b) 6.9 m/s

46. (a) 2.4×10^6 J
    (b) 0.25 kg

47. 250 m²

Chapter 8

Thermal Energy

17. $7.8 \times 10^{-6}\,°C^{-1}$

18. 32.21 m

19. 100°C

20. 6.0×10^{-2} cm

21. 1071°C

22. 5.5 cm³

23. 1.1 cm

24. 4.4×10^5 J

25. 2.73×10^4 J

26. (a) 10.9°C
    (b) 11.4°C

27. 77°C

28. 8.4×10^2 J/kg·°C

29. 65°C

30. 1.2×10^{-1} kg

31. 37°C

32. 6.9×10^2 J/kg·°C

33. 192°C

34. 6.2 min

35. 6.9°C

36. 12°C

37. 9.9×10^4 J

38. 5.6×10^4 J

39. 12°C

40. 4.1×10^{-3} kg

41. 314 g

42. (a) 1.2×10^5 J
    (b) 1.2×10^5 J
    (c) 3.1×10^5 J

43. 40°C

44. 5.2×10^{-1} kg

45. 2.3×10^6 J/kg

46. 138 g

47. 7.4×10^{-1} kg

48. (a) 4.5×10^2 kg
    (b) 6.3×10^2 m³
    (c) $1449.

49. 2.2×10^7 J

Chapter 9

Fluids

17. 7.4×10^2 kg

18. 2.1×10^5 Pa

19. 1.4×10^3 Pa

20. 11 cm

21. 10.4 m

22. (a) 2.0×10^6 Pa
    (b) 6.3×10^2 N

23. 6.4×10^3 kg, 9.0×10^2

24. 3.1×10^3 kg/m³

25. 8.18×10^3 m³

26. 7.9×10^2 kg/m³

27. 0.39 N

28. (a) 30 cm
    (b) 8.0 cm

29. 8.2×10^3 kg/m³

30. (a) 1.17×10^3 m³
    (b) 3.0×10^4 kg

31. 4.4 g

32. 5.8 kg

33. 20 m/s

34. 25 m/s

Chapter 10

The Properties and Behavior of Waves

8. 1.3 Hz, 0.77 s

9. 2.00 s

10. (a) 1.5 points/min
    (b) 3 escapes/min
    (c) 11.3 r/s

11. (a) 0.63 s
    (b) 3.9×10^{-3} s
    (c) 27.30 d

12. (a) 0.20 Hz
    (b) 1.2 Hz
    (c) 40 Hz
    (d) 4.2×10^{-2} Hz

13. (a) 0.10 s
    (b) 4.0 s
    (c) 2.00×10^{-6} s
    (d) 0.29 s

14. 4.0 cm

15. 62 m

17. (a) 3.6 cm, 1.0 cm
    (b) (i) 3.6 cm/s ii) 1.0 Hz iii) 1.0 Hz

18. 15

19. (a) B and F, A and E
    (b) 8.0 cm
    (c) 24 cm/s

20. (a) 0.93 Hz
    (b) 1.1 s
21. 2.0 m/s
22. 0.34 Hz
23. 5.0 m/s
24. (a) 2.5 m/s
    (b) 41 s
    (c) 1.5×10^2 m
25. 6.0 Hz
26. 3.8 s
27. 3.4×10^2 m/s
28. 1.1 m
29. 3.3 m
30. 2.9 m
31. 6.4×10^{-3} m
32. 1.7×10^{-2} m
38. (a) 2.6 cm
    (b) 3.1 cm/s
    (c) 1.2 Hz
39. 8.0 cm
40. 4.0 m
41. (a) 50 cm
    (b) 1.0×10^4 cm/s
42. (a) 36 cm
    (b) 3.6×10^2 cm/s
43. 15 Hz

Chapter 11

The Production and Properties of Sound

8. (a) 338 m/s
   (b) 341 m/s
   (c) 314 m/s
9. 59 s
10. 0.286 s
11. 3.44×10^3 m
12. 14 s
13. 2.1×10^3 m
14. 2.29 s
15. 9.9×10^2 m
16. 4.5×10^2 m
17. (a) 3.01
    (b) 0.501
    (c) 1.50
18. (a) 300 Hz
    (b) 300 Hz
    (c) 300 Hz
    (d) 300 Hz
19. (a) 301 Hz
    (b) 501 Hz

20. (a) 346 m/s
    (b) 338 m/s
    (c) 350 m/s
21. (a) 17 m
    (b) 1.7×10^{-2} m
22. (a) 4.15×10^{-2} m
    (b) 0.188 m
    (c) 0.631 m
23. 880 times
24. 53 vibrations
25. (a) 440 Hz, 3.8 m
    (b) 440 Hz, 0.83 m
26. 6.0×10^7 conversations
27. 4.0×10^{-9} J
28. 10^6:1
29. 3.3×10^2 m/s
30. 1.86×10^3 m
31. 6.1×10^2 m
32. (a) 12.2 s
    (b) 2.71 s
33. (a) 3.3×10^3 m
    (b) +2%
34. 6.6 s
35. (a) 338 m/s
    (b) 329 mi/s
    (c) 4.5 m/s
36. 1.7 m
37. 2.1 s

Chapter 12

The Interference of Sound Waves

26. 2 Hz beats
27. 251 Hz or 261 Hz
28. 24
29. 297 Hz or 303 Hz
30. 299 Hz or 301 Hz
31. 377 Hz
32. 397.5 Hz
33. 344 Hz
34. 0.39 m
35. 360 Hz, 300 Hz
36. (a) 800 Hz
    (b) 400 Hz
37. (a) 600 Hz
    (b) 100 Hz
38. 600 Hz
39. 19.4 cm
40. 326 Hz
41. 320 Hz
42. 808 Hz

43. (a) 1440 Hz
    (b) 1920 Hz
    (c) 960 Hz
    (d) 4800 Hz
44. 1200 Hz
45. 600 Hz
46. 4 Hz
47. 1.08 m, 346 m/s
48. (a) 143 Hz
    (b) 430 Hz
    (c) 717 Hz
49. (a) 1.20 m
    (b) 289 Hz
50. (a) 1.00 m
    (b) 338 Hz
51. 20 cm, 1.7×10^3 Hz
52. (a) 92.0 cm, 120 cm, 152 cm
    (b) 371 Hz, 284 Hz, 224 Hz
53. 1.78×10^2 Hz
54. 0.31 m
55. 0.66 m
56. 138 Hz
57. 338 m/s
58. 13 m/s
59. (a) 435 Hz
    (b) 370 Hz
60. 9.9 m/s

Chapter 13

Light Rays and Reflection

13. 58 s
14. 2.8×10^{16} m
15. (a) 1.4×10^{11} s
    (b) 4.1×10^{12} s
16. 10 a
17. 8.3 cm
18. 350 cm
19. 8.3×10^{-3}, 5.7×10^{-2}
20. 2.5 cm
26. (a) 3.0 m
    (b) 4.0 m from the image
27. 6.0 m
29. (a) 0.75 m
    (b) 0.75 m
31. 7200 lux
32. 5.2 m

Chapter 14

Curved Mirrors

14. (a) −20 cm
    (b) +2
15. −30 cm, 16 cm
16. 4
17. 11 cm, −0.67 m
18. 7.2 cm, −14 cm
19. 6.0 m
20. 2.0 cm
21. $d_o = 7.5$ cm

Chapter 15

Refraction of Light

17. (a) 1.33 (water)
    (b) 2.42 (diamond)
    (c) 1.54 (quartz or ruby)
18. 1.5
19. (a) 2.05×10^8 m/s
    (b) 1.24×10^8 m/s
    (c) 1.82×10^8 m/s
    (d) 1.84×10^8 m/s
20. 1.96×10^8 m/s, 1.97×10^8 m/s
21. (a) 1.53
    (b) 1.62
    (c) 1.41
22. (a) 1.78
    (b) 28°
    (c) 24°
23. 35°
24. 42°
25. 1.46
27. 11°
28. (a) 0°
    (b) 19°
    (c) 35°
29. 34°
30. 47°
31. 58°
32. (a) 41°
    (b) 61°
33. (a) 37°
    (b) 1.56
34. (b) 40.8°, 38.7°
35. (a) 42°   b) undefined
36. 15°

Chapter 16

Lenses and their Applications

21. −100 cm, −9.4 cm, −15 cm
22. 12 cm and 24 cm, or 24 cm and 12 cm
23. 60 cm, −10 cm
24. 42 cm
25. 17.5 mm, −30 cm, virtual
26. 9.1 cm
27. 13.3 cm, −1.0 cm, real
28. −0.57 mm
29. 3.6
30. 45 cm
31. (a) 0.13 m
    (b) −6.7 d
32. −67 cm
33. −9
34. −15.3 cm from the eyepiece,
    −31 cm

Chapter 18

Electrostatics

14. (b) 8.0×10^{-8} C
15. (a) 1.9×10^{19} Elections
    (b) 4.0×10^{-8} C

Chapter 19

Current Electricity

7. 3.6×10^2 C
8. 2.0×10^3 s
9. 1kV
10. 1.6×10^{-13} J
11. 5.0 V
12. 7.2×10^3 J
13. 1.2×10^2 V
14. 9.5 A
15. 4.5×10^4 J
16. 2.4×10^2 V
17. (a) 1.5×10^3 A
    (b) 3.0×10^9 J
18. 4.8×10^{-12} J
19. (a) 0.33h
    (b) 2.2×10^5 C
    (c) 2.6×10^6 J
20. 4.8×10^5 J

Chapter 20

Electric Circuits

12. 20 Ω
13. 0.40 A
14. 2.4×10^2 V
15. (a) 1.6×10^2 Ω
    (b) 20 Ω
    (c) 15 V
16. (a) 20 Ω
    (b) 10 Ω
17. (a) 90 Ω
    (b) 2.5 Ω
    (c) 12 Ω
18. 8 Ω
19. 1.0 Ω
20. 16 Ω
21. (a) 10 Ω, 12 Ω, 4.8 V
    (b) 36 V, 18 Ω, 6 Ω
    (c) 4 Ω, 1 A, 5 A, 3.3 A, 1.6 A, 1.1 A
    (d) 3.0 A, 2.0 Ω, 6.0 Ω
    (e) 1.5 A, 1.5 A, 0.30 A, 0.90 A,
        0.30 A, 4.2 V, 1.8 V, 1.8 V, 1.8 V
22. 2.2×10^4 J
23. (a) 3.00×10^3 W
    (b) 1.2×10^3 W
    (c) 60.0 W
24. (a) 3.6×10^3 W
    (b) 3.5 A
25. (a) 8.3 A
    (b) 17 A
    (c) 4.1×10^3 W
26. $55.85
27. $5.76

Chapter 23

Electromagnetic Induction

9. (a) 0.75 V
   (b) 3.0 V
   (c) 4.5 V
   (d) 4.5 V
10. (a) 1:20
    (b) 5.0 A
11. 8.0 V
12. 16 mA
13. 30 A

Chapter 24

Investigating New Rays

15. (a) 1.0×10^5 Bq
    (b) 1.6×10^5 Bq
    (c) 44 Bq
16. 8.4×10^8 emissions

Chapter 26

Investigating the Nucleus

9. (a) $_2^4$He
   (b) $_2^4$He
   (c) $_{-1}^0$e
   (d) $_{-1}^0$e
   (f) $_2^4$He
   (g) $_{-1}^0$e
   (h) $_2^4$He
10. (a) α
    (b) α
    (c) α
    (d) β
    (e) β
11. 10, 17
12. (a) 80 g
    (b) 20 g
    (c) 5 g
13. (b) 6 h
    (c) i) 8 kBq   ii) 2 kBq   iii) 0.5 kBq
14. 800 a
15. 75.0 d
16. 8.0 d
17. (a) $_{14}^{30}$Si
    (b) $_6^{13}$C
    (c) $_4^8$Be
    (d) $_1^1$H
    (e) $_1^2$H
    (f) $_{11}^{24}$Na
    (g) $_8^{17}$O
18. (a) correct
    (b) $_{14}^{19}$Si
    (c) correct
    (d) $_9^{17}$F
    (e) $_{86}^{222}$Rn
19. (a) 141
    (b) 214
    (c) 234
    (d) 82
    (e) $_{82}^{212}$Pb
    (f) $_{90}^{234}$Th
    (g) $_{90}^{227}$Th
    (h) $_{49}^{116}$In

Chapter 27

Nuclear Energy

23. (a) 1.8×10^{17} J
    (b) 3.6×10^{15} J
    (c) 9.0×10^9 J
24. (a) 1.0 kg
    (b) 5.0×10^{-3} kg
    (c) 2.0×10^{-6} kg
25. 4.4×10^9 kg/s
26. (a) 2.5×10^{21} atoms
    (b) 8.9×10^{-4} kg
27. (a) 2.96×10^{-11} J
    (b) 1.81×10^{-12} J

Index

Van de Graaf, Robert, 548
vector diagrams, 64, 66
  in airplane navigation, 70
vector quantities, **3,** 7, 64
vectors, 3, 64
  acceleration, 138
  addition of, 65, 115
  displacement, 64
  force, 134, 138
  velocity, 66, 68
velocity, **6,** 7, 10, 20
  at a point, 19–20
  average, 16, 18
  change in, 36
  increasing, 19
  negative, 15
  terminal, **87**
  uniform, 6
velocity vectors
  in one dimension, 66–7
  in opposite directions, 67
  in two dimensions, 68
vertex, **439**
vibration, 309, 310
Villard, Pierre, 721
Volta, Allesandro, 572
voltaic cell, 674
voltmeter, **574**–5
volume expansion, **230**
von Helmholtz, Heinrich, 191

Walton, E.T.S., 767
watt, **606**
Watt, James, 178, 246
Wave Equation, **315,** 317, 355
wave interference, **323,** 325, 327
wave rays, **321**
wave theory of light, 410–2, 742
wave transmission, 311
wavefront, **320**
wavelength, **312, 314,** 355
waves, **308**
  displacement of, 323
  electromagnetic, 309, 411
  in two dimensions, 319–20
  inversion of, 318
  longitudinal, **313**
  periodic, **311**
  shock, **311**
  standing, 325
  transverse, **312**
wedge, 196
weight, **105**
wheel and axle, 196

work, **174, 181,** 571
  and energy, 175, 244
  and power, 178

X-rays, **717**
  applications of, 719
  hard, **718**
  properties of, 718
  soft, **718**

Young, Thomas, 411

Credits

Every attempt will be made to correct any errors and omissions to this credits list in subsequent printings.

Photo Research: Sue McDermott, Martha Friedman, Nina Whitney

Photo Credits
Front Matter and Table of Contents: P. i: David Leah (TSW-Click/Chicago). P. iii: t, Four by Five (Superstock); b, Ernst Haas (The Stock Market). P. iv: t, Philip Wallick (The Stock Market); m, Ocean Images, Inc. (The Image Bank); b, J. Zimmerman (FPG International). P. v: t, David Leah (TSW-Click/Chicago); b, Kevin Schafer (Peter Arnold, Inc.). P. vi: t, Joanna McCarthy (The Image Bank); b, Martin Dohrn/Science Photo Library (Photo Researchers, Inc.). P. vii: t, Bob Evans (Peter Arnold, Inc.); b, Ralph Mercer. P. viii: t, Steve Niedorf (The Image Bank); b, Eric Meola (The Image Bank). P. ix: t, Otto Rogge (The Stock Market); b, Dominique Sarraute (The Image Bank). P. x: t, Dominique Sarraute (The Image Bank); m, Peter Saloutos (The Stock Market); b, W. Warren (West Light). P. xi: t, Don Carstens (Folio, Inc.); b, Manfred Kage (Peter Arnold, Inc.). P. xii: t, Richard Megna/Fundamental (Photo Researchers, Inc.); m, Lawrence Manning (West Light); b, Robert Essael (The Stock Market). P. xiii: t, Dr. S.L. Gibbs (Peter Arnold, Inc.); b, Chris Bjornberg (Photo Researchers, Inc.). P. xiv: t, Patrice Loiez/Science Photo Library (Photo Researchers, Inc.); b, Jake Rajs (The Image Bank). P. xix: Don Carstens (Folio, Inc.).

Chapter 1: P. xxii–1: Four by Five (Superstock).
P. 2: M.E. Warren (Photo Researchers, Inc.). P. 3: Charles Campbell (West Light). P. 6: Martin Rogers (Stock Boston). P. 14: Tony Freeman (PhotoEdit). P. 22: Science Kit & Boreal Laboratories. P. 25, 26: Irvin Krause. P. 27: Bob Daemmrich (Stock Boston). P. 29: NASA. P. 31: Jordan Coonrad (Imagery Unlimited).

Chapter 2: P. 34–35: Ernst Haas (The Stock Market). P. 36: NASA. P. 47: Bill Denver (Sportschrome). P. 48: Andrew Hourmont (TSW-Click/Chicago). P. 51: Mike Powell (Allsport). P. 56: Howard Sochurek, Inc. P. 59: NASA. P. 61: l, Brian Spurlock (Allsport); r, Photri.

Chapter 3: P. 62–63: Philip Wallick (The Stock Market). P. 64: Alastair Black (Focus On Sports). P. 68: Focus On Sports. P. 69: Thomas Ives (The Stock Market). P. 70: Mike Surowiak (TSW-Click/Chicago). P. 72: Ted Mahieu (The Stock Market). P. 74: Jean-Marc Loubat (Photo Researchers, Inc.). P. 78: Jordan Coonrad (Imagery Unlimited). P. 81: Birgitte Nielsen/© D.C. Heath.

Chapter 4: P. 82–83: Ocean Images, Inc. (The Image Bank). P. 84: t, Scala/Art Resource; b, Nimatallah/Art Resource. P. 85: Scala/Art Resource. P. 87: Richard Megna (Fundamental Photographs). P. 88: Richard Megna (Fundamental Photographs). P. 96: Peter Lamberti (TSW-Click/Chicago). P. 99: John Tudyk.

Chapter 5: P. 100–101: J. Zimmerman (FPG International). P. 102: t, Ralph Merlino (Allsport); b, NASA. P. 105: NASA. P. 113: Bill Ross (West Light). P. 118: James Sugar (Black Star). P. 119: Steve Smith (West Light). P. 122: NASA. P. 124: NASA.

Chapter 6: P. 126–127: David Leah (TSW-Click/Chicago). P. 128: Scala/Art Resource. P. 129: Science Kit & Boreal Laboratories. P. 130: Robert Macnaughton. P. 132: GM Proving Ground. P. 136: Irvin Krause. P. 140: Clyde H. Smith (Peter Arnold, Inc.). P. 148, 149: Dr. Harold Edgerton, MIT, Cambridge, MA. P. 152: Ben & Miriam Rose (The Image Bank). P. 154: Paul Kennedy (Leo de Wys, Inc.). P. 158: Mark Tomalty (Masterfile). P. 165: GM Proving Ground. P. 170: Estes Industries.

Chapter 7: P. 172–173: Kevin Schafer (Peter Arnold, Inc.). P. 174: John W. Mayo (Unicorn Stock Photography). P. 175: Irvin Krause. P. 176: l, Allsport USA/Vandystadt; r, Voscar (F/Stop Pictures). P. 182: Phil Habib (TSW-Click/Chicago). P. 183: l, James S. Steinberg (Photo Researchers, Inc.); r, Paul Silverman (Fundamental Photographs). P. 184: l, David Cannon (Allsport); r, Mike Mazzaschi (Stock Boston). P. 196: Carolyn A. McKeore (Photo Researchers, Inc.). P. 199: Harry Wilks (Stock Boston). P. 202: Craig Aurness (West Light). P. 203: t, Bob Hahn (Taurus Photos); b, David Hiser (Photographers/Aspen). P. 204: Jeff Zarub (TSW-Click/Chicago). P. 207: Kevin Schafer (Peter Arnold, Inc.) P. 208: Chuck O'Rear (West Light). P. 209: t, Lowell Georgia (Photo Researchers, Inc.); b, T.J. Florian (Rainbow). P. 211: Irvin Krause. P. 213, 214: Robert Macnaughton. P. 215: Christine M. Robertson/United Engineers & Constructors. P. 219: Kachaturian (International Stock Photography). P. 221: Brian Drake (Sportschrome). P. 222: Tony Duffy (Allsport).

Chapter 8: P. 224–225: Joanna McCarthy (The Image Bank). P. 226: The Bettmann Archive. P. 230: Richard Choy (Peter Arnold, Inc.). P. 231: Irvin Krause. P. 246: General Electric. P. 252: Tom McHugh (Photo Researchers, Inc.). P. 253: t, Robert Perron (Photo Researchers, Inc.); b, Steve Allen (Peter Arnold, Inc.). P. 254: Science Kit & Boreal Laboratories. P. 261: M. Timothy O'Keefe (Southern Stock Photos). P. 262: Clifford Hausner (Leo de Wys, Inc.). P. 264: Mike Powell (Allsport).

Chapter 9: P. 266–267: Martin Dohrn/Science Photo Library (Photo Researchers, Inc.). P. 268: Makoto Iwafuji (The Stock Market). P. 271: Giraudon/Art Resource. P. 272: Annie Griffiths (West Light). P. 276: WHOI. P. 280: Phil Degginger. P. 291: E. Masterson (H. Armstrong Roberts). P. 295: Steven E. Sutton (Duomo). P. 302: Hasler & Pierce, NASA/Science Source (Photo Researchers, Inc.). P. 305: Birgitte Nielsen/© D.C. Heath.

Chapter 10: P. 306–307: Bob Evans (Peter Arnold, Inc.). P. 308: Vince Cavataio (Allsport). P. 309: Robert Mathena (Fundamental Photographs). P. 313, 317, 318: D.C. Heath. P. 319: Science Kit & Boreal Laboratories. P. 320–328: D.C. Heath. P. 330, 331: Ken O'Donoghue/ © D.C. Heath. P. 339: John S. Shelton. P. 345: Martin Dorn (Photo Researchers, Inc.). P. 347: l, Deni McIntyre (Photo Researchers, Inc.); r, Peter Menzel (Stock Boston).

Chapter 11: P. 348–349: Ralph Mercer. P. 353: PLI (West Light). P. 356: Courtesy of AT&T Archives. P. 358: Jean-Claude LeJeune (Stock Boston). P. 359: Brad Bower (Picture Group). P. 361: t, Ontario Science Center; b, Ken Biggs (The Stock Market). P. 362: Tony Freeman (PhotoEdit). P. 363: t, NASA/Science Source (Photo Researchers, Inc.); b, Howard Sochurek (Woodfin Camp & Associates). P. 364: Dave Bartruff (Photo File). P. 365: t, Richard Pasley (Stock Boston); b, Courtesy of AT&T Archives. P. 367: Birgitte Nielsen/© D.C. Heath. P. 370: W. Warren (West Light). P. 373: Stephen Dalton (Photo Researchers, Inc.).

Chapter 12: P. 374–375: Steve Niedorf (The Image Bank). P. 385: Robert Macnaughton. P. 387: AP/Wide World Photos. P. 395: r, Comstock. P. 397: The Association of Universities for Research in Astronomy Inc./Kitt Peak National Observatory. P. 405: Richard Gross (The Stock Market). P. 406: Tony Freeman (PhotoEdit).

Chapter 13: P. 408–409: Eric Meola (The Image Bank). P. 410: Garry D. McMichael (Photo Researchers, Inc.). P. 411: t, Georges Seurat, French, 1859–1891, Sunday Afternoon on the Island of La Grand Jatte, oil on canvas, 1884–86, 207.6 x 308 cm, Helen Birch Bartlett Memorial collection, 1926.244, detail, photograph © 1990. The Art Institute of Chicago. All rights reserved; b, Royal Society, London/Bridgeman Art Library. P. 412: NASA. P. 413: The Bettmann Archive. P. 415: Richard Megna (Fundamental Photographs). P. 423: t, Dr. Jeremy Burgess/ Science Photo Library (Photo Researchers, Inc.); b, David M. Phillips (Visuals Unlimited). P. 424: t, Phil Degginger; b, Richard Megna (Fundamental Photographs). P. 427: Leonard Lessin (Peter Arnold, Inc.). P. 430: Comstock. P. 431: t, NASA; b, National Optical Astronomy Observatories. P. 432: Yoav Levey (Phototake). P. 433: Superstock.

Chapter 14: P. 436–437: Otto Rogge (The Stock Market). P. 439: Ken Kay (Fundamental Photographs). P. 440: E.R. Degginger. P. 444: t, E.R. Degginger; b, Leonard Lessin (Peter Arnold, Inc.); r, Paul Silverman (Fundamental Photographs). P. 449: l, Robert Macnaughton; r, Custom Medical Stock Photo. P. 450: Roger Ressmeyer (Starlight). P. 451: l, Gazuit (Photo Researchers, Inc.); r, E.R. Degginger. P. 454: Judith Aronson (Peter Arnold, Inc.). P. 460: California Association for Research in Astronomy. P. 461: Telegraph Colour Library (FPG International); inset, NASA.

Chapter 15: P. 462–463: Dominique Sarraute (The Image Bank). P. 464–465: Robert Macnaughton. P. 470: Ken Kay (Fundamental Photographs). P. 472: Ron Slenzak (West Light). P. 473: t, E.R. Degginger; b, David Parker (Photo Researchers, Inc.). P. 474: Ken O'Donoghue/ © D.C. Heath. P. 475: Stephen Frisch (Stock Boston). P. 476: Phil Degginger. P. 478: T, DPI; b, Robert Macnaughton. P. 480: Robert Macnaughton. P. 481: Darlene Gallerani. P. 482: Hank Morgan (Rainbow). P. 487: Richard Megna (Fundamental Photographs).

Chapter 16: P. 488–489: Dominique Sarraute (The Image Bank). P. 492: Richard Megna (Fundamental Photographs). P. 493,499: Bruce Iverson. P. 501: Barry L. Runk (Grant Heilman Photography). P. 502: E.R. Degginger. P. 505: main photo & top inset, © Eli Peli, Eye Research Institute of Retina Foundation; bottom inset, Allergan Optical. P. 511: The Telegraph Colour Library (FPG International). P. 512: Jim Cummins (Allstock). P. 514: George East/Science Photo Library (Photo Researchers, Inc.).

840